THE GENERALISSIMO

蔣

The Generalissimo

Chiang Kai-shek and the
Struggle for Modern China

Jay Taylor

THE BELKNAP PRESS OF
HARVARD UNIVERSITY PRESS
Cambridge, Massachusetts
London, England

The character 蔣 is Chiang Kai-shek's surname.

First Harvard University Press paperback edition, 2011

Library of Congress Cataloging-in-Publication Data

Taylor, Jay, 1931–
    The generalissimo : Chiang Kai-shek and the struggle for modern China / Jay Taylor.—1st. ed.
        p.   cm.
    Includes bibliographical references and index.
    ISBN 978-0-674-03338-2 (cloth : alk. paper)
    ISBN 978-0-674-06049-4 (pbk.)
    1. Chiang, Kai-shek, 1887–1975.   2. Presidents—China—Biography.
3. Presidents—Taiwan—Biography.   4. China—History—Republic, 1912–1949.
5. Taiwan—History—1945–   I. Title.   II. Title: Chiang Kai-shek and the struggle for modern China.
    DS777.488.C5T39   2009
    951.04′2092—dc22
    [B]   2008040492

To John Taylor, my son, editor, and best friend

Contents

IV The Island

Maps

Acknowledgments

Extensive travel, interviews, and research in Taiwan and China over five years made this book possible. Among the many scholars with whom I consulted in Taiwan were Chang Ruide, Chen Cungong, Chen Liwen, Chen Pengren, Chen Yongfa, Huang Zejin, Liu Weikai, Qin Xiaoyi, Zhu Hongyuan, Shao Minghuang, Yu Minling, and Zhang Suya. Special mention must also be made of the contribution of Professor Yang Tianshi, former head of the Chinese Modern History Institute in Peking. I also relied heavily on the work of numerous American and other Western scholars who, drawing on archives in China, Taiwan, and elsewhere, have provided impressive new insights into various China issues, foreign and domestic, relevant to Chiang's career.

Until the middle of 2006, my primary source for Chiang's extensive diaries was the twelve-volume collection put out by the Kuomingtang Party Historical Office, *Zong tong Jiang gong da shi chang pian chu gao* (Preliminary Draft of President Chiang's Chronological Biography), Taipei, 1978–2004. The editor of this extensive project, Qin Xiaoyi, in 2003 kindly presented me with a copy of this then hard-to-find collection. Beginning in 2006, the Chiang family began slowly to make available photocopies of the original diaries for public access at the Hoover Institution Archives at Stanford University. By the time I had finished the final draft, the diaries through 1954 were available. Checking the translations in the Qin Xiaoyi collection against the original diaries, we found no major discrepancies.

Assisting in this five-year work were outstanding associates, most especially Lilian Chu, who, during more than four years, in addition to research and translation also expertly arranged and managed my visits to Taiwan. Doria Spichak turned up fascinating documents in Moscow and Jean Israel did the same in Washington. Tong Xiaohua was an immensely valuable associate, travel companion, and assistant during my earlier visits to the mainland, and subsequently provided valuable research material. Outstanding graduate-student assistants at various times in the United States and Taiwan who succeeded one another over the years were Ray Wang, Jian Zhang, Hui-min Ng, Wang Xiang, Cheng Hsin-syi, Lin Wei-yu, and Wang Jian-jiun. During the last year, May Miao provided exceptional work on the original Chiang Diaries in the Hoover Institution and many other matters, and Stefan Hahn played a valuable role in collecting the photos in Taipei.

Funding for this wide-ranging travel and research came from an advance from Harvard University Press, along with generous grants not only from the Smith-Richardson Foundation administered by the Asia Society, but also from the Himalaya Foundation and the Chiang Ching-kuo Foundation. All of the foundations involved in the project fully carried out their commitment to have nothing to do with the contents of the book or the judgments it might express.

My principal editor was my son John Taylor, who did a Herculean job of carefully trimming tens of thousands of words and hundreds of pages and suggesting reorganization here and there, thus making the original text much more cogent. Likewise, manuscript editor Julie Carlson's fine-tuning, corrections, and suggestions were invaluable. Joyce Seltzer, my principal editor at Harvard University Press, was also a key adviser whose professional input and personal encouragement were essential. Among the readers who provided insightful and critical comments were Fredrick Chien, Alice Lyman Miller, David Dean, David Lampton, Charles Martin, and Robert Sutter, but as customary I bear full responsibility for the final work. Finally, my wife, Betsy, supported me with affection, care, endurance, and inspiration.

Note on Romanization

The two common ways to Romanize Chinese names into English are the Wade-Giles system used on Taiwan and the pinyin system employed on the mainland. Readers and editors strongly recommended that I switch to the pinyin system, which increasingly is being adopted on Taiwan. I have thus employed pinyin with some important exceptions, including the familiar names of the Chiang Kai-shek and Charles Soong families and Sun Yat-sen; idiosyncratic personal names such as Wellington Koo, H. H. Kung, C. K. Yen; and names of authors writing in English like Tang Tsou, Hung Mao-tien, Ray Huang, and many others, including my graduate-student assistants who have their own preferred spelling of their names. The English-language editions of books originally published in Chinese will show the names of the authors as they appear on these editions—for example, the *Memoirs of Li Tsung-jen*. Other exceptions are traditional well-known names in English of prominent places and features in China, including, of course, "China" as well as Manchuria, Inner Mongolia, Harbin, Mukden, Port Arthur, Peking, Nanking, Chungking, Quemoy, Matsu, Taipei, Amoy, Hong Kong, Macau, Canton, Tibet, Swatow, Gobi, Yangtze, and Yellow River. As I noted in a previous book, *The Generalissimo's Son,* the Chinese have sensibly chosen not to change their traditional names for foreign places, like Jiujinshan (Old Gold Mountain) for San Francisco.

Every duty is a charge, but the charge of oneself is the root of all others.

Mencius

Prologue

When Chiang Kai-shek died in April 1975 at the age of eighty-seven, I was China desk officer in the U.S. State Department responsible for political affairs regarding the People's Republic of China. I was traveling in China at the time, and since a separate office dealt with Taiwan, I did not pay much attention to the passing of the old Kuomintang leader. I had shaken hands with him two or three times at receptions in the early 1960s when I was a young Foreign Service officer stationed in Taipei. He had seemed small and frail, and I was surprised that he had such a weak handshake.

At the time of his death, my view of Chiang was similar to that of many China specialists. He was best known as a brutal dictator who ruled for almost fifty years and as a failed military leader who, in a grand reversal of fortune, lost the mainland to Mao Zedong. As far as I knew he had no redeeming qualities except for being considered personally honest; even so, he tolerated widespread corruption among his supporters. He seemed like a man who had possessed no authentic principles or ideals and had few if any achievements. Among the books that had influenced me in my view were Harold Isaacs's *The Tragedy of the Chinese Revolution*, Graham Peck's *Two Kinds of Time*, André Malraux's novel *Man's Fate*, and Barbara Tuchman's *Sand against the Wind*.

When almost twenty years later I was writing *The Generalissimo's Son*, a biography of Chiang's son and successor, Chiang Ching-kuo, I found that the elder man was not the cardboard figure often portrayed in the West and certainly not the icon described in the hagiographies that were so prevalent in Taiwan until the 1980s. But still, in my biography of his son, I portrayed the father by and large in the usual manner. When asked by Harvard University

1

Press to follow up my biography of Chiang Ching-kuo with a book on the Generalissimo, I thought long and hard about what promised to be a challenging and lengthy project. Although my view of Chiang was mostly negative, as a moderate liberal and foreign policy pragmatist I thought I could bring an open mind to the subject.

I was further encouraged by several scholars who confirmed my impression that no comprehensive Western biography of Chiang had been written that took serious advantage of the mountains of new archival material gradually becoming available not only in Taiwan and China, but also in Russia, Japan, and the United States. Drawing on this material, China scholars were producing hundreds of perceptive and balanced studies both of specific events and of the domestic and international dynamics involved in Chiang's long tenure on the mainland and Taiwan. Soon, moreover, the Chiang family was to begin a phased release of the Generalissimo's original diaries spanning fifty-six years.

New, anticipated interviews along with earlier ones conducted for *The Generalissimo's Son* meant that I could draw on hundreds of discussions with relevant individuals, including many who knew Chiang Kai-shek—though the window for such conversations was rapidly closing due to their advancing age. Pulling all this together seemed like a fascinating and worthy project. I also saw this new work, like my biography of the son, as a distinctive vehicle for telling the story of China's painful, erratic, and often brutal transition from a decaying, medieval, foreign-led dynasty at the turn of the twentieth century to a country one hundred years later marked by peace, stability, and rapidly growing prosperity and strength.

In the course of my travel, research, and interviews for this project, I came to see Chiang as a highly contradictory figure. He was a modernizing neo-Confucian who supported women's rights and had no trouble with an openly cross-dressing lesbian who was his wife's niece and close companion. He was a strong nationalist, extremely bitter about Western humiliation of China in the past, yet he was not bothered a bit by the fact that all his grandchildren—except two born out of wedlock—were Eurasian. He had little charisma and was generally not liked by his peers, but his determination, courage, and incorruptibility led at times to wide popularity. He was an inhibited man, yet one with a commanding personality—a staid, seemingly humorless individual who had a terrible temper but also smiled easily, sobbed deeply at times, and, judging by his diary, was a devout Christian. Yet in response to a threat to the nation's survival, its unity, or his own rule, he could justify atrocious acts—and in his journals he at times fell into paranoid rants. But during times of crisis he was usually calm and analytical, reflecting an understanding of the dynamics and possibilities of the matter at hand. At certain times on the mainland he had an impressive military record, but in 1948–1949 it ended in a debacle. Unconsciously or not, he also set the stage for Taiwan's development of a vigorous democracy.

Chiang's diaries cast new light on major historical events, including his surprising rise to leadership of the Kuomintang, his early leftism, his bloody purge of the Communists in 1927, the repeated warlord rebellions, his appeasement of the Japanese for five years while building up his army, his famous 1936 kidnapping in Xi'an, his united front with the Communists and its breakdown, and his long, unique relationship with Zhou Enlai. New insights also emerged into his military strategy at Shanghai and afterward, his and Stalin's mutual efforts to involve the other in war with Japan, his long struggle with General Joseph Stilwell, and his serious military commitment to the Allied cause after Pearl Harbor—a steadfastness that was marred by the repeated failure of the Allies to live up to their commitments to him and his calculated but unwise reaction to those failings.

Dramatic postwar events included the doomed Marshall Mission to China, Chiang's disastrous decision to stake everything on the battle for Manchuria, and his plans as early as 1946 to retreat to Taiwan. Finally, Chiang's journals and other new material also provided a wealth of previously unknown facts about his long reign on Taiwan after his retreat to the island, such as his brutal and senseless intimidation and suppression of potential opposition from the native Taiwanese, unhappiness with his leadership within the KMT, his pessimistic views of the wars in Korea and later in Vietnam, his private recognition early on that he would not live to see the "recovery of the mainland" even while publicly announcing that "counterattack" was imminent, his use of such warnings to receive special treatment from Washington, his success likewise in turning to his advantage the two near-nuclear Quemoy crises, and his turndown of a risky proposal by Eisenhower that could have led to a U.S.-China war.

Other critical events followed, but in Chiang's last great crisis he responded pragmatically—among other things hiding his great loathing of Nixon, whose détente with Mao he apparently learned about first from Zhou Enlai. Among major world leaders in modern times, the duration of Chiang's uninterrupted, active engagement at the highest levels in transformative world events may well be unsurpassed. For this reason, however one judges Chiang Kai-shek's mixed record over this tumultuous period, his story is a compelling one.

I

REVOLUTION

1

A Neo-Confucian Youth

It was late on the morning of August 15, 1945, in the battered and steaming city of Chungking, when an aide brought a shortwave radio into the large but spare office of the leader of China, Chiang Kai-shek, and tuned in Radio Tokyo. A few minutes later, Chiang, who understood Japanese, listened quietly as the Japanese people for the first time in history heard Emperor Hirohito, the "Voice of the Crane." The incarnate divinity embodying the soul of Japan was telling them to "bear the unbearable." In order to save innocent lives from the "cruel" bombs of the enemy, he had accepted the Potsdam Declaration of the Allied leaders. In other words, the great samurai nation had accepted unconditional surrender.

Finally, it was over. Under Chiang's leadership, the Chinese people had fought an eight-year bloody war, half the time virtually alone. The war of resistance had actually been raging on and off since Japan's seizure of Manchuria in 1931. By the end of the fourteen-year conflict, at least three million Chinese soldiers had been killed or wounded, and perhaps another million or more had died of disease and malnutrition.[1] The vast majority of those soldiers killed—over 90 percent—had been in Chiang's armies, not those of the Chinese Communists. Nine million Chinese civilians, too, died in the war— bombed, shot, burned, starved, or drowned. Tens of millions had been refugees for various periods, with huge numbers dying in camps or while on the move. Middle-class families who had fled Shanghai and other cities had seemingly lost everything. Millions of farm families, victims of the Japanese Imperial Army's policy of "burn all, destroy all, kill all," were destitute, and whole cities had been burned to the ground—some, like Changsha, more than once.

* * *

Early that evening, Chiang went to a stifling hot broadcast studio in Chungking to announce the news to the Chinese people. He stood before the microphone, straight and erect as usual, dressed in a simple military uniform. His secretary, Chen Bulei, was sick, so he had written the speech himself. He adjusted his horn-rimmed glasses and spoke to the nation in his clear, high-pitched voice, reporting the surrender, praising the Chinese for their heroic struggle, but also giving credit to the Allies.[2] "The truth that justice must overrule force," he began, "has finally been proved . . . the historic mission of our national revolution has been achieved." Most Chinese could hardly understand his thick Ningbo accent, but they knew what he was saying. Then he spoke about the future: "I believe all our compatriots as well as the people of the world must hope that this will be the last war all the civilized countries have to fight. If so we will not count the price we have paid and the time we have wasted, although we all have suffered indescribable cruelties and humiliations." Then in a concluding, oblique reference to the internal enemy, he said, "The current peace procured by our armed forces is not the full realization of eternal peace. Only when our enemies are also conquered in a battlefield of reason, become thoroughly repentant, and are transformed into peace lovers like us, can we say that we have reached the final aim of this war—human peace in eternity."[3]

Repeated first by those few with radios, the news spread by shouts and runners through all the cities and towns of China. Most villages had no radios but virtually all seemed to hear the report within an hour. In cities from Shanghai to Chungking and in rural areas almost everywhere, women, men, and children—a few hundred million—poured into the streets yelling and cheering, while Japanese soldiers remained in their barracks in a daze. Millions upon millions of firecrackers crackled through the night and into the next day. In Chungking, Americans joined the celebration, and crowds "clutched at their uniforms, cheered them, and suffocated them, shouting 'Mei guo ding hao!'" (America is the very best!)[4] It was arguably the biggest celebration in human chronicles and the greatest moment in Chinese history. The fact that the Americans and the atom bomb had defeated the Japanese did not distract from the sense of a great Chinese victory. After all, the Chinese felt that they had done their part all those years, tying down more than a million Japanese soldiers and as many as a thousand enemy warplanes.

In his radio address, Chiang told his countrymen that the people of Japan were not their enemy and "not for a moment [should Chinese] think of revenge or heap abuses upon the innocent people of Japan."[5] As he left the radio studio that night, the American reporter Theodore White observed that for a fleeting moment "the smooth exterior of this contemporary mandarin was punctured, the weariness and strain of the years broke through." Then the lapse was gone. "Nodding but unsmiling, the Generalissimo, as Westerners called him, passed through the cheering crowd and returned to his command center."[6]

Some five hundred miles to the north, in Mao Zedong's headquarters in the dusty town of Yan'an, the celebration of V-J Day was muted. The American team at the CCP base noted that the Communists welcomed the news with a seemingly hastily organized, spiritless demonstration. No doubt the CCP leaders recognized that people throughout China perceived the triumph as Chiang Kai-shek's victory.

But neither Chiang nor Mao was celebrating that night. The Chinese Nationalists and the Communists had been fighting off and on for almost twenty years to see which party and leader would guide China toward fulfilling its dream of becoming a great nation restored. Both leaders talked of engaging in negotiations to achieve a peaceful and united China, but they each knew that in fact a battle to the death had begun. Steel determination and a stubborn stoicism had seen both men through grave defeats and long periods when their respective enemies were much stronger than they. At this moment, Chiang seemed to have every military and economic advantage and he was more popular and powerful than he had ever been. Indeed, the Americans were in the process of completing the training and arming of thirty-nine government divisions, offering Chiang his best hope in the coming struggle. But Mao was more optimistic than Chiang. The presence of the Americans in Yan'an symbolized a dormant but grave problem for Chiang—the disdain for his leadership within the U.S. government. At the same time, Chiang himself had long privately believed that Communist officers and troops as well as Communist civilian cadre were on the whole more dedicated and disciplined than their Kuomintang counterparts—a conclusion that darkened his outlook even at this moment of triumph.

Chiang sent a telegram to Mao assuring him that "eternal peace was on the horizon" and "sincerely" inviting him to "our temporary capital" to discuss problems of "critical importance to our nation."[7] Mao clearly viewed the invitation not only as a stratagem in the Nationalist-Communist contest to appear the most desirous of unity and peace, but also as a demonstration of what he had long seen as Chiang's disingenuous but strong belief in his own benevolent and moral character—not to mention Chiang's skill at political manipulation and crisis management.

The story of Chiang's rise is one of persistence, loyalty, physical courage, personal honesty, and a willingness to acknowledge that much of the tragedy that befell him and China was outside his control. He evolved from a narrow-minded military officer with only one year's training at a military preparatory school into a national leader with a strategic vision who understood the dynamics of Chinese and world affairs and, often, how best to play a weak hand. He also rationalized coldhearted strategic and political decisions on the mainland and ruthless acts of military as well as secret-police suppression on Taiwan—acts that cost the lives of thousands—by citing the exigencies of a terrible war and the need to achieve national goals. He was as hypocritical as the next undemocratic powerful leader, but he was not a cynical man. Like others at the time, including the Communists, for a long period he had important connections with a secret political and criminal society, and taxes on the opium trade in part financed his government on the mainland. Still, he thought of himself as a moral, sincere, up-to-date Confucian Christian, and he was motivated less by the desire for personal power than by a vision of a unified, modern, independent China. Mao, of course, justified the killing of a million land owners and other atrocities in a similar manner, pointing to the need for a violent destruction of the old order to achieve the transcendent goal of an egalitarian, utopian society.

I

In the late nineteenth century, Chiang Kai-shek's paternal grandfather, Jiang Yubiao, owned 30 mu (about five acres) of farmland outside Xikou, a small hamlet in the coastal province of Zhejiang, 150 miles south of Shanghai. Misty mountains with dramatic names like "Tiger Killing" and "Hole in the Snow" rose in the near distance and sparkling waterfalls cascaded into the valleys. Local teas such as "Wuling" were and still are among the most popular and expensive teas produced in China.

The Chiang property in Fenghua County consisted of hillside bamboo, terraced rice paddies, and some tea bushes. Those five acres made the Chiangs economically one of the top five families in the Xikou area and thus part of the rural elite, though not of the rural gentry.[8] A few years after the end of the bloody rebellion against Manchu rule in the 1860s by the messianic, crypto-Christian Taiping, Jiang Yubiao rented out his agricultural land and opened a salt shop in the village. Salt was a government monopoly and Chiang obtained his license through some connection or service, perhaps related to helping end the Taiping Rebellion.

The store did not begin to prosper until Kai-shek's father, Jiang Suan, took over the business and procured a license to sell wine, another official monopoly. The three generations of Chiangs lived together in the rooms above the store just across the road from Shan Creek, a usually placid stream that regularly flooded in the spring and on occasion submerged the first floor of the salt shop. Suan's first wife left behind a son, Xuhou, and a daughter, Ruizhun. His second wife died without having children, and in 1886, Suan took as his third wife a young woman named Wang Caiyu, who was twenty-two when she wed the forty-two-year-old widower with children. A close relative of both the Jiang and the Wang families recalls that Caiyu came from a "very poor village of hillbillies" whose principal crop was bamboo, and like many Chinese women of the day, she hobbled about on bound feet.[9] (Originally an affectation of the rich, by the late nineteenth century a good percentage of Chinese parents—though not the ruling Manchus—were tightly strapping the feet of their daughters, a painful practice that bent the instep and reduced the length of the foot by about a third.) Nonetheless, Caiyu was intelligent and shrewd and would prove ambitious for her children.

On October 31, 1887, a year after her marriage, Caiyu bore a son in a room above the salt store. The grandfather gave the boy his generational name, Ruiyuan (good omen), and his official name, Zhongzheng (balanced justice). In keeping with the Chinese custom, Ruiyuan eventually was given an honorific name—Jieshi, literally "upright stone." Decades later, the revolutionary leader Sun Yat-sen would call him by the Cantonese pronunciation of this name, and the outside world would also come to know him as "Kai-shek."

The Jiang's general store thrived and in 1889 the family moved into a two-story merchant's house a hundred feet or so down Wu Ling Street. Two new daughters soon appeared, but only one, Ruilian, survived infancy. In 1894, the grandfather, Jiang Yubiao, died, and that same year Caiyu gave birth to a second son, Ruiqing, a beautiful boy with a lovable disposition who became his mother's favorite. Kai-shek, her first born, was neither handsome nor academic, and grew to be rebellious and temperamental. According to his own account, his mother had "to use the birch repeatedly in order not to spoil me."[10] Yet he was articulate and had a volatile and commanding disposition. In 1896, Kai-shek's fifty-year-old father, Suan, suddenly passed away and afterward Suan's brother adopted Kai-shek's older half-brother, Xuhou, who inherited the salt shop. The nine-year-old Kai-shek inherited the house, the bamboo grove that produced forty to fifty (probably Mexican) silver dollars a year, and the rice paddies.[11] The women in the family received nothing substantial.

The young Kai-shek's early education consisted of sessions with a series of neo-Confucianist tutors, men who had passed only the lowest-level exam to become a "Shengyuan." Before he was nine, he was said to have read "the four books"—*The Great Learning, The Middle Way (The Doctrine of the Mean)*, the *Analects*, and *Mencius*.[12] All these texts, however, were written in classical Chinese characters, and Chinese contemporaries recalled in their memoirs that they were mostly "gibberish" to the students, who spent hours a day "squawking [the words] out loud in unison."[13]

When he was fourteen, Kai-shek's mother, a strong-willed widow, decided for several reasons that it was time for her son to have a wife. As a relative suggests, Caiyu wanted a strong and willing daughter-in-law for herself and a servant for her son.[14] For the bride, his mother chose a young, rather plain nineteen-year-old named Mao Fumei with only partially bound feet from a nearby poor village called Yandou. The wedding was sometime in the winter of 1901–1902, after which Fumei moved into the Chiangs' two-story upper-class merchant's house.[15] That Fumei did not become pregnant until eight years later suggests the marriage went unconsummated for a long while.[16]

In 1903, Chiang took the new civil service examination and failed. This did not deter his mother, who promptly enrolled her son in the Phoenix Mountain Academy, a small Confucian school in Fenghua, the county capital. The curriculum was heavily classical, but included lessons in English and mathematics.[17] And while Fenghua was a small town it was far more sophisticated than Xikou; it was there that Kai-shek saw his first "big-nosed" foreign missionary—and where he began to regard as an embarrassment his illiterate peasant wife who kept house for him.[18] According to various reports, Fumei complained to her friends that Kai-shek frequently beat her.[19] But according to local lore, she retained her warm and friendly nature, perhaps because, as Chiang later recorded in his diary, his mother often sided with her against him.[20]

Kai-shek, the very filial son, and his ambitious mother, Wang Caiyu. Courtesy KMT Party History Institute.

II

Two distinct forces shaped Chiang Kai-shek's identity and outlook during these formative years. The first influence was Confucianism and even more importantly, neo-Confucianism, which originally was a reaction to the catastrophe of the Mongol invasion of China in the thirteenth century. After that calamity, Chinese scholars and officials were obsessed with restoring and safeguarding the cultural heritage of China, and by the late nineteenth century, when Chiang was a student, art, music, and arithmetic were considered far less important than rote learning of the more than two-thousand-year-old

Chinese classics and preparations for writing the infamous "eight-legged" essays on these ancient collections.

But the aspect of neo-Confucianism that most affected the young Chiang was its emphasis on character development, self-discipline, and the conscious cultivation of the self, along with a sense of duty, courage, honor, and activism rather than passive contemplation. The concept of the superior man emerged from the nurturing of these principles. At the same time, the neo-Confucianists promulgated the traditional Confucian concepts regarding moral behavior and the hierarchy of obligations in society. The Confucian approach to morality was based on the political order and had a political objective—the creation of a harmonious, orderly society. It was an ethos shaped by millennia in which extended families lived in crowded, clan-based agricultural communities where survival depended on a combination of independent, household farming and communal maintenance of infrastructure and order.

The second force that shaped the political views and career of Chiang Kai-shek, and virtually all other Chinese leaders of the twentieth century, was the extraordinary loss of sovereignty, territory, and self-respect that China—the center of world culture in the eyes of its people—had suffered during the previous sixty years. When Kai-shek was born, once nomadic Manchus from north of the Great Wall had been ruling China for some 250 years. But while the foreign rulers maintained their own Tungusic tongue and forbade intermarriage with ethnic Chinese (the Han), they adopted most other aspects of Chinese culture. Like other foreign dynasties before them, their system of rule depended on the cooperation of the Chinese mandarins as well as the rural elite and gentry. But in the 1840s, the Qing dynasty endured a series of mortifying military defeats and humiliations at the hands of Westerners, who not only did not look Chinese, but also did not accept the benevolent supremacy of Chinese culture as had the Manchus and other barbarians surrounding China.

The ensuing record of defeat, dishonor, and loss of sovereignty was astonishing. Over the last half of the nineteenth century, military routs at the hands of the Western powers forced China to accept, among other humiliations, the import of opium, and by the early 1900s, millions of Chinese—possibly tens of millions—were smoking the drug. The weakened dynasty was also compelled to surrender all legal, including criminal, jurisdiction over Westerners in China to their respective embassies or consulates, and to open specified "treaty ports" to Western traders and missionaries, who received special rights and privileges that even the richest Chinese did not enjoy. In addition the powers took over management of China's customs collections in order to extract payment for the brief punitive wars that they had been "forced" to wage against China.

The British, French, Germans, and Russians all gained separate special rights, leases, or concessions over Chinese territory. In the American West, anti-Chinese riots broke out and the U.S. Congress banned Chinese immigration. Then Japan, only forty years out of its medieval isolation, joined the feeding frenzy. After a short war it forced China to pay a large indemnity and cede Taiwan to it "in perpetuity." The Chinese were stunned that the "dwarf pirates," who had derived their culture from China, now possessed a modern army and navy like those of the European powers. Even some ossified mandarins realized that drastic changes had to be made, but the powerful empress dowager and the Manchu court brutally suppressed the "One Hundred Days of Reform" begun by the young Emperor Guang Xu.

In 1887, the year of Chiang Kai-shek's birth, a twenty-one-year-old medical student in Hong Kong named Sun Yat-sen embraced the idea of creating a modern, democratic China. Sun, who had spent some years in his youth living with his brother in Hawaii, earned his medical degree in 1892, but two years later decided to become a full-time rebel dedicated to the overthrow of the Qing dynasty.[21] Sun's first uprising in Canton ended abruptly in failure and he fled the country, eventually taking up exile in Japan. There he was supported by Japanese liberals and radical nationalists, both of whom foresaw a Sino-Japanese alliance against the West. Sun also thought Japan was China's natural ally.

Kai-shek was an impressionable thirteen-year-old when China's humiliation reached a new low with a patriotic but ludicrous and bloody antiforeign movement that burst on the scene. The Boxers, who engaged in martial exercises called "harmonious fists" and were dedicated to the extermination of all foreigners in China as well as Chinese Christians, brutally butchered tens of thousands of converts and several hundred foreign missionaries, including women and children. The empress dowager feared the Boxers but she hated the foreigners even more, and the initial success of the Boxers convinced her they did indeed have magical powers, so she sided with them.

But a joint expeditionary force put together by the foreign powers, including Japan and America, easily routed both the messianic warriors as well as the Manchu Army and arrived in Peking just in time to save several thousand Chinese converts and foreigners. The occupying troops then went on their own rampage, killing, looting, and raping, and the powers forced China to pay a staggering indemnity—about $5 billion in 2002 U.S. dollars—and to agree that it would not establish defenses along its own coast.[22]

Most Chinese, including the most obscurantist mandarins, the Manchu court, and the illiterate majority, now understood that the West and Japan were not only militarily stronger than China, but also far ahead in science, technology, medicine, education, public services, and standards of living. A stream of edicts from the Forbidden City called for, among other things, a new system of government schools featuring mathematics, engineering, and modern science. Implementation of the reforms, however, was painfully slow.[23]

By this time Japan and Russia were vying for control over China's Northeastern provinces, the region Westerners called Manchuria. This vast homeland of the Manchus was four-and-a-half times the size of Great Britain, rich in mineral resources, and despite the supposed ban on migration, was populated with far more Han Chinese than ethnic Manchus. In 1905, Japan and Russia went to war in the region, and in May the Japanese fleet under Admiral Togo Heihachiro annihilated a large Russian fleet that had sailed from the Baltic to do battle.

To informed Chinese, this defeat of a European power was a stunning and encouraging development, and it was probably a principal catalyst in young Chiang Kai-shek's decision to make the military his career and to do so as a Chinese republican revolutionary, not as a defender of dynastic China. In February 1903, he transferred to the Golden Arrow Academy in Ningbo.[24] Mao Fumei made the move with him, but after a few months Chiang, irritated with her country manners, sent her back to Xikou to live with his mother.[25]

In February 1906, Chiang decided to transfer to an academy back in Fenghua called the Dragon River School, apparently attracted by a neo-Confucian but modern teacher named Gu Qinglian. Gu encouraged his new student's fascination with the scholar-generals—Wang Yangming (1472–1529) from Zhejiang and Zeng Guofan (1811–1872) from Hunan. Wang had taught that self-understanding was the key to moral action, and that ethics only had meaning when converted to direct, decisive, and spontaneous action. But as a "Confucian gentleman," he also stressed rectitude, integrity, honesty, and loyalty.[26] The philosophy seemed to resonate with the young Chiang Kai-shek. Hollington Tong, a teacher at Dragon River with a room on the same floor as Chiang, recalled that every morning the eighteen-year-old student would rise early and stand erect on the veranda in front of his bedroom for half an hour, with his lips tightly pressed, a determined look in his eyes, and his arms folded, concentrating on his goals for the day and in life.[27] It was a ritual he would continue as long as he could rise from his bed.

After only a few months at Dragon River School, young Chiang informed his family he was going to Japan. In a dramatic demonstration of his anti-Manchu views he cut off his queue or pigtail, an act that alarmed his relatives and neighbors. At eighteen, Chiang was already a revolutionary.

III

A year earlier, leaders of various anti-Manchu organizations and a group of students had met in Tokyo and formed a new revolutionary movement called the Alliance Society (Tongmenghui), electing Sun Yat-sen as "Zong Cai" or director-general. By then, Sun had developed his synthesis of major trends in modern political theory and practice—the Three People's Principles (San min zhu yi), emphasizing nationalism, democracy, and the people's livelihood. It was a centrist and moderate platform that reflected the intellectual currents of the day in the West.

Again leaving his estranged wife behind, the young Chiang from Xikou lived several months in the Chinese community in Tokyo, studying Japanese at his own expense and getting to know this extraordinarily clean and orderly country where everything seemed to run efficiently—the tram system, the police, the utilities—and of course, the army.[28] Chiang's self-support at this time indicates that in addition to property he had inherited a modest or more than modest nest egg, probably in Mexican silver dollars. But he was getting nowhere in his hoped-for military career, and he returned home to take the highly competitive exam for the Central Army School at a place called Baoding near Tianjin. He passed the exam, spent about a year at Baoding, and then passed another exam that allowed him, and a few other cadets, to go to Japan for training. Back in Tokyo, he entered the Shimbu Gakko, a school set up especially for Chinese students wishing to attend a Japanese military academy.

Chiang was aloof, which caused resentment among many of his fellow students, but he did have a few companions, including another former Baoding cadet from Sichuan named Zhang Qun, who would remain his closest friend

On right, Chiang in Japan, ca. 1909, with his friend, Zhang Qun, with whom he would be close for the next sixty-six years. Courtesy KMT Party History Institute.

through life, and an intense young man from Guizhou named He Yingqin, one of Chiang's key future generals. On free nights, Kai-shek and his companions passed their time drinking in cafes and sometimes visiting favorite Japanese girls in selected brothels. It was at this time that Chiang developed his penchant for beautiful and expensive prostitutes, women with whom he would often become infatuated.

On liberty days from the school, however, he also kept up his contacts in Tokyo with Chen Qimei, a fellow provincial from Zhejiang and an important activist in Sun Yat-sen's Alliance. Chiang had met him during his earlier stay in Japan. Under Chen's auspices, Chiang and his friends joined the Alliance and Chen became Kai-shek's mentor and "big brother."[29] Chiang also became friends with a Chinese law student at Japan University named Dai Jitao, a precocious and determined young man whose passion for restoring China's national integrity greatly impressed Chiang.[30]

During these years, Chiang read *Min Bao* (People's News), the revolution-ary paper of the Chinese exiles in Japan, which introduced him to Western thinkers from Jean-Jacques Rousseau to John Stuart Mill. Two of the editors and key writers of *Min Bao* were Wang Jingwei and Hu Hanmin, Cantonese men who were both destined to play a major role in the future Kuomintang. Wang, a graduate of Japan University's law school and a gifted polemicist and thinker, was, along with Dai, one of the golden young men among the revo-lutionaries in Japan. The *Min Bao* advocated not only the overthrow of the Manchus through any means, including assassination, but also the national-ization of land and support for the revolutionary cause around the world.

This decidedly leftist world view adopted by many Chinese studying abroad, including Chiang, became a cause of growing concern to the ruling oligarchs in Japan, and in 1907 the government asked Sun Yat-sen to leave the country. For their part, many of the Chinese students were becoming alarmed at the steady march of Japanese imperialism, particularly in Korea. The Alliance leaders, however, were not prepared to criticize Japan and still made cooperation with Japan a key objective of the party. Before his depar-ture, Sun had even intimated in a speech in Tokyo that he would have no complaint if Japan felt it deserved northern Manchuria in return for its assis-tance to the revolutionary cause.[31]

That same year, Chiang's mentor, Chen Qimei, moved from Tokyo to Shanghai where he set up a secret headquarters to prepare for uprisings in Ji-angsu and Zhejiang, provinces that were adjacent to Shanghai. During his summer vacations Chiang joined Chen in the city and worked on various projects. In the summer of 1909, Chiang decided to break up with Mao Fumei, but his mother had learned from a fortune-teller that her son's first wife would bear a son who would become a high-ranking official. Caiyu took matters into her own hands and escorted her daughter-in-law to Shanghai. When they arrived in the city, Kai-shek at first refused to go along with his mother's plans, but after she wept and threatened to kill herself, Chiang agreed to do his duty. Fumei lived with Kai-shek over the hot summer months. When she told Chiang she thought she was pregnant, he sent her home.[32]

On April 27, 1910, Fumei delivered their son. Very likely it was Caiyu who, recalling the fortune-teller's words, chose the boy's name "Ching-kuo" (save or manage the county). The character *kuo* henceforth would be the gen-erational part of the given name of any children Kai-shek might have.[33] On Ching-kuo's first birthday, his father took no note of the event.[34] His lack of attention to his new heir reflected not only his estrangement from the boy's mother, but also his increasingly deep involvement in the movement led by Sun Yat-sen.

After graduating from Tokyo's Shimbu Gakko in November 1909, Kai-shek and his friend Zhang Qun received orders to report to the 19th Field Artillery Regiment at Takada in order to gain real army experience—a requirement for entering the Japanese Military Academy for combat officers. Life in the barracks was spartan, the training was severe and demanding, and the troops often performed their drills in the snow. Chiang responded positively to the challenge, but he was still considered standoffish, known for his temper, and by his own admission, "cantankerous."[35] His seriousness and dedication may have won him grudging respect, but he did not stand out as a cadet; he finished only fifty-fourth among the sixty-two Chinese students in his academy preparatory class.[36]

The Japanese officers and sergeants who knew Chiang in the regiment, however, remembered his willingness to submit to rigid discipline and to render absolute loyalty. A sergeant recalled his "impressive and forbidding expression."[37] Some twenty years later, after Chiang had taken over leadership of the KMT and purged the Communists, he visited his old division commander in Japan, General Nagaoka. Upon leaving this meeting, Chiang left the general four characters on a panel, which loosely translated read "Do not be ungrateful for the instructor's teaching." That summed up the secret of Chiang's success, Nagaoka thought: "loyalty and gratitude."[38]

In the summer and fall of 1911, Chen Qimei was busy planning uprisings in cities throughout the Yangtze Valley, including the city of Wuhan up the Yangtze in Hubei province. One of the plans that Chiang was involved in as a junior assistant was the projected revolutionary takeover of his home province of Zhejiang, but he was back in Japan when on October 9, an explosion in one of the rebels' secret bomb factories in Wuhan alerted the authorities to the plot. The police seized a Revolutionary Alliance membership list and began arresting suspected soldiers. On "Double Ten Day" (October 10, the anniversary of the 1911 revolution), rebel officers and sergeants in the Eighth Division responded by shooting loyalist officers.

The revolution was on.[39] In many provinces, senior military officers of the dynasty's New Army broke away and became the de facto political leaders or military governors. In a few cases, bandit chiefs in alliance with army units

Chiang as a trainee in a Japanese artillery regiment just before the 1911 Revolution, which he and Zhang Qun rushed to join. Courtesy KMT Party History Institute.

seized control. With this, the "warlord period" began, although it did not yet have that name. When Chiang Kai-shek heard about the events in Wuhan, he, Zhang Qun, and 120 other Chinese cadets immediately left their barracks, mailed their uniforms back to their base, and began searching for a quick passage home.

Now twenty-four years old, Chiang had spent almost three years in Japan and he spoke and read Japanese fairly well. He had no real Japanese friends, having stayed in Chinese circles except for women of the night, but Japan had had a major influence on him, strengthening what were presumably natural proclivities of temperament. He left with a strong sense of military discipline, revolutionary fervor, and deep loyalty to his cause and its leader, all of which combined to give him an extraordinary sense of both political commitment and personal courage and honesty. He saw the samurai's "bushido" code of honor unto death as the principal reason for Japan's military success, but he also believed that critical to Japan's modernization was the disciplined efficiency of most things in Japanese life, from the train system to education to manufacturing. For the rest of his life he would believe that patriotism and national spirit—most especially identity with the mother country above family, possessions, and one's life—were the keys to restoring China's dignity and its place in the world. The problem was that China seemed to lack the public strength of mind and character and the fervent nationalism necessary to build such an army. As Sun Yat-sen lamented, China was "a heap of sand."

Sailing from Nagasaki on a Japanese freighter, Kai-shek and Zhang Qun disembarked at a wharf in the Japanese area of Shanghai. Foreign concessions controlled three-quarters of the city, but the population was still 95 percent Chinese. The main avenues—like the principal foreign business street called the Bund along the Whangpoo River, and commercial Nanking Road—were bustling with a diverse population of Chinese, including *compradors,* who dealt with foreign firms, and local merchants—all in pigtails and wearing long white or gray gowns topped with high-collar mandarin jackets. Also in the mix were Western bankers and Japanese traders in black Western suits, a few in newfangled automobiles that competed for space with coolies who were balancing loads on bamboo poles, pulling rickshaws or carts, or pushing big wheelbarrows. But the lifelines of Shanghai were its hundreds of narrow, winding *hutongs* or alleys, where at any one time until around midnight a hundred thousand or so shoppers, laborers, housewives, craftsmen, students, clerks, and the unemployed crammed past endless rows of fruit stalls, noodle or dumpling stands, workshops, food markets, tea houses, and other outlets. Proprietors in shorts and shirtwaists sat on stools and gossiped with their neighbors and passersby. As they hurried along in the human torrent, the two friends were disappointed, for in no way did it look like a great revolution was under way.

When they arrived at the secret Alliance headquarters, Chen was in the midst of planning attacks on the arsenal in the Chinese part of Shanghai and on the provincial government headquarters *(yamen)* in Hangzhou, the Zhejiang capital about ninety miles away. In Hangzhou, pro-revolutionary army officers were ready to move. Chen put Chiang in charge of an armed "dare-to-die" contingent made up of Fenghua county fishermen reinforced by members from both the Green and Red gangs of Shanghai.[40]

These "secret societies" or gangs were clandestine, revolutionary, quasi-religious fraternities of sworn "brothers." Decentralized and autonomous, the gangs became involved in and ultimately dominated what today would be called "organized crime," while also often running legitimate businesses. But the strong anti-Manchu roots of the gangs kept them committed to the goals of Chinese nationalism. Their membership included prominent merchants, bankers, and other respectable citizens. Sun Yat-sen himself had deep ties to the Triads in Guangdong province, one of the largest anti-Manchu societies in south China.

Chiang was ecstatic with his first combat assignment. He had dreamed of this moment, and he wrote his mother to tell her "I have sworn to give my life for the revolution" and to ask her forgiveness for "neglecting my filial duties."[41] But Kai-shek played only a minor role in the overthrow of the Qing regime in Zhejiang. On November 4, 1911, the turncoat New Army regiments seized the key public buildings in the provincial capital, and while the small "dare to die" corps led by Chiang took part in the attack, there was little or no resistance: the Qing governor had already fled to Shanghai and the Qing provincial army commander at the last minute joined the revolution. Kai-shek probably performed well, but provincial gazetteers of the day, who reported in detail on the planning and execution of the coup, did not even mention him.[42]

The day before the attack in Hangzhou, Chen Qimei's forces, including 3,000 members of the Green Gang, seized the governor's *yamen* in Chinese Shanghai, the police headquarters, and the Jiangnan arsenal. "Five-colored flags" of the Shanghai revolutionaries suddenly appeared in thousands of windows and rooftops, while euphoric crowds thronged the streets. Soon a half million shorn pigtails lay on the ground.[43]

Chiang returned to Shanghai from Hangzhou to find that his mentor, Chen Qimei, had become *dudu* or military governor of Chinese Shanghai. Chen reportedly appointed Chiang commander of the Fifth Regiment, but with so many graduates of the Japanese Military Academy available who had also participated in the uprising, it is more likely he simply told the young Chiang to retain as many of the fishermen and secret society members in his "dare to die corps" as he could, recruit others, and try to transform them into a disciplined outfit. Chen instructed his commanders to raise their own money to maintain their units.[44]

On a cold, damp Christmas Day, Sun Yat-sen, who had been in the United States on October 10, arrived in Shanghai by ship and went directly to a house in the French Concession where he was visited by supporters. Among them was a young Australian correspondent for the *New York Herald* named William Henry Donald, who had been an adviser to the Revolutionary Alliance since 1908. The visionary and idealistic Sun and the pragmatic Donald immediately formed a close relationship. Decades later, Donald said his role was to "guide" Sun and "talk to him like a Dutch Uncle," but ranking KMT officials described Donald as primarily involved in public relations. Some suspected he was secretly reporting to the British.[45] At a minimum, he would be a close and interested witness to events over the next twenty-five years.

On December 29, the revolutionaries convened a provisional national assembly in Nanking, which was dominated by the Revolutionary Alliance. Tao Chengzhang, head of the rival Restoration Society, wanted to be the new governor of Zhejiang but Chen Qimei was determined the job would go to an Alliance supporter.[46] The dispute grew more hostile until Tao, fearing for his life, tried to back out of the dispute and hid in a hospital. Chiang, however, identified the address and Chen dispatched assassins, who on January 12 sneaked into Tao's room and killed him. Chiang implied that he was not the person who orchestrated the assassination but "took responsibility in order not to get Chen Qimei in trouble." Gazetteers and newspapers of the day did not mention Chiang in connection with the murder, which suggests he was probably not present when the event occurred.[47]

On January 6 the new National Assembly in Nanking inaugurated Sun Yat-sen as the provisional President of China. At this point, a prolonged political standoff seemed likely between Sun and Yuan Shikai, the Manchu-appointed prime minister and former army grand marshal who controlled North China. All the foreign powers except Japan were pushing for Sun to step down. Then in a surprise development, Sun, only sixteen days after achieving his lifelong ambition of becoming President of a republican China, suddenly offered to resign in favor of Yuan. Sun was willing to make this painful concession in order to achieve national unity under a coalition government, a grand and selfless gesture that reflected both high idealism and naiveté. While Chiang Kai-shek, like Chen Qimei, strongly disagreed with Sun's decision to give up his position, the resignation of a leader who put the cause ahead of himself and the acclaim he received as a result impressed Chiang mightily; he would resort to this technique several times in his long career. On March 12, Yuan Shikai officially became President but exercised clear authority over only half of the old Manchu Army. In what would in retrospect be a major mistake, Sun agreed that the capital should be in Peking and the provisional government should move there.

Chen Qimei stayed on as military governor of Shanghai—one of the most important provincial-level positions—and Chiang continued to drill his troops in the city while seeking funds to keep them fed. But the revolutionary excitement had ended and the young officer spent much of his time discussing politics with Qimei, Dai Jitao, and a few other colleagues from his Japanese days. Chiang's quick temper was a matter of growing legend. Qimei's home was on Mohawk Road near the race course in the International Settlement (essentially the British sector, where Americans and Japanese also lived and did business). One day, Chiang went to visit Qimei and when a sentry would not let him in, he hit the fellow. Qimei strongly admonished his young protégé about this bullying behavior and "some people" urged him to get rid of the young man. But Chen Qimei apparently believed that such bellicosity had its usefulness in a military leader. Chiang himself saw his quick temper as a problem: he continued to chastise himself for displaying anger toward ordinary people like rickshaw pullers.[48]

There were several important developments in Chiang's personal life during this period. One night at a brothel, Chiang met a strikingly attractive young woman named Yao Yicheng, a native of Suzhou, a town renowned for its ancient canals and its beautiful women. He fell in love with her and took her to live with him in his small flat in the French Quarter.[49] And around this time, Chiang became friends with Qimei's nephew and aide, a frail eighteen-year-old named Chen Guofu, as well as Guofu's twelve-year-old brother, Lifu, both of whom were staying at the house on Mohawk Road. Years later, the two Chen brothers would constitute the famous (or infamous) "C-C Clique" in the KMT. Through Qimei, Chiang also got to know the antique dealer Zhang Renjie, a fellow Zhejiangese and stalwart Sun supporter. Zhang was a diminutive man with a deformed foot, the scion of a wealthy silk merchant, but an intellectual anarchist rather than a right-wing conservative. This connection brought Chiang closer into the inner circle, but still he had not come to the personal attention of Sun himself.

Meanwhile, the most intellectual of Chiang's friends from his Japanese days, Dai Jitao, had become the Tom Paine of the postrevolution period, producing a newspaper called *Min Quan Li* (People's Rights) that became "the conscience of China's new republican politics."[50] After Sun's withdrawal from office, Dai continued attacking Yuan Shikai, as well as the emerging de facto political order in which self-interest and provincialism seemed quickly to be overriding the national cause. Dai leaned distinctly to the left, stressing not only economic development but also anti-imperialism and evolutionary socialism. Chiang was an avid reader of *Min Quan Li*.

Sun's Alliance Party now amalgamated with four others to form the Kuomintang (Nationalist Party) or KMT. Under the leadership of Song Jiaoren, a close comrade of Sun and a hero of the struggle both in Canton and Wuhan, the new KMT enjoyed a majority in the National Assembly. Nonetheless, in August, after four weeks of talks in Peking, Sun declared that Yuan should be President for ten years and promptly accepted a position in his government as head of railway affairs.[51]

At this point, Chen Qimei gave up his powerful position as civil and military chief of Chinese Shanghai and together with Chiang sailed off to Japan. The two men may have feared assassination.[52] While they strongly disagreed with Sun's cooperation with Yuan Shikai, they had asked for and received Sun's permission to leave the country. Chen and Chiang were already thinking of the need for a second revolution, but it seemed that the political arrangement between Yuan and Sun might hold for several years. Chiang returned briefly and secretly to Shanghai, found Miss Yao, and brought her back with him to Japan.[53]

IV

In March 1913, the KMT in general elections won control of the National Assembly and tensions with Yuan Shikai increased, ending in the assassination of the acting President of the KMT, the energetic Song Jiaoren, apparently by agents of the Yuan government. The fragile coalition quickly collapsed and Sun Yat-sen's "second revolution" now began. Chen Qimei and Chiang returned secretly to Shanghai and pulled together as many fighters as possible, including Chiang's old "regiment." The Green Gang, bought off by Yuan's side and perhaps the European authorities in Shanghai as well, this time declined to join in the revolution. After all, its members were anti-Manchu, not pro-democratic, and the Manchus were gone. Attacks by the rebels on the arsenal and the Woosung forts failed and, according to heroic accounts by friendly biographers, Chiang was almost captured, but he and his men escaped and in disguise fled down the river. Yuan then began a terror campaign in which he executed thousands of KMT supporters, including KMT members of the National Assembly. He ordered the complete dissolution of the KMT and the arrest of Chen Qimei and other KMT leaders. Chiang Kai-shek was still too little known to make the list.[54]

Chiang and Chen fled back to Japan and in August 1913, with his once high-flying optimism in tatters, Sun himself escaped to Yokohama. He assumed his old Japanese name, Nakayama, and established himself in secret quarters provided by Toyama Mitsuru, the head of Japan's ultranationalist Black Dragon Society. Sun immediately began to draw up plans for a rejuvenated, disciplined, and clandestine movement to be called the Chinese Revolutionary Party. Members were to swear an oath of loyalty to Sun as the undisputed director-general of the party and commander in chief of the revolutionary army. Wang Jingwei and others refused to accept this condition and left Japan, but Chen Qimei and Chiang Kai-shek agreed on the need for total commitment and took the oath. The new platform adopted Sun's original idea that, after the revolutionary movement attained power, democracy could be introduced in China only after an indefinite period of "tutelage" under the Revolutionary Party and military rule. In other words there would be an authoritarian, military regime of some indefinite tenure.[55]

Among Sun's supporters who fled to Japan was the remarkable Charles Jones Soong. Soong had spent eight years working and studying in America, earning a degree in divinity at Vanderbilt University. Back in China, he worked for several years as a Methodist missionary, then went into Bible publishing, and finally mass-produced and marketed dried noodles. The noodle business made him a fortune, and he soon became a key financial backer of Sun Yat-sen. After Soong and his family arrived in Japan, his eldest daughter, Ai-ling, a graduate of Wesleyan College in Macon, Georgia, who had become Sun Yat-sen's secretary in Shanghai shortly after the formation of the Republic, resumed this role.

In December, Chiang Kai-shek had his first meeting with Sun, who was impressed with his dedication and soon sent him on a dangerous mission back in China.[56] Soong Ai-ling noticed the slim officer with the thin mustache, high forehead, and thick Ningbo accent. She asked her sister, Chingling, who had just returned from America as another Wesleyan graduate, if she would be interested in a match with Kai-shek. Chingling said no.[57] Unknown to Ai-ling, Sun had developed a deep attachment to her and one day declared his feelings to Ai-ling's father and asked for her hand. Like Chiang Kai-shek, Sun had been married as a youth to a simple farm woman and she was with him in Tokyo. They had two grown children. For a Chinese man, a divorce was as easy as snapping one's fingers, but Sun and the Soongs were Christians—Ai-ling's father, aghast at the proposal, adamantly refused.

Some months later, Ai-ling married H. H. Kung, the head of the Tokyo Chinese YMCA. He came from a distinguished family of merchants and bankers in the Northwestern province of Shanxi, held degrees in economics from Oberlin and Yale, and like all Chinese named Kung was supposedly a direct descendent of Confucius.[58] As a youth, Kung had become a Christian, and a few years later, relatives hid him when Boxers descended on his hometown of Taigu and slaughtered his friends—Chinese converts as well as missionaries and their families. After returning from America, Kung did not take up one of the lucrative family businesses but instead accepted a job as head of a mission school. Following the revolution of 1911, Kung became an adviser to the twenty-eight-year-old Shanxi military governor, Yan Xishan. Then, apparently unhappy with Yan's cooperation with Yuan, he resigned his position and took the YMCA job in Tokyo—confirming that money and power were not his preoccupation in his early manhood.[59]

The twenty-one-year-old Ch'ing-ling, more slim and alluring than her sister, eagerly took over her job serving the revolutionary hero, and he promptly lusted after her.[60] Sun Yat-sen did not declare himself either to Ch'ing-ling (who was twenty-six years younger than he) or, knowing his attitude, to her father. Ch'ing-ling's affection for her boss remained purely political and platonic.[61]

At this point, Charlie Soong, possibly sensing Sun's affection for his second daughter, decided to take his family back to Shanghai. Ch'ing-ling resisted going, but her father insisted. Shortly after they arrived home, she smuggled out a letter to Sun, who wrote back saying he needed her help urgently in Tokyo. With the aid of a maidservant, who put up a ladder against her window, she escaped one night and was soon on a Japanese ship headed to Yokohama.[62] When Sun Yat-sen greeted her in Tokyo, he had already gone through simple divorce proceedings and he proposed to her. Startled, she nevertheless agreed and they were married the next day. She was barely twenty and he was forty-eight. She resumed her work as his English-language secretary and also began doing his secret coding and decoding. Charlie Soong disowned his daughter and swore he would have nothing ever to do with Sun Yat-sen again.[63]

In the spring of 1914, Sun sent Chiang to Shanghai to try to pull together the scattered and demoralized revolutionary underground. Several of Chiang's men were arrested, and after another narrow escape he returned to Japan.[64] The very next month, Sun dispatched him to explore the possibilities of ties with one or more of the warlords in Manchuria.[65] The Chinese generals in that region, nominally under Yuan Shikai, were cool to Chiang's suggestions of a third revolution, and he prepared to sail back to Tokyo. But before he did so, he wrote a letter to Sun predicting that with the outbreak of the new internecine European war of unprecedented scale, Japan would exploit the situation to advance its position in East Asia.[66]

On January 18, 1915, Tokyo secretly delivered the Twenty-one Demands to Yuan Shikai, which included de facto Japanese economic control of Manchuria and cession to Japan of the previous German rights in Shandong and Fujian, the province opposite Taiwan. Other demands would have made China effectively a semi-colony of Japan.[67] Outrage spread across China and among Chinese overseas, but Sun Yat-sen, oblivious to this sentiment and still hoping for large-scale Japanese aid, submitted to Tokyo a series of proposals that seemed to surrender even more Chinese sovereignty than Japan had asked for. The Peking government accused Sun and his revolutionaries of selling out the country, and again many Sun supporters left Japan.[68] When Yuan Shikai continued to stall on the Twenty-one Demands, Japan mobilized its troops. Yuan then yielded, authorizing a treaty incorporating most of the twenty-one requirements.[69]

Again deserted by many of his close followers, Sun was at the lowest point in his career, and he valued more deeply than ever the loyalty of the few who stuck with him. Chiang understood and supported Sun's view that the ouster of Yuan Shikai and the creation of a unified and modernizing government took precedence over Japan's transgressions. This was another lesson that Chiang would remember: "First pacify the interior then resist the external [threat]" *(Rang wai bi xian an nei).*

Despite Sun Yat-sen's loss of much support, Chiang and Chen Qimei were soon once again in Shanghai hiding out in the *hutongs* of the French Concession, plotting new ways to promote the revolution. As a first step, they planned the assassination of the hated defense commissioner in Chinese Shanghai, Zheng Ruzheng. On November 10, two gunmen intercepted Zheng's car on Garden Bridge and killed him with a fusillade of shots. Next, an attack on police headquarters by "dare to die" teams led by Chiang and Chen Qimei went badly, and Chen and Chiang barely managed to escape.[70] The attempted putsch was widely considered a debacle and Sun Yat-sen's reputation sank further. Exhausted, Chiang fell ill. His mother came to Shanghai to be with him, and under her care he recovered.[71]

In February, Chen Qimei and Chiang Kai-shek—with a Japanese loan to Sun of US$700,000 and again protected by the Green Gang leader in the

French Concession, Huang Jinrong (also known as Pock-marked Huang)—
tried once more to rebuild the Chinese Revolutionary Army in Shanghai.[72]
But a group of assassins, probably paid by the Northern warlords, gained access to Chen's office on a ruse and shot and killed him and his bodyguards.
Two days later, Chiang, dressed in a white mourning robe, gave a eulogy that
was as much about himself as his fallen leader. "Who is there beside myself,"
he asked rhetorically, "to continue your work?"[73] In another telling comment,
he noted that some people had tried to "persuade you [Chen] to get rid of
me" and "you believed lies about me." But Chiang declared he did not care
about this betrayal and just wanted to have a clear conscience "after you are
dead."[74]

The graveside speech revealed that the twenty-eight-year-old revolutionary
was already entertaining high ambitions, a side to his character he had until
then kept in check, at least in public. Chiang, however, was well aware of his
flaws and in the diary that he began keeping in 1918 he listed a plethora of
traits he hoped to eliminate from his personality. These included being "ruthless and tyrannical; irritable; conceited; stubborn; wicked; . . . extravagant;
jealous; stingy; lascivious; arrogant; full of sorrow and indignation," and finally, given to "public spectacles, and boasting of wealth."[75]

Yuan Shikai ended the political crisis on June 6, 1916, by suddenly dying.
The Vice President, Li Yuanhong, who had been a mere figurehead, recalled
the elected National Assembly with its KMT majority, and Sun Yat-sen and
his wife returned to Shanghai and settled down at 26 rue Molière in the
French Concession.[76] During the next two years, Sun's circle of hardcore supporters stayed near each other in the relative haven of the French Concession.
When he was in Shanghai, Chiang Kai-shek now stayed sometimes with the
wealthy once-anarchist antique merchant Zhang Renjie, who had replaced
Chen Qimei as his principal patron and "teacher."[77] Chiang's concubine, Yao
Yicheng, had returned from Japan with him and he set her up in a house
in Ningbo, where he also spent some of his time. In September 1917, he
submitted to Sun a then seemingly far-fetched military blueprint for taking
Peking and uniting the country—a plan he called the Northern Punitive
Expedition.[78]

After Chiang's hectic involvement over four years in one adventure after
another for the party, little is known about his activities during the years
1916–1917. In his diaries, which begin in 1918, Chiang added brief recollec-

tions some time later for those years. In one entry for the spring of 1917, Chiang reports that Sun Yat-sen, who had left town for Guangdong, ordered him to collect—presumably from the German consulate—one million yuan that the German government had agreed to lend the movement.[79]

In copies of the original diaries for the years 1918–1922 and released by the Chiang family in 2006 to the Hoover Institution Archives, more than a hundred passages have been redacted—some by family editors but others decades ago by Chiang Kai-shek or his son. Given the ninety-year age of some of the deleted passages, they most likely related to behavior or opinions considered by the Chiangs to be embarrassing or incriminating, and as such they virtually demand speculation.[80]

It is conceivable that Chiang during this time was engaged in criminal activities with the Green Gang. In 1914, the British defense commissioner of Shanghai issued a warrant for Chiang's arrest in connection with an unspecified "crime in the Xiao sudo District." This charge probably related to the failed underground activity in Shanghai by Chiang and Chen Qimei about that time. In October 1917, the northern regime's military governor of Chinese Shanghai submitted a warrant to the British Settlement police charging that Chiang had been involved in the murder of a "prominent Chinese resident of the Settlement in 1910," that is, seven years earlier. This was possibly a mistaken reference to the murder of Tao Chengzhang in January 1913. In 1910, Chiang was spending only his summer months in Shanghai and there are no other reports of such a crime. Then in July 1918 the same Chinese military governor alleged that Chiang was "concerned in [an] armed robbery on Seward Road [in the Settlement] on October 18, 1917." The British authorities, perhaps believing the alleged events were part of the ongoing civil war between the Chinese parties and suspecting political motives on the part of the Chinese military governor, never arrested Chiang on these charges.[81]

A member of the family in 2008 stated categorically that no redactions made by the family refer to the Green Gang, criminal activity, or political matters but related to "personal," nonpolitical issues. References in the first category, however, could have been deleted by Chiang himself or his son, Ching-kuo.[82]

Beginning in 1918, Chiang began writing at least one diary page every day in classical Chinese rather than the vernacular. He continued the practice until 1972 when bad health finally put an end to it. As well as the main events of the previous twenty-four hours and his ruminations on them, he recorded the time he rose and went to bed, the temperature, and the weather.

The daily list of his own flaws, which continued well into the 1920s, was in part for Confucian effect, but they also seemed to reflect Chiang's recognition of the immaturity in his personal behavior. Yet he still did little to reform. Sun Yat-sen, for one, saw Chiang's serious shortcomings but also his valuable qualities as a tenacious activist and loyalist who had the dare-to-die spirit—a spirit undampened by the defeats and narrow escapes in which he had been involved.[83] The setbacks and dangerous escapades simply added to his sense of personal destiny.

After Yuan Shikai's death, political confusion reigned again in China, with one warlord coup in Peking following another. In 1918, KMT members of the National Assembly fled to Canton and together with Sun Yat-sen launched a "constitution protection movement," which entailed, in part, organizing a provisional military government with Sun as *da yuan shuai* or grand marshal of the Chinese Army and Navy.[84] The southern military rulers of Guangdong and Yunnan pledged their support, including a key Cantonese leader, Chen Jiongming, who commanded the loyalty of a major fighting force in the south, the Guangdong Army.[85] Despite his august titles, Sun Yat-sen did not have unchallenged authority even over the new Canton political establishment, which was split into factions.[86]

In March, on Sun's orders, Chiang Kai-shek joined Chen Jiongming's army as senior operations officer for an attack on the warlord of Fujian province.[87] Sun's fragile coalition in Canton, however, once again quickly unraveled as some of the southern warlords demanded more authority in the new government. Sun resigned as leader and went back to Shanghai.[88] Chen Jiongming and his 30,000-man Guangdong Army remained solidly behind Sun, and in July, Chiang Kai-shek successfully rallied units to recover a key town in Fujian. Soon afterward, his sharp temper and rigid personality created resentment among the Cantonese officers, and he briefly resigned, but Chen asked him to return and take up command of the Second Detachment, a force of some one thousand men.[89] Chiang trained the unit of raw recruits as best he could and led them over perilous mountains deep into enemy-controlled territory.[90]

A momentous event affecting China's and the world's future took place in November 1917 when the Bolshevik forces led by Vladimir Ilyich Lenin seized power in Petrograd and much of Russia. The next year, also in November, World War I ended and at the Paris Peace Conference the Chinese delegation, composed of representatives from both the Peking and the Canton governments, sought to recover all of Germany's ill-gotten rights in China now in the hands of the Japanese. President Woodrow Wilson supported the Chinese position, but, outvoted by the Europeans, settled for a compromise in which about half of the former German territorial rights in China were formally given to Japan.[91] When the provisions of the Treaty of Versailles became known in China on May 4, 1919, students, intellectuals, and most informed Chinese were furious. Mass demonstrations started at Peking University and spread to other universities, high schools, and factories. The "agitation against Japan," Chiang wrote, was "unprecedented," and demonstrated "the Chinese people's fighting spirit and patriotism." At last, he thought, the "revival of China" seemed certain.[92]

Before 1911, the focus of revolutionaries in China had centered on putting an end to China's backwardness and humiliation—conditions blamed on the alien Manchu dynasty. Now, as a Chinese-run republic, the nation had splintered into warring fiefdoms, was weaker than under the Qing, was raked over by internal wars, and continued to be exploited by the foreign powers. Reform-minded Chinese condemned the foreign imperialists for many of China's ills but also demanded a profound change in Chinese culture and national character that would enable their nation finally to stand up in the world. Dai Jitao was one of those who harped on this theme. The most famous, however, was the writer Lu Xun, who charged that Chinese tradition bred a regressive, stultifying culture and moral cowardice. Sun Yat-sen also had long been calling for a new breed of unselfish, patriotic, and heroic Chinese, a kind of a people, he believed, they had never been before. Chiang agreed, but his optimism about this transformation happening anytime soon was short-lived. He noticed that while the spirit of the people seemed on the upsurge, most Chinese were illiterate, and he feared it would be difficult to carry out a revolution in the character of the country within ten years. In terms of national fortitude, Japan was "way ahead."[93] Chiang would remain pessimistic on this score for the next twenty-six years.

While the May Fourth or New Culture Movement of 1919 gave yet another breath of life to the followers of Sun Yat-sen, it also provided a dramatic boost to the infant Marxist movement in China and its academic leaders, Chen Duxiu and Li Dazhao. An intellectual but politically ineffectual "third force" was also emerging, inspired by the writings of John Dewey–pragmatists like Peking University's Hu Shi, a Columbia University philosophy Ph.D. Virtually all Chinese, including the warlords, endorsed the goals of the May Fourth movement. The question was which party or faction or warlord would lead China as it sought to realize the common dream of national restoration and modernization.

Although Sun Yat-sen believed that Marxist class struggle was not relevant to China, he was increasingly inspired by news of the Russian Revolution and its ideals of a classless society and a worldwide end to imperialism. So was his officer from Xikou, Chiang Kai-shek, who had begun reading "A Chronicle of the Russian Revolution." He wrote in his diary that he would forever "admire" this great event in history, a "new epoch" in human affairs. Short entries like "reading Russian" and "studying Russian" repeatedly appeared in his diary, and he became a fan of the Communist *New Youth* magazine, reading it sometimes in the morning and then again in the afternoon.[94] These readings further stirred up Chiang's strong anti-imperialist sentiments directed at the West. The appeal of the Russian Revolution in China soared when Moscow announced it would relinquish its special rights in Manchuria and would cancel all the "unequal" tsarist treaties with China. To the long-suffering Chinese, this was a thunderbolt of goodwill.

At this time, Chiang was still in the field leading his detachment of the Guangdong Army. He was not attracted to the girls of Fujian, he wrote, but he could not get sex off his mind: "If I don't stop my desire, there will be no progress in my lifetime."[95] In March 1919, he took a break from the front lines and returned to Shanghai. There he stayed with a new lover he called "Jiemei." Judging by his passion for her, she was another beautiful woman. He had become estranged from his concubine Yao Yicheng because of her frequent gambling, and now was desperately in love with Jiemei. According to his diary, at one point he was at the dock, ready to return to his post in Fujian, but could not bear to leave her and so stayed behind several more days. He even wanted to marry her, but according to a letter she wrote him, even though she wanted to stay with him forever, she did not want to be bound by a formal marriage contract.[96] During this time, despite their estrangement, Chiang continued to stay off and on with Yao Yicheng in Ningbo.[97]

One consequence of Chiang's promiscuous lifestyle was that he believed he had become sterile because of diseases passed on to him by one or more sexual partners over the years. As a result, he became more attentive to his only biological child. On his way back to the front in Fujian, he stopped in Fenghua and asked his old Confucian tutor, Gu Qinglian, to spend time with Ching-kuo, now nine, and assess the boy's potential. In Chiang's first letter to Ching-kuo, he reported that Gu had said the boy was "not brilliant" but "liked to study very much." Chiang then sent his son off to Fenghua to attend his old school, the Phoenix Mountain Academy.[98]

At the same time, Chiang informed his mother and Fumei that his concubine, Yao Yicheng, would be arriving in Xikou with a handsome three-year-old boy he had adopted. The boy, whom Chiang had named Wei-kuo, was the son of Chiang's friend Dai Jitao and Dai's former Japanese mistress. Yicheng and Wei-kuo took up residence in the Chiang home, but Fumei and Yicheng did not get along, and eventually Chiang Kai-shek's uncle took in the boy and his foster mother.[99] Judging by the letters he sent the two boys, Kai-shek felt more affection for his fine-featured adopted son than his biological heir, who was less handsome. In the spring of 1920, Chiang brought his mother to the city for medical treatment, but shortly thereafter he himself came down with a bout of typhoid. Recuperating, he had more time to lament at length in his diary about his need for self-improvement.[100]

Inspired by his increasingly leftist thinking, Chiang's writings during this period turned to the "cunning and snobbery" of businessmen and capitalists. "If we don't restrict private capital," he wrote, "laborers will never have the chance to enjoy pleasure and freedom." After a landlord tried to cheat Yao Yicheng, he remarked, "The rich do nothing but embezzle others."[101] But when on July 1, 1920, the new Shanghai Securities and Commodities Exchange, set up by party supporters to provide funds to the KMT, officially began, he leaped into investment as a sideline. With various loans, Chiang and Chen Guofu formed an investment firm "to speculate in stocks." After an initial drop, the original capital of 3,000 silver dollars (probably Mexican) soon soared to 30,000, and in early December his rich patron, Zhang Renjie, purchased shares for him worth 3,500 silver dollars in another investment company. The market, however, quickly started to slide downward and by the end of the year, Chiang confessed to his diary that he had lost seven or eight thousand dollars, an amount he apparently owed.[102]

But Chiang had little time to devote to following the market. On September 30, 1920, Sun appointed him chief of staff of the Second Guangdong Army, the highest position Chiang had held. In his diary Chiang promised that "in order to diminish people's doubts about me, I am not going to take any [political] position," implying that he would stick to military matters and not cause resentment by his outspoken criticism of others and his volatile temper. By the time Chiang reported for duty as chief of staff, Sun Yat-sen's Guangdong Army, supported by sympathetic bandit gangs, river pirates, and

10,000 coolies, was gradually gaining ground against the southern warlords who had forced Sun's resignation back in 1918. Throughout October, Chiang was almost constantly on the move with his battalions, "winning one victory after another."[103] But the pressure of combat frayed his temper and again he frequently lashed out at his fellow officers, who nicknamed him "Big Gun."[104]

In a letter that fall, Sun sternly upbraided him for his provocative temperament:

There are but few in our party today who have the dual qualities of military expertise and political dedication. Only you, my elder brother, are with us, you whose courage and sincerity are equal to those of Zhu Zhixin [a heroic officer who was killed in battle in August] and whose knowledge of war is even better than his. But you have a fiery temper, and your hatred of mediocrity is too excessive. Thus it often leads to quarrels and renders cooperation difficult. As you are shouldering the great and heavy responsibility of our party, you should sacrifice your ideals a little and try to compromise. This is merely for the sake of our party and has nothing to do with your personal principles. Would you, my elder brother, agree with this? Or would you not?[105]

Chiang did agree, but he still seemed unable to change. After he and Dai got into a fierce argument, he wrote an apologetic but defensive note to his "Elder Brother": "When a man has been so lacking in self control and so rude, how can he have the face to see his beneficent teacher and helpful friend again?"[106] In his reply, Dai reiterated his deep affection and admiration for Chiang but then described him as "extremely self-willed to an almost incorrigible extent." Chiang wrote back accusing his friend of sharp words, prejudice, and sentimentality, and in a revealing passage, complained: "The trouble with me in society is that I go to extremes. Therefore, I have [a few] lifelong sworn, intimate friends but no ordinary boon companions or social acquaintances."[107] Chiang's strong points—the intensity of his commitment to the cause and doing the job right, and not suffering fools lightly—were also his weaknesses.

In late October, Chen Jiongming and the Second Guangdong Army entered Canton, where a "huge welcoming crowd greeted him."[108] Chiang was still in the field fighting remnants of the Guangxi forces, but he returned to Shanghai on November 12 to brief Sun Yat-sen, then left the next day for Zhejiang and home because of his mother's poor health.[109] The following month, Sun Yat-sen, supported by the Chinese Navy's First Fleet, arrived in Canton from Shanghai, and almost immediately he and Chen Jiongming disagreed about the direction of the new Canton government. Sun favored a strong central government and plans for an early launching of the military expedition to overthrow the Northern warlords, while Chen wished to concentrate on making Guangdong a model province and seeking a peaceful agreement on a federal framework for all of China.[110]

Chiang, in his dispatches from Xikou to Sun Yat-sen, pushed for an early military campaign to capture all of Guangxi province as the first stage in preparing for the Northern Expedition. When Sun again urged him to report for duty, he replied with some impudence, "Sir, you have been in Guangdong for fifty days, but not a single order has been issued for mobilization. That is what I am waiting for. As soon as the date for the start of the campaign is decided, I will come to serve you without waiting for your call."[111] In late April 1921, with the support of the Peking government, a Guangxi warlord army again invaded Guangdong. On May 10, Chiang belatedly arrived in Canton to join Sun Yat-sen and the Second Army, but on the night of May 24, he dreamed of a landscape of "white and boundless" snow. He felt this portended ill for his mother and hastened back home.[112] His foreboding proved correct and his mother died on June 4.

General Xu Chongzhi led the Second Army against the Guangxi interlopers, who panicked and whose commanders deserted. A few wobbly biplanes of the Cantonese air force had no bombs but instead dropped logs on the fleeing enemy soldiers.[113] General Xu pursued the invaders deep into their home province and soon, to the surprise of many, the Guangdong Army and officially the Canton government controlled all of Guangxi's major cities. Sun, who had been made President again on May 4, believed it was now time to launch the long-promised Northern Expedition to unify the country. He moved his headquarters to exotic Guilin, the Guangxi capital city surrounded by gorgeous peaks made famous by Chinese artists over the centuries.

V

Despite the victory in the south, Chiang remained in Xikou, enacting all the traditional rituals of a Chinese son mourning the death of a parent. He planned the funeral and selected the burial site. Halfway up the winding path to Hole in the Snow Monastery, he built a small cabin for himself with a stunning view. There he spent many days in meditation, ignoring pleas from Sun to join him in Guilin. It was during this time that Chiang came to a "more mature understanding of his personal strengths and flaws."[114] As he frequently detailed in his diary, his personality and behavior were deeply flawed. Although often introverted, he could be a bully, self-righteous, and arrogant. His demanding leadership style and short temper alienated his peers as well as his subordinates. His superiors saw the steel will of a commanding personality but they could also be irritated by his abrasive manner. In addition, he lusted after prostitutes even after he had taken a concubine. While this was not unusual behavior for a young military officer, it was not what a Confucian scholar-soldier would do.

Walking in the mountains, Chiang drew up a new life plan, promising to adhere in practice and not just in theory to the ideals of neo-Confucianism—sincerity, rectitude, serenity, constancy, and determined action. In his mind, morally rearmed, it was "evident what will ensue."[115] Though only thirty-four years old and a mid-ranking officer in Sun Yat-sen's forces, he now had no doubt as to his mission—he would be one of modern China's great men of destiny. At this point he probably saw his sacred mission as eventual commander of the military forces under Sun, leading the Northern Expedition to victory and unifying the nation. The idea that he could also be the successor to the fifty-eight-year-old, apparently healthy Sun also lurked in the back of his mind, but the prospect must have seemed far in the future. To prepare for this leadership role, he would need to rein in his temperamental, impetuous, and judgmental nature through self-criticism, self-discipline, and conscious character development.

During this time Chiang drew closer to his two sons than ever before. Wei-kuo was now five years old and thus still at an age when parental indulgence was in order, but Ching-kuo, at eleven, was the object of strict discipline. Still there were moments for father-son bonding. The young officer and his elder son visited the Hole in the Snow Monastery and hiked around the Thousand League Falls. Chiang found Ching-kuo to be a "very teachable boy" and the adopted Wei-kuo "lovable."[116]

In early September, Chiang finally started back south to join Sun in Guilin. Along the way he stopped in Shanghai to review with Chen Guofu a recent downward plunge in their investments. Only a few months before, Chiang had felt "terrific" about the way the market had recovered since the previous December. But brokerage firms in Shanghai were now closing their doors every day, brokers were going bankrupt, and some, including one of Chiang's friends and co-investors, were committing suicide.[117] He himself seems to have made and then lost 200,000 (possibly Mexican) silver dollars between his initial investment in 1920 and the end of the collapse in 1922.[118] Chiang's creditors were soon harassing him for the 2,500 silver dollars that he still owed. Sun sent a certain amount to help and the rest was written off through a friendly intervention.[119] The gang leader, Huang Jinrong, invited Chiang's "fifty or so creditors" to dinner and told them to consider the young officer's debts to be his (Huang's). The guests were impressed and, according to Huang, quickly forgave the arrears, and as a result Chiang became his "disciple."[120] Chiang blamed his financial losses on his own lack of attention and experience, but concluded there was "nothing regrettable" about the matter. As with military and political defeats, he could accept the blame for this large personal loss and then completely put it out of his mind.

But the experience in business made Chiang even more leftist in his thinking than before—as well as more committed to the revolution and his military career. Soon thereafter he tried to set up some sort of a school at Xikou for local children but, according to his diary, the gentry for some unexplained reason thwarted the effort. He swore he would never return home until this rural elite had died.[121] Another time, he observed that the reform of the nation required an end to a government of gentry and merchants. In fact, throughout his long career, Chiang would have no special affinity for capitalists and capitalism. Still, he consistently believed that Communism could not be carried out in China and that class struggle was a disastrous concept; like warlords and secret societies, the moneyed elite and the wealthy gentry were realities of power that had to be dealt with and utilized.[122] As for his own revolutionary career, he now believed it was "enormous and bright."[123]

While in Shanghai, Chiang ran across a young girl, Chen Jieru, with whom he had become infatuated two years earlier when she was thirteen. According to her account, Chiang met her while attending a meeting at the house of her father, a paper merchant who supported the KMT. A few days later, Chiang managed to arrange a lunch with her. Afterward he lured the teen to a hotel room but she ran away. He then tried to persuade her mother to let Jieru become his concubine or—as she would insist in her memoirs—his wife.[124] Before receiving an answer, Chiang returned to Xikou for the final burial of his mother.

Chiang had waited until his mother's death to divorce Mao Fumei, his wife of twenty years. "For the past ten years," Chiang wrote his brother-in-law, Mao Maoqing, "I have not been able to bear hearing the sound of her footsteps or seeing her shadow . . . Enlightened and wise as you are, I think you may be able to plan for my happiness, freeing me from a life-long suffering."[125] After divorcing Fumei, Chiang also made a continuing monetary commitment to Miss Yao. He could have simply abandoned her, but he was grateful that she wanted to raise young Wei-kuo, and she and the boy went to live in Suzhou, her hometown on China's ancient Grand Canal. Meanwhile, Chen Jieru's mother reputedly agreed to her daughter's marriage (or more likely, concubinage) to Chiang Kai-shek. The wedding, Jieru claims, was on December 5, 1921.[126] Six years later, when Chiang was leader of the KMT and wanted to marry Soong Mayling, he would publicly assert that Jieru had been his concubine and not his wife.[127]

Whenever and how it began, by Jieru's account it was an unusual union. She asserts that she contracted a venereal disease on their honeymoon, not an experience she would likely invent. Chiang, she declares, in repentance swore never to drink alcohol, coffee, or tea again. From this time on, but not religiously, he usually drank boiled water rather than either wine or tea. Other aspects of his new austere lifestyle probably began about this time, including apparent faithfulness to Jieru; simple meals of everyday Ningbo food; a daily habit of early to bed, early to rise; and with notable ceremonial exceptions, usually dressing in a basic officer's uniform without insignia or ribbons—just a Pershing-like belt across the chest—or else in a traditional gown and a Sun Yat-sen jacket. These habits left a strong but always neat if severe ascetic impression and were meant as symbols of a new maturity, self-control, and seriousness—traits that did become more evident in his behavior.

Chiang was soon back as chief of staff to the Second Guangdong Army, busy with preparations for the planned advance north into Hunan and Jiangxi. But tensions increased between Sun and Chen Jiongming, and when Sun removed him as Guangdong governor and commander of the Guangdong Army, Chen's forces in Canton tried to seize power, forcing Sun to flee Canton in the dead of night. He escaped to the gunboat *Yong Feng,* which steamed down to the island of Whampoa. From there he dispatched a radiogram to Chiang Kai-shek, who was back in Xikou, addressed as a cover to Chiang's adopted son Wei-kuo. It simply said, "Emergency! Hope you come quickly."[128] In this crisis, Sun turned to the most determined man of action available.

Chiang hurried to Shanghai where he contacted Yu Xiaqing, president of the Shanghai general chamber of commerce and a longtime Sun supporter. Yu advanced Chiang 60,000 silver dollars (of unspecified type) for the cause. Carrying a huge trunk of silver, Chiang then sailed to Hong Kong where he rented a launch to take him up the Pearl River. On June 29, 1922, he joined Sun on the *Yong Feng,* which lay at anchor off Whampoa.[129] Chiang assumed tactical command of the gunboat, and under his direction it proceeded down the river. For five weeks, as the fighting raged between the Second Guangdong Army and Chen's troops, the *Yong Feng* anchored off a sweltering river port called Bai-e-tan. But then those on the ship learned that Chen Jiongming had defeated Xu Chongzhi as well as Sun's Yunnan and Guizhou allies.[130] On August 9, a British warship agreed to take Sun and his party to Hong Kong from whence they sailed on to Shanghai.

Chiang's time alone with Sun aboard the *Yong Feng* was the turning point in his career. Clearly, Sun was more impressed than ever. Chiang had performed well as a tactical military officer in the field, chief of staff in a multidivision unit, urban guerrilla, and clandestine operative involved in two assassinations and other covert assignments. He seemed the quintessential loyalist, but one not afraid to disagree strongly with the supreme leader. Moreover, despite Chiang's limited education, he was a thinker who kept abreast of world affairs, talking knowingly, for example, about the new society in Russia, and early on submitting a blueprint for the Northern Expedition. He was courageous and apparently honest. It was a great advantage that Chiang had no base of support except one wealthy patron, the diminutive Zhang Renjie. He had a few interesting friends like Dai Jitao and Zhang Qun, but no network of influence or, in the Chinese phrase, *guanxi*—no conflict of interest or personal source of power that could compromise his total devotion to Sun and the movement. This asset was to be key to his rise.

Seemingly defeated again, Sun was optimistic—he had a new promising source of support, the most important ever. The previous year, a Comintern agent with the code name Maring had met with Sun and suggested Soviet cooperation with the newly renamed Kuomintang (KMT) or Nationalist

Party in a united front with the new Chinese Communist Party (CCP), a small group that had formed earlier that year in Shanghai.[131] When Maring promised the KMT large-scale Soviet assistance in the form of military arms and supplies, Sun, who had long sought such aid from Japan and the Western powers, was delighted.[132]

Although Sun refused to form a united front with the Communist Party, he would permit CCP and Socialist Youth Corps members to join the KMT. For its part, the CCP, at the Comintern's insistence, reversed itself and agreed to accept a united front as a "bloc within the KMT."[133] The Soviet decision reflected the hope that with socialist-minded leaders like Sun Yat-sen, the KMT could be open to Communist influence. The Russians also felt they needed a strong, united, and friendly China serving as a bulwark against both Britain and Japan, and the KMT clearly was the more likely party to bring this about. At that point, the CCP had only 123 members and Maring did not consider it a serious organization. The KMT itself had only a few thousand members, but they included career military men, writers, teachers, and scholars, as well as the new and growing class of patriotic Chinese merchants and bankers. Most importantly, the KMT had an army.[134] Dual membership in the KMT, the Soviets argued, would provide the small group of Communists with respect and credibility.[135]

On January 17, 1923, Adolph A. Joffe, a ranking Soviet diplomat, visited Sun in Shanghai and set out a detailed plan of cooperation that covered the quantity of Soviet weapons, ammunition, and cash that Moscow would provide, the admission of Chinese Communists to the Kuomintang, and the radical reorganization of the KMT along Marxist-Leninist lines.[136] At this time, Chiang wrote a long letter to Sun setting out his views on political strategy. During the fight for unity and national leadership, he said, the KMT should emphasize power over principle, that is, it should be prepared to make unsavory but temporary allegiances, meaning with patriotic warlords willing to cooperate.[137] Sun agreed. When he returned to Canton, which Chen Jiongming had abandoned, Sun resumed the title of grand marshal or generalissimo instead of President. Military methods, he believed, were now to be paramount in the struggle.[138]

Sun appointed Chiang as Xu Chongzhi's chief of staff, and after Chiang arrived in Fujian in October, one of his first recommendations was to send more secret agents to bribe Chen Jiongming's senior officers. Chiang had long been involved in covert operations for the party and this was another example of the importance he gave this branch of service.[139] But the chief of staff position was a short assignment for Chiang to raise his status; Sun soon named him to lead a KMT mission to Russia to study its military and party systems. This was a plum assignment given the high priority Sun was now giving his relations with the revolutionary Soviet Union. Sun wrote Lenin and Trotsky introducing Chiang as his "most trusted deputy," and in mid-August Chiang and three other Chinese delegates, including two CCP members, departed on a steamer headed to Manchuria.[140] Taking a train from Dalian, the group crossed the Sino-Soviet border at Manzhouli and transferred to the Trans-Siberian Railway.[141]

With his three companions, Chiang spent almost three months in the USSR, inspecting units of the Red Army as well as naval and air bases. He also visited various organs of the Communist Party of the Soviet Union (then called the All Union Communist Party), military schools and academies, and even a chemical weapons factory. Chiang's main mission, however, was to seek Soviet support for a new Northwest military strategy he himself had devised and Sun had approved. This strategy called for a Soviet-supported KMT military base in the far Northwest region of China from which the KMT could attack the Peking government.[142] In a meeting with E. M. Sklyansky, deputy chairman of the Revolutionary War Council, and L. B. Kamenev, chief of staff, Chiang stressed that whichever plan was followed, the KMT was bent on early military action to eradicate the warlords and unite China. But the Russians were not happy. They did not want a Soviet-supported revolution to provoke the Japanese; moreover, early military action would not give the small Chinese Communist Party time to gain strength. Sklyansky told Chiang that military operations in China would only be possible after a great deal of political work; otherwise it would be an adventure "doomed to failure."[143]

Leon Trotsky also explained to Chiang that while the Soviet Union would provide the national revolution in China all the help that it could in the form of weapons, advisers, and economic aid, it would not send troops.[144] After these meetings, Chiang wrote that the Russian Revolution had succeeded because the workers knew it was necessary, the farmers desired a socialist system, and its leaders had allowed the nation's 150 ethnic groups to form a federal system to govern themselves. On November 25, the Comintern invited Chiang to address its Executive Committee. In his remarks, he implied that Communism was a possible goal for the next stage in China's revolution, but an open embrace of Communism by the KMT would undermine its primary objective—uniting all Chinese in the struggle to expel the imperialists.

At first, this seemed to imply that the KMT, as a matter of tactics only, could not for the moment embrace Communism, but then he told the committee directly that "proletarian revolution was not appropriate" for China.[145] After hearing Chiang, the Comintern's Executive Committee passed a resolution on the national liberation movement in China, stressing the role of the proletariat and the peasantry.

Chiang was upset by this direct contradiction of his explanation of the unity line and of Sun Yat-sen's rejection of class struggle.[146] In his diary, he called the Soviet government "conceited and autocratic" as well as "credulous, and hesitating." During a visit to Petrograd, he found the city "desolate," the citizens depressed, and their morale low.[147] He also noted that nationalization resulted in excessive centralization and a lack of qualified managers. In addition, "the equitable distribution of benefits" in socialist Russia was "difficult."[148]

But after requesting an opportunity to address a Red Army group, he spoke to four hundred soldiers, saying he was a revolutionary like them and his purpose was to learn from and unite with the Soviet Union in the struggle to defeat imperialism and capitalism. As he spoke, "his voice rose and his hands trembled." In mid-October, Chiang's delegation submitted a written report to the Comintern on the revolution in China. "Unless we [the world's people] overthrow world capitalism and imperialism," it stated, "it will be impossible for China to have real independence."[149] Although the concept of a world revolution against the hated imperialists appealed to him, for Chiang this statement was largely rhetoric. Nevertheless, he was sold on the Red Army's corps of political commissars, a system he would incorporate into the KMT armies, and on Komsomol, the youth organization of the Communist Party. "This [the Komsomol] is the best policy of the CPSU," he wrote.[150]

The trip to Russia played another critical role in Chiang's career, suddenly making him the party's principal expert on the powerful and still mysterious country to the north that was now seen as the key to the Kuomintang's success. When Chiang got off a Russian freighter in Shanghai on December 15, he was met by Liao Zhongkai, the KMT's financial chief, and the man selected by Sun to reorganize the party along Marxist-Leninist lines. Some KMT officials were deeply worried about Moscow's intentions, and Chiang assured them that the Soviet Union was sincere in its offer to help the KMT (although years later he was at pains to assert that he had returned home extremely alarmed about Soviet intentions, that was clearly not the case).[151]

Chiang finally arrived in Canton on January 12 and gave a written report to Sun.[152]

By this time, the Comintern's new resident political adviser to the Kuomintang, Mikhail Borodin, was in Canton reorganizing the KMT along Leninist lines. Under Sun's orders, KMT members now called their new CCP and Soviet allies "comrade." Nonetheless, Sun told the January 1924 KMT Congress that there were no marked class distinctions in China. Everyone was very poor or slightly poor, he said, which contradicted the Communist view of the need for a drastic social revolution. Sun was more susceptible to Soviet influence when it came to the military. He knew they would be pleased when he appointed Chiang Kai-shek to the Military Council and then to head the new school for training military officers. In June 1924, with Chiang on the platform beside him, Sun presided over the opening of the Whampoa Military Academy, made possible by a Russian gift of 2.7 million Chinese yuan plus a monthly stipend of 100,000 yuan. In his address on the occasion, Sun declared that the goal was to create "a new revolutionary army" modeled after the Soviet Red Army.[153]

At Chiang's request, General Vasiley K. Blucher, commander of Soviet Far Eastern forces, whom he had met in Siberia and immediately liked, arrived to serve as his chief of staff.[154] A few other Russian officers also joined the academy.[155] Instituting what he had learned in Moscow, Chiang appointed Dai Jitao as head of the political or commissar department, and under Dai as deputy director the CCP nominated a twenty-seven-year-old member named Zhou Enlai, who had just returned from two years of study in Japan and almost four years in France. Zhou was a Zhejiangese and he and Chiang easily conversed. As good-looking as a silent film star, Zhou was also good-humored, dignified, and polite, erudite and self-confident but modest and respectful. He was, in Chiang's eyes, a sincere man. Over forty-seven years of competition, struggle, and violent conflict between the KMT and the CCP, an unusual relationship would develop between the two men, including a mutual respect that during times of bitter interparty conflict would sporadically manifest itself.

The academy inculcated the *bushido* spirit, including the slogan "Love your comrades" *(ch'in ai ching-cheng),* as well as a code of honor that meant never retreat and death before surrender. These values could justify "defense

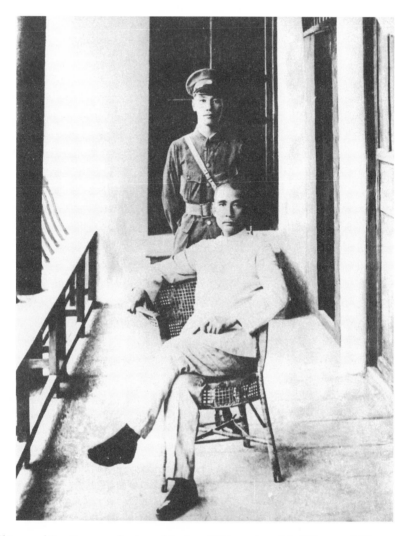

Chiang and Sun Yat-sen at the time of the June 1924 opening of the Whampoa Military Academy, which Chiang commanded and which would provide him a minority coterie of loyal officers for the next twenty-five years. Central News Agency, Taipei.

to the last man of untenable positions, attacking regardless of losses, and obeying orders without question." The ethos also incorporated the idea of collective security *(lien tso fa)*. All members of a unit accepted punishment for the failure or misdeed of one of them.[156] Classes on military tactics and weaponry comprised only a quarter of total class time. Most of the lectures consisted of political indoctrination, which at Whampoa meant focusing on the Three People's Principles but also driving home a Marxist-Leninist view of imperialism and an image of China as a splintered and exploited semi-colony. Despite the long classroom hours, the training was demanding and rigorous, requiring total and unquestioning commitment.

The CCP was given the right to nominate a certain number of candidates for each class, but the KMT recruiters signed up the majority—7,000 prospective cadets, mainly sons of middle- and upper-middle-class urban families or landed gentry.[157] From these lists, Chiang personally selected the first classes of about five hundred each.[158] It was an intensive three-month program—similar in length to a U.S. Army officers' candidate school for college graduates—turning out some 2,000 new officers in one year. This "Whampoa clique" would provide Chiang with his core supporters over the next twenty-five years.

The previous year, a prestigious group of eleven party veterans for the first time had warned Sun of growing Communist influence, including secret cells at all levels. Now, in June 1924, some of the same members submitted a petition for an order of censure against the CCP. The group confronted Borodin with CCP documents showing how the Communists secretly intended to use the KMT to achieve their revolutionary purposes, either by taking over the senior party or abolishing it. But the top KMT leaders in Canton, including Chiang Kai-shek, were not concerned. Chiang believed that "at this critical moment . . . ranks must be closed and members of the KMT must fight hand-in-hand with the Communists against the common enemy."[159] In one speech, Chiang praised the Russian Bolsheviks, who, he said, "work for the welfare of their country and the common people, not solely for their private interest."[160] Meanwhile, on October 7, 1924, the first shipment of 8,000 Soviet rifles arrived, soon followed by another shipment of 15,000 rifles, along with machine guns and artillery pieces.[161] By the end of the year, Moscow had about 1,000 military and political personnel working in China, and was providing the KMT 35,000 Chinese yuan a month, plus other subsidies.[162] From this point until 1960 the Soviet Union would—except for Japan's role as an invader and occupier and America's role as an ally during the war years of 1941 to 1945—be the decisive foreign influence in China.

As Soviet weapons were being stacked on the Canton docks, the Canton Merchant's Association and the KMT right wing formed a volunteer militia of 9,000, and, with the connivance of the British, Chinese conservatives in

Hong Kong sent a shipload of arms for this group. Hearing of this activity, Chiang assembled his cadets into a fighting corps, marched into town, and seized the arms. When the merchants threatened a general strike and the British in Hong Kong stoked up the engines of their gunboats, Sun ordered the weapons returned, but then fighting broke out between the militia and KMT forces. Sun finally authorized Chiang to suppress the militia, and Chiang completed the task within a few days.

Meanwhile, a new ruling coalition of the Northern warlords had invited Sun Yat-sen to Peking to talk about the future of the nation. Sun, whose health was slipping fast, felt this was his last opportunity for peaceful unification. But after his arrival in Peking, he became terribly ill and doctors diagnosed advanced and incurable cancer. He died on March 12, 1925, only fifty-eight years old.[163] Until that moment, Chiang had not been thinking in terms of political leadership as a near-term goal, but he had certainly considered the eventual possibility. Two years before, he quoted in his diary the words of the nineteenth-century scholar-general Zeng Guofan: "Profound change first of all depends on one or two persons who manage deeply, delicately, and silently, then their successors join in and God responds to their call." Rhetorically he asked, "Can you believe that I regard myself as one of those one or two persons?"[164]

At the time of Sun's passing, Chiang was still not in the KMT Central Standing Committee—the equivalent of the Soviet Politburo—and most insiders did not consider him among the contenders for leadership. Chiang also had enemies (during this period, he always carried a pistol).[165] But his image as a forceful military commander was spreading rapidly. His following among junior military officers and among the majority of ordinary party members was probably greater at this stage than that of any of the top post-Sun political leaders. To them, Chiang was not only an impressive soldier, he was also second to none as a disciple of Sun Yat-sen, a strong but independent leftist who seemed personally incorruptible, and one who had pursued his aims with "fortitude, confidence, and complete singleness of purpose."[166] Chiang was also thought of as an officer who knew the Soviet Union and was trusted by the Soviets. The burgeoning Soviet role in China had played a major part in Chiang's sudden rise in the KMT, and he knew it would play an even greater role over the next few years.

2

The Northern Expedition and Civil War

During the spring of 1925, foreign powers continued to act with impunity in China, but the Chinese people were increasingly unwilling to tolerate these affronts. In May, two months after the death of Sun Yat-sen, guards shot and killed striking workers at a Japanese-owned textile mill in Shanghai—and when student demonstrations broke out, British-led police killed eleven demonstrators. In Wuhan, British volunteers turned a machine gun on "thousands of rioting coolies" and when rioters burned down the Japanese and British consulates in Jiujiang, British and French marines rushed in reinforcements.[1]

The police attributed the disorders in Shanghai to "Chinese Bolshevik" activities, particularly "the radical branch of the Kuomintang."[2] A *New York Times* correspondent warned that "the radical party" (KMT) was determined to terminate "all special foreign positions, privileges and extraterritorial treaties" and lamented that unlike the powers' response to the Boxer Rebellion, now there was no consensus over how to deal with the challenge. Even Japan, the *Times* reporter warned, might "side with the position of the yellow world against the West."[3]

As spring turned to summer, the rioting grew worse. On June 23, 1925, a huge parade of anti-imperialist protesters, including boy scouts and Whampoa cadets, passed by the foreign enclave of Shamen Island. Someone fired a shot, and British troops on the island opened up, killing fifty-two people and wounding more than a hundred.[4] When Chiang learned that the dead included twenty of his Whampoa cadets, his hatred of the British surged to a new level. "The stupid British," he wrote, "regard Chinese lives as dirt." He took to writing daily some new anti-British dictum, such as "How can we emancipate mankind if we cannot annihilate the English?" At one point, he added, "The United States and France should also not be neglected."[5] Chiang's anti-imperialism was as strong as his Chinese patriotism, because he saw the two causes as symbiotic.

On July 1, the KMT proclaimed a National government at Canton and elected Wang Jingwei chairman of a new ruling political council. The two other key members of the council were Liao Zhongkai, the most leftist of the ranking seniors, and Xu Chongzhi, the top KMT general. Reinforcing his image as a noble, selfless officer, Chiang declined to be a member of the political council because he felt it was improper for a soldier to take part in the operations of a government.[6] Instead, he was again appointed to the new Military Council and at his suggestion, all military units, including those of the allied warlords, were now simply to be called the National Revolutionary Army. In addition he put himself in the forefront of those KMT leaders insisting on an early launching of the military campaign to unite the country, calling for the creation of seven armies or corps, the construction in Guangdong of several arsenals, and the incorporation of Guangxi into the revolutionary movement. This last goal meant integration into the Revolutionary Army of the new dominant force in Guangxi, the First Guangxi Army. This army, led by thirty-four-year-old Li Zongren, had by the end of 1925 impressively suppressed all rival warlord armies in the province. After prolonged negotiations, Li and his two close colleagues, Huang Shaohong and Bai Chongxi, formally agreed to join the National Revolutionary Army, but in fact they retained effective control over both the Guangxi Army and their entire province.[7]

Li, Huang, and Bai were not only warlords, but also unusually effective military leaders for their day, strongly committed to the restoration of China's unity and strength. Their Guangxi Clique, as it came to be called, would possess one of the best-led, most efficient, and—via taxes on opium passing through the province—well-fed and funded of all Chinese armies. The Guangxi Clique had no special interest in social or economic reform and would always seek to retain its independence.[8]

Chiang declared that a major goal in preparing for the Northern Expedition was to deal with corruption in the military. "From now on," he ordered, "the military supply bureau will directly provide funds to the divisions and no military unit can manage its money."[9] He intended to make his Revolutionary Army not only highly disciplined but also a modern institution run honestly and efficiently like the Japanese Imperial Army and the Soviet Red Army.[10] This was one of the reasons he gave high priority to the role of political commissars, and was willing to accept that they would be mostly Communists, an early sign that even at this stage he recognized that CCP members were generally more disciplined, dedicated, and honest than their average KMT counterparts. The other functions of the commissars would be to assure the loyalty as well as the honesty of the commanders and other line officers, as well as guarantee the relatively humane treatment of the enlisted ranks and civilians.

Unfortunately, the majority of Chiang's army commanders simply rejected his proposal to centralize military financial matters—and Chiang soon realized that he had to give the fight against corruption much lower priority than that of retaining cohesion and loyalty among his disparate supporters and allies, both civilian and military. He had no choice. Significantly, however, his aborted effort to implement this basic financial reform as soon as he had obtained command of the Revolutionary Army in 1925 does suggest that he was aware of endemic corruption on the mainland (and its dire consequences), even if he did not succeed in combating this vice until after he retreated to Taiwan in 1949.

On August 20, 1925, when Liao Zhongkai stepped out of his car on his way to a meeting of the KMT Central Executive Committee in Canton, several men leaped out from hiding and killed him with a volley of pistol bullets. Chiang received a call telling him of the event, and in his diary that night, he wrote that the British must have been behind the murder.[11] At Borodin's suggestion, the National government organized a special committee to handle the investigation, consisting of Wang Jingwei, Xu Chongzhi, and Chiang Kai-shek. Chiang was suddenly in the KMT's top triumvirate, although the junior member—while Hu Hanmin, considered the most conservative of all the top leaders, was excluded. In fact, it soon turned out that a prime suspect in the murder was a cousin of Hu, who fled Canton before he could be questioned.

The investigation also discovered an alleged plot by a group of conservatives in the KMT and the Guangdong Army to liquidate the leftists in Canton. The Political Council ordered the execution of several senior officers under General Xu Chongzhi, one of the investigating threesome. Xu was not directly implicated in Liao's death, but soon another charge emerged—he was suspected of secret contact with Chen Jiongming. On the morning of September 20, Chiang and a handful of soldiers surrounded the residence of General Xu. Chiang demanded that the general, nominally still his superior, leave Canton for three months.[12] Xu was known to be corrupt, and the Political Council agreed on his immediate departure for Shanghai. With the council's approval, Wang and Chiang then dispatched the anti-Communist Hu Hanmin to Moscow where he was soon ironically named the official KMT representative to the Comintern.[13]

Authority for the direction of the KMT now lay with two men. Wang Jingwei was the government leader, the chief party representative in the Revolutionary Army, and the most prestigious of the old anti-Manchu KMT revolutionaries. Chiang was the subordinate military chief and concurrent Whampoa and Canton garrison commander. Both men seemed to stand firmly on the left flank of the KMT. Wang was outgoing and expansive, while Chiang was introspective and formal. According to Borodin, Wang could understand people and "the trend of things once informed of the facts." But when asked "to shoulder responsibilities, he would often retreat."[14]

Wang had a very persuasive manner but also "an irrepressible desire for power and personal fame." Borodin, Li Zongren, and others believed that Wang was untrustworthy and lacked firmness. By contrast, Borodin said Chiang had limited knowledge but was "brave about shouldering responsibility." Li, writing decades later after their fourth and final breakup, described Chiang as "narrow, partial, stubborn, crafty, suspicious, and jealous," but acknowledged, "He loved to make decisions."[15]

Stubbornness (or firmness) and decisiveness were in fact widely assumed to be Chiang's principal attributes. He deliberately cultivated, practiced, and projected these traits to the world, even as over the years he also proved to be a pragmatic compromiser, backing down and making concessions to warlords, Japanese, Communists, and Americans in negotiated settlements that he considered tactically wise. Craftiness and suspicion are the usual mark of successful political leaders in Chiang's circumstances, and he had his share of such characteristics and developed them further as he went along. Nonetheless, his strong belief in his own sincerity as well as shrewdness made him susceptible not only to flattery and praise, but also to gestures of respect and goodwill—as well as offers of compromise. He was not at heart a cynical man.

Until the ouster of General Xu, Chiang had risen steadily without any real or suspected political machinations on his part. He had not up to this point tried to create a faction (except for the very young Whampoa graduates) to accumulate political allies, or to lobby for political position. In addition, Chiang seemed to be a powerful man with unusual restraints on his ambitions. Among his political handicaps was the fact that he was a Zhejiang man, while the vast majority of the men and officers of the Revolutionary Army, except for the First Corps with its many Whampoa graduates and cadets, were from Guangdong, Guangxi, Yunnan, and Hunan.

The removal from the scene of the senior veterans Liao Zhongkai, Hu Hanmin, and General Xu Chongzhi, as well as the continued rise of the Communists, opened a breach in the KMT. In the summer of 1925, Dai Jitao published two pamphlets charging that the Communists represented an alien radicalism that "mocked Chinese values and threatened its social order."[16] Dai also wrote Chiang a long letter reiterating his fear of the consequences of Communist penetration of the KMT. Chiang was outraged. He lamented that Dai and other old friends had become "decrepit and behind the times."[17]

Chiang was increasingly enthusiastic about the mobilization work of his mostly Communist political officers, now led by Zhou Enlai. Chiang even appointed Zhou as chief commissar in the First Division of the most loyal First Corps. Like his diary entries of the time, this appointment suggests that Chiang was in fact still very much leftist in his thinking, believing in a comradely relationship with the Soviet Union in pursuit of their common interests—the destruction of global imperialism and the unity of China—but unwilling to accept any role for the Comintern in Chinese domestic matters. This attitude was underscored when, in October, he quickly approved the request of his fifteen-year-old son Ching-kuo to study at the University of the Toilers of the East in Moscow. That same month, after a final victory over Chen Jiongming at a celebration party with Chinese and Russian officers, Chiang praised the Russian national spirit and the strength of the Comintern and its mission of revolution against imperialism. The Chinese revolution would fail, he said, if it did not unite with all the revolutionaries of the world.[18]

But the breach within the KMT was widening. In November, a number of the disaffected KMT veterans, including Dai Jitao, met in the Western Hills near Peking in a rump plenum of the Central Executive Committee. They voted to expel the Communists from the Kuomintang, fire Borodin, and dissolve the Political Council. In a private letter, Chiang blamed the failure of the revolution to date on just such "arrogance and corrosive jealousies" as demonstrated by the Western Hills group. The same month he told the Whampoa cadets, "I will die for the Three People's Principles, namely for Communism."[19] Meanwhile, among young Chinese, Chiang's charisma was becoming apparent. In January 1926, when the KMT convened its Second National Congress in Canton, he appeared before the delegates wearing a debonair cloak over his shoulders that "attracted great attention." To one of the Communist leaders, Zhang Guotao, Chiang conveyed the picture of "an important military bulwark," and cast a figure that was in "a class by itself."[20]

For the first time, the Congress, which was one-third Communist, elected Chiang a member of the Central Executive Committee.[21] Of the KMT party workers, 70 percent were Communists, with 75 percent of the 876 commissars in the Revolutionary Army members of the CCP as well.[22] According to Comintern documents, when Whampoa was selecting its first classes, Chiang even suggested to the Russian advisers that all the slots for political commissars be given to Communists even though they represented only a fraction of the rest of the Revolutionary Army, including line officers and enlisted ranks.[23] One Russian adviser warned his superiors that Chiang's favoritism toward the CCP aroused the "indignation of the KMT commanding officers of all ranks" and might backfire.[24]

At the same time, the official Russian advisory group's own presence in Canton was rapidly expanding. Six Soviet ships were regularly bringing oil, weapons, and even disassembled aircraft to Canton.[25] The Russian South China mission boasted in its report to the Soviet embassy in Peking that it actually acted as chief of the General Staff of the Revolutionary Army. "The Kuomintang as it now exists," the report said, "was created by us . . . and there has not been a case yet when a measure we proposed was not accepted . . . by the Government." A general named N. V. Kuibyshev, known as Kisanka, replaced Blucher in November as head of the Soviet military advisers. Kisanka hinted at the ultimate goal when he reported to Moscow in January that it was not yet possible "to obtain complete control" of the Revolutionary Army.[26]

One Russian adviser characterized Chiang as "conceited, reserved, and ambitious" but concluded that much could be obtained from him if he were "praised in a delicate manner" and dealt with "on the basis of equality and never showing that one wants to usurp even a particle of his power." Nonetheless, Kisanka was openly disdainful of his Chinese military colleagues, writing that they were "completely ignorant of the arts of war."[27] Conflict was inevitable. As early as January 1926, Chiang began to record his resentment of the new chief Russian adviser and his deputies: "I treat them with sincerity but they reciprocate with deceit." After Kisanka had "ridiculed" him, Chiang again complained that the Russians were deceitful, suspicious, and envious.[28]

One matter of discord was Chiang's all-out planning for an early launch of the Northern Expedition. While the National Revolutionary Army had 85,000 soldiers with about 60,000 rifles, the warlord adversaries could claim ten times as many troops. Chiang was confident that spirit and commitment would still win the day. Stalin, however, opposed the early start to the campaign: he still feared the Japanese reaction and knew the Chinese Communists needed to gain time.[29]

Meanwhile, members of the Western Hills faction in Shanghai were spreading rumors trying to fuel suspicions in Canton of a plot by the CCP, Wang Jingwei, and the Russians to get rid of Chiang.[30] Members of Chiang's staff informed him that leaflets denouncing him, evidently written by the Communists, were appearing in Canton. Chiang himself now began to write critically of the Communists in his diary, noting on one day, for example, that the Communist members within the Kuomintang "are not open and they do not deal honestly with us." Soon Chiang began to feel that he "was single-handedly fighting tigers in front and wolves behind." Political life, he wrote, "is Hell."[31]

It was at this point that Wang Jingwei directed him to travel to Moscow and discuss with the Soviets his plans for the Northern Expedition as well as his problems with Kisanka. Chen Lifu, brother of Guofu, a recent U.S. graduate, and now a new confidential secretary to Chiang, later wrote that Chiang did not want to go to Moscow but felt he had to accept the KMT's and Sun's principle that the party (meaning Wang) controlled the military (himself).[32] Then, as Chen Lifu tells the story, after midnight on March 18 a Zhejiang member of the CCP Central Executive Committee passed a secret warning to Chiang that the Communists and the Russians were conspiring to oust him.[33]

The next day, a gunboat of the Revolutionary Navy called the *Zhongshan*, captained by a CCP member, made movements reported to Chiang that he thought suspicious, and Wang Jingwei twice called asking about Chiang's schedule that day.[34] According to Chen Lifu, Chiang became worried about a "trap" and decided to go by car to a site outside of Canton where elements of the loyal First Corps were camped. On the way he resolved to fight the Communist threat against him.[35] He and senior officers in the First Corps discussed the matter all night and at 4:00 a.m. on March 20 he placed all of Canton under martial law and arrested both the captain of the *Zhongshan* and about fifty other Communists, including Zhou Enlai. His First Corps troops, for their part, disarmed the Communist worker pickets in Canton and took the weapons of the guards at the compound of the Russian advisers.[36] In the afternoon, the widow of the murdered Liao Zhongkai, He Xiangning, burst into Chiang's headquarters. "Have you gone mad?" she asked. "Or do you want to capitulate to imperialism?" Knowing that Sun Yat-sen had been confident in his acceptance of civilian rule, Chiang "bent across the desk and wept like a child."[37]

Subsequent Soviet reports on the affair seem to confirm that Chiang had reason to be suspicious about Wang. Moscow itself at that stage would not likely have been trying to topple Chiang. Every indication was that Stalin and Borodin saw him as a sort of Jacobin, a near-Communist who accepted the authority of the Comintern on international matters but not domestic ones, and who might someday go the last mile. When the Manchurian marshal Zhang Zuolin seized the Soviet embassy in Peking in early April 1927, there would be no indication among the documents seized of a Soviet plot against Chiang in March of 1926. An internal Russian report concluded that the Soviet advisers had moved too quickly in asserting authority and had incited resentment, but also noted suggestively that Wang Jingwei had been "a member of the anti-Chiang Alliance in and after the March 20th incident."[38]

Despite the uncertainty, and his later belief that the gunboat captain was not involved, Chiang had seized the opportunity not only to assert the KMT's full authority in China over the Soviet advisers and to put a stop to Communist infiltration of the KMT, but also to secure his own leadership of the Kuomintang and thus of the revolutionary movement. He hoped to avoid being seen as having achieved these goals through a coup, however, since this would violate Sun Yat-sen's principles as well as his own vows of sincerity and honor—and threaten future Soviet aid. Thus he immediately acted to assure the Russians that nothing had changed. In the afternoon of the very day of the "incident" he withdrew his troops from the Soviet compound and sent an apology. He also pulled back his soldiers from the offices of labor organizations and released most of the other detained Communists, including Zhou Enlai. Wang Jingwei was furious and thought he could rally all but the First Corps to oppose Chiang, but to his dismay, the corps commanders, with one or possibly two exceptions, were strongly anti-Communist; they welcomed Chiang's restrictions on the CCP and the Russians.[39]

In short order, the KMT Executive Committee approved Chiang's actions, including his takeover of the chairmanship of the Military Council from Wang. Moreover, the committee formally proposed that "in view of the present situation, the comrades of the left should temporarily retreat." Wang, pleading sudden illness, quickly departed for Shanghai and then France.[40] Chiang assured Solovyev, the senior Soviet diplomat in Canton, that his efforts were not aimed at halting KMT cooperation with Moscow or with the Communists. He asked for the early return of both Borodin, who had temporarily returned to Moscow, and Blucher. Solovyev agreed and said he would dismiss Kisanka.[41]

Chiang also arrested some conservative KMT officers, and sent the Whampoa cadets an open letter stating that, like Sun Yat-sen, he believed the revolutionary front would not be united without an accommodation with the Communists.[42] The leader of a Soviet study commission who happened to be in Canton, A. S. Bubnov, concluded that Chiang was willing and able "to work with us."[43] Although the CCP now had 30,000 members, it still had no prospects of seizing power in the short term, and Stalin and the Comintern agreed it should continue its united front with the Kuomintang.

Chiang dutifully requested that the KMT Executive Committee punish him for the events of March 20, but to no one's surprise the committee refused to oblige and instead resolved to entrust the revolution to him.[44] On June 5, Chiang was named commander in chief *(zong si ling)* of the National Revolutionary Army and the Northern Expedition, and one month later he assumed office as Supreme Commander. As it had with Sun Yat-sen, the Western media referred to him as "Generalissimo."[45] Working closely with his brother, Lifu, and Chiang's patron, Zhang Renjie, Chen Guofu, who was then director of the KMT's Organizational Department, set off to purge most CCP members from all positions of leadership in the party. Chen also began to infiltrate his own clandestine "political units" into labor unions, farmer associations, and even the army commissar corps.[46]

Chiang was now even more determined to launch the Northern Expedition at an early date, calculating that a series of early victories would unite the Chinese political, intellectual, and business worlds behind him. He also knew that although the Russians and the Chinese Communists considered him a man who had "just emerged from obscurity" and a "self-crowned Napoléon," they would have no choice but to support him once he launched the campaign. Chiang had three corps—the First, the Seventh, and Fourth—that would do most of the serious fighting on the long and difficult road north. All except for the First Corps had their origins as traditional warlord forces. An Eighth Corps was suddenly added in June when Tang Shengzhi, the commander of the largest division in the army of the anti-KMT Hunan warlord, defected to the Revolutionary Army with his troops.

Chiang's strategy was to take Hunan, capture the Wuhan cities three hundred miles to the north on the Yangtze, link up with the Christian and now leftist warlord Feng Yuxiang (famous for baptizing his troops by water hose), and then advance on Peking. An American missionary doctor in Changsha, Phil Greene, reported in his letters home that Hunan was divided into many "little kingdoms," each with its own military chief and hordes of loafing soldiers.[47] There were in fact twenty-three separate warlord units in the province and as the Revolutionary Army advanced, they all withdrew or joined the Kuomintang. Chiang's officers reported there was "no one to fight."[48]

On July 11, the Revolutionary Army marched into Changsha followed by a long procession of students. One day the following month, the Yale-in-China Xiang Ya Hospital, where Greene worked as a surgeon, received a summons from army headquarters: "Send dentist at once to attend the Generalissimo." The hospital's Western-trained Chinese dentist had long since fled to Shanghai, so Greene answered the call. After the American had waited several hours, "in came a man . . . dressed in an ordinary white shirt, gray pants, and Chinese shoes." Greene thought he was an orderly and when he asked his name the patient answered simply, "Chiang." Greene explained that while he was not a dentist he could take out the offending tooth. "Then take it out," Chiang said. Chiang did not engage in what Greene called "the usual Chinese custom of discussing and re-discussing a matter before acting." All the Americans were impressed when three days later the Generalissimo opened a new, well-equipped two-hundred-bed army hospital across the street from Xiang Ya. It was a hopeful sign. Maybe the dream was coming true, Greene thought—a fully sovereign China, its self-respect and dignity restored, welcoming foreigners who wanted to help.[49]

Chiang ordered the Revolutionary Army to press ahead immediately into Hubei province. In the several battles for Wuhan that followed, Li Zongren, no admirer of Chiang, marveled that the commander in chief "calmly" stood out in exposed areas "as bullets screamed by us . . . in the darkness."[50] By the end of October, the Revolutionary Army had destroyed the warlord forces in Hubei and occupied Wuhan. Meanwhile, He Yingqin's First Corps captured

Seeing Chiang and General V. K. Blucher (chief Soviet adviser) off to Changsha on the Northern Expedition, 1926. *Left to right:* Mikhail Borodin; unidentified man; Fanny Borodin; widow of Liao Zhongkai; Chen Jieru, Chiang's concubine; Blucher; Chiang; Chiang's son Wei-kuo; the writer Dai Jitao; *sitting,* Zhang Renjie, Chiang's longtime patron. Courtesy KMT Party History Institute.

Fujian and moved into Zhejiang. In both provinces local warlords quickly declared allegiance to the KMT and Chiang dutifully appointed them new commanders in the Revolutionary Army.[51] As he would time and again, Chiang sought to achieve military victory by embracing allies of convenience, leaving for later the task of dealing with any consequent political problems. It was a policy that Sun Yat-sen had followed and it would come back to haunt Chiang, but at this juncture he again felt he had no option.

During the advance, Chiang and his headquarters staff accompanied the main force of the army, often traveling by horseback or sedan chairs carried by coolies because there were virtually no trucks. Wherever he was, Chiang continued his morning meditations and exercise. Rising at 5:00 a.m., he first would shadowbox, slowly stretching, tensing, and relaxing his muscles in the traditional dreamlike motion, then he would breathe in deeply and exhale slowly. Facing each day's challenges he asked himself what course would have been taken by his neo-Confucian models Zeng Guofan and Wang Yangming, and the ancient strategist Sun Tzu.[52]

The challenges were enormous and Chiang added to them by micromanaging. Because he did not have confidence in the competence of most of his generals—or trust them—he sometimes communicated directly with regimental commanders.[53] The collection of his military directives and correspondence in the archives in Taipei consists of an astonishing seventy-eight volumes.[54] He often personally allocated to individual units ammunition and equipment, at one time doling out four trench mortars, one hundred artillery shells, and four hundred hand grenades. Given the desperate shortage of equipment, ammunition, blankets, food, and of course money, sometimes the question of where to send four trench mortars was a political as well as a military issue. Every allocation by Chiang of scarce supplies, every tactical deployment of units, affected other units and created resentment or jealousy. World War I artillery batteries were an especially precious and scarce asset, and sometimes Chiang personally decided where to deploy the few cannon the army had.

Clearly, Chiang commanded a complex array of military forces with an extremely wide range of training, experience, dedication, dependability, and loyalty.[55] He often listened to General Blucher and Bai Chongxi, but he felt that in the end he could only trust himself and a few classmates from his Japan days like He Yingqin and Zhang Qun. While the Communist commissars at first had helped reduce vice and abuse in the army, after the gunboat incident of March 20, Chiang removed Communist political officers from his most reliable unit, the First Corps. (Li Zongren had never permitted them in the Seventh Corps.)

Chiang's life with Chen Jieru during this time was tempestuous. He missed her when they were apart, sent for her from various locations during the campaign, and became angry when she did not appear as scheduled. They had frequent fights, which he usually regretted. Back in June 1926 when Chiang was in Canton, he had gone to pay his respects to the three Soong sisters at the house of H. H. and Ai-ling Kung. Three days later he returned to call on Mayling alone. The differences between the youngest Soong woman and Jieru—not to mention Chiang's other previous female companions—were striking, and he began to complain about Jieru's "bad housekeeping" and poor education.[56]

Chiang had first met Soong Mayling in December 1921 at a Christmas party at Sun Yat-sen's home in Shanghai. He was reputedly so taken with her (and no doubt also her connections) that at the time—despite his then quite recent arrangement with Chen Jieru—he asked Sun and Chingling if they thought Mayling could be persuaded to accept him. They reportedly said "no" in no uncertain terms.[57] Mayling herself sent back word she was not interested.[58] Five years later, in August 1926, when Chiang returned briefly to Canton on business, the Kungs invited Chen Jieru and Chiang to dinner. The Kungs, Jieru believed, clearly had their eye on the suddenly preeminent Kai-shek as a marriage partner for Mayling. With the men out of the room, the two sisters questioned Jieru about life with Chiang, and the subject of his notorious temper came up. "But a man with a bad temper," Mayling said, "is better than a man without a temper."[59] Chiang's prospects as a suitor had dramatically improved and after that meeting he and Mayling began to exchange the occasional letter. She also sent him a message of congratulations on the capture of Wuhan.[60]

As units of the Revolutionary Army moved through the countryside, they often took with them the local militia, normally paid and controlled by the gentry and other landowners. Consequently, in many areas, local officials lost control to the new CCP-created farmer associations that followed behind the army. As described by Mao, the young CCP cadre usually turned over leadership of the new associations to the dispossessed of the village—the unemployed, dropouts, beggars, and mercenaries. The "so-called 'riff raff,'" as Mao approvingly described them, led bands of the poorest farmers in killing landlords and other class enemies. Trials of "local bullies and evil gentry" were carried out at mass rallies.[61] In his "Report on the Farmer Movement in Hunan," Mao wrote, "A revolution is not a dinner party, but an act of violence by which one class overthrows another." "To put it bluntly," he said, "it was necessary to bring about a brief period of terror in every rural area."[62]

Christian missions were also attacked and looted. Several missionary friends of Phil Greene and his wife, Ruth, escaped into Changsha "with their clothes, their skins, and little else." On January 26, the American consul in

Chiang with General Blucher and other senior Soviet military advisers during a pause in the Northern Expedition, November 1926. Courtesy KMT Party History Institute.

Changsha, John Carter Vincent, urged the Greenes and their four children to make their way secretly at night to a tugboat that would take them down the river to a British steamer. Aided by the school's medical students, the American family completed a midnight escape, but vowed to return.[63]

The CCP Central Committee tried to stop the premature excesses in the countryside but had no real success.[64] Soviet officers in Hunan expressed alarm at the outbreak of attacks by destitute farmers against the landed gentry and against the Revolutionary Army. Many corps commanders in fact replaced Communist commissars with non-Communists, suppressed poor farmer uprisings, and reversed land seizures.[65]

By the end of 1926, Chiang Kai-shek had taken control of the vast region of China from Guangxi province on the Vietnam border, westward to Sichuan where the ruling warlords had officially joined the Revolution, north to the Yangtze River at Wuhan, and eastward to northern Fujian. Chiang's surprising defeat of the warlords during this period has been attributed to the "spontaneous rising of the people that gave the Kuomintang armies little more to do than occupy" already seized territory.[66] But the press in China at the time, both Chinese language and Western, described civilian support for the Revolutionary forces as being "unorganized, mainly spontaneous, and passive in nature." The success of the expedition against ten to one odds was primarily a military victory made possible by the far better discipline of the Revolutionary Army.[67] Chiang moved his military headquarters to Nanchang.

Meanwhile in Canton, KMT liberals on the party's Central Executive Committee, including Soong Chingling and her brother T.V., feared that with Chiang's growing military success and prestige, he would inevitably establish a military dictatorship. What upset them were the moves Chiang had made immediately after the *Zhongshan* gunboat incident, including his election as chairman of the Central Executive Committee and the continuing removal of CCP members from KMT departments and organs. Otherwise Chiang, who understood that the anti-Communist commanders were also leery of his taking dictatorial control, had taken no additional steps to strengthen his power. Together with its CCP members, the left faction now controlled the committee and in October, it passed resolutions implicitly critical of Chiang's concentration of personal political power immediately after the gunboat incident. Moreover, in November it voted to move the committee and KMT headquarters to Wuhan, where they would be closer to the action and in a pro-union environment. In his diary, Chiang at first welcomed the move, presumably not wanting to aggravate the situation further.[68]

Two months later, the pro-Chiang and non-Communist wings of the KMT met at Lushan, a mountain resort towering over the southern bank of the Yangtze River in Jiangxi province. With its dramatic peaks, cragged cliffs, and cascading waterfalls, Lushan would be Chiang Kai-shek's favorite conference site. Again apparently to dispel concern about his possible ambitions, Chiang seconded a proposal at the meeting to eliminate his key position as chairman of the Central Executive Committee and, as he had earlier, called for Wang Jingwei to return and resume leadership of the party. Perhaps he was being totally cynical in these gestures, but judging by his diary and his earnest temperament he probably hoped a compromise could unite the non-Communist elements in the KMT, including Wang—a necessary step before bringing the Communists into line one way or the other. He wrote that he was anxious to unite "the downstream area of the Yangtze" so as to stabilize Wuhan and develop the economy.[69]

Then, on January 11, in a bold move that again implied his good faith, he put himself in the hands of the KMT leftists and the CCP by visiting Wuhan and trying to persuade the Central Executive Committee to move to Nan-chang. At a banquet for Chiang given by the committee, Borodin made sev-eral biting allusions to dictators and power-seeking militarists.[70] "Almost im-mediately" Borodin feared he had gone too far.[71] Soon afterward, the Soviet agent sent a message to Li Zongren suggesting that he replace Chiang as com-mander in chief. Li, fearing the ouster of the new KMT leader would result in a takeover by the CCP, declined. Because he abhorred the Communists and to cover himself in case Borodin's message had been intercepted, he most likely informed Chiang.[72] Chiang now became so worried he could not sleep and over the next few days, four times he wrote that he had thought of sui-cide as a way to "arouse the whole country to realize the dangerous situation." On February 1 he wrote that he had "made up [his] mind to move the Gov-ernment to Wuhan," but he seemed unlikely to do so as long as Borodin—whose "iniquity" was "beyond description"—was in the country.[73]

At this point, the road to Shanghai lay open to the Revolutionary Army. The Wuhan KMT, the Communists, and the Soviet advisers wanted the army in-stead to advance north to link up with Feng Yuxiang, who, judging by his recent behavior and statements made on a visit to Moscow, was believed to be firmly in the left camp of the Kuomintang. Chiang, however, insisted on taking Shanghai and Nanking first, because this would give the new Na-tional government a capital in Nanking, direct access to Shanghai's large fi-nancial resources, and probably foreign recognition. The Lushan conference approved Chiang's strategy. But on March 1, 1927, the Wuhan Central Ex-ecutive Committee formally placed Chiang under the authority of a new military council it had named. The meeting also transferred Chiang's key party posts to the absent Wang Jingwei and issued a secret order for Chiang's arrest. Chen Guofu probably learned of this secret edict, and it is likely that at this time Chiang made up his mind that a purge of the Communists was necessary.[74]

The Revolutionary Army marched on toward Shanghai, and Communist and KMT unions in the city staged joint strikes as part of the revolutionary surge. Two hundred workers died in the ensuing violence, but on March 22, the warlord garrison commander defected to the KMT as did the Fujian Naval Fleet, giving Chiang control of the "Long River" (the Yangtze).[75] Bai Chongxi's forces entered Shanghai on March 22. General Zheng Qian, who had moved his forces into Nanking, received Wuhan's order for the arrest of Chiang but ignored it; in fact, to protect himself he almost certainly told Chiang about the order when, on March 24, the Generalissimo reached Nanking on one of his newly acquired warships, the *Zhi Dun*.[76] Upon his return to Shanghai two days later, he found that workers and students were holding daily rallies demanding that the foreign concessions be seized. Many Westerners doubted that Chiang Kai-shek had either the will or the power to control the situation.[77] Zhou Enlai was the leader of the Communist elements in the city.

Then, on April 6, Wang Jingwei arrived on a Soviet ship. Most of the KMT leaders in the city, including Chiang Kai-shek, requested that Wang stay in Shanghai, assume leadership of a united Kuomintang, expel Borodin, and "restrain" the Communists. Given the strong majority in favor of Wang's return, including all the corps commanders except He Yingqin, Chiang must have felt he had to accept Wang's return to the political leadership. If Wang had agreed and acted against the Communists, there is no telling what would have happened, but he could well have consolidated his control, bringing most of the left KMT back into the fold. If so, this could have put off indefinitely or perhaps permanently Chiang Kai-shek's rise to political leadership of the KMT. But Wang declined, insisting that there had to be a plenary meeting of the Central Executive Committee in Wuhan to decide such a serious matter.[78]

The next day, Chiang sent a telegram to all commanders announcing "Chairman" Wang's return in flattering terms and stating that all military, civil, financial, and foreign matters should be centralized under Wang's direction. Chiang then met privately with Wang and personally stressed the necessity of sending the meddlesome Borodin home and purifying the party of its Communist members. Chiang thought that Wang reacted positively. But that same day, the CCP leader Chen Duxiu unexpectedly arrived in Shanghai, and he and Wang quickly published a joint statement denying that the Communists intended to subvert the Revolutionary Army or overthrow the KMT—albeit ending with a Marxist injunction that what was needed was a democratic dictatorship of all oppressed people's to deal with the counter-revolutionaries of the world. Wang and Chen then secretly boarded a steamer and sailed for Wuhan, leaving Chiang leader of all the anti-Communist forces in the Revolutionary Army and the Kuomintang.[79] Chiang instituted martial law, ordered the disarming of all civilians bearing arms, then steamed off in his warship back to Nanking.[80]

On April 6, the Supervisory Committee of the KMT—a mostly honorary body that did not have executive authority and included Chiang's key backer Chang Jieru, as well as Dai Jitao and the Chen brothers—unanimously agreed to remove Communists from the party and established a coordinating group to do so: the "Shanghai Purge Committee." The "most important objective," Chen Lifu tells us in his memoirs, was to assure that the Green Gang did not ally with the CCP, which the KMT considered a real possibility.[81]

The two principal leaders of the Green Gang, Du Yuesheng and Huang Jinrong, "for political reasons" had "stayed close to the Communist Party" as well as the Kuomintang. According to Chen Lifu, Du had direct contact with Wang Shouhua, a Green Gang and CCP member who was leader of the Communist-led Shanghai Federation of Trade Unions. Because of these ties, the CCP Central Committee did not believe the powerful Green Gang was an imminent threat. But a ranking gang member named Yang Hu, who had worked with Chiang Kai-shek in the early years of the revolution, served as the KMT purge committee's principal contact with Du Yuesheng, who was given 600,000 Chinese yuan by the committee to create a "Mutual Progress Society" of armed thugs to help carry out the gang's assigned actions. Indeed, before leaving, Chiang appointed Yang commander of Shanghai's garrisons.[82]

That same day, Manchurian marshal Zhang Zuolin's police stormed into the large Soviet embassy in Peking, arresting Russian diplomats and CCP members, and carrying off truckloads of documents that provided "persuasive evidence of the degree to which Moscow, through its agent, Borodin, controlled the CCP." Marshal Zhang ordered the strangulation of Li Dazhao and nineteen other CCP members taken at the embassy. But ruthlessness and treachery were inherent on both sides. By coincidence, also on April 6, Stalin, ignorant of events in Peking, told a meeting of three thousand party workers in Moscow that "When the [KMT] Right is of no more use, Chiang Kai-shek will be squeezed out like a lemon and flung far away."[83]

The twenty-two-year-long Chinese civil war began in Shanghai in the early morning hours of April 12, 1927. The previous evening, the Green Gang's Du Yuesheng invited his friend Wang Shouhua, the Communist labor leader, to his home for a chat. While there, Du advised Wang to quit the Communist party and join the KMT. Wang declined and as he left the house, two

Green Gang leader Du Yuesheng, an important supporter of Chiang from about 1915 to 1937 and a key participant in the 1927 purge of the Communists. Courtesy KMT Party History Institute.

assassins gunned him down. Then, after midnight, Bai Chongxi's Seventh Corps units in Shanghai took over the offices of the pro-Communist Labor Federation and shot resisting workers, while armed bands organized by the Green Gang as the Mutual Prosperity Society attacked workers' inspection corps in several localities, killing several dozen resisters. Many more, including Zhou Enlai, were arrested and sent to Bai's headquarters. Zhou was the ranking CCP official in the city, but Bai released him, very likely with Chiang's approval or on his orders.[84]

Green Gang members rooted out other Communists in hiding, reportedly killing hundreds while thousands fled. When troops of the Seventh Corps fired on a demonstration, scores more lost their lives. Similar purges took place in Canton, Guilin, Ningbo, Amoy, and elsewhere. Decades later, Chen

Lifu concluded, "It was a bloodthirsty way to eliminate the enemy within. I must admit that many innocent people were killed." According to Chen, 16,000 Communists "crossed over to our side."[85] Chiang did not mention the purge itself in his diary, but on April 14 wrote that for the time being he would "take advantage of the change in the political situation and take defensive actions to solidify the southern regions of the Yangtze."[86] In retaliation, the Wuhan leaders ordered the execution of eight veteran union leaders who had resisted Communist domination in that city. In Changsha, thirty to forty Chinese businessmen with foreign connections also fell before a Communist rifle squad.

On April 18, Chiang proclaimed the formation of a rival KMT government in Nanking chaired by Hu Hanmin, the KMT veteran who had been forced out of the top leadership after the assassination of Liao Zhongkai, and who had returned recently from Russia. Like Wang Jingwei, Hu considered himself superior to Chiang, whom he viewed as a provincial upstart. Nevertheless, in the name of the National government, Hu commended Chiang for his loyalty and courage—and ordered the arrest of Borodin and two hundred CCP members, including Chen Duxiu, Mao Zedong, and Zhou Enlai. Meanwhile in Wuhan, the Central Executive Committee, with Wang Jingwei as chair, charged Chiang Kai-shek with twelve crimes, including "massacre of the people and oppression of the Party." The committee expelled Chiang from all his posts, and offered 250,000 taels of silver for his capture and 100,000 taels if he was killed.[87]

There is no indication that prior to the purge Chiang gave any thought to the fate of his son, who had been a student in Moscow since November 1925. Ching-kuo, it turned out, had become a fervent supporter of Trotsky's radical line on revolution and when news of the purge reached Moscow, he was shocked and outraged. The next day, he publicly denounced his father as a "traitor and murderer." While the official KMT explanation was that Ching-kuo had been forced to make these statements, Chiang likely suspected the truth. His idealistic son would remain in the Soviet Union another ten years, and during all that time he considered himself a true Marxist-Leninist and his father, because of the great purge, a traitor to the people of China.[88]

I

After the Shanghai purge, Chiang's prestige rose among the warlords. He could now count on those who controlled the provinces of Zhejiang and Fu-

Chiang *(center)* with Feng Yuxiang, on his right, and Yan Xishan, 1927. These warlords threw in their lot with Chiang, then later rebelled. Courtesy KMT Party History Institute.

jian, as well as Shanghai, Nanking, and parts of Anhui and Jiangsu. Most of Guangxi, Guangdong, and Sichuan seemed safely in the hands of war-lords who were in the Kuomintang's Revolutionary Army and were anti-Communist but had only a thin loyalty to Chiang. The shifty Tang Shengzhi dominated Hunan militarily, but the Communists controlled much of the province's countryside. The Northern warlords held most of China north of the Yangtze. Feng Yuxiang, the Christian general who controlled Shaanxi, Gansu, and parts of Henan and Inner Mongolia, possessed a new arsenal of Soviet weapons and held the balance between Wuhan and Nanking.

Chiang's realm included the commercial and banking cities of Shanghai, Ningbo, and Nanking. His support from the financial leaders of these cities would not suffer from the factional rivalry and jealousy that afflicted his mili-tary base. In fact, the capitalists were given no role in the KMT and the party remained anticapitalist. Throughout his career, Chiang Kai-shek would tightly control the various organizations of bankers and merchants in these cities, milking them of funds when necessary with the unacknowledged help of Du Yuesheng's gang through such means as threats, destruction of property, and even kidnapping.[89] For the next ten years Chiang would also obtain large funds from taxes on the growth and consumption of opium, part of a control system officially intended to gradually reduce use of the drug—and a system in which Du Yuesheng would play an official part.[90]

Having decided that maintaining the momentum of the campaign made sense both militarily and politically, Chiang sent his most reliable forces across the Yangtze to resume the Northern Expedition. The loyal First and dependable Seventh Corps again took the lead, and soon, Chiang's three advancing columns had captured most of northern Jiangsu.

After the purge in Shanghai, Chiang changed the daily mantra in his diary to read, "Still, the rebels and the Great World Powers are not eliminated."[91] The Wang-led coalition of the CCP and the Left KMT exercised tenuous authority over three provinces—Hunan, Hubei, and Jiangxi. But support for the Wuhan government within these areas began to collapse almost immediately because of anger at the wanton Communist-led killings in the countryside. The Hunan and left-leaning KMT general Tang Shengzhi turned his forces on the Communists in a bloody midnight attack on CCP personnel in Changsha. The anti-CCP slaughter quickly spread to other counties in Hunan and then in Hubei and Jiangxi. Chiang watched these developments with satisfaction. Very likely he had a hidden hand in them.

The grave setback for the CCP embarrassed and provoked Stalin, who fired off a radiogram to Borodin and M. N. Roy, a newly arrived Comintern representative in Wuhan. Stalin ordered the seizure by Communists of land in the Chinese countryside, as well as "the replacement of vacillating leaders" of the KMT, the elimination of "unreliable generals," and the creation of a new army of 70,000 revolutionary workers and peasants.[92] The assigned tasks were completely unrealistic, and when the CCP leaders read the message, they did not know "whether to laugh or cry."[93] Roy inexplicably showed the message to Wang Jingwei, who understood it as a Soviet plan to purge the Wuhan government of its non-Communist leaders. He informed Feng Yuxiang, who was so alarmed he immediately sought a meeting with Chiang Kai-shek.

On June 19, Chiang and several KMT commanders waited for Feng Yuxiang at the Xuzhou railway station, about 260 miles northwest of Shanghai. They wore their dress uniforms with ungainly ceremonial swords dangling from their waists. A military band added to the importance of the expected guest. Feng's special "Flowery Train" pulled slowly alongside the platform, and the greeting party peered in the windows but saw only a few uniformed waiters. The waiters pointed to boxcars at the rear of the train. Finally, through the open door of a boxcar, Chiang saw a very tall, husky soldier, dressed in a shabby uniform, sitting on the floor. As the train stopped, the soldier stood and walked out. "Where is Commander Feng?" Chiang asked. The soldier replied with a smile, "I am Feng Yuxiang." The band played and Feng shook hands all around.[94]

The two men had a lot in common, with each espousing leftist views and each receiving large amounts of military aid from the Soviet Union. Each had a child in Moscow—Feng in fact had two. Feng was a Christian and Chiang would become one. More important, both now saw the CCP and the Soviet Union as grave enemies, and by the end of their meeting, they had reached complete agreement. Since Chiang now had access to loans and "contributions" from the principal banks of China and the opium tax, he was able to promise Feng a subsidy of 2 million Chinese dollars a month, far more than Wuhan had been sending him.[95]

Feng returned to his headquarters at Zhengzhou (the capital of Henan, about 225 miles north of Wuhan) and immediately ordered the expulsion—and in some cases execution—of the Communists in his ranks. Deng Xiaoping, a twenty-five-year-old Communist who had studied in Paris and Moscow and had been with Feng as a political commissar, barely escaped. When he heard of Feng's actions, the Shanxi warlord Yan Xishan, who had been dallying with Nanking, Wuhan, and Peking about taking sides, quickly supported Chiang and hunted down what few Communists he could find in the major cities of his province.

The Northern warlord Sun Chuanfang, by contrast, inflicted a major defeat on the Revolutionary Army at Xuzhou. Chiang insisted on personally leading a counterattack, which failed miserably, and the entire force of several corps retreated all the way back to the north bank of the Yangtze.[96] Unshaven and unbathed, Chiang returned to Nanking on August 5, furious at the defeat. He ordered the advance commander, General Wang Tianpei, executed—a punishment he usually commanded only if the officer had retreated without orders. Privately he wrote that one of the reasons for the failure was his own "underestimation of the enemy."[97]

Meanwhile, Wang Jingwei also moved against the Communists, expelling them from Wuhan and disarming the worker pickets. Some Communists caught in Wuhan were executed, but Wang carefully protected the Russian advisers, pretending that the recent turn of events should not disturb relations with the Soviet Union. The Soviets, however, decided to pull out, recognizing that their China strategy was in shambles. M. N. Roy took off across the Gobi desert in a dusty convoy of three large touring cars with gasoline cans lashed to the running boards. Borodin did not leave until late July because Northern warlord forces had captured his wife and imprisoned her in Peking. But dressed as a nun she escaped, and she and Borodin sped away on the long trip across the Gobi to the safety of Mongolia.[98]

But the Soviets were not about to give up the fight in other areas of China. The CCP Politburo, in hiding in Shanghai, followed instructions from Moscow and declared a policy of insurrection wherever possible. In August 1927 the Comintern sent an agent to Shanghai with US$300,000 for the CCP and Stalin approved the shipment of 15,000 guns, 10 million cartridges, and 30 machine guns.[99] Mao Zedong, too, returned to Hunan to revive the revolutionary farmers' movement there. In early September, Mao's military units, consisting of army deserters, village defense corps members, bandits, and the unemployed, killed local officials and landlords and attacked some towns, including Changsha. By the middle of September, however, provincial military troops had virtually destroyed the ragtag Communist forces and Mao was forced to retreat with the survivors to the famous bandit bastion in the Jinggang Mountains on the Hunan-Jiangxi border.[100]

Back in Nanking, Chiang sent emissaries to Wang Jingwei once again proposing reconciliation. Wang, however, refused any settlement until Chiang resigned. Chiang sent for Li Zongren and told him that he had decided to step down because Wang Jingwei had refused peace talks unless he did so.[101] It was evident to Li that without Chiang, it was entirely possible that the Nanking alliance would break up into warring factions, Wang Jingwei would be unable to keep the KMT united, and the Northern Expedition would sputter out. For all his faults, including his domineering and cold personality, Chiang's dedication to putting the country back together, his continuing reputation as an uncorrupt leader, and his astonishing success to date in leading the Northern Expedition still made him a unifying figure. Li also recognized that Chiang's departure would seriously curtail Nanking's ability to raise funds in Shanghai. Li "begged" him to reconsider.[102]

But Chiang believed that it was a good time to resign, and on August 12, 1927, he handed in his resignation, calling on the KMT to unite and complete the capture of North China and Peking. "Comrades in Wuhan," he implored, "Why do you hesitate?"[103] He then cleaned out his desk in Nanking and took a warship down the Yangtze to Shanghai. From there, accompanied by a bodyguard of two hundred men, he traveled on to Xikou and then walked up the steep trail to Hole in the Snow Monastery. After rising at 5:00 a.m. to the chanting of the monks and the beating of the temple drums, Chiang read and meditated. Dressed in a traditional long gray gown, he told two American reporters that he planned to spend the next five years abroad observing the customs of the other great nations of the world, among which China might soon take its rightful place.[104] Chinese reporters, meanwhile, conveyed to all the major cities of China the image of the benevolent and principled general in self-exile sitting among pious monks on a mountaintop. Chiang expected to be called back, but to gain the moral high ground he had put himself in a somewhat unpredictable situation.

II

The forty-year-old leader was contemplating more than philosophical and political issues. He and Soong Mayling had been corresponding for a year.[105] In May of 1927, nine months before his resignation, apparently by correspondence, he asked her to marry him. Having reportedly refused in 1922, this time she was pleased to accept. He was now famous and she was twenty-nine, a worrisome age for any unmarried Chinese female of the day. But Mayling's mother was opposed—after all, one of her daughters had, in an unfilial manner, rushed off without permission to marry a divorced KMT leader three decades older than she, and the union had produced no children. But at least Sun Yat-sen had been highly educated and a Christian, while Chiang was neither Christian nor college educated. Most troubling of all, he had been married at least once, had had several concubines, and had sired only one child. Interestingly, there were few references to Mayling in his diaries during the summer of 1927. But on October 1, 1927, he wrote, "Recently, night and day, there is nothing in my heart but San Mei [Soong Mayling]."[106]

In late September, after several weeks at the monastery, Chiang put aside his gown, came down from the mountain, and sailed to Shanghai. Upon his arrival, he explained to reporters that his only purpose was to obtain the consent of Mayling's family to their marriage. Madame Soong, however, was staying at a health resort in Japan with Mayling and Ai-ling. Chiang caught up with her in the city of Kamakura, declared his intentions, and presented papers showing his divorce from Mao Fumei. He also promised to read the Bible and study Christianity, but said he could not give a guarantee of conversion. Madame Soong finally agreed to the marriage. Chiang told the press that he had "paid off" Chen Jieru as he had a previous "concubine [Miss Yao]."[107]

On December 1, 1927, Chiang Kai-shek and Soong Mayling were married in what was Shanghai's social event of the year. A small Christian ceremony was held in the Soong home in the French Concession followed by a Chinese ceremony in the grand ballroom of the Majestic Hotel. Mayling wore a beaded gown of silver and white and Chiang a morning coat and tails, striped pants, and a wing collar.[108] The couple bowed three times to Sun Yat-sen's portrait draped in Kuomintang flags, then Chiang read a statement grandiosely declaring that the wedding was "a symbol of the reconstruction of Chinese society . . . [and] the foundation of the Revolution."[109] The marriage certificate was read aloud and sealed, and the bride and groom bowed to each other and then to the official witnesses. A "tea party" for several thousand guests followed, after which the couple set out for their honeymoon at a borrowed villa on Mokan Mountain in Zhejiang.[110]

Chiang's marriage promised to be an excellent one in every respect. His wife was an attractive, even beautiful, woman who had been educated in the United States; she was cosmopolitan, articulate, intelligent, and wealthy. During the long, terrible years of resistance against the Japanese, she would convey to the world and to her own people an image of Chinese dignity and bravery. She knew her role and how to play it, including at least superficial and perhaps serious engagement in good works such as the YWCA and efforts to protect child workers. Completely unlike her husband, she did not have an austere, private lifestyle; rather she strove to appear moderately glamorous. She always wore makeup and a traditional *qi pao* dress with the slit stopping at the knee (albeit without expensive jewelry). Throughout her life, she enjoyed her wealth, about which she had no embarrassment. She had a full-time tailor, who made her a new *qi pao* every three or four days.[111] She took numerous servants for granted and sometimes traveled with an entourage of sixty or more. Luxury and constant attendance by personal servants, however, do not necessarily ruin prospects for a serious life. Churchill all his life was dressed and undressed by someone else.[112]

Mayling liked Western music and cigarettes, and before her marriage, parties and dancing. She was always a night person, reading and writing until midnight, even as Chiang went to bed early and rose before dawn. She was an avid reader; a student of Chinese—and world—history and politics; and by all accounts, a truly devout Methodist. She was politically determined and

Wedding photo of the Chiangs, December 1927. Chiang, having officially resigned, was urgently called back from the couple's honeymoon. Courtesy KMT Party History Institute.

often a shrewd behind-the-scenes manipulator, and she passed the test for personal courage on numerous occasions, often joining her husband in camp during his war campaigns, living in tents or railway cars. She was talkative and easygoing, in stark contrast to the stuffy and humorless Chiang, who was shy but emotional, and for a Chinese male wept easily. He tried to change his taciturn image. For some while, perhaps since his mother's death and as part of his conscious effort to soften his public persona, he had begun to show a more benign public face, often smiling gently throughout interviews and often in photos.

Chiang and Mayling's life as a couple was an interweaving of profound differences, mutual irritations, a common grand cause, genuine affection, and perhaps passion. When Mayling was twenty-one she wrote to an American woman friend, "There is nothing disgusting about it [sex] if you consider it in conjunction with the other elements that make up love."[113] This obscure comment on the subject may not reflect an enthusiastic view of sex, but stories that the marriage was purely political and even unconjugal are not believable. Chiang possessed a high libido, but he had always been involved with women intellectually and socially beneath him. The new object of his desire had attributes that he had never encountered in a woman—independence, intellect, and power—and they must have been exhilarating. Mayling called him "Darling," and, abbreviating the English word, he called her "Da." He picked flowers for her and held her hand in public, a shocking gesture to most Chinese.

Soong Chingling, who disliked Chiang but was close to her sister Mayling, said it became a "love match."[114] He had a bad temper but so did his wife. She thought she was much smarter than he and certainly more sophisticated, and his stubbornness and faithfulness to those loyal to him frustrated her. But still she thought he was a great man.

Mayling and Kai-shek became the symbol of China, and they came to think of their own destiny as inherently linked with that of their county—a tendency shared to varying extent by democratic wartime leaders and eventually to a pathological degree by Mao and his wife, Jiang Qing. Until Chiang Kai-shek's son returned from Russia and won his father's confidence, Mayling would be the Generalissimo's confidante, exerting a liberalizing influence and acting as his interpreter of both the English language and the ways of the West. That she was wealthy, Christian, and in many ways highly Westernized did not seem to bother most Chinese. In a biographical note for the Comintern files written in May 1941, Zhou Enlai commented that Mayling could influence her husband on international and financial matters, was more democratic than Chiang, and supported the war of resistance as well as the united front with the CCP.[115] She probably contributed positively to Chiang's image in China, at least until the collapse of the economy—and morale—in the postwar period.

Chiang now believed that the imperial ambitions of Japan, not Great Britain, posed by far the greatest peril to the new China. In June, while still in office, he had responded to new Japanese pressures in Shandong by launching the League for the Rupture of Economic Relations with Japan. This boycott movement, supported by the Green Gang, enlisted an army of beggars acting as spotters to threaten targeted merchants selling Japanese goods and to extract large "fines." During his visit to Japan to pursue his courtship of Mayling, Chiang had abandoned Sun Yat-sen's position on Manchuria and told Prime Minister Tanaka Giichi that his intention was to reassert China's sovereignty, including over Manchuria. Tanaka urged Chiang to stay south of the Yangtze and not to become entangled with the warlords of the north—Japan's sphere. Undaunted, Chiang asked that the Japanese government not interfere but rather aid the Northern Expedition so as to dispel the notion that it was on the side of the Manchurian, Marshal Zhang Zuolin.[116]

Chiang greatly admired aspects of Japanese society, but he also was aware of the cruelty and the will to dominance that lay at the samurai heart. At this early date, he feared Japan would do everything it could to prevent China from becoming unified.[117] There was, however, at this time only one country that for a price was willing to help out. While still "out of office," Chiang welcomed the foreign military adviser he had sought from Germany, Max Bauer, a one-time chief of operations for Field Marshal Erich Ludendorff. Over the next ten years, Bauer and forty-six other German officers would draw up extensive plans for modernizing China's Central Army in a thirty-year program and begin to implement it. The Germans also would institute a general staff that would put every phase of military operations and policy in the hands of Chiang Kai-shek when and if he returned as commander in chief.[118]

Without Chiang Kai-shek, the Nanking government encountered numerous difficulties, particularly financial ones, since the bankers and other wealthy capitalists of Shanghai were no longer under pressure from the Green Gang to lend and contribute funds. Not surprisingly then, shortly after Chiang's return from his courtship trip to Japan, KMT officials had preliminary conversations with him in Shanghai about rejoining the government. After the first day's meeting, Chiang stopped off at the residence of Huang Jinrong to pay his respects on the sixtieth birthday of the éminence grise of the Shanghai gangs, the man who had solved Chiang's debt problems six years before.[119]

While Mayling and Kai-shek were getting to know each other in the mountains of Zhejiang, a flurry of cables from warlord and Whampoa officers called on him to resume his office. Wang Jingwei finally proposed that Chiang pick up where he left off with his former duties, and the Central Executive Committee unanimously agreed. The next month, traveling in an armored train, Chiang returned to Nanking with his new bride and five days later resumed his duties as chairman of the Military Council and commander in chief of the Northern Expedition. Wang Jingwei, acknowledging that he had lost face, abruptly returned to France, leaving Chiang more or less in charge of the government and the military.[120] The Revolutionary Army's Soviet weapons and supplies were depleted, but Chiang was determined to keep up the momentum and to launch the next stage of the Northern Expedition without waiting for further resupply. With new prestige and power in hand, he admonished himself to be "tolerant and magnanimous."[121]

As part of this newly tolerant outlook, Chiang forgave his Harvard-educated, thirty-three-year-old brother-in-law T. V. Soong his previous association with the leftist KMT, and named him minister of finance. Like his youngest sister, Mayling, T.V. was a Westernized Chinese, straightforward and gregarious, but like his sister also prone to deep spells of moodiness. He was a Harvard man, a liberal and a reformer like his other sister, Ch'ing-ling, whom he favored, but a conservative in fiscal matters. He was relatively tall for the times, slicked down his black hair in pompadour style, had a rather imperious walk, and usually wore a Western suit, which Chiang Kai-shek (with maybe two exceptions in his life) never did. Whenever T.V. removed his jacket, his holstered pistol was on display. He would develop a condescending attitude toward his boss and future brother-in-law and, with foreigners, refer to him as "Gissimo." But he was also somewhat in awe of Chiang.[122]

The bankers trusted T.V. and very soon the flow of revenue exceeded what it had been the previous summer. As an emergency measure, merchants and factory owners were expected to purchase notes or bonds equal to one month's payroll. A wave of kidnappings of Shanghai businessmen, probably orchestrated by the Green Gang, was believed to be related to victims' failure to contribute sufficiently to the government. But for all the largesse they provided the new regime and the critical role of these funds in the coming military campaign, the Shanghai capitalists once again gained little or no influence over Chiang's political decisions.[123]

Chiang now turned his attention to the battlefield, launching his offensive against the combined force of the Northern warlords, which still numbered 600,000 men. The remnant troops of warlord Sun Chuanfang briefly put up stiff resistance in Shandong, then fled across the Yellow River. The way lay open to the provincial capital of Jinan. Some 2,000 Japanese civilians lived in Jinan, and Prime Minister Tanaka had asked that the Revolutionary Army avoid the city, but Chiang needed control of the north-south rail lines through the town. The cabinet in Tokyo, sensing danger to their compatriots, approved the dispatch of 5,000 soldiers under General Fukuda Hikosuku "to protect Japanese nationals and their property."[124]

Chiang was so anxious about the risks involved in occupying Jinan that as the Revolutionary Army approached the city in April 1928, he tossed and turned in bed, unable to sleep.[125] On the evening of May 1, dressed in his simple field uniform, Chiang rode into the city in a staff car to discover Fukuda's 5,000 soldiers camped both inside and outside the city walls.[126] He had a reassuring meeting with General Fukuda, but in parts of the city soldiers of the new Chinese Fortieth Corps were tearing down Japanese flags and inevitably confrontations occurred. The next morning, the Japanese fired artillery shells into parts of the city, killing hundreds of civilians. On May 5, Chiang informed Fukuda that he would take all his military personnel across the river and leave only a few in the city to keep order.[127] But the Japanese arrested the head of Nanking's foreign affairs office in Jinan, claiming shots had been fired at them from his office. When the man refused to kneel or identify the alleged shooter, the Japanese cut out his tongue, gouged out his eyes, and then fatally shot him and more than ten of his staff members. That night, in his diary, Chiang for the first time used the old Chinese pejorative expression for Japanese: "dwarf pirates."[128]

Chiang's staff, including Feng Yuxiang's liaison officers, pressed him to bring up his old artillery and take on the Japanese. The Revolutionary Army with 100,000 men in the area far outnumbered the Japanese, but Chiang knew that Japan's armed forces with their warplanes, tanks, heavy artillery, and heavy machine guns were far superior to his and that Tokyo would send however many armies it took to wreak revenge. "The dwarf pirates are displaying this kind of perverse tyranny," he wrote. "To my loyal and faithful soldiers and civilians, who are extremely angry, I can only, with a mind of great sincerity, exhort them to calm down . . . If one does not bend, how can one extend?"[129]

When news of the fighting reached Japan, Prime Minister Tanaka ordered 16,000 reinforcements from Manchuria and Korea to Jinan. Japanese warships steamed up the Yangtze and Japanese marines landed at Wenzhou in Zhejiang province. Meanwhile, Chinese around the country protested, call-

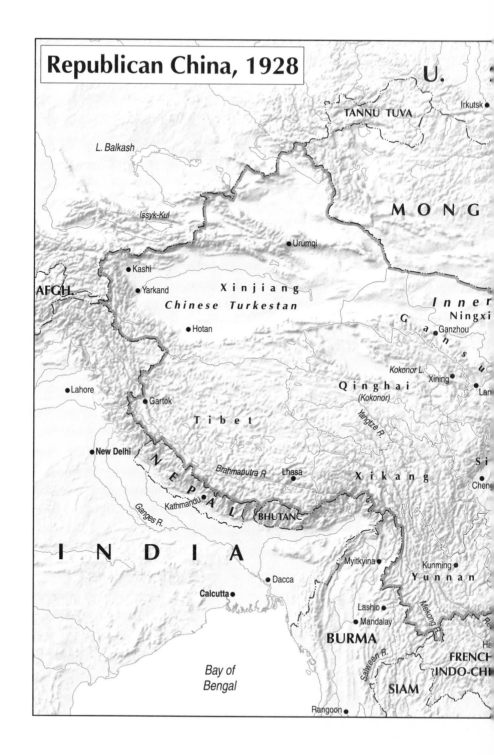

Republican China, 1928

U.

TANNU TUVA

Irkutsk

L. Balkash

Issyk-Kul

M O N G

Urumqi

Kashi

AFGH.

Yarkand

Xinjiang

I n n e r

Chinese Turkestan

Ningxi

G
a
n
s
u

Ganzhou

Hotan

Kokonor L.

Xining

Qinghai

Lan

Lahore

(Kokonor)

Gartok

Yangtze R.

T i b e t

Xikang

Si

Cheng

New Delhi

N
E
P
A
L

Brahmaputra R.

Lhasa

Kathmandu

BHUTAN

Ganges R.

Myitkyina

Kunming

I N D I A

Y u n n a n

Dacca

Calcutta

Lashio

Mandalay

Mekong R.

Re

BURMA

Ha

Salween R.

FRENCH
INDO-CH

Bay of
Bengal

SIAM

Rangoon

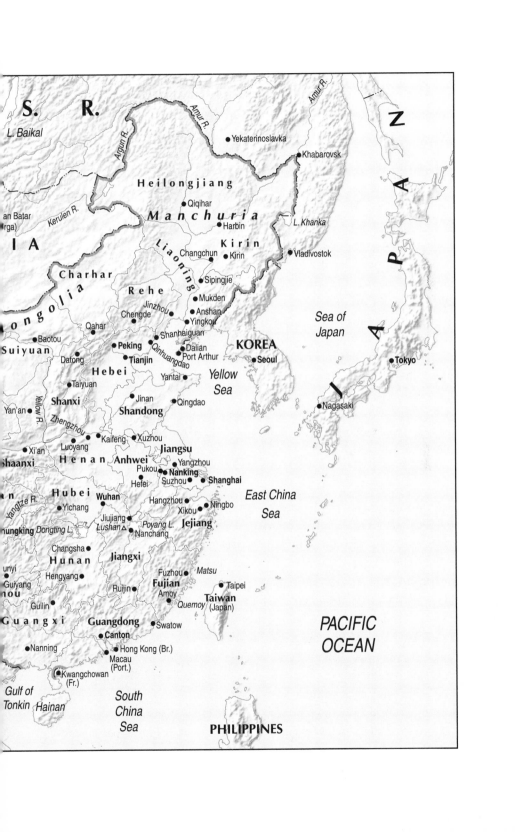

ing on the Nanking government to break diplomatic ties with Japan and institute a boycott of Japanese goods. "The people are in high spirits," Chiang remarked in his journal, "But . . . it is not easy to maintain [this spirit] over the long term and in a deep and thorough manner."[130] He ordered most of his troops to evacuate Jinan and proceed north across the Yellow River well west of the city, leaving behind two regiments totaling 5,000 men. But Fukuda demanded that the Chinese withdraw completely from the city, and the next day, asserting that his demands had not been met, the Japanese attacked the remaining Chinese soldiers. Chiang ordered his two regimental commanders left inside Jinan to break through the Japanese lines and retreat. With heavy losses, they did so. According to various estimates, the Japanese killed 2,000 to 11,000 Chinese civilians and soldiers, while, by their own account, losing only thirty-eight men.[131] On May 10, Chiang apologized to the Japanese and removed the Chinese commander, but he determined that in his diary he would now write down each day "a way to kill the Japanese."[132]

The world was outraged by the arrogance and savagery of the Japanese actions. Prime Minister Tanaka worried that things had gone too far, and agreed to negotiations. Almost a year later, on March 28, 1929, an accord was reached in which both sides accepted responsibility for the incident and the Japanese Army was given two months to withdraw from all of Shandong province, which it did.

Had Chiang anticipated the course of events in Jinan, he would probably have avoided confronting Japan at that time and place, but once the confrontation began, his decision to back down was probably the wisest course; the Japanese could have obliterated the young, poorly equipped Chinese Army. Further, in 1928, China would have found no meaningful support in the isolationist United States or elsewhere. Only when the threat of imperial Japan was linked to the profound peril to world order posed by the rise of Nazi Germany—ten years or more down the road—would the Western countries come seriously to care about Japanese armed expansion into China. But for the Japanese militarists the Jinan incident seemed to prove that China could be treated shamelessly without fear of consequence. In China, too, the humiliation sparked a new high priority in the Chinese Communist Party's propaganda—relentless attacks against Chiang Kai-shek for his appeasement of the Japanese.

In his daily journal, Chiang now wrote and rewrote the characters "revenge" but also "patience." Before "one can settle scores," he noted, "one must be strong. Ordinary people cannot easily endure great humiliation with patience. Thus in the end they have not the strength to take revenge."[133] Jinan had confirmed Chiang's rather new belief that Japan was China's greatest enemy, a more serious threat for the indefinite future than the European powers, the Communists, or the rebellious warlords. He gave a lecture to military students and urged them to help him wash away the shame of Jinan, but he also reminded them to conceal their hatred until the last moment, otherwise they would alert the Japanese. He believed his only course was to appease the Japanese but never officially to sign away Chinese sovereignty while uniting the country under a strong government and modernizing the Chinese military with German weapons and training.[134]

In May, as Chiang Kai-shek advanced on Peking, which was held by the Old Marshal of Manchuria, the ex-bandit Zhang Zuolin, the Japanese prime minister surprised Chiang—and the world at large—by announcing that Japan would accept the Kuomintang's takeover of China except for Manchuria.[135] Zhang knew that without Japanese help there was no hope of resistance in North China and he ordered his troops to withdraw to Manchuria. On the evening of June 2, dressed in their finest regalia, Zhang and his senior Manchurian officers steamed off in a special train bound for home. Two days later, as the train approached Mukden and passed under a bridge, a bomb exploded, sending the overpass hurtling down on the marshal's special car. Zhang was badly injured and died a few days later.[136]

The Japanese government in Tokyo did not know anything about the assassination, but Zhang Zuolin's twenty-eight-year-old son Zhang Xueliang—known as "the Young Marshal"—immediately suspected that the Japanese military in Manchuria was behind the killing. (Indeed, a group of Japanese officers in the imperial Guandong Army, unhappy with Tanaka's policies and feeling they could control the Young Marshal, had arranged the assassination.) The son secretly made his way to Mukden and after some political uncertainty assumed the title of commander in chief of the Manchurian (or Northeastern) Army. Zhang, it turned out, was a fervent Chinese patriot, determined never to sell out to Japan.[137] On June 19, he cabled Chiang Kai-shek and expressed his loyalty to the Chinese nation and Manchuria's determination to join the central government. The Generalissimo, however, was skeptical about the young warlord's prospects. "Han Qing

[Zhang Xueliang] seems to be sincere and honest," Chiang wrote in his diary, "but he has never experienced hardship . . . and he lacks an iron will and perseverance."[138]

After taking Peking, on July 6 Chiang met with his key military allies in the Western Hills outside Peking. Feng Yuxiang was his boisterous and cheerful self. Yan Xishan, by contrast, rarely laughed and maintained an attitude of great reserve. The Muslim Bai Chongxi was also an astringent and distant character not given to flattery or small talk. And Li Zongren, who was generally more outgoing, at such gatherings usually retained the posture of a detached observer.[139] The group of senior officers went together into the Temple of the Azure Cloud, where they gathered around the coffin of Sun Yat-sen. Although no foreign and few Chinese observers would have predicted it, three and a half years after Sun's death, the KMT flag flew from Peking to Canton. Chiang put his hand on the casket and wept openly. Feng and Yan also wiped their eyes.[140] The five generals each proclaimed undying loyalty to the founder and to the Chinese nation. But Chiang was the only one of the four who also adhered to Sun's fundamental tenet that to become a great nation again China had to become a highly centralized as well as a united country.

Chiang soon reached an agreement with Zhang Xueliang to raise the Nationalist flag—with its large, twelve-pointed, white star—over Manchuria. Prime Minister Tanaka sent a stern warning to Zhang not to align with the Nanking government, but the Young Marshal coolly replied that the decision had been based on the will of the people.[141] These were bold postures for the Chinese to take. On October 10, Chiang Kai-shek became the new director of the State Council *(Wei yuan zhang)*—in effect, president. He also remained *Zong Li* of the KMT and commander in chief of the armed forces. Zhang Xueliang was made a member of the State Council as well as chairman of the Manchurian Political Council, and on December 29, he pledged allegiance to the National government and raised the Kuomintang flag, now the national flag, at Mukden.[142]

By then the Young Marshal had come to fear that his late father's chief of staff, Yang Yuting, was plotting with the Japanese. On January 10, 1929, Zhang invited Yang and a close associate of the chief of staff to dinner. At some point, Zhang excused himself for a smoke of opium (or, depending on the story, a shot of morphine); guards then entered the room and killed Yang and his colleague. According to one account, Zhang had flipped a coin to decide whether he himself should kill Yang.[143]

This newest ally for Chiang Kai-shek was yet another warlord, but the wealthiest of them all as well as a playboy and an opium addict. Even more than the other regional militarists, however, the Young Marshal was a fervent Chinese partisan who nevertheless sought to hold on to a high degree of autonomy not only for his regional "kingdom," but also for himself, his big family, and his inner circle of senior officers. Yet Zhang was also a relatively liberal and modern person, an idealist willing, if necessary, to risk his legacy, fiefdom, and career in pursuit of his dreams of a great, united China. While many of the warlords still resented the baffling succession to the KMT leadership of the upstart Chiang Kai-shek, Zhang Xueliang was of a new generation. He looked up to the commander in chief, whose taciturnity and rigid personality seemed to reflect the same toughness and determination of Zhang's father. Decades later, Zhang told an interviewer, "At first I gave all my heart and soul to help [Chiang Kai-shek]."[144]

To the chagrin of the Japanese Army, Prime Minister Tanaka, despite his previous threats, tacitly accepted Manchuria's reaffirmation of its status as a sovereign part of Chinese territory. Now at last, from the Ussuri River in the far north to the border with Southeast Asia, China seemed to be fully joined, although the central government's real authority was limited to a few provinces. Against all odds and expectations, Chiang Kai-shek had defeated the warlords or brought them under the umbrella of a republican government and a single party—the Kuomintang. It was a historic and impressive achievement.

At an important military demobilization conference in January 1929, Chiang cited Germany and Japan as the models for China's armed forces reorganization, and underscored that this effort required returning military control to the National government.[145] But neither the warlords nor their extended entourages and families were interested in trading away control over millions of Chinese people and enormous pools of resources in exchange for key roles in the National government. In their minds, Chiang simply wanted to concentrate all military power in his hands at their expense. The regional lords all pretended to agree on demobilization, but when vice chairman of the Military Council Yan Xishan and minister of war Feng Yuxiang abandoned their central government positions in Nanking and fled back to their domains, Chiang realized his only option was to play the militarists off against each other, bribe them, buy out their supporters, and if necessary, defeat them on the battlefield.

Consequently there followed over the next two years a prolonged drama involving maneuverings, intrigue, and sometimes large military battles between Chiang and the various warlords looking to expand their sway or combine against him. Hundreds of thousands of troops were involved—and tens of thousands died. Most importantly, through all the intrigue Zhang Xueliang remained loyal to the Generalissimo. Espionage and covert activity, especially large bribes to various warlords, played an important part in Chiang's successes. By this time Chen Lifu, on Chiang's orders, had established an intelligence group called the Investigation Section of the (KMT) Organization Department. Later, demonstrating his style of creating overlapping and competing factions and bureaucracies, Chiang asked a Whampoa graduate named Dai Li to lead a new Bureau of Investigation and Statistics in the Military Council. The two intelligence units both engaged in covert operations, which included buying off enemies, occasional assassinations, and black propaganda, as well as the clandestine collection of information through infiltration, threats, and bribery.[146]

In the midst of Chiang's struggle with the warlords, a crisis erupted with the Soviet Union when in April 1929, the Manchurian leader, Zhang Xueliang, acting on his own he later said, seized the Soviet consulate in Harbin and its incriminating documents. Three months later, with Chiang's promise of troop support if necessary, he took over the Chinese Eastern Railway, which had been under joint administration by the two nations since 1896. The Young Marshal and Chiang naively thought that Stalin would not dare invade China because of the international repercussions, including from the Japanese—or that if he did, the Manchurian forces would be a match for the Red Army's Far Eastern divisions.[147]

Zhang and Chiang were wrong. On October 12, 1929, Soviet troops under Chiang's erstwhile friend and adviser, General Blucher, crossed the border into Manchuria and quickly routed Zhang Xueliang's best troops, capturing 8,000 men. The Young Marshal fell back to a new line of defense and cabled Nanking for assistance, but Chiang quickly backed off his earlier bold stance and proposed that Zhang Xueliang retreat. In December, Nanking and the Mukden governments negotiated the Khabarovsk Protocol in which Stalin,

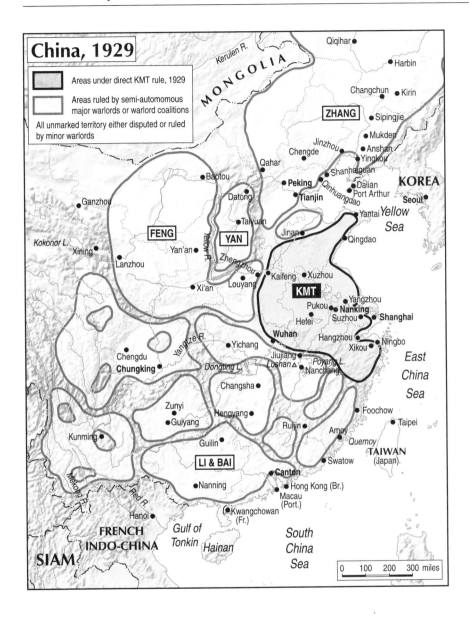

China, 1929

Areas under direct KMT rule, 1929

Areas ruled by semi-autonomous major warlords or warlord coalitions

All unmarked territory either disputed or ruled by minor warlords

not wanting to provoke the Japanese, settled for simple restoration of the Soviet position in the Chinese Eastern Railway and an additional seat on the railway company's board. The Japanese, however, took note of Chiang's renewed readiness to retreat politically and militarily in the face of superior force as well as the failure of the international community to respond to his pleas for support.[148]

III

The unprecedented world recession that began in October 1929 had a profound effect on China. As a result of the collapse of international trade, China's budding exports in silk, tobacco, cotton, and soybeans sharply declined.
In some rural areas, tens of thousands died of malnutrition. The hard times
made it more difficult for the government in Nanking—a shaky, besieged
political coalition—to institute financial and rural reforms. They also created
fertile conditions for the radicalization of youth and intellectuals, boosting
the idea that a property-free Communist society represented the wave of the
future. In addition, the circumstances convinced Stalin that an uneven but
global revolutionary upsurge was under way and China was one of its key areas. In a Comintern review of the CCP financial situation sent to Stalin on
June 11, 1928, it was reported that from August 1927 to the end of 1928 the
Soviets had provided about 1.8 million Chinese dollars to the Chinese Communists.[149]

Chiang Kai-shek often warned publicly of the Communist threat, but he
wanted first to triumph over the warlords before dealing with the guerrilla
bases. He thus delayed a major expedition to crush Mao Zedong and the
other CCP guerrilla leaders, leaving "bandit suppression" efforts up to local
and provincial military commanders.[150] Given three years to build up, however, some of the peoples' enclaves or "soviets" had grown into substantial
forces. As one CCP leader, Zhang Guotao, concluded, "the main reason" for
the growth of the CCP enclaves was Chiang's concentration on the second
phase of the Northern Expedition and then the conflicts with the warlords.
These wars had raged up and down the country, worsening already desperate
conditions, alienating country folk, and creating wandering bands of desert-
ers and defeated soldiers, who were easily recruited into the CCP. Most important of all, the wars between the KMT factions preoccupied the central
government and gave the CCP soviets, aided by Russian money and sometimes weapons, time to expand.[151]

The growth of the CCP guerrilla bases from 1927 to 1930 also reflected
the impressive dedication, leadership, and organizational skills of the young
Communist leaders who had taken to the hills in mid-1927. Chiang still
longed to imbue his party and army with the same spirit. In the Jinggang
Mountains, a young military leader named Zhu De, whom Zhou Enlai had
recruited into the Communist Party when both were in France, joined forces
with Mao's small company. Together they created the Red Army's Fourth

Route Army, "a band of soldiers, bandits, robbers, beggars, and prostitutes," the dispossessed of society who led "the most precarious existence." At this time the three CCP soviets combined had only 15,000 rifles.[152] Mao's legendary tactical slogan was key to the group's survival: "The enemy advances, we retreat; the enemy camps, we harass; the enemy tires, we attack; the enemy retreats, we pursue."

In June 1930, conflict broke out once again in China when four of the usual warlords, Li, Bai, Feng, and "Ironsides" Zhang Fakui, as well as this time Yan Xishan, all joined the returned Wang Jingwei in a new coalition: the "Movement to save China from Chiang's dictatorship."[153] The warlords were worried by Chiang's continuing efforts to create a strong central government, including his attempt to build a powerful central army with German weapons and training, and to eliminate provincial and regional currencies—all of which were essential to the emergence of a China that could stand up to Japan.

Nationwide, the anti-Chiang coalition comprised an impressive 600,000 armed men. Chiang had one million troops but a good number of these were on garrison and security duty. Zhang Xueliang in Manchuria held the balance of power. A series of bloody clashes during the summer and into the fall of 1930 laid waste once again to vast areas of Henan, Hunan, and Shandong. But Chiang's Central Army, including for the first time German-trained troops who in the end were joined by Zhang Xueliang's fur-hatted Manchurians, prevailed.[154] It was a costly war—in total 240,000 were killed or wounded.[155] Chiang did not pursue the defeated warlords into their respective home provinces and he even dropped the idea of trying to persuade or compel them to implement large reductions in their armies. Perhaps this restraint resulted from a naïve hope that his assumed sincerity and new prestige would bring them around; more likely he knew Zhang Xueliang would strongly oppose such a policy.[156] But the survival of the warlords would leave Chiang again with a giant but splintered coalition army of mixed quality and loyalty.[157]

Nonetheless, four years of warfare had established him as an accomplished military leader. With no tanks, one artillery unit with World War I cannon, frequently no maps, virtually no trucks, and only a few main rail lines, he had successfully maneuvered multiple army corps over fronts that could stretch as long as a thousand miles.[158] Foreign correspondents joined the Chinese in reporting episodes of Chiang's personal bravery.[159] He concentrated his forces in some areas, adopted defensive measures in others, and executed effective flanking moves. Against the warlords he had also continued to use divide-and-rule tactics as well as the promise of large subsidies or personal bribes—strategies that would be of no use against the Communists or the Japanese. His armies, however, were much more motivated than those of the Chinese militarists, and in his own mind and that of many Chinese his triumphs over the repeated rebellions gave evidence of a powerful destiny. He still complained in his diary of his own shortcomings—in part as an expression of rote neo-Confucian self-cultivation and ever-higher standards of behavior—but the lamentations also seemed to reflect a lack of extravagant self-delusion and a usually realistic grasp of his own and his army's weaknesses.

At the end of 1930, Chiang issued a public proclamation that the central government would now focus on reform, political rebuilding, and the reconstruction of "all business from agriculture to commerce." He admitted that during the military campaigns financial controls and economic management had been "chaotic" and pledged extensive financial reform—including a system of annual open budgets, tough accounting and monitoring procedures, a centralization of all the various currencies then in existence, and most importantly, a strong, effective, and honest central government. He was no doubt serious, for in every respect such a government was in his as well as China's interest. The so-called Nanking Decade (1927–1937) would in fact suggest to the world, and to the Chinese people, what a modern Chinese state might begin to achieve. This embryonic and mixed beginning would be accomplished despite terrible conditions created by the world depression, a collapse in exports, no foreign aid, record droughts and floods, continuing clashes with Japan and domestic rebels, enormous military budgets, traditional rampant corruption, a lack of central control over most provinces and their finances and revenues, and unending factional maneuvering within the hydra-headed KMT.

Nanking, which sits on the southern bank of the sometimes four-mile-wide Yangtze River, is a city that has been inhabited continuously for four thousand years, even if under different names. In 1931 it was still an active center of art and culture as well as industry.[160] The KMT government had taken over the old palace in the city built by the "Heavenly Emperor" of the Taipings, and the process of cutting through the city's narrow, winding *hutongs* with new wide boulevards was already well under way. With a population of only about 340,000, it was a smaller city than Shanghai and lacked big department stores, a racetrack, and other Western diversions. It was even sweatier in the summer than Shanghai, but Mayling, unlike the wives of some KMT officials, moved there, and in the Purple Mountains outside of the city she built a small mansion known as "Mayling Palace" not too far from the elaborate new mausoleum of Sun Yat-sen. She was frequently at her husband's office or out in the town making appearances with groups that were helping orphans, the wounded, and the families of dead soldiers. And she still sometimes traveled with Chiang on his military campaigns.

But Mayling was also troubled. She had suffered a miscarriage in August the previous year and afterward endured bouts of severe depression. The miscarriage, mentioned by the Generalissimo in his diary, seemed to refute the widespread assumption, including apparently his own, that he was infertile due to his past relationships with prostitutes.[161] Many years later, Madame would tell her nephews and nieces that she had wanted children but because an incompetent doctor in Nanking had bungled a procedure, she could not conceive.[162] Clearly, she had wanted a child for ordinary human reasons but also as an heir to the man who seemed destined to be considered the father of modern China. When her mother died in July 1931 another "terrible depression" settled on Mayling and she felt "spiritual despair, bleakness, desolation."[163]

Since his wedding day, Chiang had regularly read the Bible that Mayling had given him. He made up his mind to go through it twice before deciding whether to become a Christian. When he was in town, Mayling and her missionary friends sometimes conducted Bible-reading sessions with the Generalissimo, and he usually carried a Bible while traveling.[164] After three years of study he agreed to be baptized in the Soong family's church in Shanghai. Like most everything else he professed to believe in, Chiang took his Christianity seriously. According to his later pastor on Taiwan, Chiang found Christianity appealing because it stressed the conversion of moral thought to action and was consistent with the moral teachings of Confucius.[165] Chiang's philosophical and emotional preoccupation with the concept of shame also fit with his new religion's emphasis on sin and atonement. In addition, the practice of Job-like perseverance in the face of suffering, difficulty, and death was consistent with his ascetic, neo-Confucian outlook. Some of Chiang's critics at-

tacked his adoption of a foreign religion, but there is no evidence that it created any more of a problem for the eclectic Chinese people than did Mao's
embrace of a foreign ideology.

Chiang appointed the governor of Jiangxi, Lu Diping, commander in chief
of the twelve divisions that he had assigned to the first "suppression" campaign against Mao's soviet in Lu's province. The campaign began in the autumn of 1930, but about half of the Nationalist troops who trudged into the
Jinggang Mountains were killed or captured. In addition, a division commander, Zhang Huican, was taken prisoner and beheaded, a sign that, unlike
Chiang's conflicts with the warlords, this was to be a ruthless struggle to the
death.[166] In April 1931 Chiang sent He Yingqin and 200,000 Feng Yuxiang
veterans to Jiangxi on the second suppression campaign, but the soldiers were
not used to either the climate or the food and they suffered another debacle.[167] At the same time, Wang Jingwei and the southern warlords established
yet another rival national government, this time in Canton. The southerners,
however, did not immediately pose a military threat and Chiang hastened off
to Nanchang personally to command the third suppression campaign. This
was "the toughest time" the republic had faced, he confided to his diary.[168]

On July 1, with 130,000 of his best troops, including several of his own
loyal divisions from the First Army Group (an expansion of the First Corps),
Chiang sent two columns deep into the guerrilla area.[169] After fierce fighting
and heavy losses on both sides, in the last battle of this campaign the CCP's
Red Army lost one-fifth of the 20,000 men it had committed. Chiang seemed
on the "verge of success when the campaign was derailed by the outbreak of
the Manchurian or Mukden Incident."[170]

This new crisis began during the summer of 1931 when the Young Marshal's soldiers in Manchuria captured a Japanese officer out of uniform on an
intelligence mission and killed him when he supposedly tried to escape. The
Japanese ultranationalists seized on the incident, and under popular pressure,
the relatively moderate Tokyo cabinet publicly demanded a "final resolution"
of the China problem. Meanwhile, Japanese officers in the politically radical
Imperial Guandong Army stationed at Port Arthur and along the South
Manchurian Railway decided to act on their own. On the night of September
18, 1931, they set off an explosion on the rail line outside of Mukden and
fired artillery into the nearby Chinese garrison. Fighting broke out and the
Japanese commander ordered a full-scale attack. As Japanese troops overran

The "Young Marshal" of Manchuria, Zhang Xueliang *(second from left),* with Chiang Kai-shek *(second from right)* at a national leadership conference in Nanking, April 1931. The two men's bold reassertion of China's sovereignty over Manchuria would in five months lead to Japanese occupation of the entire region. On the far left is the Muslim leader Ma Fuxiang. Central News Agency, Taipei.

Mukden, Marshal Zhang asked Nanking what he should do. At that moment, Chiang was on a ship on his way back to Nanking, and the answer from the Executive Yuan was "Do what you think appropriate." The Young Marshal gathered that Nanking had no idea how to deal with the crisis and he ordered the Manchurian troops to withdraw.[171]

At this time, Japanese forces in Manchuria numbered only about 10,000, while Zhang Xueliang had 200,000.[172] In interviews long after the death of Chiang Kai-shek, Zhang took the blame for having miscalculated Japanese intentions and for having retreated once the attack had begun.[173] But the Japanese had large reserves a short train ride away in Korea and most of the Manchurian troops were actually in Hebei province. And even after Chiang Kai-shek arrived in Nanking and began communicating with Zhang Xueliang he did not command the Manchurian to counterattack nor did he send Central Army divisions to his aid. Chiang had earlier gambled that if China strongly asserted its sovereign rights in Manchuria, the Japanese would not pursue hegemony in the region. But still, in his first military meeting after the "Mukden Incident," he emphasized that at a time of domestic turmoil and inadequate preparation China must avoid an all-out war with Japan. Thus in practice he reverted to his 1928 post-Jinan strategy of "eating gall" and appeasing Japan while struggling for real national unity and over time sufficient strength to confront the Imperial Army. This policy of temporary appeasement was to last six years.[174]

The Japanese quickly moved on from Mukden and without resistance occupied Changchun and other Manchurian cities. Meanwhile, Chiang still tried to make Japan and the world believe he was truly prepared to go to war. He promoted a national boycott of Japanese goods, publicly pledged to send Central Army troops to Manchuria, discussed war mobilization with his staff, and talked about moving the capital and China's principal armies to the Northwest. He thought all this might alarm the international community into pressuring Japan. He met several times with senior Western diplomats in Nanking and in cogent presentations candidly admitted that the crisis was due indirectly to the weak attitude that the Chinese side—or in fact, he himself—had taken, but emphasized that it was now essential to deal firmly with Japan in the current crisis. "Under no circumstance," he said, would "China yield to threats of force nor negotiate in any shape or form until the Japanese troops have been withdrawn and the *status quo ante* September 18 restored."[175] In fact, Nanking would negotiate, but the accords would never be ratified at the highest level of the Chinese government. For their part, the United States and the other Western powers responded with rhetorical support but refused to send observers or aid; similarly, the League of Nations sent a powerless commission of inquiry.

Hardly deterred by verbal criticism, Tokyo signaled its readiness—even eagerness—for a wider war, sending its warships up the Whangpoo River and holding naval exercises in the Yangtze. In early October Chiang lamented, "The Japanese threat is still there but I have done nothing. How ridiculous I am."[176] At one point he told Zhang Qun and Mayling separately that he was determined to go to war, and she said she would live or die with him. But he also believed that China was so feeble it was "impossible for it to be weaker."[177]

To politically active Chinese, the refusal to fight seemed a craven performance. From the beginning of the Mukden Incident, student demonstrators poured into the streets demanding armed resistance. Twenty thousand students gathered in the capital. Of these, one thousand from Central University in Nanking broke into the office of Chiang's foreign minister, Wang Zhengting, and beat him up. Wang Jingwei's rebel opposition group in Canton, which had been on the verge of war with Nanking, called for national unity but also for Chiang's resignation.

With most of Manchuria under Japanese control, the odds of the invaders leaving peacefully seemed increasingly remote. In fact, Chiang believed that the Japanese "would rather give up the three main islands of Japan than abandon Manchuria." But in his diary he again warned that rushing into war could "cause our nation to perish instead of helping it."[178] On October 15, he wrote that he would quit, then he changed his mind. In the middle of the month, he and Mayling flew to Shanghai and met with Wang Jingwei and Hu Hanmin. The two Sun Yat-sen stalwarts, who had long been determined to oust the upstart Chiang and were now supported by warlords who wanted a weak Chinese central government, accused Chiang of not resisting the Japanese and of acting like a dictator. "They slandered and laughed at me as usual," Chiang wrote.[179] As the Chinese government evacuated the last towns in Manchuria and anti-Chiang demonstrations continued to grow, Chiang changed his mind again and informed the Canton group that if necessary to unite the country, his retirement "would not be a problem."[180]

At one point, Chiang wrote that he "hated" the students, but he continued to go forth and address them, including in freezing weather, telling them either to return to their classes or join the army to fight the Japanese. Still, the violence continued.[181] The government banned all demonstrations, but thousands of students, demanding war with Japan, flowed into the capital, again assaulting high-ranking officials.[182] The police rushed hither and yon to put down the unrest. With the situation spiraling out of control, and the criticism focusing on Chiang, he again discussed the option of retirement with his associates. Chiang confided to one official that if he did not resign, he would have to bring the country under military rule with himself as the paramount leader, that is, dictator.[183] He would not consider the option demanded by his critics of war with Japan because he believed at this time this would be disastrous.

In the midst of the ongoing turmoil, Chiang wrote probably the first affectionate thoughts he had ever expressed about his son, Ching-kuo. "I miss Ching-kuo very much," he said. "I am bad because I am not taking good care of him. I am sorry about that . . . Alas! I am neither loyal to the nation and the party nor filial to my mother nor kind to my children. I feel ashamed."[184] These sentiments may well have been inspired by a visit earlier in December by his estranged sister-in-law, the leftist Soong Chingling, who had lived in Moscow for two years after the 1927 purge. Obviously speaking with authority, she told Chiang that if he would free an imprisoned Comintern agent named Hilarie Naulen and his wife, Moscow would arrange the repatriation of Chiang Ching-kuo.[185]

From Chiang's diary entries, it appears that Mayling, hearing of Chingling's proposal, urged her husband to accept the trade. Chiang, however, wrote in his diary that over 300,000 of his men and officers, who were all "like his sons," had died in the cause; thus he could not put a personal need above the nation's interest. Releasing an enemy of the people in order to free his son was simply not an option.[186]

Chiang's decision not to intervene on his son's behalf even with a relatively minor concession added to his sense of martyrdom, which had emerged with the rising tide of criticism. He probably felt that another resignation, like that in 1927, would regain for him his lost moral authority, while probably leading eventually to a full recovery of his positions—although there were no guarantees. So on December 15, 1931, Chiang Kai-shek resigned all his posts, and the following week he and Madame Chiang left Nanking by air. They first landed on a grass field near Fenghua and from there traveled by car along a new dirt road that wound up the old sedan chair route to Xikou.

3

The Nanking Decade

Just as with his previous resignation in 1927, Chiang, on hiatus in Xikou during the winter of 1931–1932, was soon receiving messages from Whampoa generals declaring they would take orders only from him and that since his departure, funds had not arrived to pay the troops. The loss of Manchurian customs and tariffs had immediately reduced by 15 percent the government's total customs revenue—its main income source.[1] In addition, provinces withheld their salt tax revenue from the new central government headed by Sun Yat-sen's son, Sun Fo.[2] Business organizations, civic groups, and even some student associations now clamored for the commander in chief's return. Chiang also learned that Moscow, following its ploy regarding Chingkuo's return, had proposed to Nanking a restoration of diplomatic relations. Chiang could assume that Stalin wanted to boost the anti-Japanese faction in the KMT and was not sure where Chiang Kai-shek stood.[3]

In a January 1932 speech at the Wu Ling School in Xikou, published in Shanghai and elsewhere, Chiang reiterated that the government should "never surrender and never sign unequal treaties with Japan." But, he warned, given its present national strength and spirit, the nation must not act out of anger and emotion, otherwise "someday, defeated and kneeling down it will have to sign new, humiliating treaties." The result would be to "give up . . . five thousand years of civilization."[4] His words resonated with those in charge. While few of the men now running the Nanking government and none of those in opposition in Canton liked Chiang, they reluctantly accepted that in this crisis he was again indispensable, and within a month they capitulated. In January 1932, Chiang and Wang Jingwei met in Hangzhou and agreed that

Wang would become head of government, replacing Sun Fo, and Chiang would return as military commander.[5]

By then the crisis with Japan had shifted to Shanghai, where violent anti-Japanese incidents were occurring daily.[6] At the end of January, a contingent of Japanese marines landed in the city supposedly to protect Japanese citizens. When soldiers of Cai Tingkai's Cantonese 19th Group Army opened fire on the marines, Japanese planes bombed the Chinese city, killing many civilians. Chiang personally assumed overall direction of the military action and sent an open telegraph to the front saying that he would resist the invasion until death.[7] At the same time, he ordered the establishment of a temporary capital in Luoyang in Henan province to signal that the government was preparing for a long, drawn-out war. The Japanese rushed in more marines and warships, bringing the total number of Japanese troops in the city to 50,000.[8] In response, Du Yuesheng sent Green Gang sharpshooters to attack the Japanese behind the lines.[9]

According to Chiang, he warned General Cai that the enemy might land behind Chinese lines at Liuhe, on the southern banks of the Yangtze. Cai failed or was unable to send troops to defend this site, and on March 1, Japanese ships steamed up the Yangtze to Liuhe with 10,000 troops. In disorder—with 4,000 killed and 7,700 wounded since the fighting began—the entire Chinese force fell back from Shanghai.[10] Chinese newspapers, student groups, and clan, temple, and business associations demanded all-out war, but Chiang authorized a local armistice that defined a neutral zone around the city where Chinese troops were prohibited. This truce, like all his government's agreements with the Japanese, was not signed by Wang Jingwei or himself; in their eyes, they thus made the accords nonofficial. In March, Chiang resumed his positions as chairman of the Military Council and chief of the General Staff.[11]

Helped again by the huge distraction for the government of the Japanese attack on the Chinese-administered part of Shanghai, the scattered enclaves or "soviets" of the CCP had continued to grow rapidly. Mao's Jiangxi soviet was the largest, encompassing thirty counties and three million people; the second largest was Zhang Guotao's Oyuwan outpost, covering areas in central China of Hubei, Henan, and Anhui. Two campaigns by the Nationalists against the Oyuwan base failed miserably and after the fighting with Japan calmed down, Chiang in April 1932 mustered some 400,000 troops for another effort, this time building concentric rings of fortifications around the enemy. Realizing he was far outnumbered and almost surrounded, in August Zhang Guotao led most of the Communist forces in Oyuwan in a successful breakout and a march west into Sichuan on what would prove to be a four-year odyssey, one even more remarkable than Mao's Long March.[12]

In June 1932, Chiang told a military conference that "the roots of the CCP lie in the inefficiency and corruption of our government machine . . . If we don't win decisively this time [against the Communists], we will be in trouble because we cannot fight a resistance war [against Japan] while being attacked in the rear."[13] But two more suppression campaigns in 1932 and early 1933 against the Communist forces in Jiangxi failed with heavy losses and thousands of arms captured. In late May 1933, Chiang took command of his fifth "anti-bandit" campaign and, taking a lesson from the tactic used on the Oyuwan soviet, concentrated on the construction of a network of slowly advancing blockhouses.[14] This time, he assembled an 800,000-man army, most of whom were employed in expanding, supplying, and maintaining the ring of mud and brick outposts protected with interconnecting machine gun fire. Both sides suffered thousands of casualties, but by 1934, a total of 14,000 blockhouses and 1,500 miles of new roads had been constructed in the combat zone, providing an effective blockade of the Communist areas.[15]

Meanwhile, the cease-fire with Japan had applied only to Shanghai and on the first day of 1933, Japanese troops advanced out of Manchuria and occupied Shanhaiguan, the coastal gateway to Manchuria situated on the Yellow Sea at the eastern end of the Great Wall. The Manchurian troops defending the city put up a desultory resistance but were no match for the Japanese. In January, in explaining to a military conference his failure to commit Central Army troops to turn back the Japanese, Chiang used the hoary phrase "first pacify the interior then resist the external [threat]" *(kang wai bi xian an nei)*.[16] He would repeat it frequently over the next four years.

The Japanese pushed farther south, threatening Peking and Tianjin, and Chiang, supported by Wang Jingwei, abjectly agreed to a local armistice in the North—the Tanggu Truce—which declared the northern part of Hebei province a demilitarized zone, effectively ceding another huge chunk of Chinese territory to Japanese de facto (but not de jure) control.[17] Chiang told a Chinese officers' meeting that the goal of the truce was to "slow Japan down a little" and gain time "to regain North China, recuperate, and figure out what to do next."[18] Furthermore, over the next three to five years, he said, "changes in Japan's domestic policy as well as international changes" could relieve the situation and offer the opportunity "eventually to win."[19] Meanwhile, he forbade the building of new factories in the coastal areas, and ordered plans for moving heavy industries to the interior of the country.[20]

In March 1934, Chiang told a group of senior political leaders that "fewer than 1,100 days remained" before the war with Japan would begin—an estimate only about forty-three days too long.[21] His prediction that the conflict would last ten years was also fairly accurate. During this period, he said, foreign powers would eventually intervene, a world war would erupt, and finally, revolution would break out in Japan.[22]

When the Japanese overran Jehol, Zhang Xueliang resigned all his posts and entered a missionary hospital in Shanghai where a "cold turkey" treatment cured him of his opium addiction. He emerged with a renewed appetite for society—if not politics and war—and the company of women. In April, the Young Marshal and a large entourage, including both his wife and a young concubine, Alice Chao, sailed for Europe. Also among the passengers was yet another mistress, Countess Eddy Ciano, the daughter of Mussolini and wife of the Italian ambassador. She would later ask Zhang to return the letters she had written him.[23]

The Generalissimo sent the 130,000 soldiers remaining in Zhang Xueliang's Manchurian Army to Jiangxi to join the next "anti-bandit" campaign.[24] Chiang knew that military action had to be accompanied with "political measures to win over peoples' minds, attitudes, and allegiances." He told his officers that the struggle against the Communists was "70 percent political and 30 percent military."[25] Specific battles would be fruitless, he said, if "the CCP's propaganda wins the support of the people."[26] So in addition to pressing the military campaign, he would spend a great deal of time and resources on training civic action and propaganda teams, even establishing a special training camp for them at the mountain resort of Lushan in northern Jiangxi. In several speeches at the school, Chiang said land reform was "the life and death issue for the country," and the "fundamental problem of China" that would have to be carried out "under military order."[27] As with the issue of fighting corruption, however, the main question was how to carry out land reform without upsetting stability within the military and the Kuomintang.

As the ring was tightening around the Red Army, the Communist commander in Jiangxi, Zhu De, and the chief political commissar, Zhou Enlai, with an inventory of 90,000 rifles and several hundred light and heavy machine guns, tried various ways to break the blockade. Stalin was providing what aid he could. On June 2, 1933, the Comintern agent in Shanghai reported plans to purchase an airplane that "can easily reach our area" (apparently Jiangxi) to be flown by an American pilot. On November 2, Moscow instructed Shanghai to buy "heavy airplanes, gas masks and medicines" and asked whether U.S. dollars or Mexican silver dollars were required for the purchase. In 1933, CCP Shanghai reported it had "received" 3 million Mexican silver dollars at a place called Suiting, but the money was "transferred to Shanghai" for security. The CCP asked for an additional US$250,000.[28] Comintern records suggest that an uncertain but possibly a good deal of these funds would reach Mao's enclave.

Unlike Mao, Chiang was receiving no foreign military or economic aid, and was paying for weapons and training from Germany. But at this stage he could believe that his overall strategy to unify the country was working: he could appease the Japanese for the time being, while building the army and destroying the foreign-supported Communists.

The Prussian ideal intrigued Chiang; long before he ever heard of Hitler, he knew from his reading and his no-nonsense German advisers that Germany was disciplined and orderly. He especially admired the way that Germany, Japan, and Turkey had in recent years raised their respective "national spirits." Before sending his adopted son off to the *Kriegsschule* (military academy) in Munich, he told him, "Germany is the only country from which we can learn something. They can give us the base from which to develop our own style: firm and solid."[29]

But this affinity for German achievements was not a sign of craven Nazism. Unlike the Japanese, Chiang showed no interest in duplicating the key aspects of Nazi ideology: racial supremacy, territorial expansion, and hemispheric if not world conquest. In his diary he never mentioned, much less welcomed, any of the milestones of the rise of fascism in Germany such as Hitler's elevation to chancellor, the Reichstag Fire, Germany as a one-party state, or the naming of Hitler as Führer. Chiang was fascist in neither ends nor means.

During the 1930s, a semi-secret political force, the Society for Persistent Conduct (Li xing she), which came to be called the "Blue Shirts," did play a brief but infamous role in KMT China, and many writers have seen Chiang's support for this organization as evidence of his fascist proclivities. The society, like the storm troopers of the Nazi Party and their counterparts in Italy, owed its origin to a small group of frustrated and idealistic army officers dedicated to the cause of nationalism and the supreme leader Chiang. Like their Japanese fascist and Communist adversaries, the group's zeal convinced its members that their ends justified extreme means, including assassination. But unlike the Brown Shirts, who numbered two million and functioned as Hitler's private paramilitary, the exclusive Blue Shirts had only about three hundred members when it disbanded in 1938. Mass organizations affiliated with the society supposedly numbered in the several hundred thousands, but they were not used as storm troopers in the streets.[30]

The Chinese organization's main emphasis was on instilling military discipline and patriotism in the nation's schools, including loyalty to "the leader." Racism and conquest were not what they taught. Some Blue Shirts argued for a formal proclamation that Chiang Kai-shek was an infallible commander, but they did not succeed. Despite his frequent self-criticism, Chiang was certainly highly egotistical, but neither in his speeches nor in his diaries did he ever suggest that he supported adulation of himself in the manner of fascist and Communist rulers. He did not allow statues of himself. His immediate civilian staff on the mainland still called him "Wei yuan zhang" or simply "Yuan zhang," that is, director or chairman (of the Military Council), not the honorific "Ling xiu," and on Taiwan he was referred to as simply "Xiansheng" (sir) or "Zong tong" (president).[31]

In a much-cited "secret speech" reputedly given in 1932, Chiang supposedly praised foreign "fascists" specifically and declared that China "must create a dictatorship," by implication a fascist one. The quotation is purportedly documented in an undated, "specially bound" volume of 1930s Japanese government materials that cite anti-Japanese activities and covert measures against Manchuko, the Japanese puppet state of Manchuria, by the Blue Shirts.[32] It seems likely that the quotation was fabricated by the Japanese propaganda organization that printed and distributed the volume. Yet the quotation has been cited by distinguished scholars to prove Chiang's admiration of fascism.

Another probably inaccurate quotation has Chiang saying that "the success of the Japanese fascists and the Italian fascists is due" to the revival of their national spirit, and if China's revolution is to succeed, "we must create a party dictatorship." Even in this suspect quotation, after allegedly praising the two countries' "fascism," Chiang goes on to describe the national spirit that China must revive as one that embraces "loyalty, filial piety, virtue, love, harmony, peace, propriety, righteousness, purity, and a sense of shame."[33] These were not the sort of spiritual virtues that Hitler, Mussolini, the Japanese fascists—or for that matter, the Chinese Communists—sought to renew.

Chiang could be heartless and sometimes ruthless, but he lacked the pathological megalomania and the absolutist ideology of a totalitarian dictator. He was more self-delusional than hypocritical about his benevolent objectives, which he continually reaffirmed to himself, and (just as Mao and Zhou believed) he was not cynical about his claimed morality and ethics—he was an earnest man. Like Mao, however, Chiang was not a man of great human empathy. He occasionally expressed great personal anguish and responsibility for his soldiers who had died, but his diaries reflect little or no remorse over innocent lives lost by violent acts that he justified as vitally necessary. Such an absence of regret, however, is not unusual in the annals of war and politics even among democratic leaders who have felt it necessary to order horrendous military actions.

During his mainland years, unlike his fascist and other totalitarian adversaries, Chiang was required to endure frequent criticism from the press and political rivals. The Blue Shirts were often condemned in the press and their misdeeds exposed. Chiang's initial enthusiasm for the Blue Shirts reflected his recognition of the corruption, factionalism, and ineffectualness of the Kuomintang. Initially, he hoped that with the Blue Shirts he had finally found his loyal and idealistic followers, similar to those in Mao's camp. Chiang only learned of the Blue Shirts' existence in January 1932, and for several months he favored young members as assistants. But by July he was complaining of the "immaturity" of the Blue Shirts and in a letter to the newspaper *Dagongbao* asked, "How would I differ from the Communists . . . if I were to imitate the so-called fascists . . . of Italy?" By mid-1934 he had become "thoroughly disillusioned with the organization."[34]

Unlike in Communist areas, censorship of journals and newspapers in KMT China was erratic. Closing down a Chinese paper or magazine in the foreign concessions or treaty ports was especially problematic. One striking example was the anti-Chiang weekly *Life (Sheng huo)*, which consistently attacked Chiang for his appeasement of Japan. It was shut down first in 1933, reemerged as *New Life (Xin Sheng)*, was closed in July 1935, but resumed within months under another name that included the word "life." Several other newspapers critical of the government, such as *Dagongbao* and *Guang ming ri bao,* were available in the KMT areas throughout the Nanking period.[35] According to Comintern documents, the CCP secretly used Moscow's money to fund newspapers in Shanghai, Tianjin, Hong Kong, and even an unidentified city in Japanese-ruled Manchuria.[36]

Antigovernment commentaries also continued to flow from the media in warlord-controlled areas; for example, the daily *Guan cha ri bao* in Yunnan. The sensational Chinese "mosquito" press was also impossible to keep in check. While these tabloids focused on social gossip and news about celebrity sing-song girls, they also occasionally featured stories of KMT corruption and misrule—some true, some not. Even more unregulated were the *Chuan dan* (literally, sheets passed along), which were full of political harangues.[37] In most cities, Chinese readers never lacked for antigovernment and anti-Chiang material, a striking contrast to the total absence of anti-Communist writings in Communist areas.

The student movements in China spawned by the Blue Shirts were not "ultra-nationalist," a term that to most readers connotes an aggressive and malevolent temper toward other countries and peoples.[38] The Blue Shirts hated the fascist Japanese and were fiercely anti-imperialist—as, understandably, were most Chinese. They liked to claim that through intimidation they had contributed to the quieting in the 1933–1934 period of public—primarily student—demonstrations against Chiang and his regime. But none of their activities stopped the protests and the heated criticisms of Chiang and the Blue Shirts themselves, which continued to appear in English- and Chinese-language newspapers as well as in the informal press.[39]

Assassination was the most infamous activity of the Blue Shirts. Two known victims were warlord officers, one of whom was suspected of dealing with the Japanese; two others were pro-Japanese editors in Tianjin. Reflecting the strong anti-Japanese element in the group's mindset, a publication of the organization claimed that in the spring of 1933 its agents had killed forty "traitors" in Wuhan who had been collaborating with the Japanese.[40] Victims who were not pro-Japanese but liberal critics of Chiang included two members of the Chinese League for the Protection of Human Rights: Yang Xingfo, vice-chairman of the league, and Shi Liangcai, head of the Chinese Municipal Council and editor of Shanghai's most prominent Chinese-language paper, *Shen bao.*[41] Chiang may or may not have ordered these deaths, or Dai Li, as Chiang's senior intelligence chief, may have done so without checking with his boss (that way, Chiang could deny involvement). In any event, they were attributed in the press to the Blue Shirts and to Chiang himself. Significantly, even if Chiang did not know about the killings beforehand, he showed no concern over them in his diary nor mentioned that he tried to put a stop to such deeds and the bad publicity they caused.

Other than these cases, the most dramatic evidence cited by some historians linking the Blue Shirts to extensive killings is a "mysterious document" published in the *Shanghai Evening Post and Mercury* on July 19, 1933. Reputedly issued by a "'Chinese fascist organization' of Chiang Kai-shek," the document showed the names of fifty-five "Chinese leaders" on a paper titled "a death list for assassination." Harold Isaacs's magazine *China Forum* had passed this damning document to the *Post and Mercury*.[42] Isaacs, openly sympathetic to the Communist side and later the Trotskyites, was not unbiased, but he did not hide from the *Post Mercury* that the "mysterious document" had come to him from the Communist central press agency.[43] The most logical assumption, of course, is that the document was an invention of Zhou Enlai's propaganda office.

Dai Li's operatives reportedly conducted kidnappings in the international sections of Shanghai, with some charging that such crimes were committed on "a vast scale." Most of the victims were said to be "anonymous" students and workers, thus leaving no good way to estimate the numbers. The two "celebrated cases" usually cited include the writer Ding Ling and a leftist gangster assassin named Wang Yaqiao. Ding, who had joined the CCP early in 1933, was actually arrested by the concession police, not by Dai, and turned over to Nanking. She lived in that city on parole for three years before escaping—hardly draconian treatment for a serious dissident.[44] The known assassin Wang Yaqiao, for his part, was sentenced to ten years in jail.

Chiang was capable of ordering hundreds of assassinations and kidnappings if he thought such crimes were essential to the success of his regime or to China's survival, and perhaps he did. But the evidence is not clear. What is obvious is that the killings that did take place were not vast enough to significantly reduce public criticism of Chiang and his regime in the big cities of China, much less end it. Popular, pro-Communist writers like Mao Dun and Lu Xun continued to churn out literary works that excoriated the brutality and corruption of the Kuomintang as well as Chiang Kai-shek's appeasement of the Japanese. Like the allegations of mammoth corruption, stories of KMT political murders, true or false, were good news for the CCP, which amplified them and invented new ones.[45] Chiang's anti-Communist enemies, the rebellious warlords and militarists as well as non-Communist liberals, also spread and elaborated on the recurrent charges of such killings, both factual and invented.

The effect was to further lower the opinion of Chiang and his regime held by the intellectual and cultural elite of China—most particularly that of Shanghai—and to feed the growing disdain for the regime by most Western journalists, diplomats, and military attachés. Other circumstances suggest that the Blue Shirts were hardly models of ruthless effectiveness. Comintern agents secretly operating in the International Settlement in Shanghai should have been prime targets for KMT kidnappings and assassinations. KMT intelligence and covert organizations in the city, however, had limited success in ferreting out these mostly foreign agents. Archival documents of the 1930s in Moscow reveal a clandestine Comintern organization in Shanghai handling large money transfers, funding Communist youth and labor movements as well as journals and bookstores, manning radio transmitters in touch with Russia and the Jiangxi soviet ("six or eight transmitters" were in stock), running a radio operator's school with eleven students, and, as noted, even buying an airplane. Despite all this activity, Chiang's secret operatives, the British police, the French gendarme, and the Green Gang caught only a few Comintern operatives.

In a rare breakthrough, Dai Li's agents captured a man named Gu Shunzhang, who was head of the CCP's "secret service" (apparently different from the Special Department). Dai "persuaded" Gu to defect to the KMT, which led to "numerous arrests [in Shanghai] and the death of the CCP secretary-general, Xiang Zhongfa, among others." In 1931, the Politburo, "in self defense," entrusted the task of retaliation to Zhou Enlai, who ordered the killing of Gu and his entire family.[46] Zhang Guotao tells of another murder in Shanghai ordered by Zhou of a CCP Whampoa graduate suspected of wavering.[47]

From the outset, the Communists at least matched, and in some cases far exceeded, the Nationalists' ruthlessness. CCP "protection bureaus" sought out and eliminated internal enemies. A CCP "Special Department" was reported to have killed "hundreds of 'renegades,' mill foremen, detectives, guild officials, gangsters, philanthropists, key industrialists, noncooperative labor leaders, and Nationalist agents over the course of the 1930s." Zhang Guotao complained that executions of party members without approval violated party discipline, and there followed a brief respite in the "termination" of antiparty persons, but "a short time afterward the hand of the despot and the tactics of secret [CCP] agents knew no bounds."[48]

I

As the battle for Jiangxi raged between the Communists and the Nationalists, Chiang began to promulgate a mass campaign to transform the political, intellectual, and moral life of China. Some believed that this giant exercise was a ploy by Chiang as well as a debacle in terms of its goals of restoring economic life, implementing equitable land reforms, and winning popular respect.[49] More recent assessments, however, believe the effort failed but was not a sham.[50] As the Communists retreated in South Jiangxi, KMT civil action teams were sent into counties, townships, and villages to establish law and order and then introduce major reforms in agriculture and education. At an earlier Lushan conference, some officials had argued that the Communist redistribution of land provided the KMT the opportunity to reform land-holding and tenure patterns on a major scale. The best time to justify a fundamental reform that would disturb the social-economic order, they argued, was when the outcome of fighting against the advocates of much more radical methods was still uncertain. But the KMT adopted the more conservative policy of returning land to the original owners and putting off redistribution until the utterly devastated local economy had recovered. As they put out the fires of violent agrarian revolution in the province, KMT officials "had no intention of poking around in the embers any more than necessary."[51]

Still, Chiang's teams did try various ways to implement a nonconfiscatory reform of land rights, including the government's gradual purchase of land as it came on the market and the establishment of cooperatives in which the holdings of landlords could be rented out to the landless. There were enthusiastic and conscientious officials in these elite civil action units who believed that in a paternalistic framework, and by building on existing traditions, they could progress toward a more just and prosperous society. Thus revival of the traditional *Bao Jia* system of group responsibility, a favorite idea of Chiang's, was to be the key social institution not only for the promotion of law and order, but also for a new community ethos. It was hoped that along with irrigation canals and health clinics, a renewed sense of civic pride and patriotism would spring forth.

But a year after the Red Army slipped out of Jiangxi in 1934, the grand effort at grassroots reform by the Kuomintang fell apart. Or, to be more exact, hopes for a political and economic "New Deal" in Jiangxi were squashed by the return of the avaricious local village elite. These village higher-ups were unlike the more educated absentee landlords and other more cultured elements of the privileged class, who generally remained in the cities where commercial, financial, and professional ways of making money were rapidly developing; they were instead a lower rank of petty notables and land owners who rented out some of their land to tenants.[52] These petty landlords had nothing except their relatively small holdings of surplus land as a source of income, and years of violence before and during the Communist period had debased and brutalized them. As the Communists were driven out, these would-be gentry reemerged and with the help of local "bullies" reasserted their rights. Soon they dominated social, political, and economic life in the villages, exploiting and enhancing their power.[53]

Another Chiang Kai-shek campaign, the New Life Movement, began in Jiangxi as part of the fifth suppression campaign. For some time, Chiang had been thinking about how to develop a spiritual and cultural framework that would supplement and reinforce nationalism and modernization as the Kuomintang's grand causes. "Revolution," Chiang said, "meant changing the everyday pattern of behavior of individuals and societies." He believed that the basic reason for the KMT revolution's failure until that point was that "the Chinese people's habits of thinking and daily living had never fundamentally changed to adapt to the requirements of a modern state." The New Life Movement was intended to change all that.[54]

The values that the movement sought to inculcate were mostly simple neo-Confucian merits and traditional Japanese habits—frugality and conscience, simplicity, honesty, and even promptness, hygiene, and neatness. For critics, the disturbing aspect of the movement was its intention to "thoroughly militarize the lives of the citizens of the entire nation." Yet the purpose of this "complete militarization" was not to conquer other people but to cultivate "courage and swiftness, the endurance of suffering, a tolerance of hard work, especially the habit and ability of unified action." The aim was to say "farewell to yesterday's barbarian way of life, its disorderliness, lethargy, and depression."[55] These were hardly objectionable goals, especially when framed in the innocent bromides of Confucius and Christ.

And Jesus was increasingly in the Generalissimo's thoughts. His diary en-

tries often referred to the Bible, usually in the context of enduring suffering
and humiliation. On May 4, 1934, for example, he wrote, "Believers in Jesus
must control themselves, endure insults, and be patient in suffering. Every
day [they] must bear the cross along with Jesus."[56] About this time Chiang
also took to reading a collection of Christian testaments—one for each day of
the year—called *Streams in the Desert*.[57] The dominant theme was stoic perseverance and unwavering faith in the face of failure, disaster, and martyrdom.
Chiang noted down his thoughts beside each of the inspirational messages or
stories.

Madame Chiang played a major role in the New Life Movement. According to one account, she, the Australian W. H. Donald, and Chen Lifu first
came up with the idea when discussing her frustration with the abysmal lack
of hygiene in China. Mayling was "miserable about the filth of the city streets,
the happy-go-lucky dirtiness of Chinese kitchens, and the communal feeding bowl into which everyone stuck his sucked chopsticks." She even carried sheets about with her to put down on chairs or floors, and in her own
house she insisted on a set of serving chopsticks with each dish. But she had
been "unable to do anything about the hacking and spitting" of the Chinese
people.[58]

It was Lifu who suggested that the campaign also emphasize the old Confucian virtues *Li, yi, lian, and chi*—propriety, justice, integrity, and conscien-
tiousness, respectively. Chiang and his staff added the themes of austerity,
martial discipline, and patriotism. At Mayling's initiative, American missionaries joined in the campaign to promote the ideals of the movement, which
they believed were very much in keeping with Christian teachings. The emphasis on hygiene and manners also appealed to the Americans' sense of propriety and cleanliness, though the American minister in Nanking noted that
there was greater stress on the evils of tobacco—an American scourge—than
on opium.[59]

Early on, the Nanking government continued to try various ways to control
and gradually end the use of opium, but during the chaotic years of internal
conflict, taxes on its growth, distribution, and consumption continued as an
important source of income for the central regime as well as the warlords,
and little or no progress was made toward its elimination. In 1928, new laws
sought to improve enforcement, treatment, and education, but progress was
still limited because of the government's "weak authority" over the provinces.

In 1932, the Military Council, obviously with Chiang's approval, took responsibility and established a new drug control commission; applied heavier penalties, including execution; and within two years, officially banned opium entirely in seventeen provinces and municipalities. Du Yuesheng, the Green Gang leader, became a member of the commission—seemingly a bizarre appointment. But Du had accumulated more respectable sources of income and if he had really cooperated it obviously could have made a major difference.

According to an unsourced statement in an article published in 2000 on mainland China, fees and taxes on the opium trade during this period had reached more than 2 billion Chinese yuan a year, a great deal of which was no doubt siphoned off. Still the article concludes that while progress was limited, the new heavy penalties and the authority of the Military Council had laid a "solid foundation" for the next stage, a stage that was interrupted by the war. In sum, the narcotic drug habit in China continued to produce income for the government, corrupt officials, and the warlords, but some serious efforts were being made to end or reduce it.[60]

In contrast to the suppression of opium, by 1934, it was evident that Chiang Kai-shek was making significant progress in "bandit (i.e., Communist) suppression," not only in CCP enclaves like in Jiangxi but in the cities as well. According to Mao, the Chinese Red Army, which had grown to 300,000 fighters in 1929, was reduced to 25,000 by 1934–1935. At one point, when the CCP, on behalf of the Jiangxi soviet, asked the Comintern for more money, Moscow suggested creating a special "station" in southern Jiangxi for delivering supplies to the besieged soviet and even proposed setting up a firm "that could specialize in the sale of Sichuan opium."[61] Having lost all but six of its previous seventy counties in Jiangxi, the CCP leaders debated the option of breaking through the encirclement and making a long retreat to some remote area closer to the USSR.[62] Finally by shortwave radio Stalin instructed them to break out and seek a new enclave, possibly near Outer Mongolia.[63]

On October 16, the 25,000 fighters of the CCP's First Red Army tramped out of their camps in southern Jiangxi and began a long march north.[64] Only a third of them had rifles. In this multitude were thirty-five wives of the leaders, including Mao's spouse, He Zizhen. Mao himself rode out with an umbrella and a bag of books on a dun-colored horse. Like everyone else, he had a blanket and a three-day supply of rice.[65] They all survived on day four and thereafter because the group carried trunks full of Mexican silver dollars, which they used to buy supplies along the way and to bribe the warlords to let them pass. On July 25, the CCP in Shanghai reported it had sent 50,000 Mexican silver dollars "more" to the Jiangxi soviet and another 400,000 would be required before the Long March would begin in mid-October, and this could be sent in batches of 90,000 every two weeks.[66] With ten weeks left, theoretically Shanghai could have sent another 450,000 Mexican dollars.[67] This would have been in addition to any other Mexican and U.S. dollars received by Shanghai that may have arrived at the Jiangxi base. The Long Marchers also confiscated some landlord wealth along the way.[68]

Escaping the encirclement proved relatively easy. Earlier in the year, Chiang Kai-shek had pressed Li Zongren, Bai Chongxi, and Chen Jitang (the power holder in Guangdong) to take part in the fifth suppression campaign. The warlords, however, feared that Chiang wanted to force the Red Army into their provinces in order to open the way for his Central Army to move in and occupy them. Years later in an interview, Bai Chongxi said he suggested to the southerners that they make a pretense of joining in the effort to surround the Communists but essentially retain their forces in their respective strongholds.[69]

The leaders had reason to hold back. Chiang's priority objective at this time was to finish off the Communists, but like virtually all Chinese modernizers his long-term goal was to get rid of the independent armies and fiefdoms. When the Communists crossed into Guizhou, Chiang wrote in his diary that this development provided an opportunity to take over the province from warlord governor Wang Jialie.[70]

Unopposed, the Communist soldiers slipped out of Jiangxi between the staggered positions of the Guangdong Army, which was supposedly containing the Communists along the southern Hunan-Jiangxi border. In late November when Mao reached the Xiang River, Chiang himself rushed to Hunan to direct the fighting. After a week of heavy losses on both sides, the Red Army crossed the river under withering fire, then moved into Guizhou.[71] The Central Army followed the Communists there, and Chiang flew to the capital Guiyang, where he replaced the governor with the loyalist general Gu Zhutong.[72]

In January 1935, a First Red Army party summit elected Mao the CCP's senior military as well as political authority. Later, in the Sichuan-Xikang border region, Mao's army joined up with Zhang Guotao and his Fourth Red Army, which had fled Oyuwan in 1933. With differences between them unsettled, Zhang led his army west while Mao took his forces on a long trek south and then west through Yunnan province. The warlord Long Yun, probably after receiving a donation of Mexican dollars, allowed the "bandits" to pass through peacefully. Although Chiang, who had flown to Sichuan's provincial capital Chengdu again to take personal command, failed to catch up with either Zhang Guotao or Mao, the pursuit was once more politically useful as he established central control over the capital of Sichuan as well as Guizhou (although not much else). The experience also led Chiang to begin to think seriously of Sichuan as the redoubt far above the great gorges of the Yangtze to which his government and army could withdraw in a future war with Japan.

Despite the Communist retreat, China remained politically unstable, as was underscored by an incident in Nanking. On a cool autumn morning, members of the KMT Central Executive Committee lined up for a group photo at party headquarters. A news agency reporter pulled out a gun and took several shots at Wang Jingwei, seriously wounding him. Chiang had not been feeling well and was not present at the photo session, which naturally raised suspicions. Wang's wife, Chen Bijun, publicly asked KMT headquarters for an explanation. The implication of a conspiracy infuriated Chiang and he ordered Dai Li "to leave no stone unturned" in getting to the bottom of the case. Using "the cruelest torture" Dai personally interrogated the assassin, while at Chiang's request Chen Lifu conducted a separate inquiry.[73] Both Chen and Dai concluded that the shooting was the work of disaffected members of Wang's reorganization clique. When special services officers killed one alleged conspirator and arrested others, Wang's wife apologized to the Generalissimo and she and her husband sailed for Europe to seek medical treatment for his wounds. Chiang was probably not involved in the assassination attempt, but as a result he took over as president of the executive yuan or premier, and thus again gained control of the Nanking government.[74]

In September, Japanese foreign minister Kōki Hirota sent Chiang a three-point program for advancing Sino-Japanese relations: China was to accept the priority of relations with Japan over those with the West; recognize the puppet government in Manchuria; and "together with Japan devise ways and means to eradicate communism." Chiang's reply avoided the first two questions but stated that, provided Japan respected China's territorial integrity, China was prepared to discuss with Tokyo effective means for suppressing "communism on China's northern borders." Chiang informed Hirota that if all the agreements "between the two countries' militaries," including the provisions of the Shanghai Truce of 1932 and the North China arrangements of

1934 and 1935, were completely rescinded, the Manchurian issue could be put aside and China would stop anti-Japanese activities.[75]

In a telegram to his ambassador in Tokyo, Chiang reiterated that in any settlement there would be no recognition by China of the puppet government of Manchuko, but China could agree not to use military means to deal with the question provided its traditional sovereignty was otherwise honored. Most intriguing to Tokyo was Chiang's willingness to explore ways the two countries could cooperate in "fighting communism on the northern border," but again Japan would have to meet the basic conditions regarding restoration of China's sovereignty. At the same time, Chiang sought to demonstrate that he was also prepared if necessary to fight a war with Japan, holding large-scale military exercises outside Nanking, deploying troops along the Shandong-Gansu railway, and building new defense works in Wuhan.[76]

Washington, meanwhile, had finally come forward with a US$50 million "tied loan" to Nanking, and London was offering a small US$10 million credit. But the United States and United Kingdom both wanted China to be "realistic" regarding Manchuria. In September, a British envoy, Sir Frederick Leith-Ross, visited Tokyo and Nanking proposing that in exchange for China's "acknowledgment" of Manchuko, Japan respect Chinese sovereignty outside of Manchuria. After long talks in Chungking, the Englishman reported to London that Chiang's government would never surrender sovereignty over Manchuria.[77]

The record seems clear: Chiang was not prepared to compromise on the question of sovereignty.[78] Records of talks between Tokyo and Nanking during this period underscore that Chiang and his negotiators categorically insisted on China's retention of its claim to Manchuria, even if at times they proposed temporarily setting aside the issue provided Japan completely honored Chinese sovereignty elsewhere and annulled all unequal agreements that violated this principle.[79]

But the Japanese Guandong Army in Manchuria continually found opportunities to make further encroachments on China's sovereignty. Tokyo itself demanded that the Generalissimo's dual policy toward Japan—public avowal of friendship and secret preparation for war—be stopped and that all Chinese military, party, governmental, and secret service organizations and personnel be withdrawn from Hebei province as well as from Peking and Tianjin. Chiang felt that even this outrageous demand had to be accommodated, explaining to the mortified Chinese public that again Chinese acceptance was not a formal "agreement" because no documents were signed or ratified at the highest level. The next month a similar "non-agreement" accord resulted in Nanking's complete withdrawal from Chahar province in Inner Mongolia. Chiang's standing in political China dropped further but he took comfort in Mao's flight and the continued buildup of German-trained Central Army divisions—although he couldn't boast about the military buildup out of fear of provoking greater Japanese aggression.

Unsatisfied with their latest gains, Japan pushed ahead with a new plan to establish a completely autonomous North China region including five provinces—Hebei, Shandong, Shanxi, and the Inner Mongolian provinces of Chahar and Suiyuan, each of which would be headed by a collaborating Chinese general.[80] Yan Xishan and Feng Yuxiang refused to cooperate, but others accepted the opportunity. In his diary one day, Chiang impulsively wrote that now there was "no alternative but war," but in reality finishing off the fleeing Red armies and military modernization remained his highest priorities. He passively accepted but did not recognize that "North China" constituted a "special region" under Japanese-chosen Chinese "authorities."[81] In effect, China north of the Huai River, including the once proud capital of Peking, would be completely under Japanese control, although not formally independent of Nanking. Once again, angry students poured into the streets to protest the dismemberment of their country.

In October 1935, Mao and 7,000 to 9,000 men of his original force arrived at a small village called Baoan in northern Shaanxi province, just south of the Great Wall. They had traveled 3,000 miles. Taking up quarters in the dusty caves surrounding the village, Mao's group joined with a local Communist force and a long-roving Communist army from Anhui to create an army of about 20,000 soldiers. Mao told his forces that the goal was to expand their area of control until it joined up with the USSR and the Mongolian People's Republic.[82]

During the year, Mussolini invaded Ethiopia and Hitler repudiated the disarmament provisions of the Treaty of Versailles. The democracies appeared to be paralyzed, but on August 1 the Soviet Union and the Comintern called for a worldwide antifascist "popular united front," which seemed to represent abandonment of a global Communist revolution in favor of an antifascist coalition of Communists, Christian-democrats, liberals, moderate conservatives, and democratic-socialists. For China, the Comintern decreed the new watchword: "Unite with Chiang and resist Japan."

In northern Shaanxi, Mao was still out of radio touch with Moscow, but couriers or travelers apparently brought him word of the Comintern's new global united front policy. Mao and Chiang both understood that the dynamics were changing: the time Chiang had left to crush the CCP was rapidly vanishing because war was fast approaching and China's only source of arms and conceivably direct military support was the Soviet Union. Even before arriving at the new Shaanxi base, Zhou Enlai sat down and wrote an "official letter" dated September 1, 1935, to the Chen brothers Guofu and Lifu. The younger Chen was now in charge of the KMT organization department and had been recently elected to the Central Executive Committee, which finally had a majority of Chiang Kai-shek supporters. Guofu was governor of Jiangsu province. Both brothers, however, had kept their hand in intelligence and covert matters. Zhou's letter noted reports that the Nanking government was "planning to ally with Russia" and that the atmosphere in Nanking "was quite different than in the past." Cooperation between the two parties was again possible, Zhou said. The only purpose of the CCP's Red armies in the Northwest, he declared, was to defend the area against the Japanese. He asked the Chens to urge Chiang Kai-shek to cease military action at once and to unite with the Soviet Union and the CCP to fight against Japan, requesting an early meeting to begin "responsible negotiations."[83]

Chiang believed that the new Comintern policy and Zhou's letter reflected not only the escalating seriousness with which Stalin viewed looming threats to the Soviet Union from both east and west, but also the CCP's profound weakness. He instructed Chen Lifu to send a positive reply to Zhou. Chiang was determined to launch his final overpowering campaign against Mao, but he did have an incentive to consider seriously a political united-front settlement. For one thing, Mao could and probably would escape with most of his forces into the Soviet Union or Outer Mongolia. But a political settlement could open the door to large-scale Soviet military aid, which as during the Northern Expedition would be critical to Chiang's success in the coming war with Japan. After learning of Zhou's letter, Chiang called in Soviet ambassador Dimitri Bogolomov on October 18 and proposed a secret military treaty with the USSR. Moscow's response was that first Chiang had to "regulate relations with the CCP."[84] Chiang and Bogolomov then agreed that the ambassador and Zhang Qun would follow up with secret talks on the details of such a pact, which would materialize once the Chinese government and the CCP had agreed on a united front. Through intermediaries, Chen and Zhou decided that their first secret meeting would be in Shanghai in the early part of 1936.[85]

But Chiang—like Mao—believed in the strategy of *tan, tan, da, da,* "talk,

talk, fight, fight." Thus while pursuing possible détente with both the Soviet Union and the CCP, Chiang instructed Zhang Xueliang to lead his Northeast Army into northern Shaanxi, link up with the Shaanxi Pacification Commission commander General Yang Hucheng—a once illiterate bandit and former Feng Yuxiang officer—and prepare a November 1935 attack against the presumed ragtag forces in Mao's new redoubt. After Zhang Xueliang's return from Europe two years earlier, his anti-Japanese nationalism was more intense than ever, and this directive by Chiang struck him as suspicious: it meant that his Northeast Army would be posted to the Northwest, farther from Manchuria, and put under a regional commander who was a Chiang loyalist. Zhang began to believe the other warlords' charge that Chiang Kai-shek's objective after finishing with the Communists was to get rid of all the independent regional forces (which was of course true, although Chiang hoped this could be done peacefully). At some point the Young Marshal and General Yang became convinced that Chiang's objective was to bleed their armies in the upcoming action against the Communists.

The first battles proved to be another debacle for the KMT: Zhang Xueliang reported that he had lost two divisions and several thousand of his troops had surrendered. Mao's success in these initial engagements was no doubt due in good part to his organizational and tactical skills, but poor leadership and discipline on the other side also contributed. The officers and men of the Northeast and Shaanxi armies were by this time a demoralized lot. But it is also possible that even at this early stage Zhang Xueliang and Yang Hucheng did not in fact make the all-out attacks they reported to Nanking nor actually suffer all the reported casualties. Earlier, wanting to save his elite forces for the future war with Japan, Chiang had turned down He Yingqin's proposal that he send his German-trained units north to take care of the Communists.

Very likely Chiang simply wanted the two warlord armies camped in southern Shaanxi to harass Mao's forces until a large Central Army force—but not the elite units—could arrive from the south. Throwing the two warlord armies into losing battles with the Communists, however, actually strengthened Mao, giving him captured arms as well as prisoners, many of whom were taken into the Communist armies. Most importantly, the losses caused Zhang Xueliang to listen more favorably to the CCP's call to support the united front against Japan. Zhou's propaganda teams were already busy promoting the united front idea in the cities and universities of China as well as inside Chiang's various armies, most particularly the Manchurian Army.

II

In January 1936, Chiang again defended his foreign policy to a group of students and educators, saying that although he "was not afraid of Japan," China was still not strong enough to go to war with that powerful empire.[86] This position offered little emotional or ideological satisfaction to the Chinese people, but it is clear that improvements to the Chinese Army's arsenal scheduled for the next three to four years could have made a critical difference in a war with Japan. In addition, at the time the Western democracies still did not see China's integrity as being related to that of Europe or the United States and offered absolutely no hope of real help.

The next month in Tokyo, after a failed but bloody "patriotic" coup by a fanatical army faction, a new civilian regime headed by Iota Koki proclaimed a new "positive diplomacy" that, simply put, entailed Japanese dominance of all Asia. These "rational ultra-nationalists" supported preparation for war with the Pacific powers, rather than just with Russia. They also wanted to bring China to heel before the really big wars began, and the Hirota cabinet soon presented China another round of demands that included "neighborly friendship, joint defense against Communism, and economic cooperation." Chiang realized he could no longer appease the Japanese; the war would have to begin soon.[87]

Simultaneous with the coup attempt in Tokyo another key battle took place on the border between Siberia and Manchuria when the Soviet Far Eastern Army, again commanded by General Blucher, beat off a multidivisional attack by Japanese and Manchuko puppet forces. This defeat further strengthened the argument of the Imperial Navy for sailing south rather than for the Army marching north and west. Many in Washington did not understand this simple dynamic. In 1936, Japanese hegemony over China did not seem to disturb the Roosevelt administration or most Americans. The U.S. ambassador in Nanking, Nelson T. Johnson, argued that Japan's transgressions in China did not concern the United States directly. In fact, "efficient" Japanese management of Manchuria and North China, he suggested, might open up important economic opportunities for American business.[88]

Once again, Chiang ordered Zhang and Yang to attack the Communist forces to their north. Once again the engagement turned out badly: thousands more soldiers were reported killed and missing, although the figures again may have been exaggerated. Through a captured officer Zhou sent word to Zhang Xueliang that he wanted to talk with him about a united front to fight against the Japanese.[89] In February, no doubt with Yang's approval, Zhang met secretly in Xi'an with CCP officials sent by Zhou Enlai. After this meeting, Zhou and Mao, through liaison personnel, were in constant touch with Zhang, who even allowed them to set up within his army a leftist Society of Comrades for Resistance against the Japanese.[90]

In his continuing talks with the CCP, Zhang Xueliang did not have to be further persuaded. Indeed, he took the lead, insisting that it was not possible to unite with Chiang Kai-shek, whose appeasement policies, he said, had destroyed his moral authority to lead the nation. Encouraged by Zhou, Zhang proposed forming a new Northwest anti-Japanese government. Such a government would include the Communist armies and other patriotic (warlord) forces, and would employ the rallying cry "Unite with Zhang, oppose Chiang, resist Japan." Ambition as well as patriotism drove the Young Marshal's decision to turn on his commander in chief. He suggested that he himself head the proposed anti-Chiang coalition government, and Zhou quickly agreed. By this time, Mao had been officially informed that Comintern policy demanded a united front with, not against, Chiang Kai-shek. Nevertheless, the Chairman approved the contrary strategy proposed by the Young Marshal, believing the Manchurian leader's aspirations to "heroism" could be usefully employed and that Moscow would approve the decision eventually. He did not inform the Comintern of the new plan for four more months.

Unaware of these negotiations, Chiang Kai-shek's emissaries were passing through Shaanxi on their way to their own talks with the enemy at the CCP headquarters at Baoan, a small, hardscrabble market town in northern Shaanxi notable for its many cave dwellings. At this session, the CCP proposed the creation of a united KMT-CCP government devoted to national defense and a united anti-Japanese army—provided the KMT stopped the civil war and recognized the legal status of the Soviet areas. It was agreed that the Nanking government would respond at a follow-on meeting in Shanghai.[91]

In the spring, Zhang Xueliang traveled secretly through the Communist areas in the northern part of Shaanxi and met with Zhou in an abandoned Catholic Church in Yan'an, a small town then controlled by General Yang's forces. Zhou lavished praise on the idealistic and naïve Manchurian, while

Zhang told the suave and erudite Zhou that he, Zhou, was among the several people whom he admired most in modern Chinese history.[92] Although secret talks with Nanking had already begun, the CCP at this time drafted a detailed agreement with Zhang and Yang Hucheng on a dramatically new anti-Nanking alliance. About the same time, the CCP published a telegram to the nation asking for a truce and for peace talks with the KMT.

In June 1936, with radio communications restored, Mao for the first time informed the Comintern of the successful, secret agreement with Zhang Xueliang. The new anti-Chiang coalition was to be formalized in a "Northwestern Government of National Defense" and Marshal Zhang Xueliang, Mao reported, was to be the elected "chairman of this 'government'" as well as commander of the coalition "anti-Japanese army." Mao also noted that to meet its monthly payroll the Manchurian Army depended on its receipt of two million yuan (presumably in the central government paper currency, the *fabi*) every month from Nanking, but once the Young Marshal had split with Chiang Kai-shek, this large remittance would of course end. Therefore, Mao asked the Comintern if it could provide three million yuan a month to pay the Red Army soldiers as well as the Manchurian Army. Naturally, he argued, the Communist soldiers would "have to be paid the same salary" as their new allies. The message also asked for heavy artillery, airplanes, and other weapons, and promised an offensive within two months to achieve "the liquidation of Chiang Kai-shek's forces in Northwest China."[93]

When he read Mao's report, Stalin was appalled, realizing that if Chiang were to be seriously threatened by a Communist-dominated coalition of warlords as proposed, he would suspect that the Soviet Union was secretly supporting it. Such a perception of betrayal would open up all sorts of possibilities for Japan, including a common front with some of the conservative, strongly anti-Communist elements of the KMT. A development of this sort could also excite Japan's anti-Bolshevik and anti-Russian sentiments. In a curt August 13 message, Stalin completely rejected Mao's approach. In no uncertain terms he instructed Mao "immediately [to] extend an official offer to the Kuomintang and Chiang Kai-shek to enter into negotiations to cease hostilities and sign a concrete agreement about the common struggle against Japanese occupiers," which was to include "a unified command and a common military plan." Zhang Xueliang "must not be viewed as a reliable ally," Stalin declared—even his "direct betrayal" was possible. The whole idea of a united anti-Chiang front of Communists and warlords sank out of sight.[94]

Mao immediately complied. In late August, he revoked the CCP's anti-

Chiang slogans and sent a letter to the KMT Executive Committee congratulating Chiang for his "progressiveness" and expressing agreement with his policies toward Japan. Chiang saw Mao's admiration as a cynical reflection of the fact that the "Red bandit leader" was "cornered and had nowhere to go."[95] He planned for the final suppression campaign to begin in earnest before the end of the year. Acting as Chiang's envoy, Zhang Qun held a number of discussions in the spring with Ambassador Bogolomov on "joint efforts" to safeguard peace, meaning joint efforts to help China resist Japan.[96] But then Stalin, responding to Japanese subversion in both Inner and Outer Mongolia, signed a mutual defense treaty with the puppet Mongolian People's Republic, whose independence China had never recognized. In reaction, Chiang put the talks on hold.[97] Stalin responded by arranging for *Pravda* to publish a letter from Chiang Ching-kuo to his mother, Mao Fumei, that again denounced his father as "the enemy of the whole people and therefore the implacable enemy of his son."[98]

Some in Chiang's inner circle urged him to make one more appeal to Japan's anti-Communist leaders. Chen Lifu argued strongly but unsuccessfully that the leader should send Dai Jitao to Tokyo to convince the Japanese that a Sino-Japanese war would increase both the strength of the Soviet Union and the Communist threat to Asia. But Chiang understood that the imperial ethos in Japan was now unstoppable—the Japanese "hawks," who were determined to make China a subordinate country, had won out. China could attain peace only by formal acceptance of the independence of Manchuria and North China north of the Huai River. War, he said, "cannot be avoided."[99]

Addressing a huge crowd in Nanking on Double Ten Day (October 10), 1936, Chiang declared, "The remnant Communists are now encompassed in a few scattered regions and can be exterminated without much difficulty. At present, communism is no longer a real menace to China."[100] After his speech, Chiang stood and saluted as spit-and-polish military units marched by in goose step followed by row after row of powerful German weapons. Thanks to German machine tools, Chinese arsenals were now capable of producing some weapons of quality and precision. Even so, the new German adviser, Alexander von Falkenhausen, believed that China needed two more years to reach his goal of sixty well-trained, modern divisions. New German heavy coastal guns, a dozen submarines, a German cruiser, torpedo boats, and other warships were not due to be delivered before 1938. The Luftwaffe had taken over training the Chinese air force, and if things went according to plan, Chinese pilots by 1939 would be flying modern Messerschmitts and Stukas, marking a profound change in the balance of power between China and Japan.[101]

Despite continuing civil wars, the depression, depredations by Japan, and preparation for a general war, the power and authority of the Chinese central government was greater than at any time since the Taiping Uprising. In the spring, displaying military, political, and covert action skills, Chiang had quickly put down another rebellion by the Guangxi Clique and the usual dissidents in Guangdong. The rebels had again charged Chiang with appeasement and dictatorship but essentially the rebellion reflected the ongoing power struggle between the warlords and the central government. In their own provinces, the warlords were more like dictators than Chiang Kai-shek was, and within two years their preferred national leader, Wang Jingwei—at the moment still in Europe—would defect to Japan. Chiang's generous treatment of the incorrigible southerners, even sending them three million central government yuan or *fabi* in emergency aid, was an act of enlightened self-interest, which is perhaps all one can expect of a national leader.

There were many other bright spots. The rate of illiteracy among government troops had diminished from 70 percent to 30 percent.[102] Law codes had been rewritten and applied nationally. The recent extension of central financial authority over the defeated southern provinces had helped to complete the triumph of the national currency, the *fabi*. Under T. V. Soong, Nanking reduced taxes and levies on farmers by 50 million Chinese *fabi* a year, and the fall harvest produced the best grain crop in twenty years. China had somehow sloughed through the early years of the world depression. Now more Chinese villagers had more money to spend, and light manufacturing and industrial production steadily rose.[103] Even at this unfavorable time, Chinese industriousness and entrepreneurial spirit were just beginning to show what they could do. There were many failings and deep poverty prevailed, but still the distinguished China scholar Franz Michael could sum up the first decade of the National government under Chiang Kai-shek as "a time of great progress in many fields—in economic development, in social and educational transformation, in political unification, and in the elevation of China's standing in international relations."[104]

With Mao Zedong praising the Generalissimo in his recent letter, the liberal press was either quiet or joined in the new optimism. Student outrage quickly subsided. The usually unsympathetic *Dagongbao* declared, "The people's confidence seems as though it were revived from the dead." Lloyd E. Eastman, a renowned, critical scholar of the Republican period, wrote that whereas Chiang had previously been pictured as an uneducated militarist scheming for personal power, by Double Ten Day of 1936, he was being praised as "a far-seeing leader who, so long as the nation had been torn by internal struggles, had wisely avoided a confrontation with the Japanese." He had become "a popular and seemingly inexpendable (*sic*) leader."[105]

In the fall of 1936, Mao's position was also improving. He could muster only some 30,000 troops with rifles, but new Soviet aid was arriving on a regular basis. Already he had received US$200,000 from the Comintern, and in September, Stalin approved sending 15,000–20,000 guns, 8 cannon, 10 mortars, and "sufficient quantities of foreign ammunition." The next year, the Comintern promised Mao, he would receive US$1.6 million.[106] In October, Soong Chingling from Shanghai, at Mao's request, sent him US$50,000 of her own money, an amount equivalent to $704,000 in 2005 U.S. dollars.[107]

In May, with a guarantee of safe passage from Chiang, Zhou Enlai and Pan Hannian, a Comintern—that is, a Stalin—representative, met secretly in Shanghai with Chen Lifu and Zhang Qun to continue talks on a united front. The inclusion of Pan, who came with his own secret code for communicating with the Comintern, signaled that Stalin wanted the talks to succeed, and if this happened, he would follow up with Soviet military aid to the Chinese Army.[108] The Nationalists presented Zhou with a list of tough demands, the most important of which required the CCP to reduce the Chinese Red Army to 3,000 men, abolish the name "Red Army," and subject it to control by the central government's Military Council. The CCP would also have to abolish all soviets and allow democratic governments in their areas. Finally, the senior leaders of the CCP should leave their posts and depart the country for half a year—Chiang's typical punishment for defeated warlords. These demands were hardly realistic—Mao would certainly choose to retreat into the Soviet Union rather than accept them. Zhou rejected the conditions outright, insisting that the CCP would have to retain command over the Red Army. But, he conceded, the Communist force could become part of the united Chinese Army and would obey the united high command—the Military Council headed by Chiang. The talks ended for the time being.[109]

Chiang had to decide whether it was worth trying to crush the CCP if the consequence was to shut the door to the only conceivable source of arms in the coming war with Japan, especially when, if facing defeat, Mao could simply escape into Russia or Mongolia. For his part, Mao was secretly continuing the discussions with Zhang Xueliang about a coalition against Chiang Kai-shek, leading the Manchurian Zhang to believe everything was on track (and thus indirectly contributing to the coming drama in Xi'an).

On October 31, his fiftieth birthday, Chiang was back in Luoyang, Henan, where he had established his headquarters for the final campaign against Mao. Mayling flew in from Shanghai with two large cakes, and the couple posed arm in arm for photos behind the Western-style, candlelit cakes—he in his cloth cape, holding his fedora, and she in a fur cape. In the morning, 20,000 citizens gathered at the Luoyang Military Academy to pay their respects. A twenty-one-gun salute roared. The crowd cheered, then bowed three times in unison. The next day Chiang wrote a long and upbeat article: the domestic situation, he declared, had "come under control, and in October, our foreign policy became tougher." Most notably he reported that Japan had demanded a joint agreement on resisting the Communists in North China. He instructed Zhang Qun to prepare a statement declaring that China was determined to restore its sovereign territory.[110]

After the birthday party, Chiang met privately with Zhang Xueliang, who had traveled to Luoyang. Chiang was upset with Zhang over a recent letter the Manchurian had written him calling for a united front against Japan. In his stern, lecturing mode, the Generalissimo warned that anyone who talked about resisting Japan before finishing off the CCP was "an enemy of the state." Later Chiang wondered why he had said such strong words.[111] According to Zhang's later account, the Generalissimo's attitude increased his resolve to kidnap the leader, and after he returned to Xi'an and recounted the meeting to General Yang, the older warlord cited a Chinese proverb: "One should have the emperor in one's hand and then order the nobles about in his name."[112]

That month, Japan, Germany, and Italy signed the anti-Comintern Pact, and the possibility suddenly loomed that Japan and Germany could attack the Soviet Union at the same time—the worst scenario Stalin could imagine. Many suspected that He Yingqin and the absent Wang Jingwei privately favored China's joining the anti-Communist coalition. The Japanese militarists wanted quickly to bring China to heel one way or the other so they could get on with their planned aggression against the Soviet Union. A new Japanese envoy, Shigeru Kawagoe, arrived ominously in Nanking on a Japanese warship, carrying a new demand that China grant Japan the right to send troops

October 31, 1936, Chiang's fiftieth birthday (as calculated by the Chinese), celebrating at
Luoyang with his wife. Chiang's popularity was at another peak, but six weeks later he would
be kidnapped at Xi'an by Zhang Xueliang. Courtesy KMT Party History Institute.

to wherever in China government forces were fighting the Communists.
Chiang received Shigeru but refused to negotiate with him, and the envoy's
talks with Foreign Minister Zhang Qun made no progress.[113] For Stalin, reports of such events made creation of a united anti-Japanese front between
the CCP and the KMT more urgent than ever.

On November 24, Chiang, back again in Luoyang, received a message
from Zhang Xueliang informing him that the situation in Shaanxi was tense
and asking permission to report to him. "Zhang does not have the strength
of will," Chiang wrote in his diary, "to endure the last five minutes of the
[civil] war."[114] In early December, Zhang arrived and told his leader that the

troops in Shaanxi were in a mutinous mood. Despite Chiang's recent warning against advocating the united front, the Young Marshal directly argued the case and the two men quarreled for more than an hour. Chiang warned that if the KMT at this point chose to stop the civil war and instead resist Japan, it would eventually lose leadership of the nation to the CCP.[115]

Zhang urged the Generalissimo to go to Xi'an and talk to the Manchurian and Shaanxi officers and troops face to face. Chiang agreed. Once back in Xi'an, Zhang Xueliang sent a radio telegram informing Mao of the conversation. According to Zhang Guotao, Zhang did not mention the planned kidnapping, but in early November the Young Marshal had told Mao's secret liaison in Xi'an, Ye Jianying, that he intended to "stage a coup d'état." Mao replied simply: "a masterpiece."[116]

III

H. H. Kung warned Chiang that the trip to Xi'an was too dangerous, but this only made the Generalissimo more determined to go. He had exposed himself to danger before by traveling into the territory of his adversaries, and he had always returned safely with an enhanced reputation for fearlessness. So accompanied by a large contingent of ranking officials and the usual bodyguard of Fenghua County men and twenty extra soldiers, he flew off to Xi'an.

Meanwhile, Zhou Enlai and Pan Hannian, Stalin's representative, traveled secretly from Shanghai to Nanking to continue negotiations for a united front against Japan.[117] Shortly after the Generalissimo left for Xi'an, Zhou Enlai told Zhang Qun and Chen Lifu that the CCP had agreed to most of the terms required by the KMT for a united front, including abolishing the name and insignia of the Red Army, placing its forces under the government's Military Council, ceasing the confiscation of landlord property, and allowing democratic government. The only difference was in the proposed size of the Communist Army, but then the Nationalist negotiators agreed that under its new name and pending its amalgamation into the Central Army the CCP forces could consist of 30,000, not 3,000, troops. Zhou immediately accepted this more realistic figure.[118] There was no mention of the requirement that Mao and Zhu De should leave the country. According to the memoirs of Chen Lifu and Chiang Kai-shek's 1957 book, the two sides reached an understanding "on practically all issues."[119]

On the basis of these vague and easily manipulated terms, the two sides drafted a joint proclamation on a formal united front subject to approval by Chiang and Mao. But the negotiators would not have agreed to these terms, even ad referendum, unless their respective leaders had approved them beforehand. On his way to report to Mao, Zhou Enlai stopped briefly in Xi'an, but apparently he did not see Zhang Xueliang to inform him of the draft accord. Perhaps both parties had agreed to keep the draft accord secret until it had been formally approved by the two leaders. Zhang Qun, who had accompanied Zhou to Xi'an, undoubtedly briefed Chiang Kai-shek on the matter and Chiang apparently agreed in principle to the final terms.[120] Years later, Chiang said all that remained to complete the agreement was "to get his formal approval" when he returned to Nanking.[121]

If Chiang had told Zhang Xueliang this highly important news, it possibly would have aborted the Young Marshal's abduction plans. Chiang, however, was a secretive man, and from his subordinates expected obedience without explanation. Thus it is likely that he decided that unless and until there was a signed formal agreement with Mao and the final terms of a related military pact with Moscow were known, he would not inform Zhang of the "understanding." Before both sides had formally agreed to what would be an end to the civil war, Chiang also would not have wanted to diminish the already low fervor of his forces in Shaanxi to die fighting the Communists. It is possible, too, that Chiang simply had no intention of stopping his military offensive regardless of what Mao decided about the draft accord. But given the critical importance to China of Soviet military aid probably in the very near future, the presence of Stalin's representative in the talks that produced the draft accord, and the probability that Mao would escape into Russia if faced with an overwhelming attack, it seems likely that Chiang was serious.

After landing at the Xi'an airport, Chiang took up residence in a hot springs resort called Huaqing, ten miles outside the city. Huaqing was a walled compound in the countryside with numerous modest cabins, each with its own hot spring bath. There Chiang met individually with senior officers of the Northeast and Shaanxi armies, telling them, as he had Zhang, that only "the last five minutes" remained in the long bandit-suppression campaign.

On December 9, a light snow began to fall on Xi'an. That morning, the police fired on a group of students headed toward Huaqing to confront the Generalissimo and some casualties occurred. Marshal Zhang rushed to the scene and told the students that he would act as their representative in front of the commander in chief. But when he arrived in Huaqing and told Chiang what had happened, Chiang was furious. "Which side of earth are you from?"

he asked. According to the Young Marshal, Chiang said he did not fear the students, shouting, "Let them come and I can use a machine gun to kill them." This exhortation—if true—upset Zhang, who was already under the strain of the planned kidnapping. He went into the bathroom to compose himself.[122]

Chiang was scheduled to depart Xi'an on December 12, but at dawn that morning a large contingent of Zhang Xueliang's bodyguard stormed the resort. In his cabin, Chiang heard the sound of shots, then an officer rushed in and reported that soldiers wearing fur caps—headgear of the Manchurian Army—were attacking the compound. The officer urged the Generalissimo to escape to the mountains at the back of the compound, Chiang, still in his nightclothes, climbed out a window and ran up a barren hill behind the cabins accompanied by a single guard and an aide.

Looming ahead was a high wall. The three men scrambled over it and ran along a wide, dry moat on the other side. Suddenly Chiang lost his footing and fell, injuring his back and losing his dentures. Joined by a few others, the group made its way to a cave at the top of a snow-covered mountain. Early the next morning Zhang Xueliang's troops found the fugitive—cold, barefoot, and with only a loose robe thrown over his nightshirt. "I am the Generalissimo," he told his captors. "Kill me, but do not subject me to indignities."[123] "We will not shoot you," the officer said. "We only ask you to lead our country."[124]

The soldiers drove Chiang to a government office in Xi'an, where General Yang's men assumed custody of him. After some while, Zhang Xueliang came into the room, stood at attention, and addressed him as commander in chief. "Do you still call me Commander?" Chiang demanded. "If you still recognize me as your superior, you should send me to Luoyang, otherwise you are a rebel. Since I am in the hands of a rebel you had better shoot me dead. There is nothing else to say!"[125] "Your bad temper is always the cause of trouble," Zhang replied.[126]

News of the mutiny reached Shanghai that morning, but no one knew the fate of the Generalissimo. H. H. Kung informed Soong Mayling, who immediately sent for Zhang Xueliang and Sun Yat-sen's old friend and former *New York Herald* reporter W. H. Donald, and the three of them together flew off to Nanking. There, the government had received a telegram from Zhang and Yang confirming that the Generalissimo was in their care. "With tears in our eyes," the two generals said, they had tried to explain the reasons for their actions to the Generalissimo but were "repeatedly chastised" by him. The two warlords then set forth eight demands, described as "points of national salvation," which they hoped the Nanking authorities would adopt "so as to open a lifeline for the future."[127]

The points included formation of a united "National Salvation" government, immediate cessation of the civil war, release and pardon of all political prisoners, and a guarantee of political freedom. The KMT Executive Committee and the Political Council responded by naming Kung acting president of the Executive Yuan and He Yingqin as overall troop commander. General He immediately began preparations for a military expedition against Xi'an, sending a Shaanxi provincial regiment to capture the pass at Dongguan. He also wired Wang Jingwei in Italy asking him to return as soon as possible. Central Army troops began to move toward Xi'an.[128]

The reaction throughout most of China to the news from Xi'an was remarkably sympathetic to Chiang. "Profound agony and concern" swept the country. In the popular view, two ambitious, dictatorial warlords were crushing the hopes of the nation and about to unleash another round of bloody civil wars. Soldiers and citizens reportedly wept and illiterates harried those who could read to tell them the latest news.[129] Among the warlords the reaction was split. Some, like Feng Yuxiang, called for the Generalissimo's release, while others such as Li Zongren and Bai Chongxi implicitly supported Zhang Xueliang.

The military moves added urgency to Moscow's attention to the crisis, but Madame thought the deployments provocative and argued for restraint. "Stormy conferences" followed. Setting out on her own to find a "quick, calm, and bloodless" settlement of the crisis, and even suggesting that maybe the perpetrators of the events in Xi'an had "a reasonable grievance," she sent Donald flying off to Xi'an and announced that she herself would soon follow.[130] On the same day, Chen Lifu, using CCP agent Pan Hannian's secret code, sent a message directly to the Comintern warning that if anything happened to the Generalissimo, "China would be without a leader to fight the Japanese and this would not benefit the Soviet Union."

Just before the attack at Huaqing, Zhang Xueliang had cabled Mao that he was about to act. Mao told his secretary, "There will be good news in the morning." At noon the next day, a radioman rushed into Mao's cave and handed him an urgent message from Zhang Xueliang. One by one the CCP leaders hurried into the leader's primitive headquarters to hear the news. When Mao read out the message, the cave echoed with excited laughter and gleeful voices. Zhu De, Zhang Guotao, and others wanted to see Chiang and his fellow KMT generals killed immediately. Mao, "laughing like mad," felt the same way. Nonetheless, he immediately sought guidance from Moscow, proposing that Chiang be delivered for trial by "the people." Then the Chairman sent obsequious messages to the Young Marshal, calling him the "National Leader in Resisting Japan," extolling his "world-shaking moves," suggesting there was no way a compromise could be reached with the Generalissimo, and hinting that he should deal with Chiang "resolutely."[131]

News of the kidnapping reached Moscow a few hours later, but unlike Mao, Stalin did not laugh; instead he immediately saw that the event could be disastrous for the Soviet Union. The next day, the Comintern received Chen Lifu's message and very likely read reports that He Yingqin had ordered Central Army divisions—probably the elite units—to move toward Xi'an and also had urged Wang Jingwei to rush home. The possibility suddenly loomed that the Generalissimo would be killed and Wang and He would establish a pro-Japanese government. Stalin sent a flash message to Mao telling him in no uncertain terms that the Soviet Union disapproved of the "plot"— and suggesting that it was being staged by the Japanese. He ordered Mao to hold friendly talks with Chiang, find a peaceful solution, and release the KMT leader.[132] In response to Stalin's orders, on December 15 a public telegram signed by Mao, Zhou, and Zhu announced that the CCP stood for a peaceful solution of the "Xi'an incident" and that any hasty moves would "only delight the Japanese."[133]

Stalin realized that if he and Mao could be seen as bringing about Chiang Kai-shek's release, this could tip the scales for a united KMT, Chinese Communist, and Comintern front against Japan. Stalin also knew that he had a bargaining chip. Chiang Kai-shek's son, Ching-kuo, was living with his Russian wife and infant son in Sverdlovsk where he had a job in a large industrial combine, and coincidentally, he was within days of being granted full membership in the Communist Party of the Soviet Union. It was probably Stalin himself who ordered an immediate halt to the party membership process and sent word for the junior Chiang to report immediately to Moscow.[134] Stalin then apparently cabled Zhou that in his talks with Chiang he should mention that one of the benefits of a united front government would be the probable return to China of Chiang Kai-shek's wayward son.[135]

As the crisis intensified, Zhou rode a donkey from the CCP base to Yan'an, still occupied by General Yang's troops, and from there flew back to Xi'an, which he had left only two days before. Upon his arrival, he reportedly told the Young Marshal that "not a hair of . . . [the Generalissimo's] head" was to be touched.[136] Zhou, who had negotiated the secret anti-Chiang agreement with Zhang Xueliang, now told him that China desperately needed Chiang Kai-shek's leadership.[137] Stalin and the Comintern, he said, demanded that the Generalissimo remain the leader of China.[138] Zhou told the Young Marshal he should try to convince Chiang simply to agree in principle to a united front and then release him in the hope that he would feel it necessary to follow through.[139] From the beginning, Zhou understood that Chiang would not sign any document or take any action to obtain his release, but might agree to a united front in principle, specifically the terms that he (Zhou) and Zhang Qun had agreed on just a few days before and which Chiang, as well as Mao, must have tentatively approved.

The Young Marshal now knew that the whole affair had backfired disastrously and he was in deep trouble. His goal now was to obtain as much credit as possible for the release of the prisoner, but he could not make the decision alone because Yang Hucheng controlled the city of Xi'an. Yang, saying he did not want to become "a beheaded general," was fearful of freeing the Generalissimo without firm guarantees.[140] Meanwhile, the Central Army was advancing on Xi'an, its planes bombing the railway line that climbed over the mountains to the ancient city. According to Mayling, He Yingqin was determined to attack Xi'an without further ado. She feared that this approach was putting her husband in mortal jeopardy, and she bitterly complained of "the military mind." Her diary recounting the Xi'an Incident published the next year clearly implies that General He was exploiting the crisis for his own purposes. On December 15, Donald informed her by phone from Luoyang that the Generalissimo was not being ill-treated and after first refusing had finally agreed to move to more comfortable quarters under Zhang Xueliang's, not Yang's, control. In addition, he said, the Young Marshal had admitted privately that he had acted wrongly, though with honorable motives.[141]

Meanwhile in Europe, Wang Jingwei made a stunning gesture—he flew to Berlin to confer with Adolph Hitler before returning to China. The two men discussed the possibility of China joining the anti-Communist Axis and Ger-

Wang Jingwei, Chiang's main rival in the KMT for thirteen years until he defected to the Japanese in 1939. Courtesy KMT Party History Institute.

many's willingness, if that happened, to substantially expand its aid to China. Wang then started back to Nanking, hoping that he would at last succeed Chiang Kai-shek as undisputed leader of the KMT and of China. News of Wang's meeting with the Führer must have deeply shocked Stalin and the Soviet leadership generally. A *Pravda* editorial charged that Wang and Zhang Xueliang had instigated the plot in Xi'an on behalf of the Japanese militarists.[142]

On the morning of December 20, Zhang met T.V. at the Xi'an airport and took him to see the Generalissimo. When T.V. entered the prisoner's room alone, Chiang looked up in surprise and began weeping bitterly. Sweeping over him was an overwhelming sense of frustration and utter helplessness. Ten years of fighting to neutralize the warlords and suppress the Reds had seemed only "five minutes" away from either a final military victory or an acceptable political solution, negotiated from a position of strength and guaranteed by Stalin. Now, by contrast, Chiang was in no position to negotiate with the Soviet Union, and if he agreed to the united front, it would appear he had been coerced into doing so.[143]

The economy, even Chiang's popularity, had finally turned around. In only two more years his army, he thought, would have been fully ready to confront the Japanese. Furthermore, the Anti-Comintern Pact had made it likely that Japan would in fact get swept up in Hitler's war with the Soviet Union. A new day had been dawning. But now two warlords—in Chiang's view, one petulant and ineffectual and the other corrupt and ignorant—had spoiled everything. T.V. gave Chiang a letter from Mayling. "If T.V. fails to return to Nanking in three days," she wrote, "I will come to Shaanxi to live and die with you."[144] Chiang wept again.

After regaining control of his emotions, Chiang repeated that he would not agree to anything under duress. He told T.V. that he had informed Zhang Xueliang that he could take his Northeastern Army to Inner Mongolia, presumably to be in a better position to fight the Japanese, and that General Yang could reorganize the Shaanxi government with his own appointments. The only other solution, he said, was for the Central Army to attack Xi'an. T.V. argued that if the army attacked, Zhang and Yang's forces would retreat into the Communist areas and "civil war could break out everywhere." Chiang's life, his brother-in-law said, was bound up with the life of the country.[145]

In talking with T. V. Soong, Zhang and Yang seemed unwilling to budge. And T.V., for his part, did not seem to appreciate the weakness of the two warlords' position and that a simple promise of amnesty would likely free the Generalissimo. He decided that his sister Mayling and the intelligence chief Dai Li, a representative of the Whampoa Clique, should come to Xi'an to persuade the Generalissimo to compromise.

Back in Nanking, Mayling and Dai Li were eager to return to Xi'an with T.V. Mayling was still trying to delay the attack by He Yingqin, who finally agreed to put off the bombing three more days.[146] Upon her arrival at the Xi'an airport, she shook hands with Zhang Xueliang and Yang Hucheng and asked the Young Marshal not to let his men search her baggage because she "disliked having my things messed up." Zhang looked embarrassed and replied, "Oh Madame, I would never do that."[147]

Once in the city, Mayling went in alone to see her husband, who seemed wan and ill. Tears again came into his eyes as he rebuked her for coming. Reading the Bible that morning, he said he had seen the passage, "Jehovah will now do a new thing, and that is, He will make a woman protect a man." When Chiang said he was ready to die for the good of the country, his wife told him that to save the country he must live. As the Madame left her husband, Dai Li rushed in, fell to his knees, and grasped the Generalissimo's legs, weeping and berating himself for having failed to protect his leader.[148]

Zhang Xueliang in reality was feeling increasingly desperate, and he told Mayling that he knew he had committed a grave error and was ready to release the Generalissimo immediately but that Yang and his men were not.[149] It was at this time that Mayling gave her word that if the Generalissimo was returned safely to Nanking, Zhang would not be punished.[150] Chiang, meanwhile, had decided that it was senseless to talk with Zhang and Yang. It was his former Whampoa Academy subordinate, Zhou Enlai, with whom his release had to be negotiated. If the surmise is correct that it was Chiang who freed Zhou in Shanghai in April 1927, both men were aware of the irony. On the evening of December 22 the Generalissimo asked T.V. to relay to Zhou four requests for the CCP: (1) abolish the Soviet government in China, (2) abolish the name "Red Army," (3) end class struggle, and (4) obey the Generalissimo as commander in chief.[151]

These were some of the same concessions in the united front draft proclamation that had been secretly agreed to by Zhou and Zhang Qun. But Chiang also instructed Soong to tell Zhou that "not for a minute had he forgotten the necessity of reorganizing the Kuomintang" and in three months he would call an all-parties National Congress to "hand over power to the people," that is, to end "tutelage." The key, Chiang reiterated, was that the Communists must obey him as their leader. In response, Zhou told T.V. and Mayling that the CCP had accepted all these conditions before and had not changed its position "one iota" because of the Xi'an Incident.[152]

Zhou reiterated that the CCP would fight Japan under the direction of the central government, but it would want "to retain its military system" separate from that of the Central Army. "This should not be difficult," he said, "since in any case there are so many military systems outside of the Generalissimo's own," meaning the armies of warlords. Zhou asked that T.V. emphasize to Chiang how difficult it would be for the Communists to explain to their own people the measures they had agreed on. In addition, Zhou repeatedly warned T.V. about pro-Japan functionaries in Nanking, who, he said, were at that moment "giving banquets to form cliques to take control, expecting the Generalissimo would never return."[153]

Later that day, in a family gathering with T.V. and Mayling, Chiang offered several other verbal concessions, saying that he would stop the advance of central government troops toward Xi'an, that no government troops would be stationed in Shaanxi or Gansu, and that he would provide "support" (cash subsidies and supplies) to all armies when the Sino-Japanese War began. When T.V. informed Zhou, Zhang, and Yang of these points, they appeared satisfied. The next day, when a majority of Zhang and Yang's officers insisted that some if not all of the terms should be carried out before the Generalissimo left Xi'an, T.V. explained to them that Chiang would rather die than make any concession before his release. But the officers remained adamant. Consequently, Dai Li abruptly left by airplane with Chiang's orders to He to stop the military advance toward Xi'an.[154]

That evening, Zhang Xueliang told T.V. that he had had a violent altercation with Yang, who did not want to free Chiang without concrete concessions. Zhang and T.V. discussed escaping with the Generalissimo and the Madame to the airport, but decided it was too dangerous.[155] Very early Christmas morning, Donald came into Chiang's room and placed two of his golf stockings on the mantle of the fireplace. Beneath one was a new, up-to-date portable typewriter for Madame and under the other was a steamer rug for the Generalissimo. The leader, still in his bedclothes, laughed for the first time since the affair began.[156]

Later that morning, Zhou told the Soongs that he wished to see the Generalissimo. At 8:00 a.m., accompanied by T.V., Zhou entered the room and saluted—the Red Army's first sign of obedience to the united front commander. In his Zhejiang dialect, Zhou told the distinguished captive that the Communists had for a year avoided fighting to preserve national strength and had not made any capital out of the Xi'an Incident. Their proposals to resolve the incident were the same as they had "put forward months ago [in Shanghai and Nanking]." Indicating that the Generalissimo's word would be sufficient, Zhou said the CCP wanted his personal assurance that he would stop the suppression of Communists, enroll them in the fight against Japan, and allow them to send representatives to Nanking to explain their position to him.[157] Chiang replied that if the Communists were willing to obey him as their leader he would treat them as his own troops. Most of the CCP leaders, he said, were his former subordinates and he could treat them with the same generosity as he had recently shown the rebellious Guangxi leaders.[158] Zhou then told the KMT leader that Chiang Ching-kuo would soon return to China, that he was a patriotic young man and undoubtedly "wished his father to resist the invaders."[159]

Afterward, T.V. and Mayling asked Zhou for a contact person in Shanghai. To their surprise, he told them that they could get in touch with him through their sister, Soong Chingling, who, he added, had recently sent Mao US$50,000. Later, T.V. confronted his middle sister about her gift to Mao, causing her to complain through the Comintern network in Shanghai about Zhou's indiscretion. Apparently, neither Mayling nor T.V. ever told Chiang Kai-shek that their sister was a contact person for the CCP.[160] For the Soongs, blood was thicker than politics.

At 2:00 p.m. the next day, Mayling saw a coolie carrying a suitcase cross their courtyard followed by Zhang Xueliang. The Young Marshal, who only a few days before had plotted to overthrow Chiang Kai-shek and replace him as the principal leader of China, told the group he wanted to accompany them back to Nanking to show the country that his intentions had been honorable. Suddenly T.V. appeared and said that those in command in the city had agreed they could depart. The Generalissimo said first he wanted to speak to Yang and Zhang together, and when Yang arrived, he told the two warlords that he did not bear personal grudges and that his focus was on saving the nation.[161] He said if the generals obeyed unreservedly the orders of the central government, a national calamity could be turned into a national blessing.[162] According to T.V.'s journal, Chiang specifically pardoned them for their action.[163]

The party packed into several cars and drove over the snow-covered road to the airport. The Generalissimo and the Madame left in the Young Marshal's Boeing with Chiang sitting in the copilot's seat.[164] When they arrived back in Nanking the next day, thousands of cheering citizens lined the roadway from the airport to the city, and vast strings of firecrackers popped like machine guns along the route. Chiang had left for Xi'an a popular leader, but returned a national hero.

The incident at Xi'an underscored the personal relationship between Chiang and Zhou. If Chiang gave anyone credit for his release, it was no doubt Zhou

Enlai. In 1941, Chiang would tell Owen Lattimore that he considered Zhou "personally trustworthy although he was of course under Yan'an's control."[165] Years later, Chiang, obviously referring to Zhou, wrote that at Xi'an he believed that the Communists, meaning of course Zhou, had "repented and were sincere."[166] Although sometimes Zhou echoed Mao's cynicism about Chiang's belief in his own sincerity, later events would suggest that Zhou did believe and would argue within the CCP that if Chiang lived up to his commitments at Xi'an, the Communists should give priority to fighting the Japanese under the broad but real leadership of Chiang Kai-shek.

The Generalissimo did think he himself was sincere in his professions of personal virtue in the realm of politics. Declarations of loyalty, such as those voiced by Zhou, constituted the most telling appeal that one could make to him, particularly in a situation like that at Xi'an when he was experiencing profound treachery and stress. As a strong but withdrawn and melancholic personality, Chiang, when faced with a serious setback, was inclined to see himself as a martyr who was destined to suffer. Two months later in his diary, he would compare his ordeal in Xi'an with the trials and humiliations of Jesus.[167] He probably meant it when he told Zhou that if the Communist leaders followed him he would treat them as he did his most loyal commanders. He was probably sincere in this statement because, among other things, in his mind it confirmed his magnanimous nature. But at the same time he had not lost his deep mistrust of the Communists.

After his return to Nanking, Chiang called Chen Lifu into his bedroom. "How was Zhou Enlai's attitude in Xi'an?" Chen asked. "Very good," Chiang replied. Chen then suggested that the large government force now deployed near Shaanxi finish off the Communists, but Chiang bent his head and did not answer. He had given his word. The opportunity to eliminate the Communists or drive them out of China had passed. Seeing he was tired, Chen hurried off.[168]

Without the kidnapping, if Chiang had proceeded with the offensive, Mao would likely have been forced to take refuge in Siberia or Outer Mongolia, and given the dire threats facing the Soviet Union, Stalin would probably have provided Chiang the same sort of military support he in fact would provide after the Japanese attack on China in July 1937. In this case, Chiang's hand would have been immensely strengthened in the postwar contest with the Communists. But if the kidnapping had not occurred, Mao, pushed by Stalin, would probably have agreed to a united front on the terms worked out by Chen Lifu, Zhang Qun, Zhou Enlai, and Pan Hannian—and if Stalin had then committed the Soviet Union in effect to a secret military alliance with China, Chiang would probably have called off the "last five minute" offensive and the united front would still have begun. Thus the kidnapping itself did not change history; it was Chiang's decisions that shaped events. On December 26, after arriving in Nanking from Xi'an, he had another clear opportunity to choose an all-out military solution to the Communist problem.

II

WAR OF RESISTANCE

4

The Long War Begins

After his return to the capital, despite the outrage and humiliation he had experienced at Xi'an, Chiang's decisions were measured, decisive, and audacious. Most importantly, they reflected a wish to get on with the important task of unifying China and preparing for war with Japan. As Mao's friend and biographer Edgar Snow wrote: "The terrific personal shock Chiang had suffered might have embittered and unbalanced a man less gifted with foresight and hastened him into precipitate actions of revenge—which in fact, Chiang's angry followers in Nanking demanded." But instead Chiang was a "master of compromise."[1] First, with virtually no violence, the Generalissimo succeeded in gaining control of the two mutinous camps in Shaanxi, positioned five armies to advance on Xi'an, replaced division commanders in the Manchurian Army, and redeployed all the fur-capped brigades to Jiangsu and Anhui. Loyalists quickly suppressed a mutiny by a few pro-Communist officers, and the great bulk of the officers and men from the Northeast, who only weeks before had seemed so rebellious, went quietly.

Upon the party's return to Nanking, military intelligence detained the Young Marshal Zhang Xueliang, but Mayling interceded and Chiang finally issued a pardon, placing him under "supervision."[2] This amounted to indefinite house confinement—which was to prove a half-century-long boring (but not unpleasant) experience. Zhang filled the hours playing mahjong, studying history, and collecting new pieces of Chinese art, and for a few years alternating between the company of his wife and his favorite mistress, Edith Chao. His first house of arrest was in the remote mountains above the Chiang hamlet of Xikou. Mayling offered to keep safe his valuable collection of Chinese art, and she regularly sent him letters, special foods, and other small gifts.[3] By contrast Yang Hucheng, whom the Generalissimo incorrectly believed was the prime force behind the rebellion, was sent to Europe and America on a year's tour as a "special military investigator." Upon his return in 1938, Chiang ordered his arrest.[4]

When Zhou reported back from Xi'an, Mao was aghast that Chiang had only given his word that he would halt the civil war. He feared that the hated enemy who only days before had seemed in his grasp was now free to unleash his "rapid and cruel revenge." Zhou, however, said Chiang would "probably not go back on his word," explaining—in a probably sarcastic manner—that this was "the vainglory of a self-appointed hero." Mao remembered his own previous caricature of Chiang's naiveté and agreed.[5] Chiang, he said, would again likely play the part of "Ah Q," the writer Lu Xun's literary symbol of China's self-delusion and obscurantism. Mao believed that, like Ah Q, Chiang suffered delusions about both his own virtue and sincerity and that of traditional China, and moreover, that the CCP could take advantage of this ingenuousness. With this image in mind, Mao accepted Zhang Guotao's suggestion that the Communists act outwardly humble toward the Generalissimo but inwardly vengeful, like Goujian, the prince of the fifth-century BCE state of Yue, who bided his time and "ate bile" until he could achieve complete victory.[6]

Indeed, Chiang had promised nothing publicly and after sending away the previously rebellious divisions could have quickly deployed a massive force to surround the Yan'an base area. The three Chinese Red armies in the northern Shaanxi area totaled only about 50,000 troops. Of these, 29,650 possessed guns, and there was no air force.[7] At the same time, Chiang commanded armies totaling 2,029,000, of which 300,000 were German trained, with 80,000 of those troops carrying German weapons. In addition, he possessed "314 war planes and more than 600 fighter pilots." Moreover, as Edgar Snow noted, "The tremendous popular demonstration on his safe return from captivity" confirmed that his standing with the nation as a whole was "higher than that of any leader in modern Chinese history."[8] In terms of public opinion this was the best time to strike.

But once free of his captors, Chiang never even considered the military option. As Zhou foresaw, he carried through with his promises and ended the "bandit suppression campaign." Moreover, he began to remit 200,000 to 300,000 yuan a month to the Communist forces.[9] The Comintern continued its funding as well, giving US$800,000 to the CCP in early 1937 and making the same amount available for "extra purchases."[10] At the same time, Mao told his colleagues that in carrying out the united front, the CCP, by using "this or that excuse," would prevent the KMT from reorganizing or dispersing the Red Army. When war with Japan broke out, Mao predicted, "all would be resolved smoothly."[11]

In February, the KMT Central Committee refused to endorse a united front and reiterated the need for anti-Communist vigilance. More than a few members still believed that cooperation with Japan, not the Communists, was the way for China to recover its sovereignty. But Chiang relentlessly pushed ahead, ordering the opening of trade and partial resumption of mail and telegraph services with the Red districts in the Northwest. Meanwhile, with dollars flowing into its coffers from both Moscow and Nanking, the CCP bought a fleet of American trucks and started bus services from Xi'an to Mao's new headquarters in Yan'an.[12] Chinese journalists visiting Yan'an reported that the CCP had eliminated corruption and exploitation, and hundreds, eventually thousands, of young Chinese felt the call to "Go to Yan'an."

But the agreement with Chiang also created enormous confusion in the ranks of the CCP and the Red Army. To clarify matters, the party issued a confidential communiqué to all its members declaring that its pursuit of a united front was a strategy that would permit the party to resist Japan while expanding its influence "thousands of times." Chiang saw the communiqué and wrote that it showed "the treacherous nature of the Communists," but he did not proclaim this view publicly and continued to treat the CCP as a loyal junior partner.[13] Likewise, he abandoned his efforts to weaken the warlords. He was now focused entirely on the coming war with Japan and he needed national unity and Soviet military aid.

Chiang believed that if within one year he could lead a successful resistance against the Japanese—a scenario that he had come to believe was at least possible—the Communist threat could afterward be managed one way or another. Chiang's suddenly more positive, even upbeat assessment of the balance of forces in a war with Japan reflected in good part the surprising optimism of his German adviser General Alexander von Faulkenhausen, who only a few months before had said that the Chinese armed forces needed another two years. Now he was telling Chiang that the Chinese Army was strong enough to drive "the Japanese over the Wall" and urging him both to defend the coastal areas and the Yangtze Valley and not to plan an early retreat to Sichuan.[14] In March 1937, he advised Chiang to send central army troops to Peking and Tianjin, an action that would have precipitated full-scale war.[15] Chiang had long understood the modern firepower on land, sea, and air that the Japanese military possessed—a power that could compete with that of the Europeans—but now he thought he was ready to take on that military colossus in battle.

Chiang was also probably moved by the dramatic sight of the new elite Chinese forces doing their maneuvers and by the overwhelming popular support—not only for himself and the united front, but also for the government's evident plan finally to confront the Japanese. In addition, he may have convinced himself that ending the civil war had given China the necessary unity and spirit to take on the Japanese whether in a limited or a protracted war. Whatever the reasons, his and Faulkenhausen's assessment represented a gross overestimation of the capabilities of the Chinese military at that stage.

In June, Chiang sent a semi-official KMT delegation to tour the CCP areas and make anti-Japan speeches, while the Blue Shirts were ordered to concentrate on punishing "pro-Japanese traitors." The Communist enclaves together became a "Special Area Government" nominally under Nanking, and at CCP meetings, portraits of Chiang Kai-shek were hung alongside those of Lenin, Marx, Stalin, and Mao. Even ordinary CCP members understood this was a sham. In keeping with their "promises," the CCP halted new confiscation of land but did not return previously seized property, stopped anti-KMT propaganda, and espoused Sun Yat-sen's three principles. Edgar Snow observed that these changes did "not affect the CCP's basic doctrine, program, or autonomous existence."[16] All this Chiang well knew.

On April 19, 1937, Chiang Ching-kuo, his Russian wife, Faina, and his sixteen-month-old son, Alan, arrived in Shanghai. Some weeks later, Ching-kuo entered a reception room in Hangzhou and greeted his father, kneeling and touching his forehead to the floor in a deep kowtow. The Generalissimo instructed his son to spend several months recovering his written Chinese and brushing up on the classics and the writings of Sun Yat-sen. Then he took Ching-kuo into the parlor to meet his stepmother, Soong Mayling.[17] Everyone was formal and polite and there was no discussion of the years of estrangement between father and son, except Chiang did suggest that Ching-kuo write a memoir of his almost thirteen-year experience in the Soviet Union.

Although Chiang was still suffering from his injuries at Xi'an, his political position kept growing stronger. Ambassador Johnson reported to the U.S.

State Department that there was a dominant feeling among Chinese, "irrespective of their personal or political inclinations," that the continuation of Chiang Kai-shek in power was "essential to the salvation of the Chinese nation."[18] For his part, despite continuing physical discomfort, Chiang felt "relaxed and comfortable."[19]

On the hot, moonlit night of July 7, some 135 of the mere 5,000–7,000 Japanese troops in North China were engaged in maneuvers in the area of the eight-hundred-year-old Marco Polo Bridge, ten miles from Peking. At about 10:30 that evening, soldiers of the Chinese 29th Route Army fired on armed Japanese whom they saw near the bridge. The Japanese fired back. The liaison officers on duty in each other's barracks got in touch by telephone and mutually apologized, but the Japanese brigade commander, not wishing to back down, ordered his artillery to fire on the Chinese troops. The Chinese responded with their own shelling.[20]

Chiang was at Lushan for a military conference when in the middle of the night he received the first radio report of the fighting. He was uncertain if this was another unplanned exchange of gunfire or a major Japanese provocation like the Mukden Incident. He told the 29th Army commander to negotiate but not yield "one iota of sovereignty."[21] He then sent a telegram to his military commanders and governors of all provinces and special municipalities ordering martial law and a "general mobilization to get ready for war." Most importantly, he ordered three of his best German-trained divisions to cross the Yellow River and deploy into the area of North China that the Tanggu Truce had preserved as "off limits" to the Chinese Central Army. Chiang knew that the Japanese, determined not to be seen as intimidated, were bound to respond.

Within a few hours of the first shooting, Mao and Zhu De in a telegram to Chiang and a circular message to all CCP army units declared that the Red Army was ready under Chiang Kai-shek's leadership to accept orders. Early on the morning of July 9, the two opposing commanders in the Marco Polo Bridge area agreed on a cease-fire and a mutual pullback. The Japanese Army Supreme Command instructed the Japanese commander in China not to resort to the further use of force. A frenzy of jingoism, however, now arose in Japan demanding that China be taught a lesson for its arrogance. The new prime minister, Prince Konoe, sent three divisions to the area of the "provocation."[22]

When the Japanese troops arrived in Tianjin on July 12, Chiang cabled the 19th Army: "I am now determined to declare war on Japan."[23] He immediately sent diplomatic appeals for intervention to the League of Nations and the Western signatories of the Nine-Power Pact, but, as Chiang no doubt fully expected, the United States, United Kingdom, France, and Italy only timidly urged restraint on Tokyo. To avoid irritating Japan, Secretary of State Cordell Hull even stopped a shipment of bombers purchased by the Chinese government. American missionaries promoted an embargo of strategic materials to Japan, but Congress refused to act.[24]

Ambassador Johnson found the reasons for the looming conflict between Japan and China obscure. "There can be no infallible appraisal of its causes or outcome," he advised the Secretary of State.[25] For fear of provoking "an anti-foreign outburst," Ambassador Joseph Grew in Tokyo was reluctant to convey, as instructed, Washington's restrained expression of concern.[26] On July 22 the Japanese commander in the Marco Polo Bridge area issued a deadline for withdrawal of Chinese troops, but on Chiang Kai-shek's orders, the Chinese attacked. The Konoe cabinet announced to enthusiastic popular support that Japan "was now forced to resort to resolute action to bring sense to the Nanking government by punishing the atrocious Chinese Army."[27] In the Japanese government "few were for war with China but few were resolutely against it."[28] One reason was that, like General Tojo Hideki, now chief of staff, most Japanese were supremely confident of the Imperial Army's ability to punish China with such brutal force that it would finally be compelled to accept its proper place as a satellite moon to the rising empire to the east.

On July 24, Chiang cabled Ching-kuo, who was dutifully studying Chinese history, practicing Chinese characters, and writing his memoirs in Xikou. "Do not be distracted by the Japanese invasion," his father said. "I have the means to counter them." The "means" were his German-trained divisions (especially those that were also German-armed).[29] Meanwhile, a national conference at Lushan officially declared the Communist Party a legal body, but Chiang could not get the attendees to agree on his proposed "declaration of war." So on August 7 he convened the Military Council, which declared all-out resistance as the national policy.[30] Chiang had personally rammed through the decision for war, simply ignoring the institutions of party and government. For eight years Chiang believed that he had shown willpower and courage by sticking to his policy of temporary appeasement while building military power. Now he was determined to stick to the policy of war.[31]

By the end of July, 160,000 Japanese troops had poured into Hebei province. The 19th Army commander abandoned Peking without a fight. Mao ordered his army to move across Shanxi toward Hebei to support the forces of Fu Zuoyi, a successor to warlord Feng Yuxiang. On July 31, however, showing his intention to avoid serious combat with the Japanese, Mao radioed his military lieutenants that the previous order was for propaganda purposes. In reality, he said, the troops should move slowly. In particular, they could "move 50 li [25 kilometers] each day, and pause one day after every three days."[32]

Chiang immediately deployed the highly trained and German-armed 87th and 88th divisions to the Shanghai suburbs.[33] His major objective in fighting for Shanghai was to draw enemy troops away from North China, deterring the Japanese advance on Wuhan and keeping open the potential supply route to the Soviet Union. There were other reasons he chose to make a stand in Shanghai and then to fight on long after defeat seemed certain. First, as noted, he and Falkenhausen believed they could succeed, with the German repeatedly insisting that "Shanghai must be held."[34] The North China plains, both knew, were ideally suited to Japanese mechanized units, but the streets of Shanghai and the surrounding areas were full of waterways and offered better prospects for the lightly armed Chinese.

Chiang made an all-out commitment to defend Shanghai for psychological and political reasons as well. When defeat seemed certain, rather than cut his losses, he would order his soldiers to fight on because he sought to rally the Chinese people with a heroic demonstration of sacrifice and steely determination. In addition, he hoped that in contrast to the battles in North China, fighting in Chinese Shanghai would have a greater influence on the Western signatories of the 1922 Nine-Power Pact, which (except for Germany) were to meet in Brussels beginning in early November.[35] America and Europe had strong business interests in the city and many thousands of their citizens lived in the foreign concessions adjacent to the coming battle. But given Chiang's totally discouraging diplomatic exchanges with Western governments over the previous weeks and months, pusillanimous steps by Washington to appear neutral, the preoccupation of the democracies with the economic depression at home, and the isolationist and even pacifist proclivities of their people, Chiang clearly did not expect even a strong verbal intervention from Europe and America; rather he was building sympathy for the future.[36]

To believe that Chiang sacrificed his elite forces at Shanghai primarily in order to create fear in the foreign concessions in Shanghai and thereby to elicit, against all odds, some meaningful assistance by the Western democracies lacks credibility. Yet notable Western authors have insisted that after the war began, "from first to last, Chiang Kai-shek had one purpose: to destroy the Communists and wait for foreign help to defeat the Japanese," and that the hope for such foreign intervention was behind his decision to make a stand in Shanghai—a stand that would cost him most of his modern fighting force.[37]

During the first few days of fierce street fighting, Chinese troops drove the Japanese marines who were already stationed in Shanghai into a defensive perimeter near the wharves. Powerful naval gunfire, however, held back the Chinese elite forces and over the next ten days 75,000 additional Japanese troops landed. By this time Chiang had in the Shanghai area seventy-one divisions, totaling 500,000 to 700,000 men, including almost all of the German-trained units, the army's most modern artillery, and its new combat air forces, as well as the patriotic warlord armies from Guangdong and Guangxi.[38] But the new Japanese divisions that landed on the coast near Shanghai were able, over just a few days, to reduce by half two elite Chinese divisions that had been sent to challenge them. In deadly close-quarters combat in the narrow, rubble-strewn streets and *hutongs* of the Chinese city, both sides took "tremendous losses." Two Japanese divisions in a few days suffered 4,000 casualties. The streets of Shanghai and the waters of the Whangpoo River ran red with blood.[39] Deputy Chief of Staff Bai Chongxi and Li Zongren, who were at the front, urged retreat, but Chiang, who also was often near the front lines, asked, "If we do not stand firm, how can we deter our enemy?"[40]

Yet despite his stubborn stand, Chiang did not believe the loss of Shanghai would determine the outcome of the war; for example, he ordered all universities in the coastal provinces to move immediately to the interior with their existing faculties and student bodies.[41]

While the Central Army was being decimated, the Communist forces remained virtually untouched. But there was a split within the CCP on what their strategy should be. According to Zhang Guotao, he and others, including Zhou Enlai, supported a "Victory for All" policy in which the CCP would pursue genuine cooperation in the expectation that such action would lead the KMT and other non-Communist groups along a more progressive path with a real emphasis on defeating the Japanese. Mao, however, called for a "Defeat for All" policy, meaning defeat for the Japanese but ultimately also defeat for the KMT. During an October CCP conference, a majority reportedly favored the "Victory for All" policy and Mao made rhetorical concessions, dropping the stated goal of "making Chiang Kai-shek suffer defeat."[42]

On September 23, the CCP issued a public declaration that reiterated its commitment to integrating the Communist military into the Revolutionary Armed Forces under the command of the Military Council. Chiang publicly announced that the declaration was a sign that "all Chinese now realize there is only one direction and one goal for the country." But he was already receiving reports of the failure of the Eighth Route Army, the new name of the principal Red Army, to abide by the operational orders it was receiving from the Military Council. In private, he fumed at the "opportunism and cunning" of the CCP and its lack of "credibility and morality."[43] Nonetheless, with his need for massive Soviet aid increasing rapidly and his appeals to Stalin soon to include a plea for combat troops, he had more reason than ever to avoid public criticism of the Chinese Communists.

For his part, Stalin had to balance not provoking Japan with doing everything he could to make sure that the Chinese government was able to fight on.[44] He soon had large Soviet supply convoys rolling through Xinjiang to the rest of China, while Soviet freighters, loaded with heavy military equipment, headed out on the long voyage to Canton. The first flight of Soviet aircraft arrived in China in mid-October. During the next four months, 297 Soviet attack and bomber aircraft flew into Chinese airfields, while trucks and ships delivered 290 cannon, 82 tanks, 400 automobiles, and a large supply of firearms and ammunition. Eventually the USSR would make three loans to China to pay for military aid, totaling $250 million in 1937 U.S. dollars.[45]

The Chinese Air Force, Madame's adopted service, so far had only shown it needed far more training and more modern aircraft. At the start of the Battle of Shanghai, of the air force's three hundred planes, only eighty-seven were able to fly—many of the others were covered in canvas.[46] The air force's inadequacies were, at times, nothing short of shocking. On August 14, Chiang ordered the bombing of the *Izumo,* the pre-Dreadnaught cruiser in the Whangpoo River, but the bombs hit civilian areas, killing 2,000 Chinese. The 1,500 Japanese warplanes in China continually strafed and bombed the Chinese lines unopposed. Bai protested, "There is no way we can fight without control of the air."[47] On October 23, this vulnerability was underscored.

On that day Madame Chiang, accompanied by Donald, sped from Nanking to Shanghai to boost the morale of the troops. Japanese planes strafed the car, which overturned, knocking Mayling unconscious. She suffered a broken rib and a wrenched back, but, according to Donald, she insisted that they carry on with their mission.[48]

In a repeat of the 1931 battle for Shanghai, on November 5 three Japanese divisions landed unopposed on the northern bank of Hangzhou Bay, forty miles south of Shanghai. Chiang had withdrawn troops from that area to support the city itself, a disastrous move that he later said was his biggest mistake. These Japanese forces advanced north toward the Suzhou River, threatening as in 1932 to trap the vast Chinese Army in the Shanghai triangle. On November 8, Chiang finally gave the order to withdraw.[49] In response to an urgent plea from Chiang for Soviet troops, Stalin replied that the USSR "would like to see Japan weakened but now is not the time for the Soviet Union to fight Japan."[50]

Although the Chinese Army had at least five times as many troops as the invaders and Falkenhausen reported to Berlin on their impressive bravery, they could not stand up to Japan's modern killing machine.[51] In three months 187,000 Chinese troops were killed or wounded, among them a large number of the elite forces that Chiang Kai-shek and his German advisers had spent years training and arming. A substantial percentage of the 30,000 young Chinese officers who had constituted the future of the army—mostly graduates of Whampoa and other officer training schools—were swept away. With the fall of Shanghai, the government also lost its single most important source of revenue and industrial production.

Some 400,000 Central Army and other surviving troops from Shanghai fled up the Yangtze. Chiang had decided to make the Japanese pay for their advance, but he knew it was now going to be a long, protracted war. He sent the government to Chungking and moved his military headquarters to Wuhan. By the middle of November, the Japanese were threatening Nanking, and Chiang could not decide whether to defend the city. Most of his commanders and Falkenhausen believed that to make a stand in Nanking would be an unnecessary sacrifice with no strategic gain.[52]

If Chiang's principal purpose at this early date in the war was to wait for foreign help, he probably would have taken this advice and saved an enormous number of men and arms. In the end, however, Chiang decided that because Nanking was the new capital, the site of Sun Yat-sen's mausoleum, and, with its new buildings and wide avenues, the model of the future China, the government could not abandon it without a serious fight. To do so, he believed, would forever be regarded as a cowardly decision.[53] No doubt he also saw a heroic stand in Nanking as further intensifying, after the courageous defense of Shanghai, the Chinese people's hatred of the enemy, hardening them for the long and terrible struggle ahead. Hu Shi and others continued to plead with Chiang Kai-shek for peace talks. "Scholars are old and impractical," Chiang scoffed. "After military defeat, they ask for appeasement."[54]

I

As the Japanese began shelling the city walls of Nanking, Chiang fired off another radio message to Stalin expressing his sincere hope that the Soviet Union would act decisively and send troops.[55] In a December 5 reply, however, Stalin argued with some logic that if the USSR attacked the Japanese in China, the West, still more afraid of the Bolsheviks than the Nazis, would see Japan as the victim.[56] As Chiang read this reply, artillery shells and bombs were exploding nearby. Overhead, fighter planes with Chinese markings but made in the Soviet Union and flown by Soviet pilots were for the first time engaging the Japanese.

The defenders of Nanking, led by the Generalissimo and with Madame Chiang also present, fought on for three weeks. Finally, on December 7, the couple flew out of the largely destroyed capital to Lushan.[57] Two days later, as the Japanese stormed several gates of the old city, the Chinese fought fiercely but gradually fell back. Tang Shengzhi, the former Hunan warlord who had twice betrayed Chiang but who had volunteered to be the official commander at Nanking, refused a demand to surrender. But on December 12, with only two of his three divisions intact and resistance collapsing, he gave the belated order to his troops to break out of the encirclement.

Total chaos ensued. Some Chinese soldiers were drowned or killed trying to cross the broad windswept Yangtze, others were crushed in a huge stampede at the one gate in the wall not held by the Japanese. Tang himself finally left at night in a small coal-driven launch, chugging down a river full of civilians and soldiers clinging to whatever they could find, while huge flames roared through the old city. With 70,000 dead soldiers left behind, the Chinese casualty rate was higher than at Shanghai. But this was only the beginning. In the horrible slaughter known as the Rape of Nanking, which occurred from mid-December 1937 to mid-February 1938, tens of thousands, some say as many as 300,000, Chinese were killed by the most fiendish means, including live burials, disembowelment, decapitation, impalement of babies, and sexual assault.[58] If, as seemed the case, the massive atrocity was a deliberate effort to intimidate the Chinese people, it had the opposite result. Popular support for the resistance soared.

After the fall of Nanking, Chiang Kai-shek issued a proclamation as rousing as that which Churchill would give twenty-one months later and with some similar imagery: "The war will not be decided in Nanking or any other city," he said. "It will be decided in the countryside of our vast country and by the inflexible will of our people. We shall fight on every step of the way, and every inch of the 40,000,000 square *li* of our territory."[59]

As stories of what happened at Nanking spread across the country, millions of civilian refugees fled before the advancing Japanese. Camps sprouted up across China. Confusion reigned, but somehow most survived through their own pluck and ingenuity, the help of local people along the way, and efforts by local governments (and in some cases, the Chinese Army). In the meantime, thousands of river steamers, junks, ox carts, and wheelbarrows were carrying everything from university books to huge machine tools to safer ground in Guangxi and Yunnan and up the Yangtze to Chungking. Chiang Kai-shek appointed his fellow Fenghua County native, the honest Oxford-educated Yu Dawei, to head this operation. In addition, thousands of crates containing the Palace Museum's priceless collection, which had been brought earlier from Peking to Nanking, were carried by boats and barges to the Three Gorges of the Yangtze. There they were transferred to rafts and pulled by thick ropes through the rapids by barefoot men on shore.

While officially Washington did nothing to aid China, both the American government and the public were overwhelmingly sympathetic to the country and its leaders. The world had been treated to photographs and news stories about the brave defense of China's cities and the barbaric cruelty of the Japanese, and the Chiangs came to represent everything that was noble and brave in a world sinking into savagery. *Time*'s publisher, Henry Luce, the son of China missionaries, was already a leading advocate for China and the Chiangs. The magazine chose the couple as "Man and Wife of the Year." In the cover photo the Chiangs look dignified and somber, he in a rough-hewn gown and holding a fedora and she in a simple frock. In fulsome language, *Time* praised China's First Couple: "Through 1937 the Chinese have been led—not without glory—by one supreme leader and his remarkable wife. Under this Man and Wife the traditionally disunited Chinese people— millions of whom seldom used the word 'China' in the past—have slowly been given national consciousness . . . [The Chiangs'] rise in less than a generation to moral and material leadership of the ancient Chinese people covers a great page of history."[60]

The German adviser Falkenhausen was now stressing "the severity of the war situation," and some senior Chinese officers "argued for peace, some for fighting."[61] Meanwhile Japan, which had inflicted a terrible defeat on the Chinese and occupied a large part of their country, now felt it was time to move to a negotiated settlement. Tokyo asked the German ambassador Oskay Trautman to act as an intermediary, and Chiang accepted the offer as a tactic "to slow down Japan's advance." He feared that Japan would offer soft terms in order to encourage the peace faction inside the Chinese government; he was pleased when the conditions presented through Trautman were "stiffer" than expected. Still, at a December meeting of China's Supreme Defense Conference, a majority actually supported negotiations, with some openly criticizing Chiang for being "indecisive" about opening talks. Chiang, however, knew that if peace was made with Japan, internal revolts could sweep the government out of power. More importantly, he told Wang Jingwei, "If we accept unbearable concessions, we will put an eternal yoke on our country."[62]

On the second day of the new year, Chiang rejected Tokyo's latest four-point proposal for a truce. "Japan's proposal would completely destroy us," he told his foreign minister. "It is better to fight to the death than surrender to death."[63] Tokyo then proclaimed it would no longer deal with Chiang Kai-shek; rather a new Chinese regime was needed. The first Chinese puppet government since Manchuko, the Provisional Republic of China, soon emerged. Headed by old figures from the Northern warlord period, it had supposed jurisdiction over most of North China.

Meanwhile, Wang Jingwei established an informal group of peace advocates in the KMT, while in Japan there was also a small peace faction whose members were dismayed at the quagmire into which Japan had stumbled. Chiang authorized secret talks with two Japanese emissaries from this group, Mitsuri Toyama and Nagatomo Kayano, who had been friends and supporters of Sun Yat-sen. Following Chiang's instructions, his envoy demanded the "complete withdrawal of Japanese troops," but suggested that if Japan agreed to total withdrawal from China, Chiang Kai-shek would step down.[64] Soon after these talks, Tokyo sent word secretly to Wang Jingwei that he should establish a new government that could negotiate a peace settlement. Wang, believing the war was lost, began to plan a rival regime.[65]

Chiang's military headquarters was now in Wuhan, about six hundred miles up the Yangtze from Nanking and linked by railroad to Zhengzhou directly to the north. Zhou Enlai once again took a position under Chiang Kai-shek, joining the united front government in Wuhan as vice-head of the political section of the Military Council under General Chen Cheng. Despite the terrible Chinese losses in the second half of 1937, Chiang was able in a short period to put together a force of about 1.1 million men for the coming battles in the central Yangtze Valley and in northern, coastal Shandong province. The Chinese forces, however, were even more inferior than before in terms of firepower, mobility, air cover, and equipment.

A major battle now loomed near Xuzhou, a major north-south and east-west rail junction in the northwest portion of Jiangsu near the Shandong border. Chinese forces under Li Zongren and Bai Chongxi in the Huai River area were fighting Japanese armies advancing from both the north and the south toward Xuzhou. Following Bai's plan, two Japanese divisions fell into an ambush at a railway spur line at Tai'erzhuang, forty miles from the target city.[66] After seven days of fighting, 15,000 to 20,000 Japanese soldiers reportedly lay dead, a huge number of casualties for the Japanese. The news, although exaggerated, was a tremendous tonic to the people of China.[67] Again showing an aggressive spirit, Chiang envisioned a major counteroffensive to follow up the Tai'erzhuang success and he rushed reinforcements to the area.[68] But instead of another attack, Li devised "a brilliantly executed strategic retreat."[69]

The Imperial Army, riding railroad boxcars, sped along the rail line toward Zhengzhou, two hundred miles to the west. Chiang flew to confront them in that strategic city, which was also on the north-south Wuhan-Peking rail line. Chen Guofu, at this time dean of the Central Political Training Institute (the party cadre training center), suggested that the army blow up the ancient dikes on the Yellow River, flooding a vast area of the central plains in order to stop the Japanese advance to Zhengzhou and then down the rail line to Wuhan. Faulkenhausen had earlier proposed this drastic measure.[70] Over centuries heavy sediment along the Yellow River had forced the Chinese to build ever higher dikes, and in some places even the bed of the river lay above the level of the surrounding ground. It would be a human and environmental calamity to destroy the dikes, but Chiang approved the proposal. On June 5 and 7, soldiers blew open the dikes on the south banks and the waters flowed southeast to Henan, Anhui, and Jiangsu.

The flooding covered thousands of square kilometers of farmland, extending to the Huai River, the Grand Canal, and even into the Yangtze. As a result, the mouth of the Yellow River shifted hundreds of miles to the south. Several thousand Chinese villages were swamped or destroyed, and a few million rural dwellers made homeless.[71] After the war, an official Nationalist estimate gave a staggering figure of 800,000 drowned—although the real number could have been much higher.[72] At the time, Chiang issued a statement blaming the breaking of the dikes on Japanese bombers. The flooding separated the northern and southern battlefields and made it impossible for the Japanese to reach areas west of the flooded zone for six years—Zhengzhou did not fall until April 1944. Some current-day scholars in the People's Republic believe this was a major strategic benefit for China, but many would argue otherwise.

Chiang no doubt saw the sacrifice as warranted in the context of a war for the survival of Chinese civilization, a war in which there would be many rivers of blood, but he also showed no private remorse, not mentioning the event in his diary. He spent little time expressing empathy for human suffering, but few leaders in the great war did.

The flooding did force General Hata, the Japanese commander, to change his strategy and attack Wuhan by advancing up the central Yangtze.[73] Chiang decided not to commit large forces to defend Wuhan itself but to conduct a series of positional defenses as the Japanese advanced up the southern bank of the Yangtze. Falkenhausen had joined Bai Chongxi in advocating a switch to smaller-unit mobile warfare, and Chiang in principle endorsed this new tactic.[74] But a shift almost entirely to guerrilla fighting would have allowed the Japanese to take cities and transportation links with near impunity, and if Chiang hoped to retain a substantial base of territory as a focus of loyalty for all Chinese and eventually for foreign support, it was necessary to retain a large conventional force.

Chiang believed that eventually a victorious end to China's war with the "dwarf pirates" depended on "diplomacy"—an alliance between China and the next apparent targets of Imperial Japan, that is, the Soviet Union, the United States, and the United Kingdom. When first Churchill and then Stalin's countries were swept up in the Nazi whirlwind, they too would calculate, correctly as it turned out, that victory would critically depend on American support. Mao, whose forces had still suffered little, also had decreed that "China's strength alone will not be sufficient to defeat (the Japanese), and we shall also have to rely on the support of international forces."[75] Of course, Mao was thinking solely of the Soviet Union and possibly Marxist revolutionary forces in Japan and elsewhere. In fact, for the foreseeable future, the critical relationship for China would be the Soviet Union, just as it had been at the time of the Northern Expedition and during the long survival of the CCP as an insurgent party. In May, Chiang told Stalin that China could not have sustained the war without "your help," but that the country was still "in a life or death situation." He pleaded for the quick delivery of sixty-five additional aircraft, reporting that China had only ten light bombers left. Stalin quickly replied that he would send the requested bombers for "your great war of resistance."[76]

Chiang knew that while he needed Soviet assistance more than ever, Stalin's interest in helping him resist Japan was also greater than ever. During the summer and fall, Japan and the Soviet Union engaged in more bloody skirmishes on Manchuria's borders, altercations that encouraged Stalin again to increase Soviet aid to China. Soon there would be 3,665 Russian military personnel in the country—advisers, pilots, technicians, and others.[77] A new and powerful motivation for Stalin to help Chiang was the appeasement of Hitler at Munich, where Great Britain and France agreed that Germany could annex a large portion of Czechoslovakia.

Pressed by Japan, Hitler had finally overruled the opposition of his pro-China general staff and ended the advisory mission and all arms sales to Chiang Kai-shek. Seven anti-Nazi German officers, however, resigned and stayed behind. One German who was not among the official advisers was a former intelligence officer named Walther Stennes. A former Brown Shirt leader in Berlin, Stennes had led a failed revolt against Hitler in 1931 and after escaping from a concentration camp had made his way to China—at least that was his story. He became an "adviser," in effect the leader of Chiang Kai-shek's bodyguard, and a favorite of Soong Mayling. It turned out he was also a KGB agent.[78]

The summer of 1938 was steaming hot and the Yangtze was running at its usual high level for that time of year. Consequently, Japanese cruisers were able to steam upriver and fire their big guns at short range on the dug-in Chinese positions. Sometimes using poison gas, the Japanese assaulted the Chinese strong points one by one, and more massacres of civilians took place. The invaders took three weeks to advance ten miles. Meanwhile, thousands of Chinese were still laboriously pulling thousands of heavily laden barges and rafts upstream through the swiftly flowing Three Gorges. By the end of September, the Japanese were able to move across the once flooded lands and advance on Wuhan from the north.[79] Rumors were again spreading, perhaps by the Communists, perhaps by Chiang, that the Generalissimo might sign a peace agreement with the Japanese, and Stalin rushed a message to Chiang that more aid was on the way, including equipment for sixty divisions and an additional five hundred fighter aircraft.[80]

Mao publicly predicted "a glorious future for the Kuomintang," but speaking to a closed session of the Central Committee, he stressed again for those who might have forgotten that the only way for the Communist Party to seize power was through armed struggle.[81] Political power, he reiterated, "grows out of the barrel of a gun." After the meeting, Zhou flew back to Wuhan and on October 5 brought Chiang a handwritten letter from Mao, which praised Chiang's "great leadership" and "the lasting solidarity of the two parties."[82] But Chiang knew that Mao was being cynical. If he needed confirmation, Zhang Guotao, who had left the CCP the previous April, made his way to Wuhan and declared, probably to Chiang personally, that Mao intended to exploit the war and the united front with one objective in mind—to expand the CCP's armies and base areas in preparation for the final struggle with the KMT.[83]

Chiang continued to worry—not only about the CCP's duplicity, but also about the superior political skills and motivation of its members. "Communist parties all over the world," he wrote, "have long been working underground, thus they have a tightly organized structure and an iron discipline that defies that of other parties."[84] At the same time, Chiang was becoming increasingly harsh in his criticism of members of his own party, "most" of whom he said had become "a special class" struggling for power and their own "selfish concerns." All of which, he lamented, had caused the "masses" to become "antagonistic" toward the party.[85]

This frustrated comparison would be a consistent leitmotif in the diaries until Chiang's retreat to Taiwan in 1949 and several years afterward. Chiang hated the CCP's "inhuman and deadly" ideology, its tactic of class struggle, and its obedience to Moscow, but he admired its soldiers and cadre for their idealism, commitment, and spirit, qualities that he thought were lacking by comparison in the Kuomintang. Reflecting his deep pessimism about his own party, several times in 1938 he talked to Zhou Enlai about the KMT and the CCP's forming a new, single party—but with the proviso that Mao and Zhu De take vacations abroad. He even proposed, apparently in all seriousness, that as part of the merger the CCP need not officially disband and the Kuomintang would join the Comintern. Mao suggested in response that the CCP members join the KMT as individuals just as they had done in the 1920s. In the end, neither side could make the critical compromise. Some weeks later, Zhou finally told Chiang that the idea simply was not possible.[86] As these exchanges again suggest, Chiang was not an ideologue or even a strong conservative. He was in fact a left-Confucianist and would have been comfortable in the anti-imperialist Comintern, provided it kept out of telling him what to do in China.

Almost a year and a half after the war began (when it was still officially undeclared), Wuhan remained in the hands of the Chinese. But in late October, with the Japanese buildup reaching critical levels, Li Zongren, holding the line to the north of the city, was forced to pull his forces back into the mountains. Chiang ordered the destruction of any usable facilities or plants that remained in the city, and the garrison forces and remaining government personnel then withdrew in good order. On the morning of October 24, Chiang called his senior officers and civilian aides on a field radiophone with the usual message at such times: "You can go now." Each subordinate protested that he could not leave until the commander in chief did so. "No, you must go first," Chiang always replied. "I'll leave soon after."[87]

It was 10:00 at night when he and Mayling gathered on the bombed-out Wuhan airfield. Lit by brilliant flashes of light, the field was dusted with snowflakes falling softly through the drifting smoke while heavy reports of exploding shells shook the ground. Their plane, flown by Chiang's personal American pilot, Royal Leonard (formerly Zhang Xueliang's pilot), had been delayed by false radio signals. Then a German assigned to fly the First Couple to Hengyang was ruled out because he admitted he could take off at night but not land. Finally a China National Air Corporation (civil) aircraft touched down, the Chiangs quickly boarded, and the pilot took off through a pall of thick smoke. Leonard landed a few minutes later. Upon learning that the Chiangs were gone, he crammed in forty or so Chinese from the hundreds besieging the plane and took off amid "the booming of siege guns, the crackling of flame, and the red, ghastly light of a city burning."[88] After a short stay at Hengyang, the Chiangs flew on, not to the new provisional capital, Chungking, but to Changsha, another ancient walled town. Initially settled in 221 BCE, Changsha sits by the Xiang River in the rich rice bowl of Hunan. The Chiangs stayed a few days, then flew on to the Canton front.

The American missionary doctor who worked in Changsha at the Yale-in-China Hospital, Phil Greene, wrote that when 40,000 refugees, numerous KMT generals, and then the Generalissimo descended on the Hunan capital, chaos and panic spread:

October 26: the arsenal behind the Hospital blew up just one big bang and the whole place was gone—about one hundred casualties, thirty dead. At the Hospital we just kept ahead of the patients. It took as long to dig them out as it did to fix them up.

October 28: 21,000 wounded [from Wuhan] reported in town . . .

October 29: The town is moving out fast, the doctors are sticking by . . .

November 1: People expect Changsha to fall in two weeks the Government has given us five good junks which will take about 200 tons of hospital supplies to Yuanling . . .

[Some days later]: the entire town [is] leaving by boat, train, buses, rickshaws and wheelbarrows after prayer meeting, some friends told us of having seen oil and cotton waste distributed to ward officials for setting fires. So many rumors . . .

November 11: only a small fraction of the city's half million population [remain]. I am the only doctor left [at the mission] . . .

[November 12]: uncanny stillness . . . a deserted, evidently doomed city.

That day, November 12, Governor Zhang Zhizhong received a report that Japanese cavalry were within twenty miles and he ordered an evacuation of the city. The Chinese doctors at the military hospitals said they would not move until transport was sent for the wounded in their care. Early the next morning, Greene and his remaining colleagues—he was the only doctor left—woke up to shouts in the streets and saw fires throughout the entire city that had been set by Chinese soldiers and police. The missionaries, nurses, students, and remaining staff pleaded with the soldiers not to set aflame their buildings or those just windward. "For two days and nights the roar of the fire, the pall of the smoke and the wanton destruction" went on, Greene recalled. Other missionaries who took refuge at Xiangya told of seeing the military hospital downtown in flames with the sick and wounded trying to drag themselves out the doors and windows.

But with an overextended supply line, the Japanese stopped their advance into Hunan at Lake Dongting, forty-five miles away. Setting the fires was a ghastly mistake. Perhaps Chiang ordered the deed, but he had not before called for such a total destruction of a city about to be lost nor did he afterward.[89] On Monday (November 14), the governor issued an apology, saying he had not ordered the arson. The next day, Greene received a letter from Madame Chiang, who had been his wife's classmate at Wellesley, declaring that the Generalissimo also was not responsible. On November 16 Chiang arrived to investigate, and the missionaries soon learned that the garrison commander, the regimental commander, and the chief of police had been shot. Governor Zhang, a Whampoa man, a hero of the 1932 Shanghai Battle, and a trusted follower of the Generalissimo, was dismissed but remained in Changsha. Greene sent his wife a radio message through the British gunboat anchored in the Xiang River: "All Well. Hospital running full wards; nothing [in the hospital] destroyed. Most of the city gone."[90]

The fall of first Shanghai, then Nanking, Xuzhou, and Wuhan, had not resulted in the surrender or collapse of the Chinese government as the West and Japan had expected. Instead, the prolonged and costly defense led by Chiang Kai-shek ended in a pyrrhic and limited success for Japan and the beginning of a seven-year stalemate. The Japanese would end up holding most of the major cities of China, all of Manchuria, much of Inner Mongolia, all of North China, the eastern part of the Northwest down to near Xi'an, the entire Yangtze Valley up to Wuhan, all of coastal China southward to near Wenzhou, and eventually several major ports farther south, including Amoy and Canton. But despite this huge area of occupation, three-quarters of the enormous country and probably two-thirds of the population were still in Nationalist hands—this was Free China.[91]

In November 1938 Chiang told a major military conference at Hengyang in Hunan province that the first stage of his strategy had run its course. The Chinese Army had worn down and exhausted the enemy. In the second stage, he said, the emphasis would be on improving the aptitude and fighting ability of the troops and eventually turning defense into offense. The goal of this stage, he said, was to be ready to launch a general counteroffensive within a year. Meanwhile, counterattacks could be launched when the circumstances assured victory.[92] "The Japanese are impatient and short-tempered," Chiang wrote in his diary. "Their military philosophy is German and French; that is, they emphasize a 'Blitzkrieg' type offense with strong fire power and speed. Their hope is to finish a war quickly with one first, decisive attack." Consequently, China's strategy would now be "to slow everything down, enduring, and fighting a long war of attrition."[93]

Over the next seven years, Chiang Kai-shek generally, though not always, followed this same tactic. At the same time he lay down tough requirements for any counteroffensive action. As he wrote, during the first stage of the war, the Chinese Army had employed three divisions and sometimes even six divisions to engage one Japanese division, "but still we could not win . . . From now on we must try to employ six to nine divisions to fight one of the enemy and attack their flank so we can obtain the goal of defense by offense."[94]

II

The ancient city of Chungking sits on a huge rock at the confluence of the Yangtze and the Jialing rivers. In the summer, the stone is blistering hot, and from October through April, it is wet from dripping rain or heavy fog. When in November 1938 the Chiangs and the Generalissimo's large headquarters staff arrived for their long stay, the ancient walls were still standing. Hundreds of steps cut in the rock centuries before curled down the steep cliff to the river far below. At the wharves, rusting steamers and large junks with square sails and long oars unloaded goods, which coolies laboriously carried up to the city on bamboo poles across their shoulders, joined by barefoot citizens toting buckets of water up to their shelters. Once the Kuomintang moved into town, men in blue Sun Yat-sen uniforms were everywhere. Usually taller than the average Sichuanese, they walked in the streets or rode in sedan chairs or rickshaws, their bearers or pullers shouting warnings to clear the way. Hundreds of thousands of refugees from the lower Yangtze and elsewhere reached the city and were living in matted sheds made of rice straw, scavenging for food or jobs. Engineers were dynamiting caves in the rock to serve as air raid shelters. A few million others fleeing the Japanese set up camps in different parts of Sichuan and other unoccupied areas of China.[95]

Chiang and Soong Mayling stayed in a relatively unpretentious ten-room house called Yellow Mountain (Huang Shan), outside of Chungking.[96] The house was surrounded by a high stone wall, and uniformed presidential guards and plainclothes men, specially trained by Walther Stennes, patrolled the grounds. Over the next eight years Chiang would need the long moments of meditation he was to spend in this garden. The problems he faced were enormous. Although much plant and equipment had been moved west, probably 90 percent of Nationalist China's industrial base and perhaps 80 percent of its arms industry were lost. The urban revenue on which Chiang had built his army was suddenly gone. The printing presses had been saved, however, and inflation began to rise, although surprisingly not at astronomical rates.[97]

Chiang's armies were scattered from the Mongolian border to the frontiers of Southeast Asia and as far to the east as large sections of the coasts of Zhejiang, Fujian, Guangdong, and Guangxi. As much as one can tell from that chaotic and enormous scene, Chiang's stubborn and immensely costly resistance from Shanghai to Wuhan, whether or not it had been the wisest strategy in a military sense, had forged a commitment among the Chinese people to the long and painful struggle for national survival that lay ahead.[98] Guerrilla or mobile warfare from the start may have been the better strategy in the long run, but China would have initially surrendered more productive cities to Japan and certainly would have provoked charges that Chiang was treacherously avoiding fighting the invaders. Besides, at some point Chiang would have had to take a stand.

Despite Chiang's continuing personal popularity, the foundation of his political strength had been drastically undermined since the fall of Shanghai. The hard-won dominance he had seemed to establish over the militarists by late 1936 had disappeared. With the exception of the Guangxi and Guangdong armies, the warlord forces had suffered many fewer casualties than the Central Army. And with their base areas largely unoccupied, the warlords of the south and southwest were recruiting at a much faster pace than was the Central Army. These warlords continued the old system of each unit recruiting in its own favorite hunting ground, relying on the enticements of money and freedom from drudgery, as well as appeals to regional or national patriotism, to sign up young men. After the war began, the Central Army lost most of the areas where personal and local affinities had accommodated a similar mostly voluntary method of recruitment. Abuses in recruitment practices by the Central Army gradually grew, as did resentment among the villages that had to produce a certain quota of recruits. Between 1937 and 1945, 14 million men would be conscripted. This was relatively a very low rate of military mobilization—0.4 percent of the population per year compared to Japan's 1.3 percent and Russia's 3.0 percent. Even so, as the war years dragged on, the villages resisted cooperation, and with probably most families by various means able to avoid conscription, the quality of the government armies deteriorated steadily. With funds scarce and officers remaining for long periods or even permanently in the same unit, parts of the Central Army also began to exhibit characteristics of most of the warlord forces—graft, nepotism, and other abuses of power by the senior officers.[99]

The fall of Wuhan at the end of October 1938 was followed by a "four month lull in the fighting," and during this time, Chiang Kai-shek's political priorities began to change. On January 6, 1939, he wrote that "the most urgent danger for [us] now is not the dwarf pirates but the Communist . . . expansion in our backyard." The Communist Eighth Route Army was growing in numbers and moving into new areas in North and Northwest China beyond its assigned zone. South of the Yangtze and behind the Japanese lines, the CCP's small New Fourth Army, composed of guerrilla units, was likewise expanding and also operating on the north side of its permitted boundary, the Yangtze.

The Communists had proved much more effective in organizing local regulars and irregulars in occupied areas, in setting up clandestine administrative systems, and even in bringing various secret societies into the anti-Japanese guerrilla movement. Multiplying their areas of control in the Northwest as well as behind Japanese lines, Communist membership swelled from 40,000 in 1937 to an estimated 800,000 in 1940.[100] Chiang ordered Hu Zongnan and Yan Xishan to create extended lines of blockhouses to try to keep the Communist forces in the north within their designated areas.

In March 1939, when Hitler occupied what remained of Czechoslovakia, Chiang knew that the world war he had expected was coming soon and would change the international dynamics of Japan's war in China. The tide of appeasement around the globe was rapidly receding. Stalin, meanwhile, had begun secret talks with Hitler. In May Chiang appealed to London to promptly sign a military treaty with Moscow, otherwise Germany and the Soviet Union, he stated, would conclude a similar pact. This was an insight and analysis that at the time escaped most or all other capitals.[101]

Japan was still holding back from a formal alliance with Germany that would be aimed at the West as well as the Soviet Union. Chiang believed that if Japan went ahead with such an accord, this would lock in the antagonism between Japan and the USSR and also highlight for Washington the connection between the coming conflict in Europe and the ongoing one in China. On March 16, Chiang sent Mayling to Hong Kong (under the pretext of seeking dental treatment) to meet with the old Japanese moderates Nagatomo Kayano and Heishiro Ogawa. Chiang's condition for peace was, once again, complete restoration of China's "territorial integrity and sovereignty." Kayano and Ogawa suggested the quid pro quo would be a commitment by Chiang to attack the Communists, and Soong Mayling said a secret agreement could be reached on this basis. But Chiang in effect rejected the idea and Tokyo had no interest in giving up everything it had fought for in China, including Manchuria.[102]

In the spring of 1939, Japan launched another "shock and awe" campaign to subdue the recalcitrant Chinese. As the clouds and heavy fog of winter and early spring finally lifted, hundreds of Japanese bombers appeared over the at-best grim city of Chungking, now teeming with more than a million people. The Chinese had no real anti-aircraft guns and Japanese "Bettys" and other bombers freely pounded the city. Incendiaries and high explosives destroyed most of the office and commercial buildings scattered along its winding streets, and the government and foreign embassies moved off the rock to the outskirts north of the city.[103] Chiang and Mayling spent many hours with their staff in the large dugout behind their residence. She wrote to an American friend about the scene after one air raid: "The bombs have reduced rich and poor, wise and stupid, to one common level—pieces of burnt flesh which are extracted from the smoldering piles with tongs. Relatives and friends are still digging furiously . . . Do what you can to make your people realize that this death and havoc come to us with the help of American gasoline and oil, and materials for bombs."[104]

Both Chiangs had frequent illnesses in Chungking, but despite the strain they continued to look well. Chiang retained a naturally healthy complexion, showing few wrinkles, and looked fit. He kept on with his simple habits, ex-

The bombing of Chungking. Until 1942 the city had no air cover, but it did have an effective air-raid alert system and thousands of shelters dug in the granite. Courtesy KMT Party History Institute.

ercises, meditations, and prayers. Walking around his new garden he often hummed to himself, a habit he disliked in others.[105] He still had his private devotional period in the morning with Madame, who would then usually return to bed. In the evening he wrote in his diary, then prayed again before retiring for the night. During the day he met with the cabinet and senior military officers, pored over maps, read diplomatic dispatches and intelligence reports, and dictated voluminous orders and dispatches. He was well briefed for meetings and impressed his diplomatic callers with his knowledge of the issues at hand. He now delegated somewhat more authority than in the past, but he kept a firm grip on all decisions that were potentially important and a great many that were not.

One day, Chiang told foreign newsmen that China's strategy was to accumulate small victories, exchanging land for time. In ancient China, he said, "Chu Han lost 72 battles but won the last one."[106] In reality, however, Chiang still believed that tactical, geopolitical, and domestic circumstances required his armies to engage in large-scale defensive engagements and even some counterattacks against the Japanese—mostly as the invaders were withdrawing from limited campaigns. Keeping the bulk of southern China—one of Free China's principal rice bowls—out of Japanese hands was critical to the protracted war strategy. It also remained important that America and the Soviet Union, as well as the Chinese people, see that the leadership in Chungking was firmly committed to a life-and-death struggle against the Japanese.

Increasingly, President Franklin Delano Roosevelt did see China's struggle as part of the critical effort to maintain international order and "quarantine" the aggression of the fascist states.[107] In July, Chiang and China received the most important encouragement from abroad since the war began. Roosevelt notified Tokyo that the United States intended to abrogate the 1911 U.S.-Japan Treaty of Commerce and Navigation. Chiang saw this move as a reflection of America's growing willingness to become involved in Asia as France and Britain rapidly faded as actors in the region. "Only America," Chiang wrote, "had an idealistic approach to foreign affairs."[108]

In August 1939, Zhou submitted to the CCP Politburo a fascinating report that reflected his personal commitment to a true united front with Chiang Kai-shek. He noted that in the second period of the war difficulties and crises had arisen between the KMT and the CCP, but if handled correctly the situation could consolidate unity and enhance the war effort. Chiang Kai-shek's policies, he explained, involved alliance with the USSR and with the CCP a combination of alliance, struggle, and assimilation. Reflecting his many long talks with Chiang, Zhou suggested that while Chiang did not understand the class basis or the progress of the CCP, he "vaguely recognized its organizational skill, its real struggle, its ability to overcome life's difficulties, its persistence, and its initiative in work." Even more interesting was Zhou's balanced statement that "both parties [the CCP and the KMT] still have fears of being ousted, doubts, and narrow-minded attitudes." Furthermore, "backward aggressive elements" in both parties "could be used by other people to create provocations and the threat of a split." The CCP, he said, "should support the leadership of Chiang Kai-shek, help him when he is in a difficult situation, and reject him when he is unjust." It should not "hope for too much from him" but this "does not mean his attitude cannot be changed." Finally, he advised the Politburo that the Eighth Route Army should not invade Shandong and not penetrate into the Huai River basin. Mao must have wondered who Zhou considered the "backward aggressive elements" in the CCP.[109]

Relations between Chiang and Zhou, always polite and respectful, now became solicitous. Shortly after writing his report, Zhou fell from a horse and badly fractured his arm. George Hatem, an American doctor at Mao's headquarters, decided Zhou needed to go to Moscow for treatment. Chiang sent his private plane to pick up Zhou and his wife, Deng Yingchao, and fly them to Urumchi in Xinjiang province, where a Soviet plane took them to the Russian capital.[110]

On August 22, the shape of the coming global conflict seemed to become clear when Moscow and Berlin made the shocking announcement that they had signed a treaty of alliance. Chiang had anticipated this move, but the Japanese were stunned. The Anti-Comintern Pact was undone in a minute, replaced by an antidemocracy coalition. The Japanese Army's idea of first imposing puppet governments in control of China, and then, in alliance with Germany, dividing up Russia had turned to dust. Meanwhile, another rout of the Japanese Army by the Soviets on the border at Noumohan—an entire Japanese division was lost—further scattered on the Steppes the Imperial headquarters scheme of a Japanese empire in Siberia and points west. But the sudden turnaround also offered an opportunity for the Japanese Navy and its supporters in the cabinet. By heading to war with France and Britain—rather than Russia—Hitler had made the Far Eastern territories of these two democratic imperialists easy targets.[111]

On September 1, 1939, Germany invaded Poland, and on September 17, in keeping with a secret protocol of the Nazi-Soviet Pact, the USSR seized eastern Poland. Communist parties around the world, which the day before had fervently supported a united front to-the-death against fascism, suddenly reversed course and praised the Nazi-Soviet Pact. Mao Zedong was among those who welcomed the accord, saying it "strengthens the confidence of the whole of mankind in the possibility of winning freedom."[112]

Stalin informed Chiang that his new accord with Hitler would not affect

Soviet aid to China. In a handwritten message to Stalin after the announcement of the pact, Chiang declared that the Chinese people would never forget Stalin's "sincere help and great leadership." World peace and justice, he asserted, "depended on the Soviet Union and China."[113] In private, however, Chiang had a different reaction. This tectonic shift in world affairs, he believed, foreshadowed a similar deal between the USSR and Japan, which would eventually lead to a world war in which China would be on the opposite side from that of the Soviet Union, allied with the democracies against the totalitarians. He welcomed the possibility of eventually replacing China's current and only ally, the ideologically hostile Soviet Union, with the anti-Communist, wealthier, and stronger (but at the moment still isolationist) United States.[114] "I will have no difficulty in allying with the anti-fascist alliance," Chiang wrote, "but win or lose we will all go together."[115] He knew he had to "work actively" on diplomacy "and be ready for opportunities when they arose."[116]

Early in 1939 the American doctor Phil Greene made his way to Shanghai where he briefly joined his family in the International Settlement. Through donations he collected a new truck, five tons of medical supplies, and sixty-eight cases of food. He transported the truck and supplies on a ship to Ningbo, still held by the government, and then began an amazing thousand-mile journey back to Changsha, to assist at the hospital there. Crammed in the truck with him were two Catholic sisters, an older missionary, an American volunteer doctor, and two Jewish doctors who had fled Germany. Driving through refugee-jammed roads, sometimes ten miles behind Japanese lines, he made it back to Changsha, having spilled only one tin of aspirin. He found the city nearly empty. After the fall of Nanchang the previous autumn, Changsha had expected another attack by the Japanese, and the government was blowing up the remaining buildings and carting off railway tracks and even ties. The Yale-in-China Xiangya Hospital, however, remained open and crowded with the wounded and injured. Greene operated twenty-eight times a day.[117]

It was not until late September that General Okamura Yasuji, then commander of the Japanese 11th Army, advanced on the city. Chiang ordered the Changsha commander, General Xue Yue, to live or die with his men at their positions but explained that the plan was to lure the enemy in toward the city and then launch "a huge ambush."[118] Chen Cheng, now commander of the

Ninth War Zone, which included Hunan province, had prepositioned 365,000 troops on the flanks of the advancing Japanese force of some 30,000, and on September 27 the Chinese attacked, employing "expert tactical moves," including well-timed human wave assaults.[119] The invaders suffered heavy losses but fought their way out of the trap and escaped back toward Wuhan. Morale in China soared again following accounts of the battle, in which Chinese heroism and Japanese casualties predictably were again exaggerated.[120]

Until this point in the war, a half a million Japanese soldiers had been killed or seriously wounded, and the Japanese Imperial General Staff had for some time settled on a policy of consolidating the territory it controlled and launching punitive military expeditions outside this area. For his part, Chiang's strategy was basically defensive, but not entirely. In the winter of 1939 he ordered a general winter offensive across eight war zones. According to Japanese records, in this campaign 450,000 Chinese troops mounted 960 attacks in 1,340 engagements.[121] Basically this counteroffensive was a failure, with some Chinese field commanders only halfheartedly going on the attack.[122] But the most important factor continued to be the abysmal disparity between the two sides in weapons and equipment, a handicap that, after two-and-a-half years of fighting and the Chinese government's loss of most of the country's arms industry, was worse than ever.

As a People's Republic of China scholar of the war wrote in 2004, while "the Nationalist Government stepped up its efforts to suppress the Communism (*sic*), it did not reduce its endeavor to resist the Japanese aggression. In both the front battlefield and the battlefield in the Japanese enemy's rear, the Nationalist Government remained active." From the fall of Wuhan in October 1938 to December 7, 1941, the Chinese Army would suffer another 1.3 million casualties.[123] In January 1940, Zhou Enlai, in a secret report to Stalin, reported that more than one million Chinese soldiers had been killed or wounded in the war (apparently as of August 1939). Of this number, he reported, only 30,000 were from the Eighth Route Army and 1,000 from the New Fourth Army. In other words, halfway into the third year of the war, by the CCP's own account, the Communists had suffered a mere 3 percent of the casualties.[124] Zhou was careful to assure Stalin that the basic policy of the CCP was to support Chiang Kai-shek's leadership of the war and recognize "the key position of the Kuomintang in leading the organs of power and the army throughout the country."[125] But as is evident in the CCP record, Mao's actual policy was simply to pretend that these were his basic goals.

In his report to Stalin, Zhou Enlai also claimed that Chiang Kai-shek's government had "united all the forces of the nation" and carried out "a war of liberation unprecedented in Chinese history." "The officer corps, regardless of class origin," he reported, had "demonstrated determination, courage, and selflessness . . . [and] throughout the war there have been almost no cases of desertion at the front."[126] Zhou and Mao were seeking to impress Stalin with how hard the joint CCP-KMT forces were fighting against the Japanese, but the casualty figures they reported are likely accurate; they had no interest in understating their own losses or exaggerating those of the government. As Zhou declared, they also probably understood that most of the Nationalist officer corps had in fact fought bravely and died in huge numbers.

III

After the fall of Wuhan, Wang Jingwei had escalated his efforts to oust Chiang Kai-shek, renewing his secret contacts with Tokyo. He also directly urged Chiang to reverse his policies of war with Japan and cooperation with the Communists. When Chiang repeatedly refused, Wang fled to Hanoi, where later he publicly accepted Prime Minister Konoe's offer to join Japan's "New Order in Asia." Chiang was furious. In February 1939, he sent an officer to Hanoi with a personal message urging Wang to take another European vacation; when this failed, he sent intelligence operatives to kill him, but they bungled the job and killed Wang's nephew by mistake. In January 1940, under the protection of the Japanese, Wang would establish a puppet "National government" in Nanking.[127]

Wang's principal justification for his rival government was that continuation of the war would only lead to the extension of Soviet influence and a Communist China. In speeches and in his diary, Chiang responded that Wang's collaboration was the realization of Japan's dream of using China's massive resources and population to serve its imperial ambitions in Asia.[128] Hitler's easy victories in Europe had further excited this powerful delusion, leading Tokyo to put aside a new planned offensive in China in order to speed up realization of its new grand strategy—expansion into Southeast Asia and the Pacific. With the occupation of Canton and the collaborationist Vichy government's takeover of Indochina, the only passages into China were land and air routes from the Soviet Union that stretched as far as two thousand miles—and the new Burma Road. On Chiang's orders in 1938, in just two years 200,000 Chinese laborers and engineers with little heavy equipment had built the road, which extended from Kunming to the terminus of the Burma Railway in Lashio, Burma.

At the beginning of 1940, Chiang again noted that the CCP threat was becoming more vicious than that posed by the Chinese collaborationists.[129] The exponential growth of the CCP and its military forces was in fact causing financial problems for the CCP: such a rapid expansion required not only managerial dedication and skill but also increasingly large monetary and other resources, including arms; grain; and gold, silver, yuan, or U.S. dollars. In his long January 1940 report to the Comintern and Stalin, Zhou stated that the Eighth Route Army now numbered about 261,000 men and the New Fourth Army approximately 30,000. Communist Party membership had soared to 498,000.[130] The CCP budget for 1940 reflected a monthly deficit of US$358,000 (approximately $3.2 million in 2005 U.S. dollars). In February, Stalin approved a monthly grant to the CCP for 1943 of US$300,000 or only 8.3 percent of the Party's deficit. Perhaps more was forthcoming. In any event, in the fall, Mao would launch his very costly 100 Regiments Offensive.[131]

Ironically, the Chungking government, which itself was still receiving no foreign financial or economic support, continued its subsidy to the CCP's armed forces of US$110,000 a month. Although Chiang believed Mao had no intention of living up to his obligations in the united front, he clearly thought it was still necessary to continue this financial support to the CCP in order to demonstrate to Stalin as well as to the Chinese people that he was adhering to the united front agreement. The funds from Chungking covered another 18 percent of the Communist Party's budget. In other words, the CCP needed to provide only 40 percent of its military and other expenses through "local government organs," most likely traditional land taxes. With the subsidies provided by Stalin and Chiang Kai-shek, the Chinese Communists were able to maintain a relatively stable currency in their base areas. One small item of interest in the CCP budget for 1940 included US$20,000 in monthly subsidies to five (ostensibly independent) daily newspapers.[132]

In April 1940, the "phony war" or prolonged lull in the fighting in Europe ended. German heavy tanks skirted the Maginot Line and struck into Belgium and France, and the British Expeditionary Force narrowly escaped across the Channel. But France collapsed in a month. In London, Winston Churchill replaced Chamberlain as prime minister, the U.S. Congress passed a conscription act by one vote, and the Roosevelt administration moved closer to China and confrontation with Japan. Just before Hitler invaded Poland, Chiang had written again that the key was to link the Sino-Japanese War with the Allied cause in Europe.[133] Franklin Roosevelt understood this connection.

Recovered from his broken arm, Zhou left Moscow in March and returned to Yan'an, this time probably flying openly on a Soviet aircraft. Zhou left behind a file of "Information on the Persons Relatively Trusted by CKS," which was remarkably nonjudgmental and consistent with Zhou's upbeat Politburo report on Chiang Kai-shek's intentions.[134] Zhou took back to Yan'an a Comintern resolution that gave the CCP Central Committee more scope for making its own decisions. While Stalin still believed that Mao was strongly committed to his and the Comintern's current priority in China—support for Chiang's leadership of the united struggle against Japan—Mao interpreted the resolution as providing leeway for a more aggressive program of territorial expansion into KMT areas and behind Japanese lines. In an April 1940 letter to Xiang Ying, the deputy of the New Fourth Army (there was a nominal KMT commander), Mao emphasized that the "policy of expansion" was "not to be bound by the Kuomintang's restrictions." Instead, Mao ordered both Communist armies to expand and set up new bases "freely and independently."[135]

The result was more reports to Chungking of alleged and probably real CCP attacks on government forces and other "illegal acts." During the spring of 1940, He Yingqin and Chiang delivered more "serious warnings" to Zhou Enlai about these incidents. Nonetheless, in June, units of the Communist Eighth Route Army crossed over to the south bank of the Yellow River. In addition, for some time, most of the New Fourth Army under Xiang Ying had been operating well north of the Yangtze because that area had proven a better ground for recruitment and guerrilla action. Both actions were unambiguous violations of the original restrictions the CCP had accepted on its troop deployments.

In July, the Military Council in Chungking—no doubt instructed by Chiang—proposed that all Communist troops, both the New Fourth and the Eighth Route armies, should concentrate north of the pre-1938 course of the Yellow River. Chiang presented this to Zhou Enlai as a plan to avoid "internal fights among different military operating zones," and suggested, in the language of an order, that he "sincerely" hoped the Communists would "absolutely obey."[136] According to Han Suyin, Zhou supported the plan.[137] If true—and its veracity is supported by subsequent events—this was another striking example of Chiang Kai-shek and Zhou Enlai cooperating in trying to keep the united front going. Zhou would have seen that Chiang Kai-shek was giving up a vast contiguous area of China north of the old Yellow River bed that included Peking and Tianjin, all of the border with Manchuria, and more than half of that with Outer Mongolia, a concession that in effect would connect the CCP areas to the Soviet Union. Mao, however, rejected the plan because he wished to continue to operate not just south of the Yellow River but south of the Yangtze as well.

Zhou's difference with Mao was also evident in an August 3, 1940, letter he sent to the Comintern's Georgi Dimitrov in which he wrote that there was "no longer any prospect" of Chiang Kai-shek's capitulating to the Japanese. Zhou also explained that the National armed forces needed from the Soviet Union more military assistance, particularly airplanes. In addition, he reported that Chiang was considering sending T. V. Soong to Moscow for negotiations and had asked Zhou to join this mission. Zhou urgently asked Stalin whether he should become involved in the proposed trip. In this message, Zhou said nothing critical about Chiang, nor did he echo Mao's increasingly alarmist complaints at the time that Central Army troops were harassing or attacking the New Fourth Army and other Communist forces. On the contrary, Zhou reported that the danger of any major attacks of this sort by the government had passed.[138]

The growth of Mao's armies was so impressive that for the first time he departed from his firm rules of limited guerrilla engagement against the Japanese, rules intended to avoid provoking punitive raids. In the fall of 1940, he authorized a coordinated attack by 104 regiments against rail lines, major roads, coal mines, and other infrastructure in Japanese hands in Shanxi and Hebei. This offensive destroyed hundreds of miles of track, blew up bridges, and destroyed other weakly defended facilities, but by the end of September, the Eighth Route Army had suffered about 22,000 killed and wounded while Japanese losses were estimated at only 3,000–4,000. The Japanese threw in large reinforcements and with brutal "search and destroy" operations recovered all the lost territory. The occupiers created a vast network of fortified blockhouses and trenches and instituted their "kill all, burn all, destroy all" strategy, which meant killing all Chinese, including children, and all livestock found in rural areas where guerrillas were or had been operating; burning all the buildings; and destroying all crops, dikes, wells, and canals. The Japanese also created a system of protected villages—settlements of cooperating villagers who would not have their crops confiscated, their men dragooned into labor brigades, or all their inhabitants simply killed. Within months, the population in the Communist base areas had dropped from 44 million to 25 million.[139] Mao would never launch another major offensive against the Japanese.

As Chiang had foreseen, with the demise in September 1939 of the fascist anti-Communist Pact, the powers that be in Tokyo sought to join the anti-democratic group of totalitarian states, including the Soviet Union. Tokyo hoped this development and its own efforts at détente with Russia would lead Moscow to end its aid to China. The ultranationalists in Japan found it surprisingly easy to put aside their hatred of Bolshevism and to shift their idea of a new global order to one in which Germany and the Soviet Union would divide Europe while Japan would take over Asia. After Japan signed the Tripartite Pact with Hitler and Mussolini on September 27, Chiang told his senior officers that this so-called Axis Pact would propel forward the trend that he had predicted since 1934, pushing Japanese expansion southward—a dynamic that would inevitably put the Imperial forces in conflict with the United States as well as Great Britain and France. Japanese forces had already moved across the North Vietnamese border and the French Vichy authorities had rather quickly capitulated. But, as Chiang observed, by joining Hitler and Mussolini and even indirectly the Soviet Union, all Tokyo had really done was acquire powerful enemies in the Pacific who would be the natural allies of China.[140]

To increase China's leverage in this uncertain situation for the United States and Britain, Chiang renewed "unofficial peace feelers" to Tokyo, and in response Japan delayed recognition of Wang Jingwei's government, its own creation. This alarmed Roosevelt into considering how he might support continued Chinese resistance. In October, Chiang informed Washington that China was at the moment less worried about Japanese aggression than about "the potential collapse of [China's] national economy and society" and the "rampant Chinese Communist Party," which "if it grows big enough to worry about, will have a significant impact in the Far East Asia, even in the whole world." This was Chiang's first use of his tactic of threatening collapse if the United States did or did not do certain things—a strategy that would continue for thirty years. He warned that the Chinese government would not be able to keep fighting the Japanese unless it received substantial aid from the United States, including 500–1,000 aircraft and volunteer aviators, but he ended by declaring that China would follow American leadership "no matter how the international situation developed."[141] On November 30, the same day that Tokyo recognized Wang Jingwei's government, Washington approved a US$100 million line of credit for China.

In October, the CCP's New Fourth Army teamed up with units of the Eighth Route Army in northern Jiangsu and, according to Nationalist reports, attacked the central government's 89th Army, killing the commander and capturing thousands of soldiers. A long series of charges and countercharges ensued over what had actually happened. But whatever the facts of the particular incident, it was another example of the New Fourth Army's operating without authorization of the Military Council in two provinces, Shandong and Jiangsu, north of the Yangtze. On October 19, Chiang authorized He Yingqin, chief of the General Staff, to inform Zhu De that the New Fourth Army commander had to move all of his forces north of the old Yellow River by the end of November, including those in assigned areas south of the Yangtze.[142] Chiang in effect was seeking to implement the plan that he and Zhou apparently had agreed on in July and that the Military Council had issued— even if the plan had been vetoed by Mao.

When Mao replied to Chiang's orders to withdraw, in keeping with his commitment to follow the orders of the Military Council on troop deployments, he agreed in principle and radioed the New Fourth leader Xiang Ying to move his forces in Anhui north of the Yangtze—although with the caveat that Xiang could delay doing so for as long as two months. Mao saw Chiang's demands as threatening gains the CCP had made since the war began and limiting its future nationwide expansion. He now tried to excite alarm in Moscow about Chiang's true intentions. In a message strikingly different from Zhou's August radiogram to Dimitrov, Mao warned Stalin that Chiang Kai-shek was planning a separate peace deal with Japan and an all-out effort to drive all Communist armed forces into the old valley of the Yellow River, where he would liquidate them.[143] The Chairman proposed to launch a preemptive "counteroffensive for defensive purposes" that could "smash" Chiang's troops and "turn the political situation around." Dimitrov immediately radioed back that Mao's plan "caused us great doubts," and that Mao must delay any action pending a more complete reply. Shortly thereafter, in a fuller reply, Dimitrov strongly disagreed with Mao's assessment and said it was "essential" that the CCP not initiate military action against the central government. But there were no hard feelings. "If Chiang Kai-shek nonetheless attacks the people's armies," Dimitrov concluded, "you must strike (back) with all your might." To further show the Comintern's support, Dimitrov cabled Mao two days later to say that if he could secure the road between the CCP base and Mongolia, "it would be possible to send you a significant quantity of arms by that road."[144]

At Zhou's request, on December 9 Chiang moved forward to New Year's Eve the deadline for the Eighth Route Army's required redeployment and agreed that the New Fourth need only be north of the Yangtze by that time but still on its way to the Yellow River. On Christmas Day, while Chiang and Zhou were having dinner together—an interesting occasion given the importance Chiang attached to the holiday—Mao issued a new secret directive on military policy that said nothing about the redeployment north but declared, "We must expand the 8th Route Army and the New 4th Army in every way possible."[145] When the New Fourth began its redeployment on January 4, it moved to the south, not the north. According to the official CCP version of events, the intention of the New Fourth's leader, Xiang Ying, was to avoid Japanese troops to the north by circling down to the southeast before turning north. The CCP later claimed that Xiang had informed Nationalist general Gu Zhutong of the planned route, but CCP reports to Moscow on the New Fourth Incident do not mention any such message. Reading General Gu's reports on the situation, Chiang probably believed that the New Fourth units south of the Yangtze had no intention of proceeding to the north bank of that river, much less to the north of the Yellow River.

In all likelihood, Mao intended to use the movement of the New Fourth Army to provoke an incident that would justify his refusal to withdraw his forces from Hebei, Shandong, Jiangsu, and Anhui. The division-sized New Fourth unit south of the Yangtze was expendable for this purpose. But it is also possible that Xiang, who was "vigorous and outspoken in intraparty disagreements," was operating independently. A "semi-scholarly" novel published on mainland China in 1984 portrays Xiang as intending to return with his forces in southern Anhui to his old Communist bases in the Jiangxi area, where he planned to wage a guerrilla war against the Japanese more-or-less independent of the CCP leadership.[146]

As the New Fourth troops continued to march south, skirmishes took place with Nationalist forces. On January 7, Mao radioed Xiang not to wait too long (whatever that meant), and six days later Gu Zhutong reported to

Chiang that Xiang's soldiers had attacked the 44th Division.[147] Upon receiving Gu's report, Chiang decided he had to show that he was serious about rolling back the CCP's unauthorized military expansion. It was time, he said, "to punish those who do not obey orders."[148]

General Gu attacked the Communists with overwhelming force, killing or capturing 9,000 CCP soldiers, including Xiang Ying. But it was a pyrrhic victory; the high losses among the Communist forces fanned popular sympathy for them and anger at the victorious Nationalists. Mao had probably expected such a reaction, but the sympathetic response was far greater than he had hoped. Zhou Enlai's astute public affairs machinery went into overdrive. The Communist *New China Daily* in Chungking, a number of independent Chinese papers in the KMT areas, and "Third Force" intellectuals charged that in "the New Fourth Army Incident" the KMT had been guilty of a bloody act of treachery. Chiang Kai-shek, it seemed to many, had without reason set Chinese against Chinese during the most critical time in the country's modern history. "Never before have we had such a mass of people on our side," Mao boasted to Dimitrov. The CCP had so "stirred up public opinion in the country," he said, that even Anglo-American diplomats had reproached Chiang Kai-shek.[149]

Chiang asked Zhou to find "ways to straighten things out," and on February 1 he sent by special plane to Yan'an a proposal to form a single corps out of the surviving New Fourth units north of the Yangtze and move it to the Northwest. Mao, of course, rejected this plan and put forward a list of CCP demands including a full apology for the recent incident.[150] Chiang was not about to admit wrongdoing, but in effect he abandoned his far-reaching plan to force the CCP to withdraw north of the Yellow River. Except for southern Anhui and areas where they had been driven out by Okamura's "kill all" strategy, the Communist forces remained where they had been at the start of the year—in the Northwest, spread throughout the China plains north of the Yangtze, and in guerrilla units in various places south of the Yangtze. In the end Chiang gained nothing out of the New Fourth Incident to offset his enormous loss in the propaganda war. Henceforth, until the end of the war, he tried only to contain the CCP and prevent its further expansion.

Although Chiang's long-term concern was the Communist threat, shortly after the New Fourth Incident, he showed that his near-term priority still lay with resisting the Japanese. He pulled 200,000 troops out of the Central

Army forces blocking the Communists in the Northwest and sent them south to oppose a new Japanese offensive in Henan. This large-scale redeployment came only eighteen months or so before the beginning of repeated charges by American officials in China that Chiang had done and was doing little or nothing in the fight against Japan, and that his priorities were containing and ultimately destroying the Communists. But in reporting the Nationalist deployment to Moscow, Mao Zedong himself claimed it showed that "contradictions between Japan and Chiang Kai-shek remain the fundamental contradictions [in China]." Mao, in other words, was acknowledging that Chiang was giving clear precedence to fighting the Japanese, not the Communists. In the first stages of this campaign, General Tang Enbo's 31st Group Army lost 16,000 men. "The current moment," Mao told Stalin in February 1941, "offers us the best opportunity to gain the upper hand, and we must not lose it." But he promised he would keep open the option of reaching an agreement with Chiang Kai-shek.[151]

Meanwhile, it became clear that Japan's real ambitions lay elsewhere. When the plane of the commander in chief of Japan's South Fleet crashed over China, the confidential plans of the Japanese Imperial Navy were left in the wreckage. The recovered plans, which Chiang turned over to the Allies, laid out the blueprint for Japan's forthcoming attack into the South China Sea and Southeast Asia. It was now evident, Chiang wrote, that Japan had given up the idea of "subduing China before going southward." Japan, he wryly observed, could not use its naval power in China. "The only way is to go south." This meant Japan was now headed toward war with Great Britain and the United States.[152]

This development was good news for Chiang. Despite all the staggering defeats, failures, and losses of the past three years, as well as the stupendous problems of trying to run a government, economy, and army in exile and of virtual international isolation, Chiang had remained steadfast in his belief that he and China would eventually prevail over Japan. Because of the Soviet factor, he would never be as certain about the ultimate outcome of the struggle with Mao's CCP, but that problem could be tackled later. What was important now was that while the Fourth Army Incident and its aftermath were still reverberating inside China, the informal Sino-American alliance was developing rapidly. Most importantly, President Roosevelt had included China in his new and dramatic Lend-Lease Bill, which was intended primarily to save England through the provision of vast amounts of war matériel. The President had also decided to send a personal representative to talk with Chiang. The representative, Lauchlin Currie, played a key role in the White House on Far Eastern affairs, although his official titles of personal economic adviser and administrative assistant to the President had nothing to do with foreign affairs and he knew little or nothing about China. Currie, however, had another unusual distinction—he was a member of a group of officials in Washington whom Moscow considered its "agents of influence." Most of these men and women were motivated by personal ideals, sympathy for the Soviet Union, hatred of fascism, and liberal economic and social views. Some, like Currie, were not members of the Communist Party and probably were at most democratic-socialists, but they believed that the fascist threat overrode most other considerations and that in promoting the interests of Moscow and providing it sensitive information they were also serving the interests of their own country. They would have objected to being called "agents of influence," but at the minimum they showed atrocious judgment. After all, the Soviet Union was then allied to Nazi Germany, suggesting that their ideological motivations were not, after all, primarily antifascist.

When Chiang received Currie in Chungking on February 10, the American informed him that the United States would soon deliver to China US$45 million of arms and military equipment. After an expression of thanks, Chiang also asked for financial assistance to help stabilize the Chinese currency (the *fabi*), and assistance in improving the Burma Road. But this was only the beginning. On March 31, T. V. Soong presented Currie a comprehensive request on behalf of the commander in chief, including 1,000 military aircraft and arms for thirty divisions. Some of the airplanes were needed to equip a new Chinese Air Force unit to be led by Claire Chennault, a crusty, retired U.S. Army Air Force Captain with the "honorific" title of Colonel. Since 1937, Chennault had been advising Chiang and directing the training of what remained of the Chinese Air Force.[153]

Currie also passed on to Chiang Roosevelt's hope that the KMT and the CCP would be able to form a true united front to fight Japan. Taken aback, Chiang replied that it was his view that the CCP's principal loyalty was to the Communist International and the Soviet Union. The Communists, he said, did not want to see an alliance among China, America, and Britain. At the time, Chiang's assertion was an undeniable fact. But Currie did not agree with any of these premises and he left Chiang with the clear impression that in the coming war, the Americans would have one goal—defeat of the Ger-

"Colonel" Claire Lee Chennault and some of his pilots in the Flying Tigers. These men and their successors in the U.S. 14th Air Force were the only Americans who actually fought the one million Japanese troops inside China. Claire Lee Chennault Collection, envelope C, Hoover Institution Archives.

mans and the Japanese—and since the CCP was part of the united front against Japan, it would also be considered a friend. Chiang understood that his strikingly different view of the CCP would bedevil the most important foreign relationship he and his government would ever have. But aside from this issue, Chiang was immensely pleased by the visit—an alliance with the powerful United States seemed likely within a year.

Before leaving Chungking, Currie met privately with Zhou Enlai, who was very positive and convivial, portraying the Communists as patriotic reformers interested in democracy and full of praise for the idea of U.S. support for China against Japan. Zhou, however, warned that the KMT leader's policies could lead to a civil war and a collapse of the resistance. He was not so frank as to mention that his party at that moment continued vehemently to oppose a U.S.-China alliance, fearing that Japan's defeat by such a partnership would give Chiang a powerful claim to leadership.[154]

IV

Sometime in April, Chiang received intelligence indicating that Hitler was planning to attack the USSR in a matter of weeks. Chiang's information on "Operation Barbarossa" probably came from Walther Stennes, Chiang's personal security adviser. Stennes was in contact with Richard Sorge, the Soviet spy in Japan and correspondent for *Frankfurter Zeitung* in Tokyo who had won the complete trust of the German ambassador.[155] Sorge visited Chungking and probably briefed his fellow undercover Soviet spy and German national, Stennes, on Hitler's intent. Two months later Chiang would call in Zhou Enlai to warn him—and thus Stalin—that Germany was going to attack the USSR. He did not want to do this in April, since he feared Stalin might take certain defensive actions that would alert Hitler to his loss of surprise and thus cause him to cancel the history-changing invasion. But Chiang did want to alert Stalin.[156]

As far as Chiang knew, when he did so it would be exclusive information that might make a critical difference to the Soviet Union, the key supporter of what he viewed as his long-term enemy, the Chinese Communists. Chiang wanted Germany and if possible Japan to invade the USSR, but he did not want to see the Soviet Union destroyed and the Japanese empire established in Siberia. In addition, Chiang already understood that if after the war he was to defeat or truly absorb the Communist Party, it could only be done if the Soviets were willing to give their relations with his regime priority in China.

Since the Nazi-Soviet Pact, Chiang had suspected that a similar Moscow-Tokyo rapprochement was likely, and when on April 13 the Soviet Union and Japan signed a treaty of neutrality, Chiang was not surprised. Over the next few days, in meetings with his senior officers, he discussed in an analytical manner this latest twist in Moscow's geopolitical relations as well as its likely consequences. At one meeting he read out his prescient ten-page analysis. The treaty with Tokyo, he observed, was of course a significant victory for Stalin because it lessened the danger of a two-front war for Russia and encouraged Japan to reduce its ground strength on the Soviet and Mongolian borders. But it also undermined the basis of the Tripartite Alliance by demonstrating to Germany the unreliability of its Japanese ally, and it further encouraged the Japanese Navy "to court its own destruction" in the southern seas. Chiang explained to his generals that as a result of the accord signed in Moscow, Japan would feel secure enough to transfer six divisions from Manchuria to other parts of China. But however it used these additional troops, Chiang concluded, Japan could not defeat China, and certainly not over the next six months. "Within that time frame," he said with confidence, "the situation in the Pacific will change." Pearl Harbor was eight months away.

Meanwhile, Chiang's analysis went on, Tokyo's pact with Moscow would arouse greater awareness in the United States of Japan's long-term threat to America. Thus Japan's diplomatic move with the Soviet Union had in fact enhanced China's military and political prospects. The empire's march to the south, which would start soon, he concluded, would be the beginning of the end of Japan as a world power.[157] Still, given his knowledge of Hitler's plans to invade the Soviet Union he thought it possible that the Japanese Army would get its way and Tokyo would, after all, allow it to attack a weakened USSR. This would be the best possible outcome for China, Chiang thought, because America could not permit Japan and Germany to conquer and divide up the Soviet Union, and a U.S.-Japan war would soon follow with China being an important ally of both America and the Soviet Union. In such a case the Soviets would be weakened but in the final victory more beholden to the Americans and the Nationalist Chinese. Back in February, he had noted in his diary that he hoped the United States would not become embroiled in the Asian conflict "prematurely," that is, "before a war [begins] between Japan and the Soviet Union." He also passed his intelligence about the German invasion plan, Operation Barbarossa, to Ambassador Johnson and urged that the United States not take any action that might irritate Berlin and cause Hitler to cancel his imminent betrayal of Stalin.[158] Again he passed the thought to Washington that it would be best if the United States was not drawn into war with Japan for some time.

In May, Roosevelt issued a proclamation declaring an unlimited national emergency, among other things promising moral and material support for both the United Kingdom and China.[159] Although the promised military aid under Lend-Lease had not yet begun to arrive, Chiang was very pleased. In the eyes of the United States, the two wars were now not only linked, they were equated. Chiang believed his telegrams to Roosevelt had had an effect. For Mao's part, his propaganda was still calling Roosevelt "a warmonger."

When Chiang heard that Hitler's disciple Rudolph Hess had landed in England seeking peace between the two countries, he was further convinced that Hitler was on the brink of invading the Soviet Union.[160] On June 18, when Chiang read the translation of a Western news service report of a new German-Turkish Treaty, he immediately and correctly interpreted the item as the final sign that Hitler was covering his flank in preparation for a gargantuan onslaught against Turkey's neighbor. "There will be no more than a few days before Germany attacks the Soviet Union," he wrote in his diary.[161] According to Comintern documents, it was then that Chiang summoned Zhou Enlai to tell him the German attack on the Soviet Union would commence on June 21 and he urged that the CCP warn Stalin. On June 22, the Nazi juggernaut—some 2 million men—surged into Russia. Chiang quickly aligned China with the Soviet Union, broke relations with Berlin and Rome, warned Moscow of a possible Japanese attack, proposed a treaty of alliance with the USSR, and encouraged America to support the giant, beleaguered Communist state, which in the long term he greatly feared.[162] This reaction to Hitler's attack on Communist Russia reflected the high priority that Chiang at this time gave to the defeat of Japan.

The stage was now set for a global civil war to be fought without quarter. Grouped on one side were the rational or secular humanist strains of both the Western and Chinese enlightenments—the liberal democratic, the pragmatic authoritarian, and the Jacobin totalitarian. On the other side were the ultra-nationalism, racism, and absolutism of atavistic fascism.

As the Generalissimo had hoped, the shock of Operation Barbarossa re-excited the Imperial Army's dream of marching to the Urals "to shake hands with the Germans." Japan halted its redeployments out of Manchuria and instead concentrated sixteen additional divisions in the region.[163] In less than two years Moscow had embraced separate accords with the two leading fascist powers, but it now demanded that Communists around the world once again make antifascism their overriding concern. On the day of the German invasion, the Comintern sent urgent directives to the Chinese Communists telling them that now more than ever, their task was "to insist on cooperation with the Kuomintang" against the Japanese and to prepare military action to destroy Japanese transportation lines in China "should Japan join in the attack on the Soviet Union." The clear implication of the conditional verb form was that these violent actions against the Japanese occupiers in China were not to be launched by the CCP unless Japan attacked Russia. But it was understood that America was to be encouraged in every way possible to fight both fascist enemies, the Germans and the Japanese. In Chinese Communist propaganda, the United States overnight became a positive force in world affairs. The *Liberation Army Daily* called Roosevelt, the former "warmonger," an "enlightened bourgeoisie politician."[164]

The summer of 1941 in Chungking was, as usual, blistering and sticky. Human waste thrown out of the city's caves and mat huts into open sewers added a stench that hung over the wreck of the city. Having devastated the town in the summers of 1939 and 1940, the Japanese bombers returned with the seasonally clear skies, sometimes 150 of them in a single day. A vast system of airplane spotters spread out one hundred miles around the city used crank-powered transmitters and a simple code to give ample warning of the approach of Japanese planes.[165] But once over their target the bombers, unopposed in the air or from the ground, rained down explosives on what remained of the city, sometimes for two or three hours. There was no efficient fire-fighting establishment in Chungking, and fires simply burned themselves out. Electric lines were more or less permanently down. Most structures from the old days were heaps of stone—any surviving timber had already been carted off. But the Chinese people persevered—buses ran on alcohol made from potatoes and urine, and simple shops blown up one day would be rebuilt the next with planks of salvaged wood.[166]

Despite malnutrition in numerous areas, through 1941 there was no mass starvation in Sichuan nor in most of the other provinces that were entirely or partly under central government control. Grain, salt, and other food products were transported hundreds of miles around and sometimes through Japanese lines to government-controlled zones, including Chungking. In fact, despite the immense disruption and combat here and there, Free China continued to function. The Nationalists maintained agricultural production by making bank loans to farmers, distributing new seed varieties, settling refugee populations on fallow land, managing irrigation canals, protecting transport networks, and breeding draft animals. The result was that "until 1941 agricultural production in Nationalist China was adequate . . . and average calorie intakes . . . [were] at the same level as before the war." To hold down inflation, the regime reduced government salaries and increased taxes on both earned income and wealth. At the end of 1941, four-and-a-half years after the war had begun, average prices in Free China were twenty times higher than before the war, a high figure but low considering the extraordinary circumstances, and a rate to which the mostly subsistence society could adjust.[167]

All this could not likely have been accomplished by a wartime bureaucracy that was fundamentally dishonest or unskilled, an unnuanced characterization that General Joseph Stilwell and other Americans, including journalists, would within a year be reporting back home.[168]

In mid-July, an American scholar named Owen Lattimore flew into the Chungking airport, which was situated on an island in the Yangtze below the city cliffs. Lattimore was a specialist on China's minority regions and a former editor of *Pacific Affairs*. Lauchlin Currie had recommended him to Chiang Kai-shek as a personal American adviser with a direct link to the White House. Lattimore was to be a private employee of the Chinese government and would have no official relationship with the American embassy in Chungking—the arrangement sought by Chiang, who already did not trust the State Department in Washington or the Foreign Service officers in China.[169]

Lattimore came to know his employer quite well. One reason was that he had been brought to China as a baby and his longtime nurse spoke Chinese with a Ningbo accent like Chiang, thus he did also. Much later, Lattimore became a strong critic of the Nationalist government, so his positive views of Chiang Kai-shek in his postwar memoirs seem especially credible.[170] He considered Chiang a "genuine patriot," "highly nationalistic," and "a great man" who was "sometimes . . . more far-sighted than either Roosevelt or Churchill." For example, in the early days of Operation Barbarossa, as the German Army was rolling through European Russia, Chiang confidently told Lattimore that the Soviets would rally and eventually defeat the Germans. He understood the strength of continental-size countries. He also said Japan was bogged down in China and needed a victory of some kind; thus they would attack the colonial territories to the south and soon "create a diversion in the Pacific" that would get them into "serious conflict with the Great powers."[171] While Lattimore admired Chiang, he did not take to his taciturn personality. By contrast, like most Americans, he "very much" connected with Zhou Enlai.[172]

At the end of July, Japan took over South Vietnam, and the United States ordered both the freezing of Japanese assets and an informal but effective U.S. embargo of oil shipments to Japan. Two days before, Roosevelt had given the final authorization for the volunteer air group the Flying Tigers (to be commanded by Claire Chennault) to begin operations in China with five hundred aircraft. In August Roosevelt and Churchill met in Newfoundland and issued the Atlantic Charter, a reaffirmation of Wilsonian internationalism and a joint commitment to "the final destruction of Nazi tyranny." Chiang and most other observers interpreted the phrase "Nazi tyranny" to include the Japanese.[173]

At the same time, Chiang was suspicious that the ongoing high-level U.S-Japanese talks to resolve the two nations' differences might "sell China down the river." A counterbalance to this fear was the knowledge that Chungking, London, and Moscow all had a common interest in an increasingly tough American stance toward Japan, and of course in what this would lead to—an American war with Japan and then with Germany. Chiang kept in close touch with Churchill and in the autumn of 1941 "a little entente" developed between China and the United Kingdom with this goal in mind.[174] In early November, Chiang predicted that the U.S-Japan conflict could begin in "mid-December."[175] To relieve any Japanese worries about its western flank, Stalin assured Tokyo that the USSR intended to abide by its neutrality pact.[176]

In late summer the Japanese Imperial Navy won approval to plan a carrier attack against the U.S. fleet at Pearl Harbor. The intent, as with the all-out war on China in 1937, was to inflict an initial devastating blow that would set the stage for an eventual negotiated settlement on Japanese terms. At the same time, Japan would secure its empire in Southeast Asia and the Western Pacific, and further isolate China from foreign assistance. Prime Minister Konoe thought the plan was rash, but the military was against him. In mid-October he resigned and General Hideki Tojo took over the government.[177]

Probably warned by Mayling and T.V. of the likelihood of a wider war, Ch'ing-ling left Hong Kong and took up residence in Chungking. Soon she and her sister appeared together, visiting bombed out areas and comforting the injured. Meanwhile, the thirty-one-year-old Chiang Ching-kuo and his father exchanged their diaries for the other to read. Ching-kuo, by this time, was receiving high praise even from American journalists and diplomats for his effective work and strong but unassuming leadership as a regional administrator in southern Jiangxi. "The people adore you," his father wrote. Ching-kuo's stepbrother Wei-kuo, meanwhile, was developing his military career. He had taken part in the union of Austria and Germany (the *Anschluss*) as a German sergeant-cadet. He graduated in 1939 just before the outbreak of war, then spent a year at the U.S. Army's armored force center at Fort Knox. The Generalissimo had kept Wei-kuo's existence hidden from Mayling for thirteen years, but once he acknowledged him, she quickly came to enjoy her suave, handsome, English-speaking stepson, who was a second lieutenant in an army unit deployed against the Japanese along the Yellow River near Xi'an.[178]

In the fall, battles raged again in Hunan and at Yichang at the bottom of the Three Gorges. The Chinese again did not flee but lost tens of thousands of men, while the Japanese casualties were high enough to give the General Staff in Tokyo another rationale for a war with the Western powers—only a Japanese defeat of America, they now believed, could persuade Chiang Kai-shek's government to end its resistance war with Japan.[179]

Chiang kept up a flow of messages not only to Roosevelt but also to Navy Secretary Frank Knox and Army Secretary Henry Stimson. He learned that to buy time for their war preparations, the Americans were thinking of softening their requirements for an end to the sanctions recently imposed against Japan. A critical round of negotiations with the Japanese was scheduled to be held in Washington in December. Chiang was greatly alarmed, and immediately sent Hull, Currie, Knox, and Stimson urgent messages warning that "any relaxation of American sanctions against Japan would bring about a collapse of the resistance in China." Chiang also informed Churchill of his warning to Washington, and the British leader immediately cabled Roosevelt, supporting the Chinese stance. Roosevelt decided not to submit the watered-down proposal in the negotiations, and Secretary Hull in a November 26 note to the Japanese repeated the previous American stance—Japan should withdraw from China, including Manchuria. Chiang felt his grave warning had "saved the situation at the last moment." Threatening the end of China's resistance had also worked with the Soviets, and in the coming years he would repeatedly employ the same tactic. As he wrote about this instance, "It takes a true crisis to produce good thinking and action . . . Sometimes, in life, trouble is an excellent tonic."[180]

Owen Lattimore had been in China less than six months, but he was suffering from a persistent case of dysentery, and in early December decided to return to the United States for treatment. Chiang, however, warned him that "the situation is uncertain. As you have to fly down to Hong Kong to fly across the Pacific, it is better to wait for a while before you start." Lattimore later learned that Chiang's intelligence agents in Southeast Asia had reported that heavy smoke was coming out of the chimneys and incinerators of Japanese consulates in Singapore and other cities in Southeast Asia. The conclusion was that secret documents were being burned in expectation of war.[181]

It was one o'clock in the morning on December 8 in Chungking (on the other side of the International Date Line from Hawaii) when an aide woke the Generalissimo with the news that Japanese carrier planes had attacked Pearl Harbor. Chiang told the officer to call a special meeting of the KMT Central Standing Committee, then he dictated a letter to President Roosevelt that Mayling translated into evocative English: "To our new common battle we offer all we are and all we have, to stand with you until the Pacific and the world are free from the curse of brute force and endless perfidy."[182]

Seven hours later, at 8:00 a.m., Chiang entered the conference room in his unadorned Pershing uniform and all present stood. He looked impassive, and in his customary style he asked those present, including Lattimore, to give their opinions. Lattimore stressed that the United States would overcome the losses at Pearl Harbor and prosecute the war with vigor. The Generalissimo, Lattimore believed, was "not exactly pleased" that the Pacific War had started before the United States had much time to prepare. But more likely, Chiang was upset because the raid on Pearl Harbor virtually ended any chance that Japan would attack Russia. In any event, Chiang's political analysis had proven correct and his diplomacy successful. The powerful United States of America was at last officially an ally of China and had joined in the great war against Japan.[183]

Chiang told the meeting that he was going to propose that China, the United States, Britain, and the USSR all declare war on Germany, Italy, and Japan and pledge no separate peace until victory. Bringing the Soviet Union into the struggle against Japan, he told the group, was of special importance. After the meeting, Chiang read Roosevelt's reply to his message, which predicted complete victory and proclaimed, "I take great pride in my country's association with you and the great nation which you lead."[184]

Chiang's initial military operation after Pearl Harbor was an offensive one—the first for the Allies in the new Pacific War. He ordered the short, soft-spoken, but tough Xue Yue to send troops from his Ninth War Zone, both Central Army and Guangdong provincial divisions, toward Canton to relieve pressure on the British defenders of Hong Kong. General Okamura dispatched 60,000 Japanese troops to divert and if possible annihilate the Chinese force, but with the rapid fall of Hong Kong on Christmas Day, he decided instead to seize and destroy Changsha. For the third time, bloody battles raged around the Hunan capital. Xue received the usual stream of calls from the Generalissimo with unwelcome tactical orders, and at one point he withdrew to where he could no longer receive them. Xue surrounded the Japanese who had occupied Changsha and when they retreated, he attacked, inflicting—by his account—tens of thousands of casualties. Whatever the number of wounded and killed, the Japanese advance and then early retreat allowed Chiang to claim a major success. After the shocking string of Japanese triumphs against the Allies, the "Changsha victory" cheered the British and Americans as well as the Chinese. It also seemed to underscore the important role that China could play in the Pacific War.[185]

Chiang's jumble of armies was keeping occupied thirty-six Japanese divisions and some forty-four mixed brigades including those in Manchuria, or about 1.3 million men all together. This was almost 67 percent of the Japanese Army at that time and the Allies wanted to see that they remained tied up.[186] After Pearl Harbor, Tokyo transferred nine divisions from China to the various Pacific and Southeast Asian fronts.[187] But a million or so Japanese soldiers and airmen remained in China, including Manchuria. Since the prospect of the Soviets attacking the Japanese in Manchuria or elsewhere was nil, there was no other force than the Chinese Army, which included the Communists, keeping them in the Northeast. Chiang noted ironically in his diary that America and Britain had so far lost every battle in the Pacific, a record that, he thought, should remind them how heroically the poorly armed Chinese soldiers had fought since 1937. China's international prestige and position, he believed, were at unprecedented levels.[188]

Like the Allies, Tokyo saw that the Burma Road was a major strategic asset for the Allied cause. Consequently, on December 12, the Japanese 15th Army began moving up the Kra Peninsula toward Rangoon whose port was the indispensable starting point of supplies heading up the railway to Lashio and the Burma Road. On the first day of the new war, Chiang told the British that he was prepared to send 80,000 of his best troops—his remaining German-trained divisions—to Burma and, even more impressively, to put them under British command. He also offered to commit all of his remaining heavy motorized artillery to the campaign. Chiang was determined to do his part in the Allied cause.

At this time, the Flying Tigers—officially the Chinese Air Force's American Volunteer Group—consisted of only seventy-five or so serviceable P-40s recently received from the United States. All the pilots were American, but it was a Chinese outfit, paid for in cash by the Chinese government. Its planes were virtually all Chiang had in the way of attack aircraft, but although Chungking was being bombed daily, he assigned all of the Flying Tigers to the defense of Imperial Britain's colony of Burma.[189] This was another impressive commitment to the cause, which was going badly everywhere else. Even so, within a few months some American officials would be saying that Chiang Kai-shek was determined to do as little as possible in fighting the Japanese.

The British, meanwhile, were not anxious to have the forces of an anti-imperialist Asian power like China saving one of its Asian colonies. When one-eyed field marshal Sir Archibald Wavell, whom Churchill had relieved of command in Egypt and sent to India, arrived in Chungking, he told Chiang that he could accept only one Chinese division. According to Owen Lattimore, who was present and recorded the Generalissimo's words, Chiang was infuriated and lashed out at Wavell: "You and your people have no idea how to fight the Japanese. Resisting the Japanese is not like suppressing colonial rebellions, not like colonial wars. The Japanese are a serious great power . . . Fighting against them for many years, we Chinese are the ones who know how to do it. For this kind of job, you British are incompetent, and you should learn from the Chinese how to fight against the Japanese."[190] The British never did care for the Generalissimo, nor he for them, but ethnic enmity aside, Chiang was right—the road-bound British forces in Burma were no match for the Japanese Army's vanguard force—jungle-trained, light infantry often traveling on bicycles and using pack animals. In a message to Roosevelt, Chiang also warned that, unlike the Chinese, the colonized Burmese were not united in resisting the Japanese but might cooperate with them. He said it was time for the British to change their attitude and declare that their colonies would all enjoy self-determination after the war. He asked the President to forward these "humble thoughts" to Churchill.[191]

Chiang's anger at Wavell and his concern about British competence or perseverance, did not, however, affect his support for their rapidly deteriorating Allied military position in Burma. For ten weeks over the skies of Rangoon, thirty or so Flying Tiger pilots claimed to have shot down 217 Japanese planes and probably destroyed forty-three more. Even if the real "kills" were half those reported by the excited pilots, who had never been in combat, it was a stirring performance.[192]

Wavell soon realized how much he needed the Chinese and urgently called for help. In response, Chiang immediately ordered the Fifth, Sixth, and 66th armies to begin moving. With their unique advantage in the Chinese Army of actually possessing trucks, within weeks they were deployed 150 miles north of Rangoon near a town called Toungoo.

Meanwhile, on New Year's Eve Roosevelt cabled Chiang to say that he had already won the agreement of the Western Allies to nominate him as supreme Allied commander of the China Theater. Chiang thanked Roosevelt for the nomination and asked him to select a competent and high-ranking American general to be the China Theater chief of staff. This person, Chiang said, need not be a seasoned Asia or China expert, provided he had "a passion for the job, a good personality, and ability." Chiang proposed that the American appointed to the job would have "executive control" over Chinese units in Burma. But he also stressed that this officer would report to him.[193] The U.S. Army chief of staff, George C. Marshall, recommended for the job his closest friend in the U.S. Army, Joseph W. Stilwell.

Stilwell had become a lieutenant general and division commander in 1940 and had then suddenly vaulted up to corps commander the next year. By Pearl Harbor—six months later—he had been named the best corps leader in the U.S. Army.[194] In a meeting with Stimson, Stilwell said the success of the mission depended on whether Chiang Kai-shek would turn over any part of his army to American command. Stimson assured him that Chiang himself had proposed doing so. Two days later in a meeting with Marshall, Stilwell said the chances of success in China were good if, as he put it in capital letters in his diary, he were given "COMMAND."[195]

Stilwell, a Chinese speaker and West Point graduate who had served in China in the 1920s and 1930s, was also considered the most informed China specialist in the U.S. military. "Vinegar Joe," as he had come to be known, was a thin officer with a sharp nose and a tart tongue. Despite his small, boney frame—similar to that of the Generalissimo—he was a tough, aggressive officer who prided himself on unvarnished opinions. Like the Generalissimo, he was a man of action who believed that willpower and human energy drove the universe.

Among Western journalists and his military colleagues Stilwell's attitude was refreshing, but it would also lead him to flagrantly oversimplify complex problems and underestimate the subtleties of personalities like Chiang Kai-shek and Mao Zedong. He could be warm-hearted and generous but in judging others "his sentiments were harsh" and often spiteful.[196]

Despite his conservative political views, Stilwell—like many American observers heavily influenced by Edgar Snow, Harold Isaacs, and other writers sympathetic to the Chinese Communists—came to believe that Mao and his followers wanted only "land ownership under reasonable conditions." He also felt confident that "it was not in the nature of Chinese to be Communists" and thus the CCP was not really a Marxist-Leninist party. By contrast, Stilwell saw Chiang Kai-shek as a cruel and unthinking dictator who "changed nothing"—a holder with no goal but to hold.[197] Back in 1937, before the war with Japan broke out, it was clear that in the middle of a Great Depression and beset with costly internal wars Chiang had devoted substantial energy and resources to building up a modern armed force and defense industry with German equipment, training, and weapons—all paid for by China—and had taken other measures, such as banning construction of new factories in the coastal areas, to prepare for the coming war. Yet Stilwell as the U.S. Army attaché in China at that time reported that in terms of preparing for the inevitable conflict, Chiang had "no intention of doing a thing or else he is utterly ignorant of what it means to get ready for a fight with a first class power." In Stilwell's mind, Chiang had no values; no skills in government or generalship; no real interest in the modernization and welfare of China except to the extent it increased his power; no human qualities worth noting such as patriotism, bravery, loyalty, or a sense of duty and honor; and no valid intellectual or cultural interests.[198] For Stilwell, life was categorical, nuances nonexistent.

When informed of the candidate to be Chiang's American chief of staff, T. V. Soong, who had gone to Washington as Chiang's personal representative and head of China's military procurement office, reported to Chiang that Stilwell was a highly regarded officer. Chiang replied that Stilwell "was most welcome." Washington had proposed that the general serve not only as the chief of staff of Chiang's China Theater, but also as commander of American forces in the China-Burma-India theaters and supervisor of Lend-Lease matériel for China. Chiang told T.V. that this could create problems if, as seemed likely, differences arose between the two governments regarding prosecution of the war. Still Chiang agreed, emphasizing that the senior American military representative in China in all his capacities "must listen" (ting hua) to him, the Supreme Commander. In Chinese, "listen to my words" means emphatically "follow or obey what I say," and Soong stressed to Stimson that Stilwell "must be under the command of the Generalissimo."[199]

At the beginning of the year, Chiang observed that at last China was accepted as one of the four powers. For fear of leaks, China was not allowed to participate in the Allied Combined Chiefs of Staff, but other gestures were meant to assure Chiang of the importance that the United States attached to China's strategic role. At Chiang's instructions, T.V. requested and obtained a $500 million U.S. loan, the largest portion of which was used to back dollar-denominated securities sold to the public for *fabi*. Unfortunately the program did little to curb inflation; instead it enriched a number of the well-to-do and even some Americans in China.[200]

5

Chiang and His American Allies

At the end of 1941, only US$26 million had been shipped of the U.S. pledged US$145 million in Lend-Lease arms, supplies, and equipment (not counting a hundred P-40s sent to the Flying Tigers) that had been promised before Pearl Harbor. Much of this was piling up on the docks of Rangoon waiting to be sent north by train to Lashio and the beginning point of the Burma Road.[1] Even with the extensive pilfering that occurred over the 715 miles to Yunnan, at the time of Pearl Harbor, 20,000 tons a month were being delivered to their destination.[2]

Chiang assumed the Japanese troops would probably close the road, so his attention and concern were increasingly drawn to India. Without the Burma Road, the air route over the Himalayas from India would be China's only outlet to the world except for the uncertain journey to and through besieged Russia and then down through Mongolia and Xinjiang.[3] Alternatively, a road could possibly be cut across the mountains of northern Burma from Northeast India. But Mahatma Gandhi's Congress Party, while opposing Japanese aggression, would not support the British war effort, and radical nationalists in India even welcomed the prospect of "liberation" by Japan. Chiang wanted personally to urge Gandhi and his fellow Congress Party leader Jawaharlal Nehru to cooperate in the common cause against fascism or at least not to undermine the British fight against the Japanese. So during the critical opening phase of the Pacific War, the China Theater Supreme Commander took off for India. No one else in the Allied camp saw this as an important task or had the anti-imperialist credentials to make its undertaking feasible.

On February 4, accompanied by Mayling, Chiang stopped over in Lashio.

There he and his wife had a midnight meeting with General Hutton, the commander of the British forces in Burma. With Mayling translating, Chiang reiterated his willingness to place the Chinese troops just arriving in northern Burma under British command. But he soon changed his mind, after learning from Hutton that the British forces in Burma were on the "brink of disaster." The 17th Indian Division, trying to retreat over the Sitang River, had been cut off and lost half its men, and the way to Rangoon was now opened to the Japanese. The Generalissimo at this point lost faith in the ability of the British to defend Burma. He decided he did not want his best ground troops to become involved in "needless and wasteful combat."[4]

Chiang arrived in New Delhi on February 8. Churchill, the inveterate imperialist, was furious that the leader of China, while on an official visit to the "King-Emperor's India," would dare to propose a meeting with "near rebels" like Gandhi. The British ambassador in Chungking, Archibald Clark-Kerr, informed Churchill that Chiang Kai-shek genuinely believed that his personal influence on the two Congress Party leaders would serve the Allied cause, saying he (Clark-Kerr) had "completest confidence both in Chiang's decency and his discretion." But Churchill adamantly refused to allow Chiang to travel to Gandhi's home at Wardha, and Gandhi would not be persuaded to come to the Raj capital of New Delhi. Eventually, Chiang and Gandhi met on February 18 at a meditation center outside Calcutta. Both men were leading anti-imperialist revolutionaries and had much in common—with Soong Mayling translating, they talked for five hours.[5]

When Chiang told Gandhi it was critical that India continue to be a part of the Allied war effort, the wizened leader said he empathized with China and would not obstruct the resistance against Japan. Some months later, Gandhi sent a handwritten note to Chiang saying, "I consider the five hours of frank, sincere discussion that we had at Calcutta as the most satisfying and unforgettable experience in my life." Gandhi explained that nonviolent struggle against the British would go on, but he could "guarantee that all [his] actions [would] be so calculated so as to avoid benefiting Japan in its aggressions against China."[6] Chiang had made an important diplomatic contribution to the Allied cause—although one unappreciated by Churchill.

When he returned to Chungking, Chiang sent another radiogram to Roosevelt regarding the need for Britain and Holland to copy the American example in the Philippines and unequivocally promise full independence to all their colonies. This, Chiang said, was the only way to assure the true loy-

Worried that the likely fall of Rangoon would leave India as the sole Western supply base for China, Chiang and his wife visit Mahatma Gandhi in January 1942 and successfully urge him not to oppose the British war effort. Courtesy KMT Party History Institute.

alty of colonial peoples to the Allied cause. In this message, he quoted at length from his conversation with "an Indian friend" (Gandhi).[7] Roosevelt passed the message on to Churchill, who was not pleased.

On February 27, accompanied by his son Ching-kuo, Chiang and Madame flew back to Lashio in Burma to meet again with General Hutton. To Chiang, the British officers acted as if Burma was lost and seemed ready to retreat toward India. Less than a week later, Rangoon fell and this further destroyed what was left of the Generalissimo's belief in the wisdom of his army making a major stand in Burma. The next day, General Stilwell, on his way to Chungking from Calcutta, stopped over briefly at Lashio and received a "cordial welcome" from Chiang. As he looked on, the Generalissimo, in his usual "clipped staccato voice," told his Fifth and Sixth Army senior officers that they would in the future take orders only from General Stilwell. The general, pleased, flew on to China.[8]

Immediately after the Chiangs returned to Chungking, they had their first formal discussion with the new China Theater chief of staff. After asking Stilwell to describe his responsibilities in China as he saw them, Chiang noted that the general did not mention this position. "Are you my Chief of Staff or

The Chiangs and General Joseph Stilwell in Burma at their first meeting. It marked the beginning of what was to be a very brief honeymoon between the Generalissimo and "Vinegar Joe." Courtesy KMT Party History Institute.

not?" Chiang asked. Stilwell replied, "Yes, I am your Excellency's Chief of Staff and directly under your command." Getting to the immediate question of Burma, Chiang said he was fed up with British unwillingness to fight and was very suspicious of their motives, but the Chinese troops in Burma and on the border were waiting Stilwell's direction. Stilwell was rather amazed that Chiang had actually given him clear command of China's best armies.[9]

On March 9, the Generalissimo and Madame held a dinner in honor of Stilwell. Among the guests were air commander Claire Chennault and the two Guangxi generals Bai Chongxi and Li Zongren, who seemed to Stilwell to be "good eggs." After dinner, during a two-hour discussion on the overall strategy for Burma, Chiang put forward a plan that focused on falling back to Mandalay. Stilwell agreed they had to hold Mandalay but stressed that "above all we want Rangoon." He proposed taking the offensive in the Sittang Valley north of Rangoon, cutting off the Japanese in the south, splitting the enemy forces, and retaking the capital. Chiang thought Stilwell's idea exceedingly risky, but the general's élan impressed him, and he did not directly reject the goal of taking back Rangoon and thus opening up the port and railway that fed the Burma Road. Instead, to show his confidence in Stilwell, he said he was going to radio Roosevelt that very night and ask him to tell Churchill that Stilwell must have overall command in Burma, including over British troops—or else the Chinese forces would leave.[10]

It was a glorious start to their critical relationship. Soong Mayling was "bubbling over with good spirits." She took both Stilwell and Chennault by the arm and led them onto a terrace where the three of them strolled and talked. She said she was happy that at last China had "the help of two American military leaders." Stilwell found Soong Mayling conniving, but he liked her. He saw her as "direct, forceful, energetic, loves power, eats up publicity and flattery . . . can turn on charm at will . . . [potentially] an important ally [with] great influence on her husband mostly along the right lines." Before going to bed, Chiang cabled T. V. Soong to approach Roosevelt as soon as possible with the request that he push for Stilwell to take over command of British troops in Burma in addition to the Chinese armies.[11]

When Stilwell called on Chiang the next day, the Generalissimo was still in an exceptionally good mood. He gave a long and calm lecture to his new chief of staff about the importance of understanding the temperament and limitations of the Chinese soldier. The standard Chinese division in 1942 had a strength of from 7,000 to 9,000 men, but the rifle power of a Chinese division at full strength rarely exceeded 3,000, with the addition of a couple of hundred light machine guns, thirty to forty medium machine guns, and a few three-inch mortars. There were no artillery units attached to the average division except for a few antitank guns of small caliber. Each division possessed meager signals personnel, a staff car or two, maybe a half-dozen trucks, and a couple of hundred shaggy, ill-kept ponies. The equipment, weapons, and ammunition all came from a variety of sources and parts were not interchangeable. Generally half the men were undernourished, and there was one doctor for every few thousand men. Many died from disease.[12]

Chiang then turned to the critical operational question at hand—Burma. Chiang had had some second thoughts about the previous evening's discussion. In particular, he returned to his view that Rangoon was lost and it would be very risky to try to recover it at this time, given Japan's superior capabilities in the air, at sea, and probably on land. A full transcript of this meeting was sent to Soong in Washington. Following is an abridged version of part of Chiang's remarks on this subject to the general, who listened politely:

The Japanese command of the air and the sea and its possession of tanks and artillery make recovery of Rangoon very difficult. The 5th and 6th armies are the cream of the Chinese Army. Their loss would have a grave effect. Thus it is critical that these armies not be defeated . . . The best strategy in Burma is to hold an east-west line at Mandalay. The Chinese armies should deploy on the outskirts of Mandalay and wait for the Japanese to attack the British forces there. The Chinese might then make a thrust toward the enemy. But going on the offensive should not be a guiding principle so far as Burma is concerned.[13]

Stilwell listened respectfully, then told Chiang, "I wish to thank you most gratefully for this frank talk. You can rest assured that I attach the greatest importance to what you have told me. I realize the necessity for me to know and understand Chinese psychology. You are very generous in giving me command of the Chinese troops in Burma . . . I will do my best to carry out your orders." Nevertheless, after the meeting, Stilwell wrote in his diary that his plans remained the same: "to work toward the recapture of Rangoon: and only if this failed to fall back to Mandalay."[14]

Stilwell wanted to resist the Japanese at Toungoo, 150 miles north of Rangoon, and follow up with an all-out counteroffensive to retake Rangoon. As he and Chiang debated tactics, strategy, and the correlation of forces, it soon became clear that profound differences separated them. Stilwell, who since his early tour in China had disliked Chiang, began in his diary and in the company of other Americans to refer openly to him as "Peanut." Chiang, for his part, was put off by the American's cocky manner as well as what Chiang increasingly saw as reckless overconfidence. Stilwell, who had been on the scene only two weeks, was already vigorously challenging the Generalissimo's judgment and pressing his own views on how to deploy China's two best armies.

Meanwhile, Roosevelt was reluctant to push Churchill on the command issue in Burma, which after all was a British colony. After a visit to Chungking by General Sir Harold Alexander, Chiang agreed that Sir Harold would be in overall command of the Burma campaign, and Madame sent a note to Stilwell informing him of this decision. It was an unusual way of passing sensitive information on matters of state, but one that reflected her strong desire to establish a special relationship with the American.[15]

General Wavell had already reported to Alexander his grave doubts that he could hold Burma. Chiang also worried that the enemy was far stronger than Stilwell thought. Japanese troop strength in southern Burma and neighboring Thailand, he thought, had in fact doubled. The Japanese had almost five hundred war planes in the Rangoon area, while the Flying Tigers were down to just forty-two serviceable aircraft. Moreover, the Imperial Japanese Navy now controlled the entire Bay of Bengal.[16] Given the clear Japanese air and sea superiority and the hasty British retreats so far, a defensive strategy at this time seemed to make sense. But Stilwell was determined to go on the offensive.

As the days passed, Chiang became so worried about Stilwell's lack of experience and his temperament that he could not sleep at night. He was risking his best armies with a man he had quickly come not to trust, someone who had never actually led troops in combat or planned and executed a real multidivisional battle.[17] Stilwell seemed to Chiang oblivious to the very real danger of being trapped. Soong Mayling, displaying her own predilection for the offensive, privately told the American to "keep up" what he was doing, and Chiang reluctantly agreed that when the fighting started, Stilwell would be free to act.[18] It was a gamble he felt he had to take to demonstrate to Roosevelt his commitment to playing a major, cooperative role in the war.

On March 19, at Toungoo, the Japanese attacked the 200th Division, the Chinese Army's only unit that could move entirely by truck. The battle raged for twelve days, and by all accounts the Chinese-trained soldiers fought gallantly. Stilwell arrived at the front on March 22 and took over direct command.[19] On March 30, the 200th Division, clearly overpowered and outnumbered, retreated intact from the virtually surrounded town, while the British and Indian troops on the right flank fell back up the Irrawaddy Valley. At one point, General Du Yuming, commander of the Fifth Army, giving various excuses, ignored Stilwell's orders to attack a Japanese regiment with five of his own regiments. Later Du Yuming reported his version of events, explaining that on one occasion he had declined to attack a town because of the presence of civilians.

As was his wont, during the engagement the Generalissimo issued direct orders or "suggestions" to divisional commanders. Stilwell blamed the initial setback on this "meddling" and flew back to Chungking. The next day he stormed into Chiang's office where he "threw the raw meat on the floor" and charged that the Chinese commanders were not obeying his orders.[20] He had no confidence in these officers, he said, and wanted to be relieved. Chiang appeared shocked and promised to rectify the situation. In his diary, Stilwell confided that the disrespect and disobedience he had encountered among the Chinese commanders originated at "the highest quarters." Still he admitted that "in justice to all of them, it is expecting a great deal to have them turn over a couple of armies in a vital area to a goddamn foreigner that they don't know and in whom they can't have much confidence."[21] He was never to document such an insight again.

Meanwhile, Chiang was also surprised that until that day Stilwell had not sent him any reports on the military action in Burma and had left his command to come to Chungking "just because a division commander would not follow orders to attack a Burmese town." Further Chinese sacrifices in Burma, Chiang wrote, would not likely contribute to the war effort, but since China was a member of the Alliance, he could "only proceed with all the plans and wait for a change in the general situation."[22]

Chiang and his wife discussed how to handle Stilwell. Mayling still thought he was a capable military leader. His directness and earthiness were to her simply exaggerated forms of the typical American temperament, which she found endearing. She recognized from the start that there was a powerful personality difference between her husband and the American. But her highest priority was to maintain good relations between the Generalissimo and Roosevelt, and she thought that whatever one made of General Stilwell, it was necessary to bend over backward to make the relationship work. He was Roosevelt's man in China, and everything hinged on the tie with the United States. "In the scheme of things," she told her husband, their problems with Stilwell were "relatively small."[23] She urged "Kai" to be conciliatory and he accepted the advice.

The next day, Stilwell met again with the Chiangs at Yellow Mountain, their villa outside Chungking. Chiang told Stilwell that Lieutenant General Luo Zhuoying would be sent to Burma as Stilwell's executive. Henceforth, Stilwell would give his orders to Luo, who would send them on to the Chinese army commanders. In addition, the Generalissimo said he would travel to Burma to inform his generals in person that Stilwell was their superior and had full authority. Following the meeting, Stilwell was again optimistic. He liked General Luo. And although he saw Chiang as "not mentally stable" and surrounded by sycophants and parasites, he wrote that nevertheless the Generalissimo "is determined and forceful, and wants to get on with the war."[24]

Stilwell returned to the front on April 5. On the plane with him were the Generalissimo, Soong Mayling, and Henry Luce, publisher of the Time-Life Company. At Lashio, the party was informed that the Chinese and British forces had withdrawn from Toungoo, the British were retreating up the Irrawaddy Valley, and the Chinese were pulling back through the Sitang Valley. Stilwell proposed to draw the Japanese into a trap at a town called Pyinmana where he would launch a major counterattack. If the plan failed, the Allies would fall back to Mandalay. Chiang told Du Yuming "in plain words" that Stilwell was the boss and had full powers to promote, relieve, and punish any officer in the Chinese Expeditionary Force. Chiang, Stilwell, and the senior Chinese generals, Luo and Du, then set about planning the "decisive engagement" that Stilwell advocated. Chiang gave Stilwell his own plan of operations—"the usual crap," Stilwell thought, "but not so bad." Stilwell also reviewed the troops and called them "a fine-looking lot of soldiers."[25]

The Fifth Army had withdrawn to a site selected by Stilwell near Pyinmana, and in keeping with Stilwell's assumptions, the Japanese had rushed northward in pursuit. But the British, fearing that their Indian and Burmese troops were being surrounded, were already pulling back from their positions on the right flank of the Chinese. On orders from Stilwell, on April 12, the crack 38th Division led by General Sun Liren, a Virginia Military Institute graduate, moved south from Mandalay. Chiang, learning about the Chinese Army's exposed right flank, radioed Stilwell that "it was absolutely unallowable" to remain at Pyinmana. Stilwell described this message from his commander as full of "crap and nonsense," and he continued to prepare for the counteroffensive. But on April 18, Field Marshall Sir William Slim's polyglot First Burma Division appeared encircled on the oil fields of Yenangyaung and a sixty-mile gap had opened west of the Chinese lines. Awakened at 3:00 in the morning, Stilwell ordered the 200th Division, which was deployed on the Chinese eastern flank, as well as a regiment from Sun Liren's 38th Division, to rush to the rescue. Realizing that his plan for a counteroffensive was now totally impossible, he told the 96th to withdraw to Pyinmana, to the north.[26]

General Du, apparently opposing the move to reinforce the British, delayed sending the 200th Division; it did not arrive at Yenangyaung until late on April 21, by which time General Sun and his 38th Division had already helped the First Burma Division escape encirclement. But the day before, the Japanese, in much greater force than Stilwell or the British anticipated, had poured out of the jungles of Thailand and launched an attack with tanks as well as infantry on the east flank—the Chinese sector. The 200th was ordered immediately to return to the east to meet this threat, and the dusty, tired soldiers piled back into their trucks. But before the 200th could arrive back on the east flank, the Japanese drove through the Chinese lines and effectively destroyed the Sixth Army's Temporary 55th Division, made up of inexperienced recruits. Most of the rest of the Sixth Army fell back in disarray toward Lashio.[27]

Chiang believed that by dispatching the 200th to Yenangyaung to save the British, Stilwell had fatally weakened the Chinese left flank. The American general in his own report to Washington blamed the failure on the poor showing of the British and the Chinese 55th Division.[28] Notably, at this time he did not blame Chiang. Chiang, however, ordered his commanders henceforth not to move troops on Stilwell's orders unless the Chinese War Ministry approved.[29] He gave no direct sign to Stilwell of his displeasure, but the Chinese leader's frustration grew daily. After the collapse in the east, for one critical week, Stilwell sent not a single message to his Supreme Theater Commander on what was happening. Du and Luo, however, were dispatching daily reports and almost certainly blamed the collapse on Stilwell.

On April 25, Stilwell, along with Du and Luo, met with General Alexander at Kyaukse twenty-five miles south of Mandalay, and the group agreed on a general retreat. At one point, six Japanese bombers roared overhead and a 500-pounder burst just one hundred yards away from the British, American, and Chinese officers. Some of the men scrambled for cover but Alexander stood defiant in the garden, glaring at the fire and smoke. Not to be outdone, Stilwell leaned against the porch railing and lit a cigarette in his long Roosevelt-type holder.[30]

The Japanese seized Lashio on April 29 and the danger of a vast entrapment increased. The Japanese commander called for a lightening-swift pincer movement to surround and destroy the Allies in the Mandalay area and prevent withdrawal to Assam in India or to China.[31] Stilwell was in the town of Swebo when he received a message from Chiang ordering him to "go to

Myitkyina and *not lose time*" (Chiang's emphasis).[32] In a conversation with his assistant Colonel Frank Dorn, Stilwell said he "belonged with his troops," and he set out for Myitkyina, choosing to go by road, although Chennault had sent a plane.[33] At this point, Stilwell seemed to assume he was still in command, although unknown to him all his orders now officially had to be approved by Chiang. After four harrowing days of travel, by May 4, Stilwell and his staff came to believe that they had been cut off from retreat to Myitkyina. According to army historians, parts of the Fifth Army were still behind, that is, to the south of Stilwell. Sun Liren and his 38th Division were also not far south, fighting a desperate rear guard action.[34]

In Washington, senior officers were alarmed at the collapse in Burma. T. V. Soong passed on to Chiang a request from the U.S. Department of the Army, no doubt with General Marshall's imprimatur, asking for his assessment of Stilwell's military leadership. Sticking with the commitment he had made to his wife, Chiang told T.V. to reiterate that he had "full confidence and trust" in the general.[35] In fact, he had totally lost confidence and trust in both the American and British generals and was sending out orders without regard to either Stilwell or Alexander.

At this point, Stilwell decided he and his staff could "no longer be of much use." His officers agreed and thought "the boss should tell the Chinese to go to Hell and get out while the getting was good."[36] Stilwell sent a brief report informing Washington and the Generalissimo of his imminent departure. The Chinese divisions, he said, had broken into small parties that would make their way to India, so his "further command would be unnecessary."[37] (In fact, most of the Chinese divisions under his command were apparently at this point still acting as cohesive units.) Stilwell dispatched a radiogram to Du Yuming ordering him to retreat to India. Stilwell's men rounded up local guides, porters, and a team of pack mules, and on May 5 the party of almost eighty, including a group of nurses and British refugees, set out paddling up the Chindwin River, which they would soon abandon for a mountain trail. The Indian border town of Imphal was 140 miles away.[38]

On May 6, Du Yuming reported to the Generalissimo that he had been instructed by Stilwell and Luo to lead his troops into India. Du's report was the first time Chiang had heard that Stilwell had ordered a large part of the Chinese Expeditionary Force in Burma to seek refuge in a foreign country, and it was "completely contrary" to his order to "concentrate the entire army at Myitkyina."[39] He wondered if Stilwell was "losing his nerve because of los-

ing [the] battle."⁴⁰ Chiang countermanded Stilwell's order and instructed Du
to proceed with his troops to Myitkyina without delay. It was later that same
day that he received the message from Stilwell informing him that he and his
staff and a few others were going to India. Chiang was stunned. Stilwell, he
wrote, "has abandoned my 100,000 soldiers in foreign jungles and headed off
to India. Only then does he send me this telegram."⁴¹

Sun Liren and his well-disciplined 38th Division, following orders from
both the Generalissimo and Stilwell, headed directly for India, following a
path slightly to the south of Stilwell's track. Several times in his diary, recounting his escape to the north, Stilwell reported being "just ahead of the
Chinese horde" and the "deluge," meaning his retreating troops.⁴² Meanwhile, the 22nd and 96th Divisions of the Fifth Army and tens of thousands
of refugees continued up a ghastly trail to Myitkyina. Hostile locals and Japanese planes decimated the column as it made its way north. The 96th split off
and, supported by American parachute drops of food, conducted an "amazing march" back to China, although one marred by looting and pillaging
along the way. The crack 200th Division also made it home as a unit even
though its commanding general had been killed.

In the west, Du Yuming arrived with the 22nd Division at Myitkyina and
calculated that he could not reach the Chinese border from there as ordered
by the Generalissimo; the ferries on the Salween River were in Japanese
hands. Chiang then authorized Du and Luo to head for India, but Du soon
reported that Japanese forward units were ambushing his men along the jungle trails. Even more devastating were the ravages of malaria and dysentery.
Meanwhile, in the east, two divisions of the vaunted Sixth Army fell to pieces.
Small bands of soldiers and officers took off into the mountains, and after
fighting their way through hostile Burmese they escaped piecemeal to China.
The Flying Tigers, too, were forced to burn twenty-two damaged P-40s in
northeast Burma before fleeing.

The Japanese, meanwhile, paused briefly at Lashio and then dashed up the
road to the China border and at some points into Yunnan province. Their
movements were of grave concern to the Generalissimo, who worried that,
after their stunning victory in Burma, the Imperial Army would decide to try
to destroy the Chinese Army.⁴³ Marshall was also alarmed, fearing a threat
even to Chungking. But under Chiang's orders six Chinese divisions in Yunnan mounted a strong counteroffensive, and the Flying Tigers at Kunming
joined in the counterattack. Then calm settled over the jungle. For the time

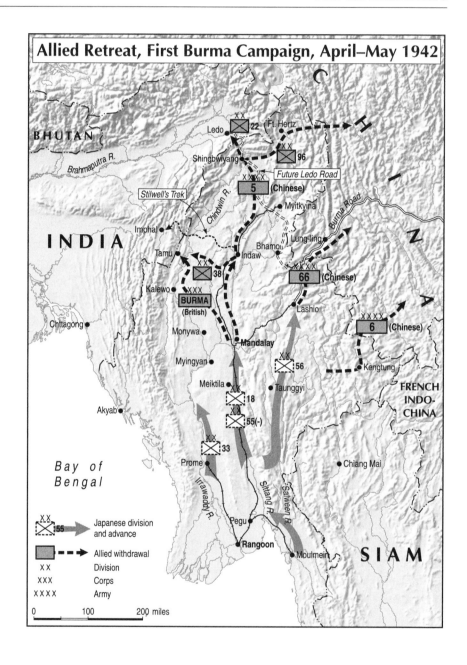

Allied Retreat, First Burma Campaign, April–May 1942

being, the Japanese General Staff was satisfied with the occupation of three-fourths of Burma, assured that the overland supply route to China was closed for the indefinite future.[44]

Stilwell's bedraggled group journeyed for three weeks in stifling heat first by raft up river, then by foot over the steep and craggy Naga Hills. The general was usually at the front of the march in his World War I scout hat, baggy shirt and pants, and rolled-up sleeves. The famous "walkout" was well recorded. U.S. Army photographers with plenty of film were part of the eighty-man expedition, as was Jack Belden, a Stilwell friend who would write dramatic *Time* features on the adventure as well as the book *Retreat with Stilwell.*[45]

It was a grueling trip but without fatalities, serious injuries, combat encounters, or even trouble with the natives. It was in fact a ramble compared to the "purgatory" endured by most of the Chinese Expeditionary Armies—which he still officially commanded—in their much longer and more deadly retreats. Stilwell's escape without any part of his army except a few Chinese guards was greeted by the American media and public as a heroic event. Likewise, after Sir Harold Alexander emerged in India at about the same time with his bedraggled and beaten forces, Radio London praised him for having "fought one of the great defensive battles of the war."[46]

When Stilwell reached India he told a press conference "I claim we got a hell of a beating . . . We got run out of Burma and it is humiliating as hell. I think we ought to find out what caused it, go back, and take it."[47] Marshall apparently had concerns but he sent commendations and Roosevelt expressed "great satisfaction over Stilwell's handling of the whole situation." Even Madame Chiang cabled Lauchlin Currie, Roosevelt's representative, to repeat to the President that the Generalissimo had "entire confidence" in Stilwell.[48] But Chiang confided to his diary that Stilwell's "abandonment of his troops" showed he "lacked the virtue and vision of a commander."[49]

The first Burma campaign was in fact an unmitigated disaster. Some 3,600 British and Indian troops were killed and about 7,000 wounded. The Chinese armies together lost approximately 25,000 of their best-trained men, with probably 8,000 or 9,000 killed. Some Chinese divisions lost a third of their strength, and most of the Chinese Army's few remaining cannon and trucks were destroyed. By contrast, although they had fought in a strange land and on the offensive, the Japanese had suffered only 4,500 killed and wounded. Stilwell blamed the defeat at Pyinmana on the Chinese generals and Supreme Commander Chiang. The British blamed Stilwell and the Chinese. And Chiang blamed the British and Stilwell.[50] All were correct, but the defeat was originally the result of a serious underestimation of enemy strength by Stilwell.

If the Allies in 1942 had from the beginning followed a defensive strategy in Burma focused on holding the line at Mandalay or Myitkyina, as Chiang had wanted, the battle at Pyinmana would have been avoided and they would have had a fair chance of success. Moreover, even if this strategy had failed, the retreat could have been orderly and China itself—as well as U.S.-China relations—would have been much stronger over the nearly four years of war to come. As it was, Chiang's position in the global alliance and within the political-military coalition he headed at home was substantially weakened by the defeat in Burma. With the loss of the Burma Road, China was now cut off from any meaningful supply by land or sea except by the long road through desert and steppe from Soviet Russia. Morale at home and in the army suffered a major setback. The defeat reinforced a defensive outlook by the Chinese commanders and the Generalissimo. It also cemented what had become perversely hostile relations between Joe Stilwell and Chiang Kai-shek.

Chiang was most outraged by what he saw as Stilwell's blatant abandonment of his troops without orders, but with the praise of Marshall and Roosevelt as well as the American press ringing in his ears, Stilwell was in no mood to placate, much less apologize to, the Generalissimo. Training of the Chinese troops under Stilwell's direction would soon begin at a military camp in central India called Ramgarh. But first, on June 2, he flew back to Chungking.

I

While the allies were collapsing in Burma, another disaster for China took shape as the U.S. aircraft carrier *Hornet* launched the famous Doolittle bombers on their mission to bomb Tokyo. For security reasons, Washington did not inform Chiang Kai-shek of the raid until about a week before it was to take place. Stilwell, too, had been told only to prepare airfields for possible landings by multiengine planes in government-controlled parts of Zhejiang province. The fields were to be landing sites for the sixteen B-25s that would head to China after completing their mission over Tokyo.

When he learned of the imminent raid, Chiang strenuously objected, predicting that the attack would spur the Japanese to overrun the airfields in east Zhejiang. He pleaded with Washington to at least delay the raid until his ground forces could consolidate defenses around the fields. He was told it was too late but was promised that the sixteen bombers involved would become an air wing of the U.S. Air Force assigned to Chiang's China Theater. The promise turned out to be meaningless. On April 18, with their fuel running out, all the Doolittle bombers except one that made it to Vladivostok were lost or crash-landed in China.

After the raid, Chiang sent an angry message to Marshall reporting that in reprisal, Japanese troops had attacked the coastal areas of China where locals had rescued the American fliers. "The Japanese," Chiang said, "slaughtered every man, woman, and child in these areas—let me repeat, every man, woman, and child."[51] In the resulting battles in Zhejiang and Jiangxi, Chiang committed thirty-four divisions against the Japanese and suffered 30,000 casualties. All of Chennault's airfields in East China were destroyed.[52] The Doolittle raid, brave as it was, did scant damage in Tokyo and, as Chiang had feared, caused great harm for China. It was a tremendous morale booster in America, however. Roosevelt gave Doolittle the Medal of Honor.

On June 4, Chiang and Soong Mayling received Stilwell, who, weak from dysentery and jaundice, was more gaunt than ever. The First Couple were "both very pleasant," and invited the general to spend the weekend at Yellow Mountain, but he politely declined. According to Stilwell, he "gave them the full story" on what happened in Burma, "pulling no punches, and naming names" of the generals he wanted court-martialed or shot.[53] According to the Chinese transcript of the meeting, however, Chiang began by asking Stilwell if in Burma he had received his messages, which were never answered. Stilwell explained that because of mistakes, presumably in coding or decoding, the messages were incomprehensible. He attributed the defeat in Burma to the fact that "the enemy was superior to us," and listed the shortcomings from logistics to air cover to intelligence. Chiang asked if the general remembered that early on he (Chiang) had told him that the Chinese army in Burma could not afford to lose. Stilwell replied that yes, he remembered, but he believed that "taking the offense would lose less than taking the defense," and if they had won the battle at Pyinmana as he had planned, the outcome would have been different. Stilwell then handed Chiang and Madame his sweeping recommendations for reorganizing the Chinese Army. These included a purge of poor commanders and unification of battlefield authority with one officer holding complete tactical command over all services.[54] Mayling remarked, "Why, that's what the German advisers told him!"[55] Later, however, she said it was necessary to be realistic: "Heads cannot be lopped off, otherwise nothing would be left."[56]

Two weeks later, T.V. informed Chiang from Washington that another American was interested in Chiang's opinion of Stilwell's performance. Secretary Stimson, T.V. said, had told him that if Chiang Kai-shek thought Stilwell was not appropriate for the job, the United States would consider a replacement. Two days earlier, Stimson and Marshall had sent a message to Stilwell reaffirming their support for him and suggesting that if conditions did not improve for his work in China they would assign him where his talents might be applied.[57] While they never said so at the time or later, Marshall and Stimson seemed to have been taken aback at what had happened in Burma and by Stilwell's scathing messages to Washington denouncing his theater commander. These messages seemed to offer the perfect opening for easing Stilwell out.

Chiang quickly replied to his brother-in-law with a list of grievances against Stilwell, including his "bad strategy in Burma," his poor organizational skills, his unfamiliarity with the job of being chief of staff, and his departure to India without permission. Yet, he told T.V., "for the sake of our Ally's reputation, I would not say much about this now." Always keenly sensitive to "face," Chiang was afraid that requesting Stilwell's removal would dishonor all American officers and seriously damage Chiang's relations with Roosevelt and Marshall. He suggested that in the future the American leaders "may learn our thinking [on Stilwell]."[58]

Chiang's repeated endorsement of the general apparently relieved any doubt Marshall and Stimson had about the wisdom of keeping Stilwell in China. Henceforth, the two would strongly side with Stilwell against Chiang, willing in the end even to risk the alliance with China to support "Vinegar Joe." For his part, Chiang now seemed to think he could yet bring the general to understand and accept his ways. He told Stilwell again that it was important to understand the mentality of the Chinese. "If you are with me closely for a few months," he explained, "you will understand the psychology of Chinese officers, and I will tell you more about their peculiarities"— apparently referring to the importance of loyalty and matters of face and honor.[59]

That month, with its three remaining principal aircraft carriers, the U.S. Navy defeated the main Japanese battle fleet at the Battle of Midway, sinking all four of Japan's major carriers. Japanese power had peaked. In the West, however, the Wehrmacht was besieging Sevastopol and Rostov, while in North Africa General Erwin Rommel and his Tiger tanks defeated the British at Bir Hacheim and advanced toward Tobruk, Cairo, and the Suez Canal. On June 26 Stilwell told Chiang that the heavy B-17 bombers of the U.S. Tenth Air Force in India, which had been assigned to the China Theater, had been dispatched to Egypt to take part in the desperate battle looming for control of the canal.

Chiang was furious. The situation in China, he told Stilwell, was as urgent as that in the Middle East. Britain had thousands of planes, yet the Allies were taking bombers belonging to his command in China. How, he asked, could this decision be made without even notifying him? Stilwell agreed that the decision was inappropriate, due to the "ignorance" of officers in Washington. Chiang told him to ask the President, "Is the U.S. interested in maintaining the Chinese theater?" Madame was more heated and provocative. "Is there any need for China to continue the war?" she asked rhetorically. Then she added even more pointedly, "The pro-Japanese element [in the KMT] is very active." Chiang added that T. V. Soong had reported that Washington was awaiting Stilwell's recommendation regarding whether it should send the promised five hundred aircraft for the Chinese Air Force. "Why have you not replied?" Madame asked heatedly.[60]

Roosevelt responded quickly to Chiang's complaint, promising future support and explaining the dire situation that had necessitated the transfer of the bombers. Chiang replied to Washington with a memo titled "Three Minimum Requirements for the Maintenance of the China Theater." These "requirements" included the stationing of five hundred airplanes in China as promised in July 1941, the flying of 5,000 tons of supplies over the Hump (the Himalayas) every month, and the deployment of three American divisions to India.

Stilwell had earlier supported nearly all of these "requirements" (he had asked for only one U.S. division). But in his messages to Washington, he described Chiang's declaration as an ultimatum—either the demanded aid would be forthcoming or "China will make other arrangements," meaning, Stilwell suggested, a separate peace with Japan.[61] Chiang, feeling he had no other leverage, was again employing the tactic of threatened collapse.

Clearly, however, Chiang had no intention of initiating peace with Japan himself or allowing others to do so. For eleven years he had sought to eradicate the shame that the "dwarf pirates'" had inflicted on China, and the image he sought to mold for history—and equally important, his deeply ingrained self-image—was built on his role as the Confucian scholar-general who would defeat China's enemies and fulfill its dream of restored greatness. As Theodore White, a strong critic of Chiang and a friend of Stilwell, wrote from Chungking in 1942, "Chiang has only one emotion: China."[62] In addition, Chiang was thoroughly convinced that the United States would eventually overwhelm Japan and that it would be the height of folly to desert the Alliance. Moreover, as Stilwell himself suggested, any attempt at a separate peace—a defection from the Alliance—would be suicide for Chiang; the uneasy coalition he ruled would not permit it.[63] Stilwell, however, did not even suggest to Washington the possibility that Chiang's threats were not real.

With the loss of Rangoon, China's Lend-Lease matériel from the United States was piling up—149,000 tons in the United States and 45,000 tons in India. As a result, the U.S. Munitions Assignments Board began to repossess the Chinese stockpiles and cut new allocations to levels that might be expected to be flown to China in the near future. In May, the total airlift fell to a mere thirty tons. Then the board, without consulting the Chinese, ordered that shipments for China were no longer to be consigned to China Defense Supplies (a Chinese government agency), but henceforth would go to the American military mission in China. In other words, Stilwell alone would have the power to distribute the matériel in China.

At this time, the Generalissimo ordered two airplanes operated by the government-controlled China National Aviation Corporation (CNAC) turned over to the Aeronautics Commission, which Soong Mayling chaired. He did so possibly to reserve the planes for Madame's and his use, or perhaps for the Chinese Air Force. But Stilwell, acting as director of U.S. Lend-Lease in China, told the American staff of CNAC to refuse the transfer. When Chiang asked for an explanation, Stilwell's memorandum reply began by explaining that the passing of title for the two aircraft had been hung up by a legal technicality, but further declared that "the real issue is of course how best to get on with the war. I will assume responsibility of saying that these planes may be used by Generalissimo whenever he considers that they may be most effectively employed to prosecute the war."[64]

The language was insubordinate and insulting. Without mentioning the new Munitions Board policy on passing title, a change about which Chiang was unaware, Stilwell was also declaring that he had the authority to decide when and where ownership of equipment would pass to the Chinese government once it had arrived in China. In the same memo, Stilwell also took the occasion to inform Chiang that in "any war council held in China" his position as the U.S. representative overrode any other status that he held, meaning any subordination to the Generalissimo as his chief of staff.[65] Appalled, Chiang sent a message to T. V. Soong reporting that Stilwell in effect had taken the position that the Supreme Commander in the China Theater "must beg of him supplies already delivered to China."[66]

To clarify matters, Soong met with Roosevelt himself, who said that in the future Lend-Lease disputes would be negotiated in Washington between T. V. Soong and Harry Hopkins, Roosevelt's senior adviser and troubleshooter. The President also explained that Stilwell represented the United States only at international military councils that might be in China, of which there had been none; thus his claim in this regard was "meaningless." When Marshall asked Stilwell to explain the situation, Stilwell called Chiang's charges "a lie." "Some bastard," he said, "is always trying to discredit me."[67]

That summer in Chungking, gray piles of rubble still littered the streets, but the Flying Tigers had effectively ended the Japanese bombing raids. Roosevelt asked Lauchlin Currie, whom he had sent to China a year before, to return to Chungking and try to resolve matters between Chiang and Stilwell. When Currie arrived in August he found the Generalissimo thinner and wearier; he also seemed to Currie to have become even more religious and austere. But Currie found "no sign of defeatism or of a desire to give up the struggle."[68] In his talks with the Generalissimo, Currie relayed the suspicion of some Americans that the Chinese government wanted to avoid fighting the Japanese; they believed that the government might be storing U.S. equipment and preserving its strength for the postwar civil conflict with the Communists. These Americans thought that the United States should not expect China to cooperate in the war effort and they advocated that the United States cut off all material aid to Chungking.

Chiang was stunned by the remarks, especially given China's huge losses in the Alliance's Burma campaign only three months earlier. Overall, between December 7, 1941, and July 22, 1942, more than 80,000 Chinese military personnel had been killed and wounded in the war, whereas total American casualties up to that point around the world were around 33,000.[69] Those who say China was not fighting the Japanese, Chiang told Currie, "will be

held responsible for anything [untoward] that happens in China's war of resistance against Japan."[70]

The Communists, however, were engaged in precisely the strategy that
Chiang was accused of pursuing. The CCP's Central Revolutionary Committee, near the end of 1941, reaffirmed that the party would engage "mainly"
in a "political offensive" against the Japanese and should "save and preserve
its strength [military and civil] and wait for favorable timing." The Communist leaders in fact decreed that "the whole army should prepare to down-
size by half"; indeed, by the end of 1942, the CCP's armies of 570,000 had
shrunk by about 100,000.[71]

Currie's main concern, of course, was the relationship between Stilwell and
the Generalissimo. Chiang expressed his pent-up grievances against Stilwell
for "recklessness . . . insubordination . . . contempt and arrogance," saying
the United States had sent him not a chief of staff but a "king of the China
Theater."[72] For his part, Stilwell recounted to Currie all the "intriguing and
lying" against him and recommended, "Either we stop fooling around and
get out of here entirely, or we should lay down certain conditions which
[Chiang] . . . must meet."[73] Currie was disturbed by the general's stark, sim-
plistic, almost flippant portrayal of the situation and of the courses open to
the United States only seven months into the war alliance.[74]

Stilwell now devised a new war plan for retaking first Burma and then Indochina, and as a peace offering proposed that it be known as the Chiang
Kai-shek plan. In fact, it was not much different from a blueprint that Chiang
had sent to Roosevelt shortly after Pearl Harbor, except that Stilwell omitted
entirely the whole question of air power. Under the plan, the Chinese divisions that had escaped from Burma and were now being trained in India and
rearmed would be called the X Force and twenty Chinese divisions in Yunnan, also trained and rearmed, would be designated the Y Force. Twelve divisions from the X and Y forces, together with one American and three Anglo-
Indian divisions supported by a strong British naval contingent, would retake
Burma, then advance through Thailand to the Indochina coast. Chiang reiterated his conditions for implementation of this strategy: clear air and naval
supremacy and arrival of the promised military aid to China—five hundred
aircraft and 5,000 tons a month of war matériel. Currie said he would lay the
plan before Roosevelt.[75]

That night in early August the two senior American generals and Currie,
along with the three Soong sisters, gathered for a pleasant dinner at Yellow
Mountain. Everyone was in a relatively good mood including Stilwell, who

Chiang and the Soong sisters in Chungking, left to right: Mayling, Ai-ling, and Chingling. Mayling and her brother, T.V., remained close to Chingling despite her open political support for the Communists. When they learned at the end of the Long March that she had also secretly sent Mao a substantial sum of money, they apparently kept the matter secret. Courtesy KMT Party History Institute.

did not know that Currie had decided to recommend he be eased out. Stilwell found Soong Chingling "the most *simpatico* of the three women and probably the deepest . . . likeable, quiet, and poised." He had had some sharp exchanges with the Madame over the past few weeks, but he still recorded mostly positive impressions of the youngest sister: "quick, intelligent . . . the executive . . . wishes she were a man. Doesn't think deeply, but catches on in a hurry. Very frank and open." His only criticism was that she "accepts . . . reports and rumors . . . that ought to be verified."[76]

Currie returned to Washington in late August and separately recommended to the President and Marshall that Stilwell be replaced. Whatever one thought of Chiang Kai-shek, Currie said, he was likely to remain the leader of China and be strongly anti-Japanese in his outlook for the foreseeable future, and Stilwell's openly confrontational approach was counterproductive. The U.S.-China alliance was at stake, and America had to work with Chiang.[77] Upon hearing Currie's report, Marshall sent out a flash message to Stilwell, who replied that he "did not understand" Currie's references to "strongly antagonistic feelings" between himself and Chiang. In recent, typical diary entries Stilwell had described Chiang as "a stubborn, prejudiced, conceited, despot" and in front of his own American staff Stilwell still repeatedly referred to him as "the little dummy" or "Peanut."[78] But Stilwell's reply satisfied Marshall, who told Currie and Roosevelt that no suitable officer could be found to replace Vinegar Joe.

Despite Chiang's problems with Stilwell, relations between himself and Roosevelt grew stronger. Both shared the goal of dismantling all colonial structures once the war was over.[79] Since Pearl Harbor, Chiang sometimes referred to "the stupidity of the British," and continually pressed the United States and the United Kingdom to drop the infamous practice of "extraterritoriality" that had made their citizens in China immune from Chinese law, even in the case of murder.[80] Finally, on National Day, October 10, 1942, Chiang announced that Washington and London had agreed to drop "extraterritoriality." To most Chinese this was a great victory. In a later speech, Chiang told the Chinese people that the old treaties had "encouraged a mood of weak surrender by which too few were ashamed." But henceforth, he said, "if we are weak, if we lack self-confidence, the fault will be ours only."[81]

Also in October, Stilwell delivered Roosevelt's formal reply to Chiang's "three requirements" message, which had originated back in late June. Although Stilwell noted that the reply was "exactly as I had recommended," it was respectful and conciliatory, promising the five hundred aircraft Chiang had requested as well as one hundred additional aircraft to fly supplies over the Hump, all to be delivered in early 1943. Tonnage over the Hump would be increased, the President promised, but the first priority was opening the Burma Road, which meant taking Rangoon—or cutting a whole new feeder road from India to Lashio. The only "requirement" expressed by Chiang that Roosevelt turned down was the request for deployment of American combat troops to India.[82] Chiang no doubt felt his threat of collapse had again paid off.

That same month, Wendell Willkie, who was on a round-the-world goodwill trip as President Roosevelt's personal envoy, arrived in China. A stocky, rumpled figure with a jovial manner and an appetite for whiskey and women, Willkie fit the Chinese stereotype of an American much more than the gaunt, severe Joe Stilwell. Before his arrival, Madame Chiang made sure that Chungking looked as presentable as possible. Beggars were cleared from the streets and flag-waving Chinese welcomed the American as his caravan drove by.

From the moment she greeted him at the airport, the exuberant American politician was infatuated with Soong Mayling. Willkie hand-carried a letter from Roosevelt to Chiang in which he expressed his hope that Madame Chiang would soon be able to visit the United States. He told the Chiangs that given Madame's "brains, persuasiveness, and moral force," she would be the perfect ambassador.[83] Mayling was in fact thinking of a trip to the United States for treatment of her skin disorder as well as her depression, which was growing deeper.

The highlight of Willkie's visit to China, if true, was a reputed one-night romantic engagement with Soong Mayling. Accompanying Willkie on his world tour was Gardner Cowles, the publisher of *Look* magazine. In his self-published memoirs written in 1982 and printed in 1985, Cowles describes how during a reception, Willkie disappeared with Mayling, and much later in the evening, Chiang burst into T. V. Soong's house, where Cowles and Willkie were staying. Chiang demanded, "Where's Willkie?" When Cowles said he did not know, the Generalissimo and his guards searched the house, then stormed off. At four in the morning, according to Cowles, Willkie appeared, and acting very cocky explained that he had spent the evening with Soong Mayling in her apartment on the top floor of the Women's and Children's Hospital.[84]

Willkie gave Cowles "a play by play account" of the claimed seduction in Mayling's boudoir, then announced that he had invited her to return to Washington with him. Cowles admitted that Mayling was "one of the most beautiful, intelligent, and sexy women" he had ever seen, but, he argued, the relationship would destroy Willkie's political career, not to mention his marriage. The next morning, Cowles reports in his memoirs, Willkie recovered enough to tell Cowles to go tell the Madame that she could not return with them. According to Cowles, when he found her in the apartment and gave her the news, she became enraged, scratching his face with her long fingernails. Cowles also wrote that weeks later in New York at a private dinner with Mayling, she allegedly proposed to support another run by Willkie for the presidency so that together they could—presumably in a poetic sense—"rule the world."[85]

Cowles was a conservative, a political supporter of the Chiangs, and not a muckraker by any means. Still, his account of the Chungking liaison raises

In November 1942 the Chiangs greet Wendell Willkie, who brought back to Washington Chennault's plan, supported by Chiang, to win the war in China mostly with air power. Courtesy KMT Party History Institute.

questions. Dozens of Chinese would have known that Mayling and Willkie spent time alone in the secluded apartment and dozens would have observed the Generalissimo's late-night search under beds in T.V.'s house. In gossip-hungry Chungking, rumors would have spread quickly. But no American or other foreigner in China at the time, including diplomats, reporters, and OSS personnel, reported this enticing item.

When in 1974 an abbreviated version of this story appeared in the book *Pearson Diaries,* the government in Taipei filed a civil action on behalf of Soong Mayling, and Gardner Cowles testified in a deposition that the alleged affair was "impossible." The publisher apologized and paid the related expenses for the Chinese government.[86] The publisher of course simply may have not wanted to go to court over the matter, and Cowles, who was the source of the story, may have felt he should cover up the affair of his prominent friend, who was by then deceased. In his memoirs written for his family twelve years later, Cowles repeated the story in detail.[87]

One possibility is that Willkie, with more than a few drinks in his system, in his ebullient and boyish manner misled his friend into thinking he had enjoyed the intimate favors of the beautiful and famous First Lady of China, and Cowles imagined the rest. But her reputed behavior and words in the two meetings with Cowles himself remain unexplained.

On November 17, accompanied by Owen Lattimore and her own doctor and nurse, Mayling flew in a U.S. Air Force Strato-Cruiser back to America, a second home she had not seen since she had graduated from Wellesley College in 1917. Harry Hopkins met her at Mitchell Field on Long Island and on the long ride into New York she talked at length about the need to give Asia priority in the global war. Forgetting her earlier support for Stilwell, she also volunteered that the general had forced Chiang Kai-shek to act against his better judgment in Burma.

Madame checked in at the Harkness Pavilion of Presbyterian Hospital, taking the entire twelfth floor. Notes from the files of Lauchlin Currie, who was the contact person for her in the White House, make clear that she was being treated for "symptoms . . . customarily associated with certain mental states."[88] In a letter to her husband, her doctors reported "prolonged fatigue and devastating emotional strain." She was discovered to have an intestinal parasite, serious sinus problems, a sedative dependency, and to be in need of extensive dental work.[89] When visitors came they found her with long and brightly lacquered nails, "perfectly made up and coiffed." To Eleanor Roosevelt, she seemed nervous and hardly able to have anything touch her body.[90]

While in China, Willkie had a long talk with General Chennault and was impressed. Like Stilwell, Chennault, at age fifty-two, was a tough, aggressive, outspoken maverick—a fighter pilot who had had many quarrels with superiors over air tactics. Upon losing his hearing, Chennault, then a captain, had taken early health retirement from the U.S. Army Air Force. He was in China in 1937 when the war began, and after meeting Madame Chiang, who was secretary general of the Chinese Air Force, was soon appointed director of advanced fighter training.[91] Chennault, son of a Louisiana farmer, was a steadfast believer in air power, whereas Stilwell, son of a Yonkers, New York, public utility vice-president, believed that warplanes were merely a minor support weapon. Stilwell despised Chiang Kai-shek even before he arrived, but Chennault respected him and thought of Madame as his "princess." Inevitably, he and Stilwell became enemies.

At Willkie's request, Chennault provided him a letter setting out his astonishingly simple strategy for how, together with the Chinese Army, he could win the war in China and eventually in the Pacific. He needed only 105 fighters as well as 30 medium and 12 heavy bombers, with 20 to 30 percent replacements per month. Back in Washington, Willkie gave the letter to the President and the War Department where it created "a major scandal," pushing into the open the struggle between Stilwell and Chennault on grand strategy in the China Theater—ground versus air power.[92]

Marshall dismissed Chennault's proposals as nonsense. He also sent a private message to Stilwell assuring him of support but also taking the occasion to suggest, gently, that he "develop more patience and tolerance than is ordinarily expected of a man and much more than is your constituent portion."[93] Stimson, for his part, asked T. V. Soong to tell Chiang that "pepper (Stilwell) was required more than molasses (Chennault)."[94]

II

The suave, engaging Zhou Enlai was a favorite contact among Western journalists and diplomats in Chungking, many of whom accepted his portrayal of the Chinese Communists as a benign reformist, even democratic, party. Zhou frequented the American embassy itself, offering his characterization of events and promoting policies that, he argued, were designed to assure a democratic, peaceful, and friendly postwar China. His influence was considerable, particularly among Stilwell's staff.[95] John Paton Davies, a young Foreign Service officer assigned as Stilwell's senior political adviser, described the Chinese Communists as "agrarian democrats," while another key officer, John Stewart Service, concluded that the CCP program was "simple democracy"—"much more American than Russian in form and spirit."[96] These men were intelligent, patriotic, and dedicated Americans who saw the early and successful prosecution of the war against Japan as the overriding priority, and if the Communist Chinese could help, so much the better.

Their generally black-and-white views of Chinese politics, which today seem curiously devoid of perspective or nuance, were a product of the times. The "old China hands" in the U.S. military and Foreign Service, as well as the American journalists in China, admired the Chinese people, their culture, and their history. They were distraught by the misery, corruption, and disparities that they saw all around them, conditions endemic in China for generations but exacerbated by the war and endlessly elucidated by the both freewheeling and self-critical Chinese society that existed in parts of Chungking. The Communist base areas, which were rarely seen by Westerners until mid-1944, were, by contrast, not crowded urban cities hundreds of years old, but communities built up from military bases in rural areas—communities that offered strict control, order, and a homogeneity of expressed views. The Americans seized upon books that explained the differences between the Chinese Nationalists and Communists in terms of villains and heroes. One early and influential work mentioned earlier was Harold Isaacs's *The Tragedy of the Chinese Revolution,* first published in 1938 with a long introduction by the then-exiled Leon Trotsky. At that time, Isaacs was himself a Trotskyite, but in the West his book for some years was considered perhaps the best work on the 1927 Kuomintang-Communist split and the early career of Chiang Kai-shek. André Malraux, another Marxist, wrote *Man's Fate,* a famous Western novel set in Shanghai at the time of the bloody 1927 KMT coup. Both authors portrayed Chiang and the Soongs as without redeeming features and completely devoid of dedication to country or principle. Perhaps most influential of all was Edgar Snow's *Red Star over China.* Snow described in positive terms Chiang's activities after the Xi'an Incident, and *Red Star* was a valuable and fascinating book, but it is essentially an uncritical biography of Mao as well as a history of the CCP and its struggle with the KMT as told by Mao and his colleagues.[97]

The recent world depression, America's engagement in the enormous war to the death against fascism, and the heroic fight of the Soviet Union all furthered a spirit of the age that made idealistic Americans more inclined to believe the claims of an egalitarian movement that espoused a world without exploitation or poverty. In addition, the handful of Communist officers chosen to deal with the Americans in Chungking, like Zhou Enlai, were not only idealists themselves but also able to dissemble in a charming, engaging way about the CCP's intentions.

In Westerners' view, one key characteristic of the KMT was growing corruption. As he had from the beginning of his leadership, Chiang privately agonized over the problem of venality and railed against it at meetings and conferences. The military academies and the advanced officer training courses at Lushan preached incorruptibility and over the years Chiang had executed a number of officials for corruption. Some general officers, like Chen Cheng, were widely considered "clean," even by the Communists. But probably most of the senior generals in the Central Army, even many of the best ones, to one degree or another took advantage of their power in ways that involved unethical or illegal misuse of funds. Other officers of course then followed suit as best they could. Even fewer restrictions or checks existed to control the financial activities of the various warlords and their subordinates. During the war, military pay after inflation, along with the quality and educational levels of new officers and men, all declined, with obvious consequences for corruption.

Chiang himself continued to try to set an example. He lived a highly comfortable and secure life mostly in villas surrounded by servants and guards, but within that cocoon his lifestyle remained notably modest or ascetic. He wanted all KMT officers and officials to uphold in practice and appearance high professional standards and private morals, but, as observed before, on the mainland he was never able to implement such an effective and simple reform as centralizing military payrolls. Corruption, he believed, was a problem best addressed in a fundamental way once peace and unity had been restored. Loyalty, for him, was the most important virtue in his generals, meaning in his mind sincerity, reliability, and steadfastness—"values that ensured predictability in an ordered system of interpersonal relations."[98] This order of values both helped keep Chiang in power and led to the toleration of corruption and ineptness. But he believed his priorities were essential to preserve the unity and thus the strength of the armed forces, which were the indispensable instrument for survival in wartime and for the eventual restoration of a great and sovereign nation.

Meanwhile, economic problems were becoming more severe. H. H. Kung reported that inflation for 1942 would be about 235 percent. This was a substantial rise from the 173 percent increase the previous year, but Chiang did not have to ask why prices were surging: as usual, the main problem was rising military costs. In 1940 Chungking had begun to increase the size of its army, which because of staggering casualties had dropped from 2.27 million troops in 1937 to a low of one million at the end of 1938. The large and growing U.S. military and civilian components operating in Free China were, by the end of 1942, also pouring into the economy tens of millions of *fabi*, bought with U.S. dollars from the Chinese government, and this stimulus to the printing presses was driving up prices and speeding up the rise of the black-market exchange rate. In addition, the closing of the Burma Road in the spring of 1940 and increased Japanese bombing of industrial facilities in Free China had reduced to a trickle the supply of already scarce everyday consumer goods such as textiles, clothing, and kitchen utensils, all of which rapidly became more expensive.[99]

In the fall of 1941, in order to deal with both the budget deficit and food needs in the army and the cities, the government nationalized the land tax and decreed that it would be collected in kind, that is, primarily in grain. This change required Chungking to set up an elaborate grain management bureaucracy to collect the new in-kind tax from millions of farmers. Most of the rural people—80 to 90 percent or more of Free China's population—had had little to do with the central government except for the conscription of their sons for the army.[100] But now Chiang ordered the creation of a coterie of "incorruptible functionaries" from the central government to take over the collection task from the widely despised local tax collectors. He thought this would actually improve the lot of the farmers and their attitude toward government by reducing abuse. The plan was successful in that huge amounts of grain were collected and, despite diversion along the way and spoilage, it mostly arrived in the cities and army and refugee camps. Organizationally, it was another impressive achievement. Politically, however, it was probably costly for Chiang. While there is no good way of verifying the charge, it is likely true that the central grain collecting bureaucracy in many cases simply became "a mantle of authority over the shoulders of the old extortionate collectors."[101]

Yet despite the horrendous problems, the Chinese people in Free China (and in Communist China as well) were probably still managing to survive at subsistence levels not much different than in the past. According to Arthur N. Young, the American financial adviser in Chungking, the Chinese public during this time even "retained a relatively large degree of confidence in the currency."[102]

As they had through the centuries, natural and manmade disasters regularly inflicted great tragedy on a portion of the Chinese population. Since 1937, it also seemed that at any given moment, some villages somewhere were being destroyed in horrific battles and in Japanese punitive campaigns. But most people in this vast country escaped such direct calamities and when less mortal troubles did arrive, they could usually be overcome with the help of family, clan, and village.

While it was easy to hear criticism and complaint, most Chinese continued to display their traditionally positive outlook on life. In the view of many Americans this represented a marked contrast with the citizens of some neighboring countries. Stilwell, when writing to his wife in December 1942, offered this interesting comparison: "Every trip from India to China I get a shock. In India, the natives are depressed, skinny, sick, unsmiling, apathetic.

In China they have their heads up, they are bright, cheerful, laughing and joking, well fed, relatively clean, independent, going about their business, [and] appear to have an object in life. India is hopeless."[103]

In November, Chiang told Stilwell that fifteen Chinese divisions would be ready for the offensive to retake Burma in the spring of 1943, and he promised to send another Chinese division to India (by air), raising the "X Force" there to three divisions.[104] Stilwell flew to India and informed General Archibald Wavell, still the overall commander in Burma, of the intention to proceed with the campaign "on the assumption that the Generalissimo's requirement of Allied naval and air dominance of the Bay of Bengal would be met."[105] But the British were not enthusiastic about any sort of attack into Burma. Like Chiang Kai-shek, the field marshal emphasized that the Allies "must not risk a second reverse in Burma." At the same time the War Department advised Chiang—in a message contravening the pledges of aircraft and other assistance that Roosevelt had given Chiang only the previous month—that because of other "urgent needs" he was not to expect any significant new support. Stilwell and Chiang were both irate. In an angry message, the general complained to the War Department that if this was the attitude of the United States, "it would be extremely difficult to persuade the Chinese to go forward in Burma."[106] "Peanut and I are on a raft, with one sandwich between us," he wrote his wife, "and the rescue ship is heading away from the scene. They are too busy for small fry like us."[107]

Once Stilwell calmed down, however, he simply adopted Wavell's plan for a campaign limited to North Burma, a plan he had previously denounced, but felt was better than nothing. Wavell's objective was similar to the one proposed as a contingency by Chiang in his visit to India in early 1942—to build and secure the land route from Ledo, India, to Myitkyina, and from there on to the beginning point of the Burma Road at Lashio, Burma. Roosevelt approved the Joint Chiefs' recommendation that Stilwell be allotted supplies and equipment sufficient to seize the target area and build the connector road in the north.

On December 2, Chiang wrote Roosevelt complaining bitterly about a drastic British retreat from its commitment to the Burma campaign. Promises during the year of eight British battleships, three carriers, and seven British and Indian divisions, he said, had been reduced to no capital ships and only three infantry divisions—and these only for a limited operation in North

Burma and at Akyab on the coast. Chiang asked the President to urge the British to meet their pledges to retake Rangoon and open the Burma Railway to Lashio and the old Burma Road. Again he declared categorically that China's nineteen divisions would be ready for the spring offensive, but there must be "enough air cover and air transport [air drop] capacity." If the requirements could be met, he said, the Allied forces could not only recover all of Burma but also "launch the all-out offensive on Japan and [not] have to wait for another year."[108] Chiang was clearly determined to carry out the large-scale Burma campaign as originally agreed, with his army contributing a large share of the ground forces.

Chiang wanted to take advantage of the fact that the momentum of the global war had shifted in favor of the Allies. General Georgy Zhukov had surrounded the entire German Sixth Army of 250,000 men in the destroyed city of Stalingrad and Field Marshal Alexander had decisively defeated "the Desert Fox" at El Alamein. Allied antisubmarine ships and planes were beginning to win the Battle of the Atlantic, while in the Pacific, since its stunning defeat at Midway, the Japanese had lost 1,800 planes and 2,362 of its best-trained and most experienced fliers and air crew.

On the second day of 1943, Roosevelt sent a message to Chiang saying he would be at a meeting with Churchill and the Combined Chiefs of Staff in Casablanca in a few days and would raise all the points made by the Generalissimo on Burma. Roosevelt, however, also wrote—in a portion of the message clearly drafted by the War Department—that northern Burma was a more important target than southern Burma. Marshall's staff at the War Department in turn was reflecting Stilwell's determination to push ahead with a spring campaign in Burma even if it was limited to North Burma, had little British support, and was undertaken with no assurance of air or naval superiority.

Roosevelt's message apparently was Chiang's first inkling that the Americans might agree to change drastically the scope of the campaign, and in his reply he reiterated his preference for a two-pronged attack to retake Rangoon. By this time, Wavell had reversed himself and was also advising that the monsoon would make holding North Burma a chancy matter, that a supply route to China could only be opened by taking Rangoon, and that such a campaign should not be attempted before the fall.[109] This was precisely what Chiang thought. Churchill went further. He believed that northern Burma was the worst place in the world for fighting the Japanese and that the laborious task of building a five-hundred-mile road across mountainous jungle from Ledo was unlikely to be finished until the need for it had passed (an observation that turned out to be prophetic).[110]

Stilwell, who had previously supported Chiang's conditions and goals for the campaign, now blamed postponement of the offensive on Chiang's supposed refusal to risk his forces. "Peanut says he won't fight," he wrote Marshall, and proposed that the United States threaten to get out of China "lock, stock, and barrel" unless Chiang committed his forces to the new Burma campaign.[111] This was not at all an accurate characterization of Chiang's position. But in any event neither the British nor the Americans could spare the ships and planes needed to support an early campaign in Burma. Consequently, at the Casablanca meeting the combined Allied Chiefs of Staff affirmed that the objective of the campaign would be to take Rangoon, but the offensive would be delayed until mid-November 1943.[112] This new dateline and parameters of the Burma operation, which was now dubbed Anakim, again accorded with Chiang's recommendations over the previous five months: assure sufficient air and naval support as well as a large advantage in ground forces, and aim for Rangoon. To make up for not having invited the Chinese leader to Casablanca, Roosevelt and Churchill dispatched a senior military team to Chungking to brief him on the decisions regarding Anakim. The team included General Henry "Hap" Arnold, commander of the U.S. Army Air Force, and the British representative in the Combined Chiefs of Staff, Field Marshall Sir John Dill.

In Chungking, the senior Allied envoys told Chiang that the objectives of Anakim were to open the port of Rangoon, the Burma Railway, and the Burma Road in order to obtain supplies and equipment for staging areas and airfields in China that would be used for offensive air operations against Japanese shipping and ultimately Japan proper. This was just what Chiang wanted and he approved the Anakim operation, while reiterating that command of the Bay of Bengal would have to be assured. The briefers said that Rangoon would be seized by January 1944. Arnold handed Chiang a personal letter from Roosevelt that again promised more U.S. aircraft for the China Theater.

Chiang, very pleased with the meeting, gave a banquet for the visitors at Yellow Mountain. The next day, in a private session with Arnold, Chiang complained that his requests and American commitments over the past year had largely been met with "excuses." Arnold told Chiang that measures were under way to satisfy his requests, including more aircraft. The principal question, Arnold said, was whether China would join the effort to retake Burma. Chiang's answer was an unqualified "yes," and he confirmed this in a follow-up letter to Roosevelt in which he said that the Chinese Army would be ready "to perform its assigned task at the specified time without fail."[113]

Stilwell was at the final meeting with the visitors, and in his account he "pinned Peanut down whether he would attack next fall in case limited naval support was not available." According to the Chinese minutes, Stilwell demanded, "Does this mean that unless the things you want are satisfied, China won't fight? Is this what you are saying?" Chiang replied, "China has been fighting Japan for six years. Even without Anglo-American assistance China would carry on on her own." Stilwell pressed on: "If what you said cannot be met, you don't fight the Japanese. Is this what you are saying?" Chiang replied, "They are not conditions. But as theater commander, this is my minimum request to secure victory."[114] In his diary, Chiang noted that during the meeting he had let Stilwell's behavior pass, but he sent T.V. to chastise the general for the insolent manner in which he had questioned him. Stilwell was not chastened. He followed up with a letter to Marshall saying that Chiang Kai-shek had been the one at the meeting who had been "irritable and hard to handle . . . upping his demands no matter what he is given." Chiang's attitude would persist, Stilwell once again warned, unless and until he was talked to in "sterner tones."[115]

Roosevelt saw the letter to Marshall and it convinced him that Stilwell had "exactly the wrong approach in dealing with Chiang Kai-shek." He also must have wondered why, when the meeting with Arnold had gone so well, Stilwell had put a negative spin on it. On March 8, 1943, the President sent a message to Marshall that was in effect a rebuke to Stilwell for his manner of dealing with the Generalissimo. It must be remembered, Roosevelt said, that "the Generalissimo came up the hard way to become the undisputed leader of 400 million people—[it is] an enormously difficult job to attain any kind of unity from a diverse group of all kinds of leaders—military men, [and others,] all of them struggling for power and mastery, local or national, and to create in a very short time throughout China what it took us a couple of centuries to attain." The President even sought to explain Chiang's authoritarian ways in the context of conditions in China. The Generalissimo, he told Marshall, "finds it necessary to maintain his position of supremacy. You and I would do the same thing under the circumstances. He is the Chief Executive as well as the Commander-in-Chief, and one cannot speak sternly to a man like that or exact commitments from him the way we might do from the Sultan of Morocco." The President made clear that Stilwell's idea of demanding quid quo pros from Chiang was wrong and would not work.[116]

Roosevelt also noted that Stilwell's letter had completely omitted any mention of air action in China in 1943. This was not the first time that Stilwell's strategic recommendations had simply ignored this key aspect of modern warfare. The President directed that U.S. policy emphasize the air strategy proposed by Chennault, and in response, the War Department transferred thirty transports from the planned invasion force for Sicily to the China Theater. A four-engine Liberator bomber group also soon arrived in India for deployment to China. The Flying Tigers became the 14th U.S. Air Force, and Chennault was made a major general and given its command as well as operational control of Hump aircraft, both separate from Stilwell's command. As a consolation, Marshall awarded Stilwell the Legion of Merit in the degree of chief commander.[117]

Private correspondence that Harry Hopkins at this time was receiving on the feud in Chungking had also stimulated Roosevelt's criticism of General Stilwell. These back-channel reports came from Chennault's new civilian assistant, Joseph W. Alsop, a young American journalist who was a distant cousin of Roosevelt and a close family friend of Hopkins. In his confidential letters, Alsop described Stilwell as "overbearing," and his manner toward Chinese in general that of "a bluff but not very affectionate uncle toward a hopelessly wayward nephew."[118] Alsop also supported the Chennault strategy for pushing the air war against Japan from China.

In mid-April the Japanese concentrated a large battle force to move up the Yangtze into Hubei and Hunan. The objective appeared to be to loot food supplies in central China, but the offensive would also keep pressure on the Chinese and could potentially disrupt the retraining of the Chinese Army and its plans to launch another campaign into Burma.[119] Chiang feared the offensive was intended to seize Chungking and had been precipitated by the decision pushed by Stilwell to transfer several Chinese armies from the central Yangtze to join the Y Force training in Yunnan for the Burma campaign. He ordered Chen Cheng, who was commander of the Y Force, to return from Yunnan to defend his Sixth War Zone, and to bring with him 70,000 troops from the Y Force to reinforce the defenders along the Yangtze. Stilwell was greatly upset at this diversion from his training program, and on April 16 he claimed to have had "a hell of a session" with Chiang. Stilwell insisted the Japanese offensive was only a "foray" intended to seize Chinese river steamers.[120]

III

In early February 1943, Soong Mayling and her entourage, including nephew David Kung and niece Jeanette Kung, checked out of Presbyterian Hospital and rode in their limousine to Hyde Park, the Roosevelt home in upstate New York. News of her hospital release after a three-month mysterious illness, along with her stay with Eleanor, provoked a wave of popular and media admiration. She spent six days as Eleanor's guest and then moved to the White House, where the appearance of Jeanette, who had dressed and groomed herself as a male since adolescence, confused Roosevelt, who called her "my boy." In meetings with the President, Mayling pleaded for the United States to send China the promised military aid, most especially the fighter aircraft. On February 18, she appeared on Capitol Hill to speak first to the Senate extemporaneously and then the House using a prepared text. She was the first private citizen and the first woman ever to address Congress. She wore a simple black *qi pao* with a high mandarin collar and a red lining that was revealed through a knee-high slit. Over her breast were the bejeweled wings of the hapless Chinese Air Force.[121] Texas congressman Sam Rayburn introduced her as "one of the outstanding women of all the Earth" and "helpmate and co-worker of one of the outstanding men of the entire world." She told the Senate that Chinese were fighting for the same cause as Americans—President Roosevelt's Four Freedoms, "which resound throughout our vast land as the gong of freedom, the gong of freedom of the United Nations, and the death knell of the aggressors." She protested the idea that defeat of Japan was not as important as defeat of Germany, but she did not explicitly mention the question of U.S. aid for China.[122]

The congressmen and the public were swept off their feet.[123] Eleanor Roosevelt reported that the men with whom Mayling conversed at White House meetings and dinners found her "charming, intelligent, and fascinating," but the velvet hand and the low gentle voice disguised a determination that could be hard as steel. When asked at a dinner table how she would deal with the troublesome labor leader John L. Lewis, Eleanor Roosevelt later recalled, "her beautiful, small hand came up and slid across her throat."[124]

After this dramatic beginning, Mayling embarked on a glorious speaking tour of America. Interestingly, at this point, Lauchlin Currie, who had strongly supported Chiang against Stilwell, now began to try to undercut support in Washington for both Chiangs. He complained to the State Department that Mayling's speeches on tour were critical of President Roosevelt's policy of defeating Hitler first—a not unusual or particularly provocative position for China's First Lady to take.[125] He also set up meetings between John Service, who was temporarily in Washington, and Drew Pearson, whose columns on China became more and more critical.[126] Currie also began to collect accusations regarding the funds that Mayling was raising for China's relief efforts—and was helped in this effort by FBI reports quoting sources of "unknown reliability," as well as obvious Japanese propaganda in radio reports from occupied Hong Kong regarding the supposed corruption of the Soong family.[127] In 1945 the FBI learned that Currie was at this time allegedly providing information to Elizabeth Bentley, the courier for KGB intelligence in New York.[128]

Despite directives from the White House, the long-promised five hundred additional fighter planes for China were still not on track, much less in the air. Marshall and Stimson remained opposed to the air strategy, and the War Department was moving slowly, perhaps deliberately so, in implementing the President's orders. At T. V. Soong's urging, Chiang wrote to Roosevelt calling for a concentration over the next few months of all resources in the China Theater with the goal of launching Chennault's air offensive.[129] Any Japanese counterattack against the bases, Chiang said, could "be halted by the Chinese Army."[130] Given how the Japanese had responded to the Doolittle raid and Chiang's assertion at the time that this reaction was predictable, such confidence was strange.

At Marshall's recommendation, Stilwell and Chennault were both invited to attend a symposium on the future direction of the war—the Trident Conference in Washington. The two generals traveled to Washington on the same chilly converted Liberator bomber. Stilwell clearly hated the idea of sharing the limelight with his adversary, a man who had retired in 1937 as an ROTC-commissioned Army Air Force captain.[131] The euphoric press, however, hailed both men as national heroes. A *New York Times* editorial declared that Stilwell was a diplomat beloved in Chungking: "From the Generalissimo down they all like him."[132]

At a separate meeting before the Trident Conference officially began,

Churchill made clear he still had no interest in attacking Burma and preferred invading Sumatra. He finally agreed, however, on the small campaign limited to North Burma, a decision that contradicted the commitment Roosevelt and Churchill had made to Chiang at the time of the Casablanca summit and that Hap Arnold had reaffirmed in his follow-up briefing in Chungking.[133] Also before the conference began, Stilwell and Chennault met with Roosevelt on April 30, 1943, to present their competing views on China strategy. Chennault's proposal, which he had rewritten on the plane to Washington, was a slightly modified version of the extravagantly ambitious war plan he had given Willkie back in October. All he required, he now explained, was a total of 255 fighters and bombers and 7,129 tons of monthly supplies. With this, the 14th U.S. Air Force would seize air superiority over East China and destroy Japanese shipping in an extensive and ever widening area. Chennault acknowledged the possibility that in reaction to such air attacks, Japan would launch a large-scale ground offensive to destroy the related airfields. But, like Chiang Kai-shek, he thought the Chinese army and his 14th Air Force could defeat such an offensive.

The craggy Chennault made a good impression on the President, who had heard glowing reports about him from Willkie, Currie, and Alsop. The record of Chennault's airmen in dogfights with the Japanese, although probably exaggerated (their kill-to-loss ratio against the Japanese seemed much higher than in other theaters), made him one of the most successful Allied air commanders in the war so far. Stilwell's performance at the meeting, by contrast, startled his supporters. He did not effectively explain his persuasive primary objection to the Chennault plan—that it would provoke a huge Japanese offensive that the Chinese Army and the 14th Air Force could not possibly contain. Instead, as his friend Marshall later described it, Stilwell "sat humped over with his head down and muttered something about China not fighting."[134] Stilwell's biographer later explained that he "did not have the tact or capacity to deal with opinions which he held in contempt, and contempt came to him easily."[135] But it is hard to believe that the articulate, outspoken, and forceful general became tongue-tied at the most important meeting of his career because he was overwhelmed by scorn for those in the room, including Roosevelt and Chennault. Stilwell had never been at a loss for words when talking with Chiang Kai-shek, the man for whom he had the utmost contempt. Roosevelt perceptively wondered if Stilwell could be ill, and asked Marshall if "a sick man should not be relieved."[136]

Shortly thereafter, Stilwell again saw the President without Chennault present and orally presented a message from the Generalissimo, which he probably freely recast, warning, in Stilwell's version, that without the promised aircraft the Japanese might just sail up the Yangtze and the Chinese Army just might desert to the Japanese. But once more Stilwell's poise deserted him and again he made a poor impression, "slipping" into his reputed "natural reserve."[137] He did prepare a memorandum for Roosevelt that outlined his views, emphasizing that priority, including air tonnage, must be given to the Burma campaign (Anakim) and that both the Chinese and the British must be held to their commitments—but he did not specify whether he was referring to the original Anakim or the greatly amended one.[138] Roosevelt, however, informed Marshall of his desire to give priority to the air offensive in China and to provide Chiang Kai-shek what he wanted as far as possible.

The discussion of Chennault and Stilwell's opposing strategies for China continued at the official opening of the Trident Conference, which began on May 14 at the White House. Stilwell once again, as Marshall described it, "shut up like a clam and therefore made an unfavorable impression."[139] The general did, however, make his basic point that the Chennault plan would provoke the Japanese into an offensive that would require fifty Chinese divisions to be stopped, and he doubted the Hump operation could deliver 5,000 tons monthly for the 14th U.S. Air Force. At one point, Roosevelt asked Stilwell and Chennault their opinions of Chiang Kai-shek, and on this question, Stilwell was not reserved. "He's a vacillating, tricky, undependable scoundrel," he said, "who never keeps his word." Chennault countered, "Sir, I think the Generalissimo is one of the two or three greatest military and political leaders in the world today. He has never broken a commitment or promise made to me."[140]

As the Trident discussions continued, the Japanese offensive—or "foray" as Stilwell saw it—in the central Yangtze Valley turned northwest into the mountains and headed for the Shipai Fortress, a vital doorway to the Three Gorges on the great river. Chiang flew to Hubei to take command of the battle. Supported by Chennault's few P-40s and Liberators, the fortress held and the Japanese began a retreat that became, in Chennault's words, a "bloody rout."[141] But when Chiang and Chennault claimed a striking victory, Stilwell's staff leaked stories refuting them. The Japanese, the leakers argued, had simply achieved their limited objectives and withdrawn as planned. While this conclusion was probably correct, the deliberate effort to scuttle an ally's victory claim, even if greatly exaggerated, suggested that the animosity Stilwell felt for the Generalissimo was clouding his judgment.[142]

During this period, Madame Chiang moved back into the White House for a brief stay, apparently at Mrs. Roosevelt's invitation. Meanwhile, her brother, T.V., who was now the foreign minister, attended one session of Trident and presented the Chinese position. The U.S. Army historians state without quotes that "Soong said that China would make a separate peace with Japan unless wholehearted operations to undertake its relief and discharge the post-Casablanca commitments began." This astounding statement by the foreign minister of China, if true, would seem to have deserved a full quotation from the historians. Moreover, according to the Chinese record, Soong instead said that Chiang Kai-shek was Supreme Commander of the China Theater and "we should not doubt his decisions. Otherwise, we would rethink whether we can continue to carry the responsibility of command of the China Theater." This was certainly a warning but a far more subtle and diplomatic one than reported by the U.S. Army historians.[143] In any event, the Combined Chiefs decided to ignore Chiang's strong preference and restrict the Burma operation to North Burma only. But after Soong protested the next day at the White House, Roosevelt again promised the plan would in fact encompass "operations in all of Burma."[144] Soong Mayling and T.V. did not coordinate their lobbying efforts. Acting independently, Mayling tried to persuade Hopkins that the President should communicate through her rather than her brother. Madame could in fact be very persuasive. During one meeting, she obtained the President's approval in principle for the Chinese government to use US$200 million of the US$500 million credit (offered in 1942) for the purchase of U.S. gold, which would be sold to the Chinese public as a way to fight inflation.[145]

Roosevelt also proposed solving the Stilwell-Chennault dispute by offering new war planes not to build up Chennault's forces but for the Chinese Air Force, a separate service that everyone, including Chennault, agreed was hopelessly ineffective. Madame rushed to the China Defense Supplies office on V Street in Washington and proclaimed to her brother that she had achieved everything the Generalissimo wanted. Incensed, T.V. sent the Generalissimo a request that he inform Roosevelt that Madame Chiang had no authority to negotiate on his behalf.[146] There is no account of how Chiang reacted, but evidently he supported T.V., for Mayling suddenly decided to return to Chungking, carrying a grudge against her brother.

Roosevelt emerged from Trident with a negative view of Stilwell, and in conversation with Hopkins in the presidential bedroom he expressed strong dissatisfaction with the way "our show is running in China." Stilwell, he said, hated the Chinese and his messages were "sarcastic."[147] T.V. produced, probably for Hopkins, a memorandum listing recent instances in which Stilwell had allegedly shown bad judgment, mostly involving his control of all Lend-Lease matériel destined for China. In colorful and insulting phrases worthy of Stilwell himself, Soong's memo concluded: "Stilwell does not smoke, drink, or chew. He would make a typical highly regarded Boy Scout leader in any country . . . [but] there can be no doubt that [he] . . . is completely unfitted to be a major military leader . . . His desire to be a Chinese Gordon is a good many years behind the time."[148] Hopkins did not need to be persuaded. He, in particular, was tired of Stilwell's "violent intransigence."[149]

Meanwhile, Roosevelt increasingly warmed to the idea that China, not the Pacific islands, would ultimately be the best theater for carrying the war to Japan, and as the American war dead piled up on the beaches of the Pacific, the American military chiefs began to come around to this view. "The best minds among American strategists," Hopkins told T.V., had come to believe that China should be "the principal base of operation [against Japan]."[150] Chiang Kai-shek welcomed this idea so long as the Chinese armies and Chennault received the massive matériel and equipment support necessary to counter a powerful Japanese reaction. In June, T.V. informed Chiang by radiogram that the United States had decided to give China three hundred brand-new P-40 fighters. Chiang was ecstatic about the "exciting news." The recent "Hubei victory," he believed, had been critical to raising the reputation of the 14th Air Force.[151]

The day after receiving T.V.'s report, Chiang cabled his wife with talking points for her farewell conversation with Roosevelt. He also suggested that she bring up the question of Stilwell, but not in "too serious a manner." He again described Stilwell's "arrogant personality," his "colonialist" denigration of the Chinese military, and despite Stilwell's "military failures," his "egotistical belief in his infallibility." In a quick response, Madame Chiang wondered if it was a good idea to mention the touchy issue with the President at that time. Chiang left the decision up to her, and apparently she did not raise the subject.[152]

When Stilwell returned to Chungking, he briefed Chiang on the Trident decisions, but in a peculiar affront, he at first refused to show Chiang, the supreme theater commander, the detailed naval plans for the Burma campaign, saying they were too sensitive—and then when Chiang insisted, he provided only a translation. Three Allied battleships and eight carriers were to take part in the campaign, another key commitment that Chiang was delighted to have acquired. On July 12, he suggested that the proposed air strength be increased, but he also formally agreed to the Trident battle plan, which accorded with his own ideas from the beginning—assured air and sea dominance.[153]

Within weeks, however, the commitments began to unravel. The next Anglo-American summit opened in Quebec on August 19 to consider strategy following the expected surrender of Italy. Chiang was angry at being excluded again. In his diary he denounced the "inequality . . . snobbishness and power" of "international society," and he fired off a telegram of complaint. As a result, the Allies invited T. V. Soong, who hurried to Canada only to cable the Generalissimo on the first day that he had "yet to meet anybody."[154] That was unusual, since at this so-called Quadrant Conference, the Allied Combined Chiefs agreed that China offered the best potential as a base for attacking Japanese shipping, for bombing Japan, and eventually for invading the Japanese home islands. According to the plan, Allied troops would land on the coast of China while retrained and rearmed Chinese armies advanced from the west. After linking up, the combined forces would march on North China. Meanwhile, the American Air Force would bomb Japan from China using the new amazing B-29s, which had a range of 2,600 kilometers and carried five tons of bombs.[155] The new British commander for India and Burma, General Claude Auchinleck, reported to the military chiefs his belief in the "futility" of any operation in Burma, and Churchill continued to grouse that it would be a complete waste.[156] Nevertheless, the chiefs affirmed that the campaign to take North Burma would begin in February 1944. They did not, however, mention taking Rangoon or refer to the substantial naval commitment made at the Trident Conference.

Although Stilwell had made a bad impression in Washington in May, as soon as he returned to Chungking he began explicitly to articulate to himself in a little "black copy book" his dream of overall command of all Chinese armies in the field, including the Communists. This would require a new position for him in the Chinese military called "field chief of staff." Such a position would give him "absolute authority" over all Chinese troops in the field while Chiang Kai-shek would only "ostensibly" be in overall charge and Chen Cheng "ostensibly" in command in the field. If Chiang did not agree to this scheme, Stilwell thought, he could "go to hell" and the United States would stop all aid to China.[157] The sixty-one-year-old Yankee who only four years earlier had been a long-serving U.S. Army colonel without combat experience now envisioned himself becoming in effect the most powerful man in the country of 400 million, usurping the Chinese icon who had led this immense and ancient country and its army for almost two decades.

Stilwell's deputy, Colonel Frank ("Pinky") Dorn, worked out the details of Stilwell's scheme in concert with "serious thinking Chinese officers" who wanted "a decided change at the top" and who had told Dorn that Chiang's control was "shaky."[158] The Chinese government would have considered these discussions treasonous. Stilwell intended to plant his bold idea informally with Marshall during the upcoming Cairo Conference, but if possible also with President Roosevelt. In August, warming up for the command he envisioned, he sent memos to Chiang proposing to employ Communist troops in a joint offensive and to reorganize all armed forces in China into national defense and local garrison forces. To Chiang these memos reflected "gross interference" in Chinese internal affairs, and he ignored them.[159]

Washington's political battle over its China strategy would, Stilwell knew, be heavily influenced by the press. Before returning from Washington after the Trident Conference, he spent time on the hill offering his views to selected congressmen. John Davies, who was in town to assist him, arranged for the publisher of the *Washington Post,* Eugene Meyer, to give a dinner for Stilwell with six or eight leading correspondents. Twenty others joined in after the dinner to listen to the general's off-the-record exposition. Unlike in his meetings with Roosevelt, Stilwell was convincing and the *New York Times* soon ran a critical article based on the reports of Hanson Baldwin entitled "Too Much Wishful Thinking about China."[160] Davies would provide the same sort of briefing to numerous individual Western journalists, diplomats, and others over the next year and a half in Chungking and the United States. It was unusual for a U.S. diplomat on his own authority to organize a major media campaign in the United States for the purpose of conveying a comprehensive indictment of a wartime ally who was still held in favor by the U.S. President, but Davies completely shared Stilwell's views.

At the same time, Chennault, Alsop, and T. V. Soong were touting the opposite views in their own backgrounders to the press and Congress. While Chennault was in Washington in May 1943, he enjoyed three private talks with Roosevelt, who told him to write personally and let him know "how things were going." This back-door route to the Oval Office was highly ir-

regular for an active-duty general and infuriated Stilwell and Stimson as well
as Marshall, who told Chennault to his face he did not trust him.[161]

On September 13, Stilwell was summoned to the Chiangs' in-town Chungking residence overlooking the river. There he met Mayling and Ai-ling. According to Stilwell's diary, the Soong women told him they were alarmed
at the Chinese Army's inadequate military preparations. Stilwell agreed with
their concerns and named those responsible for the problems—most importantly, the army's chief of staff, He Yingqin. Someone at this meeting
(Stilwell's diary is not clear who) suggested that one remedy would be to have
Mayling become minister of war, in place of He. Mayling had lobbied
strongly against Stilwell when she was in Washington and it is unclear why
she would suddenly be willing to form an alliance with him. Certainly rivalry
with her brother was a factor. She no doubt resented the way that he and the
Generalissimo had rebuked her for meddling in affairs of state in Washington
and wanted to resume her position as the key handler of American affairs for
the Generalissimo.

Without explaining their motives to Stilwell, the two women agreed with
everything he said, and the three of them "signed an offensive and defensive alliance." "They mean business," he wrote. Between October 13 and 18,
Stilwell recorded ten meetings with the sisters, who ranted against He Yingqin
("a terribly conceited little monkey"), grumbled about the difficulty of handling the Generalissimo, and took credit for pushing Chiang to resist the
Japanese in recent fighting around Yichang.[162] Mayling reputedly "let out she
has a hell of a life with the Gimo" and claimed only she could tell him the
truth.[163]

At just this time, the oldest male Soong was still in Washington and very
close at last to arranging Stilwell's removal. On August 21, T.V. met with
Roosevelt and said that if Stilwell was not transferred, there would be "cause
for concern about Sino-American cooperation." The President replied that
he was also concerned about the matter, and Soong reported this exchange
to Chiang. (Madame Chiang had probably read this exchange of messages
and subsequently called Stilwell to the surprise meeting.) In a farewell call by
Soong on September 16, Roosevelt agreed to replace Stilwell, and before he
left town Soong was also told (perhaps by Hopkins) that Marshall no longer
regarded Stilwell highly.[164]

Soong and U.S. Army Services Chief General Brehon Somervell flew to

Chungking, where on October 13, Soong cabled Hopkins saying it was agreed—the Generalissimo would raise the question of Stilwell's replacement and Somervell would formally transmit the request to Washington.[165] At this point Somervell received a War Department message that he was to remain in Chungking until he received further instructions, leading him to the alarming conclusion that he was to be Stilwell's replacement, a fate he did not desire.

Somervell did everything he could to convince the Generalissimo to give the general another chance.[166] He also privately told Stilwell that the Generalissimo insisted he be relieved and that Roosevelt had twice sought his recall. Stilwell wrote in his diary, "I guess that's that."[167] But Chiang's decision was not yet firm. In his journal he declared that his relations with the United States, the upcoming Burma offensive, and the attitude of the Chinese military should take precedence in the matter.[168] He was doubtless also afraid that if the squabble caused a crisis with the United States, his internal enemies could try to force his removal.

When T.V. returned to Chungking he learned to his astonishment that his sisters were pressing Chiang to retain Stilwell, whose forced departure, they maintained, would be a disaster for China. In the Chiang villa, an extraordinary family battle ensued, about which Alsop received nightly rundowns from T.V. He Yingqin, whom both Stilwell and Soong Mayling despised, joined the argument on the side of the women.[169] He may have thought that with Stilwell around the Generalissimo would be weakened and might retire or be overthrown before Japan's surrender, leaving the way open for himself to take power.

On October 16, Louis Lord Mountbatten, the new commander of the Allied Southeast Asia Command, flew into Chungking. When asked by Chiang, Mountbatten insisted on the retention of Stilwell, whom he had just approved as his own deputy, concurrent with Stilwell's other positions.[170] Persuaded by all these voices and afraid that Marshall and even Roosevelt might be offended despite what T.V. had been told, Chiang asked his wife to tell Stilwell that it would not be good for the general's reputation to be recalled, but if he could apologize and change his ways the Generalissimo might forgive him.[171] The two sisters urged Stilwell to humble himself, to admit that he had made mistakes, to apologize, and to promise to make amends. Stilwell reports he hesitated a long time but the women insisted and he finally agreed.[172]

Accompanied by his new female backers, he met with Chiang on the eve-

ning of October 17. According to Chinese accounts, Stilwell said he was sincere in wanting to help China and any misunderstandings were due to his
"thoughtlessness." He promised the offense would not occur again. Chiang
lectured the general on the duties of the Supreme Commander and his chief
of staff and suggested Stilwell curb his "superiority complex." Stilwell promised to be an adviser to Chiang, the principal officer.[173]

Chennault was sitting in the anteroom waiting to see the Generalissimo
when Madame rushed out of Chiang's office and announced that Stilwell had
agreed to obey his Supreme Commander. Chiang separately called in T.V. for
a breakfast meeting. Soong, in high spirits, started out by reporting that he
had at last secured the unqualified support and understanding of the U.S.
administration for Stilwell's removal. Chiang replied that he had been very
much concerned about Stilwell's unwillingness to follow orders but that
Stilwell had pledged he would in the future obey his instructions *(ting hua)*
and be much more cooperative. Therefore, he had decided to give Stilwell
another chance.[174]

Soong was upset. All for nothing he had won the approval of the President of
the United States for the recall of the man who, since he arrived, had been
the bane of the Generalissimo's existence. Soong argued that Chiang must
not pass up this chance to remove Stilwell. At one point, he demanded, "Are
you the chief of an African tribe that you should change your mind so capriciously?" At this, Chiang slammed his fist on his little breakfast table and the
dishes clattered to the ground.[175] Back at his residence, T.V. revealed to Alsop
what had happened and burst into tears.[176] But for the time being the matter
seemed settled. The next day, Stilwell, Chennault, and Somervell had tea at
the residence with the Chiangs and everyone chatted as if they had always
been friends.[177]

Mountbatten had come to Chungking to convene an official Allied military conference to discuss the Burma campaign. Held at Yellow Mountain,
this was to be the first official conference of this sort in China. On the first
day, T.V. as foreign minister escorted the distinguished visitors into the sitting room where his youngest sister was waiting. The English lord, well
known as a ladies' man, found her "most striking looking and extremely
handsome . . . [with] the most lovely legs and feet imaginable." She then carried on a rapid but low conversation with her brother, in which, Mountbatten assumed, she told him to get out, for T.V. mopped his brow, said he was

not feeling well, and withdrew, not to be seen again by the callers or virtually anyone important for many months.[178]

When the Generalissimo arrived, Lord Louis found him "a most arresting person . . . the most impressive Chinese he had ever seen." Although privately Chiang was outraged that the Combined Chiefs had sought to take Thailand and Indochina out of Chiang's theater and put them under Mountbatten, the official meetings over the next two days "could hardly have gone better." The Generalissimo and the admiral worked out a compromise in which the two countries officially remained under the China Theater but either command could operate there. Mountbatten left with "a real feeling of affection and regard" for his host.[179]

Soong wrote an abject apology to the Generalissimo but Chiang, who had been profoundly insulted when T.V. compared him to an African chief, put him under virtual house arrest. During the winter, Soong and Alsop often went for walks along the cold, empty rice paddies. Stilwell, meanwhile, was riding high and made no pretense in his diary and letters that he had been serious in promising to change his ways. He told his wife that through "the whole mess" he had felt "free as air . . . grand and glorious." He described "Peanut's" lecture on October 17 as "all balderdash."[180] In Chiang's diary and actions, by contrast, it was clear that the Generalissimo was genuinely reconciled with Stilwell. Chiang Kai-shek was not one to hold a grudge.

During that summer of 1943 Chiang had written in his diary that he did not need to force the CCP to dissolve; rather he thought his main strategy should be to employ politics and propaganda in ways that would encourage "inner rifts" among the Communists, rifts that he thought were then widening.[181] There was in fact evidence at this time of another split developing between Mao and the "internationalists" in the party, including Zhou. According to papers in the Russian archives, Georgi Dimitrov sent an NKVD (pre-KGB) agent to Chungking to make contact with Zhou's liaison headquarters and report on what was going on within the CCP. This Chinese agent, Gao Dong (whose Russian name was Godunov) met several times with Zhou Enlai and others in Zhou's office in Chungking. Drawing on these sources and apparently sending cables through the military attaché office in the Soviet Embassy, Gao reported that an anti-Chiang campaign in Yan'an was intensifying and that its principal theme was to warn of the danger of a massive KMT attack on the CCP's base area. Cartoons in the Communist papers and wall posters, Godunov reported, showed Chiang together with Hitler, Tojo, and Mussolini. The new slogan in Yan'an was the old pre-1937 shibboleth: "Struggle against Japan *and* Chiang Kai-shek."[182] Peter Vladimirov, a Soviet military intelligence (GRU) agent in Yan'an who had been consistently critical of Mao, reported that the Chairman took credit for this "vilification" of Chiang Kai-shek, saying it should have been undertaken much earlier.[183]

Stalin did not oppose this violation of the principles of the united front. With the Germans in full retreat after the great tank battle at Kursk, Stalin was already thinking about postwar China and the need to increase pressure on Chiang. Newspapers in Moscow picked up on the theme, charging that Chiang had given an ultimatum to the CCP to surrender. Hearing the accusations about a forthcoming KMT attack, Stilwell and U.S. Ambassador Clarence Gauss sent alarming messages to Washington, and Marshall cabled T. V. Soong to express grave concern.[184] Chiang saw these charges as part of a "Russian conspiracy."[185]

Interestingly, Chiang also suspected that the rumors and the CCP attacks on him were part of a "big conspiracy against Zhou Enlai." He speculated that Mao hoped to provoke him (Chiang) into attacking Yan'an and thereby provide the Chairman with a pretext to, among other things, purge Zhou.[186] Dimitrov's agent reported that the campaign in Yan'an was now criticizing Zhou and several other leaders as "right opportunists" and "internationalists" who had disseminated "illusions about Chiang Kai-shek." Mao himself told Vladimirov that the targets of the internal campaign were "defeatists" who had harmed the party by their capitulatory policy toward the KMT.[187] This criticism directly implicated Zhou Enlai.

Mao's internal campaign ended without the major split Chiang had hoped for. Instead, according to Gao's reports to Dimitrov and Vladimirov's reports to the GRU, Zhou was removed from the Secretariat of the Politburo, admitted his mistakes in accommodating the KMT, and once again aligned his thinking with Mao's.[188] In fact, Chiang soon received intelligence that Zhou, as secretary of the CCP's South Bureau, had ordered a new and intensified campaign to recruit KMT officials as underground CCP members. For Chiang this was another indicator that Mao was girding up for the postwar struggle.[189]

In September, while Chiang was still struggling with the decision on Stilwell, he was increasingly riled by CCP military provocations against government units. Stilwell's promotion of joint action with the Communists, he believed, had made the CCP "more violent and audacious."[190] In one rumination he wrote that it was best to have "a military solution" to the CCP problem and "do it before the end of the German-Russian War."[191] He informed Soong in Washington that he had not planned to use force against the CCP, but "this time, in order to correct the public's perception and to maintain the authority of the Government, I have decided to use disciplinary punishment."[192] After thinking overnight about the military and political consequences, however, the next day Chiang informed Soong that "even disciplinary measures will not be taken."[193]

On September 13, the KMT's Central Committee issued an eighteen-page booklet on the crimes of the CCP, including CCP attacks on KMT troops, its illegal expansion of military forces, the issuance of its own currency, and its alleged smuggling of opium.[194] Five days later, despite the harsh rhetoric on both sides, the Communist representative Dong Biwu attended a session of the multiparty National Political Participation Council in Chungking. Meanwhile, Mao's message—informally passed to the Americans by Zhou and others—was that despite the intensified rhetoric, including alarms about a KMT attack, the CCP was still committed to the united front and the "democratic" political process. About this time, Zhou met with Edgar Snow in Chungking and expressed the hope that American military and journalist delegations would soon visit Yan'an. Snow immediately passed this comment to the Americans. At the same time, John P. Davies, in Stilwell's office, began officially promoting to Washington the idea of Stilwell's embarking on an official visit to CCP territory.

Stalin, concerned about the reaction of both Japan and the CCP, refused to attend the next Allied summit meeting if Chiang Kai-shek was included. Chiang likewise did not want to meet Stalin, so two conferences were scheduled, one at Cairo attended by the American, British, and Chinese leaders, and the other at Tehran, where Stalin would meet with Roosevelt and Churchill. The gathering in Cairo was scheduled to begin in mid-November. Ten days before it started, FDR sent former secretary of war Brigadier General Patrick Hurley to brief the Chinese leader. Chiang was moved by this gesture of "goodwill and sincerity." The President's "chivalry and nobility," he wrote privately, had reached "a state of sublimity."[195]

Sixty-one-year-old Hurley was a tall, boisterous, strong-headed Oklahoman. He had been raised next to a Choctaw Indian Reservation, and after graduating from Indian College and then law school had become the national attorney for the Choctaw Nation. Hurley had learned the piercing Choctaw war cry, earned medals as a hero at Argonne and other World War I battles, and served as secretary of war for Herbert Hoover. A strict Republican who disagreed with everything Roosevelt was doing domestically, he was delighted to take on difficult projects abroad for the President, including trying unsuccessfully to run supplies into besieged Bataan.[196] Once in China, Hurley told Stilwell that in the United States Stilwell was viewed as "the savior of China."[197]

Beginning August 12, Hurley conferred with Chiang for three days. Responding to written questions from FDR, Chiang confirmed that he was unwilling to meet Stalin but would cooperate militarily with the Soviet Union in the war against Japan. Hurley said the American postwar policy would be to oppose all forms of imperialism, including that of the British, and to favor a free, strong, and democratic China as the predominant and stabilizing force in Asia. Chiang told Hurley that he was grateful for President Roosevelt's "great moral leadership."[198]

While preparing his own briefing points for Cairo, Chiang, in his diary, stressed adopting a "high moral position," specifically by not asking for material aid.[199] Before leaving, he approved the broad proposals that Stilwell had drawn up for presentation at Cairo, including an "all-out" Allied effort in early 1944 to reopen a truck route to China through Burma, using land, air, and naval forces; American arms and equipment for ninety Chinese divisions; and 10,000 tons a month over the Hump to support air operations in China. This was essentially what Chiang had been advocating for the Burma campaign for eighteen months—overwhelming force. But Stilwell, with emphasis, jotted in his diary that day the word "VICTORY," as if he had wrung this agreement from Chiang.[200] Taking his cue from Stilwell's reporting, Marshall made the remarkably incorrect statement that it was "the first time since the war began that the Generalissimo had shown an active interest in the improvement and employment of his Army."[201] From the beginning, Chiang had tried to relieve Hong Kong, volunteered his best armies to fight in Burma, supported Stilwell's training of the X Force in India and the Y Force in Yunnan, fought major battles at Changsha and Ichang, lost 30,000 men resisting Japanese punitive campaigns following the Doolittle raid—and now he was ready, even eager, to send a total of eighteen divisions into the second Burma campaign provided there was air and sea dominance. At this time, Chiang also agreed to Stilwell's proposal for appointing an American commander for a joint Sino-American force if and when MacArthur landed troops in South

China. This concept, however, was far different than Stilwell's idea that he himself command all Chinese armies in the field.

Ai-ling reported to Vinegar Joe that Chiang was in "a jubilant state of mind" about the upcoming Cairo summit. From his diaries it is evident that Chiang was starting a new, positive chapter in his relations with Stilwell. But this effort was not repaid in kind. Displaying his new trust in his American chief of staff, Chiang requested that Stilwell make the report for China at the Cairo meeting. But after hearing this, Stilwell went back to his room and wrote, "I heard him rattle his tail."[202] Stilwell's diaries had in fact become increasingly mean-spirited. Before leaving for Cairo and his expected meetings with Roosevelt, for example, he referred to the American President as "rubber legs."[203]

Stilwell arrived in Cairo ahead of the Chiangs to meet with Marshall, who suggested that Stilwell leave China because he was so mistreated there. When Stilwell said he wished to remain, Marshall ordered, "Then stop your outrageous talking!" Immediately understanding what Marshall meant, Stilwell protested that he had not called Chiang "Peanut" openly. "My God," retorted Marshall, "You have never lied. Don't start now . . . Stop talking to your staff about these things."[204] But Stilwell did not stop.

6

The China Theater

At dawn on November 21, 1943, the Generalissimo and Madame Chiang arrived by plane in Cairo for the conference with Roosevelt, Churchill, and assorted brass. Chennault, who had not been invited by the War Department and was attending as chief of staff of the Chinese Air Force, met the First Couple and escorted them to their villa. Madame Chiang was suffering from conjunctivitis and fatigue from the long journey and did not participate in a brief morning call on Churchill and Mountbatten, but at 6:30 in the evening both Chiangs had a meeting with the prime minister. Churchill was irritated with Roosevelt's idea that one of the four powers in the postwar world would be the poor, huge, anti-imperialist, anticolonialist, non-European nation of China, and he wanted to do as little as possible militarily in the Burma campaign. Still, Churchill recorded that he "was impressed by [Chiang's] calm, reserved, and efficient personality" and found Madame "most remarkable and charming."[1] Chiang, after his initial encounters with the prime minister, pronounced him "calm and resolute" and thought, "No wonder he is the vanguard against Japan and the Communists." But after four days of talks he would change his mind.

The conference opened the next day at the old Mena Hotel with its striking view of the pyramids. At the first plenary meeting of the three leaders, the Combined Chiefs, and various staff members, the only woman was Chiang Soong Mayling. The British chief of staff, Field Marshal Lord Alanbrooke, reports that as she shifted her legs about under her slit skirt he thought he heard "a suppressed neigh" coming from the younger officers. By contrast, Alanbrooke described her husband, the Chinese leader, as "a cross between a pine marten and a ferret" and on day one concluded he had "no grasp of war in its larger prospect."[2] But Alanbrooke did not understand that Chiang believed he would resolve all the really important military and political matters affecting China directly with Roosevelt and that the other meetings were in no way decisive.

Mountbatten presented his operational plan for the offensive into North Burma, Operation Champion, which called for a much more restricted campaign than did the Stilwell plan approved by Chiang Kai-shek or what Roosevelt and others had promised the Chinese in Washington and elsewhere. Operation Champion did not come close to an "all-out air-land-and-naval effort" to open up the land route to China; instead it proposed only to secure a bridgehead across the Chindwin River and to make an airborne landing on the railway to Myitkyina. It was not at all clear what would happen next. The plan did include an amphibious landing, but only on the Andaman Islands, the occupation of which would do little to disrupt Japanese supply lines in Burma.[3] In a critique provided to Mountbatten in October, Stilwell had criticized Operation Champion as "permeated by fear," and described the invasion of the Andamans as an "abortion."[4]

During the opening session in Cairo, Mountbatten explained that Operation Champion would include an Allied force of 320,000 men, of whom 160,000 would be Indian and Burmese troops, 20,000 British special forces, 3,000 American special forces, and 137,000 Chinese soldiers from the divisions trained in India and Yunnan—the X and Y forces. Churchill surprisingly promised that the Royal Navy would send two large battleships, four large carriers, and ten small carriers to assure command of the Bay of Bengal. When it came his turn, Chiang was pleased but emphasized strongly again that a major amphibious operation and naval supremacy were essential, Mandalay rather than Myitkyina should be the target, and the Hump air transport operation should deliver 10,000 tons a months to China.[5] Hopkins later wrote that Chiang was usually reluctant to commit himself on specific details.[6] But while the Chinese leader saved his real negotiations for his talks with Roosevelt, he also seemed concise and to the point in the joint meetings, and, it turned out, prescient regarding the likely size of the Japanese forces the Allies would encounter. Here is an abridged segment of Chiang's remarks at the November 23 session: "The success of the Burma operations depends not only on the strength of the naval forces established in the Indian Ocean but on the simultaneous coordination of naval action with the land operations. If the naval forces are not assembled, the mere concentration of land troops would not bring about sure victory . . . The forces the enemy could deploy in Burma could reach ten divisions and if we do not cut his line of reinforcement, his forces could be increased."[7]

That evening, the Chiangs were Roosevelt's dinner guests at the residence of the American ambassador, where the President was staying.[8] Hopkins was the only other guest. Madame, wearing her open-toed shoes and black silk *qi pao,* greeted her old friend of the past year, the President. Both sides had interpreters sitting nearby, but Mayling frequently corrected her husband's. The long evening of frank conversation reinforced Chiang's almost reverential feeling for Roosevelt as a statesman with a "transcendental bearing."[9] Chiang's high, staccato voice and formal courtesy before an honored person of power, by contrast, did not stir feelings of camaraderie in the flamboyant, relaxed American.

In their long and serious evening discussion, however, the two men seemed to agree on virtually all matters. Chiang concurred with Roosevelt's view that Japan's future form of government should be left to the Japanese people and he proposed that reparations could be paid to China in Japanese industrial and war machinery, merchant ships, and other actual properties. He thought that America should be the largest occupying Allied power in Japan, but Roosevelt insisted that Chinese troops should play that role. Chiang also agreed with Roosevelt's "analysis of communism," stressing that Moscow could not be trusted, but said he would follow the President's lead on relations with the Soviet Union. Roosevelt firmly endorsed the return of Manchuria and Taiwan to China.[10] As they had in their earlier correspondence, they also agreed on their vision of the postwar world, especially the need to end colonialism. In addition, Chiang mentions without giving details that the two leaders discussed Soviet participation in the war against Japan and the situation in Xinjiang. Chiang summed up the talk as "exceedingly satisfactory." Roosevelt had treated him "like an old friend."[11]

The next morning, November 24, the President's son, Elliot, found his father breakfasting in bed and asked what was happening. "A lot," the President replied, "I've met the Generalissimo." When Elliot asked what he thought of the Chinese leader, his father first shrugged, and then said he had "learned more just talking to the Chiangs last night than I did from more than four hours of meeting with the Combined Chiefs."[12] But while Chiang had described at some length the poor state of the Chinese Army, Roosevelt told his son some questions remained: "why Chiang's troops aren't fighting at all," why Chiang was "trying to stop Stilwell from training Chinese troops," and why he kept "thousands and thousands of his best men . . . on the borders of

Red China."[13] In sum, the President, reflecting his briefings, remained convinced that Chiang was inexplicably resisting General Stilwell's efforts to redress the problems facing the Chinese Army. Nevertheless, Roosevelt was "determined that Cairo be a success from the Chinese [that is, Chiang's] point of view."[14]

The next day, Mountbatten called on the Generalissimo and Madame to explain why the more ambitious plan aiming for Mandalay was not possible for logistical reasons. Decades later, Mountbatten told Stilwell's biographer, Barbara Tuchman, that the Generalissimo evidently had not understood the term "monsoon," and that Madame Chiang had explained that the Generalissimo "does not know about monsoons." Tuchman refers twice to this story and asserts that China did not have monsoons, "*ergo,* he [Chiang] knew nothing of them," and further, that this exchange was "enlightening proof" of "Stilwell's difficulties with the Gimo."[15] But Chiang's memos, letters, and diaries on many occasions refer to the "rainy season" *(yu ji)* in Burma and its obvious military implications. It seems that he was simply not familiar with the Portuguese-origin word "monsoon." In such a manner do seemingly revealing but totally misunderstood statements become part of a historic legend if they fit a preconceived stereotype. That afternoon, Mountbatten reported to the Combined Chiefs that Chiang had accepted the implication of reduced air support, was highly pleased with the British fleet that was to be made available, and would give the campaign his enthusiastic support.[16]

But as with the word "monsoon," Mountbatten had also misunderstood Chiang, mistakenly believing that the Chinese leader was now enthusiastic about the overall British plan. Part of the problem was probably Mayling Soong's interpreting, in which she tried to make Chiang's remarks as positive as possible. Mountbatten's confusion was confirmed an hour or so later when Chiang had a private lunch with Marshall. In a level-headed discussion, Chiang told the American that he opposed the British plan because he was convinced it "would lead to heavy losses and possibly defeat." He repeated his call for an amphibious landing and added that the Chinese troops from Yunnan—the Y Force—should not advance beyond Lashio. The U.S. record did not report any disagreement by Marshall.[17] In fact, throughout the Cairo Conference, Marshall and the other American service chiefs would strongly support Chiang's insistence on the full implementation of the amphibious landing in Burma, Operation Buccaneer.[18]

That evening, Churchill entertained the Chiangs at dinner. The prime minister surprised his guest by saying that the attack by sea could not take place before May 1944, by which time the rainy season would have begun. Otherwise, however, the dinner was another totally agreeable affair. That same evening Hopkins visited the Chiangs with the U.S. draft of the communiqué of the summit meeting. Chiang found in the draft "every opinion" he had mentioned to Roosevelt the previous night. He wrote that he was moved by Roosevelt's sincerity as expressed in the favorable communiqué.[19]

On Thanksgiving Day, November 25, Chiang and his wife sat in white wicker chairs in the American ambassador's garden for their famous photographs with Roosevelt and Churchill. The Chiangs and Roosevelt then had tea and later, at 5:00, with only Elliot present, the three met again, this time for seventy-five minutes.[20] Roosevelt told Chiang that his "biggest headache" was Churchill. "Britain," he said, "simply does not want to see China become a power." Roosevelt and Chiang again agreed that in the new world order the British would have to abandon their empire.[21] In regard to Burma, the two men confirmed their accord on the need for an amphibious operation and the need to persuade the British to arrange an earlier time for the deployment of their naval forces.[22] Pressed by Roosevelt, Chiang said he would establish a unity government with the CCP while the war was still going on, provided the United States (1) assured that in the future the Soviet Union would respect China's sovereignty in Manchuria, and (2) supported the ending of British "Empire rights" in Hong Kong and elsewhere in China.[23]

Chiang told Roosevelt that his personal opinion on a unity (KMT and CCP) government in China was off the record—that is, for the President's reference only—but that their views on the subject were the same.[24] Roosevelt then informed Chiang that the United States would provide American arms and training for a full ninety Chinese divisions, just as Chiang desired.[25] The meeting was another highly successful one for the two Presidents.

According to Stilwell, after Roosevelt's meeting with Chiang, which went on until sometime between 6:15 p.m. and 6:30 p.m., the President informed Marshall and Stilwell that Chiang was ready to carry out "the Burma plan," including sending in the Y Force, on the two conditions, which Roosevelt fully supported—assured control of the Bay of Bengal and a simultaneous amphibious operation.[26] At this point, the story becomes confused with allegations that Chiang within an hour or two completely reversed himself "on every single point" as well as strong evidence that this was not true. It is worth examining this incident in its brief but excruciating detail as another example of how distortions in history are perpetuated and how General Stilwell did business.

Stilwell relates that late in the evening of November 25, Hopkins sent for him—"got there at 10:30, band played—whoopee—talked to Churchill," and finally, "Hopkins says G-mo as of 6:00PM does not like the plan [for Burma]."[27] The plan Hopkins was referring to was almost certainly the British one, a plan that Mountbatten had mistakenly thought Chiang had, in their conversation early on November 24, come to support. Chiang's agreement, however, was not with Mountbatten but with Roosevelt, as confirmed in Chiang's conversation with Marshall immediately after seeing Mountbatten on the morning of November 24 and in his 5:00 p.m. to 6:15 p.m. session with Roosevelt on November 25 as the President immediately thereafter reported to Marshall and Stilwell. Hopkins's statement "as of 6:00PM" should have made all this clear. But Stilwell's reaction in his diary to Hopkins's comment was "My God. He's off again," implying that Hopkins had said Chiang had reversed the position he had taken with the President. Actually, the President's log for that day records that at 10:30 p.m. that same evening, Stilwell had a meeting with the President, and Elliot Roosevelt, who was present, records that the general discussed his "difficulties with Chiang" but nothing about the Generalissimo going back on his agreements with the President on Burma—a subject that would certainly have been raised had it happened. In his diary, Stilwell strangely reports nothing about this meeting with Roosevelt, which may have been an informal one in a recreational setting ("the band").[28]

The next morning, November 26, Marshall, according to Mountbatten, told him that "in the evening" the Generalissimo had had another meeting with Roosevelt at which he had "gone back on every single point to which he had agreed to before lunch." Chiang's recent meeting "before lunch" was on November 24 with Mountbatten, not Roosevelt or Marshall, and thus what Chiang had allegedly gone back on was his supposed approval of the British plan as Mountbatten had misunderstood him to say. Thus it seems evident that the story of the reversal emerged from Mountbatten's confusion as to what Chiang had told him at their morning meeting and possibly by Stilwell's misreporting of Hopkins's remark. The President's log at Cairo reports no other meeting between Chiang and Roosevelt after their 5:00 p.m. to 6:15 p.m. session, and Roosevelt, Chiang, Hopkins, Churchill, and Elliot Roosevelt in their various papers or conversations never mentioned a late meeting between Roosevelt and Chiang on November 25 or the Chinese leader's supposed reversal of position.[29]

To conjecture, Stilwell very likely heard from Mountbatten's staff or from

Mountbatten himself that Chiang had surprisingly approved their plan, but on November 25, sometime after 10:30 p.m., Hopkins told Stilwell that Chiang did not in fact like the British plan. Stilwell's report of this conversation must have mistakenly led Marshall to assume that the reversal was about the American-Chinese plan and that there must have been a second unsatisfactory Roosevelt-Chiang meeting in the evening. Upon hearing Marshall pass on the secondhand version of what Hopkins had told Stilwell, Mountbatten "dashed around to Hopkins" who gave him the unspecified "lowdown," that is, the news that Chiang had indeed rejected the British plan.[30]

In his diary, Stilwell does not offer a substantially different account than Chiang's regarding events on November 26. Although he starts off by noting, vaguely, "Louis [Mountbatten] in at 11:00 to spill the dope [presumably about the reversal]. He is fed up on Peanut. As who is not," Stilwell surprisingly makes no further reference to Chiang's dramatic supposed turnaround the previous day. On the morning of November 26, Chiang did have a session with Stilwell and a group of other American generals on the "Hump tonnage issue," and Chiang records that "the atmosphere" was good—in part, he had "heard," because Roosevelt had praised his "abilities" at a meeting (among Americans) the previous night. Stilwell reports that Chiang finally accepted the generals' promise simply to try to meet his tonnage target.[31]

According to Mountbatten's account, Roosevelt and Churchill, after hearing of Chiang's supposed complete turnaround of the previous day, had tea with the Chiangs on the afternoon of November 26 without a note taker. Chiang records that he visited Roosevelt at 3:00 p.m. and they discussed a U.S. loan to China, Outer Mongolia, and Tibet. On the subject of the date of the British amphibious landing, Chiang wrote only that Roosevelt "agreed again" on advancing the date and that only Churchill disagreed. Chiang assumed that he and Roosevelt were in complete accord—and they were. Meanwhile, the Combined Chiefs had met at 2:30 p.m. without the Chinese, during which time Marshall said it was "essential" that the amphibious operation (Buccaneer) go forward because the forces were available, it was vital to operations in the Pacific, it was "acceptable to the Chinese," and for "political reasons could not be interfered with." This was a strong statement of support for the Chiang-Roosevelt plan. The presidential log reports the single Chiang-Roosevelt get-together on November 26 as a 4:30 p.m. conference between all three national leaders, Madame Chiang, and others during which time the communiqué was approved, and various subjects were discussed, including the economic situation in China, postwar security in the

Pacific, equipment for ninety Chinese divisions, and postwar international organization. After this session, Churchill and Madame Chiang told Mountbatten that Chiang was in agreement on every point, which he had been since his meeting with Roosevelt the previous day.[32]

Another curious report by Stilwell the next day sheds more light on the conundrum. Chiang and his wife rose early on November 27 and made a dash to the pyramids, then headed for their airplane for the long flight home via India. Before boarding, however, Chiang asked Stilwell to stay behind to be present when the Combined Chiefs officially endorsed the amphibious operation.[33] After politely seeing off the Chiangs, Stilwell rushed to see Mountbatten. He "staggered" the Englishman, saying—according to the South East Asia Command Diary—that he had been ordered "to stay put and protest. I am to stick out for Toreador [the code word for an airborne assault on Mandalay] and 10,000 tons a month." Mountbatten in his own diary, however, reports a more sweeping assertion taken down by his aide. In this version, Stilwell said he had been ordered "to obtain a complete reversal of every point," almost the same characterization that Mountbatten had heard from Marshall the day before. The new charge that Chiang had again totally reversed himself came entirely and directly from Stilwell, but Stilwell in his own diary does not even mention his having heard Chiang that morning go back on "every point" or having related this to the "staggered" Mountbatten.[34]

On his way home, writing in his journal, Chiang was euphoric—Cairo was "an important achievement" in his "revolutionary career." He expressed great pride in his preparations and how "the various negotiations had brought about the anticipated results." There was nothing about any last-minute demand he had instructed Stilwell to pursue. It appears that neither in effect nor in fact did Chiang reverse himself in any significant way during either of these two days."[35]

It has been suggested that once Stalin agreed during the Tehran meeting to enter the war against Japan after the defeat of Germany, Roosevelt's interest in Chiang and China's role in the war quickly waned.[36] But it was Churchill, not Roosevelt, who argued that with the Soviet pledge to attack Japan, the question of whether China remained in the war was immaterial.[37] Roosevelt made no such argument. In fact he warned Churchill that they should not assume that the Soviets would definitely carry out their promise to attack Japan after the defeat of Germany.[38] With construction soon to begin on the mammoth airfields in Sichuan province, Washington's strategic interest in China had hardly waned. Roosevelt commented to Elliot that Chiang's armies were "not fighting at all" in China and he criticized the KMT leader's internal policies, but Roosevelt's recorded remarks in Cairo on Chiang's analysis of world affairs and global strategy, including Burma, were positive. While some have written that Roosevelt found his meetings with Chiang "discouraging," the two men fully agreed on a postwar program of decolonization and on a new world organization to promote global peace. Roosevelt was impressed that when he asked Chiang if China "wanted Indochina," the Chinese leader immediately replied, "under no circumstances." Roosevelt also thought that Chiang's agreement to a unity government with the CCP was a historic achievement.[39]

After the summit in Tehran, Roosevelt and Churchill flew back to Cairo to finalize plans for the Burma campaign. Roosevelt, in his words, fought "stubbornly as a mule" with Churchill on Chiang's behalf for the required British naval support. Hopkins noted that "feelings were high [among the Americans] that Chiang's conditions should be met with more than mere words." Only eighteen to twenty landing craft would be required for the desired naval landing in Burma, but with the massive invasion of Europe just months away, Churchill refused to contribute any British boats to the Burma campaign.[40] Despite the unqualified commitments he had made to Chiang Kai-shek on the subject, Roosevelt reluctantly overrode his own Joint Chiefs, finally agreeing that the British could postpone their amphibious landing for a year.[41]

On the way home, Chiang and Mayling stopped in Ramgarh to inspect the Chinese troops being trained there by Stilwell's men. The Chinese Army in India (the X Force) numbered some 33,000, all healthy and each one carrying a modern weapon—a unique experience for a Chinese army. In his screeching voice, Chiang harangued the troops, who seemed eager for battle, and promised the American officers quick replacements to make up for expected losses. General Frank D. Merrill's 3,000-man American Special Forces unit (called Merrill's Marauders) was ready to support the Chinese. With Spitfires and other new aircraft, the Allies now finally enjoyed complete air superiority in North Burma, including the ability to supply entire divisions by parachute and to disrupt the railway from Bangkok to Rangoon. Soon, Chiang believed, the British Navy would also control access to Burma's coastline. All this presented a totally different situation from the one that had existed before Stilwell's spring offensive of 1942.

One similarity with the first Burma campaign, however, was faulty intelligence. Several battalions of the Chinese 38th Division under Sun Liren had pushed some fifty miles ahead of construction of the new supply road, which had already begun in Ledo, India. In the Hukawng Valley, the 38th Division encountered an entrenched Japanese force, the veteran 56th Regiment of the 18th Division. Stilwell's headquarters—all American officers—had given no hint to General Sun that Japanese forces were in the area. Following Sun's reports of hot firefights, General Hayden Boatner, acting commander in Stilwell's absence, refused to admit that the enemy was present in strength.[42] It turned out that Boatner, misled by Stilwell's G-2 (intelligence office)—which was run by Stilwell's son, Lieutenant Colonel Joseph W. Stilwell Jr.—had in fact underestimated the Japanese force. After another engagement, the Chinese withdrew to their lines and waited for General Stilwell's return.[43]

On December 1, the Cairo Declaration, signed by the United States, Britain, and China, was formally announced. Among other historic pronouncements, it pledged to return all territories that Japan had stolen from China, most importantly Manchuria and Taiwan. On December 3, Chiang wrote that the "the whole world treated Cairo as a great victory for China." The picture of the Chiangs sitting beside Roosevelt and Churchill made an enormous impression on the Chinese people. For the first time in more than a century, the leader of China had been treated as an equal to the leaders of the West. Chiang gave much of the credit to his wife, who had worked twelve-hour days and personally negotiated an important financial issue with Roosevelt (though not with the success that the Chiangs believed at the time). He awarded her the Grand Cordon of the Blue Sky and the White Sun, China's highest honor.[44]

The supposed financial breakthrough in Cairo had taken place on the last day, November 26, when Soong Mayling, on instructions from her husband, paid a separate call on Roosevelt. Exhilarated over the other agreements he had achieved with Roosevelt, the Generalissimo had forgotten his pledge to himself not to ask for financial aid from the American leader, and he asked his wife to raise with the President the possibility of a loan of US$1 billion to solve China's inflation problem. When she returned from the meeting, she reported to Chiang that Roosevelt had said he "completely understood the

The Cairo Conference, November 1943, was a "great diplomatic victory" for China that soon turned sour. Claire Chennault, then commander of the 14th Air Force in China, is behind Chiang while Stilwell is behind Roosevelt. The two generals were bitter rivals. Courtesy KMT Party History Institute.

plight of [the] Chinese economy" and had "readily agreed" to the request.[45] The Generalissimo could not believe his and China's good fortune. Accompanied by the Madame, he hastened over to see the President to express his gratitude. Whatever the nearly always amenable Roosevelt said at that meeting allowed the Chiangs to remain convinced that a loan would be forthcoming.[46]

When Roosevelt was back in Cairo on December 6, however, he told Stilwell a different account: that the Chiangs had wanted a loan of a billion dollars but he had told them it would be difficult to get Congress to agree. Instead, he told Stilwell, he planned to bring down inflation in China by buying up Chinese yuan with 50 million or 100 million U.S. dollars.[47] One can only guess that Roosevelt had told the Chiangs he thought another loan was a good idea but had cautioned that it could be difficult to get Congressional and Treasury approval—and that the Chiangs believed that if he had in principle agreed personally to support the loan request, it was bound to happen.

Stilwell's December 6 meeting with Roosevelt lasted only twenty minutes. In his diary, he described Roosevelt as "a flighty fool."[48] At one point, according to Stilwell's account, Roosevelt asked the general out of the blue, "How long do you think Chiang can last?" Stilwell replied, "The situation is serious and a repetition of last May's [Japanese offensive] might overturn him." Roosevelt then said, "Well, then, we should look for some other man or group of men to carry on." To which Stilwell remarked, "They would probably be looking for us." "Yes, they would come to us," said the President.[49] On two sheets of paper, Stilwell jotted down his impression of the President's wishes. One says: "Keep China in the war. We must retain our flank position." The other: "If CKS flops, back somebody else."[50]

Elliot Roosevelt gives a brief but different account of this meeting with the man whom Chiang had naively left behind to represent him. Stilwell voiced his dissatisfaction with "the politics of the Generalissimo," Elliot wrote, and charged he was "storing up all his strength to use against the Chinese Communists after the war." But the President had "other things on his mind," including "his agreement with Chiang and his subsequent agreement with Stalin." He said little beyond "urging that Stilwell work things out as best he could."[51]

Back in Chungking, Chiang confessed to his journal that despite "the greatest triumph in the history of China's foreign affairs [the Cairo summit]," his inner feelings were strangely dominated by "fear and worry."[52] There was ample bad news on the home front. One was the continuing Japanese thrust into Hunan and Hubei. The other was Dai Li's discovery of an alleged plot by young generals to seize the Generalissimo when, returning from India, he landed at the airport. Dai had arrested the alleged conspirators, graduates of the army's staff college who said they were not seeking to overthrow the Generalissimo but simply wished to compel him to rid the government and the army of corruption.[53] Chiang ordered their execution or imprisonment. Conceivably, some were among those with whom General Dorn had discussed a "change at the top."[54]

The so-called Young Generals Plot was ominous enough, but Chiang's major worry was the potential disloyalty of the powerful military commanders and provincial power holders. Before he left for Cairo, there had been reports that the frequently mutinous Cantonese general Li Qishen, who had a nominal position in Guilin, was forming a group of southern generals as a contingency in the event the Chungking government collapsed. Toward this end, Li was reported to have reached an understanding with Yu Hanmou, Zhang Fakui, and Xue Yue, commanders of the Seventh, Fourth, and Ninth war zones, respectively. When Chiang ordered Li to Chungking to take a new position, he simply refused.[55] This was symptomatic of the delicate situation Chiang faced in dealing with many of his commanders (and to some extent, all of them). The other generals allegedly involved continued in their posts.

Over the next eighteen months, Stilwell, like Dorn, probably spoke privately with Chinese generals he trusted and let them know his negative views of Chiang. If so, a number of these conversations may have been overheard by Dai Li's technicians or reported by cooperating officers. This sort of intelligence capability was suggested when Chiang met with Bai Chongxi one day and suggested he be "more cautious when speaking." Later the same day, Bai sent the Generalissimo a note in classical Chinese expressing gratitude for the leader's suggestion.[56]

Despite his key jobs in Chungking as deputy chief of staff, director of military training, and chairman of the military inspection board, Bai was still one of the three leaders of the Guangxi Clique who apparently maintained some secret contact with the Communists, although after the war he would prove among the most anti-Communist senior officers. In his February 1940 memorandum to the Comintern, Zhou Enlai reported that the commanders of Guangxi and Zhejiang had "the closest contacts" with the CCP. Zhou recounted that "more than half" of China's military leaders were "grouped around CKS."[57] But even some of these were loosely grouped and for insurance were keeping secret ties with the Communists.

I

Stilwell returned to Kunming on December 11 and the next day visited his trusted subordinate, General Dorn. According to Dorn's memoirs, Stilwell told him he had been shocked by a verbal order he had received at Cairo. The instruction, he said, was "to prepare a plan for the assassination of Chiang Kai-shek." "Big Boy," Stilwell said, had told him "in that Olympian manner of his: 'if you can't get along with Chiang and can't replace him, get rid of him once and for all. You know what I mean. Put in someone you can manage.'" The order, Stilwell went on, was not to kill the Generalissimo but simply to prepare a plan. He doubted anything more would come of it. "The United States doesn't go in for this sort of thing," he said. But still, he instructed Dorn to "cook up" a workable scheme and await orders.[58] Dorn and two other officers concocted a contingency plot in which, on an inspection flight by the Generalissimo to Ramgarh, the American pilot would pretend to have engine trouble. The Generalissimo would be given a faulty parachute, then helped out the door. When informed of the cartoon-like scheme, Stilwell said "I believe it would work. When orders come from the top, we [will] have no choice." That was the last Dorn heard of the plan.[59]

But this was not the first time Stilwell had ordered a contingency assassination plan for Chiang Kai-shek. According to Colonel Carl F. Eifler, the senior OSS officer in the China-Burma-India Theater who was stationed in India at the time, apparently between early August and the end of October 1943, he was called to New Delhi to see General Stilwell, who told him that in order to pursue the war "in a logical way it would be necessary to get Chiang Kai-shek out of the way." He asked Eifler to prepare a plan but did not tell him that this order had come from "the Big Boy" or anyone else.[60] In a subsequent visit to Washington on other OSS business, Eifler, after inquiring at the appropriate office, was informed that botulinus toxin would be the weapon of choice because an autopsy could not detect it. But Stilwell had not conveyed any urgency in the matter and it was not until May 1944 when, at Stilwell's headquarters in Burma, Eifler informed the general that he had found a way to carry out the assassination. According to Eifler, Stilwell "shook his head and stated that he had had second thoughts about it and had decided against doing it 'at this time.'"[61]

Both Dorn and Eifler were strong supporters of Stilwell and apparently did not know each other. As for the order to Dorn, it is conceivable that Stilwell had seized on Roosevelt's seemingly offhand comment on December 6 about looking for a new man if something happened to Chiang and took it as an order from the "Big Boy" to make a plan to kill Chiang Kai-shek. But coming to such a conclusion on such evidence would have been irrational. Roosevelt surely could not have intended for Stilwell to prepare a contingency plan to kill one of America's key allies, a man he would describe in his next "fireside chat" as a man "of great vision [and] great courage," and whose wife had twice that year been a guest at the White House. Besides, the President was not angry at the Generalissimo at this time; instead, as we have seen, he felt guilty about the repeated American failure to live up to its promises to him. In Cairo he and Chiang had agreed on everything—even a unity government with the CCP—and Roosevelt had fought "stubbornly as a mule" with Churchill for the required British naval support for the Burma campaign.[62] Roosevelt also told his son that there was no other leader to take Chiang's place and that "with all their shortcomings, we've got to depend on the Chiangs."[63]

It seems clear that Stilwell, unconsciously or otherwise, badly misconstrued Roosevelt's casual remarks. Stilwell's order to Eifler, however, came well before the conversation with either the President or Dorn and was not prefaced with any indication that it came from someone higher up. The likely timing of his talk with Eifler also raises the possibility that Stilwell first gave such an order when he was in India from October 7 to 15. This would have been after Stilwell heard a rumor in Chungking on October 2 that Chiang Kai-shek had asked for him to be relieved from his position.[64]

Upon his return from Cairo, Chiang officially assumed leadership of the battles that had been raging in Hunan and Hubei provinces in the area of Dongting Lake. The main threat was to Changsha in Hunan and beyond that possibly to Guilin and Hengyang, areas key to the Chennault air offensive.[65] In reporting the new Japanese campaign to Washington, Ambassador Gauss predicted little possibility of the Chinese mounting more than the "usual perfunctory defense."[66] But the Chinese put up a serious and costly resistance. While the warmly clothed invaders employed modern artillery, poison gas, and parachute landings, the Chinese soldiers wore their usual cotton quilted uniforms in the bitter cold and fought with old rifles and ammunition manufactured in China.[67] To combat gas attacks, the soldiers would urinate on a piece of cotton padding and press it to their faces. With little mechanized transport, these armies moved at the pace of a coolie jogging along with a bamboo carrying-pole over his shoulders.[68]

Despite the range of critical matters to be attended to, Chiang seldom worked into the night. With Mayling and relatives or friends, he would occasionally watch a foreign war film, but usually in the evenings he would labor for a while on his book, *China's Destiny,* read a bit in various histories, and then dip into his collection of Tang poems. Before retiring and saying his evening prayers, he always read from one other work—a collection of Christian testaments called *Streams in the Desert,* compiled in the 1930s by an American missionary, Mrs. Chas. E. Cowman. As he read, Chiang would jot down his thoughts beside each of the daily inspirational messages or stories. The dominant theme of this collection was the message of Job—stoic perseverance and unwavering faith in the face of disaster, tragedy, humiliation, and failure. One typical passage he probably underlined declared, "God never uses anybody to a large degree until after He breaks that one all to pieces . . . It takes sorrow to widen the soul."[69]

Near the end of 1943, Chiang and his undeclared ghostwriter, Tao Xisheng, completed *China's Destiny*, which embodied his views on China, its glorious culture and history, and its bright and shining future.[70] It was Chiang's answer to Mao Zedong's major essay on the future of China, *On the New Democracy*. As was the case in Communist areas with Mao's booklet, *China's Destiny* became required reading for students in government-controlled territory and for all officials, military officers, and KMT members. The book reflects Chiang's distinctly nationalist, highly anti-imperialist, and strictly authoritarian outlook, but on world affairs it struck a liberal, internationalist stance.

China's Destiny asserted that every Chinese had the right and "the duty" to belong to the KMT. Citizens, Chiang proclaimed, "must pay special attention to and not neglect for a moment, the duty of obeying the state's policy." Discipline and loyalty were commanded. He quoted Sun Yat-sen's dictum that "we must free ourselves from the idea of 'individual liberty'" and unite "into a strong cohesive body, like a solid mass formed by mixing cement with sand." Indeed, the political system that Chiang supported was openly authoritarian. He rejected liberalism as well as Communism and reaffirmed Sun Yat-sen's thesis that an indefinite period of political tutelage "must be followed to attain democracy." Like Sun, he made the disturbing assertion that the principle of nationalism "is the most meritorious of all human conditions," but this is as close to fascism as the book comes. He did make presumptuous but hardly malevolent claims that "the glories and scope of our ancient Chinese learning cannot be equaled in the history of any of the strong Western nations," and that the principles of the Chinese state were "propriety, righteousness, modesty, and honor." But he also declared that "theories of 'superior civilization and superior races,' must be forever eliminated."[71]

Chiang's second book, *Chinese Economic Theory*, released about the same time as *China's Destiny*, was meant to be a textbook in the KMT's Central Political Training Institute. This work calls for a mixed, planned economy; a protectionist trade policy; an emphasis on national (state) ownership of large industries; and "control of private capital." Reflecting the book's strong socialist outlook, it calls on Western economists to abandon materialism and selfish individualism in favor of a "world of great harmony" where "human nature is developed to the highest point . . . no one will be able to earn a living by sitting idle . . . no one will be unable to find work."[72] The last paragraph in the first chapter of *China's Destiny*, after referring to the long struggle of Sun Yat-sen, boasts, "I, Chiang Kai-shek, have from the beginning been identified with restarting the Republic of China on the road to freedom and independence," and then follows with three innocuous uses of the word "I." After that, Chiang does not use the personal pronoun in the book or refer to his own political or historic role.[73]

The Chinese government did not publish *China's Destiny* in English. Madame recommended against it, fearing that its prideful, socialist, anti-imperialist, and even anticapitalist outlook—which did not much distinguish among the foreign abusers of China—would antagonize Americans and especially the British.[74] The only English edition of *China's Destiny* is apparently the one produced in New York by the leftist *Amerasia* magazine and its pro-Communist editor Philippe Jaffe. It could be argued that the book's extravagant moral tone and idealization of Chinese culture represented a high degree of naiveté and self-delusion, but not a will to personal power—much less absolute power, ethnic cleansing, or territorial expansion. Nevertheless, Jaffe, John Service, and others equated *China's Destiny* with Hitler's *Mein Kampf.*

Chiang's view of the Cairo Conference as the greatest diplomatic victory in Chinese history was short-lived. On December 7, Roosevelt and Churchill sent a message to Chiang telling him that discussions with Stalin at Tehran had committed the United States and Britain to a vast combined operation in Europe in the late spring of 1944; therefore no landing craft could be spared then for an amphibious operation in the Bay of Bengal. The President offered Chiang the option of either going ahead with the North Burma campaign as planned without a landing by sea (but with a promise to maintain naval control of the bay) or postponing the campaign until November, when heavy amphibious operations could be carried out. Meanwhile the United States would concentrate on expanding the air transport route over the Hump to carry supplies for the air and ground forces in China.[75]

This reversal was not a total surprise to Chiang, who on November 30 had confided in his diary that given British treachery he would not take Roosevelt's "promise" regarding the naval matter "too seriously." Moreover, he wisely wrote, he would not "give the British any excuses by saying we won't commit our infantry unless the UK commits its naval forces." What was important, he stated, was that if the promised naval power was not available, the Burma campaign would be postponed—an alternative that Roosevelt now gave him.[76] At this point, then, Chiang could have put himself in an advantageous political position by expressing shock and sorrow at the American leader's latest reversal but not asking for further aid in this context. By simply accepting the option of delaying the campaign, Chiang would have outraged Stilwell but not inconvenienced himself strategically or any other way. But Chiang, overestimating his shrewd diplomacy and Roosevelt's sense of regret and obligation at his latest failure to live up to his promises, took a more opportunistic approach.

His reply to Roosevelt was calm in tone but expressed fear of the likely effect of the broken promise on the Chinese people and army. Further, Chiang again raised the hoary possibility of a "sudden collapse of the entire front in China." He even declared that it would be "impossible for us to hold on for six months" unless major measures were taken to dramatize "your [Roosevelt's] sincere concern in the China theater of war," referring to what the Chiangs took to be Roosevelt's commitment in Cairo. The Generalissimo suggested a billion-dollar loan, a doubling of the number of aircraft to be provided to China (raising the commitment to 1,000 planes), and an increase in Hump traffic to 20,000 tons a month. In conclusion, he warned that once the Japanese realized the United States would be occupied with a mammoth invasion in Europe, they would launch an all-out offensive to end Chinese resistance.[77]

After more than two weeks of waiting for a reply, Chiang sent another more restrained message on December 17 in which he belatedly accepted the President's "suggestion" that the campaign be postponed until the following November. He also repeated his appeal for aid, but without the previous threats. Possibly recognizing the damage his first letter had done, the next day he gave Stilwell full command of the Chinese forces in India and those already fighting in Burma's Hukawng Valley, in effect agreeing to the immediate beginning of the campaign on the western (Indian) front. Stilwell urged Washington to demand that the Generalissimo also send the Y Force across the Salween River in the east.

No doubt influenced by Harry Hopkins and indeed embarrassed by his broken promise, Roosevelt's initial reply to Chiang's December letters was restrained, saying only that the best answer to China's military and economic problems was to open a land route into the country as soon as possible. He hoped the Generalissimo would carry out his part of the operation to retake Burma, made no mention of postponing the campaign, and said the Treasury Department was looking into the loan request.[78] Chiang's next rejoinder was even more inflammatory and foolish than his first. He told the President that if the loan was not possible, the U.S. government should start paying for all expenditures by U.S. forces in China (at the official exchange rate of twenty yuan to one dollar), including construction, already under way, of the B-29 airfields near Chengdu. He went on to bluster that after March 1 "China could not be of material or financial assistance in connection with any project the American forces [in China] might have in mind." China, he wrote, would fight on "until the inevitable military and civilian collapse" and then it would "do the best possible under the circumstances."[79]

Both H. H. Kung and Chiang's American financial adviser, Arthur N. Young, tried to get him to moderate the wording of this new letter to Roosevelt, but without success.[80] Chiang had found the President's letter threatening and felt that the tone and substance of his response were appropriate. His main objective was to win some concrete concessions, which he felt China was due; he also felt the need to salvage his and his country's dignity.[81] But his threats, which to many in Washington seemed to reflect "an infuriating absence of conscience," played into the hands of Stilwell and the War Department. Somervell even suggested that the U.S. Army stop building the airfields in China and "approach Japan from another direction." Calmer minds were to prevail, however. A professional diplomat, Stanley Hornbeck, then director of the Far Eastern office of the State Department, sent around a memo stressing the extraordinary importance of what was at stake in the response to Chiang and the need for "statesmanship of the highest order." Secretary Hull backed Hornbeck, and Roosevelt rejected the War Department's proposal for a stark ultimatum to the seemingly willful Chiang.[82]

Instead, the President gently told the Generalissimo that given the distances separating them, there was a danger of failing to work out common problems and rushing into "decisions which would not be in the interests of either of our peoples." He informed Chiang that the Treasury Department did not believe the requested loan was necessary, but suggested that China send a representative to Washington to discuss the currency exchange-rate issue. Then he included a tough statement: U.S. Army expenditures in China would henceforth be limited to US$25 million a month. Thus whatever amount of Chinese currency that would buy would be all that would be spent. In reply, Chiang repeated that he would send in the Yunnan Y Force whenever the promised amphibious operation could be launched or perhaps if the X Force captured Mandalay or Lashio. After sending this message, Chiang, seeking to calm things down, had H. H. Kung advance 15 billion yuan to Stilwell's headquarters to cover expenses for the next three months. Kung then rushed off to Washington and eventually reached a compromise on the currency issue.[83]

Meanwhile, Dai Li reported that the Japanese High Command was deploying 150,000 troops south from Manchuria and North China and rebuilding a bridge over the Yellow River. The troops were presumably moving to join a major offensive in central and east China, probably sometime in the coming months. This operation, called Ichigo, would eventually involve half a million well-armed frontline Japanese soldiers, the largest number of troops ever used in a campaign in Japanese history.[84]

The reason for Ichigo was the destruction of the Japanese merchant fleet down to 77 percent of its prewar level, which was seriously restricting Japan's importation of raw materials from Southeast Asia. Strategists in Tokyo hoped to solve the crisis by creating a continental corridor linking Japanese-occupied territories from Korea to Manchuria, through North, Central, and South China down to Indochina, and then through Thailand and Malaya to Singapore. Such a corridor would require uninterrupted control of the railways between Hanoi and Peking and to Dalian in Manchuria. The plan would in effect expand Japanese-occupied China west and southwest, thereby securing the empire's rear and allowing raw materials (such as oil, minerals, and possibly food) as well as troops to be transported from China and Southeast Asia to the port of Pusan in Korea and then across the narrow Tsushima Straits to Japan. The sizable territorial gains that the plan required would also result in the destruction of Chennault's new airfields. On April 6, Chiang received intelligence reporting that Japan's goal was not just to destroy the easternmost airfields but to open up "the Big [Dalian to Hanoi] Asian Railway."[85]

Consequently, while the Germans were retreating on every front in Europe and the Japanese were falling back in the Pacific, the Imperial Army was planning its biggest offensive of the war in China, bigger than anything MacArthur had faced. In Chungking as in the other Allied capitals there was increasing talk about the possible collapse of Hitler's regime sometime during 1944. Chiang assumed that at Tehran Stalin had agreed to enter the war against Japan after Germany's surrender, although the Allies had not informed him of this. Once in control of Manchuria and possibly Peking and Tianjin, Chiang thought, the Soviets would "talk tough and ask for a regional [CCP-dominated] government and regional autonomy." But there was nothing at the moment he could do about it.[86] In Yan'an, arguments for serious CCP cooperation with the Kuomintang lost what little force they had retained among the Chinese Communists. In Politburo meetings in December, Zhou again admitted his "capitulationist" (pro-KMT) views.[87]

Meanwhile, John Davies, working at Stilwell's headquarters in India, had been sending Hopkins ominous reports on the domestic situation in China. In February 1945, he recommended dispatching U.S. military and other observers to the CCP base area to reduce the tendency of the Chinese Communists toward dependence on Russia and to check Chiang's desire to liquidate Mao's forces. On February 9, Roosevelt made the formal request to Chiang for permission to send an American observer mission to Yan'an. Chiang lamented in his diary that "young and naïve American military officers in China believed the CCP's propaganda" but, more importantly, so did "senior U.S. officers [in Washington]."[88] Chiang turned down the request but stated that a U.S. mission could visit any area in North China that accepted the authority of the central government. Roosevelt thanked the Generalissimo for his reply and, ignoring the restriction, said he would dispatch such a mission in the near future.[89] Sometime later, to placate the Americans, Chiang approved the first visit to Yan'an by a group of foreign correspondents.

During January, Stilwell and his Chinese divisions in Burma, now called the New First Army, continued to press slowly down the Hukawng Valley while a British force moved from India down the Arakan coast. But then Mountbatten's headquarters suddenly recommended that the Allies simply drop the effort to open a supply line to China and instead plan to gain a foothold in Sumatra. Stilwell was outraged and he immediately sent General Boatner to Washington to argue against the proposal. Mountbatten found out, accused Stilwell of insubordination, and asked for his recall. On Marshall's instructions, Stilwell saw the Lord Admiral and, as he had with Chiang, "ate crow." The two men formally patched things up, but both men still wished to be rid of the other.[90]

The Allied leaders rejected Mountbatten's proposal and the Burma campaign continued. Then unexpectedly, on March 8, three Japanese divisions carrying only one month's supply of rice struck the British front. Within weeks, the invaders had surrounded 60,000 British and Indian troops and their stores on the Imphal Plain and were also attacking the border town of Kohima, which commanded the pass to the Assam Valley and the U.S. airfields flying the Hump. The Japanese were suddenly only twenty miles from the Calcutta-Assam rail line and Stilwell's Chinese and American troops were about to be cut off. Stilwell and the British had again badly underestimated the Japanese. "This ties a can to us," he wrote, "and finishes up the glorious spring offensive."[91] Stilwell immediately radioed Marshall urging that more pressure be put on the Generalissimo to send in the Y Force and to dispatch posthaste another Chinese division to join the New First Army in the Hukawng Valley. "If ever I needed help," he cabled Marshall, "Now, right now, is the time." Mountbatten also asked his own superiors in London to make the same "suggestion" to Chiang "with extreme urgency."[92]

Roosevelt duly cabled the Generalissimo and expressed the hope that he would order his Y Force commanders to cooperate in what he described not as a great crisis but as "a great opportunity." Chiang replied that should China attempt something beyond its power it "could court disaster"; consequently, such an offensive by the Y Force was impossible until the British had launched their amphibious operation. Nevertheless Chiang did agree to send the Chinese 14th and 50th divisions from Yunnan to reinforce Stilwell's position inside Burma. In a record eight days, these Chinese soldiers were flying over the Hump to Assam.[93]

This partial but important response by Chiang to the Allies' pleas for help did not merit a mention in Stilwell's diary nor probably in his reports to Washington. On the contrary, a Stilwell message of March 30 predicting total defeat in Burma persuaded Roosevelt to revert to harsh language with the Generalissimo. In an April 3 radiogram the President told Chiang that the whole point of the fight in Burma was to open up a supply route to China, and it was "inconceivable that the Y Forces with their American equipment would be unable to advance against the Japanese 56th Division." "If the Y Force is not to be used in the common cause," the President continued, "then the effort to equip and train it have (sic) not been justified." The message ended with a conciliatory touch of the old school: "I do hope you can act." Chiang decided not to answer for the time being but to "let things cool down," and "patiently watch for a change in the President's attitude."[94] Stilwell then transferred to the 14th Air Force, which was supporting the campaign in Burma, all future Hump tonnage slated for the Chinese Y Force in Yunnan.[95]

Chiang accepted the inevitable and quickly devised a transparent, face-saving way out. On April 14, He Yingqin informed Marshall by radio that, consistent with its strategic and tactical calculations, China had decided it was time to move the Y Force across the Salween River to engage the Japanese. In a strained analysis, Chiang justified his painful and politically costly holdout on the grounds that it had in some measure rebuked the broken pledges made to him at Cairo.[96] He then sent the Y Force commander, General Wei Lihuang, a message with the injunction, "Succeed—or else!"[97] Stilwell resumed shipment of supplies to the Y Force, reducing tonnage going to the 14th Air Force to its previous level.

Chennault, who strongly opposed the idea of crossing the Salween River, warned Chiang that the expected Japanese offensive in central China was imminent and would eventually extend into Hunan and Guangxi. The Y Force, he thought, would be needed to resist the enormous Japanese attack. Stilwell's recurrently inaccurate intelligence office in Chungking issued an "emphatic dissent" to the prediction of a massive Japanese offensive. Stilwell informed Chennault that "the current crisis in [Imphal] India" had priority and he instructed the air officer not to send the Generalissimo "a gloomy estimate of the military situation" in China.[98] Only when Chennault's pilots spotted 239 Japanese troop trains steaming south and west did Stilwell's Chungking headquarters finally conclude that a major offensive was indeed imminent.[99] On April 17, the Japanese 37th Division, with hundreds of tanks and armored personnel carriers, crossed the Yellow River on repaired bridges and rolled across the flat Henan wheat fields. Their goal was to sweep away the Chinese forces between the Yellow and Yangtze rivers, clearing the rail lines between Peking and Wuhan.[100] The motley forces of General Tang Enbo's First War Zone fell back in disarray, but the 28th and 31st Army Groups held on at the key city of Luoyang. For good or bad, the Generalissimo was on the phone personally directing the defense. He also appealed to Stilwell, his chief of staff, for five hundred tons of gasoline from the B-29 stores to fuel Chennault's fighters supporting the Luoyang defenders, but Stilwell, believing that the Generalissimo had brought the situation on himself, declined.

The Chinese divisions in Henan fought as usual with no armor or motor pool, a few old cannon, and for every three soldiers two old, mostly Chinese-made rifles. The only advantage the Chinese fighters inside China enjoyed was tactical air support from the ninety or so operational planes of Chennault's 14th Air Force that had been assigned to Chinese army operations inside China. The Luoyang defenders resisted for fifteen days, losing 21,000 Chinese soldiers and officers before Chiang's withdrawal order came.[101]

II

During the night of May 11, as the collapse in Henan proceeded, the 72,000-man Y Force waded across the Salween River in western Yunnan province to link up with Stilwell. According to the American liaison officers, the Chinese expedition, with its up-to-date equipment and extensive tactical air support, fought well and bravely. Scattered downpours soon merged into the near constant torrential rain of the monsoon. But U.S. planes dropped supplies and ammunition and the Chinese slogged on. At the same time, Stilwell's Chinese divisions and Merrill's Marauders, all battling mud and floods, reached the outskirts of Myitkyina.[102]

Despite the rains, Stilwell was hopeful that his five Chinese divisions could soon link up with General Wei's twelve "Y" divisions to the east. But in mid-June, Wei's effort to seize Long Ling, the center of the Japanese line on the Salween front, collapsed when a counterattack by only 1,500 Japanese troops drove back 10,000 Chinese fighters. Chiang was extremely angry and demanded that Wei "spare no effort" to renew the attack and capture Long Ling. Chiang ordered two more Chinese armies from North China to join Wei's force in Burma. These armies were desperately needed in the Ninth and Fourth war zones, which were awaiting the next phase of the grand Japanese offensive. By diverting them south, Chiang again demonstrated his commitment to an Allied victory in Burma.[103]

American pilots continued to report that elite Japanese units from Manchuria were still pouring down the newly occupied rail line into Wuhan. Chennault again appealed to Stilwell to use his emergency authority to divert supplies, transport capacity, and combat elements of the B-29 command to meet the emergency in East China. Stilwell responded that "until the emergency is unmistakable, the decision will have to wait." Two days later, the Japanese Sixth Army surged out of the Wuhan bulge into Hunan while smaller forces advanced from Canton and Vietnam. This second stage of Ichigo threatened to seize most of Hunan, which was the main rice bowl for

Free China, as well as the bases of the 14th Air Force in Hunan, Jiangxi, and Guangxi. The pilots of Chennault's 23rd Group flew three to four missions a day through and under the weather. They wreaked havoc among the Japanese, but their losses were horrendous—equaling or surpassing that of U.S. bomber groups in Europe. Nearly half the pilots of this group of three squadrons were killed or taken prisoner that summer, among them three squadron commanders.[104]

From his jungle tent in Burma, Stilwell dictated a message to Marshall, insisting that without a wholesale shakeup in the British Command in India, there was no chance of a successful attack on Burma from India in the fall of 1944. This was in effect a suggestion that his superior, Mountbatten, be relieved (a man before whom, to save his job, Stilwell had recently "eaten crow" and pledged professional loyalty). Likewise, Stilwell continued, given the "present Chinese high command," that is, Chiang Kai-shek, the most the proposed Burma offensive could hope for was to seize and hold the Myitkyina air base. Opening the land route all the way to China, he concluded, would require an American corps. In other words, the slow advance in the Burma campaign was the fault of Mountbatten and Chiang Kai-shek, and had nothing to do with Stilwell's as well as Mountbatten's sizable underestimation of the enemy's strength.

Meanwhile, the battle for Burma was determined not in the Hukawng Valley but in raging combat in northeast India, where the Japanese had committed 120,000 of the emperor's best troops. By early May, Mountbatten had achieved a significant victory, breaking the Japanese siege of the two Indian towns Imphal and Kohima. The Royal Air Force flew or parachuted in 19,000 tons of supplies and 12,000 reinforcements, and launched 29,000 air sorties against the enemy. This impressive and decisive use of air power far overshadowed anything available to Chennault and the Chinese. The Japanese full-scale retreat would begin in July and end in the largest defeat to date for the Japanese Army, which suffered 55,000 casualties with 13,500 killed.

III

Stilwell's deeply pessimistic assessment of Allied prospects in Burma probably influenced the new decision by Marshall and the Joint Chiefs to try to defeat Japan without a major campaign on the mainland of Asia. In a May 27 reply to Stilwell, Marshall informed him of the new grand strategy. Thereafter, the highest priority for the United States in China and Burma would be to build up the air effort and increase Hump tonnage for this purpose—more or less the Chennault strategy. Significantly, the Americans seem not to have discussed this matter with the Supreme Commander of the China Theater: Chiang Kai-shek.[105]

The same day that Marshall's message arrived, Chinese troops and American Marauders under Stilwell's direction finally seized the airfield at Myitkyina. The Japanese, however, with only 3,500–4,000 men, would hold the town for another three months. Stilwell and his Chinese officers and soldiers, including those without U.S. training but with new U.S. weapons, had fought with valor and remarkable stamina, and probably no other American general in the war was so literally in the trenches for as long as was Stilwell. But this was a relatively small-scale battle. By contrast, a combined almost million Chinese and Japanese were then battling each other in East China, and the fighting on the Sino-Indian border was also on a grander scale than Myitkyina—and was a more critical battle for the war. The American press, however, gave Myitkyina (and Stilwell) far more attention than they did Changsha or Imphal. When the town held by a few thousand Japanese was finally taken, Marshall hailed Stilwell's effort as a "brilliant victory."[106]

That very day, Stilwell took the time to ask Marshall by radiogram to relieve Chennault as commander of the 14th Air Force because of "insubordination"—contrary to Stilwell's orders, Chennault had reported to Chiang Kai-shek that the Japanese were preparing for a huge offensive in East and South China. The War Department—no doubt Marshall himself—replied that to remove Chennault before the expected Chinese collapse in East China could open Stilwell to charges that he had caused it. Chiang Kai-shek believed that "in seven years of war the military situation was never so serious as today." He appealed personally to Roosevelt for an increase in monthly deliveries to the 14th Air Force and assignment to Chennault of the entire inventory of U.S. tactical warplanes and aircraft ordnance at Chengdu. He also appealed to the President for 8,000 rocket launchers.[107]

But the following week, Stilwell received a report from General Dorn reporting that the Chinese could not account for seven million rounds of ammunition given to them, that some antitank rifles and radios were apparently still in Chungking, and that the Chinese had cannon and supplies for five battalions of field artillery in Kunming. The complaint was misleading. Actually little U.S. military equipment or ammunition had gotten into the hands of the Chinese Army aside from that received by the X and Y forces, both of which were committed to the Burma campaign. The cannon in Yunnan, for example, had almost certainly been allocated to the Y Force.

According to the Chinese War Ministry, since the fall of Rangoon, from May 1942 through September 1944, 98 percent of U.S. military aid over the Hump had gone to the 14th Air Force—and, the ministry could have added, to the B-29 operation and the upkeep of the large and increasing number of U.S. military personnel in China. The United States had provided the two million or so men who were in the Chinese army but not in the X and Y forces a total of 351 machine guns, 96 mountain cannon, 618 antitank rifles, 28 antitank guns, and 50 million rounds of rifle ammunition. Of these items, only 60 cannon, 50 antitank rifles, and 30 million rounds of ammunition were provided before the June 1944 battle of Changsha; the rest afterward.[108] Further, the War Department had decreed that the new Z Force of thirty Chinese divisions to be retrained and armed by the United States (as the second group of the ninety total divisions that Roosevelt had promised to support) would receive only 10 percent of the total Lend-Lease allotment for China. The American team assigned to this project calculated that if divided between thirty new divisions, these supplies of arms and ammunition would in each case amount to "practically zero."[109]

Without asking Chiang for an explanation regarding the unaccounted-for matériel, Stilwell took Dorn's report as confirmation of his decisions not to assist the Chinese ground forces with significant supplies and to refuse to take emergency measures in response to the Japanese offensive in Hunan. In early June, Stilwell was back in Chungking and discussed the military crisis with Chiang and later in Kunming with Chennault. Both repeated their earlier requests for a B-29 raid on Japanese depots at Wuhan. Stilwell promised to forward them to Washington, but when the department replied in the negative, he sent back a brief acknowledgment to Washington: "Instructions understood and exactly what I had hoped for . . . Pressure from the Generalissimo compelled me to send the request." After his meeting with Chennault, Stilwell also stuffed into his pocket and then promptly forgot Chennault's request that the two hundred fighters of the 14th Air Force assigned to protect the B-29s be deployed against the looming offensive in East China.[110]

According to Stilwell, on June 5 in Chungking Chiang told him "the situation in East China" (the expected offensive into Hunan) was to be solved by air attacks and asked him to "suspend shipment of arms and ammunition over the Hump" in order to concentrate on shipment of fuel, parts, and ordnance to the 14th Air Force. Stilwell promised Chiang that he would assure that the 14th Air Force received 10,000 tons a month in supplies but he also seemed to interpret Chiang's instructions as an order not to use U.S. transport to deliver from any location arms and ammunition to any of Chiang's armies resisting the Japanese in East China.[111] It is doubtful that Chiang was as categorical as Stilwell recounts in suggesting air power alone would "solve the situation," and Stilwell himself does not quote him as saying no American or Chinese arms and ammunition should be sent to Chinese forces in East China. In his diary, Chiang simply reports that he and Stilwell "discussed fuel supply and weapons distribution" and Stilwell "politely promised to do as I wished. His attitude was the same."[112] Actually only a "trickle" of American arms had been going to Chinese forces not related to the Burma campaign, but Chiang believed he had a compelling reason to control and even to stop any future American arms from going to his commanders in East China. At that moment Xue Yue, commander of the Ninth War Zone in Hunan, and General Zhang Fakui, commander of the Fourth War Zone in Guangdong and Guangxi, had come under increased suspicion of disloyalty—reports about which Stilwell's headquarters believed were true.

By apparently directing at least that shipments over the Hump be entirely devoted to supplies for the 14th Air Force and failing to insist that the Americans send arms and ammunition to the Chinese forces in Hunan—especially the threatened cities of Changsha and Hengyang—Chiang showed that concern over disloyalty among his generals was more important to him than the successful defense of these cities. As vividly expressed in his diaries, he had enormous political and military interest in defeating the Japanese in these looming battles—he knew the outcome would have a great effect on American and domestic support for him. Thus he would take strong measures to try to defeat the Japanese in Hunan, but, fearing supplies would fall into the hands of Xue Yue, he apparently would not ask the 14th Air Force to drop even Chinese-made ammunition and weapons to the defenders, nor did he discuss the air-supply issue with Chennault.[113]

Chennault was outraged with Chiang for not aiding Xue, but he did not raise the matter with him, apparently assuming the effort would be futile. But if Stilwell, who never hesitated to oppose Chiang's decisions, had had any question about the wisdom of Chiang's orders as he interpreted them, he could have sought clarification, or urged him to reconsider. This would have been useful at least for the record. But Stilwell, like Chiang, had his own potent political motives in these decisions. As will be seen, over the next two months he clearly preferred that Chiang suffer a serious defeat in Changsha and elsewhere in East China in order to enhance his own prospects of taking over command of the entire Chinese Army. Chiang and Stilwell would both bear some responsibility for the coming fall of Changsha and Hengyang.[114] Perhaps because of this, in his diary Chiang would not later blame Stilwell for these specific defeats.

Xue Yue's headquarters was some distance away from Changsha and as the Japanese tightened their noose around the city, Chiang concentrated on helping and directing General Zhang Deneng, whose Fourth Army comprised the defenders. Chiang continued to press for increased logistical support of the 14th Air Force's attacks on the Japanese attackers and lines of supply and he ordered six armies from four war zones to deploy immediately to Hunan. When it became clear that these units would arrive too late and Changsha would fall, General Zhang, on June 26, without orders evacuated the city with 4,000 of his men and trucks reputedly filled with his personal effects. Chiang had him shot, although he was one of his favorite generals.[115] The Japanese occupied what remained of the wasteland of the city that had avoided its fate for so long. Most of the population had long fled, including the American and Chinese staff of the Xiangya Hospital. The loss of Changsha exposed Hengyang and Guilin to the south and to the northwest, Chungking. Stilwell's headquarters in the provisional capital began planning for evacuation. Roosevelt quickly dispatched Vice President Henry Wallace to China to "calm" Chiang Kai-shek and promote cooperation between the Kuomintang and the Communists.[116]

The Chungking summer was at full blast when the Generalissimo met Wallace at the Chungking Airport. Also in the welcoming party were the rehabilitated foreign minister and now also premier, T. V. Soong, along with his sister, Mayling, who remained in the car.[117] Chiang now believed that he had made a horrible mistake the previous October; he should have followed T.V.'s advice and insisted on Stilwell's dismissal. Chiang blamed not only his wife but also the Kungs and He Yingqin for backing Stilwell. Mayling would attend the meetings with Wallace but she was to be unusually quiet. This time T.V., whom she had rudely expelled from the conference with Mountbatten and Stilwell in October, would do the interpreting.

Chennault and his bright, ambitious young aide Joe Alsop were also standing on the apron to welcome the Vice President. The remarkably connected Alsop knew Henry Wallace socially and professionally, and the Vice President gladly accepted Chennault's suggestion that Joe act as his "air aide" during the visit.[118]

Only two weeks before Wallace's arrival, the *New York Times* published one of the first dispatches from the American journalists whom Chiang had agreed could visit Yan'an. In his first interview with the Americans, Mao declared that the CCP had "never wavered from its policy of supporting Chiang Kai-shek" in the war of resistance. All the serious problems of China could be summed up, he said, in the one phrase—"lack of democracy." The *Times* report was enthusiastic, even euphoric about what the writer had seen and heard. The unidentified correspondent, presumably Brooks Atkinson, reported that the formerly barren Yan'an was "a Chinese Wonderland City." Communist soldiers, he reported, fed "themselves without imposing any burden on the people," and Japanese prisoners were not held in camps but voluntarily helped the Communist Army. Russia had "never shown any interest in the Chinese Communists," Atkinson assured his readers, but the CCP's armies were tying down four-fifths of all the Imperial forces in China.[119]

Such news reports reflected and reinforced the views of most American officials in Chungking and Washington that the Chinese Communists were a politically benign and popular (if not yet fully democratic) organization; that they were determined to employ their full strength against the Japanese if only they were freed to do so by the government; and that even without such freedom, they were already carrying the heaviest burden of the war. The corollary was that the Kuomintang regime was disintegrating and not interested in fighting the Japanese, and if only it would cooperate there could be a peaceful, democratic settlement with the Communists. The State Department's talking points for Wallace to use with Chiang mirrored these opinions.[120]

The Vice President enjoined Chiang to make better use of the Chinese Communist Army and to begin this process by approving an American military fact-finding mission to Yan'an. He also said Chiang should take steps to increase cooperation with the Soviet Union. The Chinese leader replied that American critics were forever urging him to come to terms with the Communists but never talked about the key necessity of the Communists' acceptance of a true unified command under him—the fundamental condition of the united front that they claimed to have accepted.

In vivid terms, Chiang then told Wallace that he lacked confidence in Stilwell's judgment and requested that the President appoint a personal representative who would handle both political and military matters. He blamed the flight of his army in Henan on lack of equipment, war fatigue, and demoralization caused by the suffering of the soldiers' families and the failure to receive significant help from abroad. The situation in Burma, he said, was a result of the Allies' failure to execute as promised his all-out strategy.[121]

Owen Lattimore was in Wallace's party and on his second morning at the Yellow Mountain villa he joined the Generalissimo for a pre-breakfast walk in the garden. When Chiang asked bluntly what the Vice President's trip was all about, Lattimore explained that good relations with the Soviet Union were a key aspect of U.S. postwar policy and it was best for both the United States and China to have a clear understanding with Moscow before the Soviet Union came into the war. In response to Lattimore's questions, Chiang said he thought the Soviet Union would enter the Pacific War as soon as it "was assured of its position in the West." The Soviets, he predicted, would attack straight through Mongolia-Manchuria and their victory would be quick. In a separate, private talk, Madame Chiang told Lattimore that she was planning to go abroad due to ill health, and she pulled down her stockings to show him her skin disease. She asked him to have the Vice President express concern to the Generalissimo about her health, implying that she was not sure she could otherwise get away for treatment.[122]

Wallace's other talks in Chungking were confusing and pessimistic. T. V. Soong complained that his boss was "bewildered," that "there were already signs of disintegration," and that for the Chinese government it was "five minutes to midnight." But Soong Chingling emphasized the Nationalist regime's lack of popular support, and, echoing the CCP line at the time, excused her brother-in-law, saying he did not know what was going on.[123] After leaving Chungking, Wallace and his party stopped in Kunming, where he drafted a preliminary report to Roosevelt that warned that all of East China could soon fall in Japanese hands, nullifying the U.S. military effort in China and possibly causing a disintegration of the Chungking regime. The Generalissimo, he said, had put himself into a hole by "an unenlightened administration supported by landlords, warlords, and bankers." Chiang was "so prejudiced against the Communists," Wallace said, that there was "little prospect of a settlement with them." While it was necessary to back the Generalissimo for the time being, he concluded, the United States "should be on the lookout for any other leader or group that might come forward offering greater promise." Yet although he was highly skeptical of Chiang's long-term survival, Wallace not only supported Chiang's request for a personal presidential representative but even recommended that Stilwell be replaced in China by General Albert Wedemeyer.[124]

Chiang did not know from whom next to expect bad news—his American allies, his Japanese enemies, his temporary warlord allies, his adversaries within the KMT, the Chinese Communists, or the Soviets. He spent long hours following and trying to direct the battles in Hunan and northeastern Burma, but he also had serious distractions in his personal life. His wife was undergoing another spell of depression. Moreover, she had heard rumors or perhaps knew about an affair the Generalissimo had allegedly had with a Miss Chen Ying. Various stories described Chen as a nurse, a teacher, or a daughter of Chen Bulei, the Generalissimo's confidential and influential aide. Chungking was a hothouse of lurid tales of corruption and sin within the establishment. John Service reported the many rumors regarding the Chiangs, while noting that they might be "nothing more than malicious gossip." According to one story, Mayling discovered in Kai-shek's bedroom a pair of high heels that she'd never seen and angrily threw them out the window, where they struck a guard on the head. Another story had Mayling hitting her husband with a vase.[125]

Rumors of the affair gained such currency that, after Wallace's departure, the Chiangs held an unusual tea party for foreign journalists during which Chiang categorically denied the stories that were circulating and said that they jeopardized the revolution. His wife declared that "never for a moment did I stoop or demean myself to entertain doubts of his uprightness." The extraordinary public denial, however, only drew more attention to the rumors and suggested to many that there was some truth to them.[126]

The Generalissimo's possible dalliance added to Mayling's desire to get away from Chungking. In addition to her emotional state, she had other health problems, including an eye malady and her recurrent skin disease. Mysteriously, she went first to Brocoio Island, Brazil, accompanied by Ai-ling, who had also lost her standing with the Generalissimo. The two sisters stayed in Brazil for almost two months while Mayling was under medical care, and while Ai-ling reputedly was busy examining Kung family holdings and investment possibilities.[127] In September, the party left Brazil for New York where Mayling again entered Presbyterian Hospital—and as before, took over an entire floor in the Harkness Pavilion. There she received treatment for "a severe state of exhaustion" while visitors like Eleanor Roosevelt came to see her.[128]

IV

Marshall not only rejected Wallace's recommendation that Stilwell be replaced; he gave the general a dramatic promotion. Following suggestions planted over the previous year by Stilwell, Marshall, again without asking the Chinese, offered Stilwell the command of the Chinese Army, later clarified to include the Communists.[129] Immediately after reading the message, Stilwell sat down in his sweltering tent outside the destroyed town of Myitkyina and wrote a reply, agreeing that "only a quick and radical" solution could save the desperate situation in China. But, he warned, Washington would have to force the Generalissimo to give him "complete authority" over the Chinese Army. Once in command, Stilwell explained, he would launch a counteroffensive against the Japanese from Shaanxi with the participation of the Communists, who, he said, "two years ago offered to fight with me." Marshall agreed. His first step was to promote Stilwell to full general, a rank shared with only Marshall himself, Eisenhower, MacArthur, and Arnold.[130]

The Joint Chiefs sent a July 3 memorandum to the President calling on him to send an attached letter to Chiang Kai-shek urging him to give Stilwell command of all Chinese armed forces in the field, including the Communists.[131] Apparently without consulting with any other senior officials who might have had a different outlook, Roosevelt made only a few softening remarks to the War Department letter and the historic message was soon on its way to Chungking.

Ironically, Roosevelt by this time had seemingly put aside or forgotten the events since Cairo and his respectful feelings in regard to the Generalissimo had returned. A few days before the War Department draft message arrived on his desk, Roosevelt received H. H. Kung, who delivered a letter from the Generalissimo declaring that he saw the President as "an older brother as well as a friend." Roosevelt responded affirmatively, telling Kung "confidentially" that he hoped to arrange a four-power conference by the end of the year, including Stalin as well as Churchill, Chiang, and himself. The President laughed and suggested that perhaps "Stalin, Chiang, and I can bring Brother Churchill around [on decolonization]."[132]

Marshall passed along to Stilwell key passages of the President's letter to Chiang asking Stilwell be given command of the Chinese Army, but added the admonition that the support of the President and of Chiang Kai-shek had been withheld from Stilwell for so long because of "the offense you have given, usually in small affairs, both to the Generalissimo and to the President." Marshall warned that Stilwell had to do everything in his power to avoid offending Chiang. In response, Stilwell simply promised "as a country boy" to tackle his new assignment "to the best of his ability." He admitted no fault in his previous dealings with the Generalissimo and vaguely promised that he would "consistently and continuously avoid unnecessary irritations." In his diary, however, he wrote, "The cure for China's trouble is the elimination of Chiang Kai-shek."[133]

Stilwell's man in Chungking, Brigadier General Benjamin G. Ferris, delivered to Chiang Roosevelt's "recommendation" regarding Stilwell's appointment. Roosevelt's polite additions asserted there was "no intent" on his part "to dictate on matters concerning China." But, the President's message explained, China was "on the brink of collapse" and if nothing was done, the "common effort would suffer a major setback." Roosevelt acknowledged that he was fully aware of Chiang's view of General Stilwell, but he believed Stilwell was the best qualified military leader to save the situation. He recommended that Chiang bring Stilwell back and "directly under you . . . give him real military authority," including over the Communist forces.[134]

For Chiang the proposal was stunning in its audacity. There had been nothing like it in the sovereign history of China, except when foreign dynasties had conquered the country.[135] Chiang of course saw the demand as a dire threat to his own power and to China's independence, dignity, and self-respect, but instead of immediately and angrily rejecting it, he knew it was important to remain calm. He saw three choices: "refuse; accept; or postpone and see." He decided to delay.[136] The next day he replied with due politeness and reasonableness to the proposal. In fact his reply would have been almost as shocking to the neutral observer as the American request: he agreed to it. "In principle, I fully agree with your suggestion that directly under me General Stilwell be given the command of all Chinese and American troops in this theater of war," Chiang wrote Roosevelt. "But I would like to call your attention to the fact that Chinese troops and their internal political conditions are not like those of other countries. Furthermore they are not as easily directed as the limited number of Chinese troops who are now fighting in North Burma. Therefore if this suggestion is carried out in haste it would not only fail to help the present war situation here but would also arouse misunderstanding and confusion which would be detrimental to Sino-American cooperation."[137]

Chiang then appealed to Roosevelt as he had to Wallace for appointment of an influential personal representative with "full power . . . to constantly collaborate with me and also . . . [to] adjust relations between me and General Stilwell." He then followed up with another message to the President contradicting his own regular warnings that resistance in China was on the verge of collapse. "China is not on the brink," he said. "Although the situation is quite dangerous . . . based on my seven years experience in this war I can guarantee victory."[138]

Kung again succeeded in seeing the President to pass on this message. After reading it, Roosevelt said that at the time of his own July 7 radiogram it was reported that China was indeed on the brink of military collapse. Kung then described the different personal and regional loyalties and allegiances in the Chinese military that required subtle leadership. General Stilwell, he said, "either due to his subjective attitude or lack of knowledge of this tradition or both, has run into disputes with Chinese military and political officers." But, Kung went on, "the question is whether or not General Stilwell can successfully carry out his duties once all Chinese troops are under his control. Chiang Kai-shek is doubtful . . . Not all professional soldiers have the necessary political and diplomatic experience and skill. Consequently, at the very beginning of this personnel decision, we must try to avoid misunderstandings, which in turn could have a negative impact on the future of China's political reconstruction."[139] After the friendly meeting, Kung reported back to Chiang that Roosevelt had agreed with the Generalissimo's analysis.[140]

Before leaving on his trip to Honolulu, the President wrote to Admiral Leahy: "There is a good deal in what the Generalissimo says." He also sent another letter to Chiang urging him to arrange Stilwell's assumption of command "at the earliest possible moment," but accepting the idea of first sending a senior political representative to Chungking.[141] For Chiang, Kung's report and Roosevelt's latest letter were highly encouraging. He wrote a journal entry portraying himself as the calm, noble, superior man in the best neo-Confucian tradition: "All I can abide by is the heavenly principle and the eternal law . . . I [shall] take the worsening of the American attitude, the upheaval in our morale, and the military setback as beneficial, not harmful to me. Even the American policy of making use of the Chinese Communists, if we can maneuver it to our benefit, may not necessarily be disadvantageous to us."[142] But another blow quickly followed.

While Roosevelt was in Hawaii conferring with MacArthur and Nimitz, the War Department sent him another message for Chiang that was in striking contrast to the President's seemingly understanding and cordial discussion with H.H. only a few days earlier. "Should our common goal of fighting Japan unfortunately be stifled by your decisions," the letter warned, "the United States and China would have limited opportunity for further cooperation." The unabashed threat was in effect to end not just American aid but the alliance itself. Upon receiving the letter, Chiang assumed that the words were not "literally" those of the President. Still, he wrote in his diary, "we must be psychologically prepared to fight this war alone."[143]

Roosevelt then sent Chiang a separate letter urging him to reach an agreement with the CCP for joint military efforts against the Japanese because doing so would greatly improve Sino-Russian relations. Chiang suddenly suspected that the United States wanted him to recognize Mao's control in Northern China in order to create a "two Chinas" situation—which in turn would reduce the possibility of a postwar U.S.-Soviet quarrel over China. He again felt "disconcerted and humiliated."[144]

At this time came the almost simultaneous news of the attempt on the life of Hitler and the resignation of the Tojo cabinet in Japan. Tokyo's surrender, Chiang thought, would "not be long" in coming. He believed that if he could avoid a break with the Americans by temporarily giving Stilwell command with some controls, the crisis with America would pass and after the war the aggressiveness of the Russian and Chinese Communists would eventually push the United States into opposing them.[145]

But immediately Chiang was to start down the path toward another defeat that would strengthen Stilwell's hand and perhaps encourage his warlord opponents. Having lost Changsha, victory in Hengyang, a hundred miles due south of Changsha, would, Chiang felt, be "Heaven's blessings" and would "dissolve the diplomatic crisis and deliver us to safety."[146] The idea that the

Nationalist Army was about to collapse would be eliminated by such a victory. Again, Chiang did not want to support Xue Yue, the war zone commander involved—so instead, as at Changsha, he directly conducted the defense of Hengyang with loyal forces in the city and elsewhere, which added to the chaos. But this time he had a general, Fang Xianjue, who was willing to fight.

In his mission to save the city, Chiang relied heavily on Chennault's close air support. The tactic worked well at first. For a period in early July, fighters and bombers of the 14th Air Force so disrupted Japanese supply lines that the attack on the walled city ground to a halt. Then for one week, lack of fuel grounded the American pilots. In accordance with Stilwell's wishes, the War Department still refused to allow Chennault to use aviation fuel from the B-29 depot in Chengdu.[147]

Meanwhile, on the ground, Fang repulsed three waves of Japanese assaults on Hengyang, reportedly killing 7,602 Japanese soldiers. But he lost most of his regulars—19,380 men—and by mid-July mostly auxiliaries and service troops were in the front lines.[148] Resupply became a critical issue. Chiang again did not fly or parachute in supplies, and Chennault, without telling Chiang, again requested that Stilwell authorize a single air drop of ammunition (presumably Chinese manufactured), in this case at Hengyang. Stilwell refused, saying he was concerned this would set a precedent for further demands that could not be met.[149] On July 20, Stilwell's new chief of staff in Chungking, General Tom Hearn, suggested authorizing Chennault to drop a "token" of two hundred tons of ammunition into the city, but Stilwell in his reply recalled with satisfaction what he said was Chennault's old promise "to beat the Japs with air alone." In fact, neither Chennault nor Chiang had ever claimed they could beat the Japanese without the Chinese Army playing a key defensive role. But Stilwell went on to tell Hearn that if Chennault "now realizes he cannot do [this], he should inform the Gissimo, who can then make any proposition he sees fit." This part of the message was inadvertently not passed to Chennault by Stilwell's staff. But in a segment of the same message that did make it to Chennault, Stilwell, turning aside a request for supplies for Hengyang from Bai Chongxi and clearly thinking of his own imminent takeover of the Chinese Army, grumbled, "I do not see how we can move until a certain big decision is made." He added sarcastically: "You can tell the Chinese we are doing our best to carry out the plan the Gissimo insisted on."[150]

In reply to Stilwell, General Hearn indicated that he was aware of "the pending big decision" (Stilwell's new appointment), but he recommended that in the meanwhile "drastic action" be taken "immediately" to aid the Chinese in southeast China. Chennault had offered to convert one thousand tons of his Hump quota to arms and ammunition for the besieged forces with or without Chiang Kai-shek's approval. Stilwell turned down these proposals as well as additional pleas for supplies from Xue Yue and Bai. In yet another clear reference to U.S. pressure on Chiang for his command of the Chinese Army, Stilwell told Hearn: "The time for half-way measures has passed. Any more free gifts such as this will surely delay the major decision and play into the hands of the gang. The cards have been put on the table and the answer has not been given. Until it is given let them stew."[151] The meaning was apparent. Hearn informed Chennault that Stilwell agreed that in order to restore the situation in the east, a "real operation" was required, but "he is working on a proposition which might give this spot a real face-lifting and is loath to commit himself to any definite line of action right now. Consequently, we must hold off in making any proffers of help to the ground troops until things precipitate a bit more."[152]

Bai Chongxi once again urged Chiang to pull back from a besieged city, in this case Hengyang, and concentrate on attacking the enemy's lines of communications. But Chiang still thought it was necessary to show the Chinese people as well as the Americans that the Chinese military was fighting the enemy head on and could win. Still, as at Changsha, the imperative to win at Hengyang was not strong enough to compel Chiang to insist that ammunition and other supplies be flown to the defenders. Chiang told General Fang inside Hengyang to keep fighting and ordered nearby armies to try to relieve the city. Stilwell's U.S. Army observers reported that the 62nd, 69th, and 37th armies did in fact take heavy casualties trying to break through the Japanese forces surrounding the city, while three other armies also suffered severe losses while attacking Japanese supply lines. Hengyang was finally secured by the Japanese on August 1.[153] After the war, the government built a memorial of 5,000 skulls collected from unburied Chinese soldiers.[154] The Chinese armies were not winning, but no one could say they were not fighting.

V

On August 10, Roosevelt notified Chiang that with his concurrence he was again dispatching General Patrick Hurley as his personal representative to China. He also suggested Donald M. Nelson, former chairman of the War

Production Board, as a presidential agent to study China's economy. Again, he urged Chiang to hand over command of all troops to Stilwell "without delay." Chiang mused in his journal, "What [I] must do is accept the humiliation and wait for my opportunity . . . all depends on my self-reliance, self-scrutiny, self-mastery, and self-strengthening . . . If it comes to the worst, there will be no alternative except to unsnarl the [ball of] twine with a sharp knife."[155] Chiang seemed to be thinking that at some point he would have to risk a break in the alliance with the United States.

Meanwhile a "United States Army Observer Group," unofficially called the Dixie Mission (a reference to the rebel side in China), arrived in Yan'an and set about determining what the Communists' goals were. The most influential of its reports were written by John Service, who was highly impressed by what he saw and heard. In his conclusions and comments, he occasionally put matters succinctly into perspective: "We cannot say with certainty that the Communist claims of democratic policies are true" and "[once the Communists are] the strongest force in China . . . they will then be free, immediately or gradually as circumstances dictate, to revert to their program of Communism." But such qualifiers were overshadowed by his sweeping praise of the CCP and its leaders in Yan'an: "There is no criticism of Party leaders . . . there is no tension in the local situation . . . there is no feeling of restraint or oppression . . . there is no hesitation in admitting failure . . . there are . . . no beggars, nor signs of desperate poverty . . . [and there is] total . . . unity of army and people." The Communist political program, he declared, "is simple democracy . . . much more American than Russian in form and spirit."[156]

Service did note something unusual: "In their thinking and expressions there is a noticeable uniformity." This sameness of opinion, he suggested, "may be the result of training in Communist thought and of Party discipline. But it may also, partly at least, be due to the fact that the Communist Party has not had to be a catch-all like the Kuomintang. Those who dissented have been free to leave . . . In some cases they have been expelled. Those who are left do seem to really think alike." Service seemed to imply that the remarkable homogeneity of thought in Yan'an was a positive if mysterious trait.[157] Service and the head of the mission, Colonel David D. Barrett, both recommended that the United States begin a program to supply arms and equipment to the Communists—otherwise "the chances of civil war would increase and Mao would return to his close alliance with the Soviet Union."[158]

Curiously, at this time, deep within the Stimson War Department a group of analysts in the Military Intelligence Division (MID) were producing a book-length study of the strength, nature, and intentions of the Chinese Communist Party. The analysts examined 2,500 military intelligence reports, interviews, histories, and other documents both friendly and unfriendly toward the CCP. They read all the reports from Stilwell's headquarters since 1942, including the reports of Davies and Service and the continuing dispatches from the Dixie Mission. Their study concurred with some of the sweeping and often superlative conclusions of Service and Davies. But the democracy of the Chinese Communists, the study concluded, followed "the pattern of the Soviet Union," where "real opposition groups are summarily repressed as 'traitors.'" It may be necessary, the report said, for America to "establish military cooperation with the Chinese Communists . . . [but] it is completely unrealistic to deal with [them] on the assumption that they are not Communists." The MID researchers also were devastating in their judgment of the KMT's corruption, disunity, and "lack of sincerity, as with the CCP, in its stated willingness to share power."[159] The report was released in 1945 just as the war was coming to an end, and it had no influence on thinking at the time, but it does show that there was an informed view in Washington of the CCP—one that was far more realistic than that held by most of the China specialists in the Foreign Service and the Department of the Army, the U.S. news media and academia, and many American political leaders.

By this time, Chiang had come to believe he would have to offer Stilwell overall command, even as he made it clear that the general would remain under his authority and he would have the right to dismiss him. Remarkably but not surprisingly Chiang did not appear totally cynical about negotiating this extraordinary arrangement with the United States. He even wondered once again if by careful management the difficult affair could even "change weal to woe and defeat to victory."[160]

On the morning of September 7, Roosevelt's envoy, Patrick Hurley, arrived in Chungking accompanied by the economist Donald Nelson. Hurley had gotten along well with both Chiang and Stilwell on his first mission to China (before the Cairo Conference). When the two Americans met for the first time with the Generalissimo that same day, Hurley said President Roosevelt proposed that Stilwell's authority be similar to the Anglo-American integrated command headed by Eisenhower in Europe. The unspoken difference of course was that Americans made up the great majority of Allied ground as well as air forces in Europe, while the Chinese Army was all Chinese. Hurley stressed that Stilwell would have to have "the full authority and confidence of the Generalissimo in undertaking his new assignment."[161] Chiang agreed, indicating that he even saw the decision on Stilwell as possibly an opportunity for carrying out other reforms in the Chinese military with American personnel. But Chiang also stressed that the authority for receiving and distributing Lend-Lease supplies should be taken out of Stilwell's hands and any Communists serving under Stilwell would have to accept the Generalissimo's final authority.[162] Chiang was reassured by Hurley's central message that President Roosevelt was not demanding anything; rather he was trying to satisfy Chiang's "needs."

Chiang was doubly pleased to find Hurley "very sincere," quite different, he thought, from "American officials in the past."[163] After the meeting, in another indication that Chiang was taking the matter seriously, he requested a briefing from the British military representative in Chungking on the command setup in Europe with Eisenhower.[164] The next day, he set down in his journal the "protocols" of Stilwell's imminent assignment: under the Supreme Commander of the China Theater, who was Chiang himself, Stilwell would be "the vanguard commander-in-chief in charge of frontline military action in all war zones." Notably, Chiang did not include the Military Council as an intervening authority. All war zone military troops, he wrote, would be under Stilwell's command—including Hu Zongnan's divisions, which were guarding against CCP expansion in the Northwest. But he added a new, steep price: the United States would "provide all the supplies required by the War Zone troops."[165]

On September 15, Hurley and Stilwell were called to a meeting by Chiang. Stilwell had just returned from a visit to the nervous city of Guilin, which Chiang had ordered its commander to defend to the death. Stilwell was almost certainly right that this was not the best strategy, although the Generalissimo's "do-or-die" order, like many similar ones he had given in the past, defied Stilwell's standard complaint to Marshall that Chiang Kai-shek "would not fight."

Before Chiang could talk about his concerns over what was happening on the Salween front, Stilwell, according to Chiang's diary, spoke in "defiant words" about the defeat of government troops at Quanzhou in Guangxi. More of Hu Zongnan's armies blocking the Communists, Stilwell insisted, should be dispatched immediately to the front line in Guangxi. Chiang was embarrassed by Stilwell's tone, but he moved on to his immediate worry—the persistent Japanese counteroffensive against the Chinese Y Force in Burma at the village of Long Ling. Chiang asked that the X Force now at Myitkyina immediately attack to the east in order to relieve pressure on Long Ling. Stilwell refused to do so, saying the X Force troops needed to rest. Chiang countered by saying that if this strategic movement could not be made, he would pull the Y Force back across the river to defend Kunming. Stilwell was "appalled." He declared that such a deployment would torpedo the entire Burma campaign.[166]

After the meeting, Stilwell did not confer with Hurley but rushed to inform Marshall by radio that Chiang Kai-shek, whom he called a "crazy little bastard," was about to cause a total reversal of the situation in Burma.[167] He blamed the defeats in Guangxi directly on Chiang, who he said regarded "the South China catastrophe . . . as of little moment," and he charged that the talks on his appointment as commander of all Chinese forces "were dragging."[168] He implied to Marshall that Chiang was deliberately not sending replacements to the beleaguered Y Force, although Stilwell should have known that the Generalissimo had rushed the 200th Division and 10,000 replacements to support those troops.[169] Stilwell's warning by radiogram was relayed to Quebec where Roosevelt, Churchill, and the Combined Chiefs were meeting, and provoked extreme alarm.

After learning of a positive breakthrough by the reinforced Y Force on the Salween front, Stilwell did not send a follow-up report informing Marshall that the question had been overtaken by events. Instead, Stilwell moved further to stir up a quarrel on the command issue, sending a memo to T. V. Soong declaring that he had "been delayed, ignored, double-crossed, and kicked around for years" in his attempt "to show the Chinese how they can hold up their heads and regain self-respect." This patronizing note proposed who should be the Chinese minister of war and who should be named chief of staff—Chen Cheng and Bai Chongxi, respectively—and demanded for himself "nothing less than full power" over the Chinese Army. If his demands were not met, Stilwell wrote, he would recommend that the United States withdraw from China and "set up its Asiatic base in the territory of the Soviet Union."[170]

Meanwhile in Quebec the Allied leaders were still under the impression that the situation in Burma was dire and that Chiang's inactivity was to blame. Marshall's staff drafted a letter for the President to send to Chiang that was more insulting and threatening than any in the past. Even Marshall penciled in some moderating changes before passing it on to the White House. Hopkins was still absent while Secretary Hull was also ill and soon to resign. Months later, Roosevelt disclaimed authorship of the note and left Hurley with the impression that he, the President, had simply initialed it when it was presented to him in a pile of other official papers. But Roosevelt himself almost certainly added the incongruously friendly concluding passage: "I trust that your far-sighted vision, which has guided and inspired your people in this war, will realize the necessity for immediate action." The very same day that this message went out, Roosevelt also signed off on a polite and friendly joint communication with Churchill to Chiang Kai-shek describing the developments at the Quebec summit, including the intention of the Allies to liberate Burma and a seaport on the Chinese coast.[171]

In the first message, drafted by Marshall's staff, the President told Chiang in no uncertain terms not to pull back the Y Force from Burma and instead immediately to send reinforcements to that front. It ended with the warning that if the Generalissimo failed to act in Burma as the letter demanded, "you must yourself be prepared to accept the consequences and assume the personal responsibility." On the question of Stilwell's appointment the message added no new requirement to the set of remarkable powers that Hurley was already on the verge of obtaining for the general; the startling parts were the President's hectoring tone and the clearly implied threat that all American aid would end unless Chiang "immediately" reinforced the Salween armies and "at once" placed Stilwell "in unrestricted command of all your forces."[172]

Stilwell received the radio message "to be delivered in person" early on the morning of September 19 and immediately saw it was "hot as a fire cracker." In great excitement he rode in his jeep to Chiang's residence at Yellow Mountain. At that moment, a critical meeting was under way in the residence conference room regarding the final terms of Stilwell's new position. Chiang and Hurley were present along with T. V. Soong, He Yingqin, Bai Chongxi, and several other members of the Military Council. On the table were the draft commission for Stilwell, the draft directive by the Generalissimo, and a simple draft diagram of command channels. Hurley had asked Stilwell not to come to the meeting, but an orderly came into the room about 5:30 p.m. and informed the Generalissimo that the general had arrived. "Ask General Stilwell to join us for tea," Chiang said. "We will be glad to have him."[173]

Stilwell sent back word that he wished first to see General Hurley alone, and Hurley joined him on the long veranda. Stilwell said that he had received a message from the President to the Generalissimo and, moreover, Marshall had directed that since the communication was "in the nature of an ultimatum" he was to deliver it in person. Hurley read the message. "No chief of state," he told Stilwell, "could tolerate such an insult as this letter." He then informed Stilwell of the progress in the talks that had been achieved that morning. Chiang Kai-shek, he said, had agreed to all the necessary conditions for Stilwell's appointment as field commander of the armed forces of China under Chiang's leadership. Chiang had also accepted every demand in the letter that Stilwell was just preparing to deliver. In addition, Hurley said, the Generalissimo "is ready to bring down troops from the north to reinforce you on the Salween front" and "is going to appoint you commander-in-chief."[174]

When Hurley pleaded for Stilwell to delay delivering the message, Stilwell refused. Hurley then asked that at least, before handing over the letter, Stilwell acknowledge to the Generalissimo that he (Chiang) had already agreed to its main points. According to Hurley, Stilwell replied, "No Pat, the President sent this message to me to deliver to the Peanut, and I'm going to give it to him right now." Hurley made a last appeal: "Joe, you have won this ball game, and if you want command of the forces in China all you have to do is accept what the Generalissimo has already agreed to." But Stilwell was determined. The two men rejoined the group. The Generalissimo was about to sign over command of the Chinese Army to a foreigner, but nonetheless seemed in a good mood. "I have a message from the President of the United States to the Generalissimo," Stilwell said, handing the English text to the interpreter.[175]

At that moment, wanting to minimize the embarrassment to Chiang, Hurley stepped forward and took the paper, saying that there was a Chinese-language version. He then asked Stilwell for the translation and gave that paper to Chiang, who proceeded to read it in silence. T. V. Soong later told Alsop that the Chinese version was even more insulting than the English one. After a few moments, Chiang put down the letter and inverted his empty tea cup. "I now understand," he said. Stilwell asked in Chinese, "That gesture still means, I presume, that the party's over?" A Chinese staff officer nodded, "Yes."[176] According to Hurley, as he and the American general walked out onto the porch, Stilwell, unaware that he had ruined his chances for the command he had dreamed of, said he hoped Hurley had not been offended at being bypassed in the deliverance of the message. Hurley said the potential for disaster was so serious the question was "insignificant."[177]

Everyone in the meeting, except T. V. Soong and Chiang Kai-shek, followed the Americans out of the conference room. Once alone with his brother-in-law, Chiang burst into "compulsive and stormy sobbing." After collecting himself, he told Soong that he was sure the letter was General Stilwell's doing. Stilwell, he said, would have to leave China. Chiang then set about drafting a reply to Roosevelt. T.V. telephoned Alsop in his lodgings across the river to come to Yellow Mountain immediately and the eager young aide appeared early that evening at the Chiang compound. T.V. showed him Roosevelt's letter as well as Chiang's quickly drafted reply translated into English. Alsop was astounded. The Generalissimo's letter was addressed to "The hope of the world and the light of the West."[178]

T.V. and Alsop rewrote the message, dropping the fawning salutation and making the substance and tone much tougher. This draft declared Stilwell persona non grata and blamed him for "China's fearful situation."[179] Early that night the Generalissimo wrote in his diary that the event that afternoon had been "the most severe humiliation I have ever had in my life." He then sent a message to Hurley asking him to come to a late, private dinner. The distraught envoy, who had returned to his quarters, hurried back to the residence. Chiang was somber. During the light meal, he said he was deeply offended by the letter's tone. Most importantly, he declared there could be no further discussions "while Stilwell remains in China."[180] Chiang showed Hurley the draft reply to Roosevelt that Alsop and Soong had written. Hurley was aghast. He felt it was far too strong and pleaded with Chiang to reconsider. His mission, Hurley thought, was facing a total failure. All he could do was try to calm everyone down.[181]

The next day, Chiang told T.V. to tell Hurley that Roosevelt's message represented the lowest point in the history of the U.S. leadership of the Alliance. Of the Chinese troops serving at that time, he said, 30 percent had been participating in the Chinese Revolution and war of resistance since 1936 and even 1922. No Chinese soldier would accept the "patronizing attitude" of General Stilwell. Then Chiang warned that if Stilwell "did not show due diligence, his life could be in danger at any time and any place."[182] The same day Chiang called Hurley again to Yellow Mountain and repeated the notion that the Chinese people, both military and civilian, would no longer bear Stilwell's humiliating behavior. But he still delayed sending his reply to the President.

In the meantime, apparently attempting to demonstrate to Hurley and Roosevelt his willingness to be cooperative, Chiang approved a military plan to save Guangxi that Stilwell had submitted. Chiang also ordered the execution of the commander of the 93rd Army, who had given up Quanzhou without a fight. Bai confirmed that Chiang planned to move another six divisions from the Northwest to help defend the South and Southwest. Finally, Chiang, as he had in June, asked Bai to take command of the Fourth and Ninth war zones—replacing Xue Yue in the Ninth—and this time Bai agreed.[183]

Meanwhile Stilwell, probably believing that his assumption of command would take place any day, at last ordered General Timberman in Kunming to fly about two hundred tons of ordnance to Guilin and Liuzhou. This was the first significant provision of supplies by air that he (and ironically, Chiang) had authorized for the ground forces that had been resisting the Japanese offensive in Hunan and Guangxi for five months.[184]

But Chiang had told Hurley that Stilwell had become an insuperable obstacle to cooperation between the two nations. The day after his meeting with Chiang, Hurley saw Stilwell and told him about the Generalissimo's angry reaction to the letter and to Stilwell's delivery of it. Hurley did not tell Stilwell that Chiang was determined to have him recalled. Stilwell thought it was funny and seemed to assume the Generalissimo's wrath was a sign of his imminent submission. That night the general wrote his wife that he had "played the avenging angel," and he dashed off a bit of doggerel for her:

> I have waited long for vengeance—
> At last I've had my chance.
> I've looked the Peanut in the eye
> And kicked him in the pants.
>
> The old harpoon was ready
> with aim and timing true
> I sank it to the handle,
> And stung him through and through.
>
> The little bastard shivered,
> And lost the power of speech.
> His face turned green and quivered,
> As he struggled not to screech
>
> For all the weary battles,
> For all my hours of woe,
> At last I've had my innings
> And I laid the Peanut low.
>
> I know I've still to suffer,
> And run a weary race,
> But oh, the blessed pleasures!
> I've wrecked the Peanut's face.[185]

Servants and staff members had undoubtedly heard the Generalissimo's sobbing after the meeting of September 19, and rumors spread through the city. "Rejoice with me," Stilwell told his wife, "We have prevailed . . . his head is in the dust. The dope is that after I left, the screaming began and lasted into the night."[186] On September 23, Hurley drafted an optimistic report to Roosevelt only hinting at trouble by saying that he was advising the Generalissimo not to make a response to the letter of September 19. He did not mention Chiang's anger. At Stilwell's request, Hurley deleted from his report a comment that Stilwell and the Generalissimo were "fundamentally incompatible." He included, however, a paragraph that Stilwell had asked to be inserted: "The necessity of safeguarding American interests [has] put General Stilwell frequently in a position where he has had to differ with the Generalissimo and stand alone in telling him the truth. This had in the past led to friction." Hurley wished to accommodate Stilwell, who had just given him a paper laying out an agenda for renewing talks with the Generalissimo. According to Stilwell, Hurley thought the paper "would knock the persimmons off the tree."[187]

Stilwell's proposed agenda started off with an imaginative arrangement for dealing with the Communist issue: the CCP would accept Chiang's authority exercised through Stilwell; CCP military forces would receive equipment and supplies for five divisions; the "Red Armies" would "be employed" north of the Yellow River; and the KMT and the CCP would drop their discussion of political matters until the Japanese were beaten. Stilwell's agenda also conceded that Lend-Lease matériel would be turned over to the Generalissimo upon delivery in China with the understanding that the X and Y forces would have priority, with second preference divided equally among the remainder of the first thirty new government divisions to be trained by the United States, the "Reds," and the proposed Guiyang or Z Force in East China. In his haste, but not for the first time, Stilwell completely forgot about the air force. He seemed, however, to be proposing that the United States eventually arm sixty central government and five Communist divisions.

Hurley told Stilwell that it was not Stilwell's role to solve China's internal problems. Hurley saw this as his own task.[188] Hurley also persuaded Stilwell to say once again that he would in the future change his behavior in dealing with the Generalissimo.[189] The next day, however, during a five-hour meeting, Chiang made it clear to Hurley that the general had to go. Stilwell, he said, had never tried "to maintain good personal relations." More importantly, while Stilwell "is a professional, works hard, is resolute, and good at his own military doctrine, which is to attack . . . he has no strategic thinking

. . . [or] basic political skills . . . [and] he is very arrogant." Chiang said that President Roosevelt had had "very good intentions" in nominating Stilwell for the command position, but he (Chiang) had lost his "last drop of confidence" in the general.[190] The U.S. government, Hurley conceded, must reconsider its decision, and on Stilwell's "new agenda" paper, he wrote, "Too late."[191] In a last-minute effort to save his job, Stilwell proposed dropping "the matter of the Communists" entirely and concentrating on building up government forces. But Chiang was unmoved.[192]

The next day Chiang gave Hurley a formal letter in which he said he simply could not trust Stilwell as the overall commander of Chinese forces but he would welcome any other qualified U.S. general to fill the position. He also welcomed the Americans' taking over the Chinese military logistics command. Hurley, however, found segments of the note insulting toward Roosevelt and said the language would have to be changed or he personally would not forward it to the White House. After T. V. Soong reworked the text, Hurley found it acceptable and it was sent on to the President.[193]

Rumors about what had happened at the September 19 meeting continued to circulate, and Chiang worried that his reputation, even his position, was in jeopardy. It was the lowest point in his career, worse even than the Xi'an kidnapping. "My heart is broken," he wrote in his journal on September 30, 1944. "It is difficult to go on . . . [I am] facing such insults within the Party and suffering laughing scorn at home. The humiliation . . . [has] put me in an embarrassing situation that I have never faced before." Nonetheless, he declared that he had to carry on or else how could he "face the martyrs who have laid down their lives?" After all, he wrote, despite all the losses, all the destruction, all the calumny heaped on China, "There is no cause for worry if I maintain my self-confidence and refuse to be shaken."[194] If the United States "cut off all aid and support," he told the Central Executive Committee, Free China could "once again hold out absolutely alone . . . if necessary . . . in [only] four provinces."[195]

After Washington received Chiang's note asking for the recall of Stilwell, Roosevelt, with Hopkins again by his side, rejected Marshall and Stimson's suggestion that he push the crisis over the brink by cutting off all U.S. aid. He gave way, however, to Marshall's insistence that the United States not name an American commander of all of China's field armies if Stilwell was not to have the position. Marshall also vetoed the President's proposal that Chennault replace Stilwell, but then he pushed the odd idea that Stilwell, the four-star general, should at least be allowed to continue to lead operations

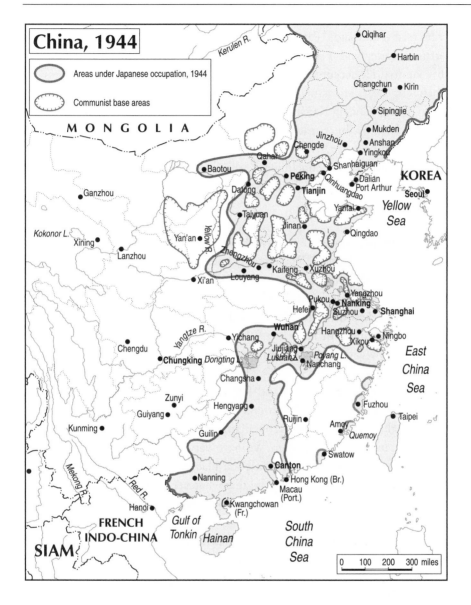

China, 1944

Areas under Japanese occupation, 1944

Communist base areas

MONGOLIA

to complete the Ledo Road across North Burma. Stilwell seemed willing to take this demotion, calling the suggestion "encouraging," but Chiang rejected it.[196]

That night Hurley was unable to sleep. He had done everything possible to save the situation for Stilwell, but at 2:00 a.m. he dictated a message to the President, strongly recommending Stilwell's recall. At daybreak, in a gesture of openness, he took the message to Stilwell. He showed it to the general, who read it and said, "Pat, that must have been a difficult message for you to write." Hurley said it was the most disagreeable service he had ever rendered his country. He accepted some of Stilwell's suggested changes to the message, then sent it off. The issue, he wrote, came down to a choice between Stilwell and Chiang. Chiang Kai-shek, he said, "reacts favorably to logical persuasion and leadership, [but] reacts violently against any form of coercion." And Stilwell, he went on, "is incapable of understanding or cooperating" with Chiang. Hurley then concluded: "Stilwell's every act is a move toward the complete subjugation of Chiang Kai-shek."[197]

Roosevelt finally agreed that Stilwell would be recalled at once and he nominated General Albert C. Wedemeyer, one of the three generals Chiang had proposed (at Alsop's suggestion), as the new China Theater chief of staff. Two days later, Stilwell declined the Generalissimo's offer of the Grand Cordon of the Blue Sky and the White Sun award ("Told him to stick it up his——!"), then in a meeting with Theodore White, Brooks Atkinson, and Harold Isaacs, who was now with *Newsweek,* he gave a scathing indictment of Chiang Kai-shek, his army, and his regime.[198] That afternoon Stilwell paid a farewell call on the Generalissimo. Hurley and T.V. were there. Chiang, who was wearing a dark blue Sun Yat-sen jacket over a black Chinese robe, was neither vindictive nor gloating. Adopting a conciliatory tone, he said, "It is very unfortunate we cannot work together. We have very different personalities and it may be good for us to work in different places for the same common goal." In a dignified response, Stilwell said that whatever the Generalissimo thought of him, he hoped he would remember "my motive was only China's good."[199]

In his last hours in China, Stilwell dashed off several notes, including "a very decent letter" to Chennault, but the flier did not know that his removal—at Stilwell's request—was pending in Washington. Stilwell also wrote the Communist general Zhu De a few words expressing his "keen disappointment" that he was not to be associated "with you and the excellent troops you have developed." Apparently he wrote none of the Chinese generals, including Sun Liren, who had fought long and bravely with him.[200] To the end he considered himself blameless in the breakup with Chiang. "At all times," he wrote on an undated piece of paper, "my relations with Chiang Kai-shek were on an impersonal and official basis, and although we differed often on questions of tactics and strategy, once the decision was made, I did my best to carry it out."[201] He left China on October 27.

Two days after Stilwell returned home, the *New York Times* carried Brooks Atkinson's long article on the general's recall. Atkinson had not bothered to seek out Hurley, T. V. Soong, Joe Alsop, or anyone else who might have given some balance to Stilwell's account. Atkinson described Chiang as becoming hostile during negotiations over the command question and as issuing a "personal ultimatum" to the Americans that Stilwell must go, without mentioning Stilwell's delivery of Roosevelt's prior ultimatum. Chiang, Atkinson reported, demanded personal control of Lend-Lease resources and declared he would "not be coerced by Americans into helping unify China by making terms with the Chinese Communists." Atkinson declared that "Uncle Joe" Stilwell was "more intimately acquainted with the needs and capacities of the Chinese army than the Generalissimo." He also wrote that Stilwell was "commonly regarded as the ablest field commander in China since 'Chinese Gordon,'" implying that in eight decades the two generals in China best able to lead Chinese troops were both Anglo-Saxon. Stilwell's ouster, Atkinson concluded, "represents the political triumph of a moribund, corrupt regime that is more concerned with maintaining its political supremacy than driving the Japanese out of China."[202]

Chiang read the translations of these and the other articles that followed Stilwell's return to the United States. The Communist bandits, he wrote, were taking advantage of this "perverted propaganda" to "stir things up." He insisted his mind was at peace, but he knew the fallout from the Stilwell affair would continue "for some time."[203] Actually, it would go on for decades, for Stilwell had won the battle of words, a loss from which the Generalissimo and his regime would never fully recover.

7

Yalta, Manchuria, and Postwar Strategy

Four days after Stilwell's departure, Wedemeyer assumed all of his predecessor's positions. The tall, Kansas-reared general, like Stilwell, had never served in combat prior to World War II, but before joining Mountbatten as his chief of staff, he had played a major role under Marshall planning the Normandy invasion.[1] Wedemeyer was a self-confident, tactful, and observant officer who during his first meeting with Chiang found him to be a "small, graceful, fine-boned man with black piercing eyes and an engaging smile." The Generalissimo, wearing his Pershing-style uniform, constantly fluttered a small fan and seemed to be nervous and shy though "keenly alert." Yet despite Wedemeyer's respect for the Generalissimo and his position, he saw the same deep flaws in Chiang's various armies as Stilwell did. Wedemeyer's first impression was that "the Chinese [officers]" were "apathetic and unintelligent" and devoted to "political intrigue and false pride." Chinese officials were afraid to report conditions accurately, "lest their own stupidity and inefficiency" be revealed. A few days after his first meeting with Chiang, he concluded that the Generalissimo and his military officers were "impotent and confounded."[2]

Wedemeyer also found the command structure in China shockingly chaotic. There was no overall general in charge of operations in East China. The Chinese staff in Chungking issued orders that might have nothing to do with what was happening on the ground. Deployments were piecemeal. There was no coordination between senior commanders in adjacent territories. Division-level command was "at best mediocre." There was no working system for replacing unit casualties with new personnel, and there was a lack of basic equipment, arms, supplies, and food.[3] The general noted in particular that after three years of alliance with the United States, Chungking still had no heavy anti-aircraft guns.[4]

Unlike Stilwell, however, Wedemeyer believed that the Nationalist government, "far from being reluctant to fight," had shown "amazing tenacity and endurance in resisting Japan." Industrialized and united France, he noted, had surrendered in six weeks, while China was still resisting after more than seven years and nearly three million total casualties.[5] Also, most unlike Stilwell, Wedemeyer had no illusions about the intentions of the Chinese Communists.

As he had promised in his message to Roosevelt, Chiang appointed an American—Major General Gilbert X. Cheves—as commanding general of the enormous and chaotic Chinese supply corps. Soon the logistics system was "beginning to work fairly well."[6] The most immediate issue, however, was the continuing Japanese offensive. After taking Guilin and Liuzhou in Guangxi province, the Japanese seemed likely to drive on to either Kunming or perhaps even Chungking. Chiang assured Wedemeyer that the Chinese Army would hold in Guilin, but in November both cities were evacuated. Wedemeyer's new defensive plan "Alpha" concentrated on saving Kunming by deploying most of the X and Y forces from Burma to defend the city. In December, Western news dispatches from Chungking reported that the next few days could determine whether China would be "knocked out of the war." Wedemeyer, fearing a Japanese paratroop and glider attack on Chungking, recommended moving the capital to Kunming. When Chiang replied that he intended to stay, Wedemeyer said in that case he would remain as well. This steadfastness impressed Chiang, who did not believe the Japanese would risk moving deeper into China, but if they did, wanted to make his "last stand" in Chungking, "to survive or perish."[7]

The attack never came. Meanwhile, in Leyte Gulf, an American naval armada destroyed most of what was left of the Japanese Navy, eliminating Japan's ability to ship significant tonnage to and from Southeast Asia. A few Japanese Army trains actually made the run from Saigon to Changsha to Dalian, but it was all in vain. Chennault's planes dominated the skies south of the Yangtze and their bombing of bridges and railways soon made the corridor of little use.[8]

The Japanese Ichigo campaign boosted Mao politically and militarily but cost his armies virtually no casualties. According to a Comintern report for December 1944, in the seven-and-a-half years of war until that point, a total of 103,186 men in the Communist Eighth Army had been killed. The CCP's guerrilla-oriented New Fourth Army had very likely lost a few thousand men, but more than a million government soldiers had died. In other words, between Zhou's earlier cited report to the Comintern in January 1940 and the December 1944 report—a time when Stilwell and others were insisting that the Communists were carrying the main burden of the war and that government forces were doing nothing significant—only about 70,000 Communist soldiers were lost.[9]

General Hurley replaced the irascible Clarence E. Gauss as the U.S. ambassador to China. Before leaving, Gauss told Wedemeyer, "We should pull up the plug and let the whole Chinese Government go down the drain."[10] Hurley, while supportive of Chiang, also proceeded to carry out the second mission Roosevelt had given him—bringing about cooperation between the Nationalists and the Communists. Usually an exuberant optimist, Hurley believed that the key was to earn the goodwill and trust of the Communist leaders as he had done with the Generalissimo. He was still convinced that the CCP leaders were in fact not real Communists but "radish" in nature, as Stalin and Molotov had described them—red only on the outside—and if treated fairly, would happily subordinate themselves to Chiang Kai-shek in a democratic coalition government.

When Hurley asked permission to visit Mao in Yan'an, Chiang reluctantly approved. Hurley landed at the Communist base on November 7 and as he strode down the steps from the plane, he let out his Choctaw war cry to the bemusement of the waiting Mao Zedong. He carried with him a five-point peace accord, and after much "pulling and tugging," he reached agreement with Mao on a revised version. The new draft put the KMT and the CCP on equal legal and political footing in a reorganized coalition government. All Chinese forces were to carry out the orders of the Military Council, but the CCP units were to remain intact, and supplies from foreign powers were to be shared equally. In return for these unprecedented gains for the CCP, Mao verbally pledged that the Communists would uphold Chiang's leadership both as president and as chairman of the Military Council. After Hurley departed Yan'an, the Communist Chairman was in a cheerful and jesting mood.[11] The American envoy had given him virtually everything he could have hoped for—equal status in what in effect would be a territorial division of China but one with no real restrictions on either CCP expansion or its monopoly of political power in its areas.

Hurley too was pleased. He believed that Mao's private pledges that the Communists would accept Chiang Kai-shek's leadership constituted a great breakthrough. But back in Chungking, Chiang lamented that Mao had "fooled" yet another American. T.V. told Hurley, "The Communists have sold you a bill of goods."[12] The fact that the amiable Hurley had approved Mao's draft of the five points suggested to Chiang that there would probably be no respite in U.S. pressure to force a coalition government with the Communists. The United States, he concluded, was still asking for concessions that, if implemented, would sacrifice his government as well as his "personal dignity." Again, he would show his "bottom line" in the negotiations with Zhou Enlai and Hurley, which was that the KMT would accept legalization of the CCP only after its military forces had been fully incorporated into the Central Army. This was to be the nub of the stalemate in the negotiations over the next two years—the Communists would only disband their army after a coalition government was established, but the Nationalists would not agree to a coalition government with any armed party. In a meeting with Chiang, Zhou declined to take the Generalissimo's "unacceptable" position back to Yan'an, but, he said, negotiations should continue and he would ask for Mao's ideas. Chiang detected that Zhou, the one Communist in whom he had any trust, "no longer appeared as deferential as before."[13]

Seeking to encourage the Americans' benign view of their party, Mao and Zhou sent a joint message to Wedemeyer asking him to pass on to the White House their desire to meet with President Roosevelt.[14] Mao also told Colonel Barrett of the "Dixie Mission" that the CCP army "would serve with all our heart under an American General with no strings or conditions attached."[15] Chiang likewise began the New Year with pronouncements intended to please the Americans. He promised adoption of a constitution at an early date, a return of government to the people, and immediate steps to liberalize and cleanse the administration. At a January conference including Zhou En-lai, Chiang's representative Wang Shijie proposed creating a war cabinet that would include CCP members; convening a committee of three composed of American, Chinese government, and CCP representatives to work out details on the incorporation of Communist troops into the Central Army; and appointing an American Army officer to command the Communist armies for the duration of the war under the Military Council. Chiang believed that he could propose such a decisive role for the Americans since they had accepted that the goal was to absorb the Communist forces into the government armies. In answer to these proposals, Zhou stressed that the CCP would submit its troops only to a new national coalition government.[16]

Although President Roosevelt had talked with H. H. Kung about an Allied summit including the Generalissimo, when the subject came up among the Big Three, the United States did not raise the question of Chiang's attendance. Roosevelt wanted to do nothing that might irritate Stalin, since the President's main goal at the summit was to formalize the Soviet commitment made at Tehran to take part in the Pacific War. At the time, the Pentagon and the White House, still uncertain when and if the atom bomb would work, believed the Japanese would wage a desperate fight on the home islands that could take another hundred thousand or more American lives. The previous fall, in meetings with W. Averell Harriman, the American ambassador to the Soviet Union, Stalin had confirmed that the USSR was prepared to fight the Japanese but his government had certain claims regarding Japan, Outer Mongolia, and Manchuria that had to be satisfied. Roosevelt and Hopkins seem to have accepted without much discussion the idea that they would negotiate Moscow's claims regarding China without even informing Chiang, who doubtless would want to argue with them that the Soviet Union was in fact eager to enter the Pacific War and thus no serious concessions were necessary.[17] The American President and his chief adviser followed their game plan, no doubt believing that their own good intentions as well as military realities justified it. Stalin, however, had no such fears about any disagreements coming from Mao; one day before the summit began, he informed the CCP chairman of the event and its objectives.[18]

The Big Three decided to meet at Yalta in Soviet Crimea, some eighty miles from Sevastopol, an area recently devastated by the advancing and then retreating German armies. Seeing the territory gave the Westerners some idea of the price Russia had paid in the war. As the formal unannounced sessions began on February 4, 1945, Chiang, still unaware of the meeting, had just sent Washington his proposed agenda for bilateral talks between his government and the Soviet Union, requesting U.S. suggestions and advice. In a great irony, the Far Eastern Bureau of the State Department, also uninformed about Yalta, curtly replied that the United States of course could not act as a mediator or adviser on matters between China and Russia.[19]

In addition to the Soviet Union's intervention in the war, the American President's goal was to assure China's recovery of all the territories seized by Japan, including Manchuria, which the USSR was to occupy temporarily. In exchange for the concessions Stalin sought, Roosevelt asked that the USSR respect Chinese sovereignty, withdraw from Chinese territory after the war, and not interfere in China's internal affairs. Stalin readily agreed. Roosevelt also pushed the related idea of a joint U.S.-Soviet effort to promote a KMT-CCP coalition regime in order to prevent a civil war.[20]

In a secret attachment to the Yalta Agreement, signed on February 11, the Soviet Union agreed to enter the fight against Japan within ninety days after the defeat of Germany. In return it would receive the Kurile Islands and return of the southern part of Sakhalin Island off the Siberian coast; a joint Soviet-Chinese commission to operate the Manchurian railroads; lease of Port Arthur as a military base; internationalization of the commercial port of Dalian; and an understanding that in Manchuria "the preeminent interests of the Soviet Union shall be safeguarded." The agreement also guaranteed the status quo in Outer Mongolia—in other words, that region's nominal independence under Soviet control. As for China, the document stated that the Chinese "shall retain full sovereignty in Manchuria." In addition, Stalin agreed that the provisions concerning Outer Mongolia and the ports and railroads in Manchuria would "require the concurrence of Generalissimo Chiang Kai-shek" and this would be achieved through a pact of friendship and alliance between China and the USSR.[21]

But Stalin also obtained a declaration by the three powers that the claims of the Soviet government [regarding China] "shall be unquestionably fulfilled after the defeat of Japan." In other words, Chiang Kai-shek would be compelled to concur in the decisions made without his knowledge. Roosevelt also agreed not to tell Chiang of the secret accord until twenty-five Soviet divisions had completed, in "three or four months," their move to the eastern frontier.[22]

Immediately after the conference, Stalin briefed Mao: The Soviet Red Army was coming! The Chairman cabled Zhou in Chungking right away, telling him to terminate the CCP-KMT talks under Hurley's mediation and return immediately to Yan'an.[23] Mao issued a call to all Communists to prepare for a harsh and bloody struggle against America and Chiang Kai-shek ("Mei-Chiang").

When Roosevelt agreed to the secret commitments at Yalta affecting China, he thought that somewhere down the road he could "straighten the whole thing out with Chiang Kai-shek." Besides, he was tired and anxious to avoid further argument. The critical assumption was that the Soviet Union was prepared, even eager, to cooperate in the postwar world as a "normal, status quo power" and not as a revolutionary state determined to create an empire of ideological satellites.[24]

Following the public announcement in February of the Yalta meeting—but not of course the secret agreements—Chiang felt "fear and suspicion" that something was being hidden. Yet as usual in dealing with the three powers, there was nothing he could do—except, in extremis, threaten collapse.[25] But at home, things were going well. Wedemeyer soon presented Chiang his plan for taking the offensive in July or August against the Japanese. The American general was optimistic not only about the fight against the Japanese but about dealing with the Chinese Communists as well. The following month, he would tell the Joint Chiefs in Washington that he thought the Communist rebellion in China could be put down with "comparatively small assistance to Chiang's government."[26] Hurley likewise believed that the military strength of the Communists was greatly exaggerated. His and Wedemeyer's views encouraged Chiang's own guarded optimism about the postwar period.

The Generalissimo and Hurley, however, soon heard reports about a "betrayal" of China at the Black Sea conference, and Hurley decided to fly back to Washington to find out what had happened. Before Hurley departed, Chiang asked him to assure Roosevelt that, whatever the Chinese Communists did, the central government intended to convene the promised national assembly and establish a constitutional government. As for the Soviets, he believed that if the United States took a tough stand against Soviet interference in China, the Russians would have to "think twice before they would supply the CCP with arms."

Rumors continued to circulate about the secret agreements at Yalta, and after much pressure, Chiang's ambassador in Washington, Wei Daoming, met with Roosevelt, who confessed to the secret accord and showed him part of the record. Upon reading the ambassador's report, Chiang's first reaction was outrage. China had been "sold out" and the war of resistance had been waged "in vain!"[27] The concessions on Manchuria themselves were not what distressed him; in less than a year he would be willing to offer Stalin even more in that region. More galling to Chiang was the insult to himself and

China in the way the Anglo-Saxons had assumed the right to give away China's sovereign rights.

But again Chiang quickly realized that he had no alternative but to accept the fait accompli. Consequently, his first decision after receiving the news was to ask Washington to receive a visit by his foreign minister, T. V. Soong, to obtain President Roosevelt's advice about "our joint strategy" in dealing with Soviet Russia and the Communists. The White House turned down the request, administering another insult, but a few days later, Chiang did hear from Stalin suggesting that they set a date for Soong to meet in Moscow with Molotov.[28]

In Washington, Hurley stormed over to the White House where Roosevelt's physical condition shocked him. The President's "skin seemed to be pasted down on his cheek bones." Roosevelt denied that China had been betrayed in any way at Yalta, but after several more calls, the President agreed to let Hurley examine the full, secret Yalta file. After doing so, Hurley was stupefied. He saw the concessions on China as a serious violation of the Atlantic Charter's principle that territorial adjustments must be in accord with the wishes of the peoples concerned. Feeling increasingly guilty about the matter, Roosevelt said he understood Hurley's concerns. The President and other high officials in Washington were in fact also having second thoughts about the entire Yalta agreement and overall relations with the Soviet Union. Moscow's aggressive actions in imposing a Communist government in Poland were especially disturbing. Influenced by his astute deputy, George Kennan, Harriman belatedly warned that Stalin's goal was "the establishment of totalitarianism."[29]

Meanwhile, Hurley read a State Department paper dated February 27 that called for U.S. commanders to arm the Chinese Communists if U.S. landings were made on the China coast and stated that the unification of China did not necessarily have to occur under the Generalissimo. Hurley was incensed that a draft of the paper had not been shown to him for comment. The recommendations, he charged, violated the policy of the President. He rushed back to see the ailing President, who agreed that the core of America's China policy was support for Chiang's government. Roosevelt trusted Hurley far more than he did either the State Department or the War Department. But Roosevelt also told Hurley, "Now, make it as easy as you can on [the Communist Chinese] and say everything favorable you can . . . don't destroy the basis for a possible unification of the armed forces by peaceful means."[30]

On April 2, Hurley held a press conference in Washington. On the basis of his meetings with the President, he declared that the United States would recognize and support only the central government of China. A few days later, as Hurley departed for Europe to consult with Allied leaders on China policy, Mao ordered a propaganda attack on "American imperialism."[31] At No. 10 Downing Street, Hurley got into a disagreement with Churchill, who said the U.S.-China policy was "the Great American illusion"—but he promised to support it.[32]

At 6:00 p.m. on April 13, Chiang was taking his evening stroll in his garden when an aide rushed out with an urgent message from the Foreign Ministry: Franklin Roosevelt had died of a cerebral hemorrhage. Chiang's reverential attitude toward Roosevelt had faded after the Cairo Conference, the demands regarding Stilwell, and then Yalta, but he still respected and honored the American leader, who had shared Chiang's dream of China as a great power allied to the United States. Consequently, Chiang worried that after Roosevelt's passing, U.S. policy might be "more influenced by Britain." He had no idea if Truman was a "sincere" man.[33]

Despite Hurley's many strong disagreements with the Foreign Service officers in Chungking over Chiang Kai-shek, he persisted in believing, like them, that the CCP was not truly Communist and therefore Stalin had no special interest in it winning power in China. In Moscow, after a series of meetings, Hurley was delighted to report to the new U.S. President that Stalin and Molotov had agreed to completely support America's China policy, including unification of the armed forces of China under the leadership of Chiang Kai-shek.

In the spring, Chiang convened the initial session of a preparatory commission for the inauguration of a constitutional government. In an important public speech he said that no one "conscious of standing at the bar of history would wish to plunge the country into civil war."[34] The Kuomintang, he promised the commission, would return "supreme power" to the people but only through the instrument of an elected peoples' assembly. Meanwhile, he said, the Kuomintang would be willing to admit other parties into the government. Back in January, Zhou had agreed in principle to holding the preparatory commission, but now he immediately sent a letter to Chungking and a message to Hurley complaining that Chiang had unilaterally proclaimed the political blueprint for the future. Zhou called Chiang's declaration "deceitful, China-splitting and one-party controlled."[35]

The Kuomintang also held its Sixth Party Congress, the first since 1938. The assumption that victory over Japan was soon coming excited the delegates and even Chiang's political enemies were willing if not happy to follow his lead. He submitted resolutions that the congress quickly passed: decreeing the imminent end of the period of tutelage or one-party rule; endorsing the passage of new laws to give legal status to all political parties; and calling for multiparty, direct elections to local and provincial assemblies in which all adult citizens, regardless of education or wealth, would have the right to vote. The delegates set November for the opening of a national assembly that would draft a democratic constitution to include all these and other provisions. The Sixth Party Congress was notably reformist as well as democratic in its edicts. It declared, for example, that the party had decided on measures to reduce agricultural rent, to resolve the questions of land tenure and land taxation, and to introduce sex education as well as an eight-hour work day. Chiang made sure, however, that the congress selected executive and supervisory committees that would put the democratization process under his control.[36]

Some old KMT veterans, like the Guangxi stalwart Bai Chongxi, argued that the constitution should not be put into effect until the Communists had been destroyed.[37] Free, direct elections, they warned, would not be possible so long as the CCP controlled a great deal of territory and people.[38] Chiang recognized the risks but felt that the critical need for good relations with the Soviet Union and the United States justified them. In his own mind, he probably believed that he had enough leeway, popularity, and power to keep control during a period of political liberalization. Improving the lives of average Chinese was consistent with his political values and interests. Just as he had no strong tie or commitment to the capitalists of his country, so he felt no strong identity with the landed gentry. Thus he was very likely serious in supporting the verbal commitment of the congress to land reform. Moreover, during the congress, he tolerated widespread attacks on corruption and incompetence within the government, the party, and the military, complaints with which he agreed.

At the party meeting, members of the KMT Youth Corps, led by Chiang's son, Ching-kuo, were among the most outspoken critics of general malfeasance in the party and government.[39] Without question, father and son sanctioned these attacks, believing that the openness to criticism would give credence to Chiang's proclamation that democracy was around the corner but also might have some effect. Foreign and independent Chinese journalists, however, took such candidness as simply confirmation of rampant corruption.

The Generalissimo also decided at this time to disband the political or commissar department of the Chinese armed forces. He did so partly in response to American criticism, but also because the commissars starkly conflicted with Chiang's demands that in a new accord with the Communists there would be only one, nonpolitical army in China—the National or Central Army. Mao, of course, never made even a symbolic move to depoliticize his armed forces, and when the next month he convened his own Seventh Party Congress in Yan'an, the Chairman, unlike Chiang, heard no criticism of his party or administration, its army, or its policies.[40] To the contrary, in the new CCP Constitution there was an increased centralization of power.[41]

I

After Ichigo, Wedemeyer ordered the building of new 14th Air Force bases northwest of Wuhan as part of his plan to retake the rice bowls of Hunan and Guangxi and then to seize a number of coastal ports, including Canton and Hong Kong. By the spring of 1945, with 1,050,000 Japanese troops south of the Great Wall, the Japanese commander in China, General Okamura Yasuji, attempted to preempt this offensive with attacks of his own into Hubei province in central China.[42] With Wedemeyer taking the lead, Chungking deployed sixty-seven divisions with 600,000 troops supported by two hundred 14th Air Force fighter-bombers. In three months the Chinese turned back the attack, proving that "with good commanders, modern weapons and vehicles, and a steady supply of food and ammunition"—as well as a sizable advantage in numbers—the Chinese Army could successfully defeat a large multicorps Japanese force. At one point Chiang, without notifying Wedemeyer, sent orders to He Yingqin, who was commanding the Chinese troops. When the American general strongly yet respectfully objected, Chiang, as he had on similar occasions with Stilwell, explained that he was only sending General He an opinion; but Chiang did not interfere thereafter. According to Wedemeyer, when confronted with "honey rather than vinegar," Chiang "was eminently willing to accede to planning in which he had primarily an onlooker's part."[43]

While these battles were raging, Hurley returned to Chungking and reported on his conversations in London and Moscow. Chiang, however, gave little weight to Stalin's professions of good faith—and the Englishman, he assumed, would pursue his colonial agenda after the war. Chiang was still brooding about Yalta and hoped to negotiate with the Soviets on tsarist "rights" in Manchuria that Roosevelt had "returned" to the Soviet Union, as well as on the bigger issue—the restoration of the Nationalist government's sovereignty over the whole region. So when he learned that Truman had informed Churchill and Stalin that every agreement made by Roosevelt would be "scrupulously supported," he was "outraged." Truman's blanket declaration had seriously undercut his leverage with Moscow.[44]

Around that time Stalin ordered the Red Army's 88th Brigade in the Far East to get ready to move into Manchuria. The 88th was an ethnic Chinese brigade made up of Chinese Communist resistance forces that the Japanese had driven into Siberia in the early 1930s. In constant training for some fourteen years, this unit, with its Chinese-speaking Soviet officers, had been waiting for the opportunity to return.[45] On April 6, Stalin formally abrogated the Soviet-Japanese Neutrality Pact.

Two weeks later, news reached Chiang that Hitler had blown his brains out and the Third Reich had unconditionally surrendered. Two American journalists described the reaction in China to the news as profound relief, "a winding horn to a beleaguered garrison heralding armies marching to lift the siege." The next day, Chiang told his senior generals that the Soviet Union would soon enter the Pacific War and occupy Manchuria, and he again pressed Hurley on America's support for China's territorial sovereignty over Manchuria. The American assured him that the United States would insist on "the principle that China's sovereignty and territorial integrity must be guaranteed." An American "guarantee" was what Chiang wanted most of all, but his main concern now was how to encourage both Washington and Moscow to live up to their separate promises.[46]

After Hurley informed Chiang that the Soviets planned to attack the Japanese in Manchuria sometime in August, Chiang issued urgent instructions to his civilian ministries as well as the military to prepare for an end to the war, possibly before the New Year. The bureaucracy that had been in hardscrabble exile for eight years was suddenly tasked with planning the takeover of all civil affairs, including the maintenance of law and order in the Japanese-occupied areas (which were home to close to 150 million Chinese), the return of millions of refugees from their long internal exile, the handling and repatriation of two million Japanese civilians, the replacement of puppet officials, and the preservation and transformation of banking and economic activity in the occupied areas.[47] Meanwhile, military officers, with their tiny inventory of trucks and destroyed rail lines, wrestled with a seemingly impossible task—the transport of hundreds of thousands of troops throughout occupied China in order to accept the surrender of a million Japanese troops rapidly enough to preempt the Communists. Chiang's government would be ready with plenty of plans—the difficulty as usual would lie in carrying them out.[48]

Meanwhile, Mao concentrated not only on preparing his troops for the CCP's movement into Manchuria behind the Soviet Red Army but also on seizing as much Japanese-occupied territory as possible in North China and elsewhere. On June 23, Chiang received a message from Yan'an that Mao was ready to resume negotiations. At the same time, Chinese Communist forces were attacking government troops in the mountains of Henan and even attempting to occupy Lihuang, the wartime capital of Anhui. Other troops from the Eighth Route Army in the North continued to move south across the Yangtze. In July, too, Mao wrote three articles attacking America. He predicted an ideological and political confrontation in the immediate future between America and the Soviet Union, and proclaimed the CCP's "lean to one side" policy.[49]

T. V. Soong, still premier as well as foreign minister, was irritated that Chiang included his own Russian-speaking son Ching-kuo as an adviser on the delegation going to Moscow to negotiate a key treaty with the Soviet Union. But Chiang now viewed Ching-kuo as his principal Soviet expert, and they had worked out their strategy for the negotiations. Already, conservatives in the KMT were demanding that there be no surrender on the issue of Russia's satellite, Outer Mongolia, which China still claimed. Chiang was ready to accept independence for Outer Mongolia via a referendum, although he knew that what Stalin proposed was "fake independence." Still, he understood this was the price that had to be paid if there was to be any chance of success for his postwar strategy.[50]

The Sino-Soviet talks began at the Kremlin on June 27. During a break in the negotiations, Stalin invited Chiang Ching-kuo to a private meeting in his office. Afterward Ching-kuo optimistically reported back to his father that Stalin had assured him the Soviet Union would support the National government in its efforts to unite China. Stalin also told Soong that all military forces in China must come under the control of the government, and that Soviet forces would begin withdrawal from Manchuria within three weeks of the Japanese surrender.[51] The Moscow talks temporarily adjourned for the final Allied summit, which opened at Potsdam in Soviet-occupied East Germany, again without the presence of China's leader.[52]

Although the atomic bomb had been successfully tested the day before the conference opened, the United States curiously remained anxious for Soviet intervention in Manchuria to end the Pacific War. During the meetings, in fact, General Marshall sent a warning to MacArthur, Nimitz, and Wedemeyer to prepare for a sudden Japanese surrender, while Truman and his new Secretary of State, James Byrnes, drafted an Allied declaration that offered Tokyo either unconditional surrender or "prompt and utter destruction." Truman dispatched the draft "Potsdam Declaration" to Chiang Kai-shek for his signature. Once again the Allies had not given the Chinese leader an opportunity to participate in the preparation of a critical Allied document. But Chiang, without complaint, approved it immediately.

Meanwhile, African-American army engineers finally completed the Ledo Road from Assam, India, to the Burma Road at Lashio, although from the halfway point of Myitkyina it was only a one-lane road and a pipeline. In February, the first Ledo Road deliveries arrived in Yunnan—1,111 tons of cargo. Oil did not commence flowing until April. The last full month of the conflict the Road delivered merely 5,900 tons of cargo. This was a fraction of the astounding 71,043 tons that American C-47 pilots flew over the Himalayas that same month.[53] But 73 percent of that airlifted tonnage went to support the more than 30,000 American military personnel in China at the time—each G.I. required almost two-thirds a ton of supplies each month.[54] The recapture of North Burma and the building of the Ledo Road had engaged China's best divisions through most of the war, consumed the great bulk of America's Lend-Lease supplies to China through 1944, cost thousands of Allied lives, and profoundly distressed Sino-American relations, but in the end it played little role in China's resistance against Japan or the defeat of the empire. Churchill and Chennault—and at one point, Roosevelt—had all argued in vain that this would be the case. Yet it is hard to fault the American Joint Chiefs and General Stilwell for the priority they gave this project in 1942 as the best means to open up a supply line to China. As it turned out, virtually all the arms that Chinese forces inside China received from the United States during the war came via the Hump airlift. With no apparent irony, Chiang suggested the route should be named the "Stilwell Road" to honor the general whose "strong will" made it possible.[55]

While the other Allied leaders were in Potsdam, Chiang, in Chungking, set down his thoughts about the postwar world. Like Mao, he foresaw the coming Cold War, writing that Russia had seized half of Europe and thereby taken America as its main "potential enemy," but would need as long as twenty years to revive its economy and its military. China, of course, was also "exhausted" but with its "great manpower and huge landmass" in the Far East, Chiang thought, it would "be on a par" politically with the Soviet Union, the United Kingdom, and the United States. But if the Nationalist government tried to suppress the Chinese Communists militarily, he concluded, Russia would support Mao and the military outlook would be "bleak." Fighting Russia would be "much more difficult than fighting Japan." In effect, Chiang was conceding—for the first time—that a civil war in Manchuria and North China between the central government and a CCP army supported behind the scenes by Moscow would most likely end in a Communist victory.[56]

To respond to these realities, Chiang concluded, China would need to focus on friendly and cooperative relations with the Soviet Union. But at the same time, Stalin would have to believe that Nationalist China had the determination and the military strength if necessary to take on the Chinese Communists, no matter how "bleak" the outcome. There was the rub. If China could develop into a "self-reliant country with a neutral foreign policy," Chiang wrote, then the USSR would "allow an independent [non-Communist] China to exist." But if China was weak—that is, unwilling or unable to take on the Communists in Manchuria—the Soviets would support the CCP, no matter how accommodating the Nationalist government might be to Soviet interests. One possible solution, he wrote, was to cooperate with the United States in "inner China" and with the Soviets in northern Xinjiang and Manchuria, as well as on the Outer Mongolian issue. It meant "focusing on economic relations with the U.S. and with Russia on political relations and the Chinese Communist problem."[57]

Ching-kuo's cautious optimism after his talk with Stalin, Hurley's strong assurances regarding a U.S. "guarantee" on China's recovery of Manchuria, and Wedemeyer's confidence in the Nationalist army's ability to deal with the Communists all played a role in Chiang's new assessment. Although he questioned the assumptions behind these judgments and he had only recently expressed again his deep skepticism about Stalin's intentions, he still made a great leap to conclude that because of global dynamics, Moscow could now "support the KMT rather than the CCP to unify China."[58]

Chiang knew that a massive U.S. airlift of government troops and supplies would be necessary for his forces to take over key occupied territories. Also, completion of the U.S. program to arm at least thirty-nine of his divisions and hopefully the ninety Roosevelt had promised would be critical to his strategy of persuading Stalin to pursue a collaborative policy. Assurances of American assistance were in fact on the way. Three days after Chiang set down his thoughts on postwar policy, Wedemeyer, following a directive from Marshall, discussed with him U.S. plans to occupy temporarily certain sites in China following Japan's surrender. Chiang welcomed the news and requested that after the surrender, the United States transport several hundred thousand government troops into Manchuria and North China. The Chinese government, he said, would assume responsibility as soon as possible for civil affairs in all areas, and the American units involved should avoid as far as possible any cooperation with Communist forces. Optimistic about Nationalist military prospects against the Communists, Wedemeyer agreed.[59]

Meanwhile, Chiang vetoed any possibility that General Stilwell might land in China with the U.S. Tenth Army, which he now commanded. The War Department concurred. Then, only two weeks before V-J Day, Marshall implemented Stilwell's recommendation and relieved Chennault of his command. During the entire war, Chennault's Flying Tigers and then his 14th Air Force were the only American forces actually fighting the one million Japanese inside China. Their achievements, while not living up to Chennault and Chiang's extravagant early promises, were nevertheless impressive. Chiang gave a farewell banquet in Chennault's honor and presented him the Grand Cordon of the Blue Sky and the White Sun, a medal Stilwell had refused.[60] During the announced farewell drive of the American known as "Old Leather Face," thousands (some claimed "millions") of cheering Chinese so crowded the street that the driver turned off the engine and the multitude pushed the car through Chungking for four hours.[61]

By August, the Stilwell-Wedemeyer program to train and arm thirty-nine divisions was more than halfway to its goal. When completed, this would be an imposing force of almost 400,000 men who were well fed and in above-average health for mostly poor, rural Chinese. Wedemeyer suggested adding forty more U.S.-sponsored divisions for a total active duty army of 120 divisions, including forty-one for local security.[62] Seventy-nine top flight divisions would transform the regime's military capability and dramatically enhance the government's advantage over the Communists. Wedemeyer's reports and recommendations continued to encourage Chiang to believe that his postwar strategy was feasible—his army could defeat the forces of Mao Zedong in Manchuria and anywhere else in China provided Stalin did not grossly interfere. Keeping Stalin at bay would require heavy American pressure, but U.S. involvement in the modernization of the Nationalist Army and in discouraging Soviet intervention would make it difficult for Chiang to convince Stalin that he was pursuing a friendly, increasingly neutral foreign policy toward the USSR.

On August 6, a B-29 dropped an atomic bomb on Hiroshima and some 78,000 Japanese perished—most in an initial bright flash of time. Early the next morning, the USSR declared war on Japan, and almost 750,000 Red Army soldiers stormed into Manchuria. The elite units of Japan's famous Guantong Army had already left to fight in China or defend the home islands, and within five days the Soviets were deep inside northern Manchuria and moving toward the Chinese and Korean borders. The Chinese Communist officers in the Soviet Red Army's 88th Brigade, mostly Northeasterners, began to disperse to fifty-seven locations all over Manchuria where they would act as commanders of city garrisons and administrative heads.[63]

On August 9, a second atomic bomb exploded, over Nagasaki. The next day, around 8:00 p.m., Chiang and other Chinese officials were having dinner with the Mexican ambassador when they heard loud applause and then the sound of firecrackers coming from the nearby former middle school that served as a U.S. military headquarters. The Japanese government had announced its acceptance of the terms of surrender in the Potsdam Declaration. Chiang finished the banquet and then convened a meeting with senior military officers. He immediately ordered the dispatch of a radiogram instructing all Chinese military commanders to warn enemy units to surrender only to officers of the Army of the Republic of China. He also dispatched a message to General Okamura in Nanking ordering him to cease all military activity, refrain from destroying assets, and accept the orders of General He.[64]

Next, the Generalissimo met with Wedemeyer and officially requested American help in disarming and demobilizing the Japanese forces in China. Wedemeyer cabled Washington, asking that seven American divisions land in key Chinese cities to take the Japanese surrender and preserve order until government troops could arrive. The American Joint Chiefs confirmed their

Chiang broadcasting news of the Japanese surrender and telling the Chinese people not to seek vengeance, August 15, 1945. Courtesy KMT Party History Institute.

previous instruction that the Generalissimo would have jurisdiction over the surrender everywhere in China except Manchuria and Hong Kong, and they instructed Wedemeyer to assist the central government in deploying its forces rapidly to essential sites, assuring they would arrive before the Communists. In a seemingly contradictory statement, Wedemeyer was also told that while helping the National government take control of occupied China, he should strictly adhere to "the basic principle that the American Government would not support the Chinese Government in civil war."[65]

On August 11, Chiang sent a message to Zhu De and Peng Dehuai, commanders of the Communist Eighth Route Army (now called the 18th Route Army by the CCP), telling them that they should follow the orders of their Nationalist war zone commanders and that their troops should not move until they received orders from the Military Council. In his reply, Zhu De proclaimed the right of his forces to accept the surrender of the Japanese and puppet troops opposing him. The same day Chiang wrote Mao: "The eternal peace of the world is on the horizon . . . I hereby sincerely invite you to come to our temporary capital as soon as possible [for talks]."[66]

II

The day that the Soviet Red Army invaded Manchuria, negotiations on a Sino-Soviet treaty resumed in Moscow. Stalin's new demands at the previous meeting for military rights over most of Manchuria's Guantong Peninsula had finally alarmed the Americans, and in Moscow, Ambassador Harriman advised T. V. Soong that he should reject them. Harriman also made strong representations directly to Stalin, and Truman sent a letter asking that the Soviet leader not press the Chinese for further concessions. But in keeping with his decision to maximize good relations with Stalin, Chiang authorized T.V. to give the Soviets what they wanted on this issue.[67]

On the key question of noninterference in Chinese internal affairs, Soong accepted the ominously less-than-comprehensive wording of the Soviet pledge that "the Government of the USSR" would provide support and aid only to the central government of China. This left open a huge back door—the Communist Party or some other "nonofficial" body in the Soviet Union could provide assistance to the CCP. Secretary Byrnes had sent word to the Chinese via Harriman that the Soviet language on this subject ought to be so explicit that there could be no future misunderstanding. But again Chiang gave in because of his hopes for Stalin's cooperation on the big issues; if China had insisted on more explicit language there might have been no treaty and Soviet troops would still have completed their occupation of Manchuria. By not taking advantage of the U.S. backing for tougher language that Byrnes offered, Chiang lost an opportunity to try to formalize an American guarantee of Soviet nonintervention in Manchuria. As it was, the treaty was initialed without such a firm guarantee and Molotov saw Soong off at the airport with a guard of honor.[68]

Chiang Kai-shek told Hurley he was "generally satisfied" with the outcome in Moscow, and for his part the American envoy saw the document as vindication of his dogged faith in Stalin. The U.S. Embassy in Moscow, however, noted that despite Soviet pledges to turn over Manchuria to the Chiang Kai-shek government, "the scope and discipline of the Soviet military position in the region" would "make it easy for the Soviet Government to remain master of the situation—in all essential respects."[69]

Mao's actions in the period just before and after the Japanese surrender reflected his readiness "to seize the golden cudgel" when revolutionary opportunities arose and—with bold, unexpected strokes—smash the existing order. On August 10, Mao ordered all guerrilla units in China proper to regroup into regiments and divisions, to expand their territory, and to seize major cities and railways in Northern and Central China. Shanghai, Peking, and Nanking were special targets.[70] Three days later, he told a meeting of Communist cadres that civil war on either a small or a large scale was certain. He dismissed the importance of the atom bomb and refused Chiang's invitation for talks.[71] For a week, Mao believed that through a combination of his own audacity, the weakness and division of the Chiang regime, and Washington's confidence in the moderation and good intentions of the CCP, he could seize control of many of China's key occupied cities. If he succeeded, he and the Chinese Communists could then be seen by the world and most Chinese as the real liberators of China.

That part of Mao's strategy was a gamble, but the outcome in Manchuria was clearly in his favor. Three days before the Japanese surrender, Zhu De ordered four armed groups to move into Manchuria and coordinate with the Soviet Red Army. Principal among these were 100,000 troops of the Eighth Route Army under Lin Biao.[72] Mao had finally linked up with the Soviet Red Army, a goal that he had pursued for nine years. He also dispatched the CCP's native Manchurian troops under General Wan Yi to march north to the home region they had not seen for fourteen years. Zhang Xuezhi, brother of Zhang Xueliang, the Manchurian hero under house arrest, led another small group of Northeasterners back home. Meanwhile, Chiang Kai-shek rejected the advice of Bai Chongxi and others that he bring back the Young Marshal and give him a prominent role in Manchuria.[73]

On August 15, Emperor Hirohito announced to the stunned but as always obedient Japanese people that the war was over—the Americans were coming.[74] That same day, the newly appointed Allied Supreme Commander in Japan, General MacArthur, issued General Order Number One, which the emperor also signed, specifying that in China, except for Manchuria and areas whose status was in dispute such as Hong Kong, Japanese forces were to surrender only to the forces of the China Theater Supreme Commander, Generalissimo Chiang Kai-shek. He Yingqin directed Nationalist forces in the field where possible to advance quickly into Japanese-occupied areas except for Manchuria. But most government troops were in the Northwest and Southwest and the commanders lacked trucks or access to working railways, which meant they required weeks of marching to reach the most important Japanese garrisons.[75] Bai Chongxi urged Chiang to accept Okamura's official surrender of Japanese troops in China only after Chinese government troops had taken over each garrison. That would have freed Japanese troops to fight aggressively, not just defensively, against Communist forces trying to take over territory the Japanese controlled.[76]

Instead, Chiang arranged a formal surrender date with Okamura, who agreed that the various Japanese garrisons in China, until relieved of their duty by government units, would resist if troops other than those of the central government demanded their surrender. In practice, what this meant was that, with few exceptions, the cities remained in Japanese hands until government troops arrived, but the Japanese garrisons did not carry out extensive patrols, and the Communists were able to move into the surrounding countryside. Within one year after Japan's surrender, the CCP had expanded its area of control from 57 to 310 counties. In North China and the northern part of Jiangsu, stiff battles resulted as Communist units attacked Japanese garrisons and forts in some smaller cities and along rail lines. Some 7,000 Japanese were killed or wounded in these engagements, but while the Communists overran a number of Imperial garrisons, none surrendered.[77]

In the Nationalist part of Shanxi, the warlord Yan Xishan began to recruit Japanese officers and soldiers to help fight the Communists, but when Chiang heard of this practice, he told Yan that it would provide the CCP propaganda opportunities. Also the Americans "would not appreciate it." All Japanese prisoners, Chiang decreed, would be sent back to Japan as soon as possible after the government units had taken over their positions.[78] If Chiang had followed Bai's suggestion and ordered the Japanese to carry out aggressive patrolling of the rural areas they had previously controlled, Okamura, who was strongly anti-Communist, would have doubtless agreed.

Wedemeyer employed the planes and ships at his command to rush three Nationalist armies to key points in the east and north. Over the next few months, American airmen and sailors would move 400,000 to 500,000 government troops into areas south of the Great Wall. This "spectacular" sea transport and airlift probably prevented the CCP from consolidating its control north of the Yellow River or even possibly the Yangtze. Wedemeyer personally viewed Mao's party as a radical movement operating under the aegis of the Kremlin and thus a serious threat to U.S. interests in the region. Thus the general stretched his orders as much as possible, but there were strict limits on how far he could go. Against Wedemeyer's recommendations, Washington suspended all U.S. training of Chinese military units, and Wedemeyer himself reluctantly rejected some transport requests by Chungking for reasons of "non-interference" in the internal struggle. On instructions, Wedemeyer began to dismantle "the elaborate apparatus of liaison and operational control, advice, and assistance" that he and Stilwell had built over four years.[79]

Just as Mao's plan for a sweeping seizure of territory began to unfold with attacks on some Japanese garrisons, he received a message from Stalin warning that a full-blown civil war in China at this stage would be disastrous. Stalin's paramount concern was avoiding a third world war so long as America was the sole nuclear power. Because he would have exploited such a monopoly had it been his, he feared the Americans might do the same if events escalated in China. "The only way out" of this confining box on Soviet behavior, Stalin reiterated, "was to end the American monopoly on the atom bomb," which would take a few years.[80]

In China as in Korea, Stalin's immediate goal was the departure of the American military. This required an American perception of a benign Soviet posture toward China. Consequently, Stalin believed that he had to go some distance in seeming to carry out his repeated commitments that he would support Chiang as the leader of a united China—he had, for example, just signed a treaty promising to support only the Generalissimo's regime. It was thus important to Stalin that the Chinese Communists concentrate on consolidating their position in the countryside and avoid action that might provoke the Americans.

After receiving Stalin's August 20 message, Mao quickly reversed course. Two days later, the Central Committee informed all bases that with the help of the Chinese puppets, the Japanese army, and the United States, Chiang Kai-shek would soon dominate the big cities and transport routes in China. Thus, Mao declared, the new CCP strategy would concentrate on occupying small cities and villages, consolidating the liberation zone, and mobilizing the people. He told the Politburo: "For now, generally speaking, we want to follow the French [Communist Party's] path, that is, a government in which leadership is exercised by the bourgeois, but with participation by the proletariat . . . this will continue for some time. We want to bore our way in and give Chiang Kai-shek's face a good washing, but we don't want to cut off his head."[81]

In Manchuria, the CCP immediately began the process of incorporating 75,000 former Manchuko puppet troops into its forces as well as thousands of other fresh recruits from the mass of unemployed Manchurian youth and the 80,000 or so bandits roaming the mountains. Meanwhile, the Soviets were quickly turning over to the Chinese Communists a huge collection of liberated Japanese weapons and military supplies. The Red Army sent the more advanced weapons and machinery back to the USSR and kept older Japanese tanks and artillery in an arsenal on the Sino-Mongolian border at Manzhouli to be turned over later. They also gave the Chinese Communists a number of captured Japanese armament factories, and the CCP itself found several underground arsenals that the Soviets had missed.[82]

With reports probably provided by Okamura, Chiang knew how many Japanese weapons and other items the Soviets had captured. In addition to hundreds of thousands of rifles, as well as other small arms and ammunition stored in 742 Japanese depots, the take totaled over 925 fighter planes, 369 tanks, 1,226 cannon, and 4,836 machine guns.[83] Chiang of course inherited even larger arsenals, including cannon to equip 116 artillery battalions. Contrary to Mao's later insistence that after V-J Day Stalin abandoned the CCP until the fall of 1947, books from the Publishing House of CCP Historical Materials, articles in official Chinese Communist journals, as well as Soviet archival material recount at length the extensive and deep Soviet-CCP cooperation that began with the Soviet Red Army invasion of Manchuria.[84] In late August, however, Stalin kept up the charade, telling Harriman that the Red Army in its sweep through Manchuria had not encountered any Chinese Communist forces. Stalin said he expected the Chinese government would soon send troops to take over the Manchurian cities.[85]

In August 1945 Mao finally accepted Chiang's invitation for talks, and Hurley personally escorted the fifty-two-year-old Chairman on his first airplane ride ever—a flight from Yan'an to Chungking. Before leaving his base camp, Mao wrote an intraparty circular explaining that it would be necessary to make some concessions in the coming talks in order to derail the KMT's civil war plot and win world sympathy.[86] That same morning, the Generalissimo rose at 5:00 a.m. and prayed that Mao would have a change of heart and permit the country to unite peacefully. He told a meeting of senior officers, "We shall treat Mao with friendliness and sincerity," and "in the political realm we shall be generous . . . [, but] militarily the unification of [government and Communist] forces must be thoroughgoing and genuine; [on this] there can be no compromise."[87]

Mao would stay in Chungking a full six weeks, lodging in a guest house in the Generalissimo's compound. That first night, to welcome the visitor, Chiang hosted a formal reception followed by a dinner party. The two men had not seen each other for almost twenty years, and upon meeting they smiled faintly. Chiang despised Mao as an enemy of Chinese culture and a Soviet lackey, while the Chairman viewed his adversary with both intellectual and ideological disdain. Each, however, had an appreciation for the other's indomitable will.

The difference between the imbibing, expansive, and humorous Mao and the teetotaling, taciturn Generalissimo was considerable. At one point, Mao raised a glass of the fiery liquor Maotai and proposed the ancient toast once made to emperors: "President Chiang Kai-shek, ten thousand years!"[88] The talks began the next day with a team of officials from each party holding formal negotiations while Chiang and Mao stayed behind the scenes, meeting separately at least nine times, including for long private conversations that were formal but always civil. During these conversations, Chiang pressed home his points while Mao, to avoid an argument, was either vaguely agreeable or evasive. In a notable concession, the Communists dropped their demand for a coalition government and agreed to hold a political consultative conference to decide on the election of a national assembly. Chiang made a seemingly major concession himself: the CCP would be allowed to keep twelve separate army divisions for some time and to occupy one provincial governorship if the officers and troops "really follow the orders and laws of the Government."[89]

The Communist delegation, led by Zhou Enlai, at one point proposed forty-eight CCP divisions and the CCP's exclusive control of five provinces and four major cities in various parts of China. Chiang was exasperated with Zhou. "How can there be creatures of such a base and silly nature?" he asked his diary. Mao told Chiang that once agreement had been reached on the areas to be controlled by the CCP, he would completely withdraw Communist forces from elsewhere in China.[90] Chiang's agreement to even twelve CCP divisions ran counter to his pledge not to compromise on the principle of "one country, one army," but it was to be a temporary arrangement. Two days after the Chungking talks opened, U.S. transport planes flew Chinese troops into Nanking and Shanghai.

On September 2, on the forward deck of the USS *Missouri* anchored in Tokyo Bay, a collection of Japanese officials in tails and top hats or army uniforms of rough cloth signed the formal Japanese surrender. Galaxies of ex-

Chiang, declining the honor, sent General He Yingqin to Nanking to accept from General Okamura Yasuji the formal surrender of Japanese forces in China. Courtesy KMT Party History Institute.

ploding firecrackers again crackled in the streets of China. Chiang, with critical help, had fulfilled his daily promise for seventeen years to redress the humiliation and shame inflicted on himself and on the great and noble China by the "dwarf pirates." The Generalissimo, however, was not happy. "Everybody takes this as a day of glory;" he wrote, "I alone feel great shame and sorrow." Stalin and Mao, he feared, could "plunge China into chaos and anarchy."[91]

While his meetings with Mao were still going on, Chiang was sending out urgent orders to prepare for large deployments to Manchuria. Bai Chongxi argued that the odds were heavily against success. Chiang knew something of the extensive cooperation going on between the two Red armies in Manchuria and also of new Soviet troublemaking in Xinjiang, but "the top priority," he believed, had to be the effort to take over civil and military power in the Northeast. Following his July analysis, his strategy was to seek the optimum or near-optimum outcome, but be ready to retreat. This required demonstrating a commitment to an all-out military effort in Manchuria, while secretly keeping open the option of withdrawal from part or all of the region depending on how Soviet and American intentions played out in this early postwar stage.[92] He named his son, Ching-kuo, as special Foreign Ministry commissioner responsible for negotiations with the Soviets in Manchuria. Ching-kuo was initially optimistic, but Soviet obstructionism soon commenced. Moscow informed Chungking that since the Sino-Soviet treaty had defined Dalian as a commercial port in peacetime, the Republic of China could not land troops there. In addition, five hundred Nationalist officials and bureaucrats arrived in Changchun, Manchuria, with the intention of fanning out through the region to assume control of local governments, but the Soviets would not give them permission to leave the city.[93]

Behind the scenes, Soviet officers recommended that the CCP deploy most of its now 500,000 or so troops to Manchuria.[94] Mao hardly needed encouragement—for him, this was "the golden opportunity that occurs once in a thousand years." The battle for Manchuria, he told his colleagues, would "determine the fate of the revolution." While still a guest in Chiang's compound, Mao ordered the main forces of the guerrilla New Fourth Army to move from their various bases south of the Yangtze Valley to North China to block the route to Manchuria.[95]

Originally, the U.S. Navy did not plan to transport government troops to Manchuria until sometime in December. But after Chiang warned that Moscow would use the delay as a pretext to turn over the region to the CCP, Truman arranged for the navy to transport over 200,000 Nationalist troops to Manchurian ports as soon as they were ready to depart. This was another signal of the American President's keen interest in Chiang Kai-shek's occupation of the Northeast and was an important factor in encouraging Chiang to fight for Manchuria.[96]

Meanwhile, at a September 18 tea party in Chungking, Mao proclaimed, "We must stop [the] civil war and all parties must unite under the leadership of Chairman Chiang to build modern China."[97] Chiang, too, spoke in conciliatory terms. When Mao came into Chiang's parlor on October 9 to say goodbye, Chiang pleaded with him to abandon armed force and compete on political and economic policies. Otherwise, the Generalissimo said, as "culprits" of history the two of them would be answerable not only to their own country but "to humanity as well." Chiang in turn went to Mao's quarters to bid him farewell, but the Chairman asked to stay another night and leave in the morning. The two then talked until 9:00 p.m., making Chiang wonder if it was "remotely possible" that he had touched the Chairman's heart.[98]

The next day, Double Ten Day (the anniversary of the 1911 revolution),

Patrick Hurley, Chiang, and Mao Zedong, September 1945, during the KMT-CCP talks in
Chungking. The six weeks of talks included many hours of private conversation between
Chiang and Mao. Courtesy KMT Party History Institute.

Mao joined Chiang for breakfast while the official talks adjourned with the
issuance of a vague but upbeat communiqué. The two sides agreed to establish a political democracy, unify China's armed forces under the Generalissimo, and convene the political consultative conference "as soon as possible."
The devilish details were avoided. After Mao left, Chiang strolled in his gar-

den. There had been scarcely any doubt in his mind before, but now it was certain—a political settlement that avoided a divided China would not be possible unless and until Mao came to believe that militarily he could not hold what he already had because the USSR would not give him the necessary backing.[99]

Back in Yan'an, Mao told his party comrades that the agreed statement in Chungking was "a mere scrap of paper," and he informed the Soviet representative that civil war was "virtually inevitable."[100] In a telegram to the Northeastern bureau, he declared that the party was determined to mobilize all resources to take control of Manchuria and to defend its positions in North China. Within six months, the Chairman concluded, "we must smash all Chiang's military offensives . . . then we can . . . force him to recognize the autonomous status of North China and Manchuria."[101] Mao at this point was thinking of a temporary two-Chinas outcome.

With Chiang's approval, Chen Cheng began to muster out more than two million officers and soldiers of the National Army on the grounds that they were unfit to fight and wasted funds best spent on improving the quality of the stronger units. Bai Chongxi strongly opposed activating the program until after the victory over the Communists, but the Americans favored it and Chiang went ahead. In the end, demobilization created masses of angry, disaffected, and unemployed officers and soldiers. Meanwhile, unlike the Nationalists, the Communists expanded whenever possible, taking in puppet troops and bandit fighters as well as ex-Nationalist soldiers. While the Nationalists were shrinking, the Communists were growing.

General Du Yuming, who had been appointed commander in Manchuria, returned to Chungking and gave the Generalissimo his plan for taking over the region: deploying ten Chinese armies, building a local force with puppet troops and officers, and making use of former puppet civilian officials throughout the region. Chiang, still not fully committed to the struggle for Manchuria, replied that he could only dispatch two armies, but he agreed to the use of puppet troops.

In late October, General Rodin Malinovsky, the senior Soviet officer in Manchuria, again denied the Chinese government permission to land troops in Dalian and Port Arthur, suggesting instead that they land at the ports of Chuluota and Yingkou. Ships from the U.S. Seventh Fleet with Chinese troops and their commander Du Yuming on board promptly sailed to Yingkou. But the Soviet forces there had moved out and Chinese Communist soldiers were occupying the harbor. Malinovsky said the Soviets could not guarantee the safe landing of the Nationalist troops because the Soviet Union could not interfere in Chinese internal affairs.

Chiang saw the Soviet behavior as "treacherous" and "shameless," and although Ching-kuo continued to urge caution, he decided in response to carry out "an aggressive policy."[102] At Chiang's request, the U.S. Navy landed Du Yuming's troops at Qinhuangdao, south of the Manchurian border on the coast just south of the Great Wall. From there, Du began an advance "with full force and aggressiveness" into Manchuria and easily defeated Communist units in the way.[103] But Chiang, growing more pessimistic about Manchuria, worried that the Chinese people would not support a prolonged battle over the territory because the war years had "drained the economy and the peoples' will to fight."[104] He began to favor the alternative plan to concentrate on "taking Inner Mongolia and strategic places in North China," and then deal with the Northeast. He called it "curing the dead horse as if it was still a live horse," implying that recovery of most of Manchuria or all of it was a moribund idea but that he would for the moment pretend it was not.[105]

On November 12, Lin Biao's soldiers moved into Changchun, the central Manchurian city where the headquarters of the Soviet Red Army's expeditionary force was located. Ching-kuo warned that if Nationalist troops were air-dropped into the city as planned, military conflict was bound to ensue.[106] In response, Chiang informed Moscow that he was moving the Chinese government liaison office in Changchun out of Manchuria and making known to the world Moscow's failure to honor its treaty with China.[107] He told his son that they would wait for the Soviet reaction to these measures. If there was in fact "hope of retrieving the situation," he said, "we can then indicate that we really do not wish to establish our military power in the Northeast; neither do we wish to provoke anyone."[108] Chiang was apparently thinking of a compromise that might make it easier for Stalin to accept Nationalist administration of all—or at least part—of Manchuria.

III

In mid-November, Wedemeyer returned from a trip to Washington and reported to Chiang that President Truman had pledged his continuing support of the Generalissimo. The United States would complete the rearming of thirty-nine divisions and fifteen air squadrons and would establish a U.S. military advisory group in China. But, the general warned, this aid would stop if civil war broke out—a stipulation that gave the Generalissimo a strong disincentive, and Mao an equal incentive, for provoking civil conflict.[109] The Joint Chiefs, while expressing full agreement with Truman's China policy, including military aid to the Nationalist government, had at the same time instructed Wedemeyer in stronger terms than before that American forces were "not to become involved in the difficulties between the Nationalist Government Forces and the Chinese Communists." Wedemeyer warned Chiang that "arrangements in the Northeast" were to be considered strictly a matter between China and the Soviet Union, although the U.S. Navy would still transport some 200,000 government troops to the region.[110]

Then, speaking personally, Wedemeyer said that despite Truman's statement of support, in his opinion the United States could not and would not furnish the necessary military aid that would allow the Central Army to take over Manchuria. Moreover, he warned, if without such aid the government did make an all-out effort in Manchuria, it would not have the strength to reestablish itself in North China. Wedemeyer urged Chiang to concentrate on holding the territory south of the Great Wall—a suggestion with which Chiang seemed to agree. In addition, he suggested that Chiang propose a temporary five-power trusteeship of Manchuria.[111] However late, this was wise and unique counsel from an American. But it was not the official position in Washington, which wanted the Nationalist Army, not a party allied to the Soviet Union, to take over Manchuria—but also wished to avoid American involvement in a Chinese civil war. The solution to the dilemma these conflicting objectives posed was to pursue both.

Wedemeyer's new views and recommendations, blatant Soviet obstructionism, Lin Biao's increasing deployments in the Northeast, and General's Du's report that he needed ten armies to occupy the region all convinced Chiang to halt his army's tentative operations to reclaim Manchuria. Judging by his diary comments in November 1945 and his actions thereafter, however, his decision to pull out of Changchun still did not reflect a final commitment to abandon the region but rather an effort to test both American and Soviet intentions. Wedemeyer's strong words had significantly influenced Chiang toward withdrawal, and the "dead horse" analogy had been in the back of his mind at least since the summer. Nevertheless, Chiang devised a two-pronged strategy: prepare for complete withdrawal while highlighting for Washington the crisis Moscow was causing. He hoped the Truman administration would become seriously alarmed over Stalin's violation of his promises at Yalta and his other commitments to support only the Nationalist government. But he also wanted to keep open at least the possibility of moving in the direction that Ching-kuo still believed feasible—détente with the Soviets, including major economic concessions such as possibly splitting the Northeast region with the CCP, and possibly even making changes in China's relations with the United States.

Three days after his talks with Wedemeyer, Chiang informed the Soviet embassy that he was protesting to Washington Moscow's actions in Manchuria and the USSR would be responsible for the consequences.[112] He ordered General Sun Liren to stop the advance of his New First Army to Mukden, and in an important speech to high-ranking officers on November 16 said that even if he sent five armies into Manchuria they would still not be able "to gain solid local control." Under the circumstances, he said, "We had rather leave the issue of Manchuria aside . . . the policy is to control the close areas [North China] and then expand our authority to the further areas."[113] On November 17, Chiang wrote to President Truman explaining the abject failure of the Soviets to live up to their commitments.

The Soviets now suddenly changed their tune. In response to Chiang's message to their embassy, they said that the Russian government would strictly abide by the Friendship Treaty and that, in order to facilitate the Nationalist takeover of the region, they would postpone the Red Army withdrawal for another two months. Oddly, both Chiang and his son had come to believe that the postponement, which Mao very much wanted, would avoid a vacuum that only the CCP could fill. The Generalissimo became hopeful again. "So," he mused in his diary, "Russia still cares about international opinion."[114]

On November 21, Malinovsky told Ching-kuo that he was sorry the National government had withdrawn and that he was shocked to learn the Chinese Communists had surrounded the KMT's headquarters in Changchun. He agreed that the KMT-appointed mayors and other officials could take up their duties around the region, and his staff began to negotiate Manchurian economic issues in a seemingly serious manner.[115] Stalin also accepted an earlier proposal that Chiang send a special envoy to Moscow. Likewise Malinovsky readily agreed to Chiang's suggestion that the Red Army withdrawal be further delayed until February 1, 1946. Mao was delighted because he had in fact also requested the Soviets to further postpone their pullout.[116]

By early December, Ching-kuo was reporting to his father that the Soviets had "agreed to almost all of the Government's proposals, including abolishment of all non-government armed forces."[117] At Ching-kuo's urging, Chungking did not make a public case against the extravagant Soviet pillaging of equipment and factories in the region, a plundering valued by an American study at US$2 billion dollars.[118]

In his 1957 book *The Soviet Union in China,* Chiang charged that "domestic and foreign interferences" were responsible for his failing "to adhere to [his] earlier policy" not to occupy Manchuria. Instead, he wrote, he committed "his best troops to Manchuria and got bogged down there." He was apparently referring not only to Russian promises of cooperation but also to the encouragement of Washington—aside from Wedemeyer's personal advice—for a Nationalist takeover of Manchuria, including the U.S. Navy's agreement to transport six corps of Chiang's troops to the region. In 1957 Chiang lamented that in this decision he had depended on diplomacy, thus "sacrificing substance for the shadow."[119] By early December 1945, wanting to test the Soviets, Chiang ordered Sun Liren to resume his advance to Mukden. Sun did so and encountered little Communist resistance.

Back in Washington, on November 27, Hurley unexpectedly resigned in a huff, denouncing those in the State Department whom he accused of working against him. Alarmed at the turmoil around his country's China policy, Truman decided he needed an even more distinguished envoy to achieve America's goals in China before things fell apart. George Marshall had just retired from the army as one of America's three most eminent generals, but his golden years would not be occupied with horseback riding and writing memoirs—at least not yet. He and his wife, Katherine, had been back at their home in Leesburg, Virginia, for only a few minutes when the President called and said: "General, I want you to go to China for me." "Yes, Mr. President," Marshall replied, and abruptly hung up. He wanted to break the news to Katherine after she had rested, but she first heard the news on the radio: her husband had agreed to go to China and bring about a democratic coalition between the Communists and the Nationalists.[120]

When the Marshall Mission was announced, Zhou Enlai explained in several internal policy papers that in the talks with this latest American envoy, the CCP goal would be to "neutralize the United States" and make use of "internal divisions in America on China policy." Zhou was confident that the "contradictions between the U.S. and Chiang Kai-shek" and "knowledge of the ideology and value system of Americans" would allow the CCP to emerge successfully from the inevitable collapse of the coming talks.[121] All these elements would in fact be key ingredients in the dynamics of the Marshall Mission, and no one knew better than Zhou the psychology of the earnest Americans.

Meanwhile Sun Liren was on the outskirts of Mukden, but Chiang was still uncertain whether a reasonable solution with Stalin was possible. "We should follow our plan that [in the worst case] we will withdraw our headquarters from the Northeast," he wrote. "This is to avoid being hijacked by them and losing our freedom of movement . . . We must have extra caution now; there is no need for haste."[122]

On December 8, before leaving for China, General Marshall had two memorable meetings with President Truman and Secretary of State James F. Byrnes. The general said he understood that he was to do his best to influence Chiang Kai-shek to make reasonable concessions in his negotiations with the Communists, and he should imply to the Generalissimo that future U.S. aid was at stake. But, Marshall added, he was worried that if Chiang made no reasonable concessions, the talks broke down, and the United States subsequently ended its aid to Chungking, there would follow "a resumption of power in Manchuria by Russia"—meaning that China at best would, like Eastern Europe and Korea, be divided into Communist and non-Communist parts. Such an outcome, Marshall said, would result in the "defeat . . . of the major purpose of our war in the Pacific," that is, a strong and friendly China.[123]

This was a tough, realpolitik view of the matter. Truman, with his own tough-mindedness and penchant for the idea of containment, immediately agreed, but he emphasized that the United States would not in any event send additional troops to China.[124] In another meeting the next day, Marshall spelled out the policy implication that was not in his written instructions: in the event that he was unable to secure reasonable action by the Generalissimo in the interparty talks, it would "still be necessary for the U.S. Government, through me, to continue to back the National Government of China." The President said this was correct.[125] In Marshall's publicly released directive, Truman instructed the general to tell Chiang Kai-shek that "a China disunited and torn by civil strife could not be considered realistically as a proper place for American Assistance."[126] But in another public statement of December 15, the President made clear that the National government of China was the "practical instrument to achieve the unification of China." Unity in China, the President said, would require "progress toward democracy" but also concurrently the elimination of "autonomous armies" such as those of the Communists. When Chiang read this statement he was extremely pleased. This was everything he had hoped for. The U.S. President had supported the Nationalist government and succinctly endorsed Chiang's core principle in negotiating with the CCP.[127]

On December 16, Chiang visited Peking for the first time since the early 1930s. One Chinese American who was there as a boy recalls that when the government troops had arrived two months earlier, there was looting and raping. Nonetheless, when the Generalissimo drove into the great plaza of the Forbidden City, 100,000 students gave him a tumultuous greeting, a welcome that excited him. In his speech he told the young crowd that in the past "we were like a pile of sand and this triggered the aggression of enemies. In the future, if we are to complete the cause of national reconstruction, we all must gather under the flag of the Three Peoples Principles, love and respect each other, and cooperate to achieve our goals."[128]

Following his remarks, thousands rushed forward to touch his clothing or simply gaze at him. It took half an hour for his bodyguards to get him safely into his car and away. The Generalissimo kept reassuring his security men, "They are well intentioned. They mean well." A huge portrait of the thin, stern-looking Generalissimo soon went up over the entrance to the Forbidden City at Tiananmen.[129]

Chiang then flew to Nanking. From the plane he could see the great tomb of Sun Yat-sen and he must have thought of his and Mayling's last-minute escape by air in 1937 and the death and destruction the city had suffered. His heart "throbbed with a thousand emotions." In one of his increasingly Christian references, he thanked "Our Heavenly Father" for the "glorious victory" and his own safe return. From the airport, sitting stiff and erect in the back seat of a long, open limousine, he rode through the streets lined with cheering citizens and tears filled his eyes. Back in the old residence in the military academy compound, he wrote a banner in his stiff calligraphy proclaiming the house "The Hall of Christian Victory."[130]

At peak periods, unoccupied China hosted about 30 million refugees, although once the fighting and the Japanese had moved on, many returned to their homes. Several million of the long-term refugees were mostly former urban dwellers who were government and party workers of middle or higher rank and who had waited out the war in Chungking, Kunming, and other free cities. A few hundred thousand military officers with their families lived in the countryside, frequently moving, never sure what the next day would bring, surviving long and arduous times. Most had lived austere lives and survived Japanese bombings, disease, and food shortages.[131] When they returned to Nanking, Shanghai, and hundreds of other cities and towns where they had lived and worked before 1937, it was with a deep sense of triumph, self-satisfaction, and in many cases, entitlement.

Among the 150 million Chinese who had stayed behind, some had collaborated and profited from the occupation, a few had resisted, and most had cooperated to the minimum extent necessary to get by. In the minds of many former exiles, however, a cloud hung over all educated, professional, or well-off Chinese who had remained—and as for themselves, they expected preferential treatment. The Generalissimo appointed mostly KMT generals as governors and mayors in provinces and cities, and most had not grown up in the areas they were now to govern. The practice of non-native governors was a Chinese tradition, but in the postwar environment it encouraged rather than discouraged cronyism and corruption. Most immediately harmful was Chiang's appointment of southerners as governors of the Manchurian provinces.

Zhou Enlai's agents and Chiang's many other enemies exaggerated or fabricated many accounts of corruption in the postwar period, but many were true. The candor on this subject shown by the newly freed press was impressive. The papers of Shanghai, Tianjin, Kunming, Canton, Hong Kong, and other cities overnight resumed their freewheeling reporting and editorializing on the ills of the government.

Some of those close to Chiang who were not corrupt, like Ching-kuo, Chen Lifu, Chen Cheng, and Zhang Qun, also brought word to him of the corruption that was rapidly spreading throughout the society. Only two months after Japan's surrender, Chiang called in the newly appointed senior officials of Nanking, Shanghai, Peking, and Tianjin and scolded them for the bad discipline of KMT officers taking over those cities.[132] But while Chiang ranted against official dishonesty and demanded action to curtail it, he still considered it, like inflation, of secondary importance—it was bad, he thought, but not "rampant."[133] In addition, serious efforts to correct stealing by high officials posed complicated political problems; thus in Chiang's view, it was a reform that could continue being mostly put off until true political unity had been achieved.

Meanwhile, the CCP did not move into the cities nor did it take over huge bureaucracies and enterprises that offered the potential for self-advancement and enrichment. The Communists cadre in their harsh environment remained underdogs who faced possible destruction by the much more powerful KMT. After V-J Day they expected not reward for past sacrifice but greater sacrifice to come.

A special grievance arose among those Chinese who had stayed in Japanese-occupied areas when Chungking set the rate at which they could exchange their soon-to-be worthless puppet currencies for the official Chinese *fabi*. In September, one yuan in the Chungking *fabi* was worth thirty puppet *fabi*. The black-market exchange rate, which the expected collapse of Japan had sent spiraling upward over the previous year or more, was about two hundred to one. Chiang approved an official rate of exchange equal to the black-market rate, which led to stories that the government had divested millions of Chinese of their assets.[134] The *Dagongbao* newspaper, for example, editorialized that citizens awoke one morning to discover that "most of them had lost their home and property . . . Wealth which had taken generations to accumulate was transferred in a twinkling to those with gold dollars and Nationalist dollars in their hands."[135]

Subsequent scholars would cite the *Dagongbao* allegation that "most" Chinese citizens in the formerly occupied areas—that is, the majority of over 150 million people—literally lost overnight their "homes and property" as a result of the currency devaluation.[136] But this charge does not hold up to serious examination. For one thing, the black-market rate is always quickly reflected in market prices. Most importantly, however, the exchange rate for swapping the two currencies did not affect the value of land and houses, jewelry, or gold and silver—the traditional ways in which almost all Chinese saved wealth. Those few with debts denominated in puppet *fabi* actually benefited from the plunge in that paper's value.[137] For well over a year, Japan's defeat had been expected in the occupied areas, inflation and the black-market rate of the puppet currency had soared, and it was the rare Chinese who long before V-J Day had not divested himself of any substantial holding of puppet currency.

Wedemeyer and Walter Robertson, acting chief of the U.S. Embassy in Chungking, met Marshall when he arrived at Shanghai International Airport on December 18, and escorted him to his room in the Cathay Hotel. There, the famous general showed Wedemeyer his instructions from President Truman. After reading the document, Wedemeyer commented that the Nationalists still had most of the power and were determined not to give it up, while the Communists were equally determined to seize all power with the help of the Soviet Union. Peace between the KMT and the CCP, he thought, was "remote." Marshall reacted angrily, saying that he intended to accomplish his mission and Wedemeyer was "going to help" him. He continued to be upset during a private dinner that night, and Wedemeyer, apparently intimidated by the rebuke, seems to have never again frankly told Marshall his views about what was happening. Despite this bad beginning, Marshall and Wedemeyer became close over the next few months.[138]

Chen Lifu had told the Generalissimo that he should turn down the Marshall peace mission because if it failed as it probably would, the Americans would blame the Chiang government, not the Communists.[139] But Chiang rejected this advice. Continuing American economic and military assistance was critical, including troop transport, but even more important was the promise of American political pressure on the Soviets. Moreover, Truman's public statement of December 15 had dramatically underscored for Chiang that Marshall's mediation effort was starting off in the right direction.

The day after arriving in Shanghai, Marshall and his party flew to Nanking. The official capital and residence were still temporarily in Chungking, but Chiang Kai-shek and Madame waited for the distinguished envoy in the Generalissimo's small two-story brick home in the compound of the Chinese Army headquarters in the old capital. (After V-J Day, the Generalissimo's aides had proposed that he take over the palace-like residence of Wang Jing-wei, but he had declined.) Marshall arrived at Chiang's office in uniform, carrying a cane and wearing his tan British-style overcoat with its fur collar and his visored Army cap. Impressed, Chiang extended his hand and found Marshall's shake as soft as his own.[140] They had been on opposite sides in the ugly battles over Stilwell, but they shared a common temperament that allowed them easily to put aside past conflicts and hard feelings. Chiang saw Marshall as a proud professional, a man of honor and dignity, "a fine Christian gentleman" whom he might win over as he had most other special representatives whom Washington had dispatched to China over the years.[141]

Marshall and Chiang both were introspective, reserved, and formal—in other words, stiff. During Marshall's early days as U.S. Army chief of staff, when Roosevelt called him "George," Marshall had suggested to the President that they keep to their formal titles. The Generalissimo would have agreed with that. Neither man had a great sense of humor. They valued discipline, duty, patriotism, and honor—or as Chiang preferred to put it, sincerity. According to Wedemeyer, whether on trips to world conferences, hiking down from his Fort Meyers quarters to the Pentagon, or in China as President Truman's special envoy, there was always "a reserve or hint of some mysterious, unseen but always present force which had first call on General Marshall's deeper thoughts."[142] Likewise, whether meditating outside a campaign tent, staring down at the fog-shrouded Yangtze, or peering from his new portrait over the gate to the Forbidden City, Chiang Kai-shek seemed detached, as though he were attending to some inexplicable but powerful destiny.

During his first exchange with the Chiangs, Marshall said the President was "aware of the extreme difficulties in achieving successful negotiation" and that both the President and he himself understood that the solution to the problem involved the Communist Army and its refusal to surrender or relinquish its autonomy. For Chiang it was again exceedingly important to hear Marshall reiterate Truman's statement on this subject.[143]

In response, Chiang was surprisingly upbeat about the talks with the CCP, telling the new envoy that there were "signs of progress": in particular, the Chinese Communists had followed the Soviets in all matters of broad policy, and Stalin had recently appeared to reverse his "unfriendly attitude."[144] Encouraged by this first meeting, Marshall and his aides flew to Chungking, where he set up his headquarters in a villa called "Happiness Gardens." The next day, he and his staff met with the relaxed, engaging, and sophisticated yet unassuming Zhou Enlai. As usual, Zhou impressed the new group of Americans as their "kind of guy." Flattering the United States shamelessly, Zhou said China should learn from America's democracy, agricultural reform, and industrialization, to which Marshall in his reports expressed no skepticism. "This intense Communistic thing," he would tell an interviewer years later, "I was not aware of really in detail until I got over there after the war."[145] That night, Chiang Kai-shek and Mayling gave an elaborate banquet in honor of the new envoy's birthday. It was another good beginning.

The previous September, Madame Chiang had returned to China after a fifteen-month absence. During her long stay in the United States she had been almost totally out of the limelight—living mostly at the Kung residence on Long Island—but by phone she had quietly cultivated a range of Americans sympathetic to the Republic of China and Chiang Kai-shek. This nebulous and informal but powerful group of conservative congressmen, corporate executives, publishers, retired generals, and missionaries soon came to be known as "the China lobby." The ten lobbying firms that the Chiang government employed to work on its behalf were also part of the network.[146] The pro-Chiang, anti-Communist campaign in all its various manifestations created turmoil in American politics and influenced China policy under Truman, but did not change the policy's fundamental direction.

The fifty-nine-year-old Generalissimo mentioned his wife little in his diary during their long separation, but now they seemed ready to put their difficulties—the Stilwell matter, her bad moods, and his possible indiscretion—behind them. While she was away there seem to have been no major rumors in Chungking of affairs or secret arrangements. She returned seemingly determined to make the marriage work, and they resumed holding hands in public. In addition, the Generalissimo again began to rely on his wife in his dealings with the Americans, a role that gave her much satisfaction. He insisted that she be present for all his meetings with Marshall, for example, "persisting even when she was sick or tired, or tried to beg off." As had been the case with Stilwell, she often supported Marshall when he disagreed with her husband. Marshall said years later that during his China mission "Madame was on my side" and he was "confident" that she "always played fair."[147]

While Marshall was having his initial talks in China, the American, British, and Soviet foreign ministers were gathering in Moscow. Stalin convincingly assured Secretary of State Byrnes that he did not object to U.S. troops in China and he fully supported Chiang Kai-shek as head of the Chinese government. Like other senior American officials before him, Byrnes left Moscow believing that Stalin intended to live up to his treaty with China, and he so informed Marshall. Marshall worked for the next year under the belief that the CCP's only external source of major assistance, the Soviet Union, was prepared to back with appropriate pressures whatever Marshall decided on during his mission.[148]

But the Soviets continued to refuse to open the key Manchurian port of Dalian, and to ignore the new deadline of early February for the Red Army's evacuation from Mukden, Changchun, and Harbin. In addition, the Red Army continued to allow Lin Biao's CCP forces to move freely about Manchuria in the 95 percent of that huge region in which there was no Chinese government presence. Nevertheless, the government military forces were making progress. By the end of December, Du Yuming had captured most of the Manchurian ports except Dalian and Port Arthur, which the Soviets occupied under the Yalta Agreement.[149]

On Christmas Day, Chiang sent his son Ching-kuo to Moscow to evaluate Stalin's intentions, and, hoping to put Stalin in a friendly mood, he followed through on his commitment to recognize Outer Mongolia's "independence." On January 10, 1946, he opened the historic People's Consultative Conference with a keynote speech announcing that the government would immediately institute freedoms of speech, the press, religion, and assembly. Political prisoners, he said, would be released, and all political parties would henceforth be equal before the law. Elections would be carried out from "the bottom up," meaning that there would be direct elections to all representative bodies, including national ones.

III

CIVIL WAR

8

Chimera of Victory

Marshall's immediate objective during his peace mission was to arrange a cease-fire. He again proposed that one way to "reorganize" CCP troops currently occupying territory and controlling local governments would be to "mingle them with government troops," in other words, incorporate them into government units.[1] Chiang, who had long sought just that arrangement, was again elated and concluded he could "certainly trust" Marshall to head a "Committee of Three" to negotiate the terms of the cease-fire. The committee, proposed by Marshall, would include a ranking Nationalist (Zhang Qun) and a Communist (Zhou Enlai) as well as Marshall.[2] Another issue was resolved when Marshall surprisingly persuaded Zhou to accept continued U.S. transport of government troops to Manchuria, as well as a stipulation that during the cease-fire, government forces would be free to move "into and in Manchuria for the purpose of re-establishing Chinese sovereignty."[3] In only a few meetings in early January, the Committee of Three astonishingly reached an accord on military integration and a coalition government as well as a cease-fire, all with terms that favored the government. Years later, Chiang would lament that Marshall's "stand and attitude" at this time had caused him to decide to fight for Manchuria.[4]

While Mao seemed willing to agree to almost anything on paper, most important to him was what was happening on the ground. He sent another 150,000 troops to Lin Biao in Manchuria and ordered him to incorporate an additional 200,000 local forces into his main units.[5] Then, on January 13, 1946, Chiang and Mao issued orders to their respective armed forces effective at midnight to stop all hostilities and all movement of troops, with agreed exceptions—most importantly the deployment of government forces

339

Zhou Enlai *(left)* with Zhang Qun, who, along with Marshall, composed the "Committee of Three." The committee's far-reaching cease-fire and coalition proposals distinctly favored the Nationalists, so it is unlikely that Mao Zedong was serious about implementing them. Courtesy Albert C. Wedemeyer Collection, envelope KK, Hoover Institution Archives.

into Manchuria. Despite the cease-fire's apparent advantages in Manchuria for the government, Chiang—as well as his generals—thought that overall the truce would be "disadvantageous" to the government. Yan Xishan, for example, warned that the truce would only give the CCP time to regroup and expand. But Chiang felt he had no choice—to protect his relations with the United States and encourage the Soviets to cooperate in the Northeast (Manchuria), he needed to proceed with the agreement. A three-party executive headquarters, which included an American element, moved to Peking to monitor the cease-fire.[6]

Chiang's hopes for a breakthrough with the Soviets were soon to be dashed.

On January 14, Ching-kuo returned from his two-week visit to the Soviet capital, after having had two long unsatisfactory talks with Stalin. The leader of the USSR had warned that the United States was trying to use China for its own purposes, and that only if Chiang Kai-shek did not allow "a single American soldier" to remain in China would the Soviet Union tell the CCP to come to an "understanding" with the Generalissimo. Stalin suggested that he and Chiang arrange a meeting. Ching-kuo sadly informed his father that Stalin was "playing games" in Manchuria and following "his own plot."[7]

In his journal, Chiang wrote that in order to keep the country united, he could agree to sweeping economic concessions to the USSR and the departure of all U.S. troops. But he would not do so until after the Soviets had withdrawn from Manchuria and other areas in Northern China.[8] Outwardly, Chiang appeared resolved on the Manchuria issue, and did not respond to Stalin's proposal for a summit meeting.

Sure enough, the Soviet offers began to fall apart. Malinovsky officially informed Chungking that, for "technical reasons," the Red Army could not meet the new February deadline for its pullout. The Soviet general also again demanded as reparation all Japanese-owned factories in the Northeast, assets that he himself valued at US$3.8 billion.[9] These setbacks led to growing criticism within the KMT of Ching-kuo's—and implicitly the Generalissimo's—handling of Soviet affairs regarding Manchuria. Chiang, concerned, decided to take responsibility for this matter from his son and once again put the Foreign Ministry in charge.[10]

One month after Ching-kuo's return from Moscow, Stalin gave his famous February 9 speech declaring that World War II had been the "inevitable result" of "modern monopoly capitalism" and that the next war would spring from the same dynamic. Upon reading the text of the speech, Truman became alarmed and angry, and ordered James Byrnes not to "play compromise" any longer. Among other things, the President said the United States should "rehabilitate China and create a strong central government there. We should do the same for Korea . . . I am tired of babying the Soviets."[11] In China, however, Zhou Enlai continued to convince Marshall that the CCP leaders were not ideological fanatics or allies of the Soviet Union but rather political moderates committed to his peace plan.

Immediately after the cease-fire, Chiang began to receive a stream of reports of Communist attacks in North China as well as in Manchuria, where the

Soviet Red Army was reputedly supporting CCP units indirectly in some engagements. On January 18, despite the cease-fire, Communist troops took two cities in Manchuria, including the important coastal port city of Yingkou. Chiang was now beginning to suspect that Marshall was not going to favor the government's position as much as he had assumed. Marshall did not in his report to Washington note the seizure of Yingkou, an oversight that disturbed Chiang, who wrote that there had to be a point where "I need to make my final decision" in regard to Manchuria.[12]

Further complicating matters for Chiang were countercharges by the Communists of Nationalist violations of the truce. Chiang lost credibility with the Americans when he initially turned down a proposal by Marshall—one accepted by the CCP—to send monitors to Manchuria to investigate incidents there. Chiang feared the investigative teams would restrict him much more severely than they would Mao, whose rapidly growing military presence and activity in the region were mostly invisible to the outside world. Chiang's relationship with the Americans was also likely impeded by Marshall's apparent ability, with the help of his cryptographic team, to read some of Chiang's coded messages to his commanders in the field, which probably alerted him to cases where the Generalissimo was less cooperative than he pretended. Unfortunately the Americans could not read Zhou's traffic, which was encoded in "one-time pads."[13]

Despite these charges of violations of the cease-fire, the peace process, including the meeting of the People's Consultative Conference (PCC) in Chungking, went smoothly. On February 4, Marshall told Truman that "affairs are progressing rather favorably."[14] Privately, however, Chiang was becoming ever more worried about Marshall, who, he wrote, thought "he knew Chinese politics very well, but . . . does not." Marshall's remarks about the good intentions of the Communists particularly bothered Chiang, who at this early date began to fear that the situation could begin to resemble that during the Stilwell era.[15]

Marshall's optimism, however, continued unabated. He was particularly pleased with the PCC, whose members were appointed by the KMT and the CCP, and which at the end of January, following up the proposals of the Committee of Three, issued a set of five resolutions setting out a framework for an interim coalition government. All parties in the proposed coalition would be required to recognize "the national leadership of President Chiang Kai-shek," but the plan also provided a substantial check on the powers of the presidency: the State Council would be the supreme organ of the government, with half the seats going to the KMT, and although Chiang would have a veto, it could be overridden by a 5–3 council majority.[16]

Despite misgivings, Chiang believed he had to be at least as supportive of the new government plans as Zhou, who had accepted all of them. He told a group of KMT officials that the PCC resolutions would not necessarily be binding on the agreed-on National Assembly, which would draw up the constitution, but in his closing speech to the PCC he praised the plan for its principles of "peace, democracy, unification, and solidarity." Shortly before the PCC's final vote on the plan, he issued a decree setting free "all political prisoners."[17] Mao, for his part, sent word to Marshall that his arrangement of the cease-fire was "fair." "Chinese democracy," the Chairman solemnly declared, "must follow the American path."[18] Zhou reported to Mao that Marshall had told him he trusted the sincerity of the Chinese Communists but was having difficulty persuading the Kuomintang leaders. Zhou told his secretary that Marshall "reminded him of Stilwell."[19]

Popular reaction in China and in the Western press to the PCC agreements was euphoric.[20] In response to the progress being made, President Truman proposed that Congress continue the Lend-Lease program for China and instructed the State Department to begin negotiations with Chiang Kai-shek's government on the establishment of a U.S. military advisory group with a maximum of one thousand officers.[21] The Chinese army that the Americans would be advising was to be the agreed-on integrated KMT-CCP force led by the Generalissimo. But meanwhile, to provide balance and "save face" for the Communist military units, Marshall urged a separate program of American training and arms supply to the CCP's armed forces.

On February 25, Marshall, Zhang Zhizhong (the Nationalist chief commissar), and Zhou Enlai agreed on a phased reduction of the two gigantic contending armies, including the stipulation that in the interim period before complete amalgamation of the forces, the Nationalist government would be authorized to have fourteen divisions in Manchuria and the Communists only one. Under this remarkable concession by the CCP, Mao would have to reduce the then thirty Communist divisions in Manchuria to just one division, suggesting the agreement would in fact never be carried out. In another unlikely-to-be-realized provision, government forces would, in the first phase, enjoy a five to one advantage nationwide over the Communists—that is, 90 KMT divisions to 18 for the CCP.

According to the plan, these adjustments would be complete in eighteen months and full integration of personnel into the new amalgamated KMT-

CCP central armed forces would then begin. The combined force would be a nonpolitical military establishment—no more commissars of either party— with Chiang Kai-shek as commander in chief.[22]

Chiang had every incentive to carry out these military agreements, but he believed the CCP would never do so and he hoped Marshall was becoming aware of their "tricks."[23] Marshall, however, was in fact immensely pleased with the way things were going. He had accomplished the impossible—at least on paper. He complained that "certain cliques," an obvious reference to hardline KMT factions, were trying to destroy the peace process, but through the spring of 1946, he thoroughly believed that his plan could succeed—the Communists would give up their large army and territory, including their huge advantage in Manchuria, and work politically for national power under a Chiang-led government, so long as the KMT leader kept China headed down the path of American-style democracy.

Deciding to make a personal inspection trip, Marshall and his staff, including Zhou Enlai and Zhang Zhizhong, flew 3,000 miles throughout North China, visiting a dozen cities and towns. At Yan'an, crowds cheered wildly for the American general, who had long talks with Mao and Zhu De.[24] The trip, according to Marshall, "had most happy results."[25] Meanwhile, news of the Soviet pillaging in Manchuria spread in China and during the last week of February large-scale demonstrations in Chungking and other cities demanded the immediate evacuation of Soviet troops from Manchuria. Rioters sacked the Chungking offices of the CCP's *New China Daily* and the *Democratic Daily* of the Democratic League.[26] While public anger toward Moscow was no doubt genuine, Chen Lifu organized the riots. Later, Marshall would attach great importance to these short-lived demonstrations and charge that they had provoked the CCP into changing its positive and reasonable attitude toward the peace process.

It was now two years after Yalta and the Cold War was quickly and dramatically heading in a direction it would maintain for the next almost halfcentury. In March, Churchill proclaimed the descent of the "Iron Curtain" across Europe, and Ho Chi Minh and the French signed an agreement that supposedly ensured Vietnam's peaceful and united future. Chiang was skeptical: he wrote in his diary, "The Vietnamese civil war begins."[27] During this same period, George Kennan's long telegram from the U.S. Embassy in Moscow on dealing with the Soviet Union's ambitions marked the official beginning of America's containment policy.

On March 11, before returning to Washington to brief Truman, Marshall again presented his draft instructions for the three-party (KMT, CCP, and U.S.) field teams due to go to Manchuria to check on cease-fire violations. The guidelines stated that Communist troops should evacuate "any places [in Manchuria] to be occupied by government troops for the reestablishment of sovereignty" and should "not be permitted to occupy places vacated by the Russian troops." These stipulations were consistent with the cease-fire agreement to which Zhou had agreed. They also reflected Marshall's continuing belief that the Communists truly wanted a democratic settlement under Chiang Kai-shek and that, if assured of this condition, they were willing to cooperate in the government's takeover of Manchuria from the Soviets and to disband their army. This time, Chiang quickly accepted both the proposed visit of a monitoring team to Manchuria and Marshall's guidelines. Zhou now objected, however, and the team's departure was delayed.[28]

The Chinese government then formally requested the immediate withdrawal of all Soviet forces from Manchuria, but Malinovsky would not respond to this request for twenty critical days. During this time, and only three days after Marshall's departure for Washington, Soviet officers secretly told the CCP that the Red Army would indeed start withdrawing from Mukden, Harbin, and other cities—and moreover, that CCP forces should move in behind them.[29] Lin Biao's Communist forces thus marched into some towns already evacuated by the Red Army and deployed closer to the outskirts of other major cities. In the countryside, as the Soviets folded their tents and departed their garrisons, they simply turned over administration to local authorities already set in place by the CCP.[30] New Chinese Communist forces poured into southern Manchuria, but the emphasis was on the northern part of the region. Stalin wanted Mao to have firm control of at least the northern half of Manchuria by the time the last Red Army tank clanked across the Soviet-Manchurian border. Before Marshall left town, Zhou had explained that any CCP troop movement in Manchuria would simply be to maintain stability in the countryside.[31]

In Washington, Marshall appeared oblivious to the growing military crisis in Manchuria and also in nearby Shandong, where new fighting raged between the government and the Communists. In fact, he acted as if his mission's success was assured. The Nationalists and the Communists, he declared publicly, "are now engaged in the business of demobilizing vast military forces and integrating and unifying the remaining forces into a Central Army." It was "very remarkable," he said, "how we could straighten out what seemed impossible conditions . . . until we arrived, nothing could be done."[32]

As the Soviet Red Army rapidly pulled out of southern Manchuria and Lin Biao's forces moved in, Du Yuming's armies, supported by air power, moved forward quickly to assert the government's authority in the major cities and along the rail lines. In the first large-scale battle with the Chinese Communists, Sun Liren's New First Army drove the enemy away from the outskirts of Mukden and entered the city on March 13, one day after the Soviet Red Army had pulled out. Chiang believed the situation would now get "worse and worse" and that he had to pursue his goal patiently and "step by step."[33]

Two weeks later, the Soviet embassy belatedly informed the Chinese Foreign Ministry that the Soviet Red Army would be out of Manchuria by the end of April.[34] When Marshall, still in Washington, heard this news, he began to believe that the Soviets were in fact not pursuing a hegemonic strategy in China. He thus began to shift away from seeing China in the context of containment of the Soviet Union, as he had during his talks with Truman in December. Instead, he would come to perceive China as a swamp of internal strife requiring stability most of all. In his view, the CCP, at most, could be blamed for sharing responsibility for the ongoing violence with the KMT.[35] Chiang sensed this change and began to wonder if Marshall was willing to give up U.S. strategic interests in China in order to appease the Soviets. He also learned the unsettling news that Marshall wanted to provide the Communist forces U.S. military training and weapons before the reorganization of the two armies had begun and that he intended to eliminate the U.S. military headquarters in China and send home the U.S. Marines. Chiang feared that Marshall's "fame and legacy" was driving his "grandiose plans" for a peace settlement.[36]

Meanwhile, Mao told Lin Biao that the Communists had to stop Chiang's expected occupation of Changchun, in which there was only a token Nationalist force and some remaining Soviet units.[37] On April 14, Malinovsky led his last troops out of Changchun, and some 20,000 soldiers of the Communist Eighth Route Army, newly armed with Japanese weapons and some artillery, immediately attacked the Nationalist force of 7,000 in the city. Most of the government soldiers were killed. Five hundred holdouts put up "an

Alamo-type defense" in the Central Bank Building until, led by their commander, one by one, they made a last, desperate charge out of the building's revolving door.[38] Manchuria was now effectively divided into a southern area officially governed by the KMT but heavily infiltrated by the CCP and a larger, completely Communist-dominated, northern region. Chiang ordered Sun Liren immediately to press northward to take back Changchun.[39]

The State Department's 1949 *White Paper* on the fall of China called the CCP capture of Changchun "a flagrant violation of the cessation of hostilities order," but the authors did not suggest that it threatened the peace effort. Instead, they concluded that the principal difficulty this violation created was to strengthen the hand of "ultra-reactionary" groups in the Chinese government. But it was not just KMT "ultra-reactionaries" who were upset. Chiang did have to take into account the factional dynamics on the issues of war and peace, but his decisions regarding Manchuria since 1945 were his own.[40]

On April 18, Marshall arrived back in Chungking accompanied by his wife, Katherine, who had accepted Mayling's invitation to return with her husband. When the Marshalls landed at Chungking it was 100 degrees Fahrenheit. The dust, heat, and stench, Mrs. Marshall reported, were "beyond description." The day after his return to Chungking, Marshall had a four-hour meeting with Chiang Kai-shek. The talk was blunt and continued the next day at Yellow Mountain.[41] Marshall blamed Chiang and his regime for the calamity facing the peace process. He charged that the Nanking government had had an opportunity for peace in Manchuria but had not utilized the opportunity. He reeled off a long list of offenses he said Chiang's "very poor" advisers had committed. These ranged from seeking unilateral control of Manchuria to closing Communist newspapers, buzzing Yan'an with a fighter plane, and troop movements in China proper in violation of the cease-fire. Marshall described these as "stupid actions" that were of no benefit to the government and, far more serious, stimulated the CCP's "suspicion of Government intentions."[42]

Marshall correctly warned Chiang that the Chinese Communists were taking advantage of the situation and becoming stronger daily, while the National government was in a very dangerous position militarily, with overextended lines and increasingly dispersed forces.[43] In turn, Chiang provided Marshall with a long list of alleged Communist violations of the cease-fire, charging that since the January 13 truce, the CCP had launched 287 offensives and captured 13 counties and 29 cities and towns. The seizure of

Changchun and the death of several thousand government troops, he said, was a very serious violation of the accords. But Chiang failed to convince Marshall that the Communists were even partially to blame for the dramatic breakdown in the talks.[44]

When Marshall next saw Zhou he did not criticize the Communists for the capture of Changchun or for any other action, and Zhou assured him that the CCP "did not intend to monopolize Manchuria but instead desired international cooperation." The CCP, he said, wanted the fighting to stop and negotiations to begin immediately.[45] According to CCP documents, Zhou recommended that the CCP pressure Marshall to force Chiang to accept a cease-fire—to the point if necessary of reaching an "impasse" in the talks with the American. Mao, however, instructed Zhou to maintain as friendly relations as possible with the envoy in order to avoid giving the Kuomintang "a crack to crawl through."[46]

In a subsequent meeting, Chiang told Marshall it was impossible to bring about a compromise if the United States appeased the CCP after it had blatantly ignored the three-party agreements. He said he was willing to negotiate problems relating to Manchuria but only if the Communists first evacuated Changchun. This suggested for the first time in the talks that he was willing to negotiate a cease-fire line north of Changchun, leaving the CCP with de facto control of more than half the territory of the region. At the same time, Chiang made clear that he could not accept anything less than the principle that Marshall and the U.S. government had previously accepted—sovereignty over all of Manchuria rested with the National government.[47] Only when the United States fully supported the Chinese government, he said, would it be possible to include the CCP in a new administration. This was the original China policy that Marshall himself had suggested four months earlier and that Truman had endorsed.[48] Later, Chiang wrote that in dealing with Marshall, he had to "stick" to his own policy but also continue to show "sincerity" because Marshall might change his views.[49]

This meeting, particularly Chiang's implied willingness to concede northern Manchuria to the CCP, had an effect on Marshall. For the first time since his return, the American talked tough with Zhou, telling him that the Generalissimo's proposal regarding negotiations after the return of Changchun, which would have left the Communists in occupation of northern Manchuria, was a "great concession," but that Communist actions had "heavily compromised" his efforts to persuade Chiang to cooperate. He implied that if the CCP could not accept Chiang's proposal and withdraw from Changchun, he would consider that he had exhausted his resources as a mediator. Chiang was very pleased when Marshall described this conversation to him.[50] That day, April 28, the Soviets turned over Harbin, capital of Heilungkiang province bordering Russia, to the CCP, and the next day regular troop units of the Soviet Red Army in Manchuria formally pulled back into the Soviet Union.

I

On May 3, the National government moved back to Nanking. Marshall and his wife also moved, receiving the rather grand residence of the former German ambassador as their quarters. Mrs. Marshall was much happier in Nanking than in Chungking. Madame Chiang and Zhou Enlai's wife, Deng Yingchao (herself a ranking member of the CCP), saw her almost every day, some days together. Katherine wrote a friend that she and the Generalissimo had "hit off a great friendship," although all he can say is "how, how . . . good, good . . . and smile."[51]

The day after the move, Marshall had lunch at his new home with John Robinson Beal, a former *Time* magazine correspondent suggested by Washington to be the Generalissimo's adviser on dealing with the press. Beal was badly needed: Chiang had little sense about how to deal with the press or even that the press needed to be dealt with. As Marshall explained the situation to Beal (in a fanciful explanation almost certainly originating with Zhou), political commissars serving with "the Chinese Reds" had been incited by the KMT's anti-Communist agitation to take control in Manchuria, and the CCP had reacted by capturing territory in violation of the January cease-fire agreement. After lunch, as the two Americans sipped Old Fashioneds, the general, in a similarly implausible interpretation, said that since he could find "no overt act by the Russian Government" in aid of the Communists, he believed that local Soviet commanders were on their own—in other words, contrary to Stalin's orders—providing rations and Japanese munitions to the CCP forces.[52]

Perhaps Marshall did know about some Soviet support for the CCP but chose to ignore it. In a May 13 radiogram to the Central Committee, Zhou reported that Marshall had told him he was aware of "Soviet support to us" in the Northeast.[53] Presumably Marshall obtained this information through his cryptographic team and mentioned it to Zhou inadvertently, but it does indicate he probably was not entirely blind to what the Soviets were doing. Several days later, *New York Times* correspondent Henry Lieberman, and

Charlotte Ebner of the *Christian Science Monitor*, both of whom had been captured and held briefly by the Communists at Changchun, spent two hours telling Marshall that the Communists had taken over most of Manchuria with Soviet help and likely could not be dislodged.[54]

This firsthand report had no effect on Marshall. Despite his recent tough talk with Zhou, he continued largely to blame the Nationalists for the turmoil. In a report to Truman, he set out a slightly different scenario than he had to Beal. The troubles, he said, began when the Communists grew fearful of the good faith of the Chinese government in carrying out the PCC agreements (agreements that would have given extraordinary advantage to the government). Then, according to Marshall, overconfident Nationalist generals influenced the Generalissimo to "precipitate" the government into "a dangerous military position." The Communists next "seized the advantage," captured Changchun, and blocked the northerly advance of the Nationalist Army. Marshall also mentioned the CCP's "justified complaints" of Nationalist misbehavior elsewhere in China, while on the other side only noting that there had been, "of course, a number of minor violations of the agreement by subordinate commanders on both [sides]."[55]

In the meantime, the U.S. Navy was still at work fulfilling the American pledge to transport a total of 228,000 government troops to Manchuria. In late May, the last convoy was under way when Chiang asked Marshall to approve transportation by the United States of two additional armies. Marshall declined, claiming that doing so would "amount to supporting a civil war." The completed huge troop lift had of course already served this purpose, consistent with Truman's policy at the time. Then in a letter to Truman, Marshall conceded that, since the United States had already transported a quarter of a million Chinese government troops to the Northeast, it would be "most unfair" for the Americans to "as it were . . . leave them in the lurch." His concession was to approve the Chinese Defense Ministry's request for six months' supply of ammunition for its thirty-nine U.S.-trained and -armed divisions.[56]

Once settled in Nanking, Marshall was soon trying to broker another accord, this one taking account of the Communist gains of the previous two months—gains that, he believed, were either carried out without orders by CCP commissars provoked by Nationalist actions or by Communist commanders taking advantage of an opportunity provided by the overextended

Nationalists. He told Chiang that the most feasible solution of the Manchurian conflict was for Nanking to accept temporary Communist occupation north of Harbin and west toward Manzhouli on the Chinese border where Outer Mongolia, Manchuria, and Siberia meet. This was in line with Chiang's own proposal and he agreed—though he insisted the Communists not occupy Harbin.[57]

Alone with Zhou, Marshall indicated that a change in the agreed military ratio in Manchuria might also be possible, from 14:1 in the government's favor to 5:1. At that moment the ratio on the ground actually favored the Communists by 3:2, and although their main forces in the Northeast were then retreating, as their overall numerical advantage grew, they increasingly regarded negotiations as unnecessary.[58] As Zhou reported to the Central Committee, "The chances of making use of the United States and Marshall are diminishing daily . . . but we should still make every effort to delay the onset of civil war."[59]

Chiang realized that the support of Truman and Marshall for his takeover of Manchuria, once strong and clear, had evaporated, but military successes had blinded him to the reality that he had foreseen the previous July and then again at the end of the year. At those times, he had realized that even with all-out U.S. material help, if Stalin was determined to see Mao gain power in Manchuria or perhaps over all Chinese territory north of the Yellow River or even the Yangtze, it would probably be impossible for the Nationalists to win. But now he concluded that he could at least consolidate control over the southern half of Manchuria. Such a compromise, which back in November 1945 he had first thought might possibly satisfy Moscow, was also consistent with Marshall's latest idea.

On May 20, Sun Liren's American-trained divisions drove the Communists from Sipingjie northward toward Changchun. Bai Chongxi, whom Chiang had just appointed minister of defense, was convinced that Lin Biao's soldiers were in bad shape and he pressed Chiang to authorize a follow-up attack to retake Changchun.[60] The day after he talked with Bai, Chiang told Marshall he agreed that retaking Changchun at that time would be inadvisable, and he left the next day for Mukden "to get control of the situation." Although Madame Chiang was ill, he insisted that she accompany him.[61]

Despite what Chiang had told Marshall, while the Generalissimo, the unwell Mayling, and Defense Minister Bai were winging their way to Mukden in Marshall's airplane, armored vehicles attached to Sun Liren's army divisions, meeting little opposition, were streaming through the gates of Changchun.[62] As soon as Chiang and his party landed at the airport in Mukden, Du informed him that Changchun was in government hands. Following Mao's orders to avoid major encounters, Lin and his 100,000 men had pulled out of the city the previous day and retreated to the Sungari River, the last remaining natural defense line before Harbin. Chiang was delighted with the news, and over lunch in the city, Bai strongly advocated moving on and attacking Harbin. Chiang, hesitating, said he was afraid that Marshall would not be happy, but in the end he authorized Du to attack across the Sungari.[63]

Lin Biao's rapid retreat and Bai's views convinced Chiang that only a third of the People's Liberation Army (PLA) were quality troops with good Japanese weapons.[64] He wrote to Marshall informing him that government troops had retaken Changchun and reiterated his recent call for adherence to all the original agreements. He also pressed a new proposal: that American officers on the monitoring teams have the deciding voice when differences arose.[65] By radio, Marshall appealed several times to Chiang for an immediate cease-fire in order to "avoid the painful results of the previous mistakes."[66] Significantly, during Chiang's absence from Nanking Marshall "talked a great deal" with the persuasive Zhou Enlai, with one session lasting six hours.[67]

Although the Generalissimo's idea of giving the mediators in the truce teams—that is, Marshall's men—the deciding vote seemed on the surface reasonable or at least debatable, Zhou complained to Marshall that it was a "very sharp maneuver" that would allow the Nationalists "to conceive of all kinds of tricks to deceive the Americans." Marshall readily agreed and explained to Washington that positive reaction in the American press and Congress to Chiang's proposal had provoked a new, virulent CCP propaganda campaign against himself. Marshall told Chiang that the integrity of his position as mediator was coming into question because of Chiang's suggestion.[68]

According to Madame, she now tried to avoid "all participation in political activity" because the Generalissimo "did not want her to meddle in American issues." But in fact she played an important role in the talks with Marshall. In addition to interpreting, she carried written memos and messages back and forth between the two men—and as the summer wore on, she had many private conversations with the general. Despite her bad experience siding with Stilwell in 1943, she again showed "complete sympathy with and understanding for the American point of view."[69] Marshall believed she was on his side.[70] Apparently in principle she was, but she was also working for her husband, reporting Marshall's thinking back to him and probably suggesting how best to handle the American general.[71]

Chiang was increasingly frustrated with Marshall, but his understanding of the balance of power between the government and Communist armies was badly flawed: incredibly he believed that government forces had all but "crushed the main force of the CCP."[72] The New First and New Sixth Armies pursued Lin Biao across the Sungari to a line only sixty miles from Harbin, which was 300 miles south of the Amur River and Russia. Upon returning to Nanking on June 3, Chiang met with Marshall for three hours. The Generalissimo was impatient and rapidly tapped a finger on the arm of his red leather chair. But with little or no pressure from Marshall, he agreed to halt "advances, attacks or pursuits" by his troops in Manchuria for fifteen days.[73] During the cease-fire, Chiang said, the Communists would have to show their sincerity by completing negotiations with the government on full termination of hostilities throughout China and by carrying out without further delay the agreement of February 25 regarding reorganization of the armies. Chiang then told Marshall that this would be "his final effort at doing business with the Communists."[74]

Three days later, Chiang and Mao issued separate announcements of another cease-fire. As ordered, Sun Liren halted his advance and withdrew south of the Sungari. Years later, Chiang wrote that this cease-fire sapped morale and was the beginning of the government "debacle in Manchuria."[75] But even if General Sun had captured Harbin, the CCP and its troops would have escaped into the hinterland, which they almost totally controlled, and probably into Russia if necessary. The correlation of forces and circumstances would have continued overwhelmingly to favor the Communists. In any event, three hours after the declared cease-fire, government commanders in five zones reported Communist attacks. When 50,000 Communist troops surrounded the port of Qingdao in Shandung, Chiang asked for U.S. troops to transport government units to the city, but Marshall refused.[76] According to the State Department's 1949 *White Paper,* the Communist offensive in Shandong "proved to be a very disturbing factor."[77] But Zhou explained to Marshall that government provocations had caused the Communist forces to retaliate with an offensive, and Marshall seemed to accept this account.[78] In a report to Truman, Marshall cited two nonviolent actions by Chiang as provocations for the large-scale, Communist armed attacks during the cease-fire—

Chiang's absence from Nanking and Chiang's proposal to give the Americans the deciding vote in the monitoring teams.[79]

Despite his continued optimism and provocative Communist attacks during the cease-fire, in late June Chiang confirmed in his journal that he did not intend "to push very far north." He thought this strategy would avoid a confrontation with the Soviet Union and would free government troops both to deploy into the huge Manchurian landscape behind their lines and to concentrate on eliminating the Communist forces in North China.[80] On June 29, Marshall concluded that he had "no basis for further negotiations," and he warned Chiang that if the Chinese government tried to solve the problem by military means the American public would "judge that it had plunged the country into chaos by its implacable demands." Furthermore, he said, the Generalissimo was "deliberately following the dictates of [his] Army [officers] as did Japan to its ruination."[81] According to Marshall, these words had "tremendous effect on the Generalissimo," who quoted the Bible and "almost wept."[82] Interestingly, Chiang himself does not mention nearly crying on this occasion but does record that when he informed Marshall he intended to convene the National Assembly in the middle of October to return political power to the people, the American "was almost moved to tears."[83]

In a continuation of the same conversation, Marshall also had an informal session with Mayling in which he used the same strong language. She reported back to her husband that the general had been "impatient and rude . . . very insulting . . . [and] arrogant."[84] But Marshall's reaction to moves by the KMT and CCP were rapidly becoming less important to both sides. Chiang told the American general that he had made all the concessions possible, and began planning a full-scale offensive to take place between the Yellow River and the Great Wall.[85] And even as Marshall was becoming sharper in his comments to the Generalissimo, further Communist attacks in Shandong and Shanxi provoked him into telling Zhou that these actions had "undermined his efforts"—a warning that went unheeded. Three days later, he even told Zhou that many things that were happening were "merely retaliation by the Government against Communist provocations." On another occasion he described reported Communist attacks as "wholly inexcusable."[86] Chiang wondered hopefully whether Marshall was beginning "to lose confidence in the CCP."[87]

On July 2, Marshall asked Acting Secretary of State Dean Acheson (Byrnes was in Paris) for his views on the China situation. The reply represented a reformulation of what U.S. policy would be if the peace effort collapsed and full-scale civil war ensued. Truman's secret December instructions to Marshall, which Acheson may or may not have known about or remembered, had stated that for geopolitical reasons, even if talks broke down, the United States would support Chiang Kai-shek. The Acheson paper, by contrast, made no mention of this six-month-old position. Instead it suggested that if full-scale civil war broke out, the United States "could" maintain relations with Chiang Kai-shek's government but "would" end material support and withdraw its remaining military forces. This major if informal reversal in U.S. policy, which may or may not have been seen by Truman, reflected Washington's basic objective not to become involved in a civil war in China, especially since most of the officials concerned did not think the non-Communist side could win.[88]

Marshall's comments on the Acheson memo marked another major change in his view of the China situation. Despite his recently harsher tone with Zhou, he had to come to the conclusion that Chiang and his regime were mostly responsible for the failure of the peace effort and that a full-scale civil war had already begun.[89] Whatever the United States did short of massive intervention with American troops, he believed, the Communists would eventually defeat Chiang Kai-shek and his armies. To Marshall the only options seemed to be to do nothing or to continue the seemingly futile effort of pursuing a peaceful, democratic, coalition government—and he chose the latter. Neither he nor anyone in Washington considered the third option: massive U.S. material support to help Chiang hold North China or China south of the Yangtze. In fact, Chiang himself never seemed to have seriously contemplated this alternative. He was willing to divide Manchuria with Mao, but for the rest of China it would be all or nothing.

On July 11, assassins in Kunming shot and killed a prominent leader of the Democratic League, Li Gongpu. Four days later, unknown persons killed Wen Yiduo, another league leader and an American-educated poet. A wave of protests swept the universities of China and a group of Harvard professors condemned the slayings. In a letter to President Truman, Marshall gave the impression that Chiang's government, if not Chiang himself, was responsible.[90] But the tiny Democratic League was a minor nuisance to Chiang and it seems unlikely he would have risked international censure by ordering the killing of the two relatively obscure figures in Kunming. By contrast, in mid-July, when three hundred Communist soldiers ambushed a supply convoy of fifty-five Marines, killing seven, Marshall said the ambush "was definitely the work of the Communists," but he did not press Zhou on the matter of culpability. Chiang thought Marshall in the case of the Marines had acted as if "nothing had happened."[91]

Now that the cease-fire had expired, Chiang launched campaigns to open up rail lines in Shanxi and to clear Jehol of Communist armies. General Fu Zuoyi prepared to take Kalgan, the ancient gateway through the Great Wall to the Silk Route, which the Communists had occupied since August 1945.[92] Other government troops along a broad front began pushing into Jiangsu north of the Yangtze, not far from Nanking.

That month, the CCP's Red Army adopted a new name, the People's Liberation Army (PLA), and it dropped the fiction that its armed forces in Manchuria consisted purely of Manchurians (or Northeasterners). The PLA launched limited offensives and counteroffensives in numerous areas including Shanxi, Henan, Jehol, Shandong, and parts of Jiangsu, but generally outside of Manchuria the government forces seemed to be pushing back the Communists. The CCP, however, controlled all of the Manchurian borders with the Soviet Union, and train loads of goods moved in both directions. The PLA also had offices in North Korea, where it arranged the supply of military matériel for its forces in Manchuria, employing no fewer than two thousand railcars for this purpose.[93]

In the middle of July, the Generalissimo and Madame Chiang left Nanking for Guling, located in the Jiangxi Mountains near the government training center of Lushan. Western businessmen, diplomats, and missionaries had established Guling as a retreat back in the nineteenth century. At five thousand feet, it sits far above the mosquitoes and stifling humidity and heat of the Yangtze valley. Katherine Marshall went to Guling with Mayling and remained for the summer. She loved it.[94]

Marshall believed that Chiang had left in order to halt the negotiations and give his generals leeway to do what they wanted.[95] He would come regularly to the mountain retreat for short spells but resented the journey—two hours by plane, forty-five minutes by gun boat, thirty minutes by car, and then two hours via a sedan chair carried by cheerful coolies along a steep cliffside path.[96] The Marshall house at Guling was across a mountain stream from the Chiang residence. When George was absent, Katherine and Mayling would lunch each day with scenery that "made Switzerland look mild." Sedan bearers waited on the lawn all day to take them where they wished. Each evening, "in a scene out of the Arabian Nights," Chiang Kai-shek would join

Mayling and Katherine for a ride up one of several nearby peaks. Although they could not speak each other's language, Katherine taught the Generalissimo to play the German game of Chinese checkers. The Chiangs, she wrote home, had become her "wonderful friends."[97]

George Marshall, meanwhile, was "becoming more depressed every day," even though he persisted in believing that the key problem—the terms of the amalgamation of the Nationalist and the Communist armies—was "80 or 90 percent solved."[98] In early July, he decided to recommend that the White House cancel its pending nomination—which Marshall had supported— of General Albert Wedemeyer as the new U.S. ambassador to China and instead nominate for the post the missionary John Leighton Stuart. Marshall felt the Communists would strongly object to Wedemeyer, and the U.S. Senate responded by approving the appointment of the seventy-year-old Stuart, a New Testament scholar and former president of Yanjing University in Peking. The decision embittered the younger general Wedemeyer, who had already bought a civilian wardrobe for the job.[99]

Stuart viewed the Chinese with "a mixture of impatience, affection, and zealous optimism." He recognized that the Generalissimo's failure or inability to curtail corruption was a major cause of China's enormous troubles, but as a fellow Christian he had faith that Chiang understood the weaknesses of his country and his regime, wanted to correct them, and to a large extent could succeed. He also believed the CCP was a legitimate political party and that its relationship to Russian Bolshevism was "tenuous and insignificant." He worked mostly alone from his residence in Nanking, occasionally visiting the U.S. Embassy, which he did not trust. Instead, he relied heavily on his Chinese secretary, a young man he had brought from his university whom embassy officers speculated was a spy for Dai Li or perhaps Zhou Enlai.

On July 18, Marshall and Stuart made the trip to Guling, where the new ambassador presented his credentials to the Generalissimo. Marshall took the opportunity to lecture Chiang with "considerable frankness" about the "uncontrollable civil war" that loomed and the drastic effect the two recent assassinations were having on world opinion. A few days later, the government declared that the two killers were junior officers of the Kunming Garrison Headquarters Secret Police. The usual execution—a bullet to the back of the head—dispatched both men. Whether they had acted independently or on orders (as Marshall thought), or were themselves sacrificial victims, is unknown. Whatever the facts of the case, the CCP greatly benefited from the internal and international outrage it caused.[100]

Chiang's responsibility for these acts on the mainland, as with other serious abuses of human rights by the police at that time, lay mostly in his expansion over the years of the various secret services. These powerful, complex, and to some extent uncontrollable groups indulged in intrigue, rivalry, and covert, often vicious, acts of oppression and vengeance. But in the postwar years, the press was free enough to report on and denounce incidents of this sort—both true and false. As the critical *Far Eastern Economic Review* in Hong Kong noted at the time:

> Millions of words are pouring forth day by day: reports, rumors . . . scoops which run to pure imagination . . . accusations and denunciations, statements and counterstatements, melodramatic appeals . . . The reading public is eager to hear the more the better about squeeze and graft, and the leftist press is certain to satisfy this popular demand . . . there is enough material for such reporting as assassination and kidnapping occur quite frequently . . . the circulation of the liberal and leftist press has therefore risen phenomenally.[101]

II

As fighting outside Manchuria escalated, Truman, in a letter drafted by Marshall, warned Chiang that unless genuine progress was made soon toward a peaceful settlement, "it must be expected that American opinion will not continue in its generous attitude toward your nation."[102] As Chiang saw it, Marshall had leverage to use against the Nationalist government but absolutely none against the Communists, so he used what he had—his control of U.S. military aid and U.S. military sales to Nanking. Without any announcement the State Department began refusing to license military equipment for China, even sales for which the Chinese government had already paid.[103] Marshall informed Zhou that he had stopped "almost every direct support" of the U.S. government for the Nationalist military. Zhou must have been delighted at the news: he had virtually achieved his objective of neutralizing the United States in the Chinese civil war.

According to a Chinese scholar writing on the mainland in 1996, "CCP leaders [in the fall of 1946] saw clearly that the U.S. basically lacked the strength to intervene in China through military means."[104] Thus "it no longer made sense to continue purely nominal [good] relations with the United

States that were of greater harm than benefit."[105] Marshall was unaware of this new attitude. Instead, he had again explained the toughening CCP line as a sign that "liberal elements in the Communist Party" were "losing control and the radicals [were] becoming the leaders." But he continued to believe the top leaders—Mao, Zhou, and company—were still acting in good faith.[106] To Chiang, Marshall and Stuart's continuing notion that the Communists would truly compromise their revolutionary objectives was like "trying to catch a fish in a tree."[107]

By September, government forces had taken over most of those localities and railways outside of Manchuria that the Generalissimo had demanded the Communists abandon after the cease-fire. The government offensive since July had been far more successful than Marshall had anticipated, but the victories had come at a high cost. According to a Nationalist general, the government had lost "one fifth of its troops and enough U.S.-supplied ammunition and equipment to organize 18 new divisions."[108]

As the chill of autumn crept deeper into Manchuria, relations between Marshall and the Generalissimo grew testier. Marshall spoke increasingly roughly to the Chinese leader. He told him the only thing holding China together was Chiang's prestige, which was rapidly deteriorating. When Chiang questioned what a group of Harvard professors who had protested the Kunming assassinations knew about the circumstances, Marshall, obviously alluding to Chiang's limited formal education, replied that they "were more than a bunch of military high school graduates."[109]

Meanwhile, Marshall's relations with Zhou remained cordial, even close. One day, complaining to Zhou about Communist anti-American propaganda, he again inexplicably leaked an intelligence source, saying that the United States regularly intercepted weekly "propaganda orders from Moscow to the Communist units in Shanghai and Shanghai's replies." Marshall explained to Beal that he knew that as a result of this comment to Zhou the United States would "lose that [intelligence] source," but "we know it [the information] anyway."[110] Still, it was another serious slip of the tongue, reflecting the casual and relaxed relations between Zhou and Marshall.

In the middle of September, Chiang decided that after the expected capture of Kalgan (in Chahar province northwest of Peking) he would propose to Marshall a cease-fire, provided the Communists agreed to move ahead with the National Assembly and the establishment of a new State Council. He believed his armies were now deployed to more defensible lines and he could make this final gesture. If, as he fully expected, the Communists rejected this proposal, he hoped Marshall might then finally lose confidence in them.[111]

In response, Zhou insisted there had to be a cease-fire at once, and if Kalgan fell, there would be a "total national split." Marshall assumed that if the attack on Kalgan was called off, Mao Zedong would be willing to accept a cease-fire, and he told Chiang that the CCP would not join an assembly or a coalition unless government troops stopped their attack.[112] Chiang argued that occupation of Kalgan, only 150 miles from Peking and a gateway for both Nationalists and Communists moving into and out of Manchuria, was required to assure the security of the area south of the Great Wall.[113] Marshall, furious, sent a memo to the Generalissimo saying that he intended to ask President Truman for orders to return home.

When the two men met again on October 4, Chiang tried to talk Marshall out of abandoning his mission, saying the crisis in China was the most important in the world.[114] He asserted that he had "always treated people with sincerity" and had tried to treat Marshall in that manner as well.[115] According to Chiang's recollection, Marshall replied, "I am touched by your sincerity and your respect for me." But, Marshall went on, because the internal war had not ended, he still planned to return to the United States. That evening, Chiang learned that Marshall had indeed sent a radiogram to the White House requesting his recall. Chiang immediately called in Stuart and said he intended to order a ten-day truce with certain conditions, and Marshall quickly rescinded his radiogram.

Chiang offered a ten-day cease-fire, during which a five-man group chaired by Stuart would agree to settle two of the primary issues: representation in the State Council and announcement of the Communist delegates to the National Assembly. At the same time, the Committee of Three chaired by Marshall would decide on immediate steps to implement the agreed reorganization of the two armies, including the identification and location of the Communist divisions to be either amalgamated into the new Central Army or demobilized. Furthermore, Chiang wanted a timetable for carrying out this action.

This time, Chiang shrewdly first raised his idea privately with the two American envoys, who were highly pleased. Then, in another astute move, he suggested that the American general and the ambassador put forward the proposal as their own. Marshall and Stuart agreed.[116] Privately Chiang fully expected that the CCP would not accept the truce package, and indeed,

Zhou quickly rejected it, saying it was equivalent to asking the CCP to surrender.[117] Instead, Zhou sent a memorandum to Marshall saying that if the attack on Kalgan was permanently called off, discussions could be held on the cessation of hostilities and other issues. "Permanently" was another new condition, and Marshall became more impatient with Zhou than at any time during the year. On October 8, he and Stuart issued a joint statement detailing the latest developments, including the CCP's rejection of their most recent proposal. Marshall told Zhou that he saw no practical basis for continuing the talks.[118]

On Chinese National Day, October 10, Chiang made a conciliatory address to the nation. While the Communists, he said, had turned down the truce proposal, he would continue to seek a settlement through mediation and consultation.[119] Probably most informed Chinese believed that letting the U.S. ambassador chair a group that would decide how to end the fighting and bring about a real peace accord was a good and fair idea. But Chiang's words of compromise and reconciliation were not the only strategy employed that day. Also on October 10, government troops under General Fu stormed into Kalgan. As the Nationalist army took over the city, the Communists lost about 100,000 men and their forces in Yan'an became cut off from Manchuria.[120] Later, in announcing this and other victories, the Generalissimo predicted that the government would finish off the Communist armies in five months and confirmed that the National Assembly would be convened on November 12.

Marshall, who had not yet given up, pressed Chiang to make a new, more generous offer to the Communists now that he had occupied Kalgan and several other important cities. He reminded Chiang that in early July he had said that it was necessary to deal harshly with the Communists and later to take a generous attitude. Chiang said this was true, and he suggested he could agree to an unconditional cessation of hostilities if the Communists would simply announce their delegation to the National Assembly.[121] This was another clever move. Mayling acted as the mediator between Chiang and Marshall in the drafting of a new proposal along these lines. The final text that Chiang accepted was "very similar to what Marshall and Stuart desired" and probably what Chiang had expected. At the urging of General Marshall and Ambassador Stuart, Chiang issued it on the evening of October 16.[122] Zhou, however, refused to consider any condition on the part of the CCP in return for an immediate and unconditional cease-fire. This was the second broad proposal supported by Marshall and Stuart that in a ten-day period Chiang had accepted and the Communists had rejected—and Marshall was not pleased. During an October 26 meeting, Marshall told Zhou that Zhou's mind was "so closed" that there was "little purpose in my arguing with you regarding various aspects of the situation."[123]

That month, Marshall and Chiang received word that Joe Stilwell had died of liver disease at age sixty-three. Chiang ordered an elaborate memorial service in Nanking, and some American officers and soldiers who had served with Stilwell in Burma flew in for the occasion. Some 1,500 Americans and Chinese gathered in a large ceremonial hall, flowers covered the altar, incense smoldered, and panels of Chinese calligraphy covered the walls with tributes from leading figures, no doubt including Chiang Kai-shek. Significantly, however, Chiang's diary that day did not mention the passing of Vinegar Joe.[124]

Manchuria had remained free of major military action since the June ceasefire. Now, with the Communists having rejected two settlement proposals, Chiang ordered his troops to attack Andong on the Manchurian–North Korean border, and they took the city on October 25.[125] Chiang Kai-shek and Mayling, however, were not in Nanking that day—they had flown to Taiwan for their first-ever visit to the island. Taiwan's peace, security, and economic development deeply impressed them. In particular, 90 percent of its industry was back to prewar levels of production and almost all of the major manufacturing and processing facilities, previously Japanese property, were now owned and operated by the new Taiwan provincial government.[126] With a separate currency, the island's inflation rate was serious but only a fraction of that on the mainland.

Although military and political developments in China proper seemed to be going his way, even in the fall of 1946 Chiang appeared to be thinking of the possibility of some day taking refuge on Formosa (as the Portuguese called the island). That might have been the reason he authorized a separate provincial currency for Taiwan, a practice he had sought to eliminate in his long fight for national unity against provincial power holders. One evening while in Taipei, he noted in his journal that the Communists had not infiltrated Taiwan and overall it was a very politically "clean land." He promised himself that he would "increase efforts to build up the province and make it a model." In this context, he added, "Then, no matter how cunning the Russians and the Communists, how can they beat me?"[127]

On November 5, 1946, the Republicans won a sweeping victory in the American midterm congressional elections. Chiang could now expect the Republican-controlled Congress to act as a check on Truman's China policy, which was one more reason to proceed with a final concession that, he hoped, would reduce any impression that the Nationalists were largely responsible for the failure of the Marshall Mission. Two days later, Chiang handwrote an order to all government troops in China to cease fighting. He also went ahead with plans for convening the promised National Assembly. In response, Zhou charged Chiang with unilaterally convoking the assembly, which, he said, would create a "definite split in China" and meant a "slamming of the door on negotiations."[128]

The National Assembly opened with Kuomintang and a few third-party delegates sitting in the big hall, but there were many vacant seats, presumably for the Communists and the Democratic League. A huge, heroic portrait of Sun Yat-sen dominated the auditorium. One of the Generalissimo's old mentors and the temporary chairman of the assembly, eighty-two-year-old Wu Zhihui, walked onto the stage, then out of the wings came the Generalissimo in his plain military uniform—but this time with the gold collar plates of a general. His bald head gleamed. To the surprise of the American press, the delegates remained seated and offered only "mild and scattered applause." Chiang told the assembly it was the most important event in the history of the Chinese Republic.[129]

Kuomintang conservatives dominated the elected presidium of the assembly but the initial sessions were chaotic, with much hissing and heckling. Nevertheless, the delegates finally set to work and on December 25 produced a draft constitution, which, as Marshall conceded, was "in reasonable agreement" with the provisions proposed by the PCC, and also drew on Sun Yat-sen's writings and the American Constitution. The U.S. Embassy described it as "reasonable," "sound," and "generally democratic and adaptable to China's situation."[130]

While the assembly was deliberating the constitution, Marshall and Stuart had a frank discussion with Chiang during which the American general emphasized that China was approaching economic disaster. "It was useless," he said, "to expect the United States to pour money into the vacuum being created by the military leaders in their determination to settle matters by force." Presciently, he warned once again that the Communists could not be eliminated before the financial foundations of the government and its army collapsed.[131] While listening to Marshall, Chiang's jiggling foot went nervously "round and round and almost hit the ceiling."[132]

The Generalissimo dismissed the economic and financial threat with his hoary theory that China was overwhelmingly an agrarian, subsistence society and could carry on for a surprisingly long period even if the urban economy was in a state of apparent collapse. The agrarian base of China's economy, he told Marshall, would not be seriously affected for two or three more years, an estimate that would prove to be not far off the mark. And in an equally prescient judgment as that of the general, he said that unfortunately, military force had proven to be the only method by which the issue with the CCP could be finally resolved. Again reflecting a vast and incomprehensible optimism, he predicted that the PLA would be destroyed in eight to ten months but then explained that he intended to divide Manchuria with the Communists. He told Marshall that the region from Changchun south was the most valuable and the government was now strong enough to retain that area since Andong had been taken. He declared that he did not intend to advance to Harbin. Such an advance, he said, could create a dangerous Soviet reaction. Drawing the east-west line somewhat north of Changchun would actually have left approximately two-thirds of Manchuria undisturbed in the hands of the Communists.[133] Chiang believed he was being highly realistic and offering an inspired compromise.

On December 6, 1946, Zhou informed Marshall that the CCP wanted him to continue his efforts provided Chiang Kai-shek immediately dissolved the National Assembly and restored his troop positions to what they had been on January 13, 1946. Marshall took this as the end of his mediation.[134] Chiang had succeeded in maneuvering the Communists into putting the ball out of play.[135] Twelve days later, President Truman released a statement edited by Marshall that expressed deep regret that unity in China had been impossible to achieve, but it did not directly or indirectly blame the Chinese government. Instead, it simply noted that "active negotiations" had been "broken off by the Communist Party." The Chinese had to solve their own problems, the statement declared, and the United States would not interfere. But it twice asserted that the United States recognized the National government as the legal government of China, and it declared that President Truman's statement of December 15, 1945, was still "valid," although it clearly was not.[136]

On Christmas Eve, two U.S. Marines allegedly raped a Peking University female student and the press eagerly spread the news. Some five thousand young Chinese poured into the streets of Peking to protest and demonstrations spread quickly to other cities, but the authorities generally refrained from using force to suppress them. Eleven citizen organizations in Shanghai demanded the withdrawal of all U.S. troops from China. Even KMT papers were demanding punishment of the marines.[137] The same evening as the alleged crime, General Marshall with some of his staff went to the Chiangs' Christmas Eve party at the big house in the Purple Hills. (Mrs. Marshall had already returned to the United States.) The Generalissimo was dressed in his black Sun Yat-sen uniform. Madame, who wore a black silk gown with green and gold brocade, helped make the martinis. A large panda-skin rug lying before a crackling fireplace drew gasps of admiration. A lighted Christmas tree was in the corner and Christmas carols from a record player filled the room. After the turkey dinner, a Chinese Santa Claus appeared and handed out gifts. This was to be the Generalissimo's last truly merry Christmas for years to come.[138]

III

Everyone in Nanking expected Marshall to wrap up his mission soon, but still it came as a surprise when on January 7 the White House announced that he was returning to the United States the very next day. That afternoon, Marshall released a balanced statement blaming the failure of his mission on "extremists on both sides" but actually coming down harder on the CCP. In the previous few months, he wrote, the Communists had "indicated an unwillingness to make a fair compromise," and had failed to participate in the National Assembly although the constitution adopted seemed "to include every major point they wanted." Among the Communists, he said, there were "liberals" as well as "radicals" and "dyed in the wool . . . irreconcilable Communists." He found similar obstacles in the KMT, where the "dominant reactionary group in the Government" and "the dominating influence of the military" created the problems.[139]

Chiang quickly arranged a farewell dinner and during the meal the two generals toasted each other. Marshall, according to Chiang, said he was impressed with Chiang's "thoughtfulness, . . . endurance, and sincerity."[140] The

The Chiangs with General Marshall and the visiting General Dwight D. Eisenhower, 1946.
Years later Marshall told an interviewer that Chiang had "betrayed him down the river several
times," but he still was "fond" of him. Courtesy George C. Marshall Foundation.

two introverted personalities did in fact seem to end up with something akin
to mutual respect and even restrained amity. The American envoy, always an
officer and a gentleman, never attacked Chiang personally in his reports or in
conversations with his staff. Years later, he told his biographer that while the
Generalissimo had "betrayed him down the river several times . . . I was and
am fond of Chiang Kai-shek."[141]

   While Marshall was in midflight over the Pacific, the White House announced that President Truman had nominated him to be the new Secretary
of State. Chiang took Marshall's failure to inform him about this appointment before leaving as a hurtful slight. The next day, however, Marshall sent
a radiogram in which he apologized and explained that he had not learned of
the appointment until he had left China. Chiang wrote that there was no
point in knowing if this was true or not, for Marshall in any event had "kept

to the basic principles of courtesy."[142] The message confirmed for Chiang his belief that he had been successful in maintaining civil relations with Marshall and in the end had moved the general back to a more neutral position. He was convinced he had skillfully dealt with another exasperating and dangerous American experience—the result, he believed, of his patient leadership and perseverance combined with military decisiveness and a refusal to be intimidated by American threats to abandon him. This perceived diplomatic success compounded his new, misguided confidence in his ability to keep the PLA forces in the Northeast corralled in northern Manchuria while government armies, in large-scale multicorps battles, "knocked out" the powerful Communist forces in southern Manchuria and south of the Great Wall.[143]

Militarily, however, the New Year began badly. The Hsuchow command lost two battalions of American heavy artillery because it had deployed them near the front for too long, and Lin Biao's small, surprise attacks across the frozen Sungari River destroyed two regiments from Sun Liren's 50th Division.[144] Despite these initial setbacks as well as sporadic civil unrest and soaring inflation, the popularity and legitimacy of Chiang's government were at another peak. There was a sense of an expanding political order based on the new constitution, some progress in reconstruction, and the government's military successes in 1946. Some critical Western observers looking back conclude that at this point, the Chinese public's "identification of Chiang and his party with the Chinese state" was in fact at its "highest point."[145] When Chiang commissioned a review of foreign press reports on China, he was delighted to learn that the most important newspapers in New York, London, and Paris agreed that on balance he had the upper hand.

To deal with sky-high inflation, Chiang banned the selling of foreign currency and gold bullion, put a ceiling on interest rates, postponed numerous government projects, froze all wages at the January level, set prices for a number of essential goods (including wheat, cooking oil, and rice), and began supplying government workers in the cities with basic foodstuffs and cloth at fixed prices.[146] These measures worked briefly, contributing to Chiang's relatively high "approval rating," but Chiang himself said he did not know whether they could resolve the serious problems.[147]

The real cause of the financial crisis, of course, continued to be out-of-control military expenditures, which were still eating up more than 50 percent and maybe as much as 90 percent of the budget.[148] In early March, T. V. Soong and the Generalissimo had a "frank conversation" about the escalation of the war and how it was to be financed. The Generalissimo insisted on in-

The First Couple and Ching-kuo *(second row, right)*, ca. 1946, with Premier T. V. Soong *(first row, right)*, who would resign in 1947 as the national currency entered its death spiral. Courtesy KMT Party History Institute.

creased pay for the troops, but T.V. resisted and finally resigned as premier and as chairman of the Supreme Economic Council. He told Beal he was happy to leave before the bottom fell out of the country financially, but May-ling complained to Stuart, "They made my brother the scapegoat."[149] One reason Chiang may have wanted T.V. gone was a government report on gold manipulation in Shanghai, which implicated several of Soong's subordinates in "highly questionable if not unsavory activities."[150] Although Chiang appointed him governor of Guangdong, T.V.'s influence in the Chinese government had ended.

IV

Meanwhile, more reports of serious military setbacks began to appear in daily reports to the Generalissimo. Chiang even flew to Jinan to direct personally the campaign in Shandong, ordering two army groups pursuing Chen Yi's troops to carry out a north-south "sandwich strategy," but poor intelligence, even with aircraft reconnaissance, led to disaster. After a Communist ambush the Nationalist forces fled in panic and the CCP captured several generals.[151]

Chiang feared these ignoble defeats would feed "the inclination of his generals to stay in the cities."[152] This may have been one of those times, as Mayling reported to Katherine Marshall, when Chiang went up on the roof and held his head in despair, moaning that he could not give an order to his generals and make them obey.[153] In Manchuria, too, the Communist Lin Biao's huge army again crossed the Sungari ice and pushed southward, seizing several towns along the rail line and isolating Changchun and Sipingjie—until Du Yuming counterattacked with twelve divisions and drove Lin back over the river.[154] Chief of Staff Chen Cheng reassured the public that the Central Army would defeat the Communists within six months.[155]

As economic conditions worsened in the cities, labor agitation increased. Labor leaders rhetorically linked their demands to those of the students who were calling for an end to the civil war. But the protestors were not pro-Communist, and when the CCP tried to recruit large numbers of union members and students in the cities, it generally failed.[156] Chiang believed that the Kuomintang could turn rising labor activism to its advantage by pressuring industrialists and other major employers to grant better pay and working conditions. At his direction, Chen Lifu took the lead in organizing training centers for labor leaders, worker welfare associations, and paramilitary protection units. The goal was to make the workers feel that the Kuomintang was truly the protector of their interests.[157] For a while, the effort seemed to be succeeding, but then it began to conflict with the need to fight inflation and rapidly unraveled.[158]

In February, Chiang transferred Chen Lifu from the Ministry of Education back to party headquarters to work on the election of National Assembly members as called for in the new constitution. The mechanics of a general election in war-torn China, with half or more of the country north of the Yellow River in the hands of the Communists, was difficult enough, but the most vexing task for Chen was selecting the KMT members to be the party's official candidates for the 2,908-seat National Assembly. Competition for such influential and thus potentially profitable positions was fierce; thousands of senior party members and ranking military officers had been waiting years for the opportunity to achieve some national office.

Chen Lifu also continued to be concerned with the general drift of the party, and he wrote several memoranda to the Generalissimo warning that greed, corruption, and a lack of willpower were weakening the Kuomintang and the country. He declared that pernicious "foreign influences" were also at work, apparently referring to both cultural decadence and demands for

Western-style civil rights. Only by a thorough purge of corrupt and undisciplined elements, he believed, could Chiang save the KMT and himself.[159] In May, *Time* magazine ran a cover story on Chen reporting his philosophical ideals—"the essence of life is the performance of benevolence"—and his strong anti-Communism.[160] Chen Lifu's reputation for incorruptibility as well as loyalty was key to his standing with Chiang Kai-shek. His reform campaign, however, went nowhere because Chiang still believed it was not the time for sweeping out of office thousands of corrupt senior officials and military commanders.

Taiwan had seemed wonderfully stable when the Generalissimo and Madame visited there the previous October. But in the winter of 1947 in Taipei the worst civil uprising in China in many years suddenly broke out. The stage had been set eighteen months earlier when thousands of mainlander officials and officers accompanied the newly appointed Governor Chen Yi (not related to the CCP general with the same Romanized name) to the island and came to occupy virtually all political, administrative, and security posts, including control of all state-run—meaning formerly Japanese private and government-owned—enterprises, which dominated the economy. By the beginning of 1947, these Nationalist officials had taken over or absconded with an estimated US$1 billion in property and other assets.[161]

A year and a half after "liberation," resentment on the island was boiling, and on February 28, protests over the arrest of a woman selling cigarettes escalated into a major rebellion. In a radiogram to Chiang, Governor Chen blamed the violence on pro-Japanese members of the Taiwan elite along with radical elements who opposed retrocession of the island to China. Chiang thought the incident was likely a Communist plot.[162] Chen Cheng, chief of the General Staff, urged him not to send more troops to Taiwan but instead to dispatch a delegation of senior officials to confer with local leaders and restructure the provincial government, especially in order to employ many more Taiwanese in its administration. But on the island the Taiwan Resolution Committee of civic leaders demanded that the government remove the Taiwan Garrison Command and "give up all weapons to the committee." This demand, Chiang wrote, "crossed the red line of what the government can tolerate."[163] But it was only a rhetorical requirement from a powerless committee.

No doubt influenced in part by his clear perception of Taiwan as the only stable refuge for him and his army should he lose the mainland, Chiang ordered a brutal "kill the chicken to scare the monkey" sort of suppression. The 21st Division sailed immediately for the island and on March 9, as the transport ships arrived in Keelung harbor near Taipei, troops aboard began shooting anyone they saw on the docks or in nearby buildings. Disembarking, the soldiers joined the Garrison Command in rounding up listed individuals and executing them as examples. Decades later, the Kuomintang apologized for its handling of the "2/28 affair" and estimated 18,000 to 28,000 deaths.[164]

On March 13, Chiang belatedly cabled Governor Chen to report that no revenge was to be taken against the Taiwan public. But events had already produced enormous carnage and international outrage. Ambassador Stuart gave Chiang a vivid and highly critical report, and Chiang, realizing he had a political and diplomatic disaster on his hands, ordered the establishment of a Taiwan provincial government, early election of mayors and county chiefs, priority appointment of native Taiwanese as director and bureau chiefs of government offices, and privatization of certain state-owned enterprises.[165] If he had taken these steps initially, the situation would very likely have calmed. He also replaced Chen Yi with Wei Daoming, a respected educator and former ambassador to the United States. The new governor ended martial law, abolished mail censorship, affirmed the freedom of the press, and began a process of local elections. Some months later Chiang again demonstrated that for him loyalty could excuse dreadful behavior and he appointed Chen Yi governor of Zhejiang, his home province.

Meanwhile, Bai Chongxi and many other KMT veterans were unhappy with the decision officially to end political tutelage. They believed that during a desperate civil war any democracy that emerged would be so imperfect and manipulated that it would be worse than continuing with authoritarian rule. In fact, Chiang's democratic gestures did not come easily. Mayling once told Marshall that over the years she had tried to educate her husband on the subject of democracy but had only made a "two percent impression."[166] Nonetheless, Chiang had seemed to be genuinely proud of the historic document produced by the provisional National Assembly in December 1946, even pushing through party approval of a new political program that guaranteed civil liberties. At the time, he appeared sincere about this newfound cause. But as student demonstrations and other civil disorders broke out in the spring of 1947, as the military situation grew steadily worse, and as heavy politicking intensified within the KMT for nominations to the National Assembly and the new Legislative Yuan, Chiang returned to his long-held belief that China was not ready for a truly democratic society. Even so, carrying through formally with the constitutional process was important to shore up American and domestic support.[167]

On April 17, Chiang announced the long-awaited reorganization of the State Council. According to the new constitution, KMT and non-KMT participants would each have twelve seats in the council, but the five constitutional Yuan presidents were to be ex-officio members, which would give the KMT a five-vote majority. Eleven seats were left vacant for the Communist Party and the Democratic League. Ambassador Stuart and his embassy concluded that the caliber and standing of the KMT appointees indicated "real effort to place in positions of power and responsibility the most capable and modern figures" of the Kuomintang. No powerful military figures or members of Chen Guofu and Chen Lifu's notorious "C-C Clique" were on the list.[168]

At this point, Chiang took a few days off and with Mayling and Chiang Ching-kuo made a trip back to the Chiang hometown of Xikou. He was happy to see that his mother's tomb was covered by "prosperous grass and hundred-year-old [apparently transplanted] trees."[169]

Stuart supported Chiang's requests for a resumption of U.S. aid, but in his reports to Washington emphasized the deflating morale on the government side and the financial, strategic, and logistical factors that would sooner or later result in a total breakdown. Meanwhile, in Manchuria, the PLA continued to increase its capabilities thanks to successful conscription and Soviet aid. The government naval commander in Tsingtao reported that his ships had detected several Soviet freighters every week unloading armed Communist troops and weapons at Yantai, the CCP-occupied port at the northeastern tip of Shandong. The rail lines in Communist Manchuria suffered occasional air attacks but were kept humming by a 300-man unit of Soviet Army Railway troops. Soviet doctors, too, were sent to help put down an epidemic of plague in the PLA camps. To pay for the imports of supplies and equipment from Russia, in 1947, Communist Manchuria sent north by train 1.1 million tons of grain as well as other products. Yet throughout the Chinese civil war, CIA assessments kept reporting that "there was no concrete evidence the Soviet Union was currently supplying Japanese or Soviet material to the CCP."[170]

In May, Lin Biao launched yet another campaign, this time mobilizing 400,000 troops and 200 heavy guns. Government forces in all of Manchuria totaled only about 250,000, although they enjoyed the support of 130 P-51 fighters as well as a few B-25 bombers. The battle for Manchuria, which would now determine the fate of China, was not a guerrilla war but a conflict of mammoth, multicorps forces clashing in conventional style with the outcome to be determined by leadership, air support, troop strength, weapons, ammunition, logistics, intelligence, and troop morale. Lin once again achieved some early success, destroying several government regiments and for a while isolating garrisons at Changchun and Kirin. But he again suffered heavy losses in his frontal attack on Sipingjie, and Sun Liren's forces once more drove the Communist general back to north of the Sungari. A "rare published casualty figure" from the Communists revealed that they had "lost" 116,000 men in the period of March to May 1947, mostly in Manchuria.[171]

But Mao intended to keep up the momentum. In order to bolster his effort at wearing down the Nationalist ranks whatever the costs, he ordered a large-scale conscription drive in Manchuria. Like the government, the Communists assigned quotas for each locality—in their case more than 100 men per district for each call up.[172] The local CCP cadre always met their quota. During the course of the civil war, it recruited or conscripted approximately one million men in Manchuria alone.[173]

The Communists achieved a significant victory in April at Menglianggu, when Chen Yi's East China Army wiped out General Zhang Lingfu's "Most Courageous" 74th Division of 32,000 men. General Zhang, "a brave, honest, and loyal patriot," a Whampoa and a Peking University man, together with four of his generals, committed suicide to avoid capture. Just fifteen days before his death, Zhang had sent a letter to the Generalissimo lamenting that Kuomintang generals and the military's culture were "corrupt and hopeless." Chiang felt the same way and he circulated the letter to all his top generals, which may have only further discouraged both the honest and the dishonest.[174] At a ceremony commemorating those who had given their lives at Menglianggu, Chiang said the division was destroyed "most of all because our officers are reluctant to work and cooperate and instead are all thinking how to keep their troops safe and intact . . . the rescuing divisions were never where they had been ordered to be." Chiang promised that a court-martial would carefully determine responsibility.[175]

But Chiang's lesson was not over. He ordered half of all senior and mid-level officers serving in the Shandong front lines to leave the battlefield and attend a special seminar in Nanking. The Generalissimo's first speech to the group carried the blunt title: "Government Military Senior Officers' Shame and Self-Reflection." "Senior officers," he said, implying that he meant virtually all ranking commanders, had "picked up the lifestyle and mentality of warlords. They don't want to sacrifice but to protect their power, and they never seriously study military tactics and the [battlefield] situation." In a particularly biting comment, he charged that the "difference of everyday life between senior and middle level officers and soldiers is unbelievably huge, resulting in low morale." He seemed to have given up on the older commanders. "Young officers," he said, must learn from the martyrs such as General Zhang Lingfu. Afterward he wrote, "I have done my best to encourage, admonish, and enlighten our senior front line military officers." He decided to employ "tougher policies and extraordinary measures to stop the decadence and the [overall downward] trend."[176] But he did not fire a hundred senior officers to make his point, or apparently even one. This was not the time, he felt, to truly shake up his army.

By the middle of 1947, a large majority of urban youth favored an end to the war and a coalition government, regardless of the concessions that would have to be made to the Communists. Polls, however, showed that only a small fraction still favored a Communist government or a Communist way of life. As Stuart put it, "95 percent of university students opposed the KMT and 90 percent opposed the CCP." Student-led anti-government demonstrations beginning in May of 1947 escalated into a "tide" of demonstrations and strikes that swept through universities, colleges, and middle schools around the country.[177]

Chiang was determined to crack down and his first new stringent move was to ban three newspapers in Shanghai and arrest the leaders of the student movement. Police also detained two hundred persons in Chungking, and during the next two weeks internal security forces in various big cities picked up large numbers of suspected "ringleaders." Some suspects were abducted by police; others simply disappeared. When students at Wuhan University stopped a police van taking away five professors, the police fired above the heads of the students, killing three people through dormitory windows. A furor erupted across the country.

Chiang quickly backtracked away from his "tough" policy. He issued a personal statement condemning the police action and, after parents of the detained students applied for writs of habeas corpus, he released almost all of them, although many of these students, along with activist faculty members, were dismissed from their universities. The chief of the detective squad of the Wuhan Garrison Command was found drowned in the Yangtze, an apparent suicide.[178] The *Dagongbao* in Tianjin published fourteen outspoken editorials in support of the students before censorship was finally imposed and it and a number of other newspapers were banned; one editor, however, still gave speeches at three universities urging the students to expand their movement into industrial and commercial circles.[179] The far-from-draconian suppression—which was perhaps subdued in part because of the disastrous bloodbath in Taiwan—contrasted with the absolute nontoleration of public dissent in the Communist areas, where habeas corpus was either unheard of or mocked. Chiang's new crackdown was a fiasco. Inconsistently harsh and generally ineffective, it undermined the prestige as well as the authority of the regime.

Meanwhile, in the United States, Truman's China policy was coming under increasing political pressure. The State Department, now under George Marshall, lifted the de facto arms embargo on China but made it clear that the Chiang government would have to pay for any American arms it desired. It would also need approval for each purchase, which could take months. The almost $1 billion in U.S. currency collected through soft U.S. loans during the war with Japan had been spent down to between $300 and $400 million, and Chiang could have used these funds to try to buy arms.[180] He also could have dipped into the supply of gold that his treasury had hoarded primarily in state banks in Shanghai. But he wanted to keep a reserve, probably thinking even more than before of the possibility of retreating to Taiwan. On June 19, with the PLA surrounding both Sipingjie and Changchun, Chiang met hurriedly with Stuart to tell him that "the Manchurian situation was extremely serious." With Soviet support, he said, the Communists "were constantly gaining in numbers and equipment." Explaining that he had only come to appreciate the gravity of the situation three days earlier, he told the ambassador that he now anticipated losing Sipingjie, then Changchun and

Mukden. A decision on Manchuria, he stressed, "must be made in a very few days." Chiang seemed to be contemplating an immediate and total withdrawal behind the Great Wall.[181]

But the fight was not over. Instead of pulling back, Chiang mustered nine divisions from eastern Manchuria and Fu Zuoyi's military zone in North China and sent these as well as most of the five corps in southern Manchuria to attack Lin Biao's forces around Sipingjie. At the same time the three-division Nationalist garrison in Changchun burst out of its encirclement and advanced south, completing a large pincer closing in on Lin Biao's attack force at Sipingjie. The Communist troops, who had just fought their way to that city center, broke and fled north around the attacking force from Changchun. Lin once more withdrew his battered forces across the Sungari, having lost another 40,000 men. Du caught up but did not pursue across the river.[182]

Upon receiving news of the victory, Chiang perversely recommitted himself to holding the line at Changchun. Apparently still thinking only of southern Manchuria, he wrote that "without the Northeast, North China will be left defenseless." But in fact without northern Manchuria and with Siberia in pro-CCP hands, the Northeast was defenseless.[183]

V

In the first week of July 1947, General Wedemeyer entered Secretary Marshall's office on the top floor of the State Department, a few hundred yards from the Lincoln Memorial. There Marshall told him that increasingly fierce accusations from Congress and the "China lobby" that the administration was pursuing a pro-Communist policy in China were compelling "a reappraisal of U.S. policy." The recent lifting of the ban on the sale of U.S. arms to China was part of the response. But the U.S. government, Marshall indicated, was at a loss over what to do next. He asked Wedemeyer to return to China as a presidential envoy for six to eight weeks and report back to the White House.[184]

Wedemeyer assumed that his mission was a critical one and that Washington would take seriously his recommendations. Marshall, however, assured Stuart by radiogram that the visit was "a temporary expedient."[185] Chiang was of course pleased when informed of the visit. He viewed Wedemeyer as a friend as well as a frank critic who nevertheless fully understood the Communists. The Communists, for their part, claimed Wedemeyer's mission was a sign that the United States was about to reverse its policy of disengagement from the Chinese civil war and go all out in supporting Chiang Kai-shek.[186]

The general and his staff spent a month traveling around China, including Manchuria. He interviewed people from all walks of life and with widely varying opinions. He also addressed a meeting of the State Council, all the ministers of the government, Ambassador Stuart, and of course Chiang and his wife. Chiang told the envoy beforehand to speak frankly in this off-the-record talk. At the last minute, however, he called Stuart and asked him to request that the general not be too critical in his comments (a message that Stuart elected not to pass on).[187] Wedemeyer, meanwhile, felt that he had to be candid about the faults of the regime; otherwise, his planned recommendation to President Truman that he approve immediate and large-scale American aid to the Chinese government would have no credibility.[188] In his remarks, Wedemeyer described the maladministration and corruption rampant in China, failings that Chiang himself had recently, albeit privately, bemoaned. The general said that the government could not defeat the Communists by military means but had to improve the political and economic situation immediately in order to win the support of the Chinese people. Many of the KMT officials attending the talk were offended, but others said they wept because they knew what Wedemeyer had said was true.[189]

Before he returned to Washington, Wedemeyer had a six-hour meeting with Chiang, who explained at length the "objective reasons" for the faults of the Chinese government and Chinese society. Wedemeyer, however, made no apologies for his remarks and did not mention that he intended to recommend a major U.S. recommitment to Chiang's government. Afterward, consciously practicing a restraint that he very likely thought Mencius would admire, Chiang wrote in his diary, "In this world all the difficulties and humiliations are brought on by oneself, not others. But the United States at this point simply does not have a clear China policy. It is unfortunate."[190]

Once in Washington, Wedemeyer sent his confidential report to Truman recommending immediate military and economic aid to China and raising his own old proposal that the United Nations place Manchuria under a "five-power" U.N. trusteeship, which would include the Soviet Union. Marshall took no action on Wedemeyer's report and chose not to release it on the argument that the U.N. guardianship proposal, if publicized, would be highly offensive to the Chinese. Wedemeyer was incensed, believing that Marshall had suppressed his report because of Marshall's firm opposition to any military aid to China.[191]

9

The Great Failure

With his recent victory over Lin Biao still untarnished, Du Yuming was suffering another bout of bad health, and in early July after Li Zongren declined the Manchurian command, Chiang chose Chen Cheng to replace him.[1] On August 29, Chen became commander of the Northeast Headquarters, responsible for all political, economic, and military matters. Chen, now the leader of fourteen armies, persuaded Chiang to increase the total number of government troops to about 500,000. He also replaced many senior military officers as well as the chairmen of all the provincial party committees in the region, a sweep that suggested the extent of corruption and ineptness he believed existed. He arrested some of the officers and KMT officials and "deported" others back to Nanking.[2] Ambassador Stuart reported that Chen's reforms were having an "excellent effect on political and military morale." But, he added, the sixth Communist offensive was expected as soon as the roads dried, and it was doubtful these changes would have sufficient time to offset the decay.[3]

The heavy military manpower balance in Manchuria in favor of the Communists, their control of probably 90 percent of the countryside in that region, their Soviet support, and their strong position in North China made Chiang's decision to pour more troops into the Northeast a huge, irrational—in fact, a mad—gamble. In addition to low morale and other disadvantages, his American-equipped divisions in Manchuria had no likely source of ammunition, parts, or replacements for their American weapons and equipment and their inventories were running dangerously low. His thinking was perhaps revealed in one journal entry where he wrote that without the Northeast, the naval ports of Shandong would soon be lost and all of North China would be open to China's enemies. Chiang seemed to be saying that whether he withdrew from Manchuria or was defeated in an all-out effort in the region, he would in either case eventually lose all of China.[4]

Chiang's continued denigration of his army officers and KMT officials certainly underscored his previously sporadic but now prevailing pessimism about the long-term outcome of the struggle with the Communists. At a surprise plenary meeting of the Executive Committee on September 9, the Generalissimo once again told his comrades that the Communists had proved themselves "abler and more devoted" members of a revolutionary party. "Reform and rejuvenation of the Kuomintang," he declared, were "doomed."[5] On other occasions he accused senior officers of embezzling grain and money intended for the troops and expressed admiration for the discipline and morality of the Communists. As with similar harangues since early 1947, these may well have hurt rather than helped his efforts to change the officers' behavior.

Meanwhile, in Washington, the suppression of Wedemeyer's report provoked much suspicion and protest. Under increasing political pressure, in October the Department of State devised a new economic assistance program for China. Marshall told the Senate that the plan envisioned about US$25 million a month for a total of US$300 million annually, but it was uncertain when any funds would actually be available. Washington also authorized the new commander of the U.S. advisory group in China, Major General David Barr, to provide "advice on an informal and confidential basis to the Generalissimo," and agreed that China could purchase ammunition from U.S. supplies in the Pacific.[6]

On October 2, Communist general Lin Biao launched his sixth offensive against the government armies in Manchuria. Chen Cheng had had only about four weeks to implement his military and political changes, and his forces numbered approximately 300,000, not the 500,000 he had planned. This time Lin avoided frontal attacks on Nationalist-held cities. Instead he concentrated on disrupting the rail lines and the road links between them, attacking small and medium garrisons, and collecting grain from the fall harvest.

At this point, five or six Nationalist reinforcement divisions reached Qinhuangdao on the Yellow Sea—just south of the eastern end of the Great Wall. With rail lines more disrupted than ever, all the government forces increasingly relied on air transport. General Claire Chennault, retired once again, had returned to China and established a commercial airline, Civil Air Transport. His "CAT" planes were heavily involved in the daily lift of supplies into Mukden and other major government-held cities in the region.[7]

Early blizzards swept the Northeast and Lin again retired with most of his forces back across the Sungari to train and refit. His men had in total killed or wounded 68,000 government troops and probably lost more themselves—many to air attacks. But Lin's army continued to grow, surpassing 500,000 by the end of the year.

Meanwhile, in North China, the PLA continued to control Shandong and Hebei, except for the cities and some rail lines, and had opened up a whole new theater of operations in central China, threatening Nanking and even Wuhan.[8] In early November Chiang received a report that on average each of his soldiers now had only 180 bullets and insufficient daily food. "I really do not know what the future holds," he wrote.[9]

One November day, the Generalissimo was riding a black sedan to the Peking airport. Early frigid winds from the north were already blowing hard through the *hutongs* of the city, and the people trudging along the streets had their faces covered with scarves or surgical masks. As the official car passed through the West Gate, a single shot rang out. The Generalissimo heard the "thang" of the bullet ripping through the sides of the auto, just above his head. One of his aides, General Sun Lianzhong, leaped from the car and captured the would-be assassin. Ambassador Stuart was told that the shooter was a subordinate of General Mou Dingfang, formerly commander of the Fourth Army, whom the Generalissimo had ordered court-martialed for graft. When Stuart saw the Generalissimo on the evening of December 2, Chiang was in "a more depressed state of mind" than the ambassador had ever seen him, but made no mention of the attempt on his life.[10]

After talking to Chiang, Stuart again urged Washington to approve emergency military assistance for the battered and demoralized Nationalist armies. He thought the Generalissimo would agree to almost any condition Washington might impose.[11] In December, Chiang's chief commissar, Zhang Zhizhong, and Chiang Ching-kuo were separately urging the Soviet embassy in Nanking to help achieve a settlement.[12] Vice President Sun Fo publicly warned that if the United States did not provide major assistance, the Nanking government would fall into the Soviet orbit. Chiang probably saw all this as a tactic to pressure the United States, but it also was clear, as Stuart reported, that the Communists were "winning on all sides" and it seemed "inconceivable" they would accept real peace talks.[13]

Even provinces south of the Yangtze were in a precarious position. In Guangdong, Guangxi, Hunan, Henan, Zhejiang, and Fujian the Communist underground was increasingly active. On Christmas Day, Mao predicted that with the imminent collapse of "America's running dog," Chiang Kai-shek, the strength of "the world anti-imperialist camp had now surpassed that of the imperialist camp."[14]

Despite his defeats during the Communist fall offensive, Chen Cheng announced on New Year's Day 1948 that the Central Army had completed its battle preparations and that the crisis of Manchuria had passed. This was a stupefying statement. At that time Chen's heavily outnumbered Northeast Army occupied about 2 or 3 percent of the entire region, and the Communist Army was still rapidly closing the gap in weaponry and training. The total lack of air power was the PLA's main weakness, but its commanders knew how to play to its strengths. Before Chen could launch his attack and when the Arctic-like weather and thick mist severely reduced Chen's use of his warplanes to a mere twelve sorties a day, Lin Biao sent a mass assault across the ice-hard Sungari.[15] The Communist general besieged Sipingjie but sent most of his 400,000-man force south of Mukden as well as Changchun. The government's elite New Fifth Army, which had fought in Burma, moved out of Mukden but was surrounded by two columns of the PLA and two Nationalist divisions were destroyed.[16]

Chen Cheng at first blamed two commanders for not marching forward to rescue the New Fifth Army. The accused officers, however, convinced Chiang that they had not received any such orders, and Chiang concluded the fault lay with Chen's headquarters. Chiang permitted Chen to transfer back to Nanking, then prevailed upon General Wei Lihuang to take command in Manchuria. Wei, who had successfully commanded five Chinese armies on the eastern front in the Second Burma Campaign, insisted on full military, party, and government powers in the region, and Chiang agreed. As another sweetener, Chiang found an additional 100,000 troops to make up for the forces lost by Chen Cheng, and he promised to send more supplies and in the future, more reinforcements.[17]

The Communist winter offensive, however, was still gaining ground; Communist troops captured areas around Mukden and destroyed two more government divisions. After arriving in Mukden on January 22, Wei saw that he lacked secure supplies and reserves and assumed a totally defensive position. A week later, Lin Biao cut the railway to Jinzhou southeast of Mukden and stormed all the garrisons along the line, destroying three more government divisions.[18] Meanwhile, students attacked the mayor of Shanghai, factory workers went on strike, and even prostitutes were demonstrating. "The people are losing confidence everywhere," Chiang wrote on February 3, 1948.[19]

Two days later, General Wei reported that he had only about ten days' worth of "logistical supplies" and needed 200 billion yuan to purchase enough food "if the troops are to stay until the end of April."[20] But the Nationalist government itself had begun to run out of troops and supplies. Against his early instincts and common sense, which had once convinced him Manchuria was a trap, for a year Chiang had kept pouring good troops after a host of dead and wounded. This bizarre policy seems to have been fueled by Chiang's belief that after the expected military loss in the Northeast, defeat in the rest of mainland China was inevitable—thus there was no incentive to save forces in order to hold the line somewhere south of the Great Wall.

Chiang also worried that the time had passed for an orderly withdrawal from the Northeast, although that was not the case. Nevertheless, he told General Wei to pull his main forces out of Mukden and Changchun, clearing the railway as they advanced southeast to Jinzhou near the coast.[21] But Wei refused, fearing an ambush and massacre of his troops and saying he did not want to abandon the 122,000 men trapped to the north in Changchun.[22] He also said he needed to rest and re-outfit his armies in Mukden with flown-in equipment before starting out. PLA forces now enveloped the area around Mukden as well as much of the rail line to Jinzhou. In addition, Wei reported, the roads out of Mukden were thawing and would be extremely muddy until April; the rivers, too, were no longer frozen hard enough to cross.[23]

In a bizarre circumstance, for the next several months, Chiang could not or would not compel Wei to carry out his orders to withdraw while it was still conceivable.[24] General Barr, in his 1949 wrap-up report to the Defense Department on the debacle in Manchuria, emphasized that "the Generalissimo had directed General Wei Lihuang as early as the preceding winter [early 1948] to prepare plans and ready himself for an attack early in May to open a corridor from Mukden to Jinzhou . . . [and] the Nationalist Supreme G-3 [the general in charge of operations] had made six separate trips to Mukden in an effort to press preparations for this breakout offensive."[25]

From late January to early February, three major civil disturbances broke out in Shanghai culminating in outbreaks of mob violence. At the same time, the urban economy was barely functioning. Despite the economic reforms of the previous year, the exchange value of the *fabi* had fallen from about 1,500 to one U.S. dollar in August 1945 to about 180,000 to the dollar in January 1948. Foreign trade was almost at a standstill. Stuart noted a growing popular awareness that the regime was not likely to survive. The American and British embassies advised their nationals to leave North China.[26] As the deluge loomed and everyone grabbed what they could, corruption exploded. The *Far Eastern Economic Review* in January 1948 summed up the despair of China as seen from Hong Kong:

> One [cannot] cease to marvel at the extent to which in recent months sympathy with the Communists' aims and programs finds vigorous expression from the most unexpected quarters in Nationalist China. Such expressions come even from conservative Chinese business men who have no love for Russia or socialism, men who in 1945 were solid supporters of the National Government but feel now that life under the relatively honest totalitarianism of the Communists could not be worse than it is under the corrupt inefficiency of the Kuomintang.[27]

Meanwhile in Washington, following the Truman administration's promise of aid, Congress eventually approved US$463 million in economic assistance along with an additional US$100 million to be used at China's option for military purposes. There were contradictory reports on the degree to which the supplies were needed on the battlefield. General Barr reported that "no battle has been lost since my arrival due to lack of ammunition or equipment," whereas Stuart commented that in most war zones shortages of matériel had weakened government defenses.[28] The first military supplies purchased by the new American funds did not begin to arrive until November 1948, a year after Marshall had informed Congress of the aid proposal, and too late to play any role in the battle for Manchuria.[29]

One Communist success now followed another in various parts of the country. Yichuan, a city halfway between Taiyuan and Xi'an, fell, putting out of action a third of government troops in Shanxi. The eastern part of Gansu and the Northwest were now in danger and a potential corridor had opened to Szechwan. Madame Chiang told Stuart that the Communist forces had put out of action sixteen divisions, most of them American-equipped.[30] Chiang again ordered an attack out of Mukden to open the rail line to the sea, but Wei insisted that before he would risk his armies in the open countryside he had to have large reinforcements and more time for his troops to recuperate and reorganize. If his best army corps struck out for Jinzhou, he was certain it would be ambushed and destroyed. Chiang now dispatched a new deputy commander to Wei's headquarters with orders to tell Wei that, regardless of the dangers, he was commanded to move his best surviving armies out of Mukden and to concentrate on securing the rail line between that city and Jinzhou.[31] Instead of obeying, on March 31, Wei flew to Nanking for a meeting with the Generalissimo, and the argument continued, with Chiang unable or unwilling to relieve Wei of his command.

The enemy had probably taken even greater losses than the government, but there seemed to be no lack of replacements for the PLA, and captured U.S. weapons were increasingly available to arm whole Communist divisions. By this time, the government controlled a mere 1 percent of Manchuria and only 15 percent of China proper north of the Yellow River. Chiang yet again mourned the absence of officers in his government who had the "character to save the situation." "There are no such persons," he wrote, asking again, "What can I do?"[32]

The newly elected National Assembly, which opened on March 29, did not go smoothly. Some of the 2,908 members were angry at the dismissal of 120 of their loyal KMT colleagues who, despite party orders, had stood and won as independents, and thus filled all the "independent" seats.[33] Chiang gave the keynote speech, focusing on "the beginning of our democratic and constitutional history."[34] From the tenor of his address, one would have had no idea that the National Assembly, the government, and the giant armed forces all faced extinction.

The assembly elected Chiang as the first president under the new Republic of China constitution. Then, in a shocking turn of events, the legislators selected Li Zongren as vice president even though Chiang had discouraged him from running. This was a serious rebuff to the Generalissimo, who was so upset he could not sleep that night and reputedly drank a rare spot of whiskey to help.[35] Li's ascension became a rallying point for the increasing number in the party favoring a change in leadership, and after the election Chiang never invited him to participate in any important conference.[36]

A week before the National Assembly met, Chiang had an unusually frank conversation with Ambassador Stuart, admitting that he should have heeded Marshall's assessment that the government could not militarily defeat the Communists. But he believed he had been proven correct in his belief that compromise or cooperation with the Communists was impossible. Chiang told the sympathetic ambassador he "really wanted to reform but did not know how to go about it." The conversation further confirmed Stuart's long-held view that Chiang needed only good advice and a lot of material assistance to turn the situation around.[37]

In early May, during a conference at the Chiangs' house in the Purple Hills, General Barr recommended that if the attack out of Mukden could not be made soon, the government should abandon Manchuria while it was still possible. Wei's commanders, however, still insisted that a retreat was too risky. Barr was astonished that Wei Lihuang continued to get away with turning down direct orders from the Generalissimo, but Chiang agreed to another postponement.[38] By midsummer the Manchurian plain had dried out, but otherwise Wei's situation was bleaker than before in terms of supplies and morale. His one advantage, tactical airpower, was shrinking due to a lack of replacement aircraft and fuel. Chiang tried to find an officer to replace Wei, but no senior general wanted the job. Wei remained hunkered down with 150,000 to 200,000 men in Mukden and 100,000 in Changchun, the best of the government's remaining armies.[39]

On July 19, Wei Lihuang flew to Nanking for yet another critical round of meetings with the Generalissimo. To everyone's surprise, Wei now said that his troops were rested and in high spirits. He was confident he could defend Mukden, but to retreat as Chiang proposed would send morale on another downward spiral. He argued also that because the pullout might fail, defending Mukden was the safer course. Finally the Generalissimo agreed that Wei would stay in Mukden for three months longer, preparing his army for an offensive withdrawal in November. Years later, Chiang said he failed to pull out earlier because of "objections from high-ranking officers and the influence of public opinion, and politics . . . especially the tearful complaint of representatives from Manchuria."[40]

As the fall chill began to grip southern Manchuria, Lin Biao was ready to launch the CCP's biggest military offensive ever—the Liaoshen Campaign. His 700,000 troops were refreshed and ready, with some divisions trained on captured U.S. arms. From intercepted messages and probably other intelligence, Lin was certainly aware of Chiang's intent to move his best armies south to Jinzhou, where they would be close to the evacuation port of Huludao. Lin Biao's bold plan was to bypass Mukden and capture Jinzhou first, trapping the rest of the Nationalist armies in Manchuria. The pending American presidential election gave both sides a special incentive for a decisive victory in Manchuria, and the Soviets stepped up their unofficial assistance to the CCP, helping to rebuild the railway bridge across the Sungari.[41]

On September 12, the PLA assaulted the outposts around Mukden and along the rail line to Jinzhou. At the same time, with impressive speed, twenty-three PLA divisions, almost 300,000 men, created a siege wall around Jinzhou. Inside the embattled city were Fan Hanzhi's 118,000 men of the Sixth Army, half of them Yunnanese who had little ammunition and no stomach for another bitter winter under siege.[42] Barr and Chiang agreed that it was essential that Wei Lihuang order General Zheng Dongguo's First Army's six divisions to break out of Changchun and head for the coast and for the twenty-one divisions in Mukden to vacate that city and attack the Communists threatening Jinzhou. Previously, Chiang had said that one army and one division should remain behind in Mukden. Now he was ready to abandon the city entirely and concentrate virtually all government forces in Manchuria and a good many from North China on the battle for Jinzhou. Wei finally agreed to send forth a "Western Strike Force" of 90,000 men under General Liao Yaoxiang, but insisted he needed time to prepare for the bigger counteroffensive.

Chiang flew to Peking to see the warlord Fu Zuoyi, chief of the bandit-suppression headquarters in North China.[43] At their meeting the Generalissimo was highly pessimistic, suggesting that only a war between the Soviet Union and the United States could save the situation. Fu was losing confidence in the Generalissimo, but for the moment he agreed to send one army and an additional division to take part in the battle for Jinzhou.[44] Flying to Mukden, Chiang looked down on the Manchurian plain—a few hundred thousand Communist soldiers were spread out across the fallow wheat fields. During his meeting with Wei and his staff after the flight, he told them they all had to cooperate in the coming decisive battles—"otherwise, see you in the next life."[45] Yet overall Chiang now seemed or perhaps pretended to be optimistic, assuring his staff in Peking that with air power and reinforcements from North China a decisive battle could still be won.[46] He planned for two government strike forces to converge from two directions on Lin's twenty-three divisions, while the garrison inside Jinzhou counterattacked.[47] Following urgent pleas from Chiang, Washington finally agreed to the emergency delivery of 30,000 barrels of aviation fuel from Japan; Chiang promised his two strike force commanders they would receive increased air support.[48]

To slow the avalanche in the rapid fall of the yuan, Chiang's government had tried pegging wages to the cost of living, freezing prices and wages, and rationing industrial materials as well as consumer goods. But nothing worked. A standard sack of rice sold for 6.7 million yuan in June 1948 and 63 million yuan in August.[49] That month, the government announced a new currency called the gold yuan and a new law that required citizens to turn in all the gold and silver bullion they held in addition to the old currency, the *fabi* yuan. The rate of exchange was 3 million *fabi* to one gold yuan. Nanking announced that it would distribute no more than 2 billion of the new yuan and it banned wage and price increases as well as strikes and demonstrations.

Chiang appointed his son, Ching-kuo, to implement the program in the Shanghai area. Ching-kuo established control over the six or more police and intelligence organizations in the city and cracked down hard on speculators and hoarders, including prominent businessmen and those connected to the Green Gang. He arrested the head of the Finance Ministry's Currency Department in Shanghai and a number of other high officials for illegal smuggling of foreign currency and gold to Hong Kong. After that, the Shanghai banks turned over large amounts of foreign currency and gold bullion reserves. Ching-kuo, who repeatedly denounced the depredations of the rich, became a popular figure in the city. He emphasized that the KMT was the party of social revolution and his intent was not only to stamp out economic crimes, but also to end the unequal distribution of wealth.[50]

Ching-kuo's crackdown kept the new currency under control in Shanghai for a few weeks. Among those he arrested was the son of Du Yuesheng; after making a substantial payment to the government, Du was allowed to close his company and join his father, who had decamped to Hong Kong. Before leaving town, Du gave Ching-kuo a list of companies owned by David Kung —Madame's nephew, the son of Ai-ling and H.H.—that were illegally storing goods. Ching-kuo put David Kung under house arrest, but Mayling traveled immediately to Shanghai and met with the two step-cousins. "You are brothers," she said to them, "You have no reason to fight each other."[51] She then sent an urgent message to her husband. Although Chiang was in a critical military meeting in Peking on the eve of the decisive battle for Manchuria, he dropped everything and flew off to Shanghai to resolve the personal conflict, prompting General Fu Zuoyi to comment, "Chiang Kai-shek loves the beauty more than the throne."[52] After some negotiation, the young Kung reportedly turned over US$6 million to the government, then left for Hong Kong.[53] Shortly thereafter he joined his parents, who had fled to New York a year earlier.

I

On October 9, Wei ordered General Liao Yaoxiang to lead the Western Strike Force in a campaign to break through the PLA ring encircling Mukden and move down the rail line toward Jinzhou. The force out of Mukden employed only eleven divisions instead of the fifteen Chiang had ordered; once again, Wei was disobeying his commander.[54] But Wei did carry out Chiang's instructions to send the 52nd Corps on a surprise attack out of Mukden to clear the railway to the port of Yingkou—which lies at the northern edge of the Bohai Gulf about sixty miles along the coast eastward from Jinzhou—and on October 11 the Nationalists recaptured this important port.[55]

On October 12, while General Liao's Western Strike Force engaged in ferocious battles with twelve PLA divisions, Chiang ordered the strike force on the coast at Huludao to move north immediately and attack those PLA forces besieging Jinzhou. The PLA, however, stopped this strike force forty kilometers from Jinzhou, and the Western Strike Force remained stymied halfway from Mukden.[56] Meanwhile, PLA sappers blew holes in the walls of Jinzhou and the defenders fell back inside the devastated city.

"This is the life and death moment for the overall military situation in Manchuria," Chiang told his generals. Hoping against hope, he now threw everything he had into what he still believed might be the battle that would determine the fate of Manchuria and even settle China's civil war. He ordered more divisions from North China to the rescue of Jinzhou, but it was too late. Chiang was back inside the wrecked city of Mukden on October 15 when the last holdouts in Jinzhou surrendered. Of the 122,000-man garrison, 34,000 had died in the battle. The PLA marched off 88,000 prisoners.[57]

Liao Yaoxiang, still in the field between Jinzhou and Mukden, learned of the surrender and wanted to lead his eleven-division strike force to Yingkou and from there by ship out of Manchuria.[58] On October 19 Chiang held a meeting in Peking with his generals Du, Wei, and Fu. Chiang wanted to continue the fight to retake Jinzhou. Du supported Liao's call for a withdrawal to Yingkou, and Fu offered no opinion.[59] At this point, Du reports in his memoirs, Chiang became angry and suddenly leaped from his seat. "It was Marshall," Chiang grumbled, "this American, who lost us and lost China." In 1945, he told the group, he had initially intended to occupy only a small part of Manchuria north to Jinzhou, but Marshall's actions and words had encouraged him to move his best armies deep into Manchuria. The current debacle was the result.[60]

Chiang soon realized Liao's force alone could not take Jinzhou and he belatedly approved the plan to march to Yingkou for evacuation by ship. Meanwhile, however, the Communist general Lin Biao had brought up twenty-four additional divisions in forced marches to confront the Nationalist force. Realizing his troops were far outnumbered, Liao tried to turn them back to Mukden, but they were blocked at the Yao River. After a day of vicious fighting, the huge government formation broke and along with its several thousand horses ran off in all directions on the flat land. Liao and his senior officers were captured, along with 38,000 other prisoners, 22 tanks, 150 guns, 600 vehicles, and 6,000 horses.[61] Liao's corps, which Chiang considered the government's best remaining fighting force, had been destroyed at a cost of 70,000 captured and dead men (according to Chiang's own estimate).[62]

Upon hearing the news of Liao's defeat, the 80,000 troops in Changchun soon surrendered. But Wei Lihuang still insisted on the defense of Mukden and even asked for ten more divisions. On October 30, the PLA broke through the walls into the eastern part of the city. As hand-to-hand fighting raged, Wei and a number of his staff officers flew out of the surrounded airport. On November 1, the senior remaining officer went to the airport to meet the PLA and surrendered the city. On November 9, Chinese government ships evacuated 140,000 troops and equipment from Huludao.[63] The battle for Manchuria was over.

Chiang stripped Wei of all titles and posts and put him under house arrest in Nanking to await trial for disobeying orders to move his troops out of Mukden until it was too late. Years earlier, Chiang had received and apparently dismissed reports claiming that Wei was in touch with the CCP. Now there was much speculation in Nanking that Wei had been suborned by the Communists and had sabotaged the retreat. In fact, in 1955 Wei would return to Peking from Hong Kong and participate in various organizations of the People's Republic.[64] Whatever the extent of his treachery, Wei's ability to postpone for months the retreat resulted in the loss of 300,000 Nationalist troops. Of those, 246,000 were captured, and many if not most were quickly incorporated into the PLA. The next fighting they would see would be in Korea.[65] Later, Chiang would blame himself and others for not pulling out of Manchuria when he could have saved most of his armies in the region, but he never did explain why he had not fired General Wei. He accused Wei of cowardice at the end, but he did not blame him for the debacle nor mention his likely treason, perhaps because he (Chiang) had ignored early warnings about the general.[66]

The Chiangs had sponsored the construction of a new Christian church for Nanking, and on a Sunday morning after the terrible defeat, the couple, with Chiang's two sons, attended a service there. It was Mayling who had provided the money for the church and Chiang gave a little sermon himself. Drawing from Chronicles, he commented, "As for me, I had in my heart to build a house of rest for the ark of the covenant of the Lord, but God said unto me, thou shalt not build a house for my name, because thou hast been a man of war." Chiang derived the lesson: "Man proposes but God disposes."[67]

The State Department's *White Paper,* issued in 1949, declared that Chiang's government "in occupying Manchuria took steps contrary to the advice of competent United States military observers who were aware that the Government could not reoccupy Manchuria and pacify the rest of China."[68] This claim is one of the most important unexamined, and incorrect, assumptions of the Chinese civil war.[69] Wedemeyer did tell Chiang and the Pentagon in November 1945 that the Nationalists could not win in Manchuria and probably not in North China, but policymakers in Washington did not adopt this point of view. In addition, earlier that year Wedemeyer himself had been optimistic about the Nationalist Army's prospects for dealing successfully with the Communists in the postwar period, including in Manchuria. Beginning with the negotiations on the Sino-Soviet treaty in the summer of 1945 in Moscow, the United States had made clear it wanted Chiang to take a tough stand in asserting Nationalist China's sovereignty in Manchuria. After Japan's surrender, America stood ready to transport almost a quarter million Nationalist soldiers to the region for this purpose and it completed the task during the Marshall Mission. At the beginning of the mission, the firmly, albeit privately, stated policy objective of Truman and Marshall was to support Chiang's takeover of all of Manchuria while trying to prevent a civil war. To accomplish this goal, the United States sought to promote a coalition government, but did not make such a coalition a quid pro quo of U.S. assistance to Chiang. Marshall at first clearly encouraged Chiang to continue to try to assert his authority throughout the Northeast. Marshall's original peace plan

A smiling Chiang in December 1948, shortly after his disastrous defeat in Manchuria, with new Vice President Li Zongren and Ambassador John Leighton Stuart on his left, and on his right, R. Allen Griffin, special representative, Mutual Security Agency to the Far East. Courtesy R. Allen Griffin Collection, envelope mB, Hoover Institution Archives.

provided for a huge 14–1 advantage in government troop presence in Manchuria, and gave the Nationalist government the right to deploy its military anywhere in the region in order to establish its authority. Marshall even promised to find surplus winter clothing for the Nationalist troops heading north. As noted earlier, as far back as mid-November 1945, Chiang had decided tentatively to withdraw from Manchuria, but positive Soviet moves and Marshall's initial steps and statements changed his mind.

It was not until the spring of 1946 that Marshall began to tell Chiang he could not defeat the Communists in Manchuria, but even then, still believing a genuine coalition was possible, he did not urge Nationalist withdrawal from the region. Prior to Marshall's arrival, Chiang had ranged from less to more pessimistic about Soviet cooperation in Manchuria and thus about his own prospects in the Northeast, and probably he would have withdrawn if Marshall, during their first meetings, had strongly echoed Wedemeyer's advice.

If Marshall had given this counsel and Chiang had agreed, it would have saddled the United States with the responsibility for helping the Nationalists assert and maintain control along a line somewhere south of the Great Wall. America would have been caught up in the enormous civil war over whether there was to be one China under the Communists or two Chinas, and if two, where the lines between them would be drawn. Almost certainly, neither Marshall nor Truman had thought this through; they simply wanted the best of both worlds—to avoid getting caught up in the civil conflict while maintaining a united, non-Communist, non-Soviet, allied China that included Manchuria. Thus they pursued the chimera of the optimal solution: Mao's abandonment of not only his revolutionary ideology, powerful army, and large territorial and population base, but also his support from China's superpower neighbor, all in order to serve as junior partner in a democratic government and a truly amalgamated army under the leadership of Chiang Kai-shek.

Within weeks of Marshall's arrival, Chiang began to fear that the Americans were headed down the path of appeasing the Communists, and he could have easily abandoned the struggle for Manchuria. It was primarily the Nationalist military victories in 1946 that misled Chiang into thinking he could hold the southern half of Manchuria, and he proceeded to pour in more and more troops for another almost two years, even when, beginning in early 1947, he again recognized that it was highly unlikely he could succeed. During the final and decisive 1948 Manchurian campaign from September to late October, Chiang, as usual, sent detailed instructions to the field commanders and often made it difficult for his senior commanders to give their subordinate generals tactical as well as strategic orders. But according to General Barr, "in spite of this unorthodox procedure," the plans Chiang made and the orders he gave in the decisive battles for Manchuria in the fall of 1948 "were sound." Had they been obeyed, the American general concluded, "the results probably would have been favorable."[70] Barr's assessment seems highly doubtful given the powerful position the Chinese Communists with Soviet help had established in the region and the financial and moral decay within the Nationalist regime. But it does give some weight to the argument that had Chiang pulled out of Manchuria even as late as the spring of 1948, he might have had enough military strength to hold the line at either the Yellow River or the Yangtze, albeit only with large-scale U.S. military and economic aid.

On October 29, 1948, Chiang explained to an American correspondent that, in his view, government leaders would have been ashamed to give up major cities of the country without a fight and as a result "we defended too many cities, and this stretched our supply lines." China, he continued, had been left to defend the region alone. Chiang's concerns about the consequences of this defeat were prescient. The loss of Manchuria, he predicted, would "open a Pandora's Box in the Far East," and if China would fall to the Communists, Asia would become the key region for the Communist bloc, and "China will be its base."[71]

After Manchuria, the defeat of the Nationalists may have been foreordained, but the climactic struggle in the Chinese civil war was still to come. The fateful battle began in Central China only days after the fall of Mukden. The key area lay north of the River Huai, which flows westward midway between the Yellow River and the Yangtze. There 450,000 Nationalist forces under General Du Yuming, instead of withdrawing to south of the Yangtze, followed Chiang's orders and waited for the coming onslaught. Without pausing to rest and regroup, Lin Biao led his grand army of 750,000 well-armed Communist fighters down the frost-covered roads of Manchuria and past the Great Wall. On the night of November 1 they attacked and surrounded Tianjin. Government engineers countered by flooding the southern approaches to the city, submerging the surrounding network of canals and posing a serious obstacle. Undaunted, the PLA set about draining the area.

Farther south, Chen Yi's eastern armies, using captured American and Japanese cannon, enveloped ten divisions at Nienchuang, located about thirty miles to the east of Xuzhou. Chiang ordered several government armies to the rescue, including the U.S.-trained and -armed Fifth Army and its tank division, which was led by the Generalissimo's adopted son Chiang Wei-kuo.[72] The Nationalist force moved slowly toward Nienchuang and in the initial engagement PLA units drove them back. Once again the Generalissimo was caught practicing mostly static defense combined with doomed relief missions, and in this case there were no compelling reasons of national morale or international sympathy and respect to warrant the sacrifice. On November 20, as the Communists overran the Nienchuang pocket, the Nationalist commander shot himself and only 3,000 government soldiers escaped and fled toward Xuzhou.[73] Chiang got word to Wei-kuo not to let the PLA capture his one hundred American M3-A1 tanks, and the young Chiang sent most of them south to Nanking before flying out to the capital himself. There he arranged the transport of the tanks by rail and barge to Shanghai for evacuation to Taiwan.[74]

Swollen by survivors of numerous defeats, Du Yuming's government force at Xuzhou now numbered about 300,000. Even though Chiang had removed most of the Nationalist tanks from the battlefield, he planned another counteroffensive with the supposed grandiose goal of turning the war around. He ordered the 12th Army to make the long trip north from Wuhan to take part, but it was encircled. Du Yuming was instructed to leave Xuzhou with his huge force and help the 12th Army escape.

Many intellectuals and various newspapers called for peace talks with the Communists, while Hu Shi, Wu Zhihui, and Dai Jitao encouraged Chiang in his moral and military last stand against "diabolical and implacable" Communism. But Chiang had long known what he would do in these circumstances. He had seemed agitated during the final stage of the battle for Manchuria, but the unruffled calm he now displayed impressed Ambassador Stuart, who thought he seemed confident that all the disasters that had enveloped China and himself some day would pass and he would be vindicated.[75] A sense of impending calamity, however, gripped almost everyone else in Nanking. On November 13 Chiang's longtime secretary and speech writer, Chen Bulei, whose son and daughter-in-law were members of the CCP, committed suicide, writing his leader that what he had recently heard and seen made it difficult for him to live on.[76]

On November 9, 1948, news arrived in Nanking that Harry Truman had scored an astounding upset over Thomas Dewey. Chiang sent a congratulatory message but also warned the President that the free world "could very likely lose China." He made an emergency appeal for immediate military and financial support, called for a U.S. government statement supporting the Chinese government in its struggle against the Soviet-backed Chinese Communists, and asked the President to send a senior American military officer to China to study the military situation and make plans for military aid.[77] He doubtless did not expect a positive answer.

By now, most senior officers in the Central Army felt that the situation was hopeless. Some ranking officials like He Yingqin were making preparations for flight to Canton or elsewhere, and some were already heading to Taiwan. The State Council ordered nonmilitary government offices to move to Chungking and Canton. Vice President Li Zongren openly advocated a cease-fire and negotiations, making it clear that the Generalissimo was the "sole stumbling block."[78] In the gloomy atmosphere of defeat and despair, Chiang continued his Confucian calmness. Indeed, Stuart reported a baffling "self-assurance and serenity," and an almost "exaltation of spirit."[79] That week, *Time* magazine ran another cover story depicting how in "the vortex of . . . gathering disaster" Chiang "was buoyant and determined," dodging in and out of his private map room, seeing dozens of visitors, and counseling his field commanders by long-distance phone.[80] He knew where he was going.

Mayling had a standing invitation from the Marshalls to be their guest at their home in Virginia, and she and her husband agreed that, given the dangerous situation, she would leave as soon as possible.[81] On December 1, she flew to Washington and visited Secretary Marshall in the hospital room where he was recovering after removal of a diseased kidney. She made the same requests to Marshall that her husband had made to Truman, adding that Chiang had offered to step down if that was in the national interest. Mayling also visited the White House, the State Department, and the Capitol, asking for $3 billion in aid. Truman's economic envoy Paul Hoffman, however, returned from a study mission in Nationalist China and recommended against further economic assistance. At the same time, the American Military Mission in Nanking reported that "the military position of the National Government had declined beyond possible recoupment." Chiang, who certainly knew this, advised Mayling that her entreaties in the United States would not yield any result—she had best "come back and avoid any humiliation."[82]

The American Joint Chiefs and MacArthur now realized that the slim possibility that Chiang might hold the line somewhere in China had vanished. This was not entirely unwelcome news in Washington; a successful Nationalist stand at, say, the Yangtze would have led to strong calls in Congress and elsewhere in the country for large-scale American military intervention. MacArthur warned that the Soviet offensive had shifted from Europe to the Far East, but he was vague on what the United States should do about China. He made clear, however, that anyone in favor of sending American ground troops to fight on Chinese soil "should have his head examined."[83] Even the most pro-Chiang Republicans did not advocate the use of American forces to save the Kuomintang.

On December 14, the PLA surrounded Peking and Fu Zuoyi, whose government army numbered some 240,000 veterans, sent out peace feelers. Prolonged, secret negotiations soon began. Fu asked Chiang for permission to resign, but Chiang refused, telling him not to take the question of winning or losing "too seriously." Losing, he explained, "can teach us lessons and make us strong . . . It is not a personal shame."[84] Fu went back to his secret talks with Mao. Down the rail line to Taiyuan the old warlord Yan Xishan and his 100,000 men remained holed up in the fortress city with its thirty-six-meter-thick city walls.[85]

Also by mid-December, Du Yuming, down to 130,000 men, was surrounded near the Anhui-Henan border. The other remaining 100,000 or so soldiers of his several corps had been cut off in segments and liquidated or had surrendered. Surprisingly, Deng Xiaoping, who was directing overall Communist strategy in these battles, did not press the attack on Du's encircled forces, who were living in tents or in the open in below-freezing weather, kept alive by airdrops. The Generalissimo told Du not to try to break out to the south toward the Yangtze but to attack to the north, giving a "final and decisive battle." "Don't think of evading the enemy," he said, "but destroy them." This attack, he said, would be key "to turning the military situation in our favor once and for all!"[86]

Chiang knew that Du's forces were doomed as were those of Fu and Yan, but both honor in the cause as well as the need for time to prepare for withdrawal to Taiwan required that Du "fight to the last man." Chiang may also not have wanted to be the Chinese who divided the Middle Kingdom at the Yangtze. In addition, by rejecting a general retreat to the "Long River," he was also possibly trying to deny large fighting forces to his likely Nationalist successor on the mainland, Li Zongren, who once Chiang was gone might hope for some American aid. Whatever the case, Chiang clearly had excluded the option of seeking to hold the line anywhere on the China mainland. On Christmas Day, Du reported that his men were "eating tree bark and grasses and to keep warm they were burning houses, clothes and furniture." Of his hard core of 130,000 soldiers, however, only 10,000 had defected.[87]

From his Wuhan headquarters, Bai Chongxi cabled Chiang that the military campaigns north of the Yangtze had been a total disaster; he then sent an envoy asking Chiang to step down. Vice President Li put forth a similar plan, openly talking about the Generalissimo resigning. This proposal from Bai, with whom Chiang had developed a close relationship since the beginning of the war with Japan, clearly stung him. On December 31 he wrote in his journal that the Guangxi Clique was once again "plotting against me and engaging in their treacherous behavior."[88] But that same night, New Year's Eve, he issued a statement declaring, "If peace can be secured, I am not at all concerned about my own position. I will follow only the consensus of the popular feeling."[89] Meanwhile, his wife was working hard but, as he wrote, "getting nowhere" in trying to obtain American help. He recognized that the situation on the mainland was "out of control," but still he felt "at ease." In his Confucian stoicism he even believed that in the midst of this great calamity his "personal cultivation" had made much progress—he was a better man.[90]

In the end game in China for America, Ambassador Stuart was advocating U.S. support for a coalition government, this time to be led by the Communist Party, which, he said, contained "indisputable elements of progress and reform." The Foreign Service officers in the embassy at this time had totally different opinions from their colleagues in the recent past, and Stuart reported their "sincere" views that the Chinese Communists were not basically different from Communists in any other country and that a Communist-dominated government in China would be hostile to U.S. interests.[91] But in either case Washington believed that American intervention, even on a massive scale, would fail in the end.

"Reports of lost battles swirl in like falling snow," Chiang wrote at the end of the year. "North China and the below-the-wall region are on the brink of collapse." With the destruction of the railway between Kaifeng and Chengchow, he concluded, "the country is dead." Still, he wrote, he "never relaxed for a single day," taking pride that in all the turmoil there had been some success in rebuilding a railway from Zhejiang to Jiangxi and that several dams had also been constructed. "We must accomplish something," he concluded, "no matter under what circumstances . . . I do not feel guilty. I tried my best."[92] Although he had been thinking of withdrawal to Taiwan for more than two years, and as the most probable outcome for almost a year, since the debacle in Manchuria he assumed it was certain.

Nonetheless, on New Year's Day, Chiang formally reviewed in his journal the reasons he could remain in office and those that could persuade him to step down. Staying on had only vague and uncertain gains, whereas by stepping back he could "shake up the inept party, military, and government machines; break up the stalemate in politics, and be ready to regroup for a new start from zero." He told Bai that any peace would require the CCP to guarantee that "the legal framework and way of life of the Republic of China" would continue south of the Yangtze. Any sacrifice to achieve this outcome, he said, including even the two of them "hanging as war criminals," would be justified. Of course, he knew the odds of this happening were nil. By mid-January he had transferred the air force and navy headquarters to Taiwan, and by June, five-sixths of the thousand or so remaining aircraft of the Nationalist Air Force in January would be on the island.[93] Some factories and arsenals in Shanghai and elsewhere south of the Yangtze, too, had begun moving their best equipment to Taiwan.[94]

These moves could hardly be masked, but following the dictates of Sun Tzu's *The Art of War,* deception was a critical part of Chiang's end game. The objective was to confuse Mao into believing that while Taiwan was Chiang's last refuge he had other options, including making a stand in various places in south or southwest China. Mao did worry that once Chiang had stepped down and was replaced by Li Zongren, the United States would support the new government with tremendous amounts of aid, and possibly even warplanes and troops, to try to retain a non-Communist China south of the Yangtze. Mao anxiously sent word to Stalin that, according to an intelligence report, the United States intended to use atomic bombs and Japanese soldiers against the PLA.[95] Stalin was not worried. Through his British spies Kim Philby and others he had a good sense of the likely range of Anglo-American policies in China—and such an intervention was not being mentioned in Washington, not even by the Generalissimo's most ardent supporters in the "China lobby."

Already there was considerable chaos in the mainland ports from Shanghai south. Government officials, merchants, businessmen, and their families crowded aboard freighters, ferries, tugboats, and any other type of vessel available for the trip across the Taiwan Strait. Huge army units with their weapons crowded the docks as well. The ports of Keelung and Gaoxiong on Taiwan were clogged. The Generalissimo ordered Young Marshal Zhang Xueliang and his concubine, Edith Chao, packed off to the island.[96] Many well-to-do Chinese were fleeing not to Taiwan, whose future was highly doubtful, but to Hong Kong and beyond, primarily the United States. Ching-kuo thought briefly of sending his wife and children to Hong Kong or to England, but he had no funds to support them and he rejected the option of accepting support from the Soongs.[97]

Veterans of Ching-kuo's Youth Army, who were now back on active duty as commissars in the newly revived Political Department of the military, were screening the hundreds of thousands of civilians headed for Taiwan. Ching-kuo had other special roles. Late one night in mid-January, with his father's orders in hand, he and a group of armed commissars in a convoy of army trucks appeared at the Bank of China in Shanghai. Ching-kuo had picked up Yu Hongzhun, the bank president, who dutifully opened the vaults and watched as the soldiers loaded boxes of gold bullion, silver coins, and foreign currency into the trucks. Soon a navy ship with the treasure aboard was steaming down the Whangpoo and on to Amoy—not Taiwan. This was the first of two shipments to Taiwan of China's financial reserves. Sending it via Amoy was part of the Generalissimo's plan to confuse Mao as to where he intended to make a stand.[98]

At the end of 1948, Ching-kuo had also supervised the first shipment on two naval frigates of thousands of priceless objects from Peking's world-famous Palace Museum and other collections. After the Japanese seizure of Manchuria in 1931, Chiang Kai-shek had ordered the transport of these treasures in more than 19,000 crates first to Shanghai and then Nanking and finally up the Yangtze Gorges to Chungking and hiding places in the mountains of Sichuan. Since 1946 they had been back in Nanking, but the crates remained unopened. Now, in January, Ching-kuo oversaw the loading of two additional shipments of the artifacts, which with their longtime curators and guards sailed directly to the port of Keelung in northern Taiwan. In total about 3,800 crates were shipped to Taiwan, or only about 22 percent of the artworks, though the shipment represented "the cream of the collection."[99]

II

On January 6, the PLA launched its long-awaited attack on the besieged, shivering, and hungry divisions of Du Yuming at Chinglungchi in Anhui. Du radioed the Generalissimo that he had given the effort all he had and was preparing a last, desperate counterattack. He mentioned that he was also in pain from a kidney ailment, having recently given one kidney to a brother. Chiang replied that he had no other senior officer with the fighting skills and spirit to replace him.[100] In the ensuing days, Du's divisions and battalions engaged in fierce hand-to-hand fighting across concentric trenches that had been dug around their encampment by swarms of rural laborers recruited by the Communists. On January 9, Du radioed that his best armies had all been destroyed and he and the survivors could only "fight to the end." Chiang told Du that he was sending a plane the next morning to bring him out. The following dawn, however, Chiang learned that the PLA had wiped out Du's last formations and rounded up the survivors, among them Du. The commander of the successful Y Force in the second Burma campaign proved himself courageous and loyal to the end: he would remain a prisoner for the next twenty-five years. Chiang comforted himself with the thought that he had not previously stepped down as President because of the responsibility he felt for Du and his men. "In my heart I am not guilty," he again wrote.[101]

In mid-January Mao issued eight conditions for negotiations with the Kuomintang, including punishment of war criminals, especially all the Chiangs and Soongs except Chingling; abolishment of the "constituted authority"; and the "reorganization of all reactionary troops." In other words, unconditional surrender. Had the situation been reversed, Chiang would have demanded no less.

Four days later, Chiang presided over his last meeting of the Executive Yuan. When the majority present called for a cease-fire and peace negotiations, Chiang indicated he intended to give up his office. On January 21, he informally "stepped down" as president and commander in chief of the Republic of China, but he did not "retire" or "resign." Vice President Li understood the importance of this semantic distinction. Li would simply be "acting" President. Chiang also retained his position as director-general of the KMT and could count on the support of most of the surviving KMT generals.

The next morning, Chiang sat down and again penned his own brief, but remarkably candid, analysis of the failure of his once powerful regime. At this time, he did not blame Marshall or the Americans in general. Rather "the major reason for this defeat," he wrote, "is that we are in a transitional period where the old system has been abolished but the new system is yet to be built." He implied again that the fatal flaws were the incoherent, fractious, and undisciplined party and army that he led, as well as his own failure to have built a modern and effective organization. "From now on," he concluded, "the business of nation building and army reform must focus on building a system and a structure."[102]

Chiang had never stolen from the state and he did not have his own private cache of gold. To cover his immediate expenses before arriving in Taiwan, he borrowed one million of the rapidly depreciating new gold yuan (about US$10,000 at the official rate that day) from the Farmer's Bank, which was controlled by Chen Lifu.[103] That same day, in a large black sedan with security vehicles following, the Generalissimo and his son rode out to the Purple and Gold Mountains. After twenty minutes, father and son were at the tomb of Sun Yat-sen, riding under a three-arched gate engraved with two characters that Chiang had most likely selected: "universal love" *(pu ai)*. Leaving the sedan, father and son slowly walked up the eight long sections of steep stone steps, resting occasionally. Left alone by their guards, they entered the mausoleum and stood silent with heads bowed before the recumbent marble figure of China's first modern revolutionary.

The two Chiangs and their entourage then drove to the Nanking airport and flew away on a plane named "Mayling."[104] They stopped in Hangzhou where Chen Cheng, who had flown in from Taipei, joined the party as did Chingkuo's wife and four children, who had been living in Hangzhou. That night, Zhejiang governor Chen Yi, who had carried out the Taiwan Massacre, gave a dinner in the Generalissimo's honor. It was a cold affair. Not only was there no heat, but the Chiangs were intending soon to arrest and execute Chen Yi, who was suspected of talking secretly with the Communists. The Chiangs also probably hoped his execution would dispel some of the anger in Taiwan over the terrible "2/28" affair and its aftermath.

The next morning, the Chiangs' plane made the short hop from Hangzhou to a grass airfield at Elephant Mountain near Xikou. When the party arrived at the hamlet, all the residents were in a nervous state. The Chiang relatives of course had heard news of the military disasters in Manchuria and a few hundred miles away in Xuzhou and also of the President's "withdrawal" from office. Many were quickly packing up. Word spread that those wishing to leave should go to Ningbo and await instructions.[105]

The following day, Chiang read a report that in order to spare the ancient capital of China, General Fu Zuoyi had agreed to a face-saving "non-surrender" accord with the PLA, but one that Fu had honorably delayed until after Chiang's "resignation."[106] Fu's twenty-odd divisions and several artillery brigades were incorporated into the PLA, retaining their unit integrity. Some of his generals even kept their commands, at least for a while.[107] In the up-

After "stepping down" in January 1949, Chiang arrives at the town of Xikou, where, hoping to confuse Mao, he will linger for several months on his way to Taiwan. Courtesy KMT Party History Institute.

coming Communist regime, Fu, the most senior general to surrender without a fight, would become minister of water conservancy and later a vice chairman of the National Defense Council.[108]

Soon after his arrival in his home town, Chiang wrote a radio message for his wife. He advised her not to make any further speeches promoting him in the United States. He said he intended "to take two to three years to do some solid party building." In fact, he sounded so optimistic he appeared delusional. "I think that in the next twenty years," he wrote, "I will be one of the few people in the world who will be able to achieve world peace. Therefore, there is no need to seek foreign help for my career."[109]

On January 31, in a bitter north wind, the people of Peking, who three years earlier had lined the streets to welcome Chiang Kai-shek, now greeted the new liberators. A large Mao portrait replaced the one of Chiang over the gate to the Forbidden City. Mao, however, did not pass through the city wall but established his headquarters at the old Summer Palace. There he, Zhu De, and Zhou Enlai smoked cigarettes, drank tea, and continued to discuss where the Generalissimo would likely make his next stand, the best timing and place of the crossing of the Yangtze, and whether the United States might still intervene. When Anastas Mikoyan, the Soviet Communist Party's senior Politburo member, visited, Mao said he wanted to postpone establishment of a new Communist government so he would have enough time to purge the country of "counterrevolutionary elements."[110] Following Stalin's orders, however, Mikoyan insisted that the CCP take over Shanghai, Nanking, and other cities as soon as possible and form a revolutionary government—one that the Soviet Union could openly support.[111]

According to Li Zongren, the Nationalist Army still had 3.5 million men, at least half of whom had weapons and could fight. The Communists had at least 2 million fighters. But Li lacked ammunition and fuel, and Washington made plain to him that it would not even entertain the idea of sending more military supplies or financial aid. At a February war-planning meeting in Nanking, General Tang Enbo simply refused to cooperate with Li's proposal for deploying Tang's 400,000 men in defense of the Yangtze, insisting that he concentrate his defenses closer to Shanghai. This, he said, was Chiang Kai-shek's plan.[112] While Ambassador Stuart was telling Li that the United States would do nothing to help the Nationalists, boxcars loaded with Soviet supplies and special equipment were rolling regularly down the repaired rails from the Russian border to junctions close to the Yangtze.

It was probably clearer to the men in Washington than to the suspicious Mao that the Generalissimo intended only to fight brief holding actions on the mainland while he withdrew trusted troops and selected civilian personnel and their families to Taiwan. Given the strategic reasons pushed by MacArthur, domestic political considerations, and American leaders' feeling of moral obligation, the U.S. administration and the Congress came to feel that denial of Taiwan to both Mao's Communists and Chiang Kai-shek's Nationalists was the best possible outcome for the island and the United States. President Truman approved a secret policy paper that declared this the preferred outcome. At a National Security Council meeting, Acheson emphasized that it was important to conceal carefully "our wish to separate the island [Taiwan] from mainland control." One idea, the paper noted, was a U.N. trusteeship. But the most direct way to achieve the policy goal of a non-Communist Taiwan, the paper concluded, would be discreetly to promote a Taiwan independence or autonomy movement.[113]

Taiwan, however, was already crowded with several hundred thousand Nationalist troops and intelligence and security officers. This huge presence, the continuing effects of the brutal suppression of 1947, and the geographic isolation of the island made a successful Taiwanese rebellion highly unlikely—as the CIA and the U.S. consul general in Taipei, Kenneth Krentz, well knew. The Americans were mostly concerned that Chiang's generals on Taiwan might strike a deal with the Communists, as many of their colleagues on the mainland had. Although not directly stated in the policy paper, the Americans believed that a more feasible alternative to a native uprising was a takeover of Taiwan by military commanders on the island who were "liberal and efficient." Acheson assigned the counselor at the U.S. Embassy in Nanking, Livingston T. Merchant, to explore the political situation on the island. After a few days in Taipei and without talking to Governor Chen Cheng, Livingston advised the Secretary of State that Chen could not provide the "liberal, efficient" administration the United States desired. Instead, he recommended that Washington officially ask President Li Zongren to dismiss Chen and appoint as the new governor General Sun Liren, who was now deputy army commander on Taiwan and chief of training. When Ambassador Stuart in Nanking proposed this action to Li, the new acting president said only Chiang Kai-shek could make such an appointment.[114]

Meanwhile, General Sun received an invitation from General MacArthur to visit him in Tokyo. Through Chen Cheng, Sun requested the Generalissimo's permission to accept the invitation. Chiang was angry but not surprised that the Supreme Commander in Japan had not invited Chiang Kai-shek. He knew the American administration wished he would leave the scene. Nevertheless, from Xikou, he gave his approval and MacArthur sent his plane to fetch Sun. The Chinese general from Taiwan spent three days in Tokyo. According to one report, MacArthur told Sun that the Nationalist government was doomed. If Sun took over responsibility for Taiwan's security, the Supreme Commander reportedly said, the United States would support him. Sun replied that he was loyal to the Generalissimo.[115]

Afterward, Sun sent a letter to an American official in Washington whom he knew, reporting MacArthur's discussion of the possibility of a "free province" of Taiwan. Sun did not inform Chiang Kai-shek of the letter. But in Washington, a senior CIA officer called in his intelligence counterpart in the Chinese embassy and warned him that they should be wary of Sun. When Sun returned to Taiwan he reported MacArthur's proposal to Chen Cheng who informed Chiang Kai-shek. Sun then traveled to Xikou where Chiang told him to "go back to Taiwan and keep up the good work training the army."[116]

In Xikou, Chiang instructed his son to direct the air force to build an airfield on the island of Zhoushan just off the Zhejiang coast. The Generalissimo was planning a staged retreat in which Tang Enbo's troops and others from the central coastal region would not go immediately to Taiwan.[117] Ching-kuo then flew back to Shanghai. There, on the night of February 10, with another presidential order in hand, he led another group of his Youth Army veterans to the two state banks in Shanghai. They loaded the last of the bullion and other assets of the two banks onto their trucks and drove quickly to the navy yard on the Whangpoo River. A navy frigate loaded the treasure on board and sailed directly for Taiwan.[118] According to a statement made in the U.S. Congress, the total value of the two shipments of transferred assets in 1949 U.S. dollars was US$300 million.[119] Chiang had long been saving these treasures for the contingency of an escape to Taiwan.[120]

In his black gentry robe, Chiang spent many days at the small cabin on the mountain above his mother's grave. Ching-kuo accompanied him on long walks on the mountain paths, sometimes through the snow. The Generalissimo's staff believed he was spending his days thinking.[121] But he was not in isolation. A stream of visitors poured into the little hamlet—anxious generals, government ministers, governors, and senior party officials seeking instructions and encouragement. Their careers, their lives, and their families' lives seemed on the verge of extinction. Chiang gave the commanders detailed military orders on the massive multifront withdrawal to the coast and to the south and southwest. Others were told to assure that administrators kept government services going as long as possible. Breakdowns occurred, but somehow many trains kept running, some planes continued flying, and a lot of ships carried on sailing between the mainland and Taiwan. Most of the KMT military and civilian officials who continued doing their jobs would be left behind, fulfilling their duties to the end. Perhaps hundreds of thousands or more of those who made it to ports still in government hands would find that no passage was available. There was a limit. Taiwan could and would take only so many.

Back in Nanking, several senior Chinese officials, former strong supporters of Chiang Kai-shek, told Ambassador Stuart that Chiang was hampering both the peace negotiations and military preparations for the Yangtze defense line. On March 25, Li appointed Shao Lizi, Zhang Zhizhong, and others to a negotiating delegation to Peking. Behind the scenes, Chiang demanded that the Nanking government stop the peace negotiations. He was suspicious of Shao

Lizi (identified later as a secret CCP member since 1922), whom he predicted would "totally betray us."[122] Another KMT delegate, Liu Fei, vice minister of defense, had reportedly been working secretly for the CCP for many years.[123] No sooner had Zhang Zhizhong, Liu Fei, and Shao Lici reached Peking than they all defected.

The Generalissimo, Ching-kuo, and others were watching a Peking opera performance at a grammar school in Xikou when they heard the news. Li Zongren and his colleagues hurriedly met with Chiang in Hangzhou. According to Chiang, Li said the peace talks had failed and Chiang should return to head the government. Chiang ignored the request, saying, "Whatever you do, I will support you."[124] Li did not believe this for a minute. But his government made a public statement that the talks in Peking had failed and the government would move to Canton and continue to fight the Communists.[125]

When Li's government moved south, the Soviets withdrew their embassy from Nanking to Canton, but the United States chose to have Ambassador Stuart remain in Nanking—a signal that Washington wanted to keep the door open to reconciliation with the Communist regime. The CCP response was not encouraging. Mao had told the Soviets that in its foreign relations, the CCP would adopt the strategy of "cleaning house before entertaining guests."[126] When the PLA reached Nanking, soldiers were sent into Ambassador Stuart's residence and even into his bedroom where he lay ill. Mao also seized American consular offices in Peking and arrested the U.S. consul general in Mukden.

But Mao would soften his stance toward the Americans in Nanking. Pressed by Stalin and himself worried about a possible last-minute American intervention in support of Li Zongren, Mao authorized gestures to encourage Stuart to believe the CCP was in fact interested in U.S. recognition and economic aid.[127] Zhou passed this message to Stuart, who since November had been recommending that Washington pursue such a possibility. On May 30, Zhou Enlai even sent a verbal communication to President Truman via an intermediary saying that he (Zhou) headed a "liberal" faction in the CCP leadership opposed to Liu Shaoqi's pro-Soviet "radicals."[128] Many years later, a ranking CCP official told an American scholar that Mao and Zhou's only intent was to forestall an eleventh-hour U.S. military intervention.[129]

In late April, Yan Xishan's old capital of Taiyuan finally fell. Yan had flown away supposedly in search of reinforcements, but he remembered to take with him the province's gold reserves. The Japanese commander in Yan's absence, Imamura Hosaku, and five hundred public officials gathered in the governor's residence and committed collective suicide by poison.[130]

The time had come to leave Xikou. Ching-kuo sent Faina and their four children ahead by plane to Taipei and he and his father each paid their last calls at the tombs of their respective mothers. Then, with a reduced entourage, they drove to the small dock at Elephant Mountain where they boarded a navy frigate, which, to everyone's surprise, Chiang ordered to sail to Shanghai.[131] The next morning the party arrived and set up headquarters in a hostel on Rue Père Robert.[132] In a statement, Chiang promised another "Stalingrad." A great show was made of preparing for a final street-to-street battle to the death. The U.S. consulate general predicted a bloodbath that would leave the city in ruins. Meanwhile, most of Tang Enbo's soldiers were flying or shipping out to Zhoushan Island or directly to Taiwan.

On May 3, from his redoubt in Guangxi, Li sent a message asking Chiang for full authority to make all military and personnel decisions and for the return of all government assets recently sent to Taiwan. He even suggested that Chiang "go overseas to seek foreign aid." "I have fought the CCP all my life," Chiang replied, "and I will never give up this responsibility. If the country had only one inch of free land left, how could I not but stay and fight?"[133]

On the morning of May 6 in cool spring weather, the frigate SS *Kuang Jing* steamed down the sluggish Whangpoo, past the malodorous Suzhou Creek, and by an endless line of gritty workshops, boatyards, sampans, and hovels. Artillery was firing in the distance as the two Chiangs leaned against the railing. The frigate did not steam for Taiwan, but 140 miles after leaving the wide mouth of the Yangtze put in at Zhoushan Island, just off the mouth of the Yong River and not far from Fenghua County.[134] There the Generalissimo conducted an "inspection" of Tang's 125,000 troops who had come from Shanghai.[135] With eighty-two temples and nunneries and some four thousand Buddhist monks, the island was known as "Heaven of the Sea and Kingdom of the Buddhists." Chiang curiously spent several more weeks meditating and wandering about the island, visiting the temple that honored Guanyin, the favorite goddess of Taiwan. But he ordered his son to fly back to Shanghai to give final instructions to the commanders who remained in the city.[136]

By now about five thousand refugees were arriving in Taiwan each day, and Chen Cheng had already redeclared martial law, a so-called emergency measure that would remain in effect on Taiwan for almost fifty years.[137] On May 22, at the Shanghai Naval Yard, Chiang Wei-kuo finished loading his last

American tanks onto a commandeered freighter, and with his wife steamed for Taiwan. On the civilian docks, tens of thousands of people were battling to board the last ships leaving for the island. Many if not all paid for their tickets with gold they carried with them. Years later, one prominent mainlander on Taiwan recalled that the ship he and his mother and siblings boarded was so crowded that it threatened to swamp the moment it left the dock. The captain would not continue until all the passengers had thrown enough gold into the river or onto the dock that the vessel could safely steam away. Remembering that an overloaded ship fleeing Manchuria the previous year had sunk with 6,000 refugees aboard, the passengers complied.[138]

Ching-kuo joined his father on Zhoushan Island and finally they set sail for Taiwan. The PLA entered Shanghai on May 25, finding it had been abandoned in good order. Back in Taiwan, Sun Liren told American officials in Taipei that he thought Taiwan would fall as a result of internal fighting and lack of organization rather than from a massive PLA attack. He said he had little ammunition and no heavy machine guns or artillery. When the Generalissimo's frigate docked at the Gaoxiong Naval Base in southern Taiwan, General Sun was there to greet him.[139]

IV

THE ISLAND

10

Streams in the Desert

Upon arriving in Gaoxiong, Taiwan, one of the first things Chiang did was appoint an ad hoc group of ten loyal men to study measures to reorganize the party. At a meeting of this KMT reform group on July 6, Chiang decreed that the KMT must be a "revolutionary democratic party instead of a pure democratic party." This edict and Chiang's six guidelines for reorganization basically reaffirmed the Leninist, nondemocratic structure of the KMT, which was to include a supposedly enlightened authoritarian political leadership "throughout society."[1] This time, Chiang meant to see that "tutelage" included effective and pervasive dictatorship as well as good governance.

Continuing his relaxed pace, Chiang lingered almost a month in southern Taiwan. On June 25, as the semitropical summer heat settled over the region, he and his son flew from Gaoxiong to Taipei. Through the windows of their aircraft, they could see to the east most of the forty-eight mountain peaks that grace a third of the island. To the west lay a seemingly endless, flat quilt of rice paddies. After the leaders landed at the small, scorching Taipei airport, a black Japanese limousine—the departed governor's former car—carried the Chiangs up a steep, winding road to a modest house near the top of cool Grass Mountain, soon to be renamed Yangming Mountain after a favored philosopher. The house, which had previously belonged to the Japanese state-owned Taiwan Sugar Corporation, had a stunning view of the valley below.[2] For his part, Ching-kuo rented a modest house on Chang'an East Road in the city.

Since their departure from Nanking in January, Chiang Kai-shek and his son had spent many hours alone discussing how they and the Republic of China could survive. The first priority, they clearly believed, was to consolidate the government's hold on Taiwan, which would mean eradicating Communist agents and Taiwanese dissidents. Chiang gave his son broad authority over internal security, intelligence, and paramilitary organizations. While in Gaoxiong, Ching-kuo established a political action committee to coordinate the myriad intelligence and secret police bureaucracies that had crowded onto the island. During the year, internal security men arrested about 10,000 Taiwanese for interrogation and put more than a thousand to death in another horrific example of "killing the chicken to scare the monkey." Given the absence of any organized, much less violent, underground Taiwanese opposition, these killings were as malicious as those the CCP would soon carry out on the mainland to condition the populace to accept the permanence of the new order. Another key element of internal security among the KMT in Taiwan was enhanced surveillance of all senior Nationalist generals on the island no matter how trusted, including Chen Cheng and Sun Liren.

The Chiangs' second priority was intensive preparations to resist the inevitable Communist assault, which Chiang estimated would take the PLA at least a year to prepare. The priority given to the defense of Hainan, Zhoushan, Quemoy, and various other offshore islands in Nationalist hands would depend on the feasibility and benefits of trying to hold each one. Military preparations for the defense of Taiwan itself involved not only training but also an intense effort to eliminate the various abuses that had afflicted the Nationalist military for so long. The Chiangs agreed on the immediate centralization of all financial matters in the military, most especially payrolls. In one stroke this change did away with the principal form of graft as well as most "ghost soldiers" on military unit rosters.[3]

The third priority was currency stability. The island's separate currency since its liberation in 1945 had largely protected it from the tornado of inflation on the mainland. Moreover, the first postwar Chinese provincial government in 1945 had taken over vast land holdings, real estate, and business and financial assets from the Japanese government and Japanese companies, and these acquisitions had provided a huge and instant source of revenue for spending and currency support. In October 1948, Wei's provincial government, unquestionably with Chiang Kai-shek's approval, had banned the sale or transfer of food and other products from the island to the mainland, further insulating Taiwan's economy from the tribulations across the Strait.[4] Shortly after his arrival in southern Taiwan, Chiang noted that all the necessary gold and hard currency funds for monetary reform in Taiwan were in place. On June 15, the Taiwan provincial government issued a new currency, the Xin Taibi (New Taiwan Dollar).

In June, the CIA, referring to KMT-administered territory on both the mainland and Taiwan, concluded that Nationalist China was "virtually bankrupt"; the "process of disintegration and fragmentation is so far advanced as to render almost impossible the establishment of a functioning government."[5] The U.S. consulate in Taipei and the CIA predicted not only economic collapse in Taiwan, but also terrible food and housing shortages, grave health problems, and social chaos, fragmentation, and disintegration. But under the direction of Chen Cheng's commissioner of finance, C. K. Yen, and the Central Bank's O. K. Yu (who had opened the vaults in Shanghai), retail prices in Taiwan advanced only 35 percent in March over February—nauseatingly high by most standards but not at all stratospheric in the context of the mainland, where the inflation rate had risen 20 to 50 percent in a single day.[6]

Shortly after the Generalissimo's arrival in early June, C. K. Yen, a technocrat trained at the American-run St. John's University in Shanghai, pegged the New Taiwan Dollar to gold, with conversions allowed freely—a remarkable policy for a government supposedly about to "disintegrate." At Chiang's insistence in early 1950, the government set a limit on the amount of New Taiwan Dollars that could be converted to gold each month. But for six months there was no limit and the currency gained credibility.[7]

The strengthened Taiwan Garrison Command remained disciplined, and in the cities summary executions of looters, including miscreant soldiers and others disturbing the public order, took place on a daily basis.[8] Despite American predictions to the contrary, no major health problems erupted as a result of the gigantic human influx. After months of makeshift bedding and board, necessary housing was found for the refugees and the military, in large part by taking over former Japanese-owned residences, schools, military quarters, and other buildings.

During the summer harvest of 1949, with the help of the American-supported Joint Commission on Rural Reconstruction (JCRR), Chen Cheng began a major land reform. At the end of the Chinese civil war, Japanese governmental bodies, individuals, and companies together owned a stunning 66.7 percent of the land on Taiwan, including uninhabited mountainous regions. Chen Cheng sold a good part of this appropriated land—21 percent of all cultivable acreage on the island—on cheap credit to poor Taiwanese farmers. The government also mandated a sharp reduction in rural land rents to 37.5 percent of the annual yield of chief crops like rice.[9]

This reform was an instant success, made politically easy by the fact that the KMT at this point was reapportioning land that had not been in Taiwanese hands for decades, and to which the arriving mainlanders had generally not made a claim. The initial reforms immediately created a base of genuine political support for the Kuomintang among Taiwanese farmers, and the next stages would strengthen it. Although most professional, intellectual, and urban Taiwanese understandably remained viscerally anti-KMT, the party for the first time had a foundation of popular support in rural areas. Chiang strongly approved of Chen's reforms, and they eventually began to earn praise from Americans and agrarian reformers around the world.

But threats from the mainland were never far from mind. In a paper called "On People's Democratic Dictatorship," Mao reinforced American anxiety about Taiwan's falling under the Communists. The Chairman again made plain that Communist China would be a committed ally of the Soviet Union, including in war, and an enthusiastic supporter of Communist revolution around the globe.[10] After it was published, CCP police beat and arrested the U.S. vice consul in Shanghai, William Olive, who was walking on the street, and he died in detention. Washington recalled Ambassador Stuart immediately and prepared to close its various missions in China. At the same time, Liu Shaoqi, now general secretary of the CCP Secretariat, left Peking for a secret meeting in Moscow. During his talks with Liu, Stalin emphasized that the Chinese Communist Party should lead the anti-imperialist revolution in Asia, diverting and weakening the United States. The mission of the Soviet Union, Stalin made plain, would be to strengthen itself in order to defeat the imperialists when, inevitably, they began World War III. But, Stalin explained, until the Soviet Union could build up its strategic power, it would have to avoid direct conflict with the United States. It would, however, support Communists in other struggles and would provide extensive military equipment and advisory assistance in the liberation of Taiwan. Soon after Liu returned to China, large numbers of Soviet military advisers began to arrive in China and Soviet MIGs deployed into airfields near Shanghai.[11]

Chiang's truncated regime now had few foreign friends, much less a superpower ally. To strengthen what little international support he had, he and Ching-kuo flew to the Philippines and proposed to President Elpidio Quirino a Far East "union" that would include Taiwan, Thailand, Indonesia, South Korea, and possibly Indochina and Japan. The U.S. government opposed such an alliance, but Chiang was confident that "in the end" it would happen—which eventually it did with the Southeast Asia Security Treaty Organization and an informal network of bilateral U.S. security agreements with Japan, South Korea, and Taiwan.[12] While he was there, Chiang reportedly raised the possibility of transferring a portion of his government's gold reserve on Taiwan to the Philippines, just in case.[13] From Baguio, the two Chiangs flew to Canton for a meeting with Li Zongren. There Chiang told the KMT Central Executive Committee that he "shouldered a great deal of responsibility" for the defeats they had suffered, but that Canton must be held. He declined Li's requests, however, that the Nationalist Air Force return to the mainland to help in this mission.[14] A few weeks later, father and son took off for South Korea for talks with President Syngman Rhee, who had endorsed Chiang's idea of an anti-Communist alliance.

In August, back in Taiwan, Chiang read reports of the release in Washington of the State Department's thousand-page publication popularly known as the *White Paper,* which set out to explain the course of Sino-American relations from 1944 to the collapse of the Nationalist government on the mainland, to the imminent communization of China.[15] It strove to be objective, but its drafters shared a deep dislike of Chiang and the Nationalists. Except for the turnover of Japanese arms to the PLA, they did not discuss the Soviets' essential role in Mao's remarkable triumph.

Chiang himself did not disagree with the main conclusion of the *White Paper.* He had publicly admitted that the unfathomable failures of his regime were the principal cause of its own defeat—and even his first private expositions on the subject after his "retirement" took the same line. But unlike the State Department, he believed that those failures would not have led to the collapse of the KMT without the support the Soviet Union had given the Communists. He was not the only one to disagree with the *White Paper's* conclusions. U.S. Secretary of Defense Louis A. Johnson, an avid proponent of aiding Chiang, refused to have the Defense Department identified in any way with the publication. With dissenting voices like Johnson's in Washington, Chiang remained hopeful that there could be a turnaround on China policy in the United States. But with the Democrats in power for nearly four more years, something dramatic would have to happen.

On August 24, the Generalissimo and Ching-kuo flew to Chungking for a long visit with Central Army commanders in the region. The month-long stay during such critical days lent credence to Chiang's talk of establishing a final redoubt in Sichuan and neighboring areas. Mao was still concerned that the Western Allies would seek to intervene militarily from below China's southern borders into the southwest, and Chiang wanted to encourage this fear.[16]

There was also an old score for Chiang to settle during his visit. "Old Yang," General Yang Hucheng, the Young Marshal's partner in the Xi'an kidnapping in 1936, was still imprisoned in Chungking. The Young Marshal had convinced Chiang of the falsehood that Yang was behind the pair's decision to take their leader captive. Chiang would go to his death convinced that without the kidnapping, the history of China would have been completely different—and before leaving Chungking, in an unusual display of cruel personal revenge, Chiang reputedly ordered the execution not only of Yang but also his son, a daughter, a secretary, and the secretary's wife.[17]

Back in Taiwan, Chiang named Sun Liren as Taiwan defense commander, a move aimed in part to improve the image in America of the Chinese military establishment. Sun, however, felt he was powerless to do much because Chen Cheng, who was his superior, refused to give him adequate supplies or support—no doubt on orders from the Generalissimo. Sun felt the need for matériel was urgent: he predicted that the PLA could land 200,000 soldiers on Taiwan within twenty-four hours from an armada of 1,000 junks.[18]

On October 1, Mao Zedong stood on the walls of the Forbidden City in Peking and proclaimed the founding of the People's Republic of China (PRC). A few days later, the indomitable Bai Chongxi pulled out of Canton, retreating with his worn-out, mostly middle-aged soldiers to Guangxi, where they had started out a quarter-century before. Only two days later, Canton fell, and Li ordered the seat of government moved to Chungking. On October 10, from Taipei, the Generalissimo promised to fight on until he had defeated the Communists.

After taking Amoy, the PLA landed several thousand troops on the offshore island of Quemoy. Fighting from tunnels and gun emplacements dug into the island's stone hills and cliffs, Nationalist artillery men and machine gunners rained down a withering fire on the attackers. Low-level strafing of the exposed invaders on the beaches helped to break up the attack. The Nationalists killed or captured most of the Communist force.

After these small but welcome victories, a political breakthrough with the

United States occurred—or so Chiang thought. On November 3, the new U.S. consul general John J. Macdonald presented Chiang an official U.S. démarche intended to shock him out of what was assumed to be his reported delusions about possible American support. The message told Chiang in no uncertain terms that American military forces would not be coming to his rescue. In passing, the démarche also highlighted the existing "misgovernment of Formosa" and the serious unrest among native Taiwanese. It concluded with an assertion that the future American attitude toward Formosa would "depend largely on the action of the present Chinese [KMT] Administration in establishing an efficient administration which would seek to bring the people a higher level of political and economic well-being."[19] Chiang asked Macdonald to whom the message was addressed. When the American replied it was meant for the Generalissimo, Chiang seemed "very pleased." Then—anything but chastised—he served tea to the American in "a friendly and cordial atmosphere." Chiang was not shocked at all by the intended warning; instead he was delighted. He immediately called a meeting with Chen Cheng, Ching-kuo, and a few others. The United States, he told his officials, was now willing to deal with him directly and personally. He had "not been completely deserted by his old friend and ally." Chiang interpreted the message from Washington to mean that if the Nationalist government carried out sufficient reforms, America would change its attitude on military assistance to the island. Of course, Chiang was ready to agree in principle to anything the Americans wanted—except turning over power to someone else. After the meeting, which lasted into the night, he left for his retreat on Yangming Mountain to meditate.[20]

A curious interplay followed in which the Generalissimo and Chen Cheng followed up the démarche by telling Macdonald that the Nationalist leaders were full of plans for a range of reforms exactly along the lines the Americans wanted. Chiang and Chen also emphasized the threat of invasion from the mainland and asked for an enlarged economic aid program, military assistance "of a technical nature," and an American military advisory group. In his reports to Washington, Macdonald was now optimistic about the regime's possible survival. He recommended that the administration agree to the Chinese requests and do so promptly.[21]

Acheson quickly and categorically rejected this idea and refused to list any reforms on the island that might cause the United States to change its policy. He informed Macdonald that the Chiang regime had the economic and military means to save the island if it had the will and the ability, and he chided Macdonald for his suddenly optimistic reports. Finally, the Secretary instructed Macdonald to see C. K. Yen and Sun Liren and ensure that they—and through them Chiang Kai-shek—understood the intent of the U.S. policy statement: America did not intend to intervene in any way militarily to assist Taiwan.

Around this time, the KMT Central Committee still based in Chungking, including Zhang Qun and Yan Xishan, asked Chiang to return to the new provisional capital to lead the government, which in a major understatement they described as "collapsing." "For the Party and the revolution," Chiang declared, "I have to go back to Chungking."[22] Still inspired by what he took to be a new and promising American attitude and by his government's recent, minor military victory on Quemoy, Chiang was ready to show again that he personally had still not abandoned the mainland.

On November 14, he and Ching-kuo flew off to the old city on the river cliffs, now a maelstrom of despair and panic.[23] Well before they landed at the familiar airport, it was clear the situation in Sichuan was hopeless. Next door in Yunnan, Governor Lu Han, who had promised Chiang in August that he would fight to the end, was completing his surrender negotiations with CCP agents. In October, Bai Chongxi's Fourth Army had evacuated to the island of Hainan and his remaining troops had retreated into Indochina where the French had interned them. (Later, they made it to Taiwan.) Bai himself did not go to Indochina but flew to Chungking, where he told Chiang that Li Zongren, who had fled to Kunming, was going to the United States for medical treatment.[24]

Meanwhile, Liu Bocheng's and Deng Xiaoping's PLA columns were closing in on the city. Chiang delayed leaving Chungking because he wished to give the remnants of Hu Zongnan's once mighty army of more than 300,000 the chance to complete their flight from the Sichuan-Shaanxi border area to Chengdu.[25] He was outraged at the bald refusal to follow orders of some generals in the region, like Song Xilian, whose 100,000 troops "never fired a shot."[26] Chiang deployed what forces he had along the river, but on November 28 he and Ching-kuo visited the government buildings in Chungking and found them empty—all senior provincial and city officials had fled.[27] That night, Chiang's party could hear gunfire a few miles away. As in other besieged cities that he had abandoned over the years, Chiang flew out of Chungking for the last time at nearly the final hour.[28] Perhaps no other leader in modern times had escaped from so many last stands.

The Chiangs lingered at their next stop, Chengdu, for more than two weeks. Father and son paid their respects at the grave of Dai Jitao, the father of Wei-kuo. The previous February, Dai, in deep depression over the triumph of the Communists, had committed suicide with an overdose of sleeping pills. On December 8, the Nationalist government formally moved to Taipei, and the American embassy followed. Still in Chengdu, Chiang finally received reports from Taipei that Consul General Macdonald had on instruction categorically stated that the United States would not come to the aid of the Nationalists. "U.S. China policy is so unwise and so wrong," Chiang told his journal, "that I worry about the security of the United States."[29]

Chiang asked all the Nationalist generals in the area to come to a meeting to discuss the defense of Chengdu, but some simply refused.[30] From Kunming, Lu Han suspiciously suggested that the Generalissimo remain in Chengdu five more days. Expecting another kidnapping, Chiang's entourage at 2:00 a.m. on December 10 woke him and proposed that the party leave quietly through the rear gate of the army academy where they were staying. Chiang refused, saying he would leave as he came in. He and Ching-kuo, allegedly singing the national anthem, walked out the main gate and were driven to the airport.[31] They took off in a DC-4 heavily loaded with fuel. Flying by dead reckoning, the plane droned for hours over the vast territory now controlled by the Communists and landed in Taipei in mid-morning.[32]

Now that acting president Li Zongren was in the United States for an indefinite stay, party veterans urged Chiang to resume the office. Ching-kuo, however, argued that if his father took back the presidency, Li could blame the Generalissimo for any failure to win support in the United States. Chiang accepted his son's advice and postponed formally taking leadership.[33]

I

During this time, Chiang's reformist personnel appointments and progressive policies were making it increasingly difficult for Americans to contemplate a Communist takeover of the island. Taiwan's new civilian and military chiefs were in fact all progressive, American-educated men. In the midst of a reign of brutal political oppression, a meaningful land reform was under way; inflation was being significantly reined in; and the economy had returned to the peak levels reached under the Japanese. During the summer of 1949, the Provincial government placed 2,000 native Taiwanese in lower- and middle-grade jobs in the Provincial Civil Service. Regulations for local self-government, including elections for village and county chiefs, were in place, although only KMT members and independents could run for these offices. In the context of these changes, leading U.S. Republicans such as William Knowland, Walter Judd, Styles Bridges, and Joseph McCarthy accused Under-Secretary of State Acheson of "sabotage of the valiant attempt of the Chinese Nationalists to keep at least part of China free."[34]

Nearly all the old warlords who had bedeviled Chiang for four decades had no armies and absolutely no power in the party or the government on Taiwan. Bai Chongxi, who had an honorary position on the island, was the exception, even though Chiang never forgave his advice at the end of 1948 that he should resign. Even the Whampoa Clique was not what it used to be. He Yingqin, for instance, received a sinecure in Taipei and devoted himself to working with the global Moral Rearmament nongovernment group. And Chiang readily agreed with Ching-kuo's insistence that Du Yuesheng and other unsavory types associated with Shanghai gangs be kept out of Taiwan. The once powerful Soong influence had been reduced to Mayling and her niece Jeanette Kung, who remained as her aunt's close companion and something like a chief-of-staff, and in New York, to Jeanette's brother David, who continued as a close adviser, fundraiser, and coordinator in America. T.V., along with H.H. and Ai-ling Kung, had fled to America with all the other young Soong descendants. The departure of the Soongs reflected in part Chiang Ching-kuo's long-held dislike for these wealthy relatives and his skill in convincing his father to ease them out.

By the end of 1949, Chiang felt that his government had already accomplished a great deal on Taiwan. He started "to feel alive again." Acknowledging that over the past year he had suffered "total defeat" politically and militarily, he promised himself that he would make a new beginning, "create a new history."[35] He suggested to his son that they take a break at Sun Moon Lake, a stunning spot he had heard of high in the mountains of central Taiwan. On the first day of their arrival, Chiang received a message reporting the fall of Chengdu. He sat for a moment in thought. Then waving his bodyguards away, he and his son walked to the edge of the lake where a local fisherman rowed them out in his small boat. The elder Chiang cast out the fisherman's net and as he dragged it back in he saw that he had caught a very large fish. The fisherman claimed it was the biggest he had seen in twenty years. "It is a good omen," said Chiang.[36]

The Soviet Union's first atom bomb test in 1949 dramatically intensified American fears of a global Communist threat. Then in December, Mao arrived in Moscow aboard Chiang Kai-shek's old armored train. The visit for-malized the very real possibility of a huge Communist bloc extending from East Berlin and the Adriatic to the Bering Strait and then south to the South China Sea and the Himalayas—a radical and revisionist ideological and military empire. Alarmed, General MacArthur sent more cables to the Joint Chiefs stressing the importance of preventing the early fall of Taiwan. He told visiting congressmen in Tokyo that the United States should send Chiang Kai-shek five hundred fighter planes for use by American "volunteers" in the mold of the Flying Tigers. Defense Secretary Johnson also stepped up his campaign urging support for Chiang. In response, the Joint Chiefs recom-mended sending small amounts of military supplies and a military advisory group, but reiterated that they had no interest in sending American troops to the island.[37]

Acheson believed that even if U.S. aid helped postpone the fall of Taiwan for a year, it would also deepen American involvement in the island's ultimate collapse. Such a connection, he thought, would provide Moscow with mag-nificent diplomatic and propaganda opportunities.[38] Meanwhile, some voices at the State Department—such as that of George Kennan, then head of pol-icy planning—continued to advocate making Taiwan a trustee territory of the United Nations. He and others still could not explain convincingly how this could be accomplished, however, and on January 5, President Truman made U.S. policy clear in a public statement: the United States would not get involved in the Chinese "civil conflict" and it would not provide military aid or advice to any "Chinese force on Formosa."[39] Upon hearing the news, Chiang lamented that Marshall and Acheson "have done this to me, and de-stroyed the Republic."[40] On the same day, the United Kingdom recognized the People's Republic—a big blow, Chiang wrote, equivalent to "Russia's in-vasion of China" in 1945. Still, he thought, Taiwan's military and economic situations were "not that bad," and a "U.S.-Taiwan military alliance is a must—time will tell."[41]

Preparing for the Communist invasion of Hainan and Taiwan, Lin Biao was collecting thousands of junks along the Guangdong and Fujian coasts. Short in stature but long on aggressiveness, Lin would soon have more than 800,000 troops poised across the Strait for an amphibious landing that threatened to be more than three times the scale of the assault on Normandy. To resist the attack Chiang had 670,000 troops on Taiwan and Quemoy, Matsu, Hainan, and a few other small offshore islands. Only 300,000 or so were combat ready, however; the rest were old or sick or without weapons. In addition, the Generalissimo counted in his inventory a few hundred tanks and, assuming adequate purchases of parts and fuel, several hundred operational World War II aircraft. Yet despite the mismatch in forces, vast stores of ammunition for the Nationalist Army were piled up in bunkers around Taiwan, and a gargantuan battle seemed in the offing.[42]

Throughout the winter, Chiang spoke several times to the new Academy of Revolutionary Study and Practice, located on Yangming Mountain, on why the Kuomintang had lost to the Communists. Initially, he had blamed the collapse on the decay of party, military, and government structures on the mainland. Now, however, he stressed that the failure was due first of all to a lack of an effective "political and personnel monitoring system" especially in the military; that is, he blamed ineffective internal security and commissar organizations. "Traitors, collaborators, opportunists, and defeatists" flourished, he said, because there was "no strong and highly disciplined [security] organization." "The PLA sneaked in and sabotaged us," he said in one lecture, adding on another occasion that the CCP "could always get our top secret documents, plans, and strategies." Consequently, according to Chiang, "one million [of our] troops surrendered before firing a single shot."[43]

Chiang did admit to the Standing Committee that he had to be "held responsible for the loss of the . . . country in such a shockingly short period," but, he went on, "the social foundation of our party and its reputation . . . went down so quickly, there must have been deeper reasons." At times he blamed the final collapse on his having been forced to step down from the leadership and the mistakes of his successor, Li Zongren. "What I created in 20 years was wiped out completely," he said. He insisted that the reason he had failed while "so close to final victory" was that he had turned party management over to "others," meaning apparently the Chen brothers.[44] He specifically blamed his brother-in-law, T. V. Soong, for having "mishandled the country's economy and messed up the country." Later, he told one of T.V.'s young nephews that "Every time that I have done anything with T. V. Soong, it has turned out to be a bad luck business *(dao mei sheng yi)*." He chastised himself for not knowing "how to differentiate able personnel from incompetent ones."[45]

Chiang also made plain that the effort to end tutelage had been premature and was part of the problem. The elections in 1946 for the National Constitutional Assembly and then the 1948 elections to the National Assembly and the Legislative Yuan, he indicated, had resulted in "in-fighting and self-aggrandizement" among senior party members. The infighting and corruption caused by the elections constituted "the shame of his life." This was only one of the many great embarrassments he had cited over the years, but his vivid description of the malevolent consequences of the elections, which he believed represented a gross "humiliation," demonstrated how strongly he now felt that the attempt at democratization had been a disaster. (It is difficult, however, to see how the tribulations and excesses of the brief democratic experience had much of an effect, except on inhibiting, at least for a time, Chiang's efforts to crack down on dissent and ferret out spies.) He also blamed the overall debacle on rampant factionalism and a lack of loyalty to "the revolutionary leader." The Kuomintang, he thought, needed new blood and young members. To answer this need, Chiang proceeded to dismiss veterans in the civilian ranks, order several hundred incompetent generals to retire, and disperse these generals' subordinate senior officers into other units.[46]

Ching-kuo now took over active, not just pro forma, control over internal security. His highest priority was ferreting out spies and moles in the military, rather than focusing on suspected native Taiwanese dissidents. In the first half of 1950, three hundred alleged Communist spy cases were uncovered, which involved more than 3,000 people. For the first time in KMT China, one organization now knew the names of every military or civilian secret agent in the government, military, and party. Using the Communist model, security police recruited clandestine agents in every government office and major private company as well as in all military headquarters.[47]

According to Ching-kuo's deputy Wang Sheng, during this period the security forces executed about 15 percent of those arrested.[48] Following one round of arrests and executions, four hundred underground Communists reportedly gave themselves up in a single month. Among those who did not surrender but were supposedly discovered to be Communist moles were a number of army generals (some along with their wives), including the deputy chief of staff, a division commander, and an air force general. Later, Ching-kuo would claim that by the end of the year they had "eliminated almost all Communist infiltration."[49]

In December, Chen Cheng was still devoting himself to the evacuation of people and matériel from the mainland, and K. C. Wu—another favorite of both Mayling and the Americans—was made governor of Taiwan. Wu, a

Princeton Ph.D., had held many key jobs on the mainland, including acting foreign minister, and he soon began complaining to American diplomats about the detentions and executions, most of which he believed were arbitrary. General Sun also told his American friends that the thousands of intelligence personnel squeezed onto the island simply had to justify their existence. Some of these comments by the general, the governor, and others were probably clandestinely listened to by Ching-kuo's men, for the Generalissimo and Ching-kuo now launched a campaign of intimidation against the coterie of officers around Sun, some of whom had served with him since the 1937 Battle of Shanghai. Ching-kuo's officers arrested two of Sun's subordinates—both of whom happened to be "beautiful women." One was Sun's English-language secretary, the other the head of the Women's Corps. Both were sent to prison for ten years, a short tenure for "bandit agents."[50]

But serious dissent within the party now became evident. On January 12, 1950, an extraordinary meeting took place at the Academy of Revolutionary Study and Practice during which, to everyone's amazement, Chen Cheng openly criticized the leader. In his journal, Chiang wrote that Chen had shown "disagreement and unhappiness with me" and had suggested that "my talk is old fashioned." According to Chiang, Chen even accused him of "intervention and . . . interference" in Chen's work and responsibilities, which he felt had created "chaos in Taiwan." These remarks "shocked everyone in the meeting," Chiang reported, but the Generalissimo only "politely admonished" his longtime favorite for his insolence. Chen, he wrote, was showing a "completely abnormal mentality."[51]

But doubts about the Generalissimo were festering among the "most loyal" cohort who had fled with him to the island. That same day, Chiang learned that most of his top generals opposed his bizarre idea of hiring Japanese military trainers and advisers, including the infamous General Okamura Yasuji, the last commander of the Japanese Expeditionary Forces in China.[52] Very likely the main cause of the dissatisfaction, however, was the refusal of the United States to provide military aid and the assumption that if Chiang left the scene, the Americans might reconsider.

In early 1949, George Marshall resigned as Secretary of State because of illness and Truman named Under Secretary Dean Acheson to replace him. Acheson's thoughts on most matters, including China, were similar to those of Marshall. A year later, speaking at the National Press Club in Washington,

Acheson not surprisingly again put the blame for the "loss" of China squarely on the shoulders of Chiang Kai-shek. Even more upsetting to Chiang, when he read Acheson's comments, was his definition of the essential U.S. defense line in the Pacific as running from the Aleutians, through Japan, the Ryukyus, and the Philippines. South Korea and Taiwan were not specifically mentioned but both were pointedly outside the defense line—even though both countries were being threatened by Soviet-supported military forces.

Chiang wrote that Acheson's speech had left him more humiliated, depressed, and alarmed than at any time since the Jinan Incident with Japan in 1928. Even when fleeing the mainland a year before, he had believed that if he could hold out, world events would somehow turn in his favor. But now the statements of Acheson and Truman made clear that as in 1937 he again faced an overwhelming enemy alone, and this time he had no refuge up a great river or across another strait. For a moment, he was badly rattled. It seemed that soon he would face a personal choice between a martyr's death and shameful foreign exile. Unable to give up entirely his hope for American support, he blamed London more than Washington, for in his view the British example had led Acheson to give the green light to Mao Zedong to capture the last non-Communist redoubt in China. Acheson, Chiang thought, even had the looks and manners of a proper Englishman.

Mayling flew into Taipei the next evening and Chiang met her at the airport. She had been gone thirteen months—the third time she had been separated from Chiang for more than a year. Unlike her previous visits to the United States, on this last trip she apparently did not suffer from clinical depression; age had apparently tempered this affliction. Judging by the accounts of relatives and staff, an affectionate relationship between Madame and Chiang immediately resumed. For "Kai," the boy from Xikou, the old romantic, whatever the strains and difficulties, she remained a great prize.

As the couple rode back to the Shilin residence, Mayling must have briefed Chiang on the political dynamics in Washington around the China issue. The Republicans, led by Senators Knowland and Bridges, had vehemently attacked Truman's January 5 statement that the United States would not send military aid to Taiwan. Senator Joseph McCarthy was beginning his attacks on John Service and other Foreign Service officers for being pro-Communists or worse.[53] But most promising were the efforts of Senator H. Alexander Smith, a Republican from New Jersey who was arguing in strong but measured terms for U.S. engagement in the defense of Taiwan and Chiang Kai-shek. After a trip to Asia that included a talk with the Generalissimo, Smith had publicly recommended sending U.S. troops to occupy Taiwan indefinitely.

Despite this encouraging report, Chiang remained greatly troubled and frustrated. He began drafting a book entitled *The Survival of China and the Destiny of Asia.* In it he wrote that if Taiwan was conquered he would fight "to the last drop of blood and then commit suicide." He vented his rage on the "heinous English," whose goal was "to choke to death the soul and spirit of the Asian people." George Marshall, he wrote, had "never missed an opportunity to humiliate Asians" but neither Marshall's behavior nor even that of the Russians was as bad as that of the British. Acheson, he noted, was "100 percent English" by ancestry; thus he was prepared "to sell out the interests of America." As intently as in the midst of any of his past crises, Chiang envisioned himself as a martyr doomed to give his life for the cause: "I will die for the liberation of China and the Asian people." But soon calm and the faith of Job returned. In order to come back alive, he wrote, "I have to kiss the lips of death." In public, he now not only talked of a victorious defense of the island against all odds but even launched the cry heard for the next twenty years—"Counterattack the mainland!" *(Fangong dalu!)*[54]

The same day as Acheson's speech, Chen Cheng and K. C. Wu, in a meeting with Chiang, pushed for more native Taiwanese appointments, even as governor of the island (replacing Wu). Chiang found Chen "arrogant" and Wu "too easy to anger."[55] Nevertheless, the next month Chiang informed the surprised Chen that he intended to appoint him premier. To have fired the incorruptible Chen, who was credited with the land reform program, would have displeased even pro-Chiang Americans. Besides, Chen was an honest and effective administrator. So Chiang promoted him, confirming Chen's position as second in command.

Meanwhile, in Moscow, Acheson's speech confirmed for Stalin and Mao their belief that the United States would not intervene in Communist efforts to take over South Korea, Taiwan, or Vietnam.[56] Both believed that by correlating the forces of their two Marxist countries, they "had brought about definitive changes in the world power structure in favor of the Soviet-led camp."[57] The struggle in Vietnam was initially a guerrilla one and was already under way. The question was: should the next liberation effort begin in South Korea, or Taiwan?

As far back as May 1949, Mao had suggested to Kim Il-sung that he launch his planned attack on South Korea during the first half of 1950, and while in Moscow he ordered the transfer to the North Korean Army of an additional 14,000 PLA soldiers of Korean descent, along with their equipment. Mao, however, now preferred that Kim delay the military seizure of South Korea for a year because he planned for the invasion of Taiwan to take place in the late spring of 1950—only months away. Stalin left the timing of the two liberation wars up to Mao and Kim. He made clear that the Soviet Union would not participate directly in either war except for air defense and massive material aid. A Soviet air division with Russian pilots would soon be training more than a thousand Chinese pilots.[58]

At the end of January, Chiang told the Academy for the Study and Practice of Revolution that in the United States there were two policies on China. One, he said, "is the Defense Department policy, which proposes to give aid to Taiwan and include Taiwan in the U.S.-Pacific defense sphere." The other policy was that of the State Department, "which hopes that Taiwan is destroyed, the quicker the better." The State Department policy, Chiang said, would of course "embolden the Communist Chinese to attack Taiwan."[59] Two weeks later, Mao and Stalin signed the Sino-Soviet Treaty of Friendship, Alliance, and Mutual Assistance, which implicitly promised Soviet military assistance in the event the United States attacked China. The Communist leaders no doubt saw the treaty as a further deterrent to any U.S. inclination to want to help Taiwan resist an attack. But Chiang believed the accord, like the Soviet-Nazi Pact of 1939, would alarm the United States and thus do the Nationalists "a good service." At times, Chiang, like the State Department and the CIA, assumed that a massive PLA attack on Taiwan, supported by Soviet-supplied jet fighters or even Soviet-piloted MIGs, was only months away. But on other days, he grabbed at thin hopes, speculating that Stalin might "be happy to keep me alive as a force to hold Mao Zedong in check."[60]

II

Although the White House continued to block military aid of any sort for Taiwan, Chiang was able to acquire some unofficial and backdoor military assistance. Under a private arrangement, a group of retired American military officers, under retired admiral Charles M. Cooke (who had worked with Chinese intelligence during World War II), arrived on Taiwan to serve as advisers to the Nationalist armed forces. And the Defense Department may have "neglected" to inform the Department of State of some surplus items that were sold and delivered to Taiwan. In a 1996 interview, Chiang Wei-kuo related how in 1949 he was able to purchase in Hawaii for his American-made tanks a warehouse of "surplus" ammunition at a good price.[61]

On February 3, 1950, Li Zongren informed Taipei that for health reasons he had to remain in the United States, and the next day, Chiang decided in principle to resume the presidency. He thought that if he did not do so, not only would Taiwan be "destroyed but also the Chinese race as well." These sorts of narcissistic fantasies were not repeated in public nor apparently even to his own staff. Chiang sent Li a radiogram praising his service but in his diary called him "a shameless scum."[62]

As his new foreign minister, Chiang named George Yeh, a modern, pro-American graduate of Amherst and Cambridge.[63] Americans liked his exuberance, openness, and candor. Yeh's appointment meant that as war loomed ever closer, the premier, the governor, the foreign minister, the army commander, the finance minister, and the head of the Central Bank were all individuals respected by Americans, especially representatives of the U.S. government. Four of the six held American degrees; five spoke fluent English; and five were under the age of fifty-three. Another American-trained economic figure was K. Y. Yin (Yin Zhongrong), who as head of the Economic Stabilization Board and then as economic minister had played a key role in the island's growing economic stability. This was an attractive team—and all of them were close to Madame Chiang.

On March 1, 1950, Kai-shek and Mayling stood on the balcony of the Presidential Palace and waved to the crowd of some 100,000 "enthusiastic citizens" celebrating Chiang's resumption of office. Chiang wanted younger men in the Legislative Yuan and the National Assembly—men loyal to him and free of the old cliques and factions. But 470 members of the Legislative Yuan had managed to flee to Taiwan, and since they and the National Assembly members had been elected on the mainland under the 1946 Constitution, he could not alter the membership without damaging his legal claim to be the head of the constitutional government of China. Representatives of the various national bodies, more than two thousand in all, would continue to exercise their sinecures for another forty years. Chiang would have little respect for them, but often in his diary bemoaned, "What can I do?"[64]

In Yunnan, Lu Han finally defected to the CCP, but 2,000 loyal Nationalist troops in the province took sanctuary in the mountains of the Shan state of Burma. Chiang dispatched General Li Mi, a former commander of these troops, to Burma to take charge of this hardy band of "KMT irregulars," who soon took over the opium trade in northern Burma.[65] Meanwhile, 80,000 Nationalist troops under General Xue Yue and many thousands of refugees from South and Southwest China had taken refuge on semitropical Hainan, China's second largest island after Taiwan. Hainan was only fifteen miles from the mainland and, unlike in Taiwan, many CCP guerrillas were hiding out in its mountains. In March more than 100,000 PLA troops stormed ashore against light resistance. When Chiang gave the order to withdraw, 70,000 Nationalist soldiers and refugees successfully evacuated to Taiwan.[66]

Shortly after the Hainan pullout, Chiang ordered Tang Enbo's 120,000 troops from the Zhoushan islands southeast of Shanghai also to evacuate to Taiwan. Chiang was increasingly worried about the rapid development of the PLA Air Force and he wanted to concentrate all his strength on Taiwan. His senior military officers, however, including Chen Cheng and air force chief Zhou Zhirou, "vehemently opposed" this move as a blow to the morale of all the homesick mainland soldiers on Taiwan, who would see such a retreat as evidence they would never return home. Angry at the opposition, Chiang wrote that Chen Cheng, whom he had just appointed premier, had "lost the revolutionary character of a qualified military officer." On May 16 all the troops from the islands of Zhoushan were safely evacuated to Taiwan, and a few days later, in a further sign of the discord between Chen and Chiang, Chen told Zhang Qun he was determined to resign as premier because the Generalissimo "always intervened in his affairs" and the situation was "hateful."[67]

During this time, to keep the PLA off-balance and as another way to boost morale, Chiang ordered pin-prick "commando raids" along the coast, air attacks against targets on the mainland, and a nominal sea blockade of mainland ports. He also proceeded with his controversial idea of bringing Japanese military advisers and trainers to Taiwan. Western advisers, he said, ignored the importance of spirit and focused entirely on professionalism and tactics, and in the past this attitude had had an unfortunate influence on Nationalist officers and soldiers. Chinese officers also had picked up the "Western habits of free thinking and enjoyment of a rich material life." Thus, he explained, he had invited Japanese military professionals to join the Nationalist military academies to teach "the soldier's spirit—a willingness to die."[68]

The ad hoc group of ten that had been studying party reform presented its draft proposals to Chiang in mid-May. As Chiang had wished, its guidelines called for a return to the centralized, Leninist organizational model of a "revolutionary democratic" party as Sun Yat-sen had adopted in his last two years. But according to this blueprint, the Kuomintang's control would in practice be more pervasive than ever before. Chiang intended to have the real dictatorial powers he never enjoyed on the mainland. "All decisions" down to the basic level would be made through the party system. In other words, throughout the society—in government, the military, business, the media, schools, farm organizations, and churches and temples—party units would monitor and direct major decisions.[69] The blueprint suggested a quasi-totalitarian regime similar to the Communist system in its social and political control. Chiang told the group, however, that given the existing military situation he would put the plan aside for the time being. One thing he did do was to institute an oath of loyalty to himself in the senior ranks of the party, the same type of oath that Sun Yat-sen had demanded.[70]

In the spring of 1950, the Legislative Yuan surprisingly vetoed Chiang's proposal to give full emergency powers to the State Council and its chairman (that is, Chiang himself) beyond those set out in the constitution. Angry at this display of what he took to be disloyal factionalism, Chiang said Chen Lifu, who controlled a large bloc of old C-C Clique legislators, was "lying and playing dirty." At this point, in a foul mood about the cliques, Chiang decided to go ahead with "the party purge" despite the imminence of an invasion. He thought it best to proceed with the purge while "the media was under control." Military commanders were also targeted. Feeling that they were still treating their troops as "their own personal property, [reflecting] their power and status," Chiang ordered several hundred more generals to retire. And when he learned that troops of the 45th Division had committed "robberies and other crimes," he disbanded it and retired all the officers and men.[71]

The CIA estimated that 370,000 troops of the PLA's Third Field Army were now positioned on China's central coast and that at least 450,000 troops of Lin Biao's Fourth Field Army were nearby and available to support an invasion of Taiwan. The PLA had also assembled some 5,000 junks and towable craft for the assault.[72] While they did not look formidable, the junks, which had substantial wooden hulls and one-foot-thick hardwood keels, would not be easy to sink with the naval and aircraft weapons available to the Nationalists. Mao's forces were also mobilizing by air: radio transmissions indicated that PLA pilots were flying over Chinese cities for the first time.[73] According to the CIA, the PLA already possessed 100 to 150 jet warplanes—an impressive achievement on the part of the Soviet Union as well as the People's Republic.[74] Taiwan had no such aircraft.

In May, Kim Il-sung began moving his tanks and elite infantry units toward the border with South Korea. On May 13, after flying to Peking in a Russian plane, Kim told Mao that he had secured Stalin's consent to the "liberation" of the south, and he wanted to launch the invasion as soon as possible. When Mao asked for confirmation from Stalin, Moscow replied that if the Chinese disagreed, the invasion "must be postponed." Mao told the impatient Kim that U.S. involvement in a Korean conflict was possible and that he had expected that the attack on South Korea would follow the PLA liberation of Taiwan. Nevertheless, he agreed to Kim's plan and promised Chinese support.[75]

Mao could easily have insisted that the invasion of Taiwan take precedence, but he did not.[76] One explanation is that the striking defeat of the PLA's amphibious attack on Quemoy the previous September had made the Chairman doubly cautious about moving a half million men across eighty to a hundred miles of open water to attack Taiwan. Very likely the Chairman wanted to have a substantial air force with jet fighters and a large naval presence to deal with the Generalissimo's small inventory of World War II fighter planes and frigates. At the same time, the chances of a successful attack by the North Korean Army against the unprepared and much weaker army of the Republic of (South) Korea appeared high.[77] If Kim could conquer South Korea, it would demoralize the Nationalists on Taiwan, and the island might then fall without a shot being fired.

Whatever the reason, Mao's decision to agree to the early launching of Kim's invasion would have far-reaching consequences. If Kim had not attacked the South in 1950 and instead Mao had launched his junk armada against Taiwan in June, almost certainly the Truman administration would not have intervened to save Chiang Kai-shek. In addition, Mao's remarkable victory over Chiang Kai-shek on the mainland had generated an unbridled ambition in the Chairman, one that would have been fueled by a military success on Taiwan. Around the time that Kim Il-sung was in Peking, Ho Chi Minh secretly arrived to discuss the Vietminh's coming military offensive. Mao, viewing the United States "as both a hostile enemy and a 'paper tiger,'" saw three opportunities for transforming "through the barrel of the gun" the existing order in East Asia and thus in the world—Korea, Taiwan, and Vietnam.[78]

On Taiwan, the spring harvest of 1950 produced a bumper crop thanks to the initial land reform and other efforts by the Joint Commission on Rural

Reconstruction, such as supplying fertilizer to farmers via loans. The price of rice in the market consequently fell by 40 percent. In addition, despite the near-term life-or-death threat he faced, Chiang rather surprisingly insisted that the military budget remain fixed, and apparently it did during this critical year. The government was thus able to contract the local issue of the New Taiwan Dollar, preventing further price increases. All of these developments helped further stabilize Taiwanese society.[79]

In May, the Chiangs moved into their new official residence in the Shilin District of Taipei. The grounds and buildings had originally been built by the Japanese governor-general as a "gardening laboratory." It was a beautiful, quiet place situated at the base of Good Fortune Mountain, a foothill of Yangming Mountain. Paddy fields covered the plains to the west and north, through which the Keelung River snaked its way to the East China Sea. The original house was small, with many large windows providing pleasant views of the dense, tropical gardens.

Next to the residence, the Chiangs built a small chapel, which they called Triumph Song Hall after their chapel in Nanking. They attended services every Sunday, sitting in two upholstered chairs in the front. Other Christians such as Chen Cheng, Zhang Qun, and He Yingqin and their wives sat on straight-back chairs as did Ching-kuo, Faina, and their four children, Alan (15), Alex (14), Amy (11), and Edward (2). The pastor from the post-V-J days in Nanking, Chen Weiping, conducted the services.[80] Chiang himself preached a sermon on Good Friday, talking with the pastor about what he wished to say, but having no written text. Soldiers were required to listen to the sermons, which could be three hours long. For her part, Madame began holding prayer meetings in Triumph Song with a group of Christian women every Wednesday—meetings that would go on even during typhoons. At that time, Taiwan seemed in need of prayer. The CIA once again told the White House that the PLA would probably seize the island before the end of 1950.[81] Hong Kong merchants were reporting that Chinese agents were buying up five- and ten-horsepower motors to install on wooden landing barges being built for the invasion.[82] And the U.S. State Department was urging all Americans on the island to leave.

The White House continued to write off Taiwan as a lost cause, but down in Foggy Bottom, some diplomats were still searching for a way to save the island. Dean Rusk brought John Foster Dulles, a prominent Republican, on board as a special envoy to provide advice on the Taiwan issue. Dulles believed that the United States should not allow the native Taiwanese to be ruled by either the Communists or the Nationalists, and Rusk thought it was time for a total reappraisal of policy toward the island. "Formosa," Rusk believed, was "a place to draw the line [against Communist expansion]." Acheson and others, however, continued to adhere to the theory that the People's Republic of China would eventually follow the Titoist line and that keeping the door open to this probability was the best way to serve America's long-term strategic interests. According to this view, it was essential that the United States not back an independent Taiwan and thus provide Peking an issue with which to rally the Chinese people, including the mainlanders on Taiwan, against the United States. Such a scenario, it was feared, could someday even provoke a Sino-American war, but at a minimum, it would keep China closely allied to the Soviet Union.[83]

Back in March, the CIA station in Taipei had cabled Washington that General Sun was planning a coup. The next month, the American military attaché in Taiwan reported that a high-level official, assumed to be Sun, had told him that under Chiang the situation was "hopeless" and there needed to be "drastic measures to save the situation."[84] Moreover, in meetings with the Generalissimo, Sun continued to oppose the work of the political commissars, and on one occasion even boldly told Chiang that his use of Japanese officers in the military did not serve the country's nation-building goals. Then on May 6, Chen Cheng personally asked Chiang to accept his resignation, saying he no longer had the health, personality, or ability to serve longer.[85]

Chiang sensed a growing threat to his own power and reportedly at times was heard slamming objects about his office and shouting in his phone.[86] In early May, according to a top secret State Department memorandum dated May 3, 1950, General Sun "confided" to the Americans that he was "prepared to wipe the Formosan slate clean and assume full military control without losing (support of) the Chinese Air Force and Navy." The State Department paper discussed the U.S. options should Sun successfully carry out a coup. But it prefaced this discussion with a warning about Sun's "political naiveté" and an injunction that "The [U.S.] Government should in no way be involved in Sun's *coup d'état*."[87]

Dean Rusk and others at the State Department met on May 30 and drew up a new plan to present to Acheson: The United States would inform Chiang Kai-shek that the only way to avoid a bloody Communist takeover of Taiwan was for Chiang to request U.N. trusteeship, leave the island, and

Chiang inspects troops at the Nationalist Army training center in southern Taiwan with General Sun Liren, an American favorite who was already suspected of coup plotting. Courtesy KMT Party History Institute.

turn over control to the army commander General Sun.[88] The plan, however, did not involve encouragement of a coup by General Sun. Nevertheless, the State Department reportedly asked President Quirino if the Philippines would give the Generalissimo political asylum if he were to flee Taiwan. Quirino's reply: "no."[89]

In early June 1950, Rusk, who during the war in Burma had had friendly relations with Sun Liren, received a secret note from him, hand-delivered by a Chinese friend of the general. In the letter, Sun proposed to lead a coup d'état against the Generalissimo and he asked for the support or acquiescence of the United States. Alarmed that Sun would be killed if his message got back to Taipei, Rusk burned the note and reported the incident directly to Secretary Acheson, who promised to take up the matter immediately with President Truman.[90] One possibility, which Rusk did not consider, was that the letter was a forgery intended to justify Sun's early arrest for plotting a coup.

On June 23, Rusk called on Hu Shi, who now resided in New York, and apparently raised the possibility of his replacing Chiang. Hu refused. It appears that Rusk had hoped the Generalissimo would step down if Hu publicly put himself forward. At this point, Acheson apparently discussed the situation privately and off the record with the President. Then, on June 23, the same day that Rusk talked with Hu, Acheson held a news conference and announced that Truman's January 5 statement on China and Taiwan was still American policy: the United States would stay out of the Chinese civil war.[91]

Not knowing of these events, MacArthur sent in another stinging message declaring that the fall of Taiwan would destroy the military position of the United States in the Far East. Here he used for the first time the description of Taiwan as "an unsinkable aircraft carrier and submarine tender." He also allowed the Nationalists to purchase napalm bombs for their air force from supplies he controlled.[92]

III

Early on the morning of June 25, the Generalissimo's secretary, Shen Chang-huan, woke his boss to announce that Ching-kuo had come with an important message. Chiang hurriedly put on his black robe and went into his office. Ching-kuo reported that following a lengthy artillery barrage, North Korean infantry and armored units had crossed the 38th Parallel. Chiang sat down. "I knew this would happen," he said.[93] In fact, he had not anticipated the attack on South Korea, but had long predicted an eventual clash between the United States and the Soviet Union. Now, he thought, the beginning of that superpower war had probably started in Korea, and it could well save Taiwan. He would have to wait and see what President Truman would do.

That Sunday, Truman authorized MacArthur to send military supplies to the South Koreans and to use U.S. fighters to attack North Korean tanks. He also quickly appealed to the U.N. Security Council and received a resolution calling for the immediate cessation of hostilities in Korea and a withdrawal of North Korean forces to the 38th Parallel. He stressed that the United States would wait for the North Koreans to flout the U.N. resolution before taking further action. Meanwhile, Acheson proposed that the President send elements of the Seventh Fleet into the Taiwan Strait to prevent hostile action from either side. He also emphasized that the United States "should not tie up with the Generalissimo" and suggested that the status of Taiwan "might be determined by the United Nations." The President added, "or by the Japan Peace Treaty." Truman, however, said nothing about Taiwan or China in his instructions.[94] He later told an aide that he was more worried about Mohammad Mossadegh and Iran than Formosa.[95]

Chiang waited three days with no definitive word on what the United States would actually do. He and his people still did not know whether the action in Korea was to be an ominous forerunner of their own fate or a stream flowing to the river of their deliverance. Mayling fired off cables to Chiang Kai-shek supporters in Washington, while Chiang and his son closely followed military developments in Korea and ordered reconnaissance flights and sea patrols to look for any sign of a PLA flotilla gathering along the China coast.

But there was also an important internal matter to be taken care of—the threat the Chiangs believed General Sun Liren posed to their rule and thus to the survival of their exile regime. Very likely father and son feared that whether or not America intervened in the Korean conflict, the event could prod Sun and perhaps Chen Cheng into action. Thus on that very eventful day, Chiang called in Sun and warned him against "playing treacherous games." If Sun did not change his thinking, the Generalissimo said, he would be deprived of all posts. In his diary, Chiang even wrote that General Sun was "collaborating with the Communists."[96] But still, Sun remained commander of the army.

Finally, the concrete American reaction to the North Korean invasion came: on June 27, President Truman announced that he had ordered U.S. air and naval forces to support the troops of the South Korean government. Furthermore, he said, given the circumstances, Communist occupation of Formosa would constitute a direct threat to the security of the Pacific and the United States. Thus he had ordered the Seventh Fleet to repel any attack on Taiwan, called on the government in Taipei to cease all air and sea operations against the mainland, and declared that "the determination of the future status of Formosa must await the restoration of security in the Pacific, a peaceful settlement with Japan, or consideration by the United Nations."[97]

The wonderful news for everyone on the island was that America would prevent the PLA's invasion of Taiwan. Almost as welcome was Truman's decision directly to intervene to defeat the North Korean invasion of the South. And even if South Korea was eventually lost to the Communists, it was hard to envision the United States abandoning its newly proclaimed protection of Taiwan—even if only because for decades to come it would be a relatively easy commitment for the U.S. Navy and Air Force to carry out.

The bad news for Chiang, however, was that Truman's latest statement had said nothing about support for the government on Taiwan, much less for the Generalissimo. Instead, the American President had indicated that the status of Taiwan and thus of Chiang Kai-shek was unresolved. This position contradicted Truman's statement of January 5 that Taiwan was a part of China. Now it was obvious that the White House intended to develop a U.N. option for Taiwan, the first step in a legal separation of the island from China.

Chiang immediately convened a series of policy meetings in Taipei. Truman, Chiang said, had "ignored our sovereignty, treating us worse than a colonial nation." But, he realized, he had to make the best of the good news, while pushing his friends in the United States to persuade the administration to abandon the idea of an independent Taiwan. Chiang agreed that Foreign Minister Yeh would draft a statement indicating that the Republic of China was suspending its naval and air operations against the mainland as the United States had requested, but also stressing that Taiwan was an integral part of China and that Truman's declaration did "not in any way affect China's authority over Formosa."[98]

In the interest of building support for Taiwan in America, Foreign Minister Yeh also proposed that the Generalissimo offer to send 33,000 Nationalist troops to fight in Korea. Chiang at first reportedly opposed the idea but finally approved it on the condition that the United States fully equip the Nationalist soldiers involved with modern weapons and provide two years of training. According to Dean Rusk, Yeh assured the Generalissimo that the Americans would reject this offer.[99]

When Sun Liren heard of the proposal to send three Nationalist divisions to help defend South Korea, he was "very enthusiastic" and asked to lead the expedition. But Chiang wrote in his journal: "Sun's character and principles worry me very much." During a meeting with other senior commanders, Chiang told the shocked officers that Sun had no credibility and was "treacherous."[100] A few days later, political and intelligence officers reported to the Generalissimo what he wanted to hear: Sun's headquarters was "once again found to have CCP spies."[101] Still, to fire Sun or detain him at this stage would have given ammunition to Chiang's many enemies in the Truman administration. Consequently, Chiang left the general in his command. As Yeh predicted, Washington did decline Taipei's offer of troops for Korea. Truman and Acheson did not want to get "tied up" with Chiang.[102]

Meanwhile, Mao was surprised by the strong reaction of "the paper tiger."

He ordered mass propaganda and mobilization campaigns against the American imperialists and formation of a new Northeast Border Defense Army of 700,000 that would deploy near the Sino-Korean border and prepare to enter the war. The PLA rushed huge stockpiles of war matériel to the Yalu River frontier.[103] At the same time Mao increased military aid to Ho Chi Minh.

In early July, Chiang Kai-shek publicly charged that the Soviet Union had instigated the Korean War and predicted that Mao would eventually order Chinese Communist troops into the conflict.[104] Fulfillment of this prediction would put the United States and Communist China at war and fundamentally change American views of Chiang and Taiwan. But Americans as a nation and a people, he thought, were "so shallow" they were unpredictable, and in private, he grumbled that most Americans still thought that Taiwan and Chiang Kai-shek were "already gone."[105] Believing Mao would assume that the U.S. commitment to defend Taiwan was a hollow gesture, he instructed Chief of Staff Zhou Zhirou to prepare to evacuate Quemoy. Because of Truman's restrictions, Chiang said, Nationalist planes could no longer bomb PLA concentrations opposite Quemoy and this made the island more vulnerable to attack. Zhou Zhirou and Chiang's unofficial American military advisers argued against pulling out of Quemoy. They thought it would be seen as accepting the division of Taiwan and the mainland. But for the time being, the "prepare to evacuate" order stood.[106]

With Truman's approval, MacArthur rushed four occupation divisions from Japan to Korea—but they experienced one defeat after another. Perhaps it was a growing pessimism about American prospects in the new war that made MacArthur reportedly tell the Nationalist Chinese ambassador to Japan, to Chiang's delight, that he "strongly supported" the Generalissimo.[107] MacArthur, in fact, was insisting more loudly every day on all-out assistance to the Nationalists, the use of Nationalist troops, and the incorporation of Taiwan as a key strategic asset for the protection and projection of U.S. power.[108]

On July 31, the Generalissimo and Madame Chiang welcomed General MacArthur at the Taipei International Airport. MacArthur and his entourage were making the trip without having notified the State Department or the White House; in fact, Acheson was "startled" when he learned about it.[109] During the elaborate briefing prepared for him in Taipei, the renowned American soldier sat between Madame and the beaming Generalissimo, who was deeply struck by MacArthur's commanding presence and aura of certainty. The Chinese briefers set out the many serious shortages of matériel within the Nationalist armed forces but emphasized the spirit and fighting quality of their troops. The briefing greatly impressed MacArthur, and he promised, again without authorization, that Taiwan would get everything it needed.[110] Afterward the American visitors rode up Yangming Mountain to their lodgings at the President's retreat. That night, the Chiangs hosted MacArthur and his senior staff at a Chinese dinner. As the toasts were made, the President and his wife must have found it hard to believe that only six weeks before, the end had seemed near for the Generalissimo, the Kuomintang, and the Nationalist government.

Early the next morning, Chiang and his guest talked for two hours over breakfast. MacArthur promised that the U.S. government would soon have "an official policy regarding the provision of military protection for Taiwan." Chiang, for his part, offered MacArthur full command of the Chinese armed forces—the third American to whom he had proposed this honor—but MacArthur gracefully declined.[111] In a public statement issued before his departure, the American general said the two sides would "meet any attack a hostile force might be foolish enough to make" and expressed his admiration for "the Generalissimo's indomitable determination to resist Communist aggression." In an eagerly received compliment, MacArthur declared that Formosa compared "favorably with many of the democracies of the world."[112]

Chiang was jubilant. MacArthur, he wrote in his diary that night, was the "number one American political and military leader since FDR." "He is a friend in need and my best [American] friend."[113] As if to confirm Chiang's reaction, MacArthur immediately dispatched six U.S. Air Force jet fighters to Taiwan. On August 4 the planes—the first jet fighters Chiang had ever seen—put on an air show above cheering crowds in the streets of Taipei.[114] But MacArthur's gesture did not receive the same applause in Washington. The U.S. Joint Chiefs pointedly informed MacArthur that the President's intention was to defend Taiwan without stationing U.S. forces on the island, even in the event of an attack. In other words, for the time being, the Seventh Fleet alone would assure the island's defense.[115] The jets returned to Japan.

In Tokyo, MacArthur followed up his visit by sending his deputy chief of staff, Major General Alonzo Fox, with a survey group to assess in greater detail Chiang's military needs. MacArthur ordered Fox to have nothing to do with the State Department's representatives in Taipei, one of several moves by MacArthur that made clear he had dissociated himself from Truman's poli-

A month after the beginning of the Korean War, General Douglas MacArthur, Chiang's new "best friend," arrives in Taipei. Each man wrote his name on the photo. Courtesy KMT Party History Institute.

cies on Taiwan. Meanwhile, Karl Rankin, a career diplomat who had been sympathetic to the Nationalists, took over the embassy in Taipei as minister rather than ambassador—a White House effort to retain flexibility for the future. After their first meeting, Rankin described the Generalissimo as "a Chinese gentleman to whom truth, modesty, loyalty, and magnanimity are among the greatest of virtues." Chiang knew this was a U.S. Foreign Service officer he would like. Thereafter, embassy reporting would contain no more complaints about police measures on the island. In any event, as Rankin found out, martial law was not always harshly applied. When he arrived, squatters occupied half the American embassy grounds and it took two years for the police to clear them away.[116]

Ching-kuo reported to his father that the PLA had begun moving troops away from the Zhejiang and Fujian coasts and north to Shandong opposite the Korean Peninsula. In response to this news, Chiang cancelled his earlier order to withdraw from Quemoy and the other coastal islands—that is, until he received a secret radiogram from Acheson saying that the Seventh Fleet would not help defend these islands. Chiang immediately reinstated the withdraw order as "urgent." He reversed course again two weeks later, however, cancelling his evacuation order as the possibility of a PLA assault on the island dropped further out of sight.[117]

During this time, Chiang continued to build the case against Sun Liren, with additional intelligence reports again claiming that several senior officers in Sun's headquarters in Taiwan were Communist moles.[118] Chiang also initiated investigations of officers close to Chen Cheng—the second-highest-ranking official on the island. In mid-August he deprived the commander of the 19th Army of his post, noting in his journal that this officer "is a confidante of Chen Cheng and follows Chen Cheng's orders."[119] The Chiangs wanted to send a warning to Chen as they had to Sun Liren, and Chen received it, resigning his army commission on August 28.[120]

Strengthened politically by the collateral effects of the Korean War, Chiang now felt confident enough to formalize establishment of the long-planned party reform group—the Central Reorganization Committee (CRC). This project would involve carrying out the planned large-scale dismissal or retirement of party officials and the reorientation of the party, its political program, and the military. As part of this initiative, Chiang disbanded the KMT Central Standing Committee and the Central Executive Committee. He then personally selected the members of the CRC, among them Chen Cheng, whom Chiang suspected of disloyalty and had recently branded in his journal as "useless"—but who was still premier.

In addition to Chen, the Central Reorganization Committee consisted of Ching-kuo, thirteen other trusted aides and associates, and one native Taiwanese. The average age was forty-six and the oldest member was only fifty-eight—a striking departure from the senior KMT committees of the previous ten years or so. All had received college degrees or an equivalent. (In the future, even midlevel KMT cadre would be required to have graduated from college.) Five members of the committee—almost a third—came from Zhejiang. Most importantly, all had personal ties to the Generalissimo. There were no C-C Clique members in the CRC and no representatives of the warlords or the Soongs.[121]

The primary objectives of party reform, Chiang stressed to the group, were to eliminate corruption and factions, to bring in younger party members, and to focus on serving society and the masses. Party authority was to be centralized as never before in the hands of Chiang Kai-shek and his son, but the change was portrayed as essential to achieve the necessary and long-sought unity. Chiang, it seemed, was convinced that his labors would someday, probably long after he was gone, produce a rule of law; an open, prosperous, well-educated society; and a multiparty but strictly controlled representative system of governance in which stability and the welfare of the common people would be the most important goals.[122]

This was an interesting quasi-Marxist rhetorical phase for the strong anti-Communist KMT leader, reflecting in part his admiration for aspects of the Chinese Communist Party. More often than before, in his diary and his closed talks he invoked the Marxist theme about serving the "masses."[123] He openly preached within the party that it was necessary to learn from Mao Zedong in order to defeat him.[124] He even urged party members to learn the Marxist, dialectical way of thinking. "Our attitude of disdaining the dialectic," he wrote, "was the reason why we were defeated."[125]

Mobilization of the youth was another Communist priority the Chiangs were determined to emulate. Ching-kuo, not surprisingly, became head of a new youth organization with the usual overly descriptive name, the National Salvation Anti-Communist Youth Corps. Notably, the corps fell not under the Ministry of Education but the General Political Warfare Department, which provided officers to "teach and train students from elementary school to college."[126] Standardized teaching and military training, Chiang explained, were key to carrying out the party's "principles and goals."[127]

The young Chiang also assumed leadership of the Academy of Revolutionary Study and Practice, one of the Generalissimo's favorite new institutions on Taiwan. Over the years, the academy would provide messages of political indoctrination to tens of thousands of government, military, and party officers. In the Chinese manner, these graduates, no matter how short the course, would look upon their nominal "dean," Chiang Ching-kuo, as an important mentor. As the party cadre increased, so did the number of party members. In 1950 there were approximately 50,000 KMT members on Taiwan. By 1952 the membership would stand at 282,000, of whom about 50 percent were of mainland origin; in addition, 170,000 of the total were civilians, and 112,000 were a part of the military. As in the Chinese Communist Party, a new Discipline Commission was established to investigate charges of corruption, including at the higher levels.[128]

The Reform Committee would also restore the Leninist doctrine of democratic centralism as the guiding principle of the Kuomintang. The basic or lowest-level organization was to be the party cell. The new rules would require every KMT member to belong to a cell and to attend its meetings. The cell would be a working unit carrying out party policy, developing and distributing propaganda, preventing Communist infiltration, and reporting suspicious and illegal behavior. Party journals cited the Chinese Communist Party example as evidence of the advantages of using the workplace as the basic unit of party organization in the cities; and in rural areas, villages rather than towns or districts were the foundational element.[129]

For the first time, Kuomintang cells would be formed in the Legislative Yuan, and henceforth, legislators would be given their guidance or instructions via the party. KMT cells would be created throughout the government and the military. Private businesses of any size would be "encouraged" to allow party cells within their factories and offices. Every school and every nonprofit organization had party cells, and if big enough, a web of cells. Again following CCP practice, members of Kuomintang cells practiced mutual criticism, self-criticism, and investigations of loyalty and honesty. Party-conducted polls conducted by the cells sought to learn the needs and opinions of the people in order "to develop the mass line."[130]

In addition to these individual-level directives, major sectors of business, industry, and infrastructure were under government control, including steel, mining, petroleum, electric power, railways, ship building, sugar, alcohol, tobacco, and forestry. Privatization, except in connection with land reform, was not a goal.

Chiang's strong anti-Communist defenders in the U.S. Congress seemed unaware of these striking similarities with the techniques of the Communist parties of the world. Yet Chiang's aim was not profoundly to transform human relations and the world, as Mao aspired to do, or to dominate other peoples and eventually the world as the fascists intended. Instead he hoped to assure stability and unchallenged political power in order to preserve his position and the goal of national unity, defeat any attack from the mainland,

and build a modern and prosperous Chinese society on Taiwan. The values taught in the new KMT were the same as in the old New Life Movement—patriotism, loyalty, discipline, honor, benevolence, love, and anti-Communism.

When Chen Lifu sought to convene a plenum of the Central Committee to approve the reforms, he asked why the party's financial records were not open to all committee members. His request set off a flurry of alarming criticisms. In a letter to Chen's ailing brother, Guofu, Chiang described Lifu as "incompetent" and declared that he was not to participate any longer in party-building decisions.[131] "The Commander in Chief," Chiang wrote, speaking of himself in the regal third person as he now occasionally did in his diary and letters, would "take care of things for the party." According to Lifu, he learned that Ching-kuo was about to arrest him and he fled to New Jersey, where he opened a chicken farm with a loan from H. H. Kung. Like a number of senior Kuomintang veterans, whatever his sins, it seemed that Chen Lifu had not amassed even a modest fortune.[132]

IV

Truman and Acheson feared that MacArthur's endorsement of Chiang Kai-shek could provoke the People's Republic into entering the Korean War, a development that at that early stage could have been disastrous.[133] Truman sent Harriman off to Tokyo to tell MacArthur that the President did not want him "to permit Chiang to be the cause of a war between the United States and China." MacArthur promised to carry out any orders received from the President, but he made it clear that he disagreed with the administration's policy toward China and Chiang Kai-shek.[134]

On August 31, Truman, in response to a reporter's question, said that after the Korean War ended there would be no need for the Seventh Fleet to defend Taiwan. In other words, the U.S. commitment to prevent an attack on Taiwan was temporary. Chiang believed the detested English were again responsible for this "turning point" in Truman's China policy.[135] Meanwhile, the U.N. Security Council also continued to debate complaints from the People's Republic that the United States was taking an aggressive stance against China by deploying U.S. military aircraft and naval vessels to Taiwan, and that U.S. warplanes had violated Chinese territory across the North Korean border. In the course of the debate, the U.S. representative, Warren Austin, proposed that the Security Council send a team to the relevant site in

Manchuria to investigate the charges. The Nationalist representative to the Security Council, Jiang Tingfu, concluded that the next proposal would be to send a delegation to Taiwan to investigate the other charge; moreover, he feared that if his government vetoed this effort, it could set the stage for a move to give the China seat in the Security Council to Peking.[136]

Chiang became very emotional in one meeting on this subject, insisting that he would instruct Ambassador Jiang to veto any such proposal. He calculated that if the United States was determined to bring the People's Republic into the Security Council, it would do so no matter what his government did.[137] Chen Cheng then stood up and asked the Generalissimo "to calm down and be prudent." At this impertinence, Chiang became even more upset. Chen, he wrote in his journal that night, "thinks he is wiser" and a "statesman" but "his views . . . are nothing but useless comments." "They all humiliated me," he complained.[138]

On September 12, the audacity of Chen Cheng continued. Chiang heard that in one meeting Chen had called him "authoritarian and a dictator" and that for the first time with others present, he had threatened to resign. Those in the room, Chiang wrote, thought Chen "was crazy . . . but I just laugh."[139] A week later, Chen sent in yet another letter of resignation. After six months as premier, he wrote, he had made "little contribution" to either domestic or foreign affairs, and he again pleaded to be allowed to leave due to a "serious illness."[140] But Chiang rejected Chen's latest resignation just as he had the others.

V

Meanwhile, Truman had appealed successfully to George Marshall to return to government service; he was to be secretary of defense, replacing the pro-Chiang Louis Johnson. Despite their differences in the past, Chiang concluded that Marshall's appointment could benefit the Kuomintang since it signaled to the world, including the Soviet Union, that the United States was "preparing for the worst" with the Soviet bloc. Marshall, he noted, had never "smeared" him in public and the two of them had "pretty good personal communications."[141] But in America, the Republicans were taking a less sanguine view of the appointment. Some conservatives even denounced as a Communist agent the military leader who had guided America to victory in both theaters in World War II. Senator William E. Jenner called him "a front man for the traitors." This low mark in the partisan debate made it more difficult—but not impossible—for Truman and Acheson to continue holding open the possibility of a U.N. decision about Taiwan's status.

By this time, most of the North Korean Army was in the far south of the Korean Peninsula, massed around the Pusan perimeter, seemingly the last foothold of the American-led U.N. forces. Then, on September 14, MacArthur landed U.S. troops at Inchon just south of Seoul and threatened to trap the North Koreans. That day, Chiang predicted the Soviet Union would urgently press Mao to enter the war. In fact, in mid-September, Stalin cabled the Chairman asking if he could send troops to save Kim Il-sung. Mao was ready.[142]

By September 27, except for small pockets and a few snipers, Seoul was free of North Koreans. MacArthur and Syngman Rhee walked into the devastated capital and declared South Korea liberated. It had been a brutal war. In August and September, the Korean People's Army had lost 13,000 prisoners and suffered 50,000 casualties. The Communists, however, were not about to give up the fight. About 25,000 North Korean troops had escaped Seoul and marched north. And on the diplomatic front, Zhou Enlai warned publicly that China would not allow the imperialists to take "aggressive action" against its neighbor (he sent the same message to Washington through the Indian ambassador in Peking). In a meeting with Zhou at his Black Sea villa, Stalin promised that the Soviet Union would meet China's entire requirement for artillery, tanks, and other equipment if the PLA massively intervened in Korea. He added a promise to send sixteen Soviet air regiments to the PRC for use in Korea, although they would not be permitted to fly behind enemy lines.[143] From September 1950 to November 1952, the PLA Air Force would grow from about 150 to 1,400 Russian-made frontline aircraft, including 700 MIG 15s—evidence of a huge "Lend-Lease" program that could have virtually assured a successful PLA invasion of Taiwan if the aircraft had not been diverted to the Korean War effort.[144] At the end of 1950, Stalin was convinced there was imminent danger of a world war, but backing a massive intervention in Korea by China was, he thought, a gamble worth taking, especially since his British spies told him the Truman administration was determined to limit the war to Korea.[145]

In the post-Inchon euphoria, the idea of finishing off Kim Il-sung's Communists and uniting Korea seemed logical to the Truman administration and most members of the United Nations. As for the possible reaction of the Communists, MacArthur told President Truman that if the Chinese intervened, the U.S. Air Force would inflict on them "the greatest slaughter."[146]

The next night, the first regiment of "Chinese volunteers" crossed the Yalu into North Korea. By late November, despite MacArthur's bravado, the American and South Korean forces were in full retreat.

MacArthur was stunned. "We face an entirely new war," he declared. He asked permission to bomb military bases inside China and to accept Chiang Kai-shek's offer of 33,000 troops, an offer Chiang in fact had not renewed.[147] The Nationalist divisions, he said, were his command's only source of trained reinforcements that could be in action in fourteen days. With as many as 60,000 Nationalist troops, he believed, he could secure a defensive line across Korea (implying that without such support he could not hold).[148] Marshall and Acheson, however, continued to argue that using Nationalist troops in Korea or in major attacks against the mainland would cost the United States the support of critical allies, probably end the U.N. mandate that had legitimized the U.S. intervention, and very likely not contribute significantly to the war effort. The administration was determined to keep the war restricted to the Peninsula. But the Chinese "volunteers" continued to push southward, and to even Mao's surprise, in fourteen days occupied almost all of North Korea. Back in the United States there was growing alarm over the sudden reversal of fortune, and Chiang groused that "Americans never remain calm when things are not going their way."[149]

At this point, the British KGB "mole" McLean was head of the American desk at Whitehall and his fellow spy Philby was the representative in Washington of the British Secret Intelligence Service (SIS). Through the reporting of these phenomenally well-placed spies, Stalin now knew that the United States would not use nuclear weapons and hence Mao could try to push the Americans off the Korean Peninsula.[150] Interestingly, at this time, Chiang also drew the line at employing these weapons against China. It "would not help," he wrote in his journal, because "the root cause of the war is the Soviet Union."[151]

By mid-December, Communist troops, although they were taking heavy losses, were close to moving into South Korea, and the United States made clear it would accept a cease-fire at the 38th Parallel.[152] MacArthur continued to urge the use of Nationalist forces, but in a December 8 interview with CBS News, Chiang, instead of renewing his offer of troops for Korea, said that if the U.N. air and naval forces would support his government in fighting its way back to the mainland, the consequent diversion of Communist forces would mean the Korean War would be turned around in favor of the free world.[153] Chiang knew that the Americans were in no position to provide massive air and sea support for any Nationalist attack across the Strait and that his forces were hardly prepared for such a venture.

Later, Chiang would specify that before sending his troops onto the mainland, at least two years of preparation would be necessary, even if the United States promised complete air and naval support. MacArthur, too, was hesitating on a full-scale invasion. He called instead for Nationalist guerrilla raids against the China coast, claiming that such actions could "cripple" China's capability to wage an aggressive war. But conservative American politicians acted as if a grand Nationalist invasion across the Strait was a real possibility.[154] Senator Joseph McCarthy declared that Truman should be impeached if he did not accept Chiang's offer to retake the vast continental country he had lost less than two years before.[155]

In early January, as Chinese and North Korean troops stormed through Seoul and headed south, great anxiety gripped the Pentagon, the White House, and the American public. On January 10, the Joint Chiefs once more rejected MacArthur's proposal to employ Chinese Nationalist troops in his command.[156] In response, the Supreme Commander reported that given the restrictions on him he could not both hold South Korea and defend Japan, and in a stunning conclusion recommended total withdrawal from the Korean Peninsula as rapidly as tactically feasible.[157] In Peking, the Chinese were "in an exalted state of mind."[158]

Chiang told a group of KMT officials that the party could not count on a failure of the Communists in Korea to bring it success.[159] But he was most worried not about the military crisis in Korea but about a proposed cease-fire resolution in the United Nations that involved appointing an "appropriate [international] body" to discuss the status of Taiwan and China's representation in the United Nations.[160] In a hyperbolic outburst, Chiang called the proposed resolution that excluded the Republic of China from the projected meeting the "most despicable and nasty" decision by an international organization in the twentieth century, and an act portending "the doom of the world."[161]

Reflecting the rank defeatism in MacArthur's headquarters, the United States voted in favor of the U.N. cease-fire resolution, even though it would have drawn the truce line south of Seoul and represented a stunning U.S. defeat. Mao, however, wanted total victory. He immediately rejected the cease-fire and ordered his troops to continue their advance to the Korean

Strait and the Yellow Sea. On January 23, no fewer than 300,000 Chinese and North Korean troops launched a final offensive to drive the Americans and their U.N. allies into the sea. When MacArthur again warned Washington that his position on the Peninsula was completely untenable, Acheson concluded the general was exaggerating in order to win approval to extend the war into China and employ Nationalist forces.[162]

But despite skepticism in Washington about MacArthur's take on the situation, the U.S. Joint Chiefs ordered him to begin planning for a retreat from the Korean Peninsula. Chiang, too, told his generals that a total American defeat in Korea was now possible and they should expect a PLA attack on Taiwan in May and bombing raids as early as March.[163] To steady his generals, he remained impressively calm. But within a few days, Chiang's intelligence informed him of an encouraging report by senior American generals returning to Washington from an urgent inspection visit to Korea. The team, put together by Marshall, reported that the American troops on the front lines in Korea could in fact hold their positions and had no plans to retreat. Morale was said to be good.[164]

Chiang welcomed this report even as he gave orders to "plan for the worst." But the battle in Korea did in fact turn against the Chinese. The American forces met the new Communist offensive with hundreds of thousands of bombs and artillery shells, and only two days after it began, the attack ground to a halt and the Eighth Army and the U.S. Marines began to push back. Because China had rejected the U.N. cease-fire, the United States also proposed a resolution condemning the PRC as an aggressor. This was, of course, highly welcome news to Chiang, but he was furious when the United States also suggested that the General Assembly set up a mediation committee to continue to work with Peking on a solution to the war.[165]

Relief came the next day, however, when Chiang learned that the U.S. representative at the United Nations, Ernest Gross, had declared that the U.S. government would not discuss Taiwan in any future international conference without the presence of the Republic of China. When the U.S. Senate followed up by passing a resolution that strongly opposed the PRC's entry into the United Nations, Chiang thanked God for this "blessing on the Republic of China." Congress, he believed, had foiled the State Department's "conspiracy," and Mao had played a key role by rejecting the earlier cease-fire proposal. The next consequence of Mao's decision was passage by the U.N. General Assembly of the U.S.-proposed resolution condemning the People's Republic as an aggressor. All this seemed to be another act of providence.

"God has rewarded the Republic of China as a Christian country," he wrote, obviously referring to Taiwan's leadership. But Chiang also knew that the Truman team was keeping its options open—eight months into the war, the United States was still not providing any real military aid to Taiwan.[166]

On April 5, the Republican House leader, Joseph Martin, read a letter on the House floor from General MacArthur supporting the congressman's proposal to open a second front in China with Nationalist troops. Outraged at the general's repeated public intrusions into policymaking, Truman relieved MacArthur of his various commands. Upon hearing the news, Chiang declared that the move confirmed the "pathetic foolishness of the U.S. Government" and represented yet another step in the conspiracy of Acheson, Marshall, and the British to destroy his government. He ordered Zhang Qun to fly to Tokyo and express his deep sympathy to the ousted general.

In late April, Allied forces repulsed another PLA attack, inflicting heavy casualties and then pushing farther north. The new commander in Korea, General James A. Van Fleet, urged Washington to order the U.N. forces to pursue the enemy back to the Yalu, but to retain the support of the United Nations and its allies, the administration decided to work for a cease-fire and a truce at the 38th Parallel.[167] Washington made clear to Moscow that the cease-fire talks would not include the status of Taiwan or Chinese representation in the United Nations. Chiang welcomed this statement as "the first U.S. declaration of support for the Republic of China in the previous three years."[168] By mid-June 1951, Mao and the CCP Politburo had decided to accept a cease-fire that would restore the border at the then current line of control, which was slightly north of the 38th Parallel, and that the armistice talks need not address the status of Taiwan or the U.N. issues. On-again, off-again peace talks began in July, but the cease-fire was hardly that—rather, that month the war turned into a long and costly stalemate fought pretty much along the line of control.

Despite the political gains for the Nationalist regime, Chiang continued to fixate on the "conspiracy" by Washington and London to neutralize Taiwan and develop a Chinese or Taiwanese Third Force to replace him and his Kuomintang regime.[169] He immediately saw signs of this plot in the Washington-promoted decision that neither Taipei nor Peking would be invited to participate in the upcoming negotiations on a peace treaty with Japan. Since Chiang's regime controlled less than a hundredth of China's territory and Peking was in disrepute in the United Nations, this was a rational solution to the problem of which government would represent China—neither would. But Nationalist China led by the Generalissimo had fought Japan for eight years and lost three million citizens and soldiers in the struggle, and Chiang was overcome by deep shame and rage at the slight. He could not believe that Truman and Acheson were so "rotten and stupid" as to exclude their wartime ally from the peace conference.[170] He again found refuge in hyperbolic rhetoric: he described Nationalist China's omission from the conference as "an unprecedented and incomparably great insult" that had never happened before "in history at all times and in all countries."[171] He even insisted to his staff that he wanted to break off relations with the United States, but they talked him out of it.[172] When Governor Dewey, on a trip through Asia, discussed the subject with him, he "blew up." He and Madame "were the most furious people Dewey had met in the orient."[173]

The peace conference was held in San Francisco in September 1951. In the final wording of the resulting treaty, Japan renounced its rights to Taiwan, but otherwise the document did not refer to the status of the island: Taiwan was not "returned to China" as promised at Yalta and Cairo. The United States did, however, urge Japan to negotiate a separate peace treaty with the Republic of China. This suggestion did not mollify Chiang because he suspected that Washington and Tokyo were not serious. He thought the Truman government might be keeping open the question of Taiwan's status as "bait for a [permanent] truce in the Korean War."[174]

Washington's policy did in fact seem intended both to avoid further complicating the possibility of an acceptable peace in Korea and to keep open the possibility of a future rapprochement with China. The administration finally approved an immediate grant of $50 million for military aid to Taiwan and an additional budget of $237 million in such assistance for the 1951 fiscal year. In July, however, Chiang learned that delivery of all the promised U.S. weapons and supplies would be delayed until the next year because Korea and Western Europe were to receive priority.[175] Further discouraging news came when Chiang's old teacher, Hollington Tong, returned from a visit to America to report that Taiwan could not trust the U.S. promise of military assistance. Marshall's "personal feelings toward us might have improved," Chiang wrote, but his "policy to eliminate the Republic of China and abandon Asia has never changed."[176] Washington, he believed, was simply holding open the promise of aid as a way of "threatening or luring us into a state of collapse." The intentions of the Americans, he said, were "extremely vicious and despicable."[177]

When Washington began negotiating security treaties with Japan, the Philippines, New Zealand, and Australia, but not with the Republic of China, for Chiang it was "like waking from a bad dream," causing him to change his "views of forty years about the United States." His agitation with America now led to another bout of virtual paranoia. Marshall and Acheson, he wrote, "want to . . . eradicate us completely. So that [they] can invade new colonies to fulfill their crazy ambition to control the yellow race."[178]

Chiang's obsessive mistrust of the American agenda was further fueled when the new U.S. Military Assistance and Advisory Group (MAAG) arrived on the island and its commander, General William C. Chase, early on complained of a number of practices. Chase criticized the "Soviet-style" commissars in the Nationalist military and he was flabbergasted at the presence of Japanese advisers called "drill masters," among them General Okamura, one of the succession of Japanese commanders in China who had implemented the "kill all" liquidation campaigns.[179] In all, seventy-six former Imperial officers eventually wound up in Taiwan, some staying until 1969.[180]

Chase also strongly recommended that the Nationalists incorporate their troops on the offshore islands into units on Taiwan—in other words withdraw them—and reorganize and consolidate the still undermanned divisions in the army as a whole. To Chiang, these criticisms and suggestions were further evidence that the Pentagon, under George Marshall, was seeking to break up the Nationalist military and "liquidate" him and his administration. Likewise, he initially saw proposals by Chase and the U.S. Agency for International Development (USAID) director that American officials audit the accounts of the Nationalist military and government as "a naïve" plot to control the finances of his regime.[181]

With few exceptions, however, Chiang continued to limit his tirades on the evil forces at work in Washington to his private journals and, on rare occasions, closed in-house meetings. In the end, despite his blustering, he was pragmatic. He pulled the Japanese "drill masters" out of any training and lecturing duties that might put them in contact with the Americans, and he reversed himself on resisting American auditing of Taiwan's military and government spending, deciding after all that it would be good for the "verification of accounts." Finally, he agreed to reduce the Nationalist Army's 67 divisions to 31 and eventually to 21. He absolutely refused, however, to withdraw from the offshore islands or to eliminate the commissar corps, although he did agree to reduce the amount of time that military units devoted to political instruction. He believed American pressure to eliminate the commissars was related to their supposed desire to turn over the Nationalist military—and indeed the government—to Sun Liren.[182]

Chiang also eventually showed his basic pragmatism regarding the peace treaty with Japan. For some months he feared that Prime Minister Yoshida was trying to arrange something less than a separate peace accord with Taipei in order to keep open the door to future recognition of Peking—and Yoshida in fact probably was thinking along these lines. Despite his deep admiration of many aspects of Japanese culture, at one point Chiang wrote that the Japanese people of the day were "worse than the cunning prewar warlords," and he ranted in his diary about the return of Japanese "imperial ambition." But he also wrote that his government's future depended on cooperation among "Japan, Free China, and the United States." So in the end, he relinquished the right to compensation from Japan for war damages and made other compromises necessary for an agreement.[183]

11

Managing the Protector

While each side had considerable misgivings about the other, collaboration between the Americans and the Nationalists continued to increase steadily during the early 1950s. In Korea, Nationalist officers translated intercepted Communist Chinese battlefield communications, prepared psychological warfare leaflets, and assisted in the handling of 21,000 Chinese POWs, encouraging (and when necessary, severely pressuring) as many as possible to defect. The CIA bought Claire Chennault's Civil Air Transport (CAT) and ran 15,000 CAT flights to Korea from Taiwan, transporting and supporting Nationalist interpreters, intelligence liaison personnel, and "instructors" for the captured Chinese "volunteers."[1]

Over the longer term, however, Taiwan's most important area of cooperation with the United States would be its role in collecting intelligence on the mainland. When the Korean War started, the United States had essentially no worthwhile intelligence sources inside China. The Nationalists claimed to have many agents still operating on the mainland and unlimited potential for gaining others. Spies moving into and out of China from the offshore islands, particularly the smaller Tachens, became the most common way of getting low-level information on what was happening on the mainland. But as the Communists instigated strict population control and surveillance methods, even these agents did not survive long.

Interviews with former military, intelligence, and Foreign Service officers who served on Taiwan during the 1950s and 1960s suggest that most American officials dismissed as essentially useless the agent-based intelligence on the People's Republic produced by the Taipei government. In his memoirs, James Lilley, a distinguished CIA officer with a China background, reported that in the late 1960s, the CIA in Hong Kong learned that Peking had compromised "all" of Taiwan's intelligence operations against the mainland.[2] To many on the scene, it appeared that the huge intelligence bureaucracies on the island considered unreliable or even bad intelligence as better than no intelligence, and the effort continued.

The most useful information came from the nonclandestine Foreign Broadcast Information Service translations of mainland China radio stations, the secret interception by the National Security Agency (NSA) of China's military and civilian radio and telephone communications, airborne probes of China's coastal air defenses, and eventually flights by U2 spy planes. But neither the CIA nor Nationalist intelligence ever penetrated anywhere close to the inner sanctum of the Chinese Communist leadership even at the provincial level.

Like their ineffective attempts at agent infiltration, Nationalist harassment attacks accomplished nothing. After the Chinese intervention in Korea, Truman secretly instructed the Seventh Fleet not to interfere with small-scale Nationalist operations against the mainland and against PRC shipping. These paramilitary activities involved quick in-and-out raids to blow up a bridge, obtain local documents, or kidnap a local Communist cadre. They did insignificant damage to China's economy and military preparedness and provided no important information. But as long as the bloody war with the Chinese went on in Korea, these efforts in a very minor way punished and slightly distracted a country that the United Nations had deemed an aggressor.

The only sizable offensive operations that the Nationalists ever carried out against mainland China were undertaken by General Li Mi, whose 50,000 men had fled into Burma in 1949 and settled down in the remote Shan Hills, married local women, and taken over heroin drug trafficking from local gangs. Li Mi retained his connections with Taipei and the U.S. Office of Policy Coordination (OPC), successor to the OSS. In 1951, he carried out two Burma-based attacks into Yunnan with 2,000 men, some Nationalist Special Forces from Taiwan, and several American OPC agents. The PLA quickly scattered the invaders, who fled back to Burma, where, known as the "KMT irregulars," they resumed their control and protection of the region's heroin traffic.[3] For Chiang, even in failure the Burma operation had its good results—strengthening the hostility between the United States and the People's Republic as well as collegial bonds between Nationalist and U.S. agencies. For Truman, too, the Burma operation was a safe way to show that, as the Republicans were demanding, he was using Chiang's troops somewhere to harass the China beast. But the unfavorable mission did lead to a change in U.S. intelligence operations. The CIA director, Walter Bedell Smith, had opposed the operations as a certain debacle whereas OPC had heartily approved; the failure led to the incorporation of OPC into the CIA.

Aside from the Burma fiasco, the most important military activity that Chiang's forces ever engaged in after 1949 was interdiction of China's coastal traffic off Zhejiang and Fujian. This maritime activity, operating from the offshore islands, reached a peak in the first half of 1951 with the PLA Navy reporting 137 incidents of Nationalist "piracy." Nationalist warships and planes also interdicted sixty-seven foreign vessels trading with China, half of which were British freighters coming out of Hong Kong. For a few years, Chiang's effort to impose a blockade of two coastal provinces created some transport bottlenecks on the mainland and interrupted fishing off the East China coast.[4]

As the American presence on Taiwan grew, Soong Mayling remained her husband's principal counsel on American matters, a role she had filled since her return to the island in 1950. She was also Chiang's senior liaison with the chief of the growing CIA station and the director of the Taiwan branch of the NSA. The staffs of the CIA and NSA Taiwan bureaus soon ballooned to a total of more than six hundred Americans. One day, Kai-shek and Mayling discussed how they felt about the cloak-and-dagger Americans and found them "not easy to get along with"; they seemed "impatient and likely to show off." "We should be careful and endure them," they concluded.[5]

The couple seemed closer than ever, continuing to sleep in the same room with their beds divided by a screen, praying together, and strolling the gardens of their various residences hand in hand.[6] Part of the first couple's closeness was the ever growing importance of Christianity in their lives. Mayling had always been devout but never particularly pious. Then one day, upon rereading the story of the crucifixion, she realized for the first time that "Christ's suffering was for her." After this born-again experience, she was "not only intellectually but personally attached to God." Her health problems, however, which included neurodermatitis, insomnia, and periodic nervous breakdowns, were returning.[7] She sought solace not only in her religion but also in painting in the Chinese style. Chiang observed that she was "painting day and night," with her subjects mostly bamboo and orchids.[8] "Of all the things God gave her," a nephew said, "she was most pleased by her new found ability to paint."[9]

When she was away, Chiang missed her even more than in the past. In August 1952, she flew to San Francisco on a commercial Pan Am flight for medical treatment, and he sent her a telegram every few days, more often than on any of her previous trips. "I think about you all the time," he said in one; and in another, "I sense the feeling of melancholy in your letter. Please be patient and follow doctors' instructions. I hope you pray often."[10]

Joint U.S.-Nationalist intelligence and military operations, expanding U.S. military training on the island, growing economic aid, and other U.S.-Taiwan ties were locking the Truman administration into political and diplomatic support for Chiang's government. Chiang, however, still perceived most Taiwan-related actions by the Truman government as part of a plot to get rid of him. Thus when the U.S. Congress passed the $300 million Taiwan military aid bill, he felt there was "nothing to feel fortunate about."[11] Even the arrival in early 1952 of the first U.S. heavy weapons—one hundred and forty-two 75mm cannon—did little to change Chiang's views of the Truman team. He hoped that Eisenhower would win the U.S. presidency, and to help, he instructed Ching-kuo's secret police to turn over to supporters of Joseph McCarthy raw and some apparently forged material from old Chinese security files on those anti-Chiang State Department officials serving in China during World War II and immediately after, such as John Service and John P. Davies.[12] The Communist threat was a central theme in the brutal American political campaign, during which Eisenhower declared that he would repudiate the Yalta agreements, roll back the Iron Curtain, end the war in Korea, and "unleash" the Generalissimo against "Red China."

During the Truman period, Chiang did not press on the Americans his increasingly high-decibel domestic theme of promising an early "counterattack" to recover the mainland. In July 1952, he finally showed his mainland invasion blueprints to the visiting U.S. Chief of Naval Operations, Admiral William N. Fechteler, who, after examination back in Washington, declared them "totally impractical."[13] But Chiang continued talking up the "counterattack" for military and mainlander civilian morale as well as because it was central to his rationale for ruling over the island. He thought "recovery of the mainland"—one way or the other—was destined some day, but he did not

expect the "counterattack" in his lifetime. "Realistically," he wrote, "the restoration of our country is almost impossible in the [foreseeable] future. My
confidence in the revolution and restoration of our country, however, has
never swayed . . . From now on every plan must be designed for the success of
my successors, not for my own success." He carefully kept this realistic appraisal from the Americans as well as his own people.[14] Likewise, in his mind,
the military debacles in Korea and the continuing long-grinding stalemate
there confirmed that he had been right in avoiding sending troops by attach-
ing conditions that always made such a deployment appear a long-term possibility at best. When in 1952 Admiral Arthur W. Radford, the new commander of the Pacific Fleet, asked him if 50,000 Nationalist troops would be
available, Chiang said he could only agree to one division or about 10,000
troops. The subject was never pursued.[15]

After Eisenhower won the November election, Mayling, who had moved to
the Kung's Long Island estate, wrote the President-elect, "As you may well
imagine, we are indeed delighted."[16] Chiang, however, cautioned her not to
overdo the embrace and raise suspicions. In his diary he concluded that if
Eisenhower actually carried out the confrontational policies in Europe, Korea, and elsewhere that he had promised during the campaign and the Soviets
had resisted, Moscow's "only option would be war."[17]

Shortly before Eisenhower gave his State of the Union message to Congress, Chargé Rankin informed Chiang that the President would order the
Seventh Fleet to continue to defend Taiwan from any mainland attacks but
lift its orders to prevent Nationalist attacks on mainland China. Rankin, obviously under instructions, then asked Chiang for a commitment that he
would not initiate action by his armed forces against the mainland without
consultations with the United States.[18] Eisenhower had "unleashed" Chiang
only secretly to chain him up again, but the restriction did not bother Chiang
as long as it was not public. He regretted that Eisenhower had not discussed
the matter with him ahead of time, but still he felt "the policy is correct and I
should praise him."[19] Following his bouts of paranoia over the intentions of
the Truman team, he now enjoyed one of his seizures of euphoria. Eisenhower, he wrote, had shifted the leadership of "the anti-Communist forces in
Asia from Japan and India to the Republic of China."[20] Chiang's jubilation
about the new administration, however, was not to last.

   To the surprise and chagrin of hawkish Republicans, the President reduced

America's military budget, opted to continue Truman's policy of "containment not liberation," and left standing the geopolitical priority of Europe first, Asia second—a longstanding grievance of Chiang Kai-shek.[21] To offset a planned reduction of U.S. conventional forces, the United States would now rely on "massive retaliation," meaning nuclear weapons. The strategy of nuclear retaliation against conventional threats profoundly raised the risk and the cost of a possible U.S. conflict with China, which ironically increased the incentive for U.S. détente with the Peking government. Chiang was not happy about any of these developments, but he made little comment on the subject.

With Eisenhower's obvious full approval, the new Secretary of State, John Foster Dulles, pursued a dual Taiwan strategy similar to that of the Truman and Acheson team. His first cluster of priorities was defense of Taiwan, promotion of the island as a free market (Chinese style), and employment of Taiwan as an intelligence platform and special operations base for pressuring and harassing the mainland. But the second broad strategic goal was to keep open the possibility of eventual U.S. reconciliation with mainland China by bringing about a mutual end to hostilities across the Taiwan Strait and then promoting some sort of two-Chinas or one-China, one-Taiwan arrangement.[22]

During his State of the Union message, Eisenhower had also hinted that, if necessary, the United States would use all the weapons available to it to end the war in Korea. The President's intentions were to let the Communist Chinese know that unless there was an armistice soon he would move "decisively without inhibition in our use of weapons" and would no longer confine hostilities to the Korean Peninsula.[23] Eisenhower followed up his State of the Union remarks with a secret message to Peking implying—but not saying explicitly—that if the fighting did not stop in Korea he would authorize the use of nuclear weapons.[24] Years later, Ike told President Lyndon Johnson that he had passed this warning to China through two private channels—Prime Minister Nehru of India and Chiang Kai-shek.[25] The Generalissimo was delighted to be entrusted with conveying such a message. He probably instructed Ching-kuo to deliver the note through secure channels to their old friend Zhou Enlai, and very likely Ching-kuo used a secret intermediary with the CCP who lived in Hong Kong, an independent journalist named Cao Juren.[26] Mao's immediate reaction to the U.S. message was to dispatch his top nuclear scientist, Qian Sanqiang, to ask Stalin to provide nuclear weapons to the People's Republic as a deterrent.[27]

On the night of February 28, 1953, Stalin told his inner circle that he had decided to advise the North Koreans and the Chinese "to get the best deal they could" in the talks. It seems that he ignored Mao's request for nuclear weapons. Five days later, Stalin died, supposedly of a cerebral hemorrhage. The next evening, Zhou Enlai was in Moscow conferring with Georgi Malenkov, Nikita Khrushchev, and the soon-to-be-executed chief of the secret police, Lavrenty Beria. The new Soviet leaders told Zhou it was time to end the war. The prisoner-of-war issue was the one remaining obstacle to an agreement, and Zhou and the Russians quickly decided the Communists would offer to let neutral independent countries determine the wishes of the POWs on both sides—the very same compromise the United States and United Nations had proposed more than a year earlier.[28]

Press reports began to indicate that Eisenhower would settle for the peace terms set out by Truman—Korea would be divided. This was a possible model for a two-Chinas solution of the Taiwan conundrum, which, of course, was anathema to Chiang Kai-shek. He asked Rankin to inquire how the American government would face "the ghosts of the American and Korean soldiers who had died in the war."[29] Dulles, Chiang now wrote, was "a purely opportunistic politician," and Eisenhower's policy toward the Republic of China was "the same as in the past"—replace Chiang Kai-shek and seek to turn Mao into another Tito.[30] By May, he had come to believe that Eisenhower did not have "common sense" and that the British simply ordered the President around as they had other Anglophile American leaders.[31]

On May 25, an agreement in principle emerged on a POW exchange and a permanent cease-fire. Three weeks later, Syngman Rhee, the President of South Korea who had bitterly fought the idea of partition, allowed more than 27,000 anti-Communist North Korean prisoners to "escape" and threatened to withdraw the South Korean Army from the U.N. Command. In response, Communist forces immediately attacked South Korean frontline units, and the peace accord seemed to be coming apart. On June 22, when Chiang received a message from Rhee describing how "the U.S. had betrayed Korea," he couldn't help "trembling and being frightened." Obviously referring to the United States, he wrote in his journal that "imperialism and power politics are birds of a feather." He had to try to help Rhee "save himself from a dangerous situation," but he was "more worried" about what these developments meant for himself.[32]

Chiang sent two telegrams to Eisenhower urging the United States to sign a mutual security treaty with the Republic of Korea (South Korea) before the Korean cease-fire accord went into effect.[33] But he also sent a sympathetic reply to Rhee along the lines of his journal comments. Washington evidently intercepted and decoded this communication, which it interpreted as encouraging Rhee in his stand. Outraged, Dulles sent a scathing message warning Chiang that if Rhee did not cooperate, U.S. troops would pull out of Korea—and moreover, if this happened, the United States would also "reconsider its policy toward Taiwan."[34] This was a startling threat. Chiang thought he had been trying to resolve the dispute, but Dulles and Eisenhower now "threatened" him.[35] Chiang prayed for Rhee "day and night," but Eisenhower sent an ominous message to the South Korean warning that unless he "immediately and unequivocally" cooperated with the peace process, the U.N. Command "would affect another arrangement."[36] The next day, Chiang cabled Rhee advising him that if he received an absolute guarantee of a U.S. security treaty following the formal cease-fire and if the United States did not ask for the return of the Korean POWs to their camps, Rhee should accept the cease-fire plan.[37]

Rhee followed this advice except he also managed to squeeze a promise out of the Americans that if he cooperated, the United States would provide South Korea a substantial increase in military and economic aid. Moreover, although the armistice went into effect on August 25, Rhee never officially signed it—a gesture that Chiang admired. He thought Rhee was a true revolutionary who "understands the U.S. the most clearly."[38]

It was evident that in an extreme situation, Eisenhower would not hesitate to cut off an important but dependent anti-Communist ally. The lesson for Chiang was obvious. Still, like Rhee, he believed it was necessary to make a show of independence, and on July 16, in the middle of the Rhee crisis, without consultation with the United States, he authorized a landing of Nationalist troops on PRC-held Dongshan, a relatively large island located between Quemoy and the mainland port of Swatow and inhabited by about 750,000 people. Chiang's intention may have been to add Dongshan to the Nationalist-held list of islands, or more likely simply to show a flash of independence just after his essential ally, the United States, had threatened to desert him. Whatever the motive, the effort was unsuccessful: the PLA soon counterattacked and drove off the Nationalist force.[39]

I

Mao could claim victory in the Korean War in the sense that his PLA forces had pushed the U.S.-led coalition out of North Korea and fought it to a standstill near the 38th Parallel. But the Communists had failed in their goal of seizing South Korea, and Mao had lost face on the POW settlement, and on having been driven out of South Korea. Moreover, Nationalist Taiwan and Chiang Kai-shek now appeared secure for the indefinite future. For the Soviet Union the Korean War was costly financially but from Moscow's perspective worth every kopeck. China was now even more bitterly estranged from America and dependent on the USSR.

Some Nationalist officials worried that the Korean settlement amounted to the collapse of the anti-Communist front, but Chiang "felt contented." With the ambivalent outcome of the Korean War, he believed circumstances made Eisenhower now "definitely" committed to the defense of Taiwan (even to building up its armed forces beyond that required solely for self-defense), as well as to making Taiwan an economic success. In addition, for the foreseeable future, the possibility had passed that Peking would receive the U.N. Security Council seat, and the defection to Taiwan of 14,000 of the 21,000 PLA soldiers captured by the U.N. Command was a huge political and moral triumph.[40]

Eisenhower's views were not so benign as Chiang thought. After the end of hostilities in Korea, Eisenhower believed that ideally the United States should reexamine its China policy, including the question of Chinese representation in the United Nations.[41] He doubted that "a strict embargo" of China made sense, and at one point even told the National Security Council that he would sell jet fighters to Mao Zedong if doing so would promote U.S. interests. But the President, along with Dulles and other senior advisers, also agreed that they "were stuck with Chiang Kai-shek."[42] This jaundiced view of the Generalissimo was not much different from that of Truman and Acheson. In a conversation with Rhee in November that in some ways epitomized the bizarre situation, Chiang suggested, apparently in jest, that if the Americans asked about their military discussions they could simply say they had agreed to counterattack at the same time. Rhee agreed.[43]

Despite the much stronger political position of the Chiangs at home and abroad, they still feared that once the Generalissimo was gone, Chen Cheng and Sun Liren would cooperate to deny Ching-kuo his legacy. Even so, Chiang promoted Sun to full general in May 1953 and the next year actually

In a moral victory for Chiang, 14,000 Chinese POWs from the Korean War who chose to go to Taiwan rather than return home march in celebration after their arrival in Taipei. Courtesy Central News Agency, Taipei.

reappointed him commander of the army—a remarkable development for an officer who allegedly had harbored Communist agents.[44] For his part, Chen Cheng remained premier and in various meetings continued to challenge Chiang, who would further disparage him in his journal but nonetheless in the coming year choose him as his Vice President and formal successor. Although these two appointments may seem odd given Chiang's misgivings about the two leaders, they were in fact impressively calculating moves that applied Sun Tzu's theory of how to deal with a popular internal enemy.

Meanwhile, Chiang's chief of staff, General Zhou Zhirou, was feuding with the Generalissimo's brother-in-law, Mao Bangzhu—sibling of Mao

Fumei. The Soviet-trained Mao Bangzhu had been appointed deputy chief of the air force in 1937 and since 1943 had been head of the (Chinese) Air Force Procurement Office in Washington. In March 1951, Mao accused Zhou of skimming off money from purchases of aviation fuel from the United States.[45] Chiang investigated and found that, despite the recent financial reforms in the military, the funds in question had in fact been deposited in Zhou's personal account in Hong Kong and that many other aspects of air force accounting involved "corrupt practices and illegality." But in key cases Chiang continued to give loyalty priority over prosecuting corruption; in this case, he decided that in order to "protect Zhirou's [and the air force's] reputation," he had to give him "immunity from legal action . . . and help him come to his senses and improve."[46] Mao Bangzhu, for his part, was also skimming off huge amounts of government funds: U.S. courts eventually awarded the Taipei government US$6 million in a judgment against him and his Swiss bank accounts. By then, Mao had fled New York and was arrested in Mexico along with his American secretary. He spent two years in jail, but was released in 1954 because the Mexican court found the charges to be "political."[47]

Although the dream of a return to the mainland and adherence to the principle that Taiwan was a part of China rationalized the control of Taiwan by the KMT, the regime existed primarily because it functioned as a police state. During the early 1950s, the threat from native Taiwanese nationalists remained insignificant, but the "white terror" continued. In the 1990s, the Ministry of Justice informed opposition legislators that the security files for that period had long since been burned, but there is an official number for all arrests under martial law from 1949 to 1986, when the decree ended —29,407. (If the same proportion of the U.S. population had been arrested during that time frame, there would have been about 615,000 detentions.)[48]

Ching-kuo's medley of counterintelligence operations continued to convict more than six hundred persons a year as spies or subversives, and when Ching-kuo visited Washington in 1953, Dulles gently suggested that he improve human rights in his country. Security arrests and convictions in Taiwan went up the next year, but finally declined in 1955.[49] Governor K. C. Wu, according to his own testimony, was among the few officials who dared criticize the political terror of the time. In January 1952, Wu later wrote, he went to the President to complain about "outrages of the secret police" and warned that if Ching-kuo continued to head the secret police he would "become the target of the peoples' hatred."[50] In his journal at that time, Chiang did not mention these dramatic charges but wrote that Wu's "threatening misbehavior is excessive . . . My worst fear is that he might be out of his mind."[51]

More than a year later, the Wu affair finally came to a head. In March 1953, Wu had sought to resign because of illness, but while Chiang told him to wait another month, in his diary Chiang claimed that Wu had been "dishonest," and speculated again that Wu was having mental problems.[52] In April, Chiang agreed to accept Wu's resignation but the next day recorded that Wu had sent a letter repenting his mistakes. According to Wu, however, Chiang made threatening statements to him and, shortly after, an automobile accident convinced Wu that there had been an attempt on his life.[53] Mayling, meanwhile, flew home from New York to intercede on Wu's behalf, and the next month, Wu and his wife received their passports and left for the United States. In articles and speeches the following year, Wu publicly broke with Chiang, charging that Ching-kuo's secret police engaged in torture and blackmail.[54] The controlled press on Taiwan claimed that Wu had fled the island because of pending corruption charges, but few believed this, especially in the United States. Later that year Chiang authorized Wu's sixteen-year-old son to leave Taiwan and join his parents. Wu's charges against the secret police activity in general were well founded, but whether his life was in danger or the charges against him had any validity is unknown. In any event the whole affair greatly distressed Soong Mayling. Mrs. Rankin visited her and found her very depressed and implying that Wu's case had contributed to her condition.[55] Soon after, Chiang persuaded her to return to the United States for more treatment. She left Taipei again and on April 29, 1954, checked into the familiar Franklin Hospital in San Francisco, reportedly suffering from allergies. Chiang wrote that one day without seeing her felt like a three-year separation.[56]

Five months after the Korean Armistice, a National Security Council policy paper approved by Eisenhower stated that the United States would, without directly involving U.S. forces, "encourage and assist the Chinese National Government . . . to raid Chinese Communist territory and commerce." The United States prohibited Nationalist attacks on ships in mainland ports and obvious nonmilitary targets such as passenger ferries, but in effect it sanctioned the continued stopping and searching by the Nationalist Navy of foreign shipping in the Taiwan Strait and the seizure of any "strategic materials" bound for China. American encouragement of such action well after the end of U.S.-Chinese hostilities in the Korean conflict and its continued defense of Taiwan by the Seventh Fleet amounted to U.S. support of the Nationalists in the mostly dormant but still festering Chinese civil war. The U.S. Military Assistance and Advisory Group came close to direct involvement, for the first time assigning its officers to the offshore islands where, together with CIA officers, they planned minor attacks and harassment against Chinese Communist elements.[57]

Chiang was pleased with this hostile U.S. policy toward the mainland, but he was cautious in terms of actual actions he permitted. His strong supporter, Karl Rankin, warned Washington that the joint raids simply amounted to "tickling the Communist tiger with a feather duster" and if China should attack the islands from which the raids were launched, world opinion might think such an attack was justified.[58] According to U.S. officers who served on the Tachens, the Nationalist covert activity essentially meant encouraging the pirates who had long lurked in the area.[59] General Chase called the officer who coordinated these activities his "Vice President in Charge of Pirates."[60] Motorized junks armed by the Americans would hijack Chinese fishing junks and other small vessels along the China coast, bring home seized food shipments, and sell durable items in Hong Kong. Sometimes the Nationalist raiders would provide a propaganda lecture to the captured fishermen before turning them loose.[61] The American marines on the islands were frustrated with the refusal of the Nationalists to organize more serious operations against the mainland and Chinese shipping. The Americans believed the Nationalists feared that if they "really hurt the Chicoms," the PLA would chase them off the Tachens, which were vulnerable to attack.[62]

As during the Truman period, for both Chiang and Eisenhower the special operations in the Taiwan Strait demonstrated to their domestic supporters that they were doing something to hurt the Communist Chinese. Eisenhower and Dulles also thought it placated Chiang in his fixation on "the counterattack." For Chiang, it again increased hostility between the United States and China, fostered the growth of important pro-Chiang components in the CIA and the U.S. military, and brought a flow of money and equipment into Ching-kuo's special operations. Finally, various agency and personal agendas were advanced by the millions of U.S. dollars made available for this covert activity. As a former CIA officer recalled, the covert relationship became "a cornucopia of money, arms, equipment, and training for the Nationalists."[63]

Given his "unleashing," it seemed beholden on Chiang to present officially to the new U.S. administration a plan for a full-scale counterattack. In June 1953, through the good offices of Ambassador Rankin, he made his first proposal to Washington for a history-shaking invasion of the mainland. Of course, Chiang knew that Eisenhower would not entertain a large-scale war against China on the eve of ending the long and costly "limited" engagement in Korea. Thus the grand attack he proposed would come only after three to six years of preparation, during which time the Americans would arm and train an additional sixty Nationalist divisions. The ultimate goal was a Normandy-like invasion of the mainland by 600,000 Nationalist troops. At first Chiang suggested that only U.S. logistical support would be necessary, but later he sometimes included U.S. air cover and naval transport as well—a substantial difference.[64] Repeatedly, he sounded his basic theme: the Far East would not be stable or peaceful until the root of conflict in the area—Communist China—was removed.[65] As recounted earlier, in private he believed that any such attack would not come in his lifetime.

In September, Chiang Ching-kuo made his first trip to the United States, touring various parts of the country, and in the capital meeting with the President, the Secretary of State, the director of the CIA, and others. Long considered in Washington to be the heir apparent to his father but a shadowy figure, he made a good impression. He did not raise the subject of the counterattack or press for aid, but called for closer relations and cooperation.

Soon after Ching-kuo returned home from his Washington trip, Vice President and Mrs. Richard Nixon visited Taipei and were also house guests of the Chiangs. The Generalissimo and the Vice President talked for seven hours, sometimes alone except for an interpreter. In his memoirs, Nixon tells us he believed the counterattack plans as outlined by his host were "totally unrealistic," but he felt he "could not tell Chiang outright that his chances of reuniting China under his rule were virtually non-existent." Instead, Nixon reported, he "made it clear that American military power would not be committed to support any invasion [Chiang] might launch."[66] This polite but

Chiang toasting his distinguished visitor, Vice President Richard M. Nixon, in October 1953. In the early 1970s Chiang would come privately to despise the American leader. Courtesy KMT Party History Institute.

supposedly categorical refusal of American participation was the most explicit rejection to date by the Eisenhower administration of any U.S. direct participation in the "counterattack." There is no record in Chiang's diary that Nixon's comment surprised or upset him, since his concern continued to be that the Americans not make such statements in public. Meanwhile, Chiang in his public speeches promised that the restoration of "freedom and light" to the mainland would come in the not distant future.[67]

As the KMT irregulars in Burma stepped up their incursions into China, the Burmese government publicly demanded that the United States do something to end the aggression. Early in 1953, Dulles pressed Chiang to withdraw Li Mi's forces, but, in his usual fashion, Chiang reacted to this "interference" by ordering an acceleration of aid to the "irregulars."[68] Eisenhower had pressed Ching-kuo on the issue when Ching-kuo was in Washington, and Dulles followed up with heated messages to the Generalissimo on the subject, but still Chiang did nothing. Finally, in December 1953, the U.N. General Assembly condemned Taipei for its activities in Burma, and following more strong pressure from Dulles, Chiang at last ordered military planes to bring out more than 5,000 KMT soldiers and dependents. Many of those who arrived in Taiwan, however, were reportedly hill people, not ethnic Chinese. Chiang and the CIA in fact kept most of the KMT fighters in Burma as a guerrilla force that was at least marginally cohesive and, they thought, potentially useful in the looming struggle to keep Indochina out of the hands of the Communists.[69]

During the Eisenhower years, Chiang would warn the Americans many times that abandonment of the offshore islands would lead to disintegration of the established order on Taiwan. But he himself did not really believe that doomsday forecast, as demonstrated by his own two "urgent" orders back in July 1950 to withdraw from Quemoy and Matsu. Eisenhower, Nixon, and others in the senior American leadership believed the Generalissimo's much vaunted "counterattack" was fantasy. But the inexplicable idea did spread in the White House and elsewhere in the administration that if the United States declined to help defend the tiny islands or tried to compel Chiang Kai-shek to abandon them, morale on Taiwan would quickly collapse and Chiang would be overthrown by his generals—or worse, he might even defect to Mao Zedong.[70]

It is safe to say, however, that it never seriously occurred to Chiang to abandon his secure life and position of power on Taiwan as well as his fundamental political and religious beliefs to live under a Communist regime. Chiang had already received more than US$500 million in American military aid and budget support in addition to US$200 million in economic assistance; another $US500 million for the armed forces had been approved and was on the way. As he would reveal in 1965 remarks to Walter Judd, he felt like God had ordained Taiwan as his sanctuary where he could finally institute the orderly and prosperous society he had always dreamed of as a future model for China. Likewise, Chiang's middle- and upper-class military officers would not abandon the stable and increasingly comfortable lives that American largesse had provided in order to put themselves under the control of a Communist state that had recently killed about a million landlords and many others of the old order. A repeated analysis by the American intelligence community during the Generalissimo's time on Taiwan concluded that as long as the U.S. pledge to defend Taiwan had credibility, the great majority of the mainlanders on the islands would "come to terms with a Taiwan future."[71]

In another scenario described in a National Intelligence Estimate in September 1954, if the Nationalists perceived that their interests and those of the United States were "increasingly divergent," this could "conceivably lead them [meaning Chiang Kai-shek] to take steps in the hope of involving the U.S. and Communist China in a war."[72] Chiang did believe a world war between the democracies and the Communists was inevitable and could result in the Kuomintang's triumphant return, but he was by no means certain of the outcome of such a large-scale conflict. He did not have faith that if such a war occurred, the American public and hence the U.S. government, Republican or Democratic, would stick it out. His views of America's China policies during the Stilwell years, the Marshall Mission, and the Truman-Acheson period, as well as his recent bitter experience with Eisenhower and Dulles over Korea and Burma, had convinced him that a U.S.-China war could end up as another stalemate and thus be a further incentive for U.S.-China détente—in which case he and Taiwan would likely end up far worse off. Several of Chiang's decisions over the next decade and more would demonstrate this firm conclusion. Nevertheless, his posturing would occasionally make it appear that he wanted to start a global conflict.

II

By the middle of 1953 Ho Chi Minh had seized control of most of the Vietnamese countryside. Chinese arms aid to the Vietminh was running at 1,000 tons a month and many PLA technical personnel and advisers were serving secretly with Ho Chi Minh's forces. With the end of the Korean War in July, Mao poured more artillery and anti-aircraft weapons into the fight. To counter this effort, American aid to the French campaign reached $1 billion. Eisenhower thought the situation "was not alarming," but Chiang looked at the French and American efforts in the Indochina crisis with a jaundiced eye.[73] In November 1953, in a moment of candor, he told Rankin and a group of visiting Americans that the United States was "expending its resources in Indochina to no purpose whatsoever." The Far East, he said, would never be stable until the root causes were dealt with—Communist China and the Soviet Union. To the astonishment of his guests, he went on to say categorically that the American attempt to save the French in Vietnam, Laos, and Cambodia was "a pure waste." Under questioning from the shocked Americans, Chiang evidently realized that he had gone too far, and he agreed that under the circumstances the United States should try to aid the French—but in fact he continued to believe the odds against success were high.[74]

In March 1954, the Vietminh surrounded Dien Bien Phu and the future of Indochina suddenly seemed to hinge on the fate of this beleaguered base. The Chinese rushed to the front more than a hundred additional cannon and 60,000 artillery shells, while from Taiwan the CIA flew CAT planes over Dien Bien Phu, dropping supplies.[75] Admiral Radford and the French military proposed using three nuclear weapons to break the siege. Nixon and Dulles seemed to agree with this idea, but to Eisenhower such a horrific action to save a colonial government in an undeclared war could not possibly be justified. "You boys must be crazy," he said in a National Security Council meeting. "We can't use those awful things against Asians for the second time in ten years. My God!"[76]

Eisenhower briefly considered asking Chiang Kai-shek to send troops but cast the idea aside because it might have provoked Chinese Communist intervention. Meanwhile, Chiang confided to his journal that the French were doomed and the U.S. strategy was in vain.[77] But he continued to cooperate as requested. Looking for a way out, the Soviets and the Western Allies agreed to a conference in Geneva to discuss Korea and Vietnam. It was the PRC's first attendance at an international conference and Zhou Enlai represented China. But to assure the final fall of Dien Bien Phu, Mao rushed to the front two more Chinese-trained Vietnamese artillery battalions and told the Chinese PLA advisers "Do not save artillery; we will supply and deliver sufficient shells to you."[78]

On May 7, 1954, while the Geneva Conference was going on, the French forces at Dien Bien Phu surrendered, and the White House indicated it could accept the idea of a partition of Vietnam. The Communists were concerned that if they insisted on total victory in Indochina and the fighting continued, the "worst case" for possible U.S. intervention was possible.[79] Chiang thought that however the conflict was concluded, it would "benefit Taiwan's preparations for the counterattack," meaning greater U.S. military aid.[80] So after several weeks of adjournment, the foreign ministers convened again and on July 21 signed an accord that divided Vietnam at the 17th Parallel into a Communist north and a non-Communist south with a national plebiscite to produce a united government within two years. Dulles, who did not sign the accord and famously declined to shake hands with Zhou, was determined from the start not to carry out the agreed elections. Chiang told the Americans that "whether . . . partition, or general elections are held, or Laos and Cambodia are recognized as neutral, the final result would be the taking over of the entire area by the Communists."[81] Twenty painful years later, he would be proven correct.

III

Ever since taking office, the Eisenhower team, without giving it much thought and departing from the Truman-Acheson policy, had been prepared to help Chiang Kai-shek defend Quemoy and the other offshore islands. In November 1953, a National Security Council paper provided that the United States, without committing U.S. forces, would "encourage and assist the Chinese National Government to defend the Nationalist-held offshore islands against Communist attack and to raid Chinese Communist territory and commerce."[82] A year later, after the ambivalent endings to the conflicts in Korea and Vietnam, the administration was even more determined than before to draw the line against any further Communist territorial advances, however tiny.

In 1954, Mao launched a propaganda campaign calling for the "liberation of Taiwan." Internal CCP documents emphasized that creating a crisis to be centered on Quemoy was meant primarily to raise the political consciousness of the Chinese people and stir up revolutionary enthusiasm for socialist construction at home.[83] Probably more important in Mao's mind, threatening the islands demonstrated that Moscow's new global posture of peaceful coexistence did not mean the Chinese civil war was over or that the PRC accepted Taiwan's separation from China.[84] The PLA began to store up supplies for a massive shelling of Quemoy and Matsu.[85] As tensions built up, Dulles told a press conference in Manila that the United States would be justified in concluding that the defense of Taiwan "comprehended" the defense of the offshore territories, implying that direct U.S. involvement in their defense might be called for.[86]

On September 3, 1954, PLA batteries fired thousands of shells at Quemoy. In response, Nationalist artillerymen rolled their American cannon in and out of deep tunnels cut in the island's granite cliffs and hills and fired back; the Seventh Fleet in Yokosuka put to sea; and capital ships of the U.S. Navy in the Atlantic streaked for the Pacific.[87] From what occurred afterward, it seems clear that Mao never intended to invade Quemoy or Matsu, which by their geographic closeness to the China coast—and the fact that they were never ceded to Japan as were Taiwan and the Pescadores—provided Chiang Kai-shek a critical political link to the mainland. The CCP leader did not want to cut these links any more than did Chiang.

The crisis focused on Quemoy, 153 square kilometers of granite that also had rice paddies and an airfield. Chiang believed that with adequate supplies the island could withstand a long siege. But without U.S. air and naval intervention, he and the Americans knew, the PLA could eventually cut off the island's air and sea support.[88] After leaving the Philippines, Dulles, on September 9, stopped over in Taipei for five hours. This was Chiang's first meeting with the powerful Secretary of State with whom he had verbally crossed swords over Burma, and he was more nervous than usual. Crossing his legs, he jiggled his foot more quickly than he typically did but continued to smile softly. When he raised the subject of a security treaty between the United States and the Republic of China, Dulles simply explained that "certain difficulties" lay in the way. But at a press conference afterward, when questioned about the PLA attacks on the islands, Dulles declared that Taiwan "does not stand alone."[89] Chiang was initially satisfied. He thought Dulles was "generally good." But a few days later he decided the short visit was an "insult," and that Dulles had not shown "sincerity."[90]

Although two American officers on Quemoy died the first day of the shelling, there were few Nationalist casualties and Ambassador Rankin described the PLA effort as "all-but ineffective."[91] In response, however, Nationalist planes bombed the port of Amoy and surrounding facilities, and raiding parties attacked along the coast.[92] On September 12, Nationalist planes hit targets fifty miles inland and two days later Taipei claimed that they had sunk a thousand-ton tanker. Curiously, the PLA's MIG-15s, piloted by veterans of the Korean War, did not challenge the far inferior Nationalist aircraft, which were mostly World War II–era F-47 Thunderbolts. Clearly Mao was not throwing everything into the Quemoy campaign, much less thinking of attacking Taiwan.

Nonetheless, U.S. defense officials, the media, and soon Eisenhower and Dulles began to think that Mao was in fact determined to take Quemoy. During various National Security Council meetings from September 12 to November 2, Admiral Radford and all the Joint Chiefs except Army General Ridgeway recommended immediately putting U.S. troops on Quemoy and the other offshore islands, joining Chiang Kai-shek in bombing the mainland, and even, if necessary, using nuclear weapons to repel the Communist Chinese. Chiang now had 40 percent of his army on the tiny offshore islands, so the fall of these locations would have been a blow to the security of Taiwan, but even then hardly a fatal one.[93]

At the National Security Council meetings, Dulles at this time stressed that the United States could only prevail in a war with China with the use of nuclear weapons, and he and Eisenhower both told the group that a general war with the People's Republic would lead to war with the Soviet Union.[94] These thoughts brought realism into the discussion of what was at stake, and although they had all approved earlier policy papers and public statements committing the United States to defending the islands, the President, Dulles, and Secretary of Defense Charlie Wilson all suddenly made it clear that they did not think Quemoy and Matsu were worth defending.

At one point, the President decreed that the United States would not in fact use its armed forces to defend the offshore islands. But at the same time, the talk of a sell-out by Chiang if he was forced to abandon Quemoy worried the President. The "Generalissimo," he fretted, if pushed too far could "quit the U.S. cold and renounce Formosa"—in other words, defect with his armed forces to Mao Zedong.[95] As late as February 1955, the President was citing CIA field reports about the "possibility that whole units of Chiang's army were ready to jump to the Communist side." Consistent with the positive National Intelligence Estimate of the morale of Nationalist military and civilian leaders, CIA analysts in Washington did not give credence to these rumors, which senior Taiwan officials had probably floated with CIA officers in the hope of shoring up more support for the KMT.[96] But in the National Security Council they were believed.

Khrushchev arrived in Peking on October 1 determined to establish a closer relationship with China. To begin with, he scrapped all the secret 1950 agreements between Mao and Stalin, including the Soviet occupation of Port Arthur, and promised to supply more arms factories and a new loan of 520 million rubles. Mao pointed to the ongoing Quemoy crisis and once again asked for Soviet help in building a Chinese nuclear weapon. The Soviet leader replied that China was safe under the USSR's nuclear umbrella but he promised to consider providing a research reactor.[97] A joint Sino-Soviet communiqué on the occasion promised "unity of action to safeguard the security of the two states."[98]

Meanwhile, Dulles encouraged New Zealand to introduce a resolution in the U.N. Security Council calling for a cease-fire in the Strait, a tactic that

Truman and Acheson had tried in vain. Chiang saw this as a U.S. scheme.[99] But as a concession to Chiang, Dulles sped up negotiation of a U.S. security treaty with Taipei, proposing that the treaty guarantee the security of Taiwan and the Pescadores only, but that it also include a phrase that other territories could be included by mutual agreement. Chiang at first objected to Dulles's proposal and even more strongly to the U.N. cease-fire idea, which, he feared, could lead to a one China–one Taiwan situation. But he quickly reconsidered: if he signed he would have an alliance with the United States equal at least in theory to a NATO partnership, and as for the New Zealand initiative, he realized Peking would not accept it.

Chiang also agreed, in a separate secret exchange of letters attached to the treaty, that the two governments would say that the use of force in the area by either party would be subject to joint agreement. Privately he thought this was "intolerable" and a humiliation, but the treaty was "a light of hope in the darkness."[100] He wrote to Eisenhower that he was satisfied with the accord but it would be good "psychological warfare" for the United States publicly to assure the Chinese Nationalists that it would provide logistical support for the defense of the offshore islands. Eisenhower declined to do so. In fact, he informed Chiang that it would be a military mistake to crowd more Nationalist troops onto the small islands.[101]

The artillery duel between Quemoy and an Amoy suburb continued, and Nationalist reconnaissance reported continued PLA ground and air force buildups in the region. In November 1954, Peking gave long sentences to thirteen U.S. airmen shot down over China during the Korean War, which provoked a storm of anti-Peking sentiment in America. Senators called for a U.S. blockade of the People's Republic and Joseph McCarthy demanded that the United States free Chiang Kai-shek to attack China's "soft underbelly."[102] But in a National Security Council policy paper in December, the administration reaffirmed the recent decision that the United States would not commit U.S. forces to defend the offshore islands "except in the event of a Communist attack on Taiwan."[103]

In the New Year, Chiang publicly predicted war "at any time" and Mao ordered an armada of a hundred planes to attack the much smaller Tachen islands, some two hundred miles north of Taiwan. On January 18, 1955, four thousand PLA troops seized the even tinier island of Yichang, seven miles from the Tachens, and Eisenhower again worried that the Chinese would actually invade Quemoy, causing another piece of real estate to be lost to the Communists during his administration, and that Chiang Kai-shek could "turn against us." Dulles also now inexplicably echoed Chiang's warning that the fall of Quemoy would have "a catastrophic effect" on Nationalist morale. The President again reversed himself. The time had come, he said, "to draw the line"—meaning fifteen miles from the China coast around small islands that before 1949 were never administered as part of Taiwan.[104]

Eisenhower and Dulles now agreed that the United States would announce that it would defend Quemoy and Matsu "as long as the Chinese Communists profess their intention to attack Taiwan," a threat that Peking frequently reiterated.[105] In return, Chiang would only be asked to withdraw from the distant Tachens with U.S. Navy assistance. Thus, just one month after the last policy had been reaffirmed, the National Security Council on January 19 approved a dramatically new course of action. When Chiang received the American proposal, he was pleasantly astounded. The U.S. government was going to make a public commitment to defend the offshore territories even at the cost of all-out war with China and possibly the Soviet Union. He readily agreed to withdraw from the Tachens. Then, at the President's request, the U.S. Congress passed a resolution giving him authority to use the armed forces of the United States to defend Taiwan and the Pescadores and "such related positions and territories" as he judged necessary to assure achievement of this goal.[106]

Complications quickly ensued. Dulles informed the British ambassador of the plan, and the next day, the ambassador rushed back to inform Dulles that Winston Churchill and his cabinet were "greatly disturbed." The United Kingdom would support the New Zealand resolution in the United Nations calling for a cease-fire in the Strait only if the United States made no commitment to defend Quemoy and Matsu. Informed of this development, Eisenhower changed his mind yet again. At a National Security Council meeting on January 21 it was decided that a return to the previous policy was the wisest course—the United States would defend Quemoy and Matsu only if the attacks on them were "presumptively . . . a prelude to [an] attack upon Formosa and the Pescadores."[107] On January 29, Dulles informed Chiang's foreign minister, George Yeh, who was in Washington, that in fact there would be no U.S. public statement regarding the two principal offshore islands. He did say that Chiang could be told privately that under "existing circumstances" the United States would in fact assist in the islands' defense, but sharply hedging this commitment, he added that it was a unilateral U.S.

decision and could depend on appropriate action by the United Nations. In addition, it could be withdrawn at any time without charge of bad faith.[108]

When Chiang learned of Eisenhower and Dulles's extraordinary backtracking, he was infuriated. Another American President had reneged on a firm pledge—and this time only days after it was made. It was yet another example, he thought, of how the United Kingdom still "controlled" U.S. diplomacy. His anger was no doubt in good part genuine, but as in the past the situation also provided an irresistible opportunity to severely chastise the Americans and stir up their fears that he would react in some extreme way. Such fears would compel the U.S. leaders to mollify him on other matters, specifically military and economic assistance and diplomatic support.

Outside the American and Nationalist leadership, only London knew of the briefly promised, unqualified but now canceled, public declaration that the United States would help defend Quemoy and Matsu. Nonetheless, Chiang told Rankin that the latest reversal could encourage the Communists to attack the offshore islands and if so, the United States would bear the responsibility. As he was fond of doing, he sternly lectured the sympathetic diplomat, talking about "honor, probity, equity, and sincerity," implying that Washington had shown none of these. The Nationalist leader was in "the most nervous state" Rankin had ever seen him. He rubbed his bald pate, wiggled his foot, and wrung his hands. He said he would not withdraw from the Tachens and if its forces were lost and even if Taiwan was lost, "China's honor would be preserved for posterity." Finally he said he assumed that in its relations with his government, "the United States knew it was not dealing with children."[109]

Chiang's indirect scolding of the President as passed on by Rankin had its effect. Eisenhower was apparently distraught over giving in to Churchill and reversing the pledge he had given the Nationalist leader. He sent a message to Chiang on January 31, 1955, in which he affirmed that the U.S. government would not make an announcement on the subject but under "present circumstances would in fact come to the aid of the Nationalists if a major attack was made against Quemoy and Matsu." This commitment was the one Dulles had made but without the heavy qualifiers.[110]

Eisenhower now accepted Admiral Radford's rather extreme view that the loss of Quemoy and Matsu would "destroy the reason for the existence" of the Nationalist forces on Formosa and this conclusion justified all-out U.S. intervention to save the islands. In a letter to Churchill, Eisenhower endorsed this thesis as well as the more cataclysmic notion that Peking's goal was to seize Quemoy and Matsu, then Formosa, then Japan.[111] U.S. interagency intelligence estimates again contradicted this far-fetched scenario, but the President this time rejected Churchill's renewed plea that the United States limit its commitment to the defense of Taiwan and the Pescadores.

Chiang proceeded with the withdrawal from the Tachens as agreed, and when Dulles saw him in Taipei in early March the Secretary of State explained that for political reasons the public position of the United States would be that since Quemoy and Matsu have a relationship to the defense of Taiwan, the President "may judge their protection to be appropriate." Chiang took this as a reiteration of Eisenhower's pledge. Then, turning negative, the Secretary addressed the question of the counterattack, telling Chiang frankly that by "constantly talking about an armed re-conquest of the mainland" the Nationalist government seemed "rather foolish" and exposed itself to "a measure of ridicule abroad." Opportunities for action might arise in the future, the Secretary went on, but the Republic of China could not create these possibilities, nor could they be predicted. Taiwan, he said, had a different role to play.

Far from being angry, Chiang said he "fully shared" the Secretary of State's views regarding the future task of the Nationalist government on Taiwan. The primary role was not that of a reconquering force but of an alternative model for China's development. Even so, he told Dulles, when "it comes to domestic propaganda . . . it is a different matter as we have the need to sustain . . . morale." This was a candid and clear explanation of the tactical and psychological reasons that Chiang felt he had continually to threaten to invade the mainland, but its import seemed to make little impression on Dulles.[112]

The same month, the fear of imminent war flared again when the U.S. National Intelligence Board concluded that the PLA had completed final preparations for an attack on Quemoy and Matsu. Dulles once again reported to the National Security Council that there was "at least an even chance the United States will have to go to war" over the islands—a war in which "we'll have to use atomic weapons."[113] Eisenhower and Dulles both then set out to try to convince the American people that atomic weapons were "interchangeable" with conventional weapons.[114] The President publicly warned that in a war in the Far East, "tactical small atomic weapons would probably be used."[115]

These remarks, breathtaking in their implications, sparked mass protests around the world and warnings of a world war and nuclear desolation—

all over two little islands, claims to which were highly debatable, and from which repeated paramilitary attacks against the mainland had been launched. A nuclear attack by the United States against China would have been immensely unpopular everywhere, including in the United States, and fiercely opposed by most U.S. allies, including probably all of NATO. Only the year before, Eisenhower had seen the moral and political disaster and probably military debacle of using nuclear weapons to try to save Dien Bien Phu.

Stung by the world's reaction to his rhetoric, Eisenhower once more reverted to his earlier position. At a classified meeting with congressional leaders on March 30, he said that if a Chinese Communist attack on Quemoy and Matsu did not seem to portend an attack on Taiwan, "the United States would stay out." There was nothing said about the psychological collapse of Taiwan or the falling dominoes he had described to Churchill. The next day in the Oval Office with his core National Security Council staff, Eisenhower confirmed that war with China over Quemoy and Matsu was "undesirable" because the Allies would not support it, U.S. public opinion would be divided, and it would have a "disastrous effect on the [U.S.] economy."[116]

Public threats by American leaders that they might use nuclear weapons in a conflict with the People's Republic gave Mao an opening to renew his plea to the Soviets that China needed assistance in constructing such weapons as a deterrent. Khrushchev, looking ahead, decided it was better after all that the Chinese have their own umbrella and themselves deter or deal with any future U.S. nuclear attack, and he agreed to build a cyclotron and reactor in China.[117] The gift was also intended to persuade Mao to support Khrushchev's new policy of détente with the West, which included discussions about a U.S.-Soviet summit and a global strategy of peaceful resolution of conflicts. The nuclear aid was the biggest present he could have given the Chinese leader, and it had the desired effect. An editorial in the March 7 *People's Daily* signaled the beginning of China's "peaceful liberation" policy, including toward Taiwan.

IV

The talk of peace from Peking and of détente from Moscow, as well as the continued absence of PLA air attacks against Quemoy, quickly deflated the war scare in the United States. But the trauma of the crisis made Eisenhower determined to get Chiang off the "infernal" little islands, as he now called them. In April, he dispatched Admiral Radford and the diplomat Walter

Robertson to Taipei with a dramatically new plan to solve the problem. In a meeting that ran on until 11:00 at night with Chiang, Soong Mayling, and Foreign Minister Yeh, the two envoys explained that President Eisenhower had categorically decided that the United States would not help defend Quemoy and Matsu because doing so would "undoubtedly require nuclear weapons" and would cause "tremendous" opposition at home and abroad.[118]

The two envoys for President Eisenhower went on to say that if the Generalissimo withdrew from the offshore islands under U.S. Navy protection, the United States would join with the Nationalist government in creating an interdiction line running four hundred miles through the South China Sea, the Taiwan Strait, and the East China Sea, from Swatow in Guangdong province in the south to the port of Wenzhou in Zhejiang province. The purpose of the joint interdiction by the two navies would be to search all ships in the area, foreign or Chinese (including junks), and seize all "contraband and war-making materials." The interdiction force would also replace Quemoy and Matsu as early defense blocks to any invasion force leaving Amoy or Foochow. The joint naval action, Radford said, would in effect be "a blockade of China's coast," and it would be difficult for Peking not to challenge it with military force, but the PLA Navy would have to fire first on U.S. Navy ships and thereby assume the burden of starting a war. Eisenhower, in effect, was offering to engage in what many would see as acts of war against China in undisputedly Chinese waters. Robertson urged the Generalissimo to give "full consideration" to "all implications" of the interdiction proposal, seeming to suggest that a conflict between the United States and Communist China would most likely result. Radford apparently assumed that Chiang would see this outcome as being in his interest.[119]

If Chiang wanted to encourage a Sino-American war, here was his chance—an opportunity offered by the American President himself, who seemed on his own to have devised this scheme so full of flawed assumptions and unpredictable and possibly profound consequences.[120] Chiang had had no idea what message Redford and Robertson intended to deliver. But instead of consulting privately with his wife and foreign minister before replying, he immediately turned down the proposal. In sorrow rather than anger, he said that his government and armed forces would defend Quemoy and Matsu with or without U.S. help. To abandon the islands would be "to lose the respect of the Chinese people." The Generalissimo and Madame Chiang then took a short break.[121]

When the couple returned to the room, Chiang calmly recounted the changing U.S. commitments to him regarding the offshore islands. He then explained that if he pulled out of Quemoy and Matsu the Chinese people would not support him, then "the United States would have to find another Chiang Kai-shek" and inevitably, the situation would lead to "pressure for a trusteeship for Formosa." But, he said, he had no wish to embarrass the United States. Where matters were in doubt, he went on, "[Nationalist] China should be the loser, not the USA." He said he had no desire to involve the United States in a war on behalf of his government and that he understood President Eisenhower's position. But he believed the Communists would not attack Quemoy and Matsu except as part of an attack on Taiwan and this would not happen until Russia was ready to order a world war. Thus there was "no need to get jittery or to worry over these two islands or the buildup on the China coast." In other words, the blockade was not needed and there was no need to risk a war.[122]

This was an improbable turnaround in Chiang's assessment of the threat from the mainland to Taiwan as well as the offshore territories.[123] The Americans must have been puzzled—that is, until a meeting the next evening. There Chiang gave Radford and Robertson what was undoubtedly his most important reason for turning down Eisenhower's offer to blockade much of China's coast. He told them that he simply "lacked faith" that after he had given up the islands, America would long continue the proposed blockade. Implicit was his calculation that if the proposed U.S. naval action threatened war with China, the United States, facing severe domestic and world opposition, would soon back down, or if a conflict actually began, the Americans would eventually seek peace and desert Taiwan. Concluding the talks on a cordial note, he asked Radford and Robertson to convey to the President his "great respect and personal faith in U.S. motives" and offered his "humble apology" for not being able to go along with the President's bold proposal.[124]

Chiang's sangfroid reaction was not repeated in his diary. He thought the Americans were "completely deceiving" and "naïve and ignorant" to think he would believe them. He also believed the proposal was a British-originated plot to get him off the offshore islands.[125]

Most people on these islands and Taiwan, military and civilian, knew that the Generalissimo had successfully resisted American pressure to withdraw from Quemoy and Matsu. Senior officers and officials also probably were aware that Chiang had rejected the stationing of an American Marine division and a U.S. Air Force air wing on Taiwan, as well as other U.S. enticements to give up the "infernal" islets. U.S. military aid continued to flow to the troops on Quemoy and Matsu, and U.S. Army advisers even continued to work there. In fact, soon after the Radford and Robertson visit, Chiang deployed another division to Quemoy without telling the Americans (General Chase objected, as did the State Department, but since the deployment was already under way, Washington acquiesced).[126] The offshore defenders and the PLA forces opposing them settled back into their tense but peaceful coexistence. Depending on the wind, each side wafted propaganda balloons toward the other, sometimes with gifts of soap attached.

In Chiang's eyes, he had achieved a moral victory over the Americans, capping the other major benefits he had wrung from the crisis—the mutual security treaty and increased economic and military aid from the United States. Mao, however, had received more—the promise of nuclear weapons from the Soviet Union. In addition, the same week that Radford and Robertson were in Taipei, events were propelling the United States and People's Republic toward their first-ever bilateral talks.

On April 23, 1955, at the Bandung Conference of Asian and African nations, Zhou publicly declared that China was willing to sit down with the United States and enter into negotiations over relaxation of tensions in the Far East, "especially . . . tension in the Taiwan area."[127] He repeated that China was willing to pursue the liberation of Taiwan by peaceful means. In response, Eisenhower announced that he was ready to talk, "if there seemed to be an opportunity for us to further the easing of tensions."[128] Dulles said that America would "not, of course, depart from the path of fidelity and honor toward our ally, the Republic of China," but Chiang read the decision otherwise.[129] If and when Peking seemed willing, Chiang clearly believed, the Republican administration would be tempted to seek peace in East Asia and weaken the Sino-Soviet bloc through détente with the People's Republic and resolution of the Taiwan issue through a two-Chinas or a one-China, one-Taiwan solution.[130]

Chiang Ching-kuo's covert action units included a special-operations group stationed in Hong Kong responsible for assassination and sabotage on the mainland. In 1955, this group reportedly recruited a worker at Hong Kong's Kai Tak Airport to plant a bomb in the wheel well of an Air India Constellation plane scheduled on April 11 to fly to Bandung, Indonesia, with the Chinese delegation to the conference aboard. The main target was China's foreign minister, Zhou Enlai. The Burmese leader U Nu, however, invited Zhou to fly with him from Rangoon to Bandung and Zhou agreed. Because the change in Zhou's travel plans was kept secret, the bombing plot went ahead as planned, and the plane blew up over the South China Sea, killing all the other members of the Chinese delegation.

There is reputed evidence that the CIA provided both the bomb and the detonator and possibly originated the operation that was carried out by the Nationalist intelligence unit in Hong Kong. According to Stephen Tsang, evidence now suggests that Zhou knew of the plot beforehand and secretly changed his travel plans. Circumstantially, it appears that Chiang Kai-shek and at least Chiang Ching-kuo must have authorized the assassination of the elder Chiang's erstwhile friend in the CCP.[131] Sixteen years later, Zhou had an intriguing discussion of the 1955 Air India bombing with Henry Kissinger. Zhou told Kissinger that the man who planted the bomb had fled to Taiwan. Zhou, however, did not accuse the Nationalists or Chiang Kai-shek of involvement—instead, he volunteered the thought that "such things are sometimes not the responsibility of [a] government, rather some individuals may do it on their own."[132] But after the 1955 incident had occurred, Chiang in his diary noted that the plane had caught fire and "all the Communists" were killed. "It's a pity," he added, "that Zhou Enlai was not on the plane."[133] This does not prove that Chiang had known about the plot beforehand—in fact, he may later have passed the word to Zhou that he had not, thus inspiring Zhou's 1971 comment to Kissinger. Nevertheless, despite his occasional secret exchange of messages before and after with Zhou, Chiang had clearly soured on him as a friend.

During this period the Chiangs stepped up their covert and paramilitary operations against the Communists, and now that their relations with Washington were more secure, they decided to move against the Generalissimo's domestic opponents as well. One morning in May 1955, Ching-kuo's security police went to General Sun Liren's residence and told him he was under house arrest. The year before, Chiang had removed Sun from all his command positions and appointed him his personal chief of staff; now the general was charged with sedition and one of his officers was accused of plotting to kidnap the Generalissimo. Chiang had long considered Sun one of the most likely generals to lead a coup against him and while the likelihood of that had sharply decreased, he increasingly seemed to fear that after his own death, Sun, possibly together with Chen Cheng, would pose the greatest threat to Ching-kuo's succession. Chiang did not think the Americans were involved, but still, he wrote, "we must be extremely cautious."[134]

When Admiral Radford in Washington heard of the arrest he was appalled. The conservative friend of the Chiangs sent word to the Generalissimo that Sun was "the most able general in the Nationalist Army; he could not possibly be a Communist"—adding that Sun "was right in his criticism of the commissars."[135] Stuck with the unpopular job of heading the commission of inquiry, Chen Cheng produced an ambivalent report, and Chiang decided there would be "no punishment" for the general but he would be kept "under observation" at his home in Taichung. Ambassador Rankin visited Sun and found him "enjoying his rose garden."[136] The house arrest turned into thirty-three years of forced seclusion.

Ching-kuo also considered his foster brother a potential rival. A few months before Sun's arrest, Chiang Wei-kuo returned from a study mission in the United States expecting to be appointed deputy director of military intelligence. But according to Wei-kuo, Ching-kuo persuaded his father to appoint him to a less sensitive post in G-3 operations.[137]

In the early 1950s, U.S. economic aid and surging new confidence in Taiwan's security began to have an effect. Between 1951 and 1964 American economic aid would total $1.5 billion, the largest such program per capita in the world. The grants accounted for approximately 40 percent of capital formation in Taiwan during these years and were mostly spent on infrastructure and human resources. The technocrats C. K. Yen and K. Y. Yin were joined by the engineer and physicist K. T. Li (Li Guoting) in managing economic and fiscal affairs. The chairman of the key Joint Commission on Rural Reconstruction (JCRR) was the distinguished Jiang Menglin, a Columbia graduate and former president of Peking University. These were men respected for their ability and integrity and they added to the list of senior officials whom the Americans admired. Below these top policymakers a large number of economists and financial specialists, many Western-trained, formed a large corps of highly capable, mostly honest, midlevel professionals and technocrats.[138]

From the beginning, Chiang pretty much allowed such capable bureaucrats to manage the island's economy and finances, including U.S. aid and land reform. Both Chen Cheng and Chiang Ching-kuo argued that raising standards of living had to have the highest priority next to security, because in the long run higher living standards were essential to the survival of the regime.[139] Chiang obviously agreed and he strongly backed Chen Cheng in continuing to push ahead with land reform. Although the regime was redistributing the land of Taiwanese, not mainland, gentry, if on the mainland Chiang had had the same tight political control, he would almost certainly have done the same there. In January 1953, the government announced the biggest step in the reform program: no landlord could own more than 7.2 acres of medium-grade rice fields. The percentage of farm families that tilled their own land rose from 36 to 65 percent and tenant families dropped to only 11 percent.[140] As compensation for their expropriated land, the landowners received stocks in four government (formerly Japanese) corporations. The biggest landlords, mostly well-educated men usually living in the towns and cities, bought up stocks from the others and they and their descendents became the first new business magnates on the island, playing a major role not only in expanding the old industrial sector but also in financing and managing the new light industries that with government encouragement sprouted up in the 1950s.[141]

The JCRR was heavily involved not only in redistributing land and promoting increased productivity and income on the farms, but also in improving rural health. Key projects included the control of tuberculosis and venereal disease and the upgrading of maternal and child care. By 1960, health workers had virtually eliminated malaria and had decreased the incidence of both tuberculosis and the infectious eye disease trachoma by 80 percent. Eventually, hundreds of provincial health stations provided basic care for all farm families on the island for modest fees.[142] This was the beginning of a stunningly peaceful revolution in the lives of a rural population in Asia, and it laid the foundation for the takeoff of Taiwan's urban economy in the 1960s.

Chiang was understandably proud of the successful land reform and other rural programs, which soon became highly praised achievements even in American liberal circles. This nonviolent and nonpunitive reform was especially commendable when compared to the million or more deaths that occurred in the 1950s when Mao confiscated land on the mainland—deaths that were considered by Mao to be an essential feature of the process of revolution. Aside from its domestic implications, the triumph in farming helps explain Chiang's success for two decades in maintaining considerable diplomatic support for Nationalist China from a good number of newly independent developing states. Beginning in the 1960s, Taipei began sending agricultural assistance teams to African countries, carrying with them Taiwan's lessons in land reform.

For Chiang Kai-shek, however, there was a problem: Chen Cheng and the JCRR received most of the credit. The glowing reputation of the program made Chen a more valuable asset for Chiang, but also increased his potential for succeeding Chiang after (or conceivably even before) Chiang's death. Ching-kuo's spies continued to watch him closely.

Chiang's primary economic goal was keeping the value of the New Taiwan Dollar and consumer price increases at reasonable levels, in order to avoid the horrible mainland experience. But currency stability continued to be relatively easy on Taiwan not only because of massive American aid and the large reserves of gold and U.S. dollars, but also because stability reigned throughout the island—creating a fertile environment for business, investment, and growth that the Generalissimo never experienced during all his time in Nanking and Chungking. By 1953, thanks to all these factors as well as rising customs revenues, the national budget deficit was down to a remarkably low 6 percent of GDP. From 1949 to 1958, wholesale prices in Taipei rose thirteen times. But if calculated from 1952, the rate of inflation was only around 6 to 7 percent a year. Meanwhile, in Chiang's first nine years on Taiwan, wages rose sixteen times, easily outpacing the inflation rate.[143]

On occasion, Chiang would personally intervene on financial matters, calling C. K. Yen and others on the carpet, complaining for example about an "excess issuance" of currency, ordering the Bank of China to take control of the New Taiwan Dollar from the Bank of Taiwan, firing directors of the bank, or demanding that his generals find new ways to save money.[144] After 1953, a further reduction in inflation required putting an end to the island's trade deficit. To achieve this objective, a new stabilization board assumed the broad role of macro-managing the economy. The technocrats soon produced the first Four Year Plan for Attainment of Economic Independence, which focused on an import-substitution strategy of industrialization and high tariffs. Among other measures, it authorized the Bank of Taiwan to give subsidized loans for new light industries that would produce everything from chemical fertilizers to textiles to soap to motor scooters. In the decade 1949–1958, the value of industrial production in real terms more than tripled.[145]

During the first half of the 1950s, Taiwan's social life reflected a wartime austerity. The government banned nightclubs and even neon lights, and Americans owned virtually all the new cars in the streets. Only one of every thousand Taiwan residents owned an automobile, and two of every ten thousand owned a motor scooter, which meant that the car-owning elite class was larger than the scooter-driving middle class.[146] Despite the marked improvement in income and living conditions for farm families, almost all still travelled to market by foot or water buffalo–drawn cart; more rarely they hitched a ride on a rickety bus or pedicab. Raincoats and roofs were made of rice straw. Most farm houses had dirt floors, and virtually no farmer had a watch or a radio. Moreover, Taiwan's rural population was increasing at a rate of over 4 percent a year, and because the land was divided by inheritance, the already tiny plots tilled by most farmers became even smaller, until by 1958 the average farmer owned less than half an acre.[147]

To keep per capita income on the island increasing, the key solution was for the urban economy to expand rapidly—and it did. The import-substitution policy of the first two four-year plans resulted in hundreds of new factories producing light manufactures, tens of thousands of new jobs for the surplus rural workforce, and a reduction in the government deficit, which allowed more spending on infrastructure. Daily life in the countryside slowly but visibly improved throughout the decade. Another important result of these changes was a lowering of income disparities. The poorest 40 percent of the population eventually enjoyed a greater share of the island's income than that offered by any other non-Communist economy in the world.[148] During those years, income grew 7.5 percent annually in constant dollar terms and 4 percent when measured by per capita growth. By the late 1950s the austerity measures were relaxed. As a result, the number of Chinese restaurants rapidly multiplied, "dance halls" returned, and neon lights were again in vogue.[149]

Soon after the 1949 retreat across the Strait, American journalists reported that foreigners, Taiwanese, and mainlanders on the island all spoke of the comparative absence of a kleptocracy.[150] To curtail corruption and tax evasion, Chiang ordered banks to provide all individual and company account statements to the tax authorities; he also raised salaries for the police and common soldiers but not for military officers.[151] Chiang still hesitated to take action against his top associates, as evidenced by the previously recounted case of Chief of Staff Zhou Zhirou, but Chen Cheng and Chiang Ching-kuo both gave high priority to punishing corruption in the government, and Chen's institutional reforms (which were approved by Chiang Kai-shek) promoted good governance. Strict audits by U.S. personnel of the accounts of both the armed services and the government played a major role in uncovering and preventing high-level graft. The centralization of military payrolls and the Combined Logistics Command's takeover of procurement for all the military services were early key reforms that Chiang supported. Zhou Zhirou had strongly objected to a separate command's buying and paying for all the supplies and equipment that the various services needed, but Chiang ordered him "to correct his thoughts," and the change was made.[152] The *New York Times,* which had reported in full on rampant KMT corruption of the 1940s, reported in 1958 that "corruption [on Taiwan] has been largely stamped out."[153] Although that statement was an exaggeration, it was clear that the scourge of corruption that had so crippled the KMT was finally under control.

V

The first Sino-American bilateral talks would be held in Geneva in July 1955. Dulles earnestly explained to the Generalissimo that the purpose of this exchange was to persuade Mao Zedong to agree to a mutual renunciation of force in the Taiwan Strait. This was hardly comforting to Chiang, who feared that such an accord would lead to a neutralization of Taiwan, U.S. rapprochement with China, and Taiwan's loss of its U.N. Security Council seat. In an unintentionally ironic diplomatic message to Dulles, Ambassador Rankin warned that a declaration by China and the United States avowing their peaceful intentions in the Taiwan area would create "a grave decline in morale on Taiwan."[154]

Until this point, Mao was just as averse as Chiang to forswearing the use of force in the Taiwan Strait. Such an accord would deny the PRC the right to use military means if necessary for the liberation of what most Chinese saw as sovereign Chinese territory—Taiwan. But after much wrangling in the Geneva meetings, Mao, almost certainly encouraged by his foreign minister, Zhou Enlai, surprisingly authorized a compromise. His envoy, Wang Pingnan, proposed a written exclusion-of-force agreement in which the record of the meeting would show that the two sides verbally agreed that such a renunciation of force would include "matters between the United States and China related to Taiwan."[155] Since the U.S. commitment to defend Taiwan was the most important matter between China and the United States related to the island, this formulation seemed to provide the United States what it wanted. The Chinese accommodation suggests strongly that at this time (1955 and 1956) Mao Zedong and Zhou Enlai quite possibly were serious about working with the United States.[156] Or possibly they saw such an offer as a tactic that might jar the Nationalist leadership into seeking a deal with them. In any event, the U.S. envoy at the Geneva talks, Alexis Johnson, urged the White House to accept the Chinese compromise.

For Eisenhower and Dulles, however, the offer was the curse of getting what they had wished for. They feared a furious reaction from Chiang Kai-shek and the Republican right wing if they agreed to such a peace accord with "Red China." They also assumed, probably correctly, that such an agreement would provoke an avalanche of nations to switch diplomatic relations to Peking, and while the great majority of native Taiwanese would welcome the accord, they may have feared that it could spark a political crisis within the mainlander regime in Taipei. Chiang, always suspicious of U.S. intentions, followed the talk closely. He prepared to send another division to Quemoy and when Washington did not oppose the move he concluded, "They don't yet have any intention to break out of the alliance."[157]

Because of these concerns, Eisenhower and Dulles did not explore the opportunity presented by Mao's offer—an opportunity that would never return. Nevertheless, Dulles continued to believe that the United States should keep the door open to normalization of relations with the People's Republic. The following year, he told a group of U.S. journalists that the time was approaching when "we must treat Communist China on the same basis as we treat the Soviet Union."[158]

The trend to moderation in Peking began with the Bandung Conference and then was accelerated by Khrushchev's famous speech in February 1956, in which he revealed the prodigious crimes of Stalin and declared that there were "different roads to socialism" and that peaceful coexistence was a "fundamental principle," not a tactical ploy. Mao's first response to this staggering speech was to try to prevent Stalin-like corruption of power in China, and he launched a campaign encouraging a "Hundred Flowers"—different points of view—to bloom.

Four months later, Zhou secretly proposed to the KMT that after Taiwan's "return" to the motherland the Kuomintang could still govern the island and a "proper position would be found for Chiang Kai-shek." This message, which Zhou sent to Chiang through the Hong Kong–based journalist Cao Zhuren, ended with the statement, "We are sincere and can be patient." Apparently there was no response from the KMT, and the Chiangs did not inform the Americans of the approach by the Chinese. In September, too, the CCP's Eighth National Congress adopted a policy of emphasizing economic construction rather than class struggle in building China's socialist society.[159]

Just as the Soviet Union was demythologizing its history and entering into the first stages of "functional rationality," the Generalissimo produced his book *Soviet Russia in China: A Summing Up at Seventy.* Chiang's secretaries and KMT historians probably did much of the research and some of the writing, but the words clearly represent the thoughts of Chiang Kai-shek. In the introduction, Chiang explains that Soviet Communism, by its promise of an ideal state through a violent upheaval of human society, became "the most powerful challenge to humanistic civilization." Thus, he tells us, he wrote the book because he owed it to his own people and the people of the world to explain why he, his party, and his government "were compelled three times" to adopt a policy of "peaceful coexistence" and cooperation with the Soviet Union and its satellite, the CCP.[160]

To deal with "the protracted war" waged by the Communists, Chiang's book calls for a free-world strategy of "total war." But he hastens to explain that this means that when the inevitable new Communist act of aggression occurs, nations of the free world should strike back at the "weak points" of the Communists, not just defend themselves. In the English edition he does not discuss the Nationalist counterattack against the mainland, but China was, in his view, clearly the main "weak point."[161]

By early 1957, there were 10,000 CIA, military, and other U.S. government personnel and their families in Taiwan. Most lived in and around Taipei. Accompanying this presence was the usual array of support facilities: hospitals, PXs, moviehouses, bowling alleys, baseball fields, schools, and non-commissioned-officer and officer clubs. Numerous military and CIA personnel on temporary duty added to the number of Americans in the Chinese city. Remarkably, there were few major conflicts between them and the local citizens, but one finally did occur.

One muggy night in the spring of 1957, a U.S. Air Force sergeant shot a Chinese intruder in his garden. There was an uproar in the local press, but a U.S. military court martial in Taipei found the sergeant not guilty of manslaughter. The acquitted sergeant and his family were quickly sent out of the country. But the matter was not settled for the Taiwanese. After the press published complaints from the slain man's wife, a demonstration by members of the China Youth Corps took place outside the American embassy. It quickly became a mob that eventually stormed over the walls. Ching-kuo, who was following the event from the Youth Corps office, declined to send in a nearby antiriot squad and instead reportedly ordered plainclothesmen to try to contain the violence. This was too little, too late, and the mob sacked and burned the embassy, although no Americans were seriously injured.[162]

In approving the demonstration, Ching-kuo probably did not plan the destruction of the American diplomatic office, but only a vigorous show of protest. Worried about his "enforcer" image in Taiwan and his future leadership role, he also would not have wanted to turn the antiriot police against members of his own Youth Corps. Eisenhower was understandably upset, but the administration wanted to get the matter over with and it accepted Chiang Kai-shek's abject apologies and compensation payments (which, ironically, came indirectly from U.S. aid). Chiang very likely found the incident satisfying. It declared that he was no puppet of the United States and seemed to support those Americans like Rankin who thought that if provoked, he could even break with Washington or defect to Mao. U.S. aid continued uninterrupted.

VI

That same year, Mao's "Hundred Flowers" campaign sparked a flood of criticism of the Communist Party and the way it had governed for seven years. In Poland and Hungary, Communist leaders, also inspired by Khrushchev's speech, had already launched movements to liberalize their respective parties and in the case of Hungary, to overthrow it. Alarmed by these events and realizing how free speech engendered by the Hundred Flowers campaign threatened his own control, Mao suddenly launched a countermovement that branded 300,000 intellectuals as "rightists," sent tens of thousands to reeducation camps, and sanctioned large numbers of executions.[163]

Other dramatic developments during the fall of 1957 convinced the Chairman that the "correlation of world forces" was beginning a dramatic shift: "The East Wind was prevailing over the West Wind." The Soviets launched Sputnik, the Earth's first satellite, then tested the first intercontinental ballistic missile capable of carrying nuclear weapons. The first American military advisers flew into South Vietnam to counter the spreading Vietcong insurgency, and in September, Russian scientists and engineers secretly arrived in China to teach the People's Republic how to put together a nuclear weapon.

Inspired by these events, Mao declared that in a sudden bound China could realize a truly Communist society. The vehicle was called the Great Leap Forward, and it involved agricultural and industrial production based on fanciful methods of crop management and manufacturing. But for Mao the drama of revolution at home also required a warlike leitmotif in foreign policy and in regard to Taiwan. As he had periodically in the past, Mao criticized Zhou Enlai for having conducted a "reactionary foreign policy" with America and advocated "peaceful liberation" of Taiwan. When Zhou resigned as foreign minister Chiang knew that a new period of extremist policies in Peking was likely, one that would probably provide opportunities for the KMT.[164]

The Nationalists had not engaged in covert special operations with the CIA in a foreign country since the Burma fiasco in 1951 and the Indochina airdrops in 1954. But in March 1958, at a meeting with Secretary Dulles, Chiang, out of the blue, proposed that the two governments secretly cooperate in assisting a rebellion by a group of Indonesian officials and military officers in central Sumatra and east Sulawesi. President Sukarno was close to Peking and the Indonesian Communist Party (PKI), Chiang argued, and it would be best for the free world if the Indonesian Army rebels could oust him or, if that was not possible, split up the huge country of Indonesia.[165] Dulles agreed on the spot. Without further deliberation of the feasibility or consequences of the policy, CIA planes from Taiwan began flying arms and other supplies to the forces rebelling against the sovereign government of Indonesia, a member of the United Nations with whom the United States had diplomatic relations.

The real complications began when the Indonesian Army shot down one of the CIA planes and captured the pilot, an incident that led China, the PKI, and Sukarno to denounce America for its blatant violation of international law.[166] The Soviet Union, too, rushed Sukarno a squadron of MIG-16s.

With the rebellion falling apart, the White House shifted to a policy of strengthening the loyal but mostly anti-Communist Indonesian Army as a bulwark against the PKI.[167] Dulles, for his part, decided Sukarno was not so bad. He was "not a fanatic like Chiang Kai-shek, Syngman Rhee, and Nasser."[168] The fear in Washington that Chiang might do mad things was useful to him.

In July 1958, when U.S. Marines landed in Lebanon to stop a civil war and British paratroopers flew into Jordan, tensions between the two superpowers again soared. Chairman Mao's grandiose ideological claims, and his media's resumption of scathing attacks on "U.S. imperialism" and Yugoslav "revisionism" greatly worried the Soviets, and Khrushchev secretly visited Peking in August to try to calm the CCP Chairman or at least attempt to find out what was going on.[169] When Khrushchev suggested that the Chairman should be prudent in dealing with the Taiwan issue, Mao suspected another two-Chinas plot and he chose not to tell the Soviet leader that the PLA was, in fact, on the verge of another major artillery offensive against Quemoy. Indeed, later that month Communist shore batteries showered 60,000 shells onto the island.[170] Around this time, the Chairman explained privately to his doctor that "the islands are two batons that keep Khrushchev and Eisenhower dancing, scurrying this way and that."[171] Back in Moscow, Khrushchev heard that Quemoy was under attack and he hastily sent Andrei Gromyko to Peking. Zhou assured him that the purpose of the shelling was to "cause more contradictions" between Chiang Kai-shek and Dulles, prove that the People's Republic was not afraid of America, and "raise the combat spirit" of the Chinese people. There would be no landing on the islands, Zhou said. For his part, Mao told Gromyko that even if the United States used tactical nuclear weapons, the USSR should not take part.[172] Whether he believed Mao was serious is unclear, but Khrushchev sent a letter to Eisenhower saying that "an attack on China would be considered an attack on the Soviet Union."[173]

A year later, Mao would tell the Soviet ambassador that in the fall of 1957 Chiang Kai-shek "wanted and requested that such a shelling be conducted."[174] Mao's comment probably came from a contact between Chiang and Zhou Enlai before the crisis exploded. Zhou had sent another message to Chiang through his secret go-between, Cao Juren, saying that Chiang could either withdraw from Quemoy and Matsu or have the Americans force him to withdraw.[175] While Mao did not in fact want Chiang to leave the offshore islands,

Zhou's approach was very likely another attempt to stir up differences between the United States and Chiang. For his part, Chiang would soon have pending with Washington his own request for nuclear weapons and guided missiles, a request to which a war crisis with the mainland would add a strong rationale.[176] Thus Chiang probably told Zhou that if Peking started a crisis it would only benefit the Nationalist cause, which it did.

Back in Washington, the new artillery attack on Quemoy did indeed bestir the administration, which was convinced that this time Mao definitely intended to invade the island. As the new shelling began, 100,000 of the best Nationalist troops were on the two islands of Quemoy and Matsu, more than in 1954–1955, which again made the sites more strategically and psychologically important than before.[177] Eisenhower complained to his colleagues that "having ignored our advice [to reduce his forces on the island, Chiang] comes whining to us."[178] Remarkably, no one at the National Security Council meetings mentioned the President's stark message that Radford and Robertson had delivered to Chiang in April 1955: at that time, the President had declared categorically that the United States would not help defend the islands. Apparently, the top leaders did not ask for a staff paper setting out the history of the previous crisis and how they themselves had handled it. Instead, repeating the past, Dulles declared publicly that U.S. forces would be used for the protection of Quemoy.[179]

In another striking lapse of memory, the most senior American leaders began once again to talk almost casually in public as well as in secret meetings of the possible use of nuclear weapons in the Quemoy crisis. Air Force general Nathan Twining, the new Chairman of the Joint Chiefs, reported to the National Security Council that seven- to ten-kiloton airburst bombs would clear away the offending Communist cannon.[180] The United States rushed to Quemoy nuclear-capable eight-inch howitzers, presumably to be controlled by Americans. And Soong Mayling, who had gone back to America in May 1958, told Meet the Press that people on the mainland were asking why Taiwan did not use nuclear weapons against the Communist regime.[181]

During these weeks, the Generalissimo, Chen Cheng, and Chiang Chingkuo held daily meetings with the American principals on Taiwan. Everett Drumwright, the new U.S. ambassador—another sympathetic Foreign Service officer—as well as the CIA station chief, Ray Cline, not only passed on to Washington the dire warnings of the Nationalists, but also added their own predictions of the terrible consequences that would occur should Quemoy fall or be abandoned. In addition, they pleaded for emergency shipments of new and more advanced weapons.[182] Dulles revived the tattered worry that if the United States pushed Chiang Kai-shek "too hard," Chiang might believe he had "no other choice" but "to make an arrangement with Peking." He and Eisenhower wrote and edited an unusual secret memorandum strictly for their own guidance that set out basic assumptions in dealing with the crisis. Reviving Eisenhower's implausible domino theory, the joint memo asserted that if the speck on the map called Quemoy either fell to an assault or surrendered, it "would probably bring about a government [in Taipei] which would eventually seek the elimination of U.S. positions on the island [Taiwan]," that is, a government that would make a deal with the Communists. As a result, the memorandum claimed, Japan and all of Southeast Asia "would probably come fully under Communist influence."[183]

The memo, extraordinary for its ignorant and far-fetched analysis, appeared to be Dulles's device for locking the President into a hardline position. It went on to foresee that once the United States had intervened to save the offshore islands, it could not abandon the project without "unacceptable damage to the free world." Thus, if required as a last resort, "extensive use of nuclear weapons and even the risk of a general war would have to be accepted."[184] The key link in the expected collapsing chain was Taiwan. But the most current National Intelligence Estimate at the time on "Prospects for Taiwan"—dated August 27, 1957—repeated earlier conclusions that if the Nationalists were confident that the United States would defend Taiwan, they would in fact accept all sorts of steps by the United States that they had long insisted were intolerable, including heavy pressure for withdrawal from the islands, cessation of U.S. opposition to PRC membership in the United Nations, and even a cut in U.S. military and economic aid to Taiwan.[185] Dulles's strong and usually prevailing views, the influence of Ray Cline's alarming "inside" reports, and possibly Eisenhower's slipping memory and willpower apparently overrode this considered analysis.

Because of the crisis, the United States provided Chiang's armed forces, over and above the amount of military aid originally slated for delivery, $350 million worth of advanced artillery, aircraft, tanks, amphibious ships, and other war matériel.[186] Among the new weapons to arrive on Taiwan were brand-new air-to-air Sidewinder missiles, which immediately gave the Nationalist Air Force a decided edge over the Communist MIGs. Chiang's response to Zhou's message was being quickly borne out.

Then, in an exact replay of what had happened in the 1954–1955 crisis, Eisenhower and Dulles, after their initial hawkish response, began to hear an array of anguished voices opposing a nuclear attack on China over the micro-dot isles off the China coast. The U.S. ambassador in Tokyo reported that if the United States employed nuclear devices against China because of Quemoy, Japan would probably demand the withdrawal of all American forces and facilities from its territory. Other allies were equally aghast. In a memo to Dulles, the Assistant Secretary of State for policy planning, Gerald C. Smith, said that should the United States employ nuclear weapons in this case, the result would be either a global nuclear war or a pyrrhic victory of mammoth proportions—an America deserted by its allies and besieged by a wave of neutralism and hostility.[187]

Most upsetting was an American intelligence document, the details of which have still not been declassified, that reported Nationalist government efforts in September 1958 "to involve the United States in a nuclear war with China."[188] From all we know about Chiang Kai-shek's thinking and his rejection of Eisenhower's blockade proposal in 1955, it seems highly unlikely that he seriously sought to provoke such a war, but the report had a dramatic effect on Eisenhower. The President and his advisers suddenly came to believe that "Chiang's goal was in fact to embroil the United States in a war with the Chicoms."[189] Finally, as he had belatedly in 1955, the American President began to take a hard look at his and Dulles's latest drift toward a nuclear war.

Meanwhile, in Warsaw, the site of the new U.S.-China talks, the Chinese side proposed that if Chiang withdrew from Quemoy and Matsu, China would "for a certain period" strive to "liberate Taiwan and the [Pescadores] by peaceful means."[190] Eisenhower and Dulles continued to insist on an unconditional renunciation of the use of force in the Strait, but Mao's offer added to doubts in the White House about the rationale for going to war over the distant islands. In another conciliatory gesture intended to allow the crisis to drag on but to complicate direct U.S. involvement, Mao, on September 21, stopped the shelling long enough to permit the Nationalists one day to land supplies safely on the pockmarked beaches of Quemoy. Eisenhower told the National Security Council he wanted something done to make Chiang "more flexible," and Defense Secretary McElroy, who had recently met with Chiang, hinted at a coup: "getting someone else into the position."[191]

Chiang was obviously feeling pleased about how the crisis had developed and how it now seemed to be ending. But on October 1, while in Gaoxiong to meet with his naval chiefs, he read a cable from George Yeh reporting his presentation of credentials to Eisenhower as the new Nationalist ambassador in Washington. Yeh highlighted the President's remark that he was confident Nationalist China shared "the deep desire of the American people" that "Communist aggression should not lead to war as a result of any failure on our part to entertain suggestions for peaceful settlement." Next, Chiang read a wire service account of a press conference that Dulles had held the same day quoting the Secretary as saying it was "foolish" to have put such large forces on Quemoy and Matsu and "it would not be wise to keep them if a ceasefire could be arranged." Moreover, Dulles said, "it would be "quite impractical and quite wrong to ask the Chinese Communists to abandon the use of force if they were being attacked by the Chinese Nationalists." The Secretary even took the opportunity to declare that "a mainland revolution would most likely be primarily under local auspices and local leadership" and the "return of the Nationalists to the mainland" was "highly hypothetical." As the *New York Times* commented, these words, if followed through with action, meant that the administration's policy toward Chiang Kai-shek had yet again undergone "a profound change."[192]

Chiang now knew the Americans were enormously frustrated with the Quemoy business. But he again felt he had to demonstrate that he was not to be moved by such admonitions coming from his sole protector and benefactor. He would stand by his principles—in this case no retreat from Quemoy and Matsu—regardless of the consequences. That day he gave an interview to the Associated Press in which he said that Secretary Dulles's reported remarks were "completely incompatible with our stand" and did "not sound like him." The Secretary's statement, Chiang said, was in any event a unilateral one and the Nationalist government was "under no obligation to accept it."[193] The next day, Dulles cabled a message to the Generalissimo saying his remarks had been misinterpreted and that America's basic policy toward Nationalist China had not changed.[194] Still, Chiang probably realized that nothing more could be gained from the crisis and he hoped Mao felt the same way.

Zhou and Mao did in fact read Dulles's statements as suggesting that the American goal was to "trade off Quemoy and Matsu for Taiwan and the Pescadores," thus "formalizing the separation of Taiwan and the mainland."[195] Mao told his colleagues it was best to leave the offshore islands in the hands of Chiang Kai-shek. "Whenever we are in need of tension [with the United States or Chiang], he explained, we may tighten the noose, and whenever we want to relax the tension, we may loosen the noose."[196] Mao then initiated the de facto cease-fire that Dulles had called for. PRC Defense Minister Peng Dehuai publicly called the Chinese on both sides of the dispute "brothers" and urged negotiations to reach a peaceful settlement.[197]

Chiang, however, was still determined to fight. On Double Ten Day, Chiang told the nation that the Republic of China had won the first round in the battle for Quemoy and would win the second battle and reconquer the mainland. Later he sent a message to Dulles, expressing his hope that the Secretary would come to Taipei so they could "fix a new policy" to cope with the changing situation. He stressed his "faithfulness" as an American ally.[198] Dulles agreed to come, but had an entirely different agenda in mind.

On October 20, 1958, the Secretary's motorcade drove through the grimy city of Taipei, past the endless rows of small shops and sidewalk arcades. Most of the streets still had open sewers, and the soot-laden air was almost as polluted as Peking's.[199] Upon his arrival, the Secretary sent word that he would like to see Chiang alone except for George Yeh, who would interpret. The next afternoon, Yeh ushered Dulles into the sitting room of the Generalissimo's "quiet and dimly lit" mountain retreat. Chiang, a few days short of seventy-two, was standing and waiting for Dulles when Yeh knocked and then opened the door. The Generalissimo greeted the American warmly and led him to the two upholstered chairs used for such occasions.

After an exchange of niceties, Dulles pulled out of his suit pocket the State Department talking points that he had edited and Eisenhower had approved. He got directly to the point. The Nationalist government, he said, was perceived abroad as "militaristic [and] . . . apt to precipitate a world war," as well as having only "a limited life expectancy." "It is doubtful," Dulles went on, "whether even the U.S. can long protect the GRC [Government of the Republic of China] under present circumstances."[200] Dulles then gave the Generalissimo a list of things the Taipei government had to do if it wished "to prevent itself [from] being liquidated," including seeking an "armistice" with the mainland regime, publicly declaring it would "not attempt forcibly to return to the mainland," avoiding commando raids and "alike provocations," and accepting "any solution of the offshore island problem" that assured that the civilian population would not be turned over to the Communists. Finally, Dulles said that Chiang's government should "review the character and perhaps the size" of the Nationalist military establishment in order to achieve greater mobility and "perhaps . . . less burden on the people of Taiwan."[201]

As Dulles talked on, Chiang listened politely. A response to this startling policy reversal would require a Taoist approach. When Dulles finished,

U.S. Secretary of State John Foster Dulles before one of his October 1958 stern lectures to Chiang about the offshore islands. Chiang emerged from these talks having won more concessions from Washington and given nothing important in return. Courtesy KMT Party History Institute.

Chiang said that he had never mistrusted the sincerity of the United States, but even the Eisenhower administration did not seem to trust him. He hoped the Secretary's visit would allow the two sides to agree on basic principles, after which they could agree on methods. He said he concurred with the principle of not taking action that "might precipitate a world war" and that the return to the mainland "would not happen until there was a real desire on the part of the people reflected by a revolution against their oppressors."[202]

But shortly after the meeting, Huang Shaogu, the new foreign minister, called Drumwright to an urgent talk. Reflecting the Generalissimo's true reaction, Huang said that the "suggestions" advanced by the Secretary appeared "to be of such a nature as almost to shake the foundation of the Republic of China." They were tantamount, Huang said, to demanding an announcement by Chiang's government that it would accept the "two Chinas idea."[203]

The next morning, undeterred, Dulles again pushed Chiang to seek some sort of formal agreement ending the conflict with the mainland, and again

Chiang avoided any comment on the Secretary's strong "suggestions."[204] That evening Dulles launched into another disturbing lecture, asserting that only nuclear weapons could take out the hundreds of Communist guns arrayed against Quemoy's western shoreline, and asking whether Chiang "wanted the United States to use nuclear weapons" against Communist China. Caught off guard by the question, Chiang paused, then replied that "the use of tactical atomic weapons might be advisable." Dulles explained that subsurface nuclear explosions with the power of the Hiroshima or Nagasaki bomb would be required to destroy the Communist guns, and the fallout could kill 20 million Chinese and everyone on Quemoy. Furthermore, if the Soviet Union came into the war as it had promised, Taiwan could suffer a nuclear attack and "there would be nothing left."[205]

Instead of arguing the point, Chiang replied that he "would not want to use nuclear weapons if this would start a world war" or "involve the United States in large-scale hostilities." Even so, the next day Dulles continued the attack, insisting that the fate of free China must not be tied to a few square miles of real estate in highly vulnerable locations. This time Chiang disagreed, strongly but calmly insisting that after the loss of Quemoy his government could not survive for five months and Taiwan would fall. Without asking for a quid pro quo, Dulles replied in part by offering to station U.S. nuclear-armed Matador missiles with U.S. crews in Taiwan, and Chiang accepted.[206]

Between the meetings, representatives of the two sides went back and forth exchanging draft language for a joint communiqué. Through his intermediaries, Dulles proposed that the Nationalist side say that the Republic of China "will never itself initiate war." Chiang refused. Dulles wanted the two governments to declare that the mutual security treaty was "a defensive treaty only." Chiang would only agree to state that the treaty was "defensive in character." Dulles brought along the text of the October 3, 1954, declaration by the Federal Republic of Germany undertaking "never to have recourse to force to achieve the reunification of Germany." Chiang refused any such language. Drumwright, Cline, and the other senior Americans on the island in private sessions warned the Secretary that he was courting disaster. In the end, Dulles totally capitulated. In the final communiqué, the Taipei side simply said that "the principal means" for restoration of freedom to the Chinese people on the mainland would be "implementation of Sun Yat-sen's Three Principles" of democracy, nationalism, and equalization of wealth, and that "the foundation of this mission resides in the hearts and minds of the Chinese people and not in the use of force."[207]

All of Dulles's verbal fireworks had achieved virtually nothing. With the Matador missile offer, the Secretary in fact had made a major new commitment to the security of Taiwan—one that would be carried out without the United States getting anything in return. The communiqué also advanced the U.S. public position and Chiang's preferred viewpoint on the principal issue, proclaiming that "under present conditions the defense of Quemoy and Matsu" was "closely related to the defense of Taiwan and the Penghus."[208]

But Dulles's harangue, while it came to naught, did reaffirm for Chiang that the Eisenhower administration was still hoping someday to improve relations with Peking in the context of a two-Chinas solution. Knowing that Mao was as opposed to such a policy as he was, he and his son thus decided to try to convince Peking to end the still-festering Quemoy crisis, which both leaders had been using for their own purposes. According to a senior official of the People's Republic speaking privately in 1994, Chiang at this time sent a message to Zhou Enlai saying that if the PLA did not stop the firing, he (Chiang) would have "to do what the Americans wanted"—withdraw from the offshore islands—and over time this move would threaten the indivisibility of China. Ching-kuo probably passed this message through the Hong Kong go-between, Cao Juren.[209]

Years later Zhou confirmed this story, telling Henry Kissinger that in 1958 the United States wanted Chiang to give up Quemoy so as to completely sever Taiwan and the mainland, but the Taiwan and mainland leaders had "cooperated to thwart the efforts of Dulles." Chiang was not willing to do what Dulles wanted, Zhou said, and "we advised him . . . not to withdraw [and then began] . . . firing artillery shells only on odd days . . . so they understood our intentions and didn't withdraw."[210] On October 25, 1958, the day after Dulles had left Taipei, Peking did in fact announce a new policy of token shelling every other day, and the Nationalist artillerymen went on the same schedule. This left open the alternate days for safe resupply of the island.

The last Quemoy crisis was over. The Nationalists and the Communists would continue to be enemies, seeking wherever possible to weaken the other, but at the highest level there was an understanding—the two sides had a common interest and commitment to Chinese unity, whereas their respective superpower allies simply wanted peace in the Strait, which for both allies meant two Chinas.

The resolution of the second Quemoy-Matsu crisis was another astonishing example of Chiang's ability to have his way with the Republican administration, which politically dared not cross him. For his part, Mao, by the normal measure of things, gained relatively little by the second offshore crisis. But in fact the Chairman was moved by revolutionary zeal and the desire to create tension for ideological, domestic, and international reasons. He succeeded in doing this and again shocking the world into realizing that China was a world player and would not let the Taiwan issue go dormant. Moreover, Mao had raised new doubts in the non-Communist world about the rationality of the U.S. government's policies toward China and the chillingly loose manner in which it had again talked about and seriously considered the use of nuclear weapons.

Because of the crisis and particularly Mao's attitude toward nuclear war, the Soviet leaders became more alarmed about his recklessness. Khrushchev began to have second thoughts about giving the Chairman a nuclear weapons capability. Thus the crisis, which Chiang had helped to fan, played a role in the coming breakup of the Sino-Soviet bloc, but of course neither Chiang nor the Americans at the time could foresee this development. The Nationalists and Americans also had their differences regarding the development of nuclear weaponry in the region. In December 1958, Washington finally rejected Chiang's request of the previous January for nuclear weapons, and as a result he approved the establishment of the first clandestine nuclear weapons research laboratory in Taiwan.[211]

12

Shifting Dynamics

In 1959, with the presidential election in Taiwan's National Assembly coming up the next year, liberal intellectuals like Hu Shi and Wang Shijie began to call on Chiang to follow the constitution and not seek another term. Early in the year, too, Chen Cheng, assuming that the President would not again stretch the constitution's term limitations, discussed the succession at a private meeting with a group of generals whom he had known for a long time. But Ching-kuo's men either had a source among Chen Cheng's military associates or had wired the meeting room. Upon learning of the meeting, Chiang moved swiftly to derail any plans, retiring or reassigning to noncommand positions the military coterie around Chen, including then chief of the General Staff "Tiger" Wang Shuming.[1] Around the same time, the Generalissimo had his adopted son, Wei-kuo, who had had differences with Ching-kuo, relieved of his command of the Armored Force, which he had resumed less than a year before, and sent to the United States on another study mission. Wei-kuo felt he had been moved aside for political reasons; he never again had a command position.[2]

Mayling returned from the United States that June. She had been busy that year as the Generalissimo's advocate in the United States, addressing the Foreign Relations Committee of the Senate, the Subcommittee on Asia and the Pacific of the House of Representatives, the American Legion, the National Defense University, the National Press Club, and dozens of other organizations.[3] She received degrees from three universities, visited the dying Claire Chennault in Washington, and attended the funeral of John Foster Dulles, who passed away in May. *Newsweek* remarked on her "personal charm, keenness of intellect, and oratorical ardor" and the Gallop poll reported she was among the most admired women in the world.[4] But her often strident speeches—in which she still favored esoteric words such as "sequacious reasoning"—provoked criticism and some ridicule. Before returning home, she lunched at the White House with Eisenhower and his wife.[5] As usual, the Generalissimo greeted her at the airport when she arrived. She had been gone more than a year, but the couple continued to show very un-Chinese-like affection in front of others.

During these years, many of the Madame's American nephews, ranging in age from nine or ten to young adolescents (there were no young nieces), were dropped off in Taipei by their parents who were on their way to Hong Kong. During the summer months, their famous aunt arranged various activities for them, inviting Ching-kuo's youngest children to participate as well in what came to be called "The Eight Immortals Club." They recall that she spent a lot of time painting and still smoked daily a half pack to a full pack of cigarettes. They also remember the Generalissimo strolling in the garden in his long robe, reciting Tang poetry and cooking a pot of fried rice for the family picnics on Yangming Mountain. (Mayling's favorite dish was southern fried chicken.) As the children scampered about, the Generalissimo would sit beside his wife and smile benevolently. She would light up a cigarette with a holder, looking to her young kin more mysterious and glamorous than ever.[6]

If Chiang appeared happy, it was with reason. The late 1950s were the happiest, most contented period of his life so far. Mao Zedong, on the other hand, was running into serious problems. China's Great Leap Forward had ended in disaster, and death from starvation was again stalking the land. In December, Liu Shaoqi replaced Mao as President of the People's Republic. Chiang started to believe that an anti-Communist resistance on the mainland might emerge within the foreseeable future after all. Zhou Enlai, however, acted as if the mainland was becoming more attractive as a retirement site, appealing publicly to the Generalissimo to come home where suitable positions for him and his colleagues would be found. According to the CIA, beginning in 1959, Peking sent one or more secret messages to Taipei; Chiang's communication to Zhou after the Dulles lecture in October 1958 may have encouraged Zhou to believe there was a chance the Generalissimo might be interested in a negotiated deal. In 1964, the CIA said it had no evidence that

Chiang in his garden on Yangming Mountain, ca. 1959, feeling satisfied with Taiwan's growth and stability, his military alliance with the United States, Mao's troubles on the mainland, and his own successful management of the crises of the decade. Courtesy KMT Party History Institute.

the Communist offers to Chiang Kai-shek and Chiang Ching-kuo had elicited any response.[7] Nevertheless, the Chiangs again chose not to inform their friend, CIA station chief Ray Cline, of these latest approaches.

In March 1959 a major rebellion did erupt in the People's Republic—but it was in faraway Tibet. The CIA, working secretly out of India and Thailand, as well as Chiang Ching-kuo's special forces in an independent operation, were providing training and support to dissident Khampa tribesmen and other groups in Tibet.[8] The large-scale uprising began when rumors spread, perhaps by CIA-supported guerrillas, that the Chinese were about to carry the Dalai Lama off to Peking. The Dalai Lama backed the rebellion and he and a large group of other lamas and prominent Tibetans fled to India. Chiang and his son pushed the Americans to allow the Nationalists to participate in the CIA operations, which now greatly expanded. But the Nationalists were unpopular among Tibetan separatists since they also claimed Tibet

as sovereign Chinese territory, and India likewise did not welcome Nationalist involvement. As a result, the CIA at first avoided a joint covert action in
Tibet with Taipei. But then Chiang threatened to drop his own supplies and
paratroopers into the region and the CIA agreed to work with him.[9]

This first real revolt against Mao was so important to Chiang that he came
close to saying he would recognize Tibetan independence, declaring that the
Tibetan people should have "the right to determine their own future."[10] Chen
Cheng and others in Taipei publicly predicted that the rebellion would spread
to China's Northwest and Southwest, and then to Central China.[11] At the
end of April, however, Allen Dulles reported to the National Security Council that the rebellion had "pretty well been knocked to pieces."[12]

Still, the CIA operation continued. When the agency sought an extension
of the program in February of 1960, Eisenhower complained that since there
was no hope the insurgency would go anywhere, the result would simply be
"more brutal [Communist] reprisals" against the Tibetan people. Nevertheless, he went along with an extension for another two years. Like all the other
covert paramilitary actions against China, this one would achieve none of its
objectives.[13]

Politically, however, the Tibetan affair had profound consequences. The
rebellion soured Sino-Indian relations and led within the year to clashes between the two countries along their Himalayan borders, which in turn would
result in the Sino-Indian war of 1962. But in 1959 this scenario was again
hardly anticipated by the Chiangs or the leaders in Washington, who for years
kept poking the dead body of the Tibetan uprising. For Mao the whole affair
had been useful—the troublesome Dalai Lama had fled to India with the
other leading lamas and "serf-owners," thus making it unnecessary for him to
jail them.[14]

In October 1959, after a successful visit to the United States, Khrushchev
was once again in the Forbidden City meeting with Mao. Basic differences
kept undermining the superficial civility—in particular, war and peace in the
nuclear age, the Chinese border clashes with India, and Mao's approach to
the liberation of Taiwan. News of this unhappy meeting soon leaked out to
the world. At this stage, only a few Western observers thought that Dean
Acheson's ten-year-old prediction—that the Sino-Soviet bloc would eventually splinter—might actually come true. Acheson himself was not among
them; he said publicly the next year that the thought of the two socialist giants fighting each other was "poppycock."[15]

In March 1960, the National Assembly reelected Chiang President and Chen Cheng Vice President and premier. That same month, rigged elections in South Korea touched off widespread protests that forced Syngman Rhee to resign, and as a mob roamed the streets looking for him, a CIA DC-4, possibly from Taiwan, whisked him away to Hawaii. Chiang was deeply disturbed. In his view, the Americans, again chasing the chimera of democracy in an undeveloped country under siege by a powerful Soviet-supported regime, had encouraged the internal opponents of a strong anti-Communist leader. No doubt he was also thinking of how many in Taiwan and America would see the fall of Syngman Rhee as a model for change on the island.

The South Korean affair intensified Chiang's determination to stamp out any sign of an organized opposition on Taiwan. On Chiang Ching-kuo's advice, he approved the arrest of the *Free China Review* publisher Lei Zhen on trumped-up sedition charges. Although Lei had risked arrest in 1957 by starting an informal opposition coordination group, the Chiangs had not moved against him then because of criticism they had received in the United States over the purging of Sun Liren and the sacking of the American embassy. Lei had long proclaimed that the only way to bring about regime change on the mainland was to make Taiwan a model democratic state, and he called the return to the mainland "hopeless."[16] The Chiangs had tolerated Lei's outspokenness for some time, but in 1960, with the backing of Hu Shi, he went beyond words and began planning the formation of a new China Democratic Party.

Vice President Chen Cheng, apparently hoping to build a future base of political support among the Taiwanese, startled political observers when he said publicly that a serious opposition party could exist so long as it was not "a party of warlords, hoodlums, and rascals." This was interpreted as tacit approval of Lei's activities.[17] In the end, Lei received a relatively light sentence of ten years, reflecting the Chiangs' desire to try to hold down criticism in the United States.[18] The hearts and minds of the developing world were becoming an ever greater prize in the Cold War, and the Democratic presidential candidate, John F. Kennedy, was calling for America to boost its moral authority in the world.

Eisenhower's State Department, also paying more attention to human rights, sent Drumwright instructions to warn Chiang that his government should not make the same "fatal mistakes" as those of the "Rhee regime." Drumwright, however, pointed out to the department that in free elections "the KMT would almost certainly be doomed," and thus the Chiangs would not likely tolerate the rise of a strong, well-organized political opposition.

Drumwright did not deliver the scolding message.[19] For the first time on the island, however, Chiang did briefly allow some public criticism of political suppression. Two out of almost five hundred Legislative Yuan members and several other independent figures, including Hu Shi, publicly denounced the "false charges" against Lei and his trial by military court.[20] The crackdown on political dissent, however, soon picked up again, with the Garrison Command suspending several publications for a year.[21]

In his last year in office, Eisenhower wanted to concentrate on ending the Cold War, but a series of setbacks dashed these aspirations, most famously the downing of the U-2 spy plane over the Soviet Union and Khrushchev's tirade and walkout at the Paris summit.[22] Then, because of anti-American riots in Tokyo, the President canceled a visit to Japan scheduled to follow a state visit to Taiwan. Chiang Kai-shek thus made a special effort to arrange a positive and massive reception in his capital for the eminent American. When Eisenhower arrived in Taipei on June 17, 1960, he received the most tumultuous welcome in the history of the city. More than 300,000 people cheered his procession along the streets of Taipei. On the second day, 300,000—no doubt many of the same people—again filled the huge plaza before the Presidential Palace to hear Eisenhower speak.[23]

Eisenhower apparently had forgotten all his distrust of the Generalissimo that the offshore crises had provoked. Frustrated in his own dealings with the Communists, he now clearly felt a closer camaraderie with the stern anti-Communist warrior of more than thirty years. Chiang told Eisenhower that it was "absolutely impossible" for the Chinese Communists to split from the Soviet Union, and Eisenhower agreed that the Soviet bloc was a "solid monolithic aggregation."[24] They obviously were not anticipating Khrushchev's dramatic shift in policy the very next month: in October 1960, Khrushchev would cancel the 1957 nuclear accords with the other half of the monolith and bring home all 1,343 Soviet military and civilian specialists—nuclear and non-nuclear.

In their talks, Chiang and Eisenhower avoided the issue of the "infernal" little islands that had bedeviled their relations. But Nationalist efforts against the mainland continued to be a focus for discussion. Chiang brought up the idea of paramilitary action against the mainland and asked that Eisenhower pro-

The Chiangs and President Dwight D. Eisenhower at a Taipei rally in June 1960. After putting aside sharp differences of the past, the two World War II warriors found common ground. Courtesy KMT Party History Institute.

vide U.S. aircraft and communications for "paradrops and other sabotage and guerrilla operations."[25] Once back in Washington, the President approved U.S. training of a limited number of Nationalist soldiers for these operations, the supply of one long-range C-130B transport plane, and, most importantly, modern F-104 jet fighters.[26]

As in 1948, China was a controversial issue in the 1960 American presidential campaign. Chiang had every reason to believe that Vice President Nixon would be even more anti-Communist in action than Eisenhower and even more supportive of Taiwan. His suspicions of Democrats were heightened when Kennedy said the United States should not defend Quemoy and Matsu simply because they were "symbols of freedom," as Nixon had declared. Chiang responded aggressively, ordering the government spokesman in Taipei to say it was "incredible that any responsible leader in the United States even in the heat of a campaign could have been so irresponsibly generous in dispensing the territory of another country." In an interview the same day, Chiang said Nationalist China would "fight to the death for Quemoy and Matsu."[27]

Then, immediately after Kennedy won, Chester Bowles, who was thought a likely candidate for Secretary of State, called for a "two-Chinas" policy, and Dean Acheson, whom Chiang reviled, proposed that the United States recognize Taiwan as a "self-contained country."[28] Chiang now expected the worst from the new White House, and indeed one of the first things the Kennedy administration did was to cancel the lone C-130B that Eisenhower had approved for the Nationalists because of the plane's "probable use."[29] Instead, they substituted one old C-54 and removed the secret nuclear-armed U.S. Army Matador missile unit from Taiwan.[30] One piece of good news for Chiang, however, was that the familiar Dean Rusk, not Chester Bowles, was the new Secretary of State. Although a Democrat, Rusk was known in Taiwan as a strong anti-Communist who believed in a militant pursuit of the Cold War. The honeymoon was short, however: Rusk almost immediately had a falling out with the Generalissimo because of yet another crisis in Burma.

To keep things stirred up and to occupy his forces, Chiang had renewed secret planning for a supposed invasion of the mainland, and again one option was an attack from Burma, where the KMT irregulars, reinforced by paramilitary teams from Taiwan, were already launching new raids across the border into China.[31] Both the Chinese and Burmese governments were tired of the KMT activities, and in a joint military operation with the PLA, the Burmese Army drove most of the KMT soldiers into Laos and captured Mong Pa Liao, the main Nationalist base in Burma. They also seized five hundred tons of American military supplies and weapons, creating an early diplomatic embarrassment for the new administration in Washington.[32] Dean Rusk sent stern messages to Chiang demanding that he pull out all KMT troops in Burma, and Kennedy wrote the Generalissimo a letter saying that the free world could "best meet the challenge of communism by strengthening its democratic institutions and making them more responsive to the aspirations of the peoples of the world."[33]

April 17, 1961, the very day Kennedy's lecturing letter arrived, the CIA-supported Cuban exile force landed at the Bay of Pigs in Cuba and Castro's Revolutionary Armed Forces quickly defeated it. In Chiang's eyes, such a small landing force was doomed, and the attempt was yet another testament to the pusillanimous nature of America's global leadership. Vice President Lyndon Johnson came to Taipei in May and assured the Generalissimo that the United States had no intention whatsoever of recognizing Communist China and, in his inimitable fashion, added that the Kennedy administration policy was "to love one's friends and hate one's enemies."[34]

In an early friendly reply to a Kennedy letter, Chiang stressed that his government would never accept a two-Chinas arrangement in the United Nations. But soon a problem arose in the United Nations regarding Nationalist recognition of Outer Mongolia. The Nationalist government in 1946, following the Soviet failure to live up to its commitments regarding Manchuria, had renounced its recognition of the Soviet puppet state, the Mongolian People's Republic. Chiang was upset when the new State Department team wanted Taiwan to abstain from using its Security Council veto to prevent Mongolia's admission into the United Nations; at stake was a threatened USSR reprisal in which the Soviet Union would veto the admission of the next third-world country in line—Mauritania. If this happened, the State Department believed, the African members of the United Nations would blame Taipei and possibly switch their vote on the China representation issue. In rather poor timing, the State Department also proposed to the White House that the United States recognize Outer Mongolia in hopes of weaning it away from Moscow. Chiang was informed of both these proposals and about the same time learned that the State Department was preparing to grant a visitor visa to Thomas Liao, a Taiwanese independence leader residing in Tokyo.

These developments convinced Chiang that it was time to come down hard on the young American President, who in Chiang's eyes, was already taking him and Nationalist China for granted. In June 1961, Chiang and Madame met privately with Ambassador Drumwright to give him a message that was bound quickly to reach Kennedy's desk. The United States, Chiang said, was treating its ties with the Republic of China as a "master-servant relationship." He warned of "very serious consequences" if this continued. He protested the pressure on the Mongolian issue. He also said that U.S. proposals for dealing with the Chinese representation issue in the United Nations were not only ineffectual but constituted a plan to bring about a "two Chinas" arrangement. The Republic of China, he warned, would withdraw from the United Nations rather than be party to such an arrangement, and "the U.S. would have to bear responsibility" for the consequences. The American government, he charged, seemed to be embarking on a calculated change of its China policy. If this should be borne out by further unfavorable developments, relations between Nationalist China and the United States "could be seriously prejudiced with unfortunate results to security and other interests of both countries." Most alarmingly, he said that Thomas Liao's admission to the United States would represent a "U.S. Government supported conspiracy against him and his regime."[35]

Drumwright hurried back to his office to warn Washington that should it admit Liao to the United States, U.S. influence on the island could be "diminished, or destroyed."[36] Another believer in Chiang's threats, Ray Cline, still the CIA chief in Taipei, reported that Chiang was deeply disturbed by U.S. policy and he was "preparing dangerous adventures" up to and including "a suicidal landing on the mainland." Although yet another National Intelligence Estimate of the time concluded that as long as U.S. economic and military support continued, Chiang's government would survive and adjust, this analysis was ignored—just as similar analyses had been passed over during the Eisenhower years, or probably never read at the highest level. Kennedy felt he could not take a chance that the Nationalist leader, being in what Kennedy perceived as an apocalyptic mood, would in fact "pull the house down on himself—and on us."[37] After the Cuban debacle, Kennedy could not risk another disastrous setback with the Communists, and he wrote Chiang informing him that the U.S. government would indefinitely delay both the granting of a visa to Liao and the recognition of Outer Mongolia. He assured the Taiwan leader that his "primary purpose" was to "support the Nationalist Government in every possible way" and to keep the Chinese Communists out of the United Nations.[38]

Chiang's threats had worked. In a secret deal with Kennedy, he promised not to veto Outer Mongolia's membership in the United Nations and in return Kennedy generously pledged that if and when the Chinese representation issue ever came up in the U.N. Security Council, the United States would use its own veto if necessary so as to "be effective in preventing Chinese Communist entry into the U.N."[39] By using his timeworn device of threatening self-destruction, Chiang had wrung a major commitment from the new American President in return for not doing something that, in fact, would have damaged his own government's interests. He thought that his brinksmanship and statesmanship had won over the young American President, whom he considered inexperienced but apparently sincere.[40] But the old stratagem was wearing thin; when Chiang next tried using it to advance his interests, he would find that he had overplayed his hand.

I

Newspapers in Taiwan were full of vivid stories of malnutrition and famine throughout China resulting from Mao's disastrous Great Leap Forward, and in his 1961 New Year's speech, Chiang proclaimed that the Nationalist Army would soon return to save the Chinese people and the world from disaster.[41] That June, he let the Americans know that he had ordered his generals to plan for the grand invasion on August 1 with or without U.S. agreement. But the deadline came and went. Over the next year, he continued to engage in much posturing about his determination to do something major militarily to help the people on the mainland. He cabled letters to Kennedy, talked with visiting American officials, and had his son, Ching-kuo, again pass alarming messages to Cline indicating that various dates had been set for the "counterattack" and that anti-U.S. riots were possible on Taiwan if the United States was perceived as holding back determined action. At one point he outlined a plan for arming two to three hundred guerrilla fighters and sending them to the mainland. On March 14, 1962, he told visiting Assistant Secretary for Far Eastern Affairs W. Averill Harriman that "unless action was taken soon he might lose control." Harriman was the first American official since 1950 directly to call Chiang's bluff, saying he had no fear the Generalissimo would in fact lose control.[42] Still, Chiang began noticeable preparations for a relatively large-scale attack across the Strait and stepped up commando raids on the mainland coast.[43]

Kennedy feared the U.S.-China lobby would get "geared up" again if he simply turned down the Generalissimo. Thus to placate Chiang and his advocates he agreed that provided there was no further public discussion in Taiwan of a return to the mainland, the United States would give the Nationalists two C-130s and train the crews, with the aircraft and crew remaining in the United States until the two governments decided jointly that an operation was feasible.[44] Chiang rebuffed the offer, saying he was ready to postpone "the date for possible action against the mainland" to October, but that was the latest date.[45] He then proclaimed an emergency national defense surtax on almost all government levies and some public utility rates for a period of fourteen months, so as to prepare for an "eventual military operation" to recover the mainland.[46] Washington was "shocked" at being presented with this fait accompli, and the director of the U.S. Agency for International Development (USAID) mission was instructed to say that such actions might force re-examination of U.S. aid programs.[47] Chiang, unfazed by this threat, continued the surtax and extended the period of required military service.[48] The world press treated these and other actions as preludes to a Nationalist attack on the mainland.

In the middle of May, Chiang passed the word that because his generals were increasingly dissatisfied, it would be difficult to postpone action against the mainland beyond October 1. If the United States could provide the Nationalist armed forces some key aircraft and naval vessels, however, he might be able to overcome this pressure.[49] He specifically mentioned five C-123s, sixteen B-57 bombers "to neutralize Chinese IL-28 bombers if hostilities broke out," and twenty to twenty-five landing ships capable of carrying tanks (LSTs). With the receipt of these items, Chiang said, he could weather further delays "more gracefully."[50] This bald effort at extortion did not go down well in Washington.

At this time, the People's Liberation Army began a major movement of troops and military aircraft into Fujian and other southern provinces. Zhou Enlai knew Chiang well enough to believe that the Generalissimo would not conceivably risk any serious military action under existing circumstances. Yet the Communists could not risk being caught off guard, and besides, the troop movements might encourage Washington to end Chiang Kai-shek's bluff regarding a military attack. The State Department's Bureau of Intelligence and Research mistakenly concluded that the PLA moves indicated Mao had in fact decided to create a new offshore crisis.[51] But this analysis served Mao and Zhou's interest because it was fear of just such a contingency that led Kennedy finally to inform both the Soviets and the Chinese that the United States had "no intention under existing circumstances of supporting a Nationalist Chinese attack on mainland China," and that if Chiang Kai-shek did attack, the United States would "disassociate itself from that attack."[52] The U.S. press and wire services reported the gist of the exchanges on this subject in Warsaw, Moscow, and (through the British) Peking. But to drive home the point, on June 27, Kennedy told a press conference that the United States opposed the use of force in the Taiwan Strait area.[53] Chiang was stunned by all these reports.

Kennedy also sent out a tough new ambassador to Taipei to handle the Generalissimo—retired Admiral Alan G. Kirk, commander of the U.S. naval armada during the Normandy landings. Kirk, Kennedy thought, had the age, the military record, and the prestige to confront Chiang Kai-shek on the military questions of the moment. Kirk arrived in Taipei in July and during their first meeting, Chiang complained that the United States had undercut its ally in its talks with Peking. He did not expect the United States to declare its support for a Nationalist counterattack, he said, but given the need to maintain the morale of the Nationalist armed forces he did not see the necessity of Washington's "declaring to the enemy that the U.S. would not help" its ally Nationalist China. Presumably following his talking points, Kirk simply lied—the United States, he said, had only, as in the past, proposed to Peking a mutual renunciation of force.[54]

Chiang clearly did not believe him. Nonetheless, he said he fully agreed that only when and if the two governments mutually decided that conditions on the mainland were suitable for an invasion would military action—that is, the counterattack—be seriously considered. Chiang then implied to Kirk that he knew very well that parachuting a few hundred men into the mountains of South China would certainly fail. But in his estimate, this sort of limited failure would be better for the authority and prestige of an exiled and minority government than inactivity. What Chiang was asking the Americans to understand—but found difficult to say directly—was that except for the uncertain possibility of a dramatic "new situation" created by a great upheaval inside the People's Republic, the whole business about a counterattack on the mainland was a question of appearances, language, psychology, politics, and domestic morale. To him, the Americans inexplicably still did not comprehend this simple reality. Two days later, he sent his ambassador in Washington to ask Rusk, "could the U.S. at least not make public statements which the Chinese Communists can exploit."[55]

In early September, Ambassador Kirk formally notified Chiang that President Kennedy had decided to send two C-123 transports to Taiwan but not the requested bombers and landing craft unless new circumstances warranted. As a token (and rather ludicrous) gesture, President Kennedy also had approved CIA support for twenty-man Nationalist airdrops into China. Chiang was not happy and one more time he gave his usual warning—if popular demands to help the people on the mainland were thwarted, eventually it would be difficult for his government to keep things under control. "The GRC is ready to abide by the treaty," he said; nonetheless, when conditions on the mainland change, "the treaty must be reconsidered." But then Chiang reverted back to a candid plea for Washington to understand that as far as the U.S. position on a Nationalist attack across the Strait was concerned, the problem was "letting the world know about it"—that is, broadcasting that under the U.S.–Nationalist China Mutual Security Treaty the Nationalist government "was not free to do this or that." Washington, he asserted, "could have said that if a large scale uprising took place on the mainland this [would be] an internal matter."[56]

What he "really had in mind," Chiang explained, was not obtaining new military equipment but simply creating "a greater area of understanding" between the U.S. and the Nationalist governments. Washington, he charged, was fostering "the idea that it was beginning to be a friend to the Chinese Communists while binding its ally [the Nationalists] hand and foot." This approach, he said, was what threatened to undermine morale and stability on Taiwan.[57] Seven days after this meeting with Kirk, the State Department sent a message to Chiang protesting terrorist bombings and other activities in China carried out by Kuomintang agents based in Hong Kong and Macau, and demanded that these operations be terminated immediately.[58] Chiang refused to receive Kirk again for the rest of the year.[59] Meanwhile, Peking shot down the first of three Nationalist-flown U-2s to be lost and easily wiped out the nine twenty-man Nationalist teams that had parachuted into South China.[60]

For some years, Chiang had suffered from difficulties with urination. According to his private physician, Dr. Xiong Yuan, in 1960 or 1961 Chiang finally agreed to have an American Army urologist from Okinawa perform an operation. The American surgeon was so nervous, presumably about the consequences of making a mistake given the eminence of the patient, that as he prepared for the operation, his hands shook.[61] The trouble recurred in 1962 and Dr. Xiong decided that another operation was required. This time, Madame Chiang arranged through her brother T.V. for a prominent New York surgeon to come to Taipei to perform the procedure. Mayling stayed in the hospital with her husband, although such visits always stirred up her hated dermatitis.[62] The second operation was largely successful, but as is often the case after such procedures, Chiang would suffer incontinence the rest of his life. For this reason, he began a routine of remaining seated at the conclusion of meetings until everyone—except his aides—had departed. He also began to show other signs of the frailty of his age. His inspirational remarks or instructions following his morning conferences were shorter than before or skipped altogether. He religiously continued to hold his Monday morning memorial service for Sun Yat-sen, but his remarks on these occasions as well as his Easter sermons were also abbreviated.[63]

The October 1962 Cuban missile crisis completely consumed Kennedy and his national security team, and was intensely followed by Chiang Kai-shek. The result of this second Caribbean confrontation in a year and a half was to intensify the search by the two superpowers for new ways to reduce the chances of nuclear war and the spread of nuclear weapons, including via a nuclear test–ban treaty. This shift fed Mao's perception that the Soviet Union and the United States were conspiring against China to deny it nuclear weapons. The same month as the Cuban crisis, after years of skirmishing on the Sino-Indian border, Mao ordered the PLA to throw the Indian Army back from the existing line of control in the disputed Eastern Himalayan region, and then, having made Mao's point, to withdraw. During the altercation Moscow sided with India, widening the Sino-Soviet rift; in addition, Mao's Himalayan adventure reinforced the image of the People's Republic as an aggressive power. The likelihood of a Chinese nuclear test within a year or so became a matter of "great concern" not only to President Kennedy and Chiang Kai-shek, but also to the Soviet leaders.[64]

At the end of December 1962, the American MAAG discovered that the Generalissimo planned to equip an additional airborne regiment and to build a hundred landing ships, using funds raised by the special military surtax.[65] After the New Year, press leaks in Taipei as well as CIA reports suggested yet again that a major attack against the mainland was in the works. The Nationalists were also caught trying to buy equipment like parachutes and rubber boats from Japan, Belgium, and elsewhere.[66] All these acquisitions were of course still pitifully small in terms of any incursion on the mainland. Allowed back in to see the Generalissimo, Kirk said flatly that the United States could not support a Nationalist invasion across the Strait and would not condone it.[67] Kirk, who never understood Chiang's thinking on the matter, returned to Washington, where he told the President that he thought the Generalissimo believed he had to fulfill his promise to invade the mainland and was hoping to drag the United States into the venture.[68]

Two very senior KMT officials, however—Defense Minister Yu Dawei, the longtime intellectual stalwart from Chiang's own Zhejiang province, and Zhang Qun, the closest and oldest of Chiang's few real friends—separately told American officials on the island that they should not take the Generalissimo seriously on this question.[69] Possibly Chiang himself was behind these candid comments. The U.S. Embassy chargé Ralph Clough was the first American diplomat to look under the surface of words and deeds and suggest that Chiang's real objective was simply to gain "the appearance" of greater freedom of action in order to benefit his public posture. What Chiang wanted, Clough concluded in a dispatch to the State Department, was possibly a formula by which the United States would only appear to agree not to oppose his taking armed action against the mainland, and to pretend that it would take a hands-off policy if such an attack did take place.[70]

By the summer, many other American officials were realizing that Chiang Kai-shek was well aware that a serious Nationalist attack on the mainland would be a calamity. After Cline's transfer out of Taipei, a CIA station report from that post summed up the new view: the Nationalist government "probably does not anticipate that either the current situation in Communist China or the current international situation favors a successful GRC attack."[71]

Meanwhile, taking a new tack, Chiang sent Ching-kuo to Washington to suggest that the American and Nationalist governments work together on a plan to destroy PLA missile sites and atomic installations. The NSA paramount McGeorge Bundy told Ching-kuo that the U.S. government would examine his proposals carefully.[72] Perhaps not coincidentally, the CIA had also recently suggested options whereby the United States could take out Peking's nuclear facilities, including through joint operations with either Taiwan or the Soviet Union.[73] Two months later, however, the administration

Chiang inspecting the island of Quemoy, ca. 1963. At the time, he was once again threatening to invade the mainland, but his senior Nationalist officials were reassuring the Americans that he was not serious. Courtesy KMT Party History Institute.

came to the conclusion that a "Chicom bomb" would have marginal strategic consequences, and it categorically rejected the idea of "strangling the baby in its cradle."[74]

In November the Chiangs learned of the military coup in Saigon and the plotters' execution of dictator Ngo Dinh Diem and his brother, Ngo Ding Nhu, head of the South Vietnamese secret police. The Chiangs had many ties to the Diem regime—Chen Cheng, for example, had visited Saigon earlier in the year and met with both Diem and Nhu. In addition, Nhu had traveled to Taiwan at least once to confer with Ching-kuo and probably the Generalissimo. The encouragement by the United States of the removal by coup of the South Vietnamese leadership was a tremendous shock to Chiang.

The coup reinforced the Chiangs' mistrust of the Americans and no doubt caused them once again to redouble clandestine surveillance of their own senior military officers. Twenty days after the death of Diem, news reached Taipei early one morning of the assassination of President Kennedy. Madame

Nhu saw Kennedy's assassination as divine retribution for the killing of her husband and President Diem, and Chiang likely shared her view. He failed to send a special delegation to the Kennedy funeral and later his government explained it was an "oversight."[75]

Two months later, in January 1964, a coup did take place in Taipei, but it was a farcical one. Chiang Wei-kuo's hand-picked successor for five years as commander of the First Armored Division, Zhao Zhihua, assembled his troops and tanks one morning and announced that they would drive to Taipei in a show of force because the Generalissimo was not seriously pursuing the mainland counterattack. The division's chief political officer shouted his support but rushed to the stage and tackled the commander, who was then arrested. After the incident, Wei-kuo fell under a cloud with his father and brother from which he never emerged.[76]

Meanwhile the threat of a widening war continued to hover over Indochina. On April 16, 1964, Secretary Rusk flew into Taipei for two days of talks. The Generalissimo gave a restrained presentation of his views—nothing like his doomsday lectures to Cline and Drumwright—even saying that he was "opposed in principle to the use of nuclear weapons particularly in resolving the China problem" and that U.S. bombing of South China would only create more hatred of the United States.[77]

Although Chiang rejected the idea of using nuclear force, in the mountains outside of Taipei the clandestine project continued—exploration of the feasibility of building a nuclear weapon. But the venture would not remain a secret to the United States. In its most successful operation aimed at penetrating the Nationalist regime, the CIA recruited a young army officer with a scientific bent who was assigned to the ultrasecret project. This agent would keep the United States well informed of its progress.

On the economic side, Chen Cheng and the technocrats had worked up an accelerated economic development program, including incentives to overseas investors such as tax holidays, unlimited remittance of earnings, and removal of laws requiring participation of Chinese (Taiwan) citizens in all foreign investments on the island. The new plan also emphasized incentives for domestic private enterprise and export-led growth. As a matter of ideology, many members of the old Kuomintang remained enamored of government enterprises, the policy of import substitution, and the discouragement of foreign investment. Washington's goals and those of the Nationalist reformers, however, were to wean Taiwan from American economic aid and lay the foundation for a surge in economic growth by the middle of the 1960s. Chiang fully supported the modernization strategy.[78]

As any first-time visitor to Taipei in the mid-1960s could see, the city ringed by mountains, though still poor, was a pleasant place not just to live, but to thrive. Per capita income was increasing almost 7 percent a year, but income distribution remained surprisingly equitable. Unlike on the mainland, there was no malnutrition. Hundreds of good Chinese restaurants, like the most popular ones along Hengyang Road, were crowded with customers, and farmers' markets were cornucopias of meat, fruit, and vegetables. Along the side streets, thousands of small shops and stalls hawked radios, noodles, electric fans, fresh fruit, hardware, and every other sort of inexpensive consumer item. Old and new Buddhist and Taoist temples were flourishing, as were hundreds of pachinko parlors (a Japanese legacy). Dozens of movie houses, some new and air-conditioned, showed movies from Hong Kong, dubbed ones from the United States, as well as new, popular Taiwanese films in the native dialect.

Television was also a part of Taiwanese life. Small black-and-white television sets were becoming affordable even in a household of average income. A government-controlled TV station broadcast hugely popular Chinese soap operas, which, it was reported, the Generalissimo and Madame regularly watched. Basketball was the most popular spectator and participant sport, with military teams providing the main competition. Baseball was a legacy from the island's Japanese as well as American experience—and it would soon become a national preoccupation.

By this time, too, more than half the people on the island lived in urban areas, and many of those who remained on the farm owned mechanical tillers that converted to three-wheeled vehicles. Most families had bicycles; some had motor scooters. Despite heavy military spending, education spending in the 1960s represented about 13 percent of the government budget, and during the decade, the government raised the age of compulsory education to nine years.

Nationalist military officers enjoyed American-style officers' clubs with bars, dining rooms, and swimming pools, while well-to-do Taiwanese had opened country clubs and were avidly playing golf. Twenty thousand Americans were now living on the island, many in local neighborhoods, and the interaction was usually positive. The popular practice of sending college graduates, children of both mainlanders and Taiwanese, to pursue graduate studies in the United States over the long term had a great influence on Taiwanese life—between 1954 and 1989 a total of 115,000 such students would make the trip, more than from any other country in the world.[79] A few American graduates were already returning and adding another protein jolt to Taiwan's economic muscle and to its emerging modern outlook on government. Among them was Lee Deng-hui, who received his Ph.D. in agriculture from Cornell University. Lee would become the first native Taiwanese governor of the island and eventually, President.

Chiang could still get mad or pretend to be angry, but now he rarely showed his famous temper. Previously known for his micromanaging leadership style, he more and more left matters in the hands of Ching-kuo, Chen Cheng, and the technocrats. In his office, his desk was always clean. He used the five brushes in a ceramic container to sign documents with his rigorous style of calligraphy, which was once described as like a fugitive frog hunkering down in a torrent.[80] Often he would simply write on each document shorthand for "can do" *(ke)* or "can't do" *(bu ke)* and his secretaries would complete the answering memo. He continued his Friday morning intelligence briefings, which included updates on any developments on the mainland, but his Thursday morning inspection tours and Saturday morning military conferences were fewer. His afternoons were usually free of state business. He would be back in the residence by 1:00 p.m., nap until 2:00, and then eat a small lunch, usually joined by Madame or if not, by Ching-kuo. Afterward, he might walk in the gardens with his dog and then, sitting by the shaded pond, clap his hands and watch the large golden carp respond. He would spend the rest of the afternoon in his study. One secretary assumed that he was thinking of the counterattack, but others assumed he was mostly reading Tang poetry, Mencius, or a book of history.[81]

There had been very few state dinners at any time during Chiang's long reign, but now there were even fewer. If visitors were to dine with the President, they usually came for an informal meal. Even at the formal dinners, Chiang ate his soft vegetables, seafood, and his one indulgence: shark fin soup prepared by his cook, a specialist in ancient Ningbo cuisine. He also treated himself to Coca Cola, which in the 1950s and 1960s came from the large U.S. military commissary not far from the Shilin residence.

At some point, Mayling's favorite niece, Jeanette Kung, took over management of Madame's many charitable organizations and other activities, including oversight of the Chinese-style Grand Hotel, which Madame chaired. Jeanette continued to sport close-cropped hair and to wear either the traditional

Chiang on Taiwan with Vice President Chen Cheng, ca. 1963. Chen was an honest general, but the Chiang family worried that as the official successor to Chiang he would interfere with the long-planned ascendancy of Chiang Ching-kuo. Courtesy KMT Party History Institute.

Chinese man's gentry gown or a Western suit and tie.[82] She had female lovers, including the mother of a close friend of the wife of Alan Chiang, Ching-kuo's oldest son.[83] Another favorite relative of Madame's was her nephew Louie Kung—now a wealthy oilman in Texas who had married the beautiful movie actress Debra Paget. Louie was active in Republican circles and by the

1960s was Mayling's key adviser on American political developments. Louie provided his famous aunt a luxury apartment in New York as a home base when she was in the United States. In the early 1980s Kung built a 40,000-square-foot nuclear bomb shelter on his Texas land.[84]

Chiang worried about his grandchildren. Alan was a convivial, handsome, and intelligent young man, but his drinking problem became serious during the 1960s and together with his inherited diabetes would eventually cause a serious health crisis. When an early effort at a military career did not work out, the Generalissimo arranged a job for him at the Taiwan Power Company. Alan married a fine-looking woman named Nancy Zi, whose mother was German, and she gave birth to Chiang's first great-grandchild, a beautiful Eurasian girl named Youmei.

Ching-kuo and Faina's daughter, Amy, against her parents' wishes, had in America married a much older man—the son of Yu Dawei, the long-time minister of defense. Living in America, she soon presented the Generalissimo with a great-grandson, Theodore. Alex, who had also inherited his father's diabetes, after some drifting went to school in Germany. The youngest of Ching-kuo and Faina's brood, Eddy, entered the Military Academy, but after two years he, like Alan, dropped out and entered National Taiwan University. The family's inclination to Eurasian unions continued as the now-widowed Wei-kuo married a woman also of Chinese-German parentage, and the couple soon had their first child, a boy named Gregory. With these new births the family gatherings again rang with the sounds of playful little children. The seventy-five-year-old Generalissimo relished his reign as patriarch with his line of descendents assured, all Eurasian except for the two undeclared sons of Ching-kuo, John and Winston, who did not carry the Chiang name, and who were discreetly supported by Ching-kuo in their university studies.

II

In 1963, Chen Cheng became ill with what turned out to be liver cancer. He took leave from his position as premier, and then, resentful of Chiang Ching-kuo's increasing power in the party and the military, officially resigned.[85] As the new Vice President, Chiang chose the accomplished technocrat C. K. Yen, who was serving as finance minister. Yen was politically a "soft" figure, close to Madame Chiang, and certainly acceptable to Ching-kuo. The Taiwanese and Americans both liked him because of his focus on development. Yen would, in effect, be the nation's chief operating officer.

Ching-kuo still managed sensitive political issues. He now tried to win over Taiwanese oppositionists, arranging light sentences for handing out illegal pamphlets and other banned activities, releasing detainees early, and offering them jobs. He could also threaten to confiscate the family property of recalcitrants, a tactic that worked with the independence leader Thomas Liao, who gave up his activities in Japan and returned to Taiwan. For local elections he allowed independents again to have poll watchers and three non-oppositionists won key mayor's races, including in Taipei, which had again become a city led by an elected leader.

Meanwhile Taiwan's international role as the locus of the government of all China was beginning to come apart. In early 1964 the French President Charles de Gaulle recognized Peking, not Taipei, as the government of China, but did not break relations with the Nationalists. Pushed by Washington, Chiang showed flexibility and did not sever relations with France until told by Paris that the Nationalist diplomatic mission there would soon lose its raison d'être. Chiang felt he had unnecessarily lost face and he would not repeat that experience.[86]

At the same time, corruption once again began creeping into what had been a comparatively honest bureaucracy. Civil service salaries had not kept up with inflation, and teachers and even military officers who were once thought to have "iron rice bowls" were said to be taking bribes—and where possible, dipping into public funds—in order to maintain their standards of living. Academics were holding down two or three jobs, and petty crime increased.[87]

III

In October, when China exploded its first nuclear device at Lop Nor, Chiang told the Americans that the irrational Chinese Communist leaders would use the weapon against their "main target"—Taiwan and the Nationalist government. The people of Taiwan, he said, felt that their American friends were now asking that "they wait for death."[88] In a letter to President Lyndon Johnson, he again urged the United States "at least" to give the Nationalists the wherewithal to destroy the Chinese nuclear installations. By now, however, the Americans were completely cynical about the Generalissimo's harangues. In his letter of reply Johnson reaffirmed the principles in the 1958 Dulles-Chiang communiqué, which stressed political means to achieve the ouster of the Chinese Communists. The U.S. government, Johnson said bluntly, had no evidence of a weakening of Communist control on the mainland, and he doubted conditions there favored military action.[89] As a gesture, he ordered the stationing on Taiwan of one or two American Phantom jets with tactical nuclear bombs as another supposed deterrent to a Chinese nuclear attack. But the real purpose of the jets and their weapons was for possible use against mainland China should Peking intervene directly and massively in the Indochina war.[90]

Meanwhile, Chiang continued to worry that the Americans were sinking into an ever deeper quagmire in Vietnam. Ten years earlier, he had predicted that the French, with or without U.S. support, could not win in Indochina. Now, in a long and notable letter to Lyndon Johnson dated November 23, 1964, he wrote that when fighting Communist insurgents, Asian nations "should individually assume the principal responsibility to prosecute the war to a successful end." Anticipating the Nixon Doctrine, he urged Johnson to provide only U.S. training in the rear, help with operational plans, logistical support, and, "at most . . . advice and supervision at the front." The worst case, he warned Johnson, was for the United States to become caught in a protracted war of attrition, which would "impoverish the people [of the country concerned], create social disorder, and . . . [lead to] hatred of Americans." Chiang also feared that the American people would have neither the stomach nor the nerves to endure such a war for long.[91] This was a perceptive analysis, albeit one that most informed Americans of the time did not share.

It followed that Chiang believed his troops would be no more welcome or successful fighting insurgents in other Asian countries than were the Americans. Nevertheless, he felt obligated to offer assistance as a U.S. ally; during various meetings with Americans, when the subject came up, he would casually say that he was willing to send troops to Vietnam if asked. But as in the case of the Korean War he never pressed the matter and when the American Joint Chiefs recommended seeking Nationalist troops for the war, Rusk rejected the idea, fearing it could provide a pretext for massive Chinese Communist intervention. Rusk also correctly pointed out that the Nationalist leaders themselves would only want to send large numbers of their forces to the Asian mainland if it was part of a war to defeat Mao. When during a visit to Taipei Secretary Rusk told Chiang that America was not going to put large numbers of its conventional troops on the Asian mainland, Chiang warmly welcomed the statement. "Vietnamese manpower," he said, "should be used in Vietnam, and Chinese manpower in China."[92]

But despite Rusk's statement and apparently against his earlier instincts, in the spring of 1965 the first of 500,000 U.S. combat troops arrived in South Vietnam and began offensive operations. Chiang, of course, had to continue to cooperate with his essential ally, and during the war of attrition in Indochina that he had predicted and feared, Taiwan provided important aid to the South Vietnamese in addition to key rear-base support for the Americans. Chiang Ching-kuo secretly sent Nationalist special forces to work with South Vietnamese paramilitary groups, including one involved in sabotage raids into the North.[93] CAT and Air America (another CIA operation with facilities in Taiwan) provided air support to CIA activities throughout the region. South Vietnam's psychological warfare and political officer programs sent teams to Taiwan to study Nationalist methods in these fields, and Taipei dispatched a military advisory group of twenty-five political officers.[94] Finally, Ching-kuo's intelligence officers, working with elements in the ethnic Chinese community in South Vietnam, played a role in the 1965 military coup in Saigon that brought in General Thieu as president.[95]

Because of his failing eyesight, the seventy-eight-year-old Generalissimo now did little reading himself, and his staff did not inform him of some things that he might have considered unpleasant.[96] But he did keep up-to-date on developments related to Washington's China policy, the Indochina war, and political machinations on the mainland (which suggested to him a developing power struggle between Liu Shaoqi and Mao). Unlike Mao, Chiang was completely comfortable with his succession arrangements. Ching-kuo, who had been named defense minister at the beginning of the year, was effectively the country's chief executive. The Generalissimo was like the aging founder of a surprisingly successful family corporation who becomes chairman emeritus and attends meetings but spends little time in the office and makes fewer and fewer decisions. Ching-kuo's key supporters now dominated the military and the party leadership as well as the intelligence and commissar establishments, a situation that seemed to assure his ascendancy.

In August 1965, Mayling returned to the United States for her last public speaking tour. In one stretch of eighteen days she gave fourteen speeches.[97] During a dinner given by Secretary Rusk, she urged the United States to provide her husband with the capability to take out China's nuclear installations. Congress held a reception for her, President Johnson and Lady Bird had her for tea, and she received New York's "key to the city" as well as various honorary degrees. But she made little diplomatic progress with the Americans.[98]

A month after his stepmother's U.S. trip began, Ching-kuo traveled separately to the United States where he met individually with the President, the defense secretary, the CIA director, and McGeorge Bundy—a reception re-

The Generalissimo, Madame Chiang, and their family—except for the then-unacknowledged twin sons of Ching-kuo and the twins' children—ca. 1965. Courtesy KMT Party Historical Institute.

flecting the Americans' assumption that their guest was the next Generalissimo. But the younger Chiang also made clear to the Americans that they would not be dealing with the same seemingly irrational advocate of war with Red China that they took his father to be. First of all he did not mention a preemptive attack on nuclear facilities. He did dutifully present a new plan to seize five southwestern provinces in China, but he made clear that it was his father's idea, not his, and that it was "not an operational proposal." He instead stressed that recovery of the mainland "depended on winning over the people and the Communist Armed Forces."[99]

The younger Chiang, however, was not completely candid with the Americans about his military plans. Three months before his trip, his father had ordered Taiwan's super-secret nuclear bomb project to move out of the research stage and into development. Before making this decision, several high-ranking Nationalist officials and "presidential advisers" reportedly told the Generalissimo that a "Manhattan Project" for Taiwan would be economically unsound, technically unfeasible, and politically unwise.[100] One likely assumption of the dissenters was that the Americans would inevitably discover the project, which they did.

Both Chiangs were worried by the drift in the public debate in America toward an assumed need for accommodation with Communist China. In April the Generalissimo told the CIA's visiting Ray Cline (who was now at CIA headquarters) that he believed some change would likely take place in U.S.-China policy "whether the U.S. now intends it or not."[101] Indeed, Washington and the West in general showed mounting signs of wishing to come to terms with the giant, nascent nuclear power that was no longer an ally of the Soviet Union. The term "containment without isolation," first employed by the China scholar Doak Barnett before the Senate Foreign Relations Committee, suggested that America's goal should be the inclusion of China in the world community. That summer, President Johnson called for "reconciliation" in Asia, while Senator Edward Kennedy demanded immediate admission of Peking into the United Nations. Meanwhile, on Taiwan, the CIA began to "minimize" its support to "unproductive, infeasible" Nationalist mainland operations, particularly paramilitary ones, and to reduce the size of its huge Taipei Station.[102] The U.S. MAAG informed Ching-kuo that the Military Assistance Program would gradually shrink to about US$30 million a year by 1970.[103] These moves reflected the diminishing importance of the relationship for the United States, but they were also indirect reflections of a growing feeling in America of the potentially huge importance of mainland China in world affairs.

From the day he arrived in Taiwan, the elder Chiang believed he would live out his life on the island—and it was becoming increasingly clear that the future of the Nationalist Party would probably be on Taiwan for decades or generations to come. In March 1966, when the National Assembly reelected the elder Chiang to a fourth term as President, it also approved a significant constitutional amendment pushed by Ching-kuo. To reflect population growth on Taiwan, the change allowed special popular elections in three years to fill new seats in the National Assembly and the Legislative Yuan. The additional seats amounted to only 5 percent or so of the total membership of the two elected bodies, but they would add both much-needed young blood to the aging institutions as well as native Taiwanese (including a few real oppositionists). This tiny but symbolically important step reflected Ching-kuo's recognition that the fundamental political challenge to the Kuomintang's future was the disaffection of the majority Taiwanese population.

For more than fifteen years, father and son had dealt with the potential challenge of disaffection in two dramatically different ways: by providing reasonably good governance and improving economic and social conditions, and by employing ruthless police methods. But by the mid- to late 1960s, Ching-kuo and his coterie of relative moderates realized that they could not continue indefinitely to rule as a communal minority exercising martial law and constantly suppressing dissent. They envisioned a transition over twenty or more years to democratic, majority-rule governance. At the time, however, most foreign observers believed that the native Taiwanese would not give the regime nearly so long to transfer power and that the entrenched mainlander minority would never surrender their dominance and accompanying privileges without a violent struggle.[104] Furthermore, the former internal security and intelligence czar, Chiang Ching-kuo, did not seem to be the kind of person who could lead a peaceful transfer of authority.

The younger Chiang almost certainly did not discuss in frank terms with his father the sensitive issue of a transition to majority rule. A number of decisions that the older man approved during his last decade, however, suggested acquiescence in the general direction that Ching-kuo wished to move the party. He probably went along with the new course primarily because he perceived it as a tactic necessary to appease the Taiwanese and the Americans. But the Generalissimo was also a serious man who was earnest about implementing Sun Yat-sen's commitment to eventual democracy, even if not in his lifetime. Thus his acquiescence in the political reforms to some degree also probably reflected this commitment.

As defense minister, the younger Chiang ordered the retirement of 500 generals and 2,000 colonels—all mainlanders. Meanwhile the number of Taiwanese in the military academies steadily grew and the first Taiwanese field-grade officers began to assume positions of leadership.[105] By 1970, of the 260,000 civil servants in Taiwan, 160,000 were Taiwanese.[106] Ching-kuo also had to deal with the 800,000 or so old soldiers who, after marching back and forth through China and fighting battles for the Generalissimo for as many as thirty years, had been brought to Taiwan almost twenty years earlier. They were effectively an ocean and a war away from their home villages. The U.S. and the Nationalist governments agreed that there was a critical need to make sure that these hundreds of thousands of ex-military men who had no wives or families did not become a threat to Taiwan's social and political stability.

With U.S. financial support, Chiang's government began the process by re-tiring about 180,000 "ineffective" members of the armed forces who were judged too old, disabled, or uneducated to be suitable for duty.[107] Every vet-eran who could work was assisted in finding a job such as a construction worker or street cleaner, or helped with small loans so he could become, say, a pedicab driver or a street vendor. Some received small plots of land from Tai-wan Sugar Corporation estates and assistance in getting started as farmers. With American money, conditions for those soldiers still serving were also vastly improved with increased pay, new quarters, and healthy food. In ad-dition, without U.S. assistance, the general Political Warfare Department opened thirty-seven "tea houses" or brothels with a thousand "hostesses" as a further effort to keep the ex-warriors content.[108]

As the Sino-Soviet split widened, Chairman Mao became obsessed with the "embourgoisement" of Soviet society and the priority of avoiding such a fate for China. His obscurantism and self-absorption had been encouraged by the idolatry that increasingly surrounded him, as well as by his persistent deep belief in the supremacy of the will and the centrality of the ruler and his doc-trine. The disaster of Mao's Great Leap Forward opened up a political rift within the CCP, which further fanned the flames of radicalization. Beginning with the purge of General Peng Dehuai, a faction led by Mao's wife, Jiang Qing, and Lin Biao sought to advance itself by catering to the Chairman's Manichean views and megalomania. In sum, an amorphous chemistry of in-ternal, external, and idiosyncratic developments combined to create a vicious storm—the Great Proletarian Cultural Revolution.

On June 16, 1966, a remarkable period of officially sanctioned chaos be-gan to sweep over China and every school, office, shop, and factory—every organizational unit of the society except for the PLA and agricultural villages, which Mao and the military leaders isolated from the troubles. Youth and workers were exhorted to use mob and kangaroo justice to cleanse their insti-tutions of revisionist, antiparty leaders, as well as others in authority such as teachers. In Xikou, the hundred or so Chiangs most closely related to the Generalissimo who had had the bad luck to stay behind were made to sweep the streets and take on the dirtiest jobs in the hamlet.[109]

In the prevailing madness, Mao and the Communists seemed to Chiang to be revealing their true natures. But unlike his reaction to the troubles in China fostered by the Great Leap, he did not call for U.S. support of an attack across the Strait; instead he told the visiting Secretary of State Rusk that in view of the recent purges and resulting "restiveness" inside China, he and his people could "afford to wait for an opportunity" to recover the mainland.[110] The Cultural Revolution seemed so irrational that almost anything could happen, even the breakup of China into warring regions. In addition to his understanding from the beginning that a counterattack was wholly unrealistic militarily, it was now apparent that a serious armed attack by the Nationalists might well unite the bitterly divided Communists. Chiang believed the best strategy was to wait patiently and enjoy the spectacle of Mao shredding his own image and that of the CCP.

By early 1967, an open power struggle seemed under way throughout China and various military and provincial leaders were successful in thwarting Mao's control in their regions or institutions.[111] The role of the PLA in putting down the Red Guards was growing rapidly. Chiang came to think that the fight would go on for a long time, possibly twenty to thirty years—far past his own lifetime and that of Mao—and that the Chinese economy would possibly suffer "disastrous results." It was also possible, he calculated, that a "reunified China under a different leadership" could eventually emerge. "In this connection," Vice President Yen told President Johnson in May 1967, "we have our aspirations."[112] Chiang liked to imagine that if Mao was ousted, the successors might look to him. But more likely, he feared, a victorious anti-Mao group led by Liu Shaoqi or some other moderate figure would restore the Sino-Soviet bloc and thus pose an even greater threat to the Nationalists and to his own position than had Mao.

By this time, American-trained scholars at Ching-kuo's think tank, the Institute of International Affairs, were providing analyses of mainland developments that the Americans thought were relatively objective.[113] Among their conclusions was the view that despite the Cultural Revolution, Communist China's military strength was continuing to grow. Each month the arms industry of the People's Republic was building new conventionally powered submarines, ground-to-air missiles, and twenty to twenty-five MIG-19s (and soon MIG-21s).[114] The growing power of the new China, the fanaticism of the Cultural Revolution, and Radio Peking's strident Red Guard propaganda made the Soviet Union view its former ally with growing alarm. In June 1967, China exploded a test hydrogen bomb and analysts expected Mao to have an intercontinental ballistic missile by the early 1970s.

During a visit to Taipei, Secretary Rusk, "in strict confidence," informed Chiang that in a recent conversation Soviet Foreign Minister Andrei Gromyko, obviously thinking of China, had told him it was regrettable there was no provision in the 1963 nuclear test ban treaty "to enforce its provisions on non-signer nations." Rusk informed Chiang that the United States would "follow up" on Gromyko's remark.[115] Meanwhile, the Soviets increased their divisions on the Chinese border from fifteen to twenty-one. All these developments reinforced Chiang's determination to lay low and let events take their course. In his 1967 New Year's message, he said Taiwan's task was to strengthen its political preparations to ensure a smooth transition in the wake of the inevitable fall of the Communists.[116]

Despite Communist China's new and multifaceted displays of extremism, public commentary in America indicated ever-increasing support for some sort of détente with Peking. Consumed by the growing tragedy in Vietnam as well as the civil rights and antiwar movements at home, Americans seemed to welcome the possibility of a friendly reconciliation with China, Communist or not. In an article in the distinguished journal *Foreign Affairs,* Richard Nixon declared simply that the United States "could not afford to have China forever outside the family of nations, there to nurture its fantasies, cherish its hates, and threaten its neighbors."[117] While few informed observers understood the import of this one-liner, Chiang saw it as a serious omen.[118] Still, it did not darken his otherwise buoyant mood.

Chiang still had strong American supporters, including Walter Judd, the former missionary doctor and conservative Republican congressman. That September, Judd came to Taiwan to see the Generalissimo. During a tea party at the Yangming Mountain residence, the Chiangs discovered it was the sixty-ninth birthday of their longtime American friend, and Mayling spontaneously invited Judd and his accompanying staffer to an impromptu birthday party that evening. During the friendly occasion, according to Judd, the Generalissimo seemed remarkably healthy, vigorous, and mentally alert. He ate heartily and, Judd observed, was in unusually good spirits. In fact, Chiang's serenity on this occasion was to result in the most unguarded and revealing statement that he ever made to a foreigner and perhaps to anyone about his loss of the mainland and his reign on Taiwan.

Twice during the evening the Generalissimo turned philosophical. From a historical point of view, he said, it would probably prove to have been "providential the mainland was lost when it was." Twenty years on Taiwan had given him "the chance to show the world, undisturbed by actual conflict with

In September 1967, Chiang met with visiting longtime American supporter Congressman Walter Judd. He told the American that losing the mainland had been "providential." Courtesy KMT Party History Institute.

the Communists, the proper path for an undeveloped nation to achieve true progress." What had been achieved on Taiwan, he explained, could never have been accomplished on the mainland under all the pressures that accompanied the Communist threat. The programs so successful on Taiwan had failed on the mainland "due to subversion and the Government's inability to give them full attention while engaged in a civil war."[119]

These fascinating remarks suggest that the profound irrationalism of Mao's Cultural Revolution had caused Chiang to think that Communism would actually fall in China sooner or later—and that his and his son's mission was to make Taiwan a model that would demonstrate to the world, especially the people on the mainland, "the proper path" for China to achieve its dream of a great nation restored.

Later, after a toast with the missionary doctor/congressman, the Generalissimo grew pensive again. Although previously he had confided to his diary that he would end his days on Taiwan, the Cultural Revolution had changed his mind: he told Judd that he would spend his ninetieth birthday on the mainland. Referring to the Cultural Revolution, he said that, in effect, Mao Zedong was doing all he could to speed the Nationalists' return. The best posture was to watch and wait. He then recited an unusual medley of one Chinese and three Western proverbs, each of which reflected his traditional and long-tested faith that despite the vagaries of history he and China were children of destiny:

> Bees steal from one flower only to pollinate another;
> Whom the Gods would destroy they first make mad;
> The mills of fate grind exceedingly slow but exceedingly fine; and
> It is always darkest before the stars come out.[120]

IV

In 1968, the United States suffered a series of setbacks that threw into disarray basic assumptions about its foreign policy. The new year had hardly begun when North Korea seized the American signal intelligence ship the USS *Pueblo* and held its eighty-three officers and crew as spies. Chiang Kai-shek was not surprised that Washington, bogged down in Indochina, made no threat of reprisals; instead the Americans engaged in lengthy negotiations to free the prisoners. A week after the Pueblo Incident, Viet Cong guerrillas aided by North Vietnam Army troops launched the Tet offensive, attacking hundreds of cities and towns in the South. For the Communists, who failed to hold any new ground, it was a military defeat but a political victory, prompting Robert McNamara to resign as secretary of defense. Then, in March, Lyndon Johnson startled the world by announcing that he would not seek reelection and by turning down the request for an additional 206,000 soldiers by the U.S. commander in South Vietnam, General William Westmoreland.

Chiang's prediction was coming true: the people of America did not have the stomach for an ambiguous, drawn-out, costly land war in Indochina against Communist insurgents. As he repeatedly had warned the Americans, the disciplined Vietnamese Communists—with a safe and enormous supply base just to the north, a superpower supporter further up the map, and the propaganda value of fighting a foreign enemy—were bound to outlast their powerful adversary. As the year went on, he did not say much to the Americans about the war and nothing specifically about the political turmoil in the United States.

But then assassins killed Robert Kennedy and Martin Luther King. Chiang saw these events as "a deterioration of the morals of day to day life" in the United States and the result of "democratic permissiveness."[121] His reaction reflected his greatest fear: that America's reversals in Vietnam would cause it to lose its appetite for the larger Cold War conflict with China. In a rare outburst in the midst of a conversation with the new American ambassador, Walter McConaughy, Chiang said that the American attitude toward the Viet Cong, North Vietnam, and China was reminiscent of "Chamberlain's attitude toward Nazi Germany." There were in fact increasingly audible voices in America calling for reconciliation with Communist China. Assistant Secretary of State William Bundy publicly said there could be no bargaining over the lives of the 13 million people of Taiwan but, he asserted, the U.S. government "fully acknowledged" that the Chinese Communists controlled the mainland. In June, a *New York Times* editorial called for American recognition of Peking as the government of China, but not of Taiwan.[122]

Inside China, the PLA was still busy restoring order and Zhou Enlai was gradually reducing the devastating influence of the Red Guards on foreign policy. Maoist propaganda had taken to accusing the Chairman's internal foes of being "KMT agents" as well as "power holders traveling the capitalist road." Chiang leaped on these words, and in his 1968 Double Ten Day speech said that Mao had been compelled to admit the role of the Kuomintang in stirring up opposition to the Maoist path in China.[123] The American embassy reported around this time that "desultory planning" for mainland recovery continued, but beginning in 1968 "top leaders" in Taipei again regularly acknowledged the obvious to their American counterparts: the Nationalist Armed Forces could not possibly carry out a major unilateral initiative against the mainland.[124]

Meanwhile, the Soviets were still increasing their troop deployments along the Sino-Soviet and Soviet-Mongolian borders. By the end of 1968, both sides had several hundred thousand troops positioned on the frontier.[125] The Soviet invasion of Czechoslovakia in August and Moscow's enunciation of the Brezhnev Doctrine of "limited sovereignty," which justified Soviet armed intervention to prevent the overthrow of a Communist government, seemed a warning to China.

Two months after the invasion of Czechoslovakia, a Russian national named Victor Louis, the Moscow correspondent for the *London Evening Star*, arrived in Taipei. Louis, clearly a KGB agent, had several conversations with one of Chiang Ching-kuo's trusted associates and then one meeting with Ching-kuo. Louis's remarkable message was that the Nationalists and the Soviets should explore ways to cooperate to bring about the downfall of Mao Ze-dong. The skeptical Ching-kuo replied that if Moscow abrogated the 1950 Soviet-PRC treaty, this "would help Taipei re-orient its mind." Later, in Hong Kong, Louis leaked the fact of his meetings in Taipei. Apparently the KGB purpose was to stir up apprehension on the mainland, which was fine with the Chiangs. In fact, Ching-kuo's man continued to meet with Louis in Europe over the next three years.[126]

Since 1945, the Generalissimo had castigated the Soviets as the source of all evil in Asia, but after Louis's visit, the Taipei press ceased derogatory references to the Soviet Union. Instead, the KMT Tenth Party Congress declared that Mao had created the border fighting with the Soviet Union to divert attention from China's internal crisis. For a period, Taiwan media also began to employ the term "anti-Mao" in place of "anti-Communist."[127] In typical fashion, the Generalissimo also tried to exploit the situation to gain additional U.S. military assistance, telling visiting American generals and admirals that Mao, fearing a Soviet attack in the north, would seek to consolidate a strong military fallback position in southern China. This in turn, he said, could mean PLA pressure on the offshore territories and possibly an attack on Taiwan. If he could not have F-4 Phantom jets immediately for his own air force, he asked that a U.S. Air Force squadron of these planes be stationed in Taiwan.

Chiang, of course, knew that Mao would probably never attack Taiwan at a time when an assault on China by the powerful Soviet Red Army was his overwhelming concern. The White House, now thoroughly inured to the Generalissimo's cries of alarm, calculated that Chiang was hoping to draw out a high-level U.S. commitment that the next administration would find difficult to overturn. But still, to placate the Generalissimo, the Pentagon proposed an intermittent and temporary rotation of four to eight U.S. Air Force Phantom jets for six days a month.[128]

Given all the uncertainties regarding China, the Soviet Union, America, and Indochina, Chiang's strategic goal was to build up a defense capability and make his government as self-reliant as possible. The Chiangs sought to buy an array of some of the most modern U.S. military equipment, including a number of conventional submarines and destroyers, over a hundred tanks, a squadron of antisubmarine aircraft, and twenty helicopters.[129] The secret work on a Nationalist nuclear deterrent had by this time developed a small reprocessing facility (a "hot lab") and was seeking to acquire a research reactor and enriched uranium.[130]

As 1969 began, Chiang was eagerly anticipating the inauguration of his friend Richard M. Nixon as the thirty-seventh President of the United States. Chiang had had a much closer relationship with Nixon than with any other American elected President. Nixon had visited Taiwan six times and each time stayed at the Chiang guest house. The two famous anti-Communists had had many hours of serious and often private conversation about the flow of human events. Chiang thought he knew Nixon quite well and that he was a strong conservative in the mold of William Knowland and Walter Judd. Nonetheless, there was the worrisome one-liner in the 1967 *Foreign Affairs* article about bringing China into the world community.

Soon after the election, Nixon asked Harvard professor Henry Kissinger to be his national security adviser. When Chiang's staff provided Chiang a brief résumé on the professor, he was not pleased to find Kissinger described as "a realist." Chiang knew that the powerful pressures in America to get out of Vietnam, combined with the extraordinary Sino-Soviet split, were steadily increasing the perception among American "realists" of the logic of a U.S. détente with China.[131]

The Chinese in Peking were also ready to be realistic. Before Nixon took office, on November 26, 1968, Peking proposed to Washington another Warsaw meeting to take place the following February. Washington agreed and the meeting was announced. Twelve days after the inauguration, Nixon told Kissinger to "encourage" the idea that the administration was "seeking rapproachment *(sic)* with China."[132] Less than a month into office, Nixon and Kissinger were informing select world leaders of their keen interest in improving ties with the People's Republic. Knowing his words would quickly get back to Peking, Nixon told French President Charles de Gaulle that it was in the U.S. interest to recognize both China and the Soviet Union as "great powers" and to build "parallel relationships with them."[133]

In an April speech, the new U.S. Secretary of State, William Rogers, declared that the United States would take "initiatives to reestablish more normal relations with Communist China and we shall remain responsive to any indications of less hostile attitudes from their side."[134] Most telling for the Chiangs were steps that Nixon and Kissinger began to take to remove military irritants to U.S.-PRC relations. In early 1969, the White House limited aerial reconnaissance of the mainland by the Nationalist-flown U-2s.[135] These statements and moves by Washington represented an astonishing gyration in America's posture toward China, and an incredible personal turnaround for the strongly anti-Communist and conservative Nixon. The Chiangs suspected there was much more going on behind the scenes, but in an unprecedented display of sangfroid, they said nothing when faced with these and other signs of a U.S. policy shift toward Peking.[136]

At the same time, Italy, Canada, Belgium, and West Germany all began talks with Peking about the establishment of diplomatic relations. These countries had also seen the obvious signs that the new Nixon administration wanted to move toward some kind of serious détente with the People's Republic, and they all wished "to get on the bus" before the Americans. In July, on a long Asian trip that significantly did not include Taiwan (an omission Chiang saw as another bad omen), Nixon stopped on Guam.[137] There the American President outlined what came to be known as the Nixon Doctrine, under which the United States would fully honor its treaty commitments but would look to each "nation directly threatened to assume the primary responsibility of providing the manpower for its defense." In essence it meant a revival of the forgotten Eisenhower pronouncement that the United States would never again send troops into a war on the Asian continent—a dictum that Chiang had preached for some fifteen years and specifically urged on President Johnson in his prescient 1964 letter.

The Nixon Doctrine and the beginning of "Vietnamization" (turning the war over to the South Vietnamese) made it clearer than ever that the President was determined to get out of the Vietnam quagmire. Initially, however, Nixon and Kissinger believed that by threatening a profound escalation of the war they could persuade Moscow and Hanoi to accept some compromise resolution short of a near-term Communist takeover of the South. They sent out dire warnings that if, by November 1, the North Vietnamese had not agreed to compromise on American terms, the United States would "take measures of great consequence and force." Should these threats fail to persuade Hanoi, then the second phase of the military escalation option would begin: dramatic military pressure consisting mainly of heavy air attacks in the far north of North Vietnam, and a mining of the port of Hanoi and other harbors. Nixon and Kissinger hoped to benefit from the enemy's perception of the President as a possible "madman" capable of anything—a tactic that Chiang Kai-shek understood well.[138]

Nonetheless, Chiang believed this strategy would not force major concessions from North Vietnam so long as it had the support of China. In fact, he still foresaw a likely debacle in Indochina, but he had to back Nixon. Chiang and his son readily conceded to every American request for cooperation in the Vietnam War effort, including, for example, extending airfields for the emergency landing of B-52s in Taiwan when and if that became necessary. At the same time, it was increasingly evident to Chiang that Nixon and Kissinger saw U.S. rapprochement with China as an element in a Vietnam exit strategy and as presenting a historic opportunity for a fundamental reordering of global politics.[139]

In the summer, Nixon lifted the ban on travel to China for seven categories of U.S. citizens. This was widely seen as a cautious step forward, but secretly the White House was intensifying its efforts to establish direct communication with the Chinese. On August 2, in Sofia, Nixon told President Nicolae Ceauşescu that the United States would welcome the Romanian leader's playing "a mediating role between us and China."[140] Twelve days later Nixon told the National Security Council that it was "against America's interests" to let the Soviet Union "smash" China "in a Sino-Soviet war." He followed up with a specific request to the Pakistani President to convey his views to the Chinese.[141]

In June 1969 Chiang named his son vice premier and the next month Ching-kuo became chairman of the two key policymaking and coordinating boards for financial and economic matters. For the first time, Ching-kuo had formal, not just informal, authority over the economy, although it was officially still under C. K. Yen's control. It was a good year to begin: the growth rate that year would be 10 percent, making a 1,000 percent total expansion of the economy since 1950. The Generalissimo had made Ching-kuo a four-star general in January 1968, a title he retained as vice premier. Ching-kuo, however, still seldom wore a uniform; he usually appeared in a business suit at work but otherwise donned a casual sport shirt. Ching-kuo made other moves to demilitarize the appearance of the regime. Since 1964, parades featuring goose-stepping troops (taught by German advisers in the 1930s), tanks, missiles, and jet flybys had not been part of the Double Ten Day celebrations in Taipei.

The junior Chiang was also still unofficial boss of the hydra-headed internal security establishment, including secret police, commissar, intelligence, and covert action units. But his frequent long walks visiting villages and small towns, and his smiling, somewhat cherubic appearance began to change his political image. On his treks through the countryside he wore frumpy clothing and a floppy, round-brimmed hat. This public image was quite a contrast to that of his father, who still dressed in uniform on formal occasions and at leisure wore his usual prim Sun Yat-sen jacket or a priest-like gentry gown.

One of Ching-kuo's first measures as vice premier was to launch a drive against spreading corruption. The campaign's initial victory was exposure of pervasive graft in the banana business. There were charges in the quasi-free press, however, that in this case and others only relatively minor figures received jail sentences while more elevated culprits escaped punishment. For example, the governor of the Central Bank, who was close to Madame Chiang, was allowed to resign following charges of malfeasance. Nevertheless, most informed foreign observers of the time credited the government as being serious in its drive against corruption. Like his father, Ching-kuo had a reputation for personal honesty, which had continued as he rose in power. Moreover, unlike his father he did not have a rich wife, old ties to a secret society or gang, nor a leadership style that gave loyalty the highest priority.[142]

During the early years on Taiwan, the Generalissimo, like most senior KMT veterans, opposed family planning because the notion of the counter-attack required the prospect of a lot of future soldiers. But in the 1960s, the Nationalist technocrats and officials from the U.S. Agency for International Development pushed a program to reduce population growth by distributing on a massive scale a new intrauterine contraceptive device called the "loop." Taking an old-line Marxist as well as a Sun Yat-sen view—the more Chinese the better—Ching-kuo made a point of opposing the program, a position that served to improve his standing with the old guard, which had long been suspicious of him. The Generalissimo, however, perhaps influenced by Mayling, approved the plan and it quickly showed results.[143]

By mid-July 1969, rumors spread around the globe that Nixon had asked Ceaușescu to mediate between the United States and Peking. State Department officials assured the Nationalists that there was "no truth to such speculation."[144] Kissinger, who was present during the meeting in Sofia, told Nationalist ambassador Zhou Shukai that there had been "no dialogue in Romania on the subject of opening talks with Communist China." President

Nixon, he told Zhou, wanted him to pass along assurances to President Chiang that there had been no change in the basic U.S. policy toward Communist China.[145]

Chiang Kai-shek, however, was an old hand at judging which rumors in the press were likely true and which were not, and he almost certainly did not believe the American denials regarding the Bucharest-sourced reports of the conversations in Romania. Nevertheless, he remained unusually relaxed as shown by his conversations with Secretary of State William P. Rogers during the Secretary's midsummer visit to Taipei. Having warned the United States not to send troops to Vietnam, Chiang now warned that it should not withdraw too quickly. But when Rogers said the temper of the American people would not permit a slow pullout, Chiang said nothing. He asked whether President Nixon was disposed to encourage Nationalist China to go back and free the Chinese people or to "freeze" its position on Taiwan. The Secretary replied that "the United States would be happy if Nationalist China could return to the Mainland by peaceful, political means, but any sort of military venture would not be realistic." This was a simple and categorical statement rejecting the "counterattack," but Chiang did not object. Instead, he assured Rogers that the Nationalist government was "not desirous of attempting an invasion of the mainland because it does not have the capability." This had been starkly true ever since Chiang fled to the island in 1949. Chiang went on to indicate that his concern was entirely with defense, not offense.[146] In addition, he noted that while the United States had supplied Taiwan Nike and Hawk missiles, it had provided only six warheads for each system, making them essentially useless.

Rogers ended by saying it was the age of compromise and the United States intended to loosen trade and travel restrictions on China. Chiang did not respond.[147] Even at this stage the Chiangs seemed to know more than some senior U.S. officials about what was going on behind the scenes, knowledge that convinced them a détente in Sino-U.S. relations pushed by a Republican President and a Democratic Congress could not be stopped. They realized there was little prospect of exciting conservative forces in the United States to reverse the ominous trend. As in other critical moments over the previous forty-five years, Chiang realized he had no good options but to go along with the flow of events and salvage whatever opportunities there might be to advance his country's interests—and his. The main challenge for Chiang and his son was how best, in light of the coming profound setback in Taiwan's relations with the United States and the raison d'être of KMT rule, to retain political and economic stability on Taiwan, continued military support and sympathy from the United States, and access to America's financial investors and open market.

Retaining confidence in the future of Taiwan both on the island and abroad would require the Chiangs to protest American moves to normalization, but also to react calmly to the coming political setbacks—the opposite of the previous tactic of raising alarms of Taiwan's total collapse or even defection if Washington even thought of pursuing any such policy. While U.S. public opinion favored an opening to Communist China, the American people seemed likely to oppose U.S. abandonment of all responsibility for Taiwan's security. The Chiangs knew that preserving this sentiment was key to Taiwan's long-term survival and to winning offsetting U.S. concessions to strengthen Taiwan's defenses.

The Chiangs' strategy for survival also focused on accelerating the advance of Taiwan's economy into more capital-intensive sectors while further improving education and levels of per capita income. As Ching-kuo told the CIA station chief, Taiwan was the only future the Kuomintang would have, and he believed a carefully managed and gradual opening of the political system, including Taiwanization, was essential.[148] To lead this undeclared political program of change, Ching-kuo, doubtless with his father's approval, appointed his longtime political associate Lee Huan as chairman of the KMT provincial committee and a technocrat, Zhang Baoshu (a fisheries expert), as secretary general of the Kuomintang. The dual objectives were to co-opt more Taiwanese into the KMT while cautiously nurturing the growth of a moderate opposition. A rapid turnover of county- and municipal-level Kuomintang executives followed in which mainlanders were replaced with Taiwanese; within a year a third of such executives were native islanders. More Taiwanese also received posts at Kuomintang headquarters in Taipei.

On Ching-kuo's advice, Chiang appointed as mayor of Taipei the anti-KMT, nonparty Henry Kao, a native Taiwanese. Kao had gone out on a limb when he had joined Lei Zhen's short-lived movement to form an opposition party, but he represented the type of pragmatic, native oppositionist whom the Chiangs wanted to encourage: one who disliked or even hated the Kuomintang but was willing to work within the system, even while pushing persistently for greater rights for Taiwanese and a multiparty democracy. That Kao was allowed to say pretty much what he wished in private was part of the approach of co-opting dissidents and allowing them to retain some credibility.[149]

In the middle of the decade, the peskiest gadfly was Li Ao, a flamboyant and plucky publisher of the outspoken *Wen Xing*. In December 1965, Li published an article calling on Chiang Kai-shek by name to remember that the country had officially entered the period of constitutionalism when the rights of the press were guaranteed. Never good at recalling such freedoms, the Garrison Command responded by closing *Wen Xing* and eventually sending Li to Green Island, the main prison for political prisoners, for four years. Although he favored eventual reunification with China, Li, once freed, was later jailed again for allegedly helping the most prominent pro-independence advocate on the island, the professor Peng Mingmin, escape to Sweden. Chiang, however, was convinced that Li Ao had nothing to do with Peng's successful flight; rather, in his view, it had been part of a CIA plan to foster a Peng-led Independence Movement abroad and a détente with the mainland based on a two-Chinas framework.[150]

One fine September morning in 1969, the Chiangs took a ride in their limousine up the steep curving road leading to the residence on Yangming Mountain. Two security cars escorted them up the mountain. As a jeep sped down the hill and swerved across the center line, the security car in front slammed on its brakes and the limousine plowed into its rear. Chiang and his wife were not wearing seat belts and the crash threw them forward. Chiang's dentures were knocked out and he was badly shaken, but he escaped without apparent serious injury. Mayling, however, suffered whiplash when she was thrown into the front seat and one of her legs was injured but not broken.[151]

After the accident, Chiang was never quite as "spirited as before." In a health check, doctors discovered murmurs in the aorta of his heart and suspected that a heart valve had been injured.[152] By mid-November, Madame still could not walk, and four months later she could not sign letters or resume her beloved painting. President Nixon offered to send an American neurologist to treat the Chiangs, but they declined "the kind offer."[153]

V

In the spring of 1969, the Soviet Red Army destroyed a PLA brigade in skirmishes on Zhenbao Island in the Ussuri River on the Sino-Soviet border. The CCP Central Committee ordered a general mobilization along the frontier and four senior PLA marshals recommended that China play "the United

States card." Marshal Chen Yi suggested to Zhou Enlai that China propose high-level talks with the United States.[154]

In August, Secretary Rogers, in answer to a question from Chiang Kai-shek, assured him that President Nixon did not "have any intention to move the Seventh Fleet" from the Taiwan Strait.[155] Three months later, however, the Pentagon informed Ching-kuo that because of budgetary restrictions and a reduction of one hundred ships from its fleet, the U.S. Navy would in fact suspend these token patrols. The Americans explained that this move would in no way affect security in the Taiwan Strait or U.S. commitments. According to archival documents the Defense Department did in fact originate this decision for budget reasons, but the White House immediately saw the positive political implications for its China strategy and quickly approved the proposal.[156] Kissinger's intention was to lead Peking to believe that the action was a conciliatory, confidence-building move by the United States, and Pakistan President Yahya Khan confidentially informed the Chinese of the decision with this explanation.[157]

For their part, Ching-kuo and his father also saw the policy change as another opportunity to pressure the United States for more advanced weapons. On November 19, Chiang dispatched a letter to Nixon warning that the decision on the Strait patrol would tempt the Communists to attack the sea lanes from Taiwan to the Pescadores, as well as the offshore islands. On these grounds he called for an immediate review of the U.S.-Nationalist contingency plan "Rochester" for the defense of Taiwan and the Pescadores. In his letter, Chiang also again endorsed the Nixon Doctrine and reiterated his request for submarines and F-4 Phantom fighters. Nixon sent back a friendly reply saying the United States would be interested in hearing any ideas Chiang had for modification of the defense plan. While Chiang did not get the F-4s or submarines, he did receive five destroyer and destroyer-escort-type vessels, sufficient additional F-104 fighters to replace all F-86 squadrons in the Nationalist Air Force, and local production of the new F-5 fighter. In addition, the U.S. Navy each month also rerouted through the Strait fifteen of its warships traveling to and from Japan.[158]

The elections for new, supplementary members from Taiwan for the Legislative Yuan went ahead in December as planned. Two of the non-KMT candidates, "Big Gun" Kuo Kuoji and Huang Xinjie, violated numerous official guidelines by demanding the end of martial law and going so far as to say that the return to the mainland was "hopeless" and the country would suffer if President Chiang remained in office for long.[159] Ching-kuo certainly had to

have approved this unprecedented tolerance and his father must have acquiesced. While newspapers did not report the stinging attacks, the independent
press criticized the KMT's huge campaign spending and its control of most
media. The two independents won seats, giving the Legislative Yuan two token but real opposition members—a first. Ching-kuo welcomed their presence.

13

Nixon and the Last Years

On December 17, 1969, at a meeting in the presidential residence in Shilin, the new U.S. ambassador to China, Walter McConaughy, relayed an oral message to Chiang from President Nixon regarding American policy on China. McConaughy began by stressing that the Chinese Communist regime posed a continuing threat to East Asia and that America "was not changing its attitude of vigilance." At the same time, he said, the U.S. government "believed that it had an obligation to take every practicable and prudent step to lower tensions" in the region. "In this era," he said, "effective contacts with all great areas and peoples of the world aimed at creating a larger measure of understanding are an imperative necessity." In this spirit, the United States was "making earnest efforts to establish a worthwhile dialogue with the Peiping [Peking] regime."[1]

The White House, McConaughy explained, was "determined to continue the search for serviceable contacts, and we feel it is right and appropriate for President Chiang as a friend and ally to be fully aware of the nature and the purposes of this policy." Speaking for the President, the ambassador then assured Chiang in "the most positive and explicit terms" that the United States stood by its mutual defense commitment to the Republic of China. Nothing related to the search for better relations with the mainland would "dilute that commitment," nor "impinge upon or be prejudicial to any essential interest of the Republic of China," nor "interfere with constructive and collaborative development efforts by our two governments in an atmosphere which we hope will be less shadowed by threats of aggression from the Mainland."[2]

Chiang listened to McConaughy's presentation "intently, with apparent deep concentration and without interruption." For almost thirty years, Chiang had been lecturing Americans on what he perceived as their extreme naiveté regarding the Chinese Communists, and for more than two decades he had believed that an important group of Americans was plotting with the British to move the United States toward the People's Republic and away from Taiwan and his government. But after hearing out the ambassador, Chiang quietly "reflected for a few moments," then simply said that he was "reassured to have the confirmation that there would be no change in the U.S. policy of strong support for the Republic of China." The only concern he raised was the deactivation of the Taiwan Strait patrol, to which McConaughy replied that Nixon had authorized him to say that this action was motivated "purely by reasons of economy." Any "unwarranted and unprovoked" Communist attack on the Republic of China's shipping in the Taiwan Strait, the ambassador continued, quoting Nixon, "would not go unnoticed." Chiang indicated his "appreciation" for this less than impassioned assurance.[3]

This conversation was another striking example of Chiang's clear understanding of the fundamental transformation that was happening in global politics, and of his pragmatic calculation that he would only create more problems for himself if he reacted in high dudgeon. In addition, he probably thought that Nixon's gambit with Mao could fall apart if it stirred up fierce opposition against Mao within the CCP and the PLA. The key issue was going to be how Nixon would deal with the status of Taiwan and how U.S. military relations with the island might change. Chiang could be confident that Mao would not accept a two-Chinas arrangement, and of course he shared Mao's views on this highly sensitive question. A two-Chinas approach, with its inevitable culmination in an independent Taiwan, was the main threat to the Chiangs and to the KMT position on the island. But in the conversation with McConaughy, Chiang did not even raise the matter.

Circumstantial evidence is strong that by this time and possibly some months earlier, Zhou Enlai was informing Chiang through the usual intermediary in Hong Kong of the secret Peking-Washington exchanges via third parties. The following spring, Ching-kuo would tell Kissinger that Nationalist intelligence "in Hong Kong had learned that the Chinese Communists may propose a change in venue for the Warsaw talks, perhaps even seeking to move them to Peking." Kissinger's assistant, Foreign Service officer John Holdridge, was very likely correct in reporting to his boss and to Nixon that

Chiang Ching-kuo was "trying to tip us off that the GRC [the Government of the Republic of China] has intelligence contacts with the Chinese Communists." Taipei's purpose, Holdridge thought, was probably "to remind us that we should not take the Nationalist Government for granted." From the Peking standpoint, Holdridge surmised, "this intelligence by-play is a useful reminder that the Communists' immediate tactical objective in the present talks is probably to see if they can slip a blade in between us and the [Nationalist Government]."[4]

Holdridge, however, overlooked what were likely the main reasons for Zhou and Mao's apparent decision to pass such sensitive information to Chiang. First, they very likely wanted to let Chiang know that he was being abandoned by the United States and thus encourage him to agree to a political settlement with the Communist party. And second, but most immediately, they probably wanted to encourage coordination with Chiang of a firm "no two-Chinas" approach. Zhou and Mao knew that Chiang was no less a Chinese nationalist than they; thus as high-level Washington-Peking talks loomed, it made sense for Zhou to send word to the Generalissimo that the Peking leadership would never accept a two-Chinas framework and it hoped Chiang would take a similar stance. Thus the stage could be set for another KMT united front with the CCP—this time a de facto and undeclared one—to protect the territorial integrity of China. Just as with the behind-the-scenes settlement of the 1958 Quemoy crisis, this cooperative arrangement would involve a mainland agreement not to use force against the Nationalists for an indefinite time.

Sometime in December, Kissinger informed Nixon that President Yahya Khan had "conveyed his impression to the Chinese" that the United States was "prepared to normalize relations with Communist China." Peking responded that it appreciated Pakistan's role in conveying that message and in response would release two American yachtsmen who, the previous February, had inadvertently sailed into Chinese waters.[5] On December 25, the State Department publicly acknowledged the change in the Taiwan Strait patrol and the White House announced that it opposed the effort in the House of Representatives to make available a squadron of F-4s to Taiwan.[6] During the January 20, 1970, meeting in Warsaw, the U.S. representative, Walter Stoessel, told the Chinese that the United States was prepared to send a high-level representative to Peking or accept a Chinese representative in the American capital. As added inducements, Nixon approved the sale of U.S. grain to China and removed most restrictions on the travel of Americans to the mainland.[7]

Kissinger told Nixon that in light of early prospects for concrete negotiations with Peking, "We may need to be somewhat franker (*sic*)" with the Nationalists about what was happening. Kissinger was concerned that the Communists were leaking distorted accounts of the Warsaw meetings to Taipei. The Americans also knew that the Polish intelligence service was monitoring the meetings. The State Department gave the Nationalist Embassy in Washington misleading briefings on the talks that left out the key elements in the exchanges, falsely implying, for example, that "renunciation of force" remained the key American *sine qua non* for any advance in United States relations with China.[8] Meanwhile Zhou Enlai, it appears, was providing Chiang a more candid account.

To the delight of Nixon and Kissinger, during the February Warsaw meeting the Chinese agreed to accept a special presidential envoy for "the further exploration of fundamental principles of relations" between the United States and China. The Chinese made it plain that the "fundamental principle" with which they were concerned was the Taiwan question and that once this was settled other issues could be resolved. They also made it clear that the resolution of the Taiwan issue could not be in the context of "two Chinas" or "one China, one Taiwan."[9] Although the sessions in Warsaw were closed, news reports included much speculation about their content, particularly because the flurry of meetings after a two-year hiatus suggested that significant progress was being made.[10]

In a March letter to Nixon, Chiang referred to the President's "well meaning policy." He also claimed not to object to the Warsaw talks as such, but then proceeded to review the record of failed U.S. attempts to negotiate with the Chinese Communists during World War II and subsequently. The Communists, he maintained, had not changed and he warned Nixon to be on guard. Confident there would not be a two-Chinas arrangement, Chiang's main concern now was the possibility that the United States might consider "accepting the so called Five Principles of Peaceful Co-existence," including noninterference in other nations' affairs, and within this framework discuss with Peking how to settle "the so-called Taiwan problem." Such an approach, he told Nixon, "would be infringing upon the sovereign rights of the Republic of China"—but his specific worry was that this principle could eventually rationalize Peking's use of force to reunite Taiwan with the motherland. All in all it was a light, almost pro forma admonition.[11]

The U.S. side in Warsaw, however, had already accepted the notion that the Five Principles could be cited in an accord that included the subject of Taiwan. Nixon replied to Chiang that he would be remiss in his "duty to the American people if I did not attempt to discover whether . . . certain of the issues which lie between us [the United States and China] may not be settled by negotiation."[12] The President, however, again reassured Chiang that the Warsaw talks "will not affect the friendship and close cooperation which has existed between our Governments for so many years."[13] From the briefings that Zhou evidently supplied, Chiang knew this was not true. But he had no way to avoid or even slow down Nixon's rush to embrace Mao Zedong, so he continued to be calm, preparing to greet whatever happened in American-PRC relations with feigned surprise and considerable resentment but mostly confidence and optimism about the future.[14] "We should forge ahead with dignity," Chiang told his staff.[15] The keys to Taiwan's success would be Nixon's continued commitment to defend Taiwan and to support the Generalissimo's rule on the island. It was critical—though given both Mao and Chiang's fierce opposition, seemingly safe to assume—that the United States would not support Taiwan independence.

When in late April 1970 Vice Premier Chiang Ching-kuo arrived in Washington on an official visit, he received a reception equal to that of a head of government. He stayed just across from the White House at Blair House, where visiting queens and presidents were lodged, and he was afforded an unusual fifty-minute meeting with the President with no other Americans present. Kissinger and the secretaries of both state and defense then joined the meeting, which went on another half hour. At one point, Ching-kuo, in a pro forma manner, told Nixon that Taiwan was "the central problem of Asia" and that the Chinese Communists were likely to launch a surprise Pearl Harbor–like attack against the island. But the President simply ignored this prediction, and Ching-kuo did not repeat it during his trip. Nor did Ching-kuo protest or complain about any of the recent developments in U.S.-China policy, except to politely suggest that for Peking the Warsaw talks were a tactic intended to alienate the United States from the Republic of China. It was at this point that Ching-kuo revealed he had learned from sources in Hong Kong that the Communists might propose changing the venue of the talks to Peking.[16] Before the meeting adjourned for an elegant dinner, Nixon again reaffirmed his support for the Republic of China. He had been a friend of the Generalissimo's nation for twenty-three years, he said, and "the United States will never sell you down the river."[17]

Although he knew what the Americans were up to, Ching-kuo revealed not the slightest doubt about the good intentions of Nixon and Kissinger. In a meeting with Ching-kuo the next day, Kissinger declared: "We believe very strongly in standing by our friends." He then spent some time explaining how President Nixon "was always four moves ahead of the game" and thus his tactical decisions sometimes looked confusing. He spelled out how he and the President went "through lots of maneuvering" before they acted because there "was no sense in tipping our hand." After hearing this expansive description of Nixon's ability to hide his intentions and deal by stratagem, the vice premier said that his President had known President Nixon for more than twenty years and "liked to think that he understood him and knew what he thought."[18]

Kissinger may have believed this was a signal that Chiang Kai-shek understood what the Americans were intending in their China ploy. To make sure, the next day Kissinger, without an interpreter, walked across Pennsylvania Avenue to Blair House for a private, English-language-only meeting with the Generalissimo's son. Ching-kuo understood English fairly well, and that was all that was required for this most likely one-way conversation. In addition to implying that the Warsaw talks would in fact eventually move to Peking or Washington, Kissinger probably assured Ching-kuo that there would not be a two-Chinas context to any U.S.-China agreement, and that the United States would fight for Taiwan's continued representation in the United Nations generally but not in the U.N. Security Council. When a Nationalist official asked Ching-kuo what else transpired at Blair House, Ching-kuo only smiled.[19]

After his meetings in Washington, Ching-kuo flew to New York to address the East-Asian American Council of Commerce and Industry. As he was entering the Plaza Hotel, two young Taiwanese men, pro-independence radicals, darted out from behind marble pillars. One got off a shot that just missed Ching-kuo before policemen tackled them both. Ching-kuo proceeded into the hotel and gave his speech without mentioning the incident, but it made him a hero in Kuomintang circles on Taiwan.

In May 1970, Nixon ordered the heavy bombing of Cambodia but at the same time announced the pullout of another 150,000 U.S. troops from South Vietnam. In retaliation, Peking cancelled that month's Warsaw meeting, though Mao's statement on the bombing was notably constrained. Also that month, Chiang Ching-kuo visited South Vietnam to assess for himself the prospects for the war. His father, he decided, had been right all these years: the Americans could not prevail in such a conflict. The South Vietnamese seemed to have the military forces and equipment necessary to hold off the North Vietnamese and the Viet Cong so long as the United States continued to provide all the material support they needed. But it was doubtful that the rulers in Saigon had enough popular support, and the army enough spirit, to win, and equally unlikely that the American Congress would be willing to keep military aid flowing. The lesson for Taiwan was clear.

Nixon had warned Kissinger that they must not seem to the Chinese to be "too eager" in reaching an accommodation, but while Mao sat back and considered the initiatives coming at him from Washington, the American President in fact continued to be extremely eager. In June, he sent another message to Peking indicating that he was ready to establish an alternative, direct channel for addressing the most sensitive matters confronting the two nations and once again suggesting that he dispatch a high-level personal representative to confer directly with the Chinese leaders.[20] During the summer, however, China seemed to be sending contradictory signals. Zhou Enlai freed the long-imprisoned American bishop James Walsh, but a Lin Biao supporter, Chinese chief of staff Huang Yongsheng, said publicly that relaxation of Sino-U.S. tension was "of course, out of the question." Around this time, too, the Chinese military attempted to shoot down an American C-130 over the high seas, an act that Kissinger saw as possibly an effort by the radicals to sabotage Zhou's efforts.[21]

As these signals indicated, an intense struggle was going on within the Chinese Communist leadership over the question of whether the Soviet Union or the United States was China's main enemy. Lin Biao and the radicals argued that to accept a Nixon envoy in Peking would shatter China's revolutionary credentials. On the other side, Zhou and his allies pointed to the Soviet divisions on China's northern borders. The matter came to a head during the Central Committee meeting in August and September 1970, when Mao proclaimed the Soviet Union to be China's main enemy and informed his comrades of the ongoing talks with the United States on restoring relations between the two countries.

At Mao's invitation, the American writer Edgar Snow stood beside him during the October 1 National Day celebrations, marking the 1949 establishment of the People's Republic of China. In a subsequent five-hour interview with Snow, the Chairman confessed to a belated recognition that his deification had been overdone, saying it was ridiculous to call him "Great Teacher, Great Leader, Great Supreme Commander, and Great Helmsman," titles bestowed on him by Lin Biao.[22] Even more interesting to Kissinger was a report that "Mao told a French delegation that China would never accept "two Chinas," but it could "live with the factual situation.""[23] An early September analysis from the U.S. Consulate General in Hong Kong noted a new direction in China's foreign policy that "may present opportunities for improving relations."[24]

In late August 1970, the Chiangs learned that exiled Taiwanese independence leader Peng Mingmin, who had been in Sweden since his flight from Taiwan in 1969, was about to go to the United States to take a position at the University of Michigan. Since Chiang was convinced the CIA had spirited Peng out of Taiwan, the professor's move to America revived his fear of a Washington-backed Taiwan Independence Movement. Despite a formal protest from the Nationalist foreign minister, Secretary of State Rogers and Kissinger approved issuance of a visa to Peng on the basis that he would sign an unenforceable commitment not to engage in political activities. To the Chiangs, it was inexplicable that this was done without any U.S. warning. After all, the two Taiwanese accused of trying to shoot Chiang Ching-kuo when he was in New York in April were allegedly associated with Peng's pro-independence organization. The Generalissimo sent a personal appeal to Vice President Agnew to intervene in the case, but U.S. officials lamely explained that under U.S. law there was no way Peng could be denied entry.[25] Believing as they did that the CIA had arranged Peng's flight from Taiwan, the Chiangs worried that a "one China, one Taiwan" conspiracy could really be at the heart of Washington's machinations. This possibility was far more dangerous for the Chiangs than was the prospect of a U.S.-China détente.

More reverses for Taiwan soon followed. First, Canada recognized the Pe-king government and broke with Taipei, an expected but upsetting move. Then the American MAAG mission informed the Nationalist Defense Ministry that military assistance program funding for the coming fiscal year would be cut further, from US$30 million to US$7 million. The Chiangs were "shocked" when informed later that all investment items, that is, new or replacement military equipment, would be eliminated and funds for operations and maintenance cut completely.[26] On October 22, Ching-kuo told Ambassador McConaughy that this totally unexpected and unilateral U.S. decision was "outrageous" and that "there had to be policy implications."[27] Ching-kuo then turned to the approval of Peng Mingmin's visa, calling it the "most abrasive event in Sino-U.S. relations in the last 20 years." The assumption in Taiwan, he said, was that the United States was sympathetic to the Taiwan Independence Movement.[28]

In fact, the truth was less complicated. The U.S. government from the top down had simply continued to attach ever less importance to the interests and feelings of its longtime Nationalist allies. McConaughy, who like Agnew was not privy to the White House's fervent courting of Peking, told the younger Chiang that "the best assurance of the steadfastness of this Administration to its commitments lay in the character, the convictions, and the wisdom" of President Nixon and Vice President Agnew. Ching-kuo replied with a straight face that his government "did indeed find much comfort and reassurance in President Nixon's and the Vice President's positions of leadership."[29]

With an eye to the coming transformation in relations with the United States, Ching-kuo replaced all his military chiefs of staff and reshuffled the cabinet, bringing in officials more closely tied to him. Internal security was again tightened and nine prominent mainlander journalists with pro-KMT media were accused of being part of an extensive Communist spy ring.[30] As the director of Taiwan's secret nuclear weapons program, Ching-kuo also arranged the establishment of a new Nuclear Energy Research Center to develop nuclear power plants for the island. The weapons project became a clandestine wing of the new center, but the undetected CIA spy remained in the operation.[31]

Ching-kuo's measured show of anger in his meeting with McConaughy did pay some dividends, however. When Premier Yen met with Nixon on October 25, 1970, the President told him confidentially that he intended to submit a supplemental spending bill to Congress that would attempt to restore "a great deal" of the military aid cut from the Taiwan program.[32] At the conclusion of their meeting, Nixon told Yen that the U.S. attitude toward Communist China had "not really changed." Washington was just keeping some lines of communication open, he said, but would do so "without any illusions."[33] Sometime after Yen walked out of the Oval Office, however, Nixon the same day met with visiting Pakistani President Yahya Khan, telling him "it is essential that we open negotiations with China" and asking him to press the idea with the Chinese of a visit to Peking by a special representative of the American President. The next day Nixon and Kissinger also urged President Ceauşescu to "act as a peace maker" with Peking.[34] In December, Mao responded by telling Edgar Snow that he would be happy to talk with Nixon, either as a tourist or as President.

A November National Intelligence Estimate of China's international posture declared that "Peking does not expect an early major improvement in Sino-U.S. relations."[35] But the U.S. Consulate General in Hong Kong continued to see a potentially more profound foreign policy change going on in China, one that both reflected a serious split in the leadership and was energizing that split.[36] Significantly, most of the relevant memos flying about the State Department and between the foreign missions to the United Nations in 1970 assumed that the China representation issue would have to be resolved through a one China, one Taiwan arrangement.

Meanwhile, the rapidly evolving changes in Taiwan-China-U.S. relations continued to excite changes in Sino-Soviet affairs. The Soviets understood the geopolitical games being played by the Nixon and Mao team, and they did not intend to be the odd man out. After Soviet gestures earlier in the year, Peking and Moscow returned their ambassadors to the other's capital and the two parties exchanged surprisingly warm messages on their revolutionary anniversaries.

I

In the fall of 1970, personal troubles beset the Chiang family. Soong Chingling, still living in Shanghai, got word out that she would like to go to Hong Kong for a family gathering, but hinted that she was unable to leave China.[37] In October, Chiang's oldest grandson, Alan, suffered a diabetic stroke and went into a coma. He recovered partially but remained in the hospital for almost five years. Because of his condition and Madame's ongoing ailments, the Christmas feast that year was subdued. Still, the Generalissimo told some of his English-Chinese puns. And not everyone in the Chiang family was having problems. Grandson Alex had met and married a young Chinese woman in Switzerland, while Eddy was doing well at National Taiwan University. Meanwhile Ching-kuo's twin sons, their parentage still not public or known by their cousins, began successful careers. John entered the Foreign Service and Winston became a law professor.

In his 1971 New Year's message, the Generalissimo warned the people of Taiwan that they faced "endless difficulty, danger and pain"—and indeed, he soon had to endure another slight from the Americans.[38] Details of the planned U.S. return of Okinawa to Japanese administration included an unpopulated group of rocky islets north of Taipei called the Diaoyutai (or in Japanese, Senkaku), which were claimed by Taipei, Peking, and Tokyo. The Chiangs were furious that the Americans had failed to even consult with them before this change in plans, especially since recent explorations indicated that sizable oil deposits might exist around the islands.[39] When anti-American demonstrations uniting Taiwanese and mainlander youth broke out in Taipei and other cities, the Chiangs allowed the protests to continue, seeing them as a unifying show of nationalism and independence. Besides, they wanted the oil, if any, for Taiwan. The Diaoyutai had long been administered as part of Taiwan and Kissinger seemed to believe the Nationalists had a good case. The White House, however, was absorbed with its secret initiative with Peking. In January it received from the Romanians a reply to Nixon's message to Zhou Enlai. "President Nixon," Zhou said, "would . . . be welcome in Peking." Nixon quickly told Kissinger: "I believe we may appear too eager. Let's cool it."[40] The next day the Americans read a Zhou Enlai interview with Edgar Snow that seemed to signal the return of "peaceful coexistence" as the general line of China's foreign policy.[41]

For the next two months, however, events elsewhere sidelined any progress.[42] In March, the Pakistani Army brutally put down the Bangladesh War of Independence, and as many as 10 million refugees poured into the poverty-ridden state of Bengal in India. A war between India and Pakistan, backed by superpower military strength, threatened to break out. Moscow supported India, the Chinese backed Pakistan, and primarily because of the Pakistani President's role as an interlocutor with Peking, Washington also took the side of Islamabad.

Meanwhile on Taiwan, Ching-kuo continued to take small steps forward toward democracy and a more open society. The Institute of International Affairs held a "Sino-American Conference on Mainland China," during which many Taiwanese as well as American scholars criticized Taipei's conventional wisdom regarding China.[43] Also in January, the government approved publication of a new journal, *The Intellectual* (*Da Xue,* literally "University"), which ran articles demanding new elections for all the central government bodies.[44] Ching-kuo made public speeches urging young people to express their opinions and criticisms, and the government cancelled a much-heralded urban development project for half a million people that had provoked large protests by farmers in the area. For the first time, the Chiang regime was reacting to popular pressures on specific issues.[45]

But Ching-kuo drew a sharp line between, on the one hand, criticizing the political structure and the leadership, and on the other, advocating Taiwan independence or trying to organize an opposition party. In March he agreed to the detention again of the mainlander writer Li Ao, and Garrison Command police rearrested Professor Peng Mingmin's two student associates and former jail mates.[46] The government also expelled an American missionary couple and a Japanese tourist charged with involvement with the Independence Movement. And at the insistence of Taipei's Foreign Ministry, the U.S. Embassy transferred off the island a junior CIA officer and four American military personnel accused of giving advice to Taiwanese dissidents.[47]

The State Department put forward various options to expand U.S.-China trade and travel, but warned that they might provoke a severe crisis in relations with Chiang Kai-shek. Nixon and Kissinger, however, paid no attention. They were looking for the right opportunity to put trade with China on the same basis as that with the Soviet Union, and finally an innocuous "triggering event" occurred in early April. Mao woke up in the middle of the night with a decision to approve an invitation to a U.S. Ping-Pong team competing in Japan to visit China.[48] In response to this pregnant move, Nixon and Kissinger immediately announced the elimination of the embargo on nonstrategic trade with China, offered to admit Chinese visitors to the United States, authorized American vessels to carry Chinese goods, and freed controls on the use of U.S. dollars in trade with China.

That same month, Nixon and Kissinger dispatched retired ambassador Robert Murphy to brief Chiang Kai-shek about Washington's official thinking on how to handle the China representation issue in the United Nations. Murphy told Chiang that because it was no longer possible to bar the Chinese Communists from the United Nations, the United States proposed that Peking be invited into the General Assembly, while the Republic of China would retain its seat in the Security Council as well as in the Assembly. Chiang, as well as Kissinger, knew Mao would never accept this solution, but despite its obvious two-Chinas cast, Chiang said he would go along if his government did in fact retain the Security Council seat. Suggesting this would not be a problem, Murphy pointed out that the Nationalists had veto privileges in the council, but then said he would check with the White House on whether this right could be assured.[49]

Murphy, however, had been misled as to the real thinking of the White House. He never got back to Chiang on the veto question and three months later Kissinger would make plain in his talks with Zhou Enlai that the United States would in fact support Peking's replacement of Taipei in the Security Council—not the other way around—thus assuring Taipei's complete withdrawal from the United Nations.

On April 24, 1971, T. V. Soong, then seventy-seven years old, choked to death on a bone in a San Francisco restaurant. While Mayling was on a flight to the United States to attend her brother's funeral, the news media reported that her sister Chingling would also be there. Chiang and his son, fearing that a chance meeting between the sisters might fan speculation of a deal between Peking and Taipei, ordered the plane to return. This probably upset Mayling. She would have been thrilled to have seen her much-beloved sister. Then she learned that, contrary to the news reports, Washington had no indication that Soong Chingling was seeking to visit the United States for any purpose.[50]

T. V. Soong had been a controversial figure, but whatever his flaws, his career was a historic one. Over the years, he had consistently pushed for fiscally responsible policies, including restraints on military expenditures. He had long harbored an exaggerated idea that he might someday succeed Chiang, but he had no base of support in the military or the Kuomintang. Many things about the Generalissimo always grated on the sophisticated Soong, including his neo-Confucian earnestness, but he admired his brother-in-law's single-minded pursuit of national unification and empowerment. T.V. himself, like his sister Mayling, had a temperament that "wavered between black depression and gay courage."[51] Perhaps not surprisingly, then, their sibling relationship was also bipolar. Like Mayling, T.V. remained closest to his leftist sister Chingling and he always kept a photo of her on his desk, which never provoked an objection from Chiang Kai-shek.[52]

For decades the large and efficient Chinese rumor mill circulated numerous stories that T. V. Soong and H. H. Kung, both of whom came from very rich families, had stolen vast fortunes while in office. When he died, Soong's estate left a net of about $2.7 million to his heirs, a surprisingly small legacy, but unknown foreign bank accounts were of course possible.[53] Some historians on Taiwan who have studied the issue believe that Soong probably did not accept bribes but did earn huge profits at certain points by having inside knowledge of the government's financial policies. When he was in private business in the early 1930s, for example, he knew the Nationalist government intended to replace gold with silver as the standard backing for China's currency, and he allegedly profited hugely from this. But the charges of criminal as distinct from unethical profiteering seem to lack concrete evidence.

While the American Ping-Pong players were still in Peking, Nixon met at the White House with the Nationalist ambassador, Zhou Shukai, who was returning to Taipei to become the Generalissimo's new foreign minister. This was the first opportunity Nixon had had since taking office to explain his intentions toward China to a ranking official close to Chiang Kai-shek. Nixon asked Zhou to tell the Generalissimo that the United States would "stick by our treaty commitments to Taiwan" and "will be very much influenced by what the Generalissimo will think." He also warned Zhou that "we will take some steps [with Peking] in the next few days that are primarily to be seen as part of our world perspective, particularly vis-à-vis the Soviet Union."[54]

That same day the ambassador saw Kissinger, who told him that pending steps toward Peking "had nothing to do with U.S. relations with the Government of the Republic of China." Kissinger asked Zhou to explain to Chiang that if the administration was "obliged to do things which caused them [the Nationalists] pain, this would be to the minimum extent possible." The message was not reassuring, even though Kissinger also promised that the American side "would do nothing without checking with the ROC." Despite these commitments, however, nothing would be checked with the Republic of China.[55]

After Ambassador Zhou returned to Taipei and briefed the Generalissimo on Nixon and Kissinger's "minimum pain" assurances, Chiang did not ask to see McConaughy or in any other way respond to these tortuous signals of American intentions. According to a ranking military aide in his office at the time, Chiang by this point had made clear to his senior staff that he despised Nixon. Chiang had always been careful not to let his subordinates hear him vent about the American presidents, but Nixon was different: he was, in Chiang's eyes, not just naïve about the Communists; he was also disloyal, insincere, and scheming. Chiang hated him even more than Stilwell.[56]

Occasionally Chiang let this anger show to those outside his inner circle. In May, he received David M. Kennedy, former secretary of the treasury, who was in town for negotiations on Taiwan textile exports. After a cordial discussion of textile matters, Chiang brought up a statement made by the State Department spokesman on April 28. The spokesman had repeated Harry Truman's declaration more than two decades earlier that Taiwan's ultimate status awaited final determination.[57] Chiang then became "increasingly agitated" and began "visibly shaking." He said that the recent statement in Washington questioned China's sovereignty over Taiwan and the Pescadores. It was, he said, a "slap in the face." Chiang then apologized, saying he felt so strongly on the subject that he was "not able to help himself."[58] Despite the emotional incident, McConaughy reported after the meeting that the cost to U.S. relations with the Nationalist government of the recent drama in Washington-Peking relations had been "moderate."[59]

In response to Chiang's numerous requests for new weapons systems and for a reduction in the drastic cuts in U.S. support for the Nationalist military budget, Nixon sent word through David Kennedy that he would send a senior military representative in August to review in "a favorable and forthcoming way" important defense possibilities. By October 1971, however, no such mission had been sent or even planned. Still, Chiang made no complaint to Washington.[60]

Around this time, Nixon accepted the avidly sought invitation for direct conversations with the leaders of the People's Republic of China, and the two sides agreed that Kissinger would clandestinely visit Peking in July 1971 to work out the details of a summit for the following year (also to take place in Peking). A week before Kissinger left for Rawalpindi and thereafter secretly to Peking, Ambassador McConaughy, still in the dark about the secret deal, returned to Washington to try to learn what he could about what was going on in U.S.-China affairs. His meeting with Nixon on June 30 was a rambling, incoherent exchange in which the rattled President alternated between rank dissembling and hints of the truth, at one point promising strangely that his administration had no intention of assassinating the Generalissimo. The ambassador began by asking if he was still authorized to say that U.S. efforts to reduce tensions with Peking "would not prejudice the vital interests of the Republic of China."

> *Nixon:* I think that's fair enough. Just say that we, that our—as far as the Republic of China is concerned that we have—we know who our friends are. And we are continuing to continue our close, friendly relations with them. As for their vital interests, what you really mean by vital interests, what you mean is, are we going to turn them over to the ChiComs, is that it?
>
> *McConaughy:* Well——
>
> *Nixon:* Is that what they're afraid of?
>
> *McConaughy:* I think they, they'd find—of course that . . . they know we wouldn't do that. I believe they think of that as just general support for their membership in the U.N.—general international backing of them.
>
> *Nixon:* We will—we will certainly in the U.N. We're not going to support any proposition that would throw them out.
>
> *McConaughy:* Yeah. Exactly.

Nixon soon turned to the core issue.

> *Nixon:* But we must have in mind, and they must be prepared for the fact, that there will continue to be a step-by-step, a more normal relationship with the other—the Chinese mainland. Because our interests require it. Not because we love them, but because they're there.
>
> *McConaughy:* Yeah. Precisely.
>
> *Nixon:* And because the world situation has so drastically changed. This has not been a derogation of Taiwan.
>
> *McConaughy:* Exactly.
>
> *Nixon:* And it's done because, as I say, because of very great considerations in other areas.
>
> *McConaughy:* Yes. Yeah.
>
> *Nixon:* It's a hard thing to sell.
>
> *McConaughy:* Yes it's a——
>
> *Nixon:* I know it's terribly difficult.

McConaughy: Yes. It's tough.

Nixon: They're going to see it in black and white. And they—my personal friendship goes back many years.

McConaughy: It does indeed.

Nixon: They sent the most beautiful gifts to our daughter's . . . [unclear] wedding and so forth. We just—that's the way we're gonna deal with it. The personal considerations here are—we'll put it this way, we're not about to engage in what the Kennedy administration did with Diem. Because they might think that way. Either physically or philosophically, we don't do that to our friends.

McConaughy: Yeah, exactly.

Nixon: You remember that?

McConaughy: Yes. Of course they——

Nixon: The Kennedy administration has Diem's blood upon its hands, unfortunately. That was a bad deal.[61]

Overnight, Nixon seemed to experience some regret over how he would be regarded as treating his old ally. In a meeting the next day with Kissinger he indicated that the talking points on the question of Taiwan for the upcoming session in Peking were "far too forthcoming," and he wanted Kissinger "not to indicate a willingness to abandon much of our support for Taiwan until it was necessary to do so." He asked Kissinger to review the entire discussion of the Taiwan issue so that "we would not appear to be dumping on our friends."[62] During his coming talks in Peking, Kissinger would totally ignore these instructions, and Nixon, in his euphoria over the historic breakthrough, would simply forget his stern directive on the subject. In addition, Nixon told Kissinger that he wanted the leadership summit in Peking to be made conditional on "certain accomplishments": the release of all U.S. prisoners of war held in China, at least some token shipments of U.S. grain to China, and, most importantly, "some progress on the Vietnam war issue."[63] These conditions were also forgotten in the excitement of developing a new U.S.-China relationship.

In the early morning hours of July 9, after much intrigue to throw off the world press, Kissinger and his small party took off from Rawalpindi in a Pakistani airliner, flew over the snow-covered peaks of the Hindu Kush, and then across the vast arid plateau of Xinjiang to Peking. Kissinger's first meeting with Zhou Enlai was later that day. Once it began, Zhou soon established an atmosphere in which the Americans were the petitioners from afar who had come to seek China's benevolent help in resolving a problem between the two morally unequal parties. Kissinger played the part eagerly. Early on in his opening remarks, he noted that "in the earlier contacts between America and China we were a new and developing country in contrast to Chinese cultural superiority."[64] When Zhou complained that Voice of America broadcasts from Okinawa to China were to continue after the island's retrocession to Japan, Kissinger, instead of defending the Voice of America, blamed the decision on the "American bureaucracy."[65] At this time, China was blatantly supporting the overthrow of numerous governments materially as well as rhetorically, but more than once, Zhou referred to America's "oppression . . . subversion, and . . . intervention" in the world and Kissinger gave no critical response.[66]

In explaining how the United States became involved with Taiwan in 1950, Kissinger told Zhou, "For reasons which are now worthless to recapitulate, a previous Administration linked the future of Korea to the future of Taiwan, partly because of U.S. domestic opinion at the time."[67] The implication of everything Kissinger said about Taiwan during his time in Peking was that the American involvement there had been a perhaps understandable mistake, but a mistake nevertheless, and that the goal of the Nixon administration was to end U.S. political and military support for the Nationalist government in a way that would minimize both the domestic repercussions and the damage to America's image abroad. Kissinger said that within a specified period after the ending of the war in Indochina by a U.S.–North Vietnamese accord, the United States was prepared to remove two-thirds of its military forces from Taiwan, possibly within a year and a half. In addition, Kissinger indicated that as U.S.-China relations improved, the United States would begin reducing its remaining forces on Taiwan—to those committed to the island's defense or to intelligence collection.[68]

In seventeen hours of talks, Kissinger only once, and only gently, suggested that unification of Taiwan and the mainland ought to be peaceful. "We hope very much," the American envoy said, "that the Taiwan issue will be solved peacefully." Zhou replied, "We are doing our best."[69] Kissinger also referred only once to a "mutual renunciation of the use of force" agreement between the United States and China, which had been the main focus of the U.S. position in all the Warsaw talks prior to the Nixon era. But now Kissinger, referring to the compromise approach to such an agreement that Mao had submitted in the 1955 Geneva talks, said that the United States was ready to sign an accord "such as you proposed in 1955." Zhou responded in a vague manner but indicated that any such agreement would now have to reflect the fact that the question of Taiwan was a Chinese internal matter.[70]

Zhou made clear that his and Mao's objective was U.S. recognition of Peking as the sole legal government of China. "I must be honest," Kissinger said. "There's no possibility in the next one and a half years for us to recognize the PRC as the sole government of China in a formal way." But, he said, the administration could "certainly settle the political question [that is, disengage from Taiwan] within the earlier part of the President's second term."[71] As for Taiwan's fate after the United States ended its military and political support, Kissinger predicted that the island's "political evolution" would likely be in "the direction" that Zhou Enlai had "indicated"—that is, reunification with the mainland. He stressed that the administration could not within a short period of time formally declare this policy goal, but "we will not stand in the way of basic evolution, once you and we have come to a basic understanding."[72]

Like the Chiangs, Mao and Zhou were especially worried about the independence option for the island. Kissinger repeatedly affirmed that the United States "would not support Taiwan independence." Zhou attached "great importance" to that statement, and he repeatedly came back to the subject, pressing particularly hard on the case of Peng Mingmin, which he had obviously followed closely. Implying that he had had contact with Chiang Kai-shek on the subject, Zhou said that Chiang was complaining about CIA involvement in the professor's flight from Taiwan.[73] As noted earlier, Chiang was convinced that the CIA had been responsible for Peng's escape but he said nothing public on the matter. No doubt reflecting Mao's geopolitical outlook, Zhou also said that Japan's economic expansion would "of necessity lead to military expansion," and he repeatedly came back to the idea that as the United States withdrew from Taiwan, Japan would try to replace it militarily and otherwise on the island.[74]

Chiang Kai-shek, Zhou said, was also opposed to a policy of two Chinas; a one-China, one-Taiwan solution; and Taiwan independence. Again indicating communication with Chiang on the subject, he said the Nationalist leader would be relieved to know that the United States would oppose any Japanese effort to fill in behind the United States militarily.[75] Zhou recalled that he had been political commissar under Chiang at the Whampoa Military Academy and thus he was "most familiar with him." Zhou seemed confident in asserting that Chiang shared Peking's views on the status of Taiwan and on the danger of Japan's role on the island once the United States had withdrawn. At one point, he said that Chiang was able to control his armed forces, but "there are those among his troops who deliberately want to make adventures—deliberately to create trouble for him and for you."[76]

After this first round of talks, Zhou immediately reported to Mao that the American position was even better than they had hoped. Kissinger did not pose any conditions for the Mao-Nixon summit, and he clearly acknowledged in so many words that the U.S. goal was termination of its military and political ties with Taiwan and recognition of the PRC as the sole, legitimate government of China. All of this could be achieved, Kissinger had said, within Nixon's second term, which would end at the beginning of 1977. Kissinger had implied that the United States would put up a show of opposing a two-Chinas resolution in the United Nations by giving Peking the seat in the Security Council and Taipei the General Assembly seat, but the American made plain that this approach would fail, and that the end result would be Taipei's withdrawal or expulsion.[77]

From Kissinger's remarks it was evident to Mao that the United States wanted badly to get out of Vietnam and, in his view, was asking only for help in arranging a face-saving interlude between its withdrawal and Hanoi's takeover. Mao commented to Zhou that it took time for a monkey to evolve into a man and that the Americans were now "in the ape stage." He told Zhou that China was in no hurry on the Taiwan issue but that fighting was going on in Vietnam and China should not give an inch on that subject.[78]

On the second day of his talks with Kissinger, Zhou accordingly adopted a harsher and more hectoring tone. He was particularly tough on the subject of Vietnam, underscoring China's moral commitment to the cause of the Vietnamese people. He made clear that, if necessary, China was prepared to continue its support despite the threat of future retaliation by a frustrated United States. In other words, Kissinger obtained no hint at all of a Chinese willingness to ease America's exit from Vietnam except for the meaningless statement that Peking favored a negotiated settlement. During Zhou's long indictment of U.S. "aggression" and "intervention" and that of its various "puppets," Kissinger continued to refer to China's "principles," to Zhou as "a man of principle," and to Mao's "great inward strength."[79] Having performed his ritual emasculation of the American envoy, Zhou proposed that the two sides decide on a date for Nixon's visit, and with little discussion an agreement was reached.

II

On July 15, Kissinger and his staff departed Peking on another Pakistani airliner, and ninety minutes later Nixon went on international TV to announce the dramatic breakthrough. An hour before the announcement, the President for the first time informed his senior diplomat, the Secretary of State, of the diplomatic tour de force in Peking. Rogers kept his vexation to himself and sent a flash cable to Taipei. The startled Ambassador McConaughy rushed to see Acting Foreign Minister H. K. Yang to tell him of the impending broadcast. After watching Nixon on TV, the officer in charge of American affairs, Fredrick Chien, quickly typed a background memo with his own thoughts for the Generalissimo and Chiang Ching-kuo.[80]

After talking with Chien, Ching-kuo drafted a mild public statement in the name of Premier Yen and carried it to the presidential residence. According to Chien, the Generalissimo was "very calm"; there was no shouting or other show of anger.[81] Chiang approved the statement, which expressed "great surprise and regret," denounced the Communists, and proclaimed that the Republic of China would not yield to any pressure or "to any violence or might."[82] The next morning, KMT and independent newspapers declared that the United States could not be trusted, and the National Assembly charged Nixon with "betrayal." But that day, and the days that followed, people on the island went about their daily business. Foreign diplomats and newsmen, as well as probably Zhou Enlai and Kissinger, were surprised at the equanimity.

In Washington, Chiang's new ambassador, James Shen, lodged a protest with Assistant Secretary Green, and, according to his memoirs, expressed dismay that the United States was secretly dealing with the Communists behind the back of the Nationalist government. This was the strongest protest any Nationalist official would make over the matter, but perhaps the ambassador exaggerated the scolding he gave Green. According to the U.S. record of the conversation, he mildly asserted that the secret visit to Peking could "hardly be described as a friendly act" and expressed appreciation for Green's reassurance that the United States continued to stand by the Republic of China.[83]

On July 17, Nixon cabled Chiang, saying he "deeply regretted" that he had been unable to inform him at an earlier date of the planned talks in Peking.

But "the people of free Asian nations," he explained, would be "the first to benefit from efforts to lower tensions in relations between the United States and the People's Republic of China." Nixon promised that the United States would maintain its ties of friendship with Chiang's "country" (not his "government") and would "continue to honor its defense treaty commitment to the Republic of China."[84] At this point, Nixon knew that Kissinger had agreed in Peking that this commitment would end by 1977 if the United States had successfully withdrawn from Vietnam. By this time, too, Chiang probably knew very well what Kissinger had promised because Zhou had already informed him of the tentative agreement.

While the people of Taiwan remained strikingly calm, there was, as McConaughy later described it, "considerable ferment" within the Nationalist leadership. Most Taipei officials except the Chiangs were shocked by the "Kissinger surprise," and at least a few believed that a "sweeping move" was needed to counter international acceptance of China's claim that it had the right "to take over Taiwan as an integral part of China."[85] Vice Foreign Minister H. K. Yang, for example, told Ambassador McConaughy that the Taipei government should declare it would henceforth be named the Chinese Republic of Taiwan and would "have nothing to do with the Mainland."[86] This was just the scenario that Chiang and Mao feared.

In their upcoming October 1971 meeting, Zhou would tell Kissinger of an interesting development related to the internal KMT division on the crisis. According to Zhou, after the Kissinger "shock," three key "pro-Japanese" KMT officials visited Japan for "a very significant talk" with Prime Minister Sato and former prime minister Kishi about Taiwan's future. The three travelers from Taipei were the President's close associate Zhang Qun; the minister of national defense, Huang Jie; and Gu Zhenggang, the arch-conservative honorary chairman of the World Anti-Communist League (WACL) in Taipei. The Japanese hosts, according to Zhou, made "some suggestions" regarding a formula to solve Taiwan's problem in the United Nations.[87] Sato and Kishi, according to Zhou's report, transmitted a "closely-guarded message" to President Chiang declaring that "the only hope" for the future of the Republic of China was to adopt a course of separation, giving up all mainland claims and pretensions—advice that accorded somewhat with the ideas of Vice Minister Yang (except for Yang's emphasis on a Taiwanization of the government).[88]

Zhou would tell Kissinger that Chiang was "following closely" this danger-ous development, implying once again that he had been in touch with Chiang on the matter and that this contact was the source of his information. Ac-cording to Zhou, Chiang "did not agree to the formula" that was proposed by Tokyo and apparently supported by the pro-Japanese KMT group because it would "turn Taiwan into a subsidiary state of Japan." Chiang was "very ill at ease" and "quite fearful," Zhou would say, about Huang Jie, who in Taiwan was considered to be a possible rival to Ching-kuo after the passing of his father. Kissinger would repeat categorically that the United States would strongly oppose any Japanese plot to overthrow Ching-kuo, but Zhou was to conclude with a warning: "So long as Chiang Kai-shek is still around, he will not permit Japanese military forces into Taiwan, but, as you know, Chiang . . . is already 85."[89]

Zhou was emphatic in recounting the Generalissimo's fears regarding the Japanese and Huang Jie in particular. Rumors were swirling in Hong Kong at this time regarding contacts in the colony between the two Chinese re-gimes.[90] Hard evidence is lacking, but given Zhou's extraordinary remarks and the Hong Kong rumors it seems likely that Chiang had assured Zhou through their usual intermediary in the colony that he would fight to the death against any Japan-centered plot, such as that reportedly suggested by Kishi and allegedly favored by Huang Jie.

But the greatest political turmoil created by the "Kissinger surprise" would occur not in Taipei but in Peking. There it led to a deadly struggle between Mao and his hand-picked successor, Lin Biao. Late in the evening of July 9, 1971, after telling Zhou to speak more harshly with the American visitors at the next meeting, particularly about Vietnam, Mao turned his attention to dealing with Comrade Lin. CCP investigators came to report that Lin's sup-porters in the PLA General Staff had failed to make "self-criticisms," presum-ably meaning confessions. "Behind them," Mao said, "is a big plot."[91] Then several weeks later, the desperate Lin (still officially "Mao's closest comrade in arms"), Lin's son, and several other senior officers were accused of plotting to assassinate the Chairman by bombing his train as he traveled south. The sup-posed plot failed, but it is known that early on the morning of September 13, Lin, his wife, and some of his key supporters rushed aboard a PLA Air Force plane to flee China. The accuracy of the official story of what happened next is of course unknown. What is certain is that a few hours later, the aircraft, which was clearly headed to the Soviet Union, crashed in Mongolia, killing all aboard. As a result of Lin's death, Zhou Enlai's position was enhanced, but the purge of yet another successor badly strained Mao's credibility as a "Great Helmsman." The Chairman now needed to ensure that the opening with the United States, which Lin had opposed, was successfully brought to fruition.

Back in Washington from his July trip to Peking, Kissinger told the delighted Nixon that the breakthrough would send "enormous shock waves around the world," panic the Soviet Union into "sharp hostility," shake Japan loose from its heavily American moorings, [and] "arouse a violent upheaval in Taiwan." Both Kissinger and Nixon were so admiring of the Chinese Communist leaders that they appeared infatuated. Kissinger claimed to recognize that the Chinese leaders "are deeply ideological, close to fanatic in the intensity of their beliefs," but at the same time believed that they displayed "an inward security that allowed them, within the framework of their principles, to be meticulous and reliable in dealing with others."[92]

Nixon assured Kissinger that no one had "less illusions about this initiative [with the Chinese]" than he himself. But at the same time, Nixon suggested that in Kissinger's talks with the media, he point out how "ironically in many ways" he, the President, has a "similar character . . . and background [as that of] Zhou." For example, both had "strong convictions . . . came up through adversity, are at their best in a crisis, are cool and unflappable . . . tough and bold . . . [and] willing to take chances [but also are] subtle . . . almost gentle."[93]

On the key matter of handling the Generalissimo, Kissinger could only suggest to the President the use of more misleading rhetoric while preparing for the traumatic break to come: "On Taiwan we can hope for little more than damage limitation by reaffirming our diplomatic relations and mutual defense treaty even while it becomes evident that we foresee a political evolution over the coming years."[94]

Kissinger told the ROC ambassador Shen that "nothing in his tenure in the White House had been more painful to him" than what had occurred in Peking and that "no people had deserved what had happened less than the ROC . . . our loyal friends." But, he explained again, what had happened had been "brought into play by general necessities, and had nothing to do with Taiwan." Kissinger further explained that the problems addressed in Peking "were not connected with Taiwan."[95] In a follow-up meeting, however, Kissinger indirectly but clearly indicated to Shen that the United States intended to establish diplomatic relations with Peking sometime during Nixon's second term.[96]

Since Truman, Chiang believed, a naïve preference for a two-Chinas solution had guided all American presidents in their views of Taiwan. But now Nixon was actually pursuing a deal with Peking that could strip the Nationalist government of U.S. diplomatic recognition and end U.S.-Taiwan military ties, even as the President continued to profess his steadfast friendship and support for Chiang and his government.

During this period of transition, Nixon sent a new Republican star, the conservative governor of California, Ronald Reagan, to represent the United States at Taiwan's Double Ten Day celebration, which recognized the sixtieth anniversary of the 1911 Revolution. Earlier that morning, during tea back at the Shilin residence, Chiang reacted respectfully to Reagan's explanation of Nixon's coming trip to Peking and his repetition of all the assurances Nixon and Kissinger had given before that the vital interests of the Republic of China would be fully protected. Reagan no doubt believed what he was saying and Chiang said he did "not question the President's good intentions," but he did indicate that he thought such a trip could not be justified unless essential to avert a major crisis, which did not exist. He said he was certain Peking would focus on extracting U.S. concessions on Taiwan and the trip would be "especially hurtful" to his government. Chiang wanted the President to know that he and his people would never permit a Chinese Communist takeover of Taiwan, and would fight to the last man if necessary to prevent it.[97]

Hoping to hold on to as much American support as possible and to avoid creating a panic in the financial and business world about Taiwan's future, Chiang felt it was essential that the Americans and the world know that the island could deal with whatever came out of the Nixon summit with Mao Zedong. Thus later in the day, Reagan was in a place of honor in the reviewing stand when Chiang and Madame, as was customary, stepped briefly onto the balcony of the Presidential Palace. A quarter million citizens cheered enthusiastically and the Chiangs as usual smiled and waved.

In September, Nixon announced that the United States would support the PRC's bid for admission into the U.N. General Assembly and the Security Council, while opposing any effort to expel the ROC from the General Assembly.[98] Nixon, however, knew that Peking would reject any arrangement that left Taiwan in the United Nations in any capacity; for this reason it was likely that even if the American plan was adopted, the General Assembly would expel Taipei within a year. Chiang and his son fully understood that once again they had no alternative. Withdrawing meekly from the Security Council in hopes of a seat in the General Assembly would only result in Taiwan's also losing that position sooner or later, doubling its humiliation. Moreover, Chiang had an informal pact with Zhou Enlai—neither Taipei nor Peking would give an inch in opposing any sort of two-Chinas solution. The prevailing feeling in the presidential offices in Taipei was summed up in the old axiom, "It is better to be a broken jade on the ground than a whole tile on the roof."[99] Consequently, on orders from President Chiang, the Nationalist delegation in New York withdrew from the United Nations on October 25 before a vote was taken on a resolution to expel it. Chiang took comfort in his belief that the United Nations had become a "shameful organization" and "a den of iniquity." Nothing had changed, the Republic of China would persevere, and it would "never permit an outside power to interfere in its affairs."[100]

The people of Taiwan again took the setback in stride. Indeed, most scarcely noticed. "Nobody got excited the day of the U.N. vote. Life went on as usual. Children went to school. *Tai Tai* [wives] did their marketing. In the evening everybody watched television, but the newscasts kept within their usual formats and there were no special programs." One member of the Nationalist U.N. delegation, upon returning home, publicly declared that the outcome was basically beneficial to Taiwan. "The withdrawal will save the country much money and manpower," he said, "We have relieved ourselves of a burden and we can do more meaningful things now." Even some foreign journalists long critical of the Generalissimo and his regime wondered how many other countries "would have appeared less bloody and more unbowed after a succession of reverses such as those the Nationalists have suffered."[101] And not all the international news was bad. Shortly before the defeat in the United Nations, the Taiwan Giants won the Little League World Championship in the United States, stirring patriotic fervor among mainlander and Taiwanese fans alike. Most of the population of ten million, including the Chiangs, watched the final game on television.[102]

Before Kissinger returned to Peking in October, he had a long meeting with the President in which Nixon tried to cover his political and moral flanks, assuring himself he had not betrayed America's Taiwan ally. He told

Kissinger they had "to remember that everything always comes out. I don't think we can have a secret deal, if we sold out Taiwan, you understand? I know what we're doing, but I want to be very careful."[103]

Once again in Peking, Kissinger reaffirmed for Zhou that the United States was "prepared to move toward a normalization of relations with the People's Republic of China, and we understand what you have in mind." The United States, he repeated, would not support or encourage the creation of a Taiwan Independence Movement; a two-Chinas framework; or a one-Taiwan, one-China strategy, and it would oppose the establishment of Japanese military forces on Taiwan. Most striking of all, he also made clear that the United States would not insist on the People's Republic using peaceful means to re-unite the island with China. "To the degree that the People's Republic can on its own, in the exercise of its own sovereignty, declare its willingness to settle [the Taiwan issue] by peaceful means, [U.S.] actions will be [made] easier," he said. After making this statement, Kissinger provided a virtual carte blanche: "But whether you do so or not [that is, pursue peaceful unification or not], we will continue in the direction which I indicated."[104] If, as seems likely, Zhou was briefing Chiang on the talks, he certainly passed along this particular exchange, which underscored the intention of the Nixon administration, once it had broken with Taipei, to tolerate a military takeover of the island by the Chinese.

After Taiwan's withdrawal from the United Nations, Vice Foreign Minister Yang spoke "privately and frankly" with President Chiang about what Yang saw as the need for a major transfer of political power on the island to native Taiwanese.[105] The Generalissimo was profoundly aware of the situation but he totally and apparently calmly rejected any such action.[106] Instead he continued to follow the defensive, against-the-odds, no-good-options strategy that he and his son had devised in late 1969, when he first understood the radical course that Nixon and Kissinger intended to take. It was a posture that involved demonstrating anger, but accepting humiliation and loss when necessary, holding on for the long term, maintaining dignity, upholding principles, expanding economic and military strength as rapidly as possible, threatening to fight to the death to prevent a Communist takeover of Taiwan, and waiting for God and destiny to intervene. In some ways it was like his strategy for dealing with the Japanese militarists before 1937, the war of resistance, the wartime alliance with America, the Stilwell imbroglio, the Marshall Mission, the certainty of defeat in Manchuria, the impending loss of the civil war and the mainland, the political dangers of the Truman-Acheson period, and the crises with Eisenhower and Dulles over the offshore islands.

In all these tense moments, despite feelings of betrayal or belittlement, the Generalissimo sought to keep relations with the United States as close as possible. In the early 1970s, while Nixon went his dissembling way, this meant continuing to provide as much support for the U.S. wars in Indochina and China-targeted intelligence as Washington wanted. It also meant fighting for every toehold diplomatically around the globe, seeking to modernize the Nationalist military, and secretly building a nuclear weapon. But equally important, the strategy called for an even greater focus than before on economic growth in Taiwan and on raising standards of living, health, and education for the population as a whole.

Chiang Ching-kuo, looking even further ahead, agreed with Yang Xikun that the setbacks looming on the horizon only strengthened the conclusion that the ultimate goal was to bring Taiwanese nationals into the government, the party, and the military, so as to eventually form a truly representative democracy that would logically be controlled by native Taiwanese. For practical as well as philosophical and nationalist reasons, he believed that a future democratic Taiwan could remain committed to the one-China ideal. Unlike Yang, Ching-kuo thought this was a process that would take a generation to complete and thus it was critical not to lose political control.

The Chiangs did not expect an ounce of truth from Kissinger about the second, October round of Sino-U.S. talks in Peking. Nevertheless, on the envoy's return, Chiang dispatched Foreign Minister Zhou Shukai to Washington to hear Kissinger's report and to indicate the Generalissimo's critical but calm reaction to events. Repeating his instructions from Chiang, Zhou Shukai told Kissinger that what was most needed on Taiwan in the wake of the loss of its U.N. seat and ongoing changes in U.S.-China relations was "a calm atmosphere" among the public and the business community. The main fear, the foreign minister said, was a sharp flight of capital or a panic in the stock market. In practical terms, he explained, if the Republic of China could withstand the initial shock, keep the economy stabilized, and maintain industrial production, the ordinary people couldn't care less whether the country was in the United Nations or not.[107]

This was a candid acceptance of the reality of U.S.-China détente and Taiwan's fall into international limbo—just what Kissinger and Nixon wanted to hear. It reflected a type of policy thinking in Taipei similar to that which

Kissinger had urged in a separate meeting with Ambassador Shen. For the present, Kissinger advised, the Nationalist government "should work hard, sit tight, . . . see what happen[s] . . . [and] not do anything precipitate." Nevertheless, Kissinger felt the need to continue to dissemble with Nationalist officials. He once more assured Shen that the United States was not going to give up its defense commitment to the Republic of China nor change its bilateral relations with Taipei.[108] As Shen was about to take his leave, Kissinger repeated that he found going to Peking an "exceedingly painful" assignment. Shen suspected these were the tears of "a crocodile . . . before devouring its victim."[109]

When the Generalissimo read Shen and Zhou's reports of their conversations with Kissinger, what probably outraged him most was the seeming assumption of the American leaders that he and his senior staff were as gullible as children.[110] He did, however, agree with Kissinger's judgment that if Nationalist China could maintain its stability over the next few years, the situation could change in a number of dramatic ways.[111] Recent events had increased the odds that Chiang's succession would be a stable one, whereas the opposite was true regarding likely events after the death of Mao Zedong. What neither Chiang nor anyone else suspected, however, was that the makings of a deus ex machina for himself and Taiwan would soon emerge from the character of Richard Nixon—whom Chiang now detested so much—at a place in Washington called "Watergate."

Preparing for his historic 1972 trip to Peking, Nixon sent the Generalissimo a letter assuring him that "I have very much in mind the interests of your government."[112] But he continued to feel guilty about his betrayal of Chiang. "We haven't sold Formosa [Taiwan] down the river," he again insisted to Kissinger in a January meeting. "We haven't at all." Kissinger hastened to agree, but then called "inconceivable" Secretary Rogers's proposal that the President should push the Chinese for a commitment not to use force in resolving the Taiwan dispute. For a brief moment, Nixon regretted that in the context of his visit to Peking the United States would not reaffirm its treaty commitment to the Nationalist government, but then he surmised that if China attacked Taiwan, "We would still have the Treaty." Kissinger said, "Oh, yes."[113]

On February 21, with the entire world watching, Nixon finally met Mao Zedong in Peking at his quarters next to the cold Forbidden City. Since

Chiang Kai-shek's days, the Communist rulers had torn down many of the old city walls and demolished the winding *hutongs* between the Front Gate and the Gate of Heavenly Peace, making Tiananmen Square a gigantic, sterile public space that was awkward for strolling but well suited for mass rallies and military parades (in which soldiers, as in Taiwan, marched in goosestep). Giant Stalinist buildings and drab worker flats of concrete slab had sprouted up near the Forbidden City, but still there were no skyscrapers, and the ancient city in spite of everything continued in some ways to look like the capital of Genghis Khan—a place where camel, not water buffalo, were familiar sights, where huge dust storms occurred every spring, and where people ate wheat dumplings, noodles, and steamed bread, not rice.

The first meeting, during which the leaders engaged in mostly formalities and small talk, was in a reception room lined with upholstered chairs and an entourage and interpreter on both sides. Nixon, usually derisive and cynical, seemed awed by Mao Zedong. "Our common old friend," Mao said, "Generalissimo Chiang Kai-shek, doesn't approve of this." A little later, he added that Chiang was an "even an older friend of ours than yours," noting that his party had cooperated with Chiang Kai-shek once, but also "quarreled with him, and fought against him." Chiang, he said, "still believes in one China. That's a good point which we can make use of. That's why we can say that this question can be settled comparatively easily."[114]

The next day, Nixon had a more detailed discussion with Zhou Enlai about the issues facing China and the United States. The prime minister recalled how in 1958 Chiang and the Communist leaders had cooperated to thwart the effort by John Foster Dulles to force the Generalissimo to withdraw from Quemoy and Matsu and thus sever Taiwan from the mainland.[115] He indicated that his government was only worried about the Taiwan Independence Movement in Japan and the United States, not in Taiwan itself, where Chiang would suppress any such effort: "That he has the strength to do."[116] Zhou came as close as he ever did in the talks to a renunciation of the use of force when he told Nixon, "You should not impose anything on us nor should we impose anything on Chiang Kai-shek."[117]

It was also best, he said, to apply the principles of one China "while you [President Nixon] are still in office." But as he had with Kissinger, he raised the issue of Chiang's likely passing from the scene: "Mr. President, you should be aware that there are not too many days left to Chiang Kai-shek." "We are not asking you to remove Chiang," he explained, "We will take care of that ourselves." "Peacefully?" Nixon asked. "Yes," Zhou replied, "We have self-confidence . . . As we ourselves solve this question, your forces, of course, may leave and that would be quite natural."[118]

Nixon responded that his goal was normalization of U.S.-China relations. "If I should win the election," he said, "I have five years to achieve it." But, he stressed, he could "not make a secret deal and shake hands and say that within the second term it will be done. If I did that, I would be at the mercy of the press if they asked the question." What he needed, Nixon explained, was "running room," which he hoped the communiqué to be signed in Shanghai would provide. That is, language that would not make Taiwan "a big issue in the next two or three months and next two, three, or four years." During the discussion of the Vietnam War, Nixon told Zhou that even with a skillful communiqué it would be said that "what the People's Republic of China wanted from us was movement on Taiwan and it got it; and what we wanted was help on Vietnam, and we got nothing."[119]

And essentially that was what happened. The famous Shanghai communiqué of February 27, 1972, employed skillful language on the issue of Taiwan: "The United States acknowledges [the Chinese text employs a good translation—*ren shi dao*] that all Chinese on either side of the Taiwan Strait maintain there is but one China and that Taiwan is a part of China. The United States Government does not challenge that position." The U.S. side then linked the ultimate objective of the "withdrawal of U.S. forces and military installations from Taiwan" to its "interest in a peaceful settlement of the Taiwan question," indirectly suggesting that a peace settlement was a quid pro quo for withdrawal. Privately, however, Kissinger had explicitly assured Zhou that this implicit conditionality did "not affect what the President has told you he will do . . . We are not setting conditions. We will do it [ending military and diplomatic ties to Taipei], as you know, in any event."[120] In his press conferences in Shanghai on February 28, Nixon stated that the U.S. commitments to Taiwan under their Mutual Security Treaty remained unchanged.[121]

As Nixon flew back to Washington, Assistant Secretary of State for East Asian Affairs Marshal Green, along with Kissinger's assistant John Holdridge, began a tour to brief American allies in the region on the visit. In Taipei, the Generalissimo sent word he wished to be briefed only by Kissinger.[122] Otherwise, Chiang hid his hatred of Nixon and what he saw as the White House team's treachery. Instead, at his instructions, the Americans received a "long and cordial meeting" with Chiang Ching-kuo. To Holdridge's surprise,

Ching-kuo was completely calm and did not berate the Americans, stressing instead that as long as the Mutual Security Treaty and American military assistance continued, he was not "too disturbed."[123]

According to Ching-kuo, the Americans assured him that while the Shanghai communiqué had indicated that the United States intended to seek a normalization of relations with Peking, this did not mean establishment of diplomatic relations.[124] Green, who had not sat in on the meetings between Kissinger and the Chinese and did not know what Kissinger had said, stated explicitly that the United States had not changed its policy toward the Republic of China and would "continue to have diplomatic relations" with the Nationalist government as well as a defense commitment to Taipei. Holdridge reported to Kissinger that Ching-kuo and the other Taiwan officials with whom they met "were concerned particularly over need for continued U.S. support for Taiwan's economic development." Holdridge's assessment was that the leaders and people of Taiwan would "try to make the best of [the] situation, and with typical Chinese determination [would] probably be able to get along quite well." "Our relationship with them," he predicted, "will continue, because they have nowhere else to go."[125]

Although the Nationalist party line was to accept that it had no good alternative except to live with the new U.S. approach toward the mainland, a brief flap did occur: in Taipei, Foreign Minister Zhou Shukai, in answering a reporter's question, said the Nationalist government might have its own "Warsaw talks" but with Moscow. Ching-kuo, however, quickly determined that this was a foolish approach to take. He ordered the release of a statement ruling out a "Soviet card," relieved Zhou as foreign minister, and ended the contacts with the Russian national and presumed KGB agent Victor Louis, who had tried to stir up rumors of Soviet-Taiwan cooperation. Ching-kuo's decisive rejection of this sort of poker game reflected his and his father's firm determination to cling as close as possible to the United States, even to the hated Nixon, while trying to build a foundation for the future.

In Washington on March 1, Ambassador Shen saw Kissinger and then Nixon and received the same assurances as in the past: the United States had made clear in Peking that it would not alter its diplomatic relations with Taipei or "scuttle" its Mutual Security Treaty with Taiwan. Shen, who was returning to consult with the Generalissimo, asked Nixon what he would do if he "were in my President's shoes." Nixon replied that, first, "I would not raise the question of whether there is a U.S. commitment. Now the moment that you raise the question you hurt your own cause. I have to say that quite candidly . . . The second point is that in terms of what he does, what you do with regard to the mainland, I frankly do not have an answer." With this bit of nonadvice, Nixon sent his best wishes to his "old friend" the Generalissimo, who, he heard, was still "just as sharp as a tack."[126]

As usual after devastating setbacks, including his forced retreat to Taiwan, Chiang would look for "streams in the desert" or silver linings in the darkening sky. There were a few to be seen in this heaviest blow since 1949, and he had seen some of them from the beginning. Although the United States had abandoned its persistent demand for Peking to forswear violence in resolving the Taiwan issue, a Sino-U.S. détente virtually guaranteed that for the foreseeable future—ten years or longer—the Communist military threat to the island would remain minuscule, which would increase investor confidence. The Chiangs could also expect that the entrance of Peking into the United Nations as one of the Big Five as well as its rapprochement with America would put an end to independence or "two Chinas" as realistic options for Taiwan and would influence Chinese foreign policy in a more peaceful direction.

Ironically, Taiwan's accelerating slide toward an unusual and increasing state of global isolation also rallied support for the regime at home. In a further twist, this situation would help the reformers around Chiang Ching-kuo convince the KMT hardliners that the crisis called for a significant advance in Taiwanization and political reform. Most student activists and other independent-minded Taiwanese began to think that for the foreseeable future a reformed Republic of China was the most that could be expected. In Michigan, Peng Mingmin, in keeping with this new ROC approach, received a special offer from Chiang Ching-kuo to return and freely take part in provincial politics as long as he did not challenge the KMT's return to the mainland dogma and its control of the armed forces. Peng declined, but a number of pro-independence exiles in Japan who had received somewhat similar offers did come home.[127]

At the National Assembly in March, the Generalissimo told the gathering, "In the light of my feelings of regret [at having failed to recover the mainland], I am sincerely requesting that you choose a new person of virtue and ability to succeed me." It was not a terrible surprise when the members ignored this plea and elected him to a sixth term as President.[128] Much more important was the expected ascendancy in May of the sixty-two-year-old

Chiang Ching-kuo to the premiership. He immediately doubled the number of native Taiwanese in the cabinet to six, appointed native Taiwanese as vice premier and provincial governor, and saw to it that three native Taiwanese were elected to the new KMT Central Committee. He also named the non-KMT mayor of Taipei, Henry Kao, as minister of communications and pushed through agreement on 119 additional elected seats in the national representative bodies, most to be filled by Taiwanese. On June 10, Ching-kuo issued to all civil servants "Ten Rules of Reform" and "Ten Taboos," which among other things banned their patronage of "girlie restaurants" and other bawdy establishments, and forbade large wedding and funeral banquets. Police checked proscribed clubs around the country and arrested patrons found to be government officials. Ching-kuo also initiated a crackdown on corruption, which resulted in a large number of arrests, including fifty officers in the Garrison Command. Convicted of corruption, the director-general of the Personnel Bureau received a life sentence and a vice director of the Customs Bureau paid with his life.[129]

At the same time, the new premier focused on nurturing economic ties with other nations regardless of their ideology or relationship with the People's Republic. Thus under his leadership, Taipei immediately (and in most cases, successfully) sought to open trade and cultural offices in those countries where it had been forced to close its embassies. As a result, even in the months after the dramatic Nixon visit to China, Taiwan's total trade from January to September rose an unthought-of 43 percent compared to the same period the year before.[130] And despite their disingenuous dealings with the Chiangs, Nixon and Kissinger seriously and successfully backed Taiwan's continued membership in key international financial institutions, including the Asian Bank and the World Bank. Kissinger and Nixon also approved U.S. Import-Export Bank loans to Taipei, including $58 million for modern steel mill equipment and full funding for two nuclear power plants.[131]

III

In the spring of 1972, the Generalissimo was still mentally alert and, considering his eighty-two years, in reasonably good health. But he was increasingly bothered by a number of physical maladies, primarily the heart trouble that had been discovered in 1969 but kept a close secret. The new, relatively small ailments included incontinence, increasing discomfort with his false teeth, sore joints, aching legs, and shrinking height. He now appeared almost always gentle and benign—usually he was in a calm mood and when in conversation, his soft smile lingered on his face. But in this time of seemingly huge international reverses, his aides sometimes saw him lose his temper, a display that had been rarely observed in the 1960s, except in his diary. His stoical discipline was also apparent. He still only took cold showers, and whether at the dinner table or in a garden chair by the carp pond, he always sat absolutely erect. Yet as always there was a façade around Chiang's persona. He had been on stage too long.

The Generalissimo's staff were unaware of the heart problem, but Xiong Yuan, his primary physician, knew that the weakened valve that had first been detected three years earlier at the time of the auto accident was getting worse. In late July, five months after Nixon's trip to Peking, Xiong was by the President's side in the residence garden when he suffered a cardiac arrest. Xiong immediately gave Chiang an injection that "saved his life" but he remained in a deep coma.[132]

The Presidential Office announced that the Generalissimo was suffering from a mild case of pneumonia, and the local press dared not speculate further. For months only Madame Chiang, Ching-kuo, Jeanette, and the medical team (which now included physician Paul Yu, chairman of the American Heart Association), visited the Generalissimo. Jeanette handled all the "trifles" concerning the patient, while Madame "barked orders" to the medical staff. But according to Xiong it was Ching-kuo and Jeanette who attended the daily medical meetings each morning and approved the recommended treatment for the day.[133] Lingering in the undisclosed coma, Chiang was absent from Taipei's October 10 celebration—the first time since coming to Taiwan in 1949 that he had missed the occasion. Government spokesmen, questioned by foreign newsmen, denied that he was in anything but top form, but the rumors persisted and foreigners and most Taiwan citizens either assumed the Generalissimo would not recover from whatever ailed him or that he had already died.

In Peking, Mao had also aged. It was harder than usual to understand him when he was speaking, and "the slightest physical activity took his breath away and he would turn gray." His mind remained clear but he was increasingly erratic and crotchety. Unlike his old enemy, who was his elder by six years, Mao was still in charge. About this time medical tests discovered Zhou Enlai's cancer, but skeptical of doctors, Mao would not give permission for surgery because if Zhou died, the camp of radicals led by his wife, Jiang Qing, a group that Mao had fostered, would have no check. Mao, who was now swinging capriciously from one side to the other in the internal struggle, decided to reinstate Deng Xiaoping, increasing the power of the moderates.[134]

During the December 1972 election campaign in Taiwan, non-KMT candidates made unprecedented criticisms "defaming" the government, even the President, and contravening the national policy of "mobilizing for the suppression of the Communist rebellion." The Garrison Command and other security bureaus recommended a crackdown, but Ching-kuo declined to make any arrests.[135] He did, however, force the editor of *The Intellectual* to step down and ordered the President of National Taiwan University to dismiss fourteen politically outspoken professors.[136] Nevertheless, politically aware native Taiwanese now believed that the transfer of power to the majority could be achieved by continuously pushing the limits of free speech.

In January 1973, six months after lapsing into a coma, Chiang inexplicably regained consciousness. To his family and staff it seemed a sign from Heaven. Soon he was able to sit in a wheelchair and, rational but extremely frail, converse with Ching-kuo. According to Ching-kuo's aides, he would generally report only good news to the old man.[137] No doubt this included the reelection of the hated Richard Nixon, which was not bad news since, as far as the Chiangs were concerned, it was far better that the politically crippled Nixon continue to manage U.S.-China-Taiwan relations than a new liberal Democratic administration.

Chiang was moved from the hospital to the Shilin residence. Mayling visited him twice a day. Ching-kuo, too, checked in every morning and then returned in the evening to have dinner with his father, usually along with the doctors Yu and Xiong. Once Xiong witnessed Ching-kuo reciting Mencius to his father, a touching reversal of times long ago when the father read the book of the ancient sage to his son.[138] By the summer, the patient was able to pose for a photo with grandson Eddy and his new bride, Elizabeth. Meanwhile, Alex's wife had left their abusive marriage and returned to Europe; under Chinese law she was unable to take their children, who remained with Alex.

Meanwhile, in Peking, the rehabilitated Deng Xiaoping received the foreign affairs portfolio from Zhou and aimed a new peace offensive at the Chiangs. But Ching-kuo rejected the approaches, believing that any serious suspicion among the population that he was seeking a settlement with the mainland would create a strong, possibly violent reaction on Taiwan—not only among Taiwanese—and send shivers down the spines of investors.

In early October, Mayling flew to New York to see her ailing sister Ai-ling. While there, a medical exam revealed that she herself had breast cancer and she returned to Taipei. Four days later, Ai-ling passed away. The sisters were both strong-willed and their husbands were rivals for power and influence, but through the years, the two had always remained close. Mayling put off breast surgery until the following year but underwent chemotherapy at Veterans Hospital in Taipei. She hid her diagnosis and treatment from her husband, telling him that she had a bad cold and could not visit him for a spell.[139] The next month, Chiang, eighty-seven and looking extremely feeble, posed for a photograph with nine Kuomintang leaders. It was his first official appearance in nearly eighteen months.[140]

That same month, Kissinger personally informed Mao that the U.S. "domestic situation"—meaning Watergate—precluded severing relations with Taiwan during Nixon's second term.[141] Less than two years into the new relationship with the United States, Mao found the earnest Americans blatantly rescinding the most important commitment they had made—the promise to end diplomatic and military ties with Taiwan within five years. For Mao, this pledge, along with his desire to counter the now diminishing Soviet threat, had provided the basic rationale for his détente with "imperialist" America— a policy that had sorely damaged his revolutionary reputation. Some in the CCP now even charged that Zhou Enlai had been taken in by Kissinger and Nixon.[142]

Meanwhile, under strong political pressure, Nixon had agreed to sell Chiang Kai-shek's government another package of modern weapons, including fifteen destroyers, two submarines, and sixty M-48 tanks. He also had approved a Northrop aircraft assembly plant in Taiwan to build one hundred modern F-5E defense fighters.[143] All this gave further ammunition to Zhou's enemies. But by this time the American and Chinese governments had "liaison offices" in each other's capitals, and the moderates led by Zhou and Deng Xiaoping were intent on maintaining the breakthrough with America.

On August 9, 1974, Nixon resigned in disgrace and lifted off from the White House lawn by helicopter. Although the final moments of Nixon's presidency occurred before dawn in Taiwan, the Chiangs probably watched them on TV. Like the assassination of John Kennedy, Nixon's disgrace surely seemed to the Chiangs to be divine retribution. In one of his first acts as the new President,

Gerald R. Ford signed off on a message for Zhou Enlai; the missive, drafted by Kissinger, promised to carry out the commitments made by his predecessor regarding Taiwan.[144] But this would not happen. In November 1974, Washington informed Ching-kuo that while the United States would continue to pursue the process of normalization with Peking, "the existing form of the relationship [with Peking] meets our needs."[145]

Chiang Kai-shek's strategy of accepting temporarily the shame of a foreign power's humiliation of himself, his regime, and his country had once more given him the best of the all-bad possible outcomes. His son could now hope for several more years to prepare for the eventual U.S. break in official relations with Taiwan, and the possibility remained that military sales at least could continue indefinitely. As for Kissinger, he had achieved his main goal in détente with China—a transformation of the "correlation of world forces" that gave the United States added leverage with Moscow and reduced the effect of a possible collapse in Indochina.

Mayling's chemotherapy was unsuccessful, and she decided to undergo a mastectomy at Taipei's Veterans Hospital. Still keeping Chiang in the dark about her condition, she told him that she was going on a trip to the United States.[146] The President and Madame Chiang still felt deep anger and disgust toward the United States and Richard Nixon in particular. While she was recovering, Mayling wrote a thirty-five-page paper charging that tense race relations, drug addiction, police corruption, violent crime, and other social evils were undermining America's "spiritual strength." Détente between the United States and "the Red Chinese," she said, simply whetted the latter's "aggressive tendencies." Chiang Ching-kuo was "surprised and dismayed" by the paper, which was released in an abridged form.[147]

IV

April 5, 1975, was the last night of the Tomb Sweeping (Qing Ming) Festival. Throughout Taiwan and traditionally in all of China, it was believed that on that night the ghosts of the ancestors milled about, preparing to go back into their newly cleaned chambers. Late that evening, Chiang's physician, Xiong Yuan, was in the garden of the Shilin residence admiring the endless scattering of stars in the clear night sky. Shortly after he returned indoors and retired for the night, the doctor on duty called him in a state of alarm. The President's heart had stopped. Xiong threw on a robe and rushed downstairs to Chiang's bedroom. He injected a stimulant into the President's heart and it resumed beating. Soong Mayling arrived and was at the bedside when her husband's heart stopped again. The doctor administered another injection. Soon afterward, Ching-kuo rushed into the room just as his father suffered another attack. Xiong was preparing a third injection when Mayling touched his hand and sighed. "Just stop," she said. It was a few minutes before midnight, and just then a dramatic rainstorm with thunder and lightning swept over the island from Taipei to Gaoxiong. Even Harvard-educated officials in the city thought this was more than coincidence.[148] The standby ambulance then moved the Generalissimo's body to Veterans Hospital, only a few minutes away.

Two hours after the Generalissimo's death, the government released a political testament that he was said to have written a week earlier. "Just at this time when we are getting stronger, my comrades, and my countrymen, you should not forget our sorrow and our hope because of my death. My spirit will be always with my comrades and my countrymen to fulfill the three people's principles, to recover the mainland, and to restore our national culture."[149]

C. K. Yen was quickly sworn in as President. According to ancient tradition, when a high official's father dies he is expected to take off three years to mourn and arrange family matters. Chiang Ching-kuo submitted his resignation as premier but the new President refused to accept it. Instead, the KMT Central Committee elected him "zong li" or director-general of the party, and Ching-kuo began a month of mourning and reflection, including the writing of a long tribute to his father. During this thirty-day period, the government required the closure of movie houses, nightclubs, bars, and other places of entertainment. No one was allowed to play golf, tennis, or baseball. Television and radio stations played only tributes and documentaries about the President, or scenes of public mourning with solemn music.[150]

Vice President Rockefeller, President Ford's personal representative, arrived in Taipei on April 15, 1975, and told reporters that friendship would continue "to characterize the relationship between us," avoiding any mention of the Nationalist government or the U.S. defense commitment to the island—subjects that President Ford had also ignored in his State of the Union speech in January. Rockefeller did not mention the new leaders of the Republic of China, but at least he was present. No other wartime ally of Chiang Kai-shek sent a representative.[151]

Former President Nixon issued a statement from San Clemente, California, calling Chiang "one of the giants of the history of our times."[152] But that was not the consensus. Most historians and journalists saw him most charitably as the man who with everything in his favor had "lost China." Russell Baker termed Chiang's defeats "spectacular" and "breathtaking." He "was to defeat as Vince Lombardi was to victory."[153] Many echoed the sentiment of the departed Joe Stilwell: Chiang Kai-shek was an arrogant, ignorant, and inept leader driven simply by a thirst for power, and he had contributed nothing to the war against Japan, to China, or to the Chinese people. The *New York Times* wrote that his death provoked the "memory of a monumental delusion in the political history of the twentieth century"—the Generalissimo's continual claim that from his little redoubt he was about to counterattack the mainland and defeat the colossal People's Liberation Army. Chiang would have taken pride in learning that so many believed for so long that he was actually serious about defeating the Communist Goliath.

The two Chiang brothers, as required by custom, wrapped the body of their father in white cloth. Following Chiang's requests, his copies of the Bible, *Streams in the Desert,* and a collection of Tang poetry were placed in the casket. Someone realized the Generalissimo had forgotten to ask also to take along *The Three People's Principles,* and a copy was put at his side. For five days, the casket lay in state at the Sun Yat-sen Memorial Hall. Chiang had presided over more than a thousand weekly ceremonies honoring the party founder who had set him on the road to leadership of the Kuomintang and China. Two and a half million people reportedly filed past the casket, including the journalist Lei Zhen, whom Chiang had imprisoned for some years. On April 15, while the Generalissimo was still lying in state, America's South Vietnamese ally collapsed just as he had foreseen. Saigon fell that day and American diplomats and marines at the U.S. Embassy fled ingloriously from the roof in helicopters.

The final service for the Generalissimo was held at the Memorial Hall on April 16, 1975, a gray, cloudy Wednesday. The Guanyin Mountains were lost in mist. The open casket was surrounded by lilies of the valley, and at the foot stood a large white cross of chrysanthemums. Madame Chiang, wearing dark glasses, bowed three times before the metal casket, as did her two stepsons and Alex Chiang, who represented the third generation. Then the coffin was closed, the Christian minister Zhou Lianhua gave a Christian eulogy, a military band struck up a funeral march and ten pallbearers carried the coffin out the building to a waiting float with white and yellow flowers in the shape of a church or chapel. Military cannon thundered a twenty-one-gun salute.[154]

Mayling, assisted on either side by Ching-kuo and Wei-kuo, walked behind the float for a few hundred yards as it moved down the road. The family then boarded limousines, and the cortege moved slowly through the warm, humid city and then onto the highway and through smaller towns. Hundreds of thousands of people lined the way: students, Boy and Girl Scouts, mailmen, nurses, reservists, people in sack cloth, Buddhist monks wearing saffron, a group of women in yellow Confucian gowns with mortar boards on their heads, and musicians playing ancient stringed instruments. Many were wailing softly in the Chinese fashion. High school and military bands played dirges and occasionally "Auld Lang Syne."[155]

In the countryside, the procession passed by hundreds of small workshops and in between green fields sprouting the first rice crop of the year. The motorcade wound through mountain passes and some sixty miles from Taipei turned into a small enclave by a quiet lake nestled among bamboo-covered hills. This was Chiang's favorite retreat, a place that reminded him of his home in the mountains of Zhejiang, where he hoped someday his body would be reburied—on Hole in the Snow Mountain near his mother's grave, just above the little town of Xikou.

V

On the day of Chiang's funeral, Mao, who knew his own time was limited, spent the day in bed listening over and over to the same stirring funeral music set to a twelfth-century poem. The poet was bidding farewell to a patriotic high mandarin whose career, like that of Chiang Kai-shek, had ended tragically and unfulfilled, and who had been exiled to a remote part of China.[156]

Epilogue

Like Mao Zedong, Chiang Kai-shek believed that China's sovereignty and rightful place in the world could be recovered only through national unity, a strong central government, and a disciplined people willing to sacrifice everything for the defense of their country. As Chiang and Mao well knew, however, the epic military fights in which they took part as allies or enemies were never just over territorial integrity or political power. Also at stake were strikingly different visions of modern China as a great nation restored. Although Mao could at times be tactically pragmatic, the absolutist tenets of Marxism-Leninism and China's ancient Legalists shaped his draconian means and utopian ends. But for Chiang, the Confucian precepts of conformity, harmony, stability, and practicality, along with Sun Yat-sen's reformist ideals and concept of political "tutelage," fashioned the Nationalist leader's authoritarian methods and his expectations of human progress.

During all his time on the mainland and Taiwan, Chiang's deep personal commitment to Chinese unity never wavered. Although he made compromises with the warlords to keep the country together, and while trying to build a modern army he appeased the Japanese for six years, he never formally surrendered China's sovereignty over any of its territory. His commitment to a unified China was probably one reason why, after his defeat in Manchuria in 1948, he made no real effort to hold on to the southern half of China. Instead, he chose to make his last stand on Taiwan, where he could at last take full dictatorial control, maintain the principle of one China, and pursue his long-held dream of creating a modern Chinese state based on Confucian—and also, as he saw them, Christian—values.

Chiang was the ultimate survivor. While holding to his fundamental principles and sometimes fighting tenaciously against heavy odds when he believed it was necessary, he shrewdly adopted the tactics of compromise, playing for time with his enemies, and with his foreign allies exploiting the weakness of his own regime. Despite occasional paranoid rants in his diaries, he was an astute practitioner of realpolitik and often a keen observer of world affairs. Contrary to impressions in the West, during his twenty-three years of leadership on the mainland, he was at times a highly popular leader, even among the educated political class. No general or large unit under Chiang ever defected to the Japanese or their various puppet governments in China. Even those Chinese commanders who did not like him respected his steel will, courage, patriotism, sense of honor and duty, and, for most, his anticommunism.

On the mainland he never possessed dictatorial control of the government, the Nationalist Party, or the army, and as I have argued, he was never a fascist. But he was only once briefly enthusiastic about representative, multiparty democracy. At times, his actions sharply contradicted the Confucian and Christian teachings that he thought he adhered to, as well as his belief in his own sincerity and moral virtue. On several occasions, he sanctioned extreme actions that amounted to staggering moral blindness or turpitude. Among these were the killings in Taiwan he ordered or permitted in 1947, his pouring hundreds of thousands of good troops after dead ones into Manchuria in 1947–1948, and the extensive executions during the first few years after his arrival on Taiwan in 1949. These acts constituted offenses against humanity and were unnecessary even in terms of Chiang's own objectives. The fact that while China was essentially at peace Mao Zedong was responsible for the deaths of innocent millions does not change that judgment.

Chiang never sought, in his diaries or elsewhere, to justify himself in regard to the extreme actions he took. If pressed he probably would have pointed to the savagery of the times—a war without mercy over the direction of world culture in which millions died, hundreds of millions suffered, and, as he put it, the survival of Chinese civilization seemed at stake. He once called himself a "man of war" and suggested that he bore a moral burden, the same burden that Truman and Churchill assumed for their decisions on Hiroshima and Dresden. But of course his most ruthless decisions also served to keep him in power, and to this he would likely claim that, as with his democratic allies, he had the mandate of his people to lead the national struggle for survival and unity and to do whatever was necessary to win.

During twenty-five years on Taiwan, operating in a microcosm of a stable and peaceful China, Chiang had his chance at nation-building, and in terms of social and economic indices he succeeded and laid the groundwork for Taiwan's leap into modernity. Three decades after his death, if he could return, Chiang would be impressed with the island's universal, state-of-the-art, and low-cost health system; its excellent schools, which perform at the highest levels on international tests; and its astonishing success as a high-tech economy. He would take pleasure in the fact that the small, once poor island had the fourth-largest foreign exchange reserves in the world and a per capita income (measured in purchasing power parity in 2007) of US$30,800, compared with US$1,200 in 1960.

Chiang's political legacy on Taiwan has also endured, but not without controversy. In 2007, the pro-independence Democratic Progressive Party government (elected democratically in 2000) set out to alter his pervasive image and removed more than two hundred busts and statues of the Generalissimo. Most of the stone figures, including one of the leader on horseback, were sheltered by supporters in a park next to Chiang's mausoleum in Tzuhu. The Chiang family, however, fearing further moves to discredit his memory, agreed that sometime in the future it would transfer the bodies of both the Generalissimo and his son back to Xikou in Zhejiang province—where apparently they would be most welcome. In her will, Mayling, who passed away at 105 in 2003, asked that when appropriate her remains be moved from New York to the Soong family cemetery in Shanghai and placed next to her sister Chingling. If this was not possible, she requested that she be placed next to her husband in Xikou. Apparently she loved her pro-Communist sister most of all.[1]

In March 2008, the old party of Sun Yat-sen and Chiang Kai-shek made a remarkable comeback. In a sweeping victory, the formerly dictatorial, communally (mainlander) based Kuomintang won back the presidency of the Republic of China—most impressively with majority support of the native Taiwanese. Also promising for democracy was the fact that the Democratic Progressive Party accepted defeat, thus ensuring the island's second peaceful transfer of power. Reflecting Taiwan's communal reconciliation, the new President on Taiwan, Ma Yingjeou, was a young mainlander and moderate pragmatist who advocated both de facto sovereignty for Taiwan and a somewhat amorphous one-China vision that included the island.

It is uncertain how closely if at all Chiang Kai-shek in his last years came

"Graveyard of the Gimos." At this resting place twenty-five miles outside of Taipei were stored the two hundred or so statues of Chiang put up during his long reign but taken down after his death by the Democratic Progressive Party government in 2007. Courtesy Stefan Hahn.

to share the view of his son that a popular democracy was the only hope for both the long-term viability of Taiwan and the historical legacy of the Chiangs. Most likely the Generalissimo believed to the end that Ching-kuo's limited democratic changes were only intended to placate native Taiwanese and American opinion. Even so, thirty years after his death, he would probably be impressed that Taiwan's democratic moves in the 1980s under Chiang Ching-kuo had led to a peaceful transition to majority rule and also influenced the concurrent democracy movement in the People's Republic, even if the mainland effort did not succeed. And he might even be convinced that in the first decade of the twenty-first century the factors most promoting the one-China ideal were the increasing people-to-people contacts across the Strait and the already astounding level of economic integration of the two economies. In 2008, tens of thousands of Taiwan businesses had over US$100 billion in investments, and almost a million Taiwanese employees of these firms and their families were living and working on the mainland.

Chiang might also believe that ultimately the best hope for China's reunification lay in the promise of the eventual political liberalization of the People's

In 2008, before the Kuomintang's sweeping presidential election victory that year, the Democratic Progressive Party government renamed Chiang's grand Memorial Hall in Taipei "Democracy Hall." Courtesy Stefan Hahn.

Republic, encouraged in part by the continuation of Taiwan's dynamic if raucous model of democracy. The old Generalissimo may have shown a glimmer of this insight when at some point he told General Wedemeyer, "When I die if I am still a dictator, I will certainly go down in the oblivion of all dictators. If, on the other hand, I succeed in establishing a truly stable foundation for a democratic government, I will live forever in every home in China," meaning on both sides of the Strait.[2]

Aside from these ruminations, early in the twenty-first century Chiang would also be struck by the transformation of the People's Republic of China into a respected nation with its own nuclear weapons and intercontinental missiles, spacecraft orbiting the moon, a prosperous family agriculture, huge foreign exchange reserves, and an overall economy expected to equal that of the United States in thirty years or so. Given the fact that all this success emerged from China's old entrepreneurial spirit and its new capitalist-driven, though still heavily state-involved and -regulated economy, Chiang would likely be confirmed in his view that without the interference of either Japan

In 2008, inside "Democracy Hall," Chiang's huge Lincolnesque statue still smiled down benignly on his honor guard. Meanwhile, the Chiang family indicated that it intended eventually to move his remains and those of his son back to the mainland in keeping with their wishes. Courtesy Stefan Hahn.

or the Soviet Union, he could have beaten the Chinese Communists, China's economic takeoff would then have started some twenty years earlier, and millions of Chinese deaths would have been avoided.

Most of all, Chiang would be pleased with what he would see as the Peking regime's unofficial but clear confirmation of his and Sun Yat-sen's belief that communism was not and is not compatible with Chinese society or temperament—or indeed with human nature. He would be especially gratified to learn that in answer to the mainland's post-Mao lack of an effective ethical philosophy, religion, or ideology, the new CCP has replaced class struggle, a propertyless society, and world revolution with nationalism and the ancient teachings of Confucius—both once again drawing on China's rich culture and extraordinary history to define the country's moral and ethical center. Thus Chiang would almost certainly see the new Chinese leaders as modern Confucianists, dedicated as he was to making China a well-regulated, harmonious, stable, and prosperous society as well as a powerful and avowedly peaceful actor on the world stage. He would also note with irony that both corruption and disparities in income in the new People's Republic are extremely high, probably higher than when he was on the mainland and far higher than during his years on Taiwan. Finally, he would observe that despite the booming economy and positive changes in mainland Chinese society, civil liberties in China have been much more limited than on Taiwan in his concluding years on the island. Thus, the old dictator would probably view new China's tightly closed order in the realm of politics as somewhat excessive.

Still, if Chiang could see modern China's nascent and slowly expanding although well-controlled civil society, its towering cities, and its other modern achievements, he might believe that his long-planned, seemingly fanciful "counterattack" had succeeded and that his successors had recovered the mainland. Truly, the vision that drives modern China in the twenty-first century is that of Chiang Kai-shek, not Mao Zedong.

Postscript to the Paperback Edition

The first Harvard University Press edition of *The Generalissimo* went to the printer in late fall 2008. By that time the Chiang family had released to the Hoover Institution Archives the original diaries of Chiang Kai-shek from 1918 to 1957. It was uncertain when the next batch of the journals would be released and whether or not all the remaining diaries would be included. I felt confident in my description and analysis of Chiang's thinking about and reaction to the stirring events of the period covered by the last fifteen years of his diaries. Consequently, my editor and I decided not to hold up publication.

The final batch of diaries, released in the summer of 2009, includes all the remaining journals and does not in fact contradict any of the reporting and interpretations in *The Generalissimo*. Rather, they strongly confirm both. For example, combined with substantial evidence provided in the Harvard University Press volume that the reader has in hand, the last batch of diaries makes it clear that at least by the end of 1969, Zhou Enlai was secretly briefing Chiang about the secret communications going on between the White House and Peking.

The following pages will briefly examine the most interesting issues that Chiang addressed in the last years of his journals. The dates of the cited diaries will be given in the notes. The diaries cited here, as in the main text, are part of the Chiang Kai-shek Diary collection donated by the Chiang family to the Hoover Institution Archives.

The present book describes on pages 498–502 the culmination of the second Quemoy crisis in October 1958. For two days John Foster Dulles had read the riot act to Chiang, charging that his policies were seen as militaristic and that the conflict over Quemoy could lead to a nuclear war. Chiang had not said much in reply. In his diary later that day Chiang was pleased that he had not "refuted" his visitor to his face. He was not, however, as composed as he pretended—rather, he was "enraged" that Dulles was in effect demanding that he "surrender" to the CCP. After the meeting, he instructed his foreign minister and George Yeh to make clear to Dulles that President Chiang understood the United States could abandon the Republic of China if it wished, but he would prefer to give up "international [that is, U.S.] aid and Taipei's seat in the United Nations if necessary to save the mainland people's belief in [him]."[1] As we repeatedly observed in the main text, the completely reliant weak partner was again threatening a severe crisis in order to bring his critical protector to heel.

As also noted in the main text, Dulles, not wanting to be the man who "lost Taiwan," capitulated. In the end, Chiang was "very satisfied" and even opined in his journal that Dulles was "conscientious and meticulous." That last evening, after dinner, he warned the Secretary about the PLA's growing air power and asked for help in "destroying the communist bandits' plot." Despite their earlier exchange about nuclear weapons, and apparently feeling emboldened by Dulles's remarkable climb-down, Chiang even asked for "some nuclear bombs to destroy the [PLA] positions."[2] Two months later the State Department formally turned down Chiang's request for nuclear weapons.[3]

A Chiang diary entry the night after Dulles left Taipei (October 25, 1958) further confirms that contact on ending the Quemoy crisis had been made between Taipei and Peking while the Secretary was in town. That evening (an odd-numbered date), Peking announced a new policy of not shelling Quemoy harbor on even dates of the months. Chiang's diary entry that same night said without explanation that this announcement was "confusing" and "contradicted [Peking's] real intentions."[4] Clearly, Chiang thought Peking (probably Zhou Enlai) in a secret exchange with him had promised not to shell the island at all on even dates. The next day, an even-numbered day, the PLA forces fired 239 shells at Quemoy but none hit the beach landing area or the airstrip. Chiang did not comment further on the shelling, which eventually ceased entirely on even days. Nationalist artillerymen went on the same schedule. This left open alternate days for safe resupply of the island.[5]

The diaries bear out the book's conclusion that Chiang was deeply disturbed by the March 1960 crisis that led to the flight of Syngman Rhee from his country. In Chiang's view, the "naïve and arrogant" Americans were again chasing the chimera of democracy in an undeveloped country under threat by a powerful Soviet-supported regime. Believing many would see the fall of Syngman Rhee as a model for change on Taiwan, he feared that U.S. aid would "bring disaster upon" the island and himself. "How can we not be alert," he wrote.[6]

As John F. Kennedy took office, Chiang seemed to feel that he might actually be able to work with this young Democrat. On inauguration day the Nationalist leader worried about "the future of the world," but still, Kennedy's rousing inaugural speech sounded to him "very positive."[7] However, yet another crisis over KMT troops in Burma erupted soon after that. Chiang was frustrated that Kennedy, like Eisenhower, did not understand his need to make a show of keeping the Chinese civil war going and that the American leader would not engage in "reasonable coordination" on this issue.[8]

Then came the Bay of Pigs debacle in April 1961, which Chiang saw as another testament to the pusillanimous nature of America's global leadership. But, he wrote in his diary, "it is not good to point out their weaknesses to [the Americans] . . . otherwise they will become furious."[9] Two months later, at the Paris Summit, Nikita Khrushchev browbeat Kennedy over the East German question. Chiang soon benefited from the American president's increasing need to avoid another appearance of weakness in dealing with the Communists. Chiang's diaries now reveal that in resolving the issue of Outer Mongolia's membership in the United Nations Chiang was able to get Kennedy to put in writing his personal pledge as president that when the Chinese representation issue ever came up in the U.N. Security Council, the United States "would use its veto if necessary."[10]

A dairy entry in October 1962 suggests that Chiang admired the way Kennedy handled the Cuban missile crisis and was highly pleased to receive a message from the White House—no doubt one of many to world leaders—requesting support during the critical standoff.[11] On the other hand, the Sino-Indian border conflict occurred at the same time, and, reflecting his strong Chinese nationalism, Chiang was irate that the U.S. government had made "a naïve and ridiculous statement that the McMahon Line in that region was an internationally recognized border."[12] This was of course also Peking's position.

The killing of the South Vietnamese leaders on November 2, 1963, "infuriated" Chiang and further convinced him that the "cruel and brutal" Americans were not to be trusted. "We must strengthen ourselves," he repeatedly wrote. Interestingly, in his journals he made no direct criticism of Kennedy in this connection, nor did he make an ironic link between the American president's own assassination twenty days later and that of Ngo Dinh Diem.[13]

When the radical Cultural Revolution burst on the scene in China in the summer of 1966, Chiang believed it was the culmination of a hidden internal crisis within the CCP that had been festering for two decades. Liu Shaoqi, China's head of state, he correctly predicted, would not "last long."[14]

Chiang had less troubled relations with the Johnson Administration than with any other presidency. This was probably because Taiwan's support for the war in Vietnam grew exponentially in importance during this time. LBJ also was clearly less personally critical of Chiang's historical record than most other Democratic Party leaders. In his diaries Chiang never commented on the American president's obvious decision not to take Chiang's earlier advice not to send U.S. combat troops to Vietnam. When Johnson in 1968 decided not to run again for the White House, Chiang's positive view of this American leader was reflected in his diary comment that this decision would harm the "whole world." But, he assured himself, it could not "affect [Taiwan] too much" because the island had its own strength. Besides, he wrote, "the communist perdition is close" and the future is in "the hands of God."[15]

Chiang had every reason to believe that his relations with Nixon would be the best with any U.S. president in twenty-four years. But he was worried by Nixon's assertion in his inaugural address that "this is an era of negotiation."[16] Three days later, after reading a speech by the new Secretary of State, William Rogers, Chiang was suddenly aghast. At this very early date he concluded that the conservative Nixonites were hoping for détente with the People's Republic. This attitude, he wrote, reflected America's "selfishness, viciousness," and refusal "to look forward with a grand vision." The Communists, he predicted, would see Nixon's inaugural address as "a sign of weakness and impotence."[17]

Still, Chiang drafted a letter to the new president saying that no other U.S. leader was "as resolute and courageous." Among other suggestions, he repeated his 1964 advice to Johnson, saying it would "be better for the U.S. not to join the [Vietnam] war directly, instead it must use some indirect strategies."[18] Possibly, he meant the United States should not escalate further its own by then direct and huge involvement but find ways to reduce it and, sooner rather than later, end it. Chiang never sent this particular letter.

In his journal Chiang described as "extremely stupid" Washington's decision, among other gestures to Peking, to limit Nationalist-flown U-2 flights over China. Nixon, he wrote, was "an unprincipled politician."[19] As recounted in the text, he suspected that there was much more going on behind the scenes.[20] The reader will recall that in one such move, Nixon, within a few weeks of taking office, on a visit to Paris, told French President Charles de Gaulle that he intended to seek detente with China. Without a doubt, de Gaulle—as Nixon wished—passed this sentiment on to Zhou Enlai, who very likely informed Chiang through their Hong Kong contact. But, as described at length in the book, in an unprecedented display of sangfroid, Chiang said nothing publicly on this subject. Faced with these and other signs of a possible U.S. policy shift toward Peking—one with grave consequences for Taiwan—Chiang also remained silent on the matter when meeting with Americans in private. He clearly realized he had no good option but to go along with the flow of events and salvage whatever opportunities there might be to reverse or stop the negative trend while praying for a favorable mutation of history.

Even before Nixon's July 1969 visit to Romania, Chiang suspected it was connected to the president's intention to ally with Peking against Moscow, which meant "abandoning Taiwan."[21] In a diary entry before Secretary Rodgers's visit to Taipei that summer, Chiang lamented Washington's "fierce and inflexible" attitude, which, he implied, would not even allow him to pretend he was preparing an invasion of the mainland. When Rodgers warned him against launching any violent action across the Strait, an irritated Chiang replied that the Nationalist government was "not desirous of attempting an invasion . . . because it does not have the capability."[22] This, of course, had been starkly true ever since Chiang fled to the island in 1949. He saw the Nixon people as naïve as he had most official Americans he had known over four decades. "Speaking honestly" with them, he wrote, "is like playing a harp before oxen."[23]

At this point—in conflict with his posture of stoic calm before a typhoon—Chiang ruminated briefly about a drastic alternative strategy for himself and Taiwan: an "alliance" with the Soviet Union. In an obscure diary entry in July he said he "was enraged by [the Americans'] intent to prevent us from discussing the [Nationalist] counterattack [against the mainland] with Russia." Presumably there is some relevant document on Washington's intervention with the Chiangs on this subject not yet released by the State Department. The next month, Chiang speculated that if "the United States and China became allies against Russia, then Russia would want to deal with China immediately before Peking could get aid from the United States. If this happened, Russia would definitely want to ally with us and attack the communists bandits. Then, even if the U.S. wanted to obstruct our action, would it be able to intervene in our alliance with Russia and our counterattack?"[24]

Chiang obviously had remembered the tantalizing visit the year before by the KGB agent/journalist Victor Louis and the subsequent meetings in Europe between Louis and one of Ching-kuo's trusted associates (all recounted on pp. 287–290). For a moment and perhaps longer, Chiang thought that maybe a new twist of history would bring about his third alliance with Stalin and make possible after all the seemingly harebrained idea of a counterattack across the Strait—but this time with all-out aid, including a massive invasion of China in the north, from a more determined ally—the Soviet Union. For Chiang, this was a highly intriguing notion. The Russians, he thought, were "Yang men," malicious and deceptive, but Nixon was a "Yin man," "deceptive, insidious, and hypocritical."[25] Probably he meant that the Soviets did not hide their intentions to ultimately destroy their ideological and national rivals, while Nixon was a sly and false friend.

Chiang's speculation was given currency by the ongoing skirmishes at that very moment across the Sino-Soviet border on the Ussuri River. Chiang and a few of his closest confidants, including Chiang Ching-kuo, probably again discussed the idea of playing a "Soviet card." The elder Chiang and apparently others in the leadership saw such a gambit as a more realistic option than it had been a year before.

The younger Chiang, however, almost certainly counseled heavily against pursuing any such grand reversal of policy. To do so—even for stories to leak out that it was being considered—would undermine the very goals that were guiding Chiang's stoic attitude toward Nixon's "treachery." As noted in the main text, these goals were to maintain confidence on the island and abroad in Taiwan's stability and to retain as much support and sympathy as possible among the American public, investors, political leaders, and the media.[26] Chiang did not again mention the dubious option of alliance with Moscow.

In December, Chiang wrote that Nixon was "secretly making preparations to meet with Mao." It was not known at the time outside Nixon and Kissinger's inner circle that, as part of his secret plan, the American president intended to visit Mao or that his policy included the diplomatic and military abandonment of Taiwan. This again suggests Zhou Enlai was passing messages to Chiang on what was going on.

At the end of 1969, Chiang spelled out in his diary even more clearly his strategy for dealing with what he saw as the coming radical shift in U.S. policy toward China and Taiwan. This came in the form of talking points he recorded in his diary for use in an upcoming meeting with Vice President Agnew, who planned to visit Taipei. Chiang intended to tell Agnew that he would continue to differentiate between comments he (Chiang) made in public regarding changes in U.S. China policy and those he would make in private. Furthermore, he would "not make trouble for Nixon nor harm our [U.S.-Taiwan] friendly relations." He also planned to tell Agnew that he "hoped the U.S. would inform me sincerely and in advance if it intends to allow the communists to enter the United Nations. If so, I will not trouble the United States."

This was a remarkable strategy acquiescing in both the inevitability and the broad scope of the coming U.S. rapprochement with China. Still, his inner feelings were the same. A few days later he wrote that Nixon's "detestable means and his lying are the most vicious." When Chiang did meet with Agnew, he did not in fact suggest that he knew what was happening nor indicate his Job-like forbearance of the inevitable. Meanwhile, he continued hoping and praying that fate would again intervene on his behalf and that of the Republic of China.

The Sino-U.S. talks in Warsaw resumed in early January 1970 after a hiatus of several years, and then, in an unusual development, other sessions followed in late January and February. Chiang records in his diary on March 16 that Chiang Ching-kuo reported that there would be an "ambassadorial meeting between the U.S. and the communist bandits" in either Washington or Peking. Two days later at the regular KMT Central Committee meeting, Chiang again "listened to [a report on] the content of the [Warsaw] meeting." This report noted that the U.S. side at the talks had "proposed some absurd suggestions for resolving the Taiwan problem."[27] At the time, it was not publicly known that the Americans and the PRC Chinese had discussed holding a meeting in Peking or Washington or that the Americans had made some suggestions regarding the Taiwan problem. Again it is logical to conclude that Zhou Enlai, with Mao's approval, had authorized a message to Taipei on the Warsaw meetings.

On hearing these secret reports, Chiang swore that as soon as the U.S. "abandons the [Mutual Security] agreement" with Taiwan, "we can implement our national policy of counterattacking the mainland." Only a few months before he had told Rodgers that Taiwan had no capability to invade the mainland. Thus what he no doubt meant was that after the break, the

United States would no longer be a check on what posturing against the mainland he might chose to unleash.[28]

In May, after Nixon began heavy bombing of Cambodia, there was a sudden but brief turnabout in Chiang's thoughts about the American leader. Despite his previous and consistent pessimism about U.S. prospects in Vietnam, he thought the "courageous" action in Cambodia meant that Nixon's anticommunist policy had not changed after all. This meant, he briefly hoped, that the idea of a grand rapprochement with Peking was now off and that Nixon understood world peace would only be assured when "we destroy the Chinese communist bandits."

Chiang tactically was a pessimist, but one who never gave up. He persisted in his goals and thus on key occasions was an artless optimist. He even wondered for the first time, also against his previous judgments, whether his army should join the struggle in Vietnam. But by the end of May he had reconsidered. Nixon, he wrote, "would play any political trick in order to achieve his own purposes . . . but . . . his anti-communism can be seen as a hope to us."[29]

Then the trickling stream in the desert quickly dried up. When the U.S. gave a visa to Professor Peng Mingmin, the pro-independence Taiwanese exile leader, Chiang returned to his characterization of Nixon as "hypocritical . . . deceptive and . . . insidious." Granting the visa to Peng, he thought, meant that the United States was "still trying to penetrate and overthrow our government." America itself, he wrote, had been "penetrated by the communists." Believing as they did that the CIA had arranged Peng's flight from Taiwan, Chiang still some times worried that a "one China, one Taiwan" conspiracy could after all really be at the heart of Nixon's machinations even if it meant killing the prospect of a U.S.-China détente. This thought no doubt contributed to Chiang's renewed interest in coordinating with Zhou Enlai resistance to any such plot.

In July, Zhou apparently resumed his clandestine exchanges with Chiang, who saw that he had been entirely wrong about the bombing of Cambodia. It had been, he thought, only a temporary political stratagem by Nixon. Likewise, he believed Nixon's announced decision to withdraw American troops from Vietnam was for domestic political effect. Once again he began to write that Nixon intended to break relations with Taipei and establish them with Peking.[30]

By January 1971, Chiang believed Nixon's intentions exceeded the malice of the Truman government. When the American ping pong team visited

China, he lamented that Americans had lost their "sense of honor and self-esteem."[31] But he kept repeating in his diary that his heart was calm and he was not afraid. He also knew, however, that the "unbelievably evil and vicious" Nixon planned to replace Taipei with Peking in the Security Council in order—as Chiang described it—to gain domestic "political capital" in the 1972 American elections. Still, he urged himself to hold on through the next year when some dramatic event could intervene and "we might be able to overcome" the great trouble that was approaching.[32] He did not mention Kennedy's written pledge that if necessary the United States would itself veto China's entry into the United Nations. It was now worthless.

Chiang was not surprised by Nixon's announcement in California on July 15, 1971, of the then just concluded Kissinger talks in Peking and Nixon's own planned visit to the Chinese capital in 1972. In his diary, Chiang noted Nixon's letter to him apologizing for not having notified him in advance of the visit, and he called the visit "a betrayal of my country." He decided not to answer "the clown Nixon."[33] But, underneath, the culmination of the expected "treachery" stirred in him a "fury" so great that for thirteen days he made no comment on the event in his diary. On July 29, he wrote that the visceral effect had actually improved rather than worsened his ill health. Purged of his fury, he decided that "to deal with the clown Nixon, I can only rely on calmness and righteousness."[34]

Faced with a vote of expulsion, on October 25, 1971, Chiang ordered the Republic of China to withdraw from the United Nations. Indeed, in his diary as well as publicly, he pretended that leaving the UN had been his "aspiration for years." Nothing had changed, the Republic of China would persevere, and it would "never permit an outside power to interfere in its affairs."[35]

As noted in chapter 13, before flying off to Peking in February 1972, Nixon wrote to Chiang assuring him that he would "very much have in mind the interests of your government." In his reply to Nixon, Chiang again practiced, as the Chinese say, "eating gall" (chi ku). He did not specifically mention the trip but simply suggested Nixon should be careful in dealing with the Communists. In his diary, however, he compared Nixon's upcoming China visit to "Granma Liu entering Grand View Garden (Da Guan Yuan)," a story in *The Dream of the Red Chamber* (a seventeenth-century Chinese novel) in which an illiterate, poor rural woman is totally captivated by the extravagant wealth of a rich family.[36]

A week before Nixon arrived in Peking in February 1972, Chiang seemed uncertain whether the U.S. and China would at that time announce an exchange of diplomatic relations. He wondered whether Taiwan "should decide whether or not" to cut off foreign relations with the U.S. after it formally acknowledges the communist bandits."[37] Of course he had no intention of doing any such thing, unless, as with the withdrawal from the UN, the end was in sight—that is, it was certain the United States intended to break all relations with Taiwan. On February 21and 22 he noted that "the clown Nixon" had arrived in Peking, "the thief Mao" had not gone to welcome him, but the two men had later met for about an hour. After Nixon moved on to Shanghai, Chiang wrote that the Communiqué bearing that city's name reflected only the views of the "bandits" and Nixon's "extremely shameless" plot with the "the bandit Zhou" to "sell out" the "Republic of China . . . forcing us to give in by gun point."[38] His only mention of the document's references to the key issue of Taiwan was to observe that the wording replaced "Republic of China" with "Taiwan." Blunt references to Zhou in the diaries at this time suggest that the Hong Kong exchanges between Chiang and the Chinese premier did not mean the Generalissimo did not see him as an enemy. He understood well Zhou's objectives in briefing him on the secret exchanges.

At this point, the diaries are replete with even more insistent calls than in the previous three years for Taiwan to rely on its own power. But as stated in the text, in reality Chiang and his son were determined to hold on to the United States, including Richard Nixon, as long as possible while building a foundation for the future and waiting for the tide to turn. The Generalissimo comforted himself with the thought that "time, geography, and people" were on his "side" and that within five years or "at the soonest half a year" the "contemptible communist bandits" and the "clown Nixon" would be defeated and "the humiliation we endure will not have been in vain."[39]

China would muddle through the rest of the Mao period and four years beyond before bursting out of its shell under the extraordinary reforms of Deng Xiaoping. But Chiang's premonition about Nixon coming to a bad end would soon prove clairvoyant. "Half a year later," American FBI agents would establish that a break-in at the Democratic Party headquarters at the Watergate complex in Washington stemmed from a massive campaign of political spying and sabotage conducted on behalf of the Nixon reelection effort.

Consumed with his own sense of destiny and martyrdom—and although he felt "old and weak"—Chiang believed he had to accept the presidency once again in order to lead the Republic through its most critical period.[40] He was furious about "clown Nixon's formless insult," but "it was an external loss not worth worrying about." In a following sentence he expressed another presentiment—this time about himself. "Moreover," he concluded, "I long ago put living or dying out of my mind."[41]

On July 20, 1972, Chiang rode in his limousine down Yangming Mountain with Soong Mayling. He felt "unhappy and vexed," but, he wrote that night, "a true man should be able to bend and stretch [whatever the misfortune]."[42] The next day he wrote the last brief entry in his diary, which he had begun fifty-six years before: "Recently, I am always tired and my mind sometimes does not work." Two days later he suffered his cardiac arrest, and his work was finished.

December 2010

Notes

Abbreviations

Boorman, *Biographical Dictionary*	Howard L. Boorman, *Biographical Dictionary of Republican China* (New York: Columbia University Press, 1968), 4 vols.
Chiang Diaries, Hoover	Chiang Kai-shek Diaries, Chiang Kai-shek Collection, Hoover Institution Archives, Stanford, Calif.
Columbia interviews	Columbia University, Chinese Oral History Project, 1990–1991
Currie Papers	Lauchin Currie Papers, Hoover Institution Archives, Stanford, Calif.
FEER	*Far Eastern Economic Review*
FOI	Freedom of Information Act
FRUS	*Foreign Relations of the United States* (Washington, D.C.: U.S. Government Printing Office, various years); http://www.state.gov/r/pa/no/frus
National Archives	National Archives and Records Administration, College Park, Md. branch
Qin Xiaoyi, *Zong tong*	Qin Xiaoyi, ed., *Zong tong Jiang gong da shi chang pian chu gao* (Preliminary Draft of President Chiang's Chronological Biography), 12 vols. (Taipei: Chungchang Cultural and Educational Foundation, various years)
RGASPI	Russian State Archives of Social and Political History, Moscow
T. V. Soong Papers	T. V. Soong Papers, Hoover Institution Archives, Stanford, Calif.
White Paper	*United States Relations with China, with Special Reference to the Period 1944–1949* (Washington, D.C.: U.S. Government Printing Office, 1949)

1. A Neo-Confucian Youth

1. Michael Clodfelter, *Warfare and Armed Conflicts: A Statistical Reference,* vol. 2 (London: McFarland and Company, 1992), p. 956.

2. Theodore H. White, *Theodore H. White at Large: The Best of His Magazine Writing,* ed. Edward T. Thompson (New York: Pantheon, 1992), pp. 118–119.

3. Text of Chiang's broadcast remarks, in Qin Xiaoyi, *Zong tong,* vol. 5, pp. 2639–2643.

4. Theodore H. White and Annalee Jacoby, *Thunder Out of China* (New York: William Sloane Associates, 1946), pp. 277–278.

5. Qin Xiaoyi, *Zong tong,* vol. 5, pp. 2639–2643.

6. White and Jacoby, *Thunder,* pp. 118–119, 277.

7. Chiang's message to Mao, August 14, 1945, in Qin Xiaoyi, *Zong tong,* vol. 5, p. 2639. The message was sent in full anticipation of the surrender.

8. In the rice areas of China in the 1890s, five acres would have ranked a household among the "rich peasants." A governmental survey in 1922 reported an average holding across the nation was 3.6 acres, but in Zhejiang only 1.2 acres. See R. H. Tawney, *Land and Labor in China* (London: Allen & Unwin, 1932), p. 40.

9. Interviews with Sun Yishu, personal secretary to Chiang Kai-shek in the late 1930s and 1944–1949, then again in the mid-1950s, Taipei, May 14, 1996, and May 30, 1996. His great aunt was Chiang Kai-shek's sister and his wife was a relative of Wang Caiyu. A Xikou local researcher, Wang Caiyu, however, reports that Wang Caiyu had been taught at home and knew some characters (interview with Wang Shunqi, Fenghua, June 19, 1996).

10. Pichon P. Y. Loh, *The Early Chiang Kai-shek: A Study of His Personality and Politics, 1887–1924* (New York: Columbia University Press, 1971), p. 7.

11. Mexican and Spanish silver dollars *(yin yuan)* were a highly valued currency of the times in China, although the dynasty also issued silver ingots (the tael) along with bronze coins. The Yuan Shikai regime minted silver dollars as did some warlords, and in 1933 the Nationalist government minted the Sun Yat-sen dollar and abolished the tael. Chiang's diaries and other material used in this book usually do not make clear to which silver dollar or yuan they are referring. See Zhaojin Ji, *A History of Modern Shanghai Banking* (New York: M. E. Sharpe, 2003), pp. 33–35, 184–185. The account of the adoption of Xuhuo and the division of the salt store and the bamboo grove comes from an interview with Chiang Wei-kuo, Taipei, June 5, 1996. Wang Shunqi adds that the Chiang family still held the rice paddy and this went to Kai-shek in the settlement (interview with Wang Shunqi, Fenghua, September 30, 1995). Mr. Wang reports that Kai-shek also inherited one or two other old houses that were next to the family home. For an excellent study of traditional inheritance in China, see David Wakefield, *Fenjia: Household Division and Inheritance in Qing and Republican China* (Honolulu: University of Hawaii Press, 1998).

12. Loh, *Early Chiang Kai-shek,* p. 14.

13. Sally Borthwick, *Education and Social Change in China* (Stanford, Calif.: Hoover Institution Press, 1983), p. 32.

14. Interview with Sun Yishu, May 14, 1996; interview with Wang Shunqi, June 19, 1996.

15. Wang Shunqi, "Jiang Jingguo nianxing he xuesheng de er zi," unpublished article, 1995, in author's possession.

16. Wang Shunqi, "Jiang Jingguo."

17. S. I. Hsiung, *The Life of Chiang Kai-shek,* trans. (London: Pete Davies, 1948), p. 41; Cheo-kang Sie, *President Chiang Kai-shek: His Childhood and Youth* (Taipei: China Cultural Service, 1954), p. 52.

18. Wang Shunqi, July 1996, answers to my written questions.

19. At a meeting on September 27, 1995, in Fenghua with a number of local researchers and others (including one distant cousin of Mao Fumei) interested in the Jiang family history, it was generally agreed that the stories of physical abuse were probably true, although no one knew of letters or accounts of the subject from family members of the time. Physical abuse of wives was not uncommon then, and is not today.

20. Group interview, Fenghua, September 27, 1995. See also Chiang Diaries, April 19, 1921, in "Jiang Jieshi bi xia de jiating yu hunyin—Jiang Jieshi Riji zhai bian," *Minguo dang an* (Nanking) 1 (1993): 3–10.

21. Harold Schiffrin, *Sun Yat-sen and the Origins of the Chinese Revolution* (Berkeley: University of California Press, 1970); Boorman, *Biographical Dictionary,* vol. 3, pp. 170–172.

22. See the compelling account of the uprising in Diana Preston, *The Boxer Rebellion* (New York: Berkley, 1999).

23. Borthwick, *Education and Social Change,* pp. 70, 86.

24. According to Mao Sizheng (1936), Chiang was expelled from the Phoenix Mountain Academy for leading a student protest over the heavily classical curriculum. Given Chiang's deep sense of discipline and fealty this story seems unlikely. See Loh, *Early Chiang Kai-shek,* p. 16.

25. Wang Shunqi, July 1996, answers to my written questions.

26. Wm. Theodore de Barry, *Sources of Chinese Tradition* (New York: Columbia University Press, 1960), pp. 571–573, 711.

27. Hollington K. Tong, *Chiang Kai-shek* (Shanghai: China Publishing Company, 1938), vol. 1, p. vii.

28. Huang Tzujin, *Jiang Jieshi Yan Zhong De Riben* (Japan in the Eyes of Chiang Kai-shek), unpublished paper based on 313 articles and lectures by Chiang Kai-shek on the subject of Japan (Taipei, 2003), p. 917: Cheo-kang Sie, *President Chiang Kai-shek,* p. 69; Loh, *Early Chiang Kai-shek,* p. 18.

29. Tong, *Chiang Kai-shek,* vol. 1, p. 15.

30. Herman Mast III and William G. Saywell, "Revolution Out of Tradition: The Political Ideology of Dai Jitao," *Journal of Asian Studies* 34, no. 1 (November 1974): 73–98; Boorman, *Biographical Dictionary,* vol. 3, p. 200.

31. Marius B. Jansen, *Japan and China: From War to Peace, 1894–1972* (Chicago: Rand McNally, 1975), p. 122.

32. Wang Shunqi, July 1996, answers to my written questions.

33. Chiang family member notes to author, February 10, 1999.

34. Ibid.

35. Huang Tzujin, ed., *Jiang Zhongzheng liu ri zue xi shi lu* (The Historic Record of Chiang Kai-shek's Study in Japan) (Taipei: Chungchang Cultural and Educational Foundation, 2001), p. 917.

36. Ibid., pp. 742–752.

37. S. I. Hsiung, *Life of Chiang Kai-shek,* p. 61.

38. Tong, *Chiang Kai-shek,* vol. 1, p. 12. Brian Crozier, *The Man Who Lost China* (New York: Charles Scribner's Sons, 1976), p. 40.

39. Edward L. Dreyer, *China at War, 1901–1949* (New York: Longman, 1995), pp. 32–39.

40. Wang Shunqi, July 1996, answers to my written questions.

41. Crozier, *Man Who Lost China,* pp. 40–41.

42. R. Keith Schoppa, *Chinese Elites and Political Change: Zhejiang Province in the Early Twentieth Century* (Cambridge: Harvard University Press, 1982), pp. 146–147. Western writers, including myself—see Taylor, *The Generalissimo's Son: Chiang Ching-kuo and the Revolutions in China and Taiwan* (Cambridge: Harvard University Press, 2000), p. 7—have generally repeated the heroic account as well as the story that Chen was so impressed that he offered Chiang the governorship of Zhejiang. Unfortunately, when I wrote the earlier book I did not check with Keith Schoppa, who has read most of the Zhejiang provincial gazetteers of the time. Schoppa reports that immediately after the uprising in Hangzhou, the gazetteers named the various individuals involved in the planning and execution of the coup but not one mentioned Chiang Kai-shek. Nor is there any mention that Chen offered him the governorship, an even more unbelievable claim. Email from R. Keith Schoppa, October 30, 2001.

43. Stella Deng, *Shanghai: The Rise and Fall of a Decadent City* (New York: William Morrow, 2000), pp. 86–87.

44. Tong, *Chiang Kai-shek,* vol. 1, p. 23. The unit he headed was reputedly the Fifth, later the Ninety-third, Regiment.

45. Earl Albert Selle, *Donald of China* (New York: Harper and Brothers, 1948), p. 111; Zhang Xueliang, Columbia interviews, vol. 19, tape 12, pp. 929–932.

46. Yang Tianshi, *Jiang Jieshi midang yu Jiang Jieshi zhenxiang* (Facts about Chiang Kai-shek from His Secret Archives) (Beijing: Social Sciences Documentation Press, 2002), pp. 1–10.

47. Ibid.; Schoppa, *Chinese Elites,* pp. 148–149; email from R. Keith Schoppa, October 30, 2001.

48. The story about the sentry comes from Chen Lifu, Columbia interviews, December 1958–February 1959, p. 61. The report of "some people" comes from Chiang's later eulogy for Chen Qimei in 1916. See S. I. Hsiung, *Life of Chiang Kai-shek,* p. 91. For "rickshaw puller" see Loh, *Early Chiang Kai-shek,* p. 33.

49. Zhang Xianwen and Fang Qingqiu, *Jiang Jieshi quanzhuan* (Complete Biography of Chiang Kai-shek) (Zhengzhou: Zhengzhou People's Publishing House, 1996), p. 55; Boorman, *Biographical Dictionary,* vol. 1, p. 320.

50. Mast and Saywell, "Revolution," pp. 73–98; see also Boorman, *Biographical Dictionary,* vol. 3, p. 200.

51. Ernest P. Young, *The Presidency of Yuan Shikai* (Ann Arbor: University of Michigan Press, 1977), pp. 87–88.

52. Boorman, *Biographical Dictionary,* vol. 1, p. 165.

53. Chiang noted that he came to collect her in late 1912. See Mao Sicheng, *Min guo shi wu nian yi qian qi Jiang Jieshi xian sheng* (Mr. Chiang Kai-shek, 1887–1926) (Hong Kong: Longman, 1965), vol. 1, pp. 4b–5b.

54. For the "old regiment" see Li Shoukong, "Chiang Kai-shek and the Anti-Yuan Movement," *Chinese Studies in History* 21, no. 1 (1987): 71; for the "Green Gang," see Ernest P. Young, *The Presidency,* pp. 131–133; for "the list" see Keji Furuya, *Chiang Kai-shek: His Life and Times* (New York: St. John's University, 1981), pp. 52–53, 55.

55. On the "Black Dragon Society" see Jansen, *Japan and China,* p. 170; for "swear an oath" see Chiang Kai-shek, "Ti-san-tzu Nanyou chun shih hui i shun-tzu" (Address to the Third Military Conference at Nanyou, Hunan), October 20, 1941; on "tutelage" see K'ung Hsiang-hsi (H. H. Kung), Columbia interviews, part 1, p. 42.

56. Furuya, *Chiang Kai-shek,* p. 56.

57. *Soong Mayling* (Soong Mayling's Century), television documentary produced by the public television foundation of Taipei, 2003.

58. Boorman, *Biographical Dictionary,* vol. 2, pp. 265–266; K'ung Hsiang-hsi (H. H. Kung), Columbia interviews, p. 4.

59. K'ung Hsiang-his (H. H. Kung), Columbia interviews, pp. 4–25; Dreyer, *China at War,* pp. 59–60.

60. Selle, *Donald of China,* pp. 139–140.

61. Edgar Snow interview with Qing-ling in Snow, *Journey to the Beginning* (New York: 1958), pp. 88–89.

62. Snow, *Journey,* pp. 88–89; Lyon Sharman, *Sun Yat-sen: His Life and Its Meaning* (New York: John Day Company, 1934), pp. 180–181.

63. Ibid.

64. Furuya, *Chiang Kai-shek,* pp. 58–59.

65. Dreyer, *China at War*, pp. 58–59; Boorman, *Biographical Dictionary*, vol. 1, p. 116.

66. Li Shou-kung, "Chiang Kai-shek and the Anti-Yuan Movement," *Chinese Studies in History* 21, no. 1 (1987): 80.

67. Edwin P. Hoyt, *Japan's War: The Great Pacific Conflict* (New York: McGraw-Hill, 1986), p. 45.

68. K'ung Hsiang-hsi, Columbia interviews, p. 42.

69. Edwin O. Reischauer, *Japan: The Story of a Nation* (New York: Knopf, 1970), p. 151.

70. Li Shou-kung, "Chiang Kai-shek and the Anti-Yuan Movement," pp. 85–93; *North China Daily Herald*, December 11, 1915. For a different version, see Tong, *Chiang Kai-shek*, vol. 1, pp. 42–44. See also S. I. Hsiung, *Life of Chiang Kai-shek*, pp. 86–87.

71. Huang Tzujin, *Jiang Zhongzheng liu ri xue shi lu*, p. 917.

72. Marie-Claire Bergère, *Sun Yat-sen*, trans. Janet Lloyd (Stanford, Calif.: Stanford University Press, 1998), pp. 264–265. The Japanese also provided funds to the southern commanders and the Manchu monarchists in Manchuria.

73. S. I. Hsiung, *Life of Chiang Kai-shek*, pp. 90–91.

74. Ibid.

75. Chiang Diaries, Hoover, January 10, 1918, box 1, folder 2; Paul H. Tai, "History Talks: How Did Chiang Kai-Shek Write His Diaries?" us.f353.mail.yahoo.com/ym/Showletter/boxan (accessed July 3, 2006). Tai is a private individual who has studied Chiang's diaries.

76. Lucian W. Pye, *War Lord Politics* (New York: Praeger, 1971), p. 18. Edgar Snow interview with Chingling in Snow, *Journey*, p. 89.

77. Boorman, *Biographical Dictionary*, vol. 1, p. 75.

78. S. I. Hsiung, *Life of Chiang Kai-shek*, pp. 97–98.

79. Chiang Diaries, Hoover, 1917, box 1, folder 1.

80. Ibid. The Chiang family has indicated that such redacted material will not be released until the year 2035.

81. Loh, *Early Chiang Kai-shek*, pp. 132–133 n.77, citing a November 29, 1926, confidential letter from the U.S. consul general in Shanghai, C. E. Gauss, to the U.S. minister to Peking, on the subject "Criminal Record of Chiang Kai-shek." At this time the Consular Corps in Shanghai was very alarmed about the triumphant march northward of the "Red General, Chiang Kai-shek." Gauss, who as U.S. ambassador to Chiang's government during most of the war years retained his disdain for Chiang, did not mention any of the anomalies of the three reports of criminal activity. Apparently none of the charges was ever followed up on by the British-controlled settlement police. In the case of the charges by the military governor, he had a strong political motive to make such charges.

82. The family source for the statement about the contents of the redaction has been involved in the release of the diaries. Source email to me, May 19, 2008.

83. Tai, "History Talks."

84. Dreyer, *China at War*, p. 66; Boorman, *Biographical Dictionary*, vol. 1, pp. 174–175.

85. Pye, *War Lord*, pp. 17–18; Boorman, *Biographical Dictionary*, vol. 2, p. 125.

86. Lloyd E. Eastman, "Nationalist China during the Nanking Decade, 1927–1937," in *The Nationalist Era in China, 1927–1949*, ed. Lloyd E. Eastman (Cambridge, Eng.: Cambridge University Press, 1991), p. 29.

87. Chiang Diaries, Hoover, March 15, 1918, box 1, folder 4; Boorman, *Biographical Dictionary*, vol. 1, p. 176.

88. Zhang Xianwen and Fang Qingqiu, *Jiang Jieshi quanzhuan*, pp. 49–51.

89. Tong, *Chiang Kai-shek*, vol. 1, pp. 50–51.

90. Zhang Xianwen and Fang Qingqiu, *Jiang Jieshi quanzhuan*, pp. 51–53.

91. R. R. Palmer and Joel Colton, *A History of the Modern World* (New York: McGraw Hill, 1992), p. 725.

92. Chiang Diaries, Hoover, September 23, 1919, box 1, folder 21.

93. Chiang Diaries, Hoover, October 10, November 2, 1919, box 2, folders 1, 2.

94. Chiang Diaries, Hoover, November 16, 24, 26, 27, 1919, box 2, folder 2; Yang Tianshi, *Jiang Jieshi midang*, pp. 38–57.

95. Chiang Diaries, Hoover, March 19, 27, 1919, box 1, folder 15.

96. Chiang Diaries, Hoover, May 22, 1919, box 1, folder 15. Chiang's diary accounts indicate that Jiemei was not a nickname for Yao Yicheng but another woman. For numerous references to Jiemei, Chiang's infatuation with her, and at least one letter she wrote to him, see Yang Tianshi, *Jiang Jieshi midang*, pp. 38–57.

97. Chiang Diaries, Hoover, May 22, 23, 1919, box 1, folder 17.

98. Mao Sicheng, *Min guo shi wu nian yi qian qi Jiang Jieshi xian sheng*, pp. 105–106.

99. This version comes from my interview with Chiang Wei-kuo, Taipei, June 7, 1996, and his memoirs, *Qian shan du xing: Jiang Weiguo de ren sheng zhi li* (Walking Alone in the Midst of a Thousand Mountains: Chiang Wei-kuo's Life Journey) (Taipei: Tian Xia Culture Publishing Company, 1990), p. 20; also my interview with local researcher Wang Shun-chi, Xikou, June 19, 1996.

100. Loh, *Early Chiang Kai-shek*, p. 32.

101. Chiang Diaries, Hoover, October 12, 1919, box 2, folder 1.

102. Chiang Diaries, Hoover, July 4, 1920, box 2, folder 10.

103. Leslie H. Dingyan Chen, *Chen Jiong-ming and the Federalist Movement* (Ann Arbor: University of Michigan, Center for Chinese Studies, 1999), p. 99.

104. Chiang Diaries, Hoover, October 10, 1920, box 2, folder 13.

105. Sun Zhongshan (Sun Yat-sen), *Guo fu zhuan shu* (Complete Works of the Founding Father of the Republic) (Taipei: Institute of National Defense, 1960), pp. 798–799; Loh, *Early Chiang Kai-shek,* pp. 34–35.

106. Loh, *Early Chiang Kai-shek,* pp. 36–38.

107. Ibid., pp. 42–45.

108. Dingyan Chen, *Chen Jiong-ming,* p. 101.

109. "Jiang Jieshi ri ji lei chao-an" (Selected Diary of Chiang Kai-shek, Part 3), *Minguo dang an* (Nanking) 2 (1999): 4–5.

110. Dingyan Chen, *Chen Jiong-ming,* p. 105.

111. Loh, *Early Chiang Kai-shek,* p. 48.

112. Chiang Diaries, Hoover, May 24, 1921, box 2, folder 20.

113. Diana Lary, *Region and Nation* (Cambridge, Eng.: Cambridge University Press 1974), p. 32.

114. Loh, *Early Chiang Kai-shek,* pp. 60–65.

115. Ibid.

116. Chiang Kai-shek, entry for March 6, 1921, Nanking Diaries, no. 2, National Archives, Nanking.

117. Yang Tianshi, *Jiang Jieshi midang,* pp. 68–69, 73; Chiang Diaries, Hoover, July 17, 1921, box 2, folder 22.

118. In July 1921, Chiang said he had "spent" 17,000 silver dollars so far that year.

119. Chiang Diaries, Hoover, May 23, 1922, box 3, folder 9.

120. Interview with Huang in a 2003 television documentary by China Central Television (CCTV) and Shanghai Television titled *Hai shang chen fu* (Fortune Bobbing on the Water), part 2, producer Chen Xiaoqing, director Song Yichang. According to the interview, in 1949, Huang made a deal with the Communists shortly before their takeover of Shanghai. The film in which he recounted this story was part of a mainland China TV documentary, so he may have simply made up the anecdote, but it would not be surprising if it were true.

121. Chiang Diaries, Hoover, March 21, 1922, box 3, folder 7.

122. *Minguo dang an* 4 (1998): 3–10.

123. Chiang Diaries, Hoover, May 23, 1922, box 3, folder 9.

124. Chen Jieru, *Chiang Kai-shek's Secret Past* (Boulder, Colo.: Westview, 1993), pp. 4–26.

125. Crozier, *Man Who Lost China,* p. 114, citing Ting (n.p.).

126. Ibid., pp. 27–42.

127. Interview with Chiang, *New York Times,* September 27, 1927. Chiang Wei-kuo also maintained during our interview of June 6, 1996, that Jieru and Chiang Kai-shek were never married. Wang Shunqi, the Fenghua researcher, likewise disputes the claim. Chen Jieru provides the text of their marriage certificate but not a photocopy. Likewise, among the photos in her book, there is not one of the wedding or the wedding party on December 5, 1921. Chiang's diaries from 1921 to 1922 de-

scribe his frequent nocturnal visits to Jieru. Later they seem to take up housekeeping, but there is nothing about a marriage in the diary entries as published.

128. For "chief of staff," see "Jiang Jieshi riji leichao-si" (Selected Diary of Chiang Kai-shek, part 4), *Minguo dang an* 4 (1999): 24–25; for Sun's escape, see Boorman, *Biographical Dictionary*, vol. 3, p. 143; Edgar Snow, interview with Ch'ing-ling in Snow, *Journey;* for Wei-kuo as the addressee, see interview with Chiang Wei-kuo, Taipei, June 5, 1996.

129. Yang Tianshi, *Jiang Jieshi midang,* p. 79.

130. Chiang Diaries, Hoover, July 2, 1922, box 3, folder 11.

131. Bergère, *Sun Yat-sen,* p. 279.

132. Conrad Brandt, *Stalin's Failure in China, 1924–1927* (Stanford, Calif.: Stanford University Press), pp. 26–27.

133. Ibid., pp. 30–32. Maring attended the CCP Central Committee plenum in August in Hangzhou and insisted on the new plan.

134. Zhang Guotao, *The Rise of the Chinese Communist Party* (Lawrence: University Press of Kansas, 1971), vol. 1, p. 247; C. Martin Wilbur, *The Nationalist Revolution in China, 1923–1928* (Cambridge, Eng.: Cambridge University Press, 1983), p. 2.

135. Xiong Yuwen, "Dang nei he zuo xing shi da ge ming de jie ju" (Achievement of Party Cooperation and the Great Revolutionary Period), *Minguo dang an* 2 (2001): 71–75.

136. Boorman, *Biographical Dictionary,* vol. 2, p. 366; Wilbur, *Nationalist Revolution,* p. 40.

137. Loh, *Early Chiang Kai-shek,* pp. 78–81. Chiang gave three options, but essentially they broke down into two choices.

138. Wilbur, *Nationalist Revolution,* p. 40.

139. "Jiang Jieshi riji leichao-si," pp. 21–31; Chiang Diaries, Hoover, October 18, 1922, box 3, folders 13, 14.

140. Yang Tianshi, *Jiang Jieshi midang,* p. 31. Loh reports that the letter was sent to the new Soviet ambassador in Peking and described Chiang as "my chief of staff and confidential agent." Chiang, it said, was "fully empowered to act in my behalf." Loh, *Early Chiang Kai-shek,* p. 88.

141. Chiang Diaries, Hoover, August 19, 24, 1923, box 4, folder 1.

142. Chiang Diaries, Hoover, September 20–23, 1923, box 4, folder 2.

143. Eugene W. Wu, "Divergence in Strategic Planning: Chiang Kai-shek's Mission to Moscow, 1923," *Republican China* 16, no. 1 (November 1990). Also see Yang Tianshi, *Jiang Jieshi midang,* pp. 35–56.

144. Chiang's diary, but for some reason not his 1957 book, refers to a September 7, 1923, meeting with "the CPSU General Secretary." See Chiang Kai-shek, *Soviet Russia in China* (1957; New York: Farrar, Straus and Giroux, 1967), pp. 16–17.

145. The text of this address was found at the Russian Archives by a Taiwan scholar, Yu Minling. See her "A Reassessment of Chiang Kai-shek and the Policy of Alliance

with the Soviet Union, 1923–1927," in Mechthild Leutner, Roland Felber, Mikhail L. Tarenko, and Alexander M. Grigoriev, eds., *The Chinese Revolution in the 1920s* (London: Routledge, 2002), p. 7. In his diaries Chiang does not discuss the contents of his remarks. See Chiang Diaries, Hoover, November 25, 1923, box 4, folder 4.

146. Chiang Diaries, Hoover, November 25, 27, 1923, box 4, folder 4.

147. Chiang Diaries, Hoover, November 24, 1923, box 4, folder 5.

148. Chiang Diaries, Hoover, September 7, 1923, box 4, folder 2.

149. Chiang Diaries, Hoover, October 9, 1923, box 4, folder 3; Yu, "Reassessment," p. 46.

150. Chiang Diaries, Hoover, November 4, 1923, box 4, folder 4.

151. Chiang's diaries for all of 1924 are missing. Possibly they were lost, but it might well be that they were destroyed because of excessive pro-Soviet sentiments. See Mast and Saywell, "Revolution," pp. 84–86.

152. According to later KMT histories, Chiang penned a letter on March 14, 1924, to Liao Zhongkai that set out very critical views about the Soviet Union. This supposed letter, first referred to in Mao Sicheng's 1937 collection, now at the Nanking Second National Archives, is the only document that contains Chiang's supposed warnings before 1927 about cooperation with Moscow and the Communists.

153. For "comrade" and "very poor" see Zhang Guotao, *Rise of the Chinese Communist Party,* pp. 331–332. For "2.7 million" see Louis Fischer, *The Soviets in World Affairs: A History of the Relations between the Soviet Union and the Rest of the World,* vol. 2 (London, 1930), p. 640, cited by Mast and Saywell, "Revolution," p. 40. Borodin gave this figure to Fisher. Also see Robert C. North and Xenia J. Eudin, *M. N. Roy's Mission to China* (Berkeley: University of California Press, 1963), p. 20. For "revolutionary army" see F. F. Liu, *A Military History of Modern China, 1924–1949* (Princeton, N.J.: Princeton University Press, 1956), p. 8.

154. The original senior military adviser, General Pavlov, accidentally drowned soon after his arrival.

155. Liu, *Military History,* p. 20.

156. Michael Richard Gibson, *Chiang Kai-shek's Central Army, 1924–1936,* Ph.D. diss., George Washington University, 1985, p. 36; Dreyer, *China at War,* p. 124. Liu, *Military History,* p. 12.

157. Chen Lifu, *The Storm Clouds Clear over China* (Stanford, Calif.: Hoover Institution Press, 1994), p. 64.

158. Tong, *Chiang Kai-shek,* p. 46.

159. S. I. Hsiung, *Life of Chiang Kai-shek,* p. 199.

160. Ibid.

161. Liu, *Military History,* pp. 14–15.

162. Ibid., p. 6, citing documents seized from the Soviet embassy in Peking in 1927 and published in "Soviet Plot in China," *Chinese Social and Political Science Review* 11 (1927): 131.

163. Sharman, *Sun Yat-sen,* pp. 303–310.

164. Chiang Diaries, Hoover, November 14, 1922, box 3, folder 15.

165. Chiang Diaries, Hoover, March 23, 1925, box 4, folder 8.

166. Liu, *Military History,* p. 10.

2. The Northern Expedition and Civil War

1. *New York Times,* June 5 and 12, 1925.

2. *New York Times,* May 31, 1925. *Shen Bao,* Shanghai, May 31, 1925, reports that seven were killed. For Ching-kuo's role, see Chiang Ching-kuo, "My Days in Soviet Russia," in *Chiang Ching-kuo Remembered,* ed. Ray S. Cline (Washington, D.C.: U.S. Global Strategy Council, 1989), p. 153.

3. *New York Times,* June 5, 1925.

4. Jonathan D. Spence, *The Search for Modern China* (New York: W. W. Norton, 1990), p. 340.

5. Chiang Diaries, Hoover, June 23, July 29, September 16, 1925, box 4, folders 11, 12, 14.

6. Chiang Diaries, Hoover, June 21, 1925, box 4, folder 11.

7. Diana Lary, *Region and Nation: The Kwangsi Clique in Chinese Politics, 1925–1937* (Cambridge, Eng.: Cambridge University Press, 1974), pp. 58–61.

8. Ibid.

9. Proposal of the Military Commission on Reform, December 15, 1925, in Qin Xiaoyi, *Zong tong,* vol. 1, p. 109.

10. Chiang Diaries, Hoover, July 23, 1925, box 4, folder 12.

11. Chiang Diaries, Hoover, August 20, 1925, box 4, folder 13.

12. Te-kong Tong and Li Tsung-jen (Li Congren), *The Memoirs of Li Tsung-jen* (Boulder, Colo.: Westview, 1979), p. 148.

13. C. Martin Wilbur, *The Nationalist Revolution in China* (Cambridge, Eng.: Cambridge University Press, 1983), p. 27.

14. Zhang Guotao, *The Rise of the Chinese Communist Party* (Lawrence: University Press of Kansas, 1972), p. 480, quoting Borodin.

15. Ibid.; Te-kong Tong and Li Tsung-jen, *Memoirs,* pp. 111, 192.

16. Chiang Diaries, Hoover, August 20, 1925, box 4, folder 13.

17. Chiang Diaries, Hoover, October 18, 1925, box 4, folder 15.

18. Yu Minling, "A Reassessment of Chiang Kai-shek and the Policy of Alliance with the Soviet Union, 1923–1927," in *The Chinese Revolution in the 1920s,* ed. Mechthild Leutner, Roland Felber, Mikhail L. Tarenko, and Alexander M. Grigoriev (London: Routledge Cruzon, 2002), p. 113.

19. Wilbur, *Nationalist Revolution,* pp. 30–31; Yu Minling, "Reassessment," pp. 108–109.

20. Zhang Guotao, *Rise of the Chinese Communist Party,* p. 479.

21. S. I. Hsiung, *The Life of Chiang Kai-shek* (London: Pete Davies, 1948), pp. 238–240.

22. Chen Lifu, *The Storm Clouds Clear over China* (Stanford, Calif.: Hoover Institution Press, 1994), p. 64. This was the KMT intelligence estimate and may have been inflated by adding those simply suspected of CCP membership or Communist sympathy. See also Wilbur, *Nationalist Revolution,* p. 36.

23. Yu Minling, "Reassessment," p. 113.

24. C. Martin Wilbur and Julie Lien-ying How, *Documents on Communism, Nationalism, and Soviet Advisers in China, 1918–1927: Papers Seized in the 1927 Peking Raid* (New York: Columbia University Press, 1956), p. 259.

25. Wilbur, *Nationalist Revolution,* p. 44.

26. C. Martin Wilbur and Julie Lien-ying How, *Missionaries of Revolution, Soviet Advisers and Nationalist China, 1920–1927* (Cambridge: Harvard University Press, 1989), p. 249.

27. Ibid., pp. 248–250.

28. Chiang Diaries, Hoover, February 7 and 11, 1926, box 4, folder 19.

29. Wilbur, *Nationalist Revolution,* pp. 45–46.

30. Ibid., p. 14.

31. Chiang Diaries, Hoover, March 17, 1926, box 4, folder 20.

32. Interview with Chen Lifu, May 29, 1996.

33. Chen Lifu, *Storm Clouds,* pp. 28–29.

34. Chiang Diaries, Hoover, March 19, 1926, box 4, folder 20.

35. Ibid. Seventy years later, Chen Lifu recalled that on that day he and Chiang were on their way not to the First Corps encampment but to board the Russian ship then in Canton. It was then that Chiang decided to go back and make a stand. Chen Lifu, *Storm Clouds,* pp. 27–28.

36. Chiang Diaries, Hoover, March 19, 1926, box 4, folder 20.

37. Yang Tianshi, *Jiang Jieshi midang yu Jiang Jieshi zhen xiang* (Facts about Chiang Kai-shek from His Secret Archives) (Peking: Social Sciences Documentation Press, 2002), p. 13.

38. Chiang Diaries, Hoover, January 12, 1926, box 4, folder 18; Yu Minling, "Reassessment," p. 114, citing a Comintern archival document—a report of A. Bubnov, head of a commission evaluating Soviet aid to the Chinese Revolution. The commission happened to be in China at the time of the March 26, 1926, incident and its report focused on the reasons for this setback. See also ibid., p. 131.

39. Yang Tianshi, *Jiang Jieshi,* p. 132.

40. Boorman, *Biographical Dictionary,* vol. 3, p. 37.

41. Ibid., pp. 134–135.

42. "Jiang Jieshi riji leichao: zhengdang yi" (Selected Diary of Chiang Kai-shek: Party and Government Affairs, part 1) *Minguo dang an* 4 (1998): 8, 9.

43. Chen Duxu, "The Policy for the Unity of the Chinese Revolutionary Forces and the Kwangchow Incident," *Guide* (Shanghai), April 3, 1926, no. 148; Yang Tianshi, *Jiang Jieshi,* pp. 140–141.

44. Chiang Diaries, Hoover, May 17, 1926, box 4, folder 22.

45. Boorman, *Biographical Dictionary,* vol. 1, p. 325.

46. Chen Lifu, *Storm Clouds,* pp. 58–59.

47. Ruth Altman Greene, *Hsiang-ya Journal* (Hamden, Conn.: Archon Books, 1977), p. 43.

48. Michael Gibson, "Chiang Kai-shek's Central Army, 1924–1938," Ph.D. diss., George Washington University, 1985, p. 56.

49. Greene, *Hsiang-ya Journal,* pp. 40–47.

50. Te-kong Tong and Li Tsung-jen, *Memoirs,* p. 183.

51. Gibson, "Chiang Kai-shek's Central Army," p. 93.

52. Chen Lifu, Columbia interviews, part 2, p. 1; Hollington Tong, *Chiang Kai-shek* (Shanghai: China Publishing Company, 1938), vol. 1, p. 180.

53. Ray Huang, *Chiang Kai-shek and His Diaries as a Historical Source* (Armonk, N.Y.: M. E. Sharpe, 1996), part 1, p. 31.

54. Zhang Ruide, "Chiang Kai-shek's War Time Directives," paper given at Wartime China Conference, Cambridge, Mass., June 27–29, 2002.

55. Huang, *Chiang Kai-shek,* pp. 30–31.

56. Chen Lifu, Columbia interviews, part 2, p. 2.

57. Emily Hahn, *Chiang Kai-shek: An Unauthorized Biography* (New York: Doubleday, 1955), p. 119.

58. Tong, *Chiang Kai-shek,* p. 186.

59. Laura Tyson Li, *Madame Chiang Kai-shek* (New York: Atlantic Monthly Press, 2006), pp. 70–72.

60. Hahn, *Chiang Kai-shek,* p. 122.

61. Zhang Guotao, *Rise of the Chinese Communist Party,* p. 605.

62. Mao Zedong, *Selected Works* (New York: International Publishers, 1953), vol. 1, pp. 26–29.

63. Greene, *Hsiang-ya Journal,* p. 51.

64. Wilbur, *Nationalist Revolution,* p. 80.

65. Conrad Brandt, *Stalin's Failure in China* (New York: W. W. Norton, 1966), pp. 88, 94.

66. Harold R. Isaacs, *The Tragedy of the Chinese Revolution* (1938; Stanford, Calif.: Stanford University Press, 1961), p. 111.

67. Donald Jordan, *The Northern Expedition* (Honolulu: University Press of Hawaii, 1976), pp. 190–207. Michael Gibson read numerous memoirs and recollections of the Chinese militarists of the period but none mentioned rural pro-KMT resistance against them as a factor in the military outcome or in their separate decisions to retreat, give up, or defect to the KMT. Gibson, "Central Army," pp. 78–144.

68. Wilbur and How, *Documents*, p. 371; "Jiang jieshi riji leichao er" (Selected Diary of Chiang Kai-shek, part 2), *Minguo dang an* 1 (1999): 4–11.

69. Chiang Diaries, Hoover, January 2, 1927, box 5, folder 8.

70. Leon Trotsky, *Problems of the Chinese Revolution* (Ann Arbor: University of Michigan Press, 1967), p. 401.

71. Robert C. North and Xenia J. Eudin, *M. N. Roy's Mission to China* (Berkeley: University of California Press, 1963), p. 47.

72. Wilbur, *Nationalist Revolution*, p. 81.

73. Chiang Diaries, Hoover, February 1 and 25, 1927, box 5, folder 8.

74. Zhang Guotao, *Rise of the Chinese Communist Party*, p. 581.

75. Ibid., pp. 570, 584–585; Edward L. Dreyer, *China at War* (New York: Longman, 1995), pp. 142; Chen Lifu, *Storm Clouds*, p. 56. The general strikes were joint KMT and CCP efforts and thus it seems unlikely, as frequently charged, that Chiang ordered the army to wait outside of the city to allow the warlord forces time to suppress the workers.

76. Wilbur, *Nationalist Revolution*, pp. 91–92; Chen Lifu, *Storm Clouds*, pp. 53–54.

77. Parks M. Coble, *The Shanghai Capitalists and the Nationalist Government, 1927–1937* (Cambridge: Harvard University Press, 1986), p. 30; Chen Lifu, Columbia interviews, part 1, pp. 27–29.

78. Chiang Diaries, Hoover, April 5, 1927, box 6, folder 10.

79. Ibid.

80. Wilbur, *Nationalist Revolution*, p. 98.

81. Chen Lifu, *Storm Clouds*, pp. 60–64. *Hai shang chen fu, er* (Upheaval on the Sea, part 2), TV documentary on the Shanghai underworld, produced by China Central Television (CCTV) and Shanghai Television, 2003; Chen Lifu, Columbia interviews, part 1, p. 29; Wilbur, *Nationalist Revolution*, p. 104.

82. Ibid.

83. Dreyer, *China at War*, p. 141. The documents also showed how the USSR aided the KMT as well as the CCP. See also Trotsky, *Problems of the Chinese Revolution*, pp. 383–384.

84. Chen Lifu, *Storm Clouds*, pp. 60–65; *Hai shang chen fu, er.*

85. Chen Lifu, *Storm Clouds*, pp. 62, 68; Wilbur, *Nationalist Revolution*, pp. 68, 108–112.

86. Chiang Diaries, Hoover, April 14, 1927, box 5, folder 10.

87. Brian Crozier, *The Man Who Lost China* (New York: Charles Scribner's Sons, 1976), p. 108; Boorman, *Biographical Dictionary*, vol. 2, p. 164.

88. *Time*, April 25, 1927; Jay Taylor, *The Generalissimo's Son: Chiang Ching-kuo and the Revolutions in China and Taiwan* (Cambridge: Harvard University Press, 2000), pp. 49–73.

89. Coble, *Shanghai Capitalists,* pp. 36, 262.

90. Ji Peng, "1927–1935: Nian guomin zhengfu jinyan pingshu" (Review of the Republican Government's Drug-Control Measures during 1927–1935), *Minguo dang an* 1 (2000): 77–81.

91. Chiang Diaries, Hoover, April 30, 1927, box 5, folder 10.

92. Brandt, *Stalin's Failure,* pp. 130–133.

93. Zhang Guotao, *Rise of the Chinese Communist Party,* pp. 636–640.

94. Te-kong Tong and Li Tsung-jen, *Memoirs,* pp. 216–217.

95. The currency promised was probably paper yuan issued by the Peking government. On April 4, 1927, the Shanghai Native Bankers Association advanced the Revolutionary Army one million silver, probably Mexican, dollars. The new Nationalist government established on April 18 did not issue its own silver-backed paper currency until 1928. See Zhaojin Ji, *A History of the Modern Shanghai Banking System* (Armonk, N.Y.: M. E. Sharpe, 2003), pp. 169–171.

96. Ibid., p. 217.

97. Chiang Diaries, Hoover, August 3 and 10, 1927, box 5, folder 14; ibid., p. 217.

98. Te-kong Tong and Li Tsung-jen, *Memoirs,* pp. 145–146.

99. Protocol no. 119 of the meeting of the Politburo of the All Union Communist Party or AUCP (later, the Communist Party of the Soviet Union), August 11, 1927, RGASPI, collection 17, inventory 162, file 5, sheets 74–79; Protocol no. 120 (special no. 98) of the meeting of the AUCP (All Union Communist Party), Politburo, August 18, 1927, RGASPI, collection 17, inventory 162, file 5, sheets 86–88. US$300,000 would be equivalent to US$3.373 million in 2005 correcting for inflation, but in terms of relative share of GDP about US$39 million in the United States in 2005 and possibly US$300 million in China today. For relative values see the Economics History website at http://eh.net/hmit.

100. Robert C. North and Xenia Eudin, *Roy's Mission* (Berkeley: University of California Press, 1963), p. 121.

101. Te-kong Tong and Li Tsung-jen, *Memoirs,* p. 221.

102. Ibid., pp. 221–222.

103. Tong, *Chiang Kai-shek,* vol. 1, p. 173.

104. Ibid., pp. 181–182.

105. Chen Jieru, *Chiang Kai-shek's Secret Past* (Boulder, Colo.: Westview, 1993), p. 210.

106. Chiang Diaries, Hoover, October 1, 1927, box 5, folder 16.

107. *New York Times,* September 27, 1927.

108. Li, *Madame Chiang Kai-shek,* p. 81.

109. Ibid. p. 80.

110. Hahn, *Chiang Kai-shek,* p. 125.

111. *Soong Mayling de Shi ji* (Soong Mayling's Century), TV documentary by the Public Television Foundation of Taipei, 2003.

112. William Manchester, *The Last Lion: Visions of Glory* (London: Little, Brown, 1983), p. 81.

113. Li, *Madame Chiang Kai-shek*, p. 57.

114. Interviews in Taipei with several of Chiang's secretaries, aides, and assistants, 1995–2003; Edgar Snow, *Journey to the Beginning* (New York: Random House, 1958), p. 85; and interview with a longtime friend and confidant of Madame Chiang, March 19, 2008.

115. RGASPI, collection 495, inventory 225, file 77, sheet 1.

116. Chiang Diaries, Hoover, November 5, 1927, box 5, folder 17; Wilbur, *Nationalist Revolution,* pp. 160–161.

117. Chiang Diaries, Hoover, November 5, 1927, box 5, folder 17.

118. F. F. Liu, *A Military History of Modern China, 1924–1949* (Princeton, N.J.: Princeton University Press, 1956), pp. 61–64.

119. Documentary: *Hai shang chen fu, er.*

120. Wang Ke-wen, "Counter-Revolution from Above," *Republican China* 15, no. 1 (1989): 49.

121. Chiang Diaries, Hoover, March 17, April 25, and April 28, 1928, box 5, folder 19, and April 25, 1928, box 6, folder 3.

122. John Robinson Beal, *Marshal in China* (Garden City, N.Y.: Doubleday, 1970), pp. 15–19.

123. Coble, *Shanghai Capitalists,* pp. 44–46.

124. Editor's note, in Qin Xiaoyi, *Zong tong,* vol. 1, pp. 203–204.

125. Chiang Diaries, Hoover, April 16, 1928, box 6, folder 3. See also Grace Huang, "The Politics of Knowing Shame: Agency in Jiang Jieshi's Leadership (1927–1936)," Ph.D. diss., University of Chicago, 2003.

126. Wang Wei, "Wang Wei Xiansheng gangwen jilu" (The Reminiscences of General Wang Wei) (Taipei: Academia Sinica, Institute of Modern History, 1996), p. 22.

127. Chiang Diaries, Hoover, May 5, 1928, box 6, folder 3.

128. Chiang Diaries, Hoover, April 27, 1928, box 6, folder 3.

129. Chiang Diaries, Hoover, May 2, 1928, box 6, folder 4.

130. Chiang Diaries, Hoover, July 2, 1928, box 6, folder 6.

131. For the best account of these events see Zhang Yu-fa, "The Shandong Battlefield during the Northern Expedition," in *Chiang Kai-shek and China,* part 2, ed. Li Yu-ning (Armonk, N.Y.: M. E. Sharpe, 1988), pp. 3–65.

132. Chiang Diaries, Hoover, March 31, 1928, box 6, folder 4.

133. Ibid.

134. Huang Zejin, "Jiang Jieshi yan zhong de riben" (Japan in the Eyes of Chiang

Kai-shek), unpublished paper based on 313 articles and lectures by Chiang Kai-shek on the subject of Japan (Taipei, 2003).

135. The Japanese Guandong Army stationed in Manchuria is not to be confused with the name of the southern province of Guangdong, home of the Cantonese and the Guangdong Army.

136. Boorman, *Biographical Dictionary,* vol. 1, p. 121.

137. Zhang Xueliang, Columbia interviews, vol. 19, tape 12, pp. 929–932.

138. Chiang Diaries, Hoover, July 20, 1928, box 6, folder 6.

139. Lary, *Region and Nation,* p. 79.

140. Te-kong Tong and Li Tsung-jen, *Memoirs,* p. 257.

141. Keji Furuya, *Chiang Kai-shek, His Life and Times* (New York: St. John's University, 1981), p. 264.

142. Boorman, *Biographical Dictionary,* vol. 1, p. 63.

143. Zhang, Columbia interviews, vol. 5, pp. 3-239 to 3-242.

144. Zhang, Columbia interviews, vol. 84, pp. 51-4152 to 51-4153.

145. Chiang's speech of January 5, 1929, in Qin Xiaoyi, *Zong tong,* vol. 1, p. 260.

146. Chen Lifu, *Storm Clouds,* pp. 66–67.

147. Zhang Xueliang, Columbia interviews, vol. 37, p. 24-1823, and vol. 7, p. 4-335; O. Edmund Clubb, *China and Russia* (New York: Columbia University Press, 1971), p. 256; Qin Xiaoyi, *Zong tong,* vol. 2, pp. 278, 282–284.

148. Chiang speech on the Northern Expedition, in Qin Xiaoyi, *Zong tong,* vol. 2, pp. 278, 282–284; Zhang Xueliang, Columbia interviews, 1990–1991, vol. 7, pp. 4-331 to 4-333; Robert C. North, *Moscow and the Chinese Communists,* 2d ed. (Stanford, Calif.: Stanford University Press, 1963), p. 123.

149. J. A. Piatnitsky to J. V. Stalin, June 11, 1928, RGASPI, collection 508, inventory 1, file 112b, sheets 1–2. The one million Chinese (probably silver) dollars were for an "extra," or emergency, fund. According to one Comintern document, in February 1928, 2.80 Chinese dollars were equal to US$1.

150. Te-kong Tong and Li Tsung-jen, *Memoirs,* pp. 262–265; J. A. Pliatnitsky to A. E. Albreht, Moscow, December 12, 1928; RGASPI, collection 495, inventory 23, file 50a, sheet 138.

151. Zhang Guotao, *Rise of the Chinese Communist Party,* vol. 2, pp. 164–165.

152. Stuart Schram, *The Political Thought of Mao Tse-tung* (New York: Penguin Books, 1967), pp. 245–246.

153. Lary, *Region and Nation,* pp. 155–156.

154. William C. Kirby, *Germany and Republican China* (Stanford, Calif.: Stanford University Press, 1984), pp. 109–110.

155. Furuya, *Chiang Kai-shek,* p. 286.

156. Gibson, "Chiang Kai-shek's Central Army," pp. 205–207.

157. Huang, *Chiang Kai-shek,* part 1, pp. 58, 60, 62.

158. Kirby, *Germany and Republican China,* p. 109.

159. Huang, *Chiang Kai-shek,* part 1, p. 61.

160. Zhu Yuanzhang made Nanking the capital of his Ming dynasty. His son moved the capital to Peking (Beijing or "northern capital") and named his father's brief capital Nanking, or "southern capital."

161. Chiang Diaries, Hoover, August 25, 26, 29, and 31, 1929, box 7, folder 2.

162. Interview with Leo Soong, Walnut Creek, Calif., May 15, 2004.

163. Li, *Madame Chiang Kai-shek,* p. 98.

164. Hahn, *Chiang Kai-shek,* p. 130.

165. Interview with Zhou Lianhua, Taipei, October 18, 2004.

166. Dreyer, *China at War,* pp. 159–160.

167. Ibid., p. 164.

168. Chiang speech, September 1, 1931, in Qin Xiaoyi, *Zong tong,* vol. 2, pp. 375–382.

169. Chiang Diaries, Hoover, August 12, 1931, box 8, folder 9.

170. Dreyer, *China at War,* p. 169.

171. Zhang Xueliang, Columbia interviews, vol. 15, pp. 8-706 to 8-708, and vol. 16, pp. 8-756, 9-793, 9-794.

172. Huang Zejin, "Jiang Jieshi yan zhong de riben," p. 124, citing *Manzhouguo and the Guandong Army* (English trans.) (Tokyo: Xin renwu wanglai she, 1994), p. 220.

173. Zhang Xuehliang, Columbia interviews, vol. 15, pp. 8-706 to 8-708, and vol. 16, pp. 9-793, 9-794.

174. Chiang Diaries, Hoover, September 20, 1931, box 8, folder 10.

175. U.S. Consul General Nanking cable (Johnson) to Secretary of State, October 18, 1931, *FRUS (1931),* vol. 3: *The Far East,* pp. 228–229.

176. Yang Tianshi, *Jiang Jieshi,* p. 352.

177. Chiang Diaries, Hoover, October 7, 1931, box 8, folder 11.

178. Qin Xiaoyi, *Zong tong,* vol. 2, p. 395.

179. Yang, *Chiang Chieh-shih,* p. 357.

180. Ibid.

181. Ibid., pp. 359–362.

182. Furuya, *Chiang Kai-shek,* p. 344.

183. Yang, *Chiang Chieh-shih,* p. 366.

184. Ibid.

185. *Jiang Jieshi ri ji* (Chiang Kai-shek Diaries), entry for January 25, 1931, Nanjing National Archives. Notes were provided in October 1996 by Yang Tienshi, former director of the Institute of Modern Chinese History and a specialist on the Republican period.

186. Yang, *Chiang Chieh-shih,* p. 367.

3. The Nanking Decade

1. Marius B. Jansen, *Japan and China: From War to Peace, 1894–1972* (Chicago: Rand McNally, 1975), p. 384; Parks M. Coble, *The Shanghai Capitalists and the Nationalist Government, 1927–1937* (Cambridge: Harvard University Press, 1986), pp. 88–96.

2. Coble, *Shanghai Capitalists,* pp. 88–96.

3. Robert C. North, *Moscow and the Chinese Communists,* 2nd ed. (Stanford, Calif.: Stanford University Press, 1963), p. 161; O. Edmund Clubb, *China and Russia* (New York: Columbia University Press, 1971), p. 269.

4. *Shen Pao* (Shanghai), January 15, 1932; Chiang speech of January 11, 1932, in Qin Xiaoyi, *Zong tong,* vol. 2, p. 421.

5. Chen Lifu, *The Storm Clouds Clear over China* (Stanford, Calif.: Hoover Institution Press, 1994), pp. 111–112.

6. U.S. Consul General Nanking cable (Peck) to U.S. Legation, Peking, January 24, 1932, *FRUS (1932),* vol. 3: *The Far East,* p. 79.

7. Zhang Heng and Lue Lun "1–28 Kangzhan qijian Guomindang nei de he yu zhan zhi zheng" (Negotiation or Fighting Back: Argument in the KMT about the January 28 Incident), *Minguo dang an* 1, no. 27 (1992): 111. The telegrams are in the Nanking Second National Archives.

8. Keji Furuya, *Chiang Kai-shek: His Life and Times* (New York: St. John's University, 1981), pp. 351–355.

9. Parks M. Coble, "CKS and the Anti-Japanese Movement in China: Zou Taofen and the National Salvation Association, 1931–1937," *Journal of Asian Studies* 44, no. 2 (February 1985): 296.

10. Furuya, *Chiang Kai-shek,* pp. 356–357.

11. Boorman, *Biographical Dictionary,* vol. 3, p. 150.

12. Edward L. Dreyer, *China at War* (New York: Longman, 1995), pp. 186–187.

13. Chiang speech "Eradicating the Communists and Reforming the Military," July 2, 1932, in Qin Xiaoyi, *Zong tong,* vol. 2, p. 465.

14. F. F. Liu, *A Military History of Modern China, 1924–1949* (Princeton, N.J.: Princeton University Press, 1956), p. 102.

15. Jonathan D. Spence, *The Search for Modern China* (New York: W. W. Norton, 1990), p. 400.

16. Chiang Diaries, Hoover, June 1, 1933, box 36, folder 13.

17. Editor's notes, in Qin Xiaoyi, *Zong tong,* vol. 2, pp. 515–553, 583, 585.

18. Chiang Diaries, Hoover, June 1, 1933, box 36, folder 18.

19. Chiang speech, April 12, 1932, in Qin Xiaoyi, *Zong tong,* vol. 2, p. 552.

20. Appendix to Fourth KMT Central Executive Committee Plenum, in Qin Xiaoyi, *Zong tong,* vol. 2, p. 652.

21. Chiang speech, March 18, 1934, in Qin Xiaoyi, *Zong tong,* vol. 2, p. 670.

22. Chiang Diaries, Hoover, August 21, 1935, box 38, folder 4.

23. Zhang Xueliang, Columbia interviews, vol. 86, p. 52-4289; Boorman, *Biographical Dictionary,* vol. 1, p. 65.

24. Wang Chi interview, July 26, 2003, Washington, D.C. Wang's father, General Wang Xuchang, was a longtime senior commander under Zhang Xueliang and a classmate in Japan of Chiang Kai-shek.

25. Chiang speech at the Wulan School in Xikou, January 10, 1932, in Qin Xiaoyi, *Zong tong,* vol. 2, p. 465.

26. Chiang cable to Wang Jingwei, August 21, 1933, in Qin Xiaoyi, *Zong tong,* vol. 2, p. 610.

27. Chiang speech on land reform, December 15, 1932, in Qin Xiaoyi, *Zong tong,* vol. 2, pp. 500–503.

28. CCP telegram to Moscow, November 14, 1933, RGASPI, collection 495, inventory 184, file 54, sheet 57. On November 18, Moscow reported it was sending the U.S. dollars in batches of $50,000, RGASPI, collection 514, inventory 1, file 759, sheet 105. For other relevant Comintern/CCP messages see p. 630, n. 66.

29. William C. Kirby, *Germany and Republican China* (Stanford, Calif.: Stanford University Press, 1984), p. 147; Chiang Wei-kuo interview, Taipei, June 5, 1996.

30. Joseph J. Heinlein Jr., "Political Warfare: The Chinese Nationalist Model," Ph.D. thesis, American University, 1973, pp. 303–312.

31. April and October 2003 interviews with various assistants and secretaries of Chiang Kai-shek, going back to mainland days. His Whampoa students called him "Hsiao Chang," meaning principal or (school) director; military personnel called him "Xiansheng" or "Zong si ling" (commander in chief).

32. Lloyd E. Eastman, "Fascism in Kuomintang China: The Blue Shirts," *China Quarterly* (January–March 1972): 1–31. The material is said have appeared in something called "Toyo Bunko." The same citation also lists a Japanese foreign ministry document by Iwai Ichii. One wonders if Iwai's source could be the "specially bound" document. Significantly Professor Eastman, in a review article written fifteen years later—"The Rise and Fall of the Blue Shirts: A Review Article," *Republican China* 13, no. 1 (November 1987)—notes that new material has corrected some of his previous views on this subject, and he does not repeat the alleged quotation from Chiang Kai-shek.

33. Wilbur Burton, "Chiang's Secret Blood Brothers," *Asia* (May 1936): 309. I am unable to locate this publication in the Library of Congress or elsewhere to check Burton's own citation. Healthy skepticism seems warranted. Burton's quote is cited by Frederick Wakeman Jr., "A Revisionist View of the Nanking Decade: Confucian Fascism," in *Reappraising Republican China,* ed. Frederick Wakeman Jr. and Richard Louis Edmonds (Oxford, Eng.: Oxford University Press, 2000), p. 141.

34. Eastman, "Rise and Fall of the Blue Shirts," pp. 34–35, 40.

35. Hsu Ch'o-yun interview, Taipei, October 16, 2004.

36. CCP Central Committee to the Executive Committee of the Comintern, Shanghai, October 20, 1930, RGASPI, collection 495, inventory 19, file 117, sheets 35–37a.

37. Hsu Ch'o-yun, e-mail, June 10, 2004.

38. Wakeman, "Revisionist View," p. 149.

39. Kirby, *Germany and Republican China*, p. 176.

40. Eastman, "Rise and Fall of the Blue Shirts," pp. 31–32.

41. Frederick Wakeman Jr., *Spymaster: Dai Li and the Chinese Secret Service* (Berkeley: University of California Press, 2003), pp. 279–280.

42. Ibid., p. 177.

43. Comintern archival papers show that the Comintern at least once secretly gave Issacs US$500 for his journal. See Comintern memo, Moscow, April 9, 1932, RGASPI, collection 495, inventory 4, file 182, sheets 8–9, and collection 514, inventory 1, file 707, sheets 56–59, 63–66.

44. Boorman, *Biographical Dictionary*, vol. 3, p. 274.

45. Wakeman cites numerous articles and biographies from the mainland and Taiwan. A full assessment would require looking at the sources cited by these writers.

46. Wakeman, *Spymaster*, pp. 178–179.

47. Zhang Guotao, *The Rise of the Chinese Communist Party* (Lawrence: University Press of Kansas, 1971), vol. 2, pp. 150–151.

48. Ibid.

49. Mary Wright, *The Last Stand of Chinese Conservatism* (Stanford, Calif.: Stanford University Press, 1957).

50. Stephen C. Averill, "The New Life Action: The Nationalist Government in South Jiangxi, 1934–1937," *China Quarterly* 88 (December 1981): 595.

51. Ibid., pp. 606–607.

52. Ibid., pp. 626–628.

53. Ibid.

54. Chiang speech, February 17, 1934, in Qin Xiaoyi, *Zong tong*, vol. 2, pp. 660–662.

55. Eastman, "Fascism," pp. 1–31.

56. "Shilue kao pen" (Draft Manuscripts), May 4, 1934, ed. Yuan Huizhang, Archives of President Chiang (Chiang Kai-shek), Academia Historica, Xintian, Taiwan.

57. Mrs. Chas. E. Cowman, *Streams in the Desert* (Los Angeles: Oriental Missionary Society, 1931).

58. Emily Hahn, *Chiang Kai-shek: An Unauthorized Biography* (New York: Doubleday, 1955), p. 72.

59. U.S. Legation in Peking to Secretary of State, radiogram, August 6, 1934, *FRUS (1934)*, vol. 3: *The Far East*, p. 217.

60. Ji Peng, "1927–1935 Nian guomin zhengfu jinyan pingshu" (Review of the Republican Government's Drug Control Measures during 1927–1935), _Minguo dang an_ 1 (2000): 77–81.

61. RGASPI, collection 495, inventory 184, file 47, sheets 81, 130.

62. North, _Moscow,_ p. 164.

63. Michael M. Sheng, _Battling Western Imperialism: Mao, Stalin, and the United States_ (Princeton, N.J.: Princeton University Press, 1997), p. 23.

64. Mao gave this figure in his March 31, 1956, conversation with Soviet Ambassador P. F. Yudin. See Yudin Journal, entry April 5, 1956, no. 289, Woodrow Wilson Center International Cold War History website. Mao told Edgar Snow the number was "estimated at 90,000" and did not include "thousands of Red peasants." I have chosen to use the number he gave Yudin and correspondingly reduced the usual numbers given along the route of the Long March.

65. Ross Terrill, _A Biography: Mao_ (New York: Random House, 1980), p. 121.

66. Telegram from CCP Shanghai Bureau to Comintern, RGASPI, collection 495, inventory 184, file 61, sheet 58. On September 4, the Comintern informed the CCP in Jiangxi that it was sending a foreigner to set up an apparatus for purchasing and transporting arms and ammunition for the Jiangxi soviet: see collection 495, inventory 184, file 48, sheets 9–10.

67. In 1903, one Mexican silver dollar was reportedly worth 38 U.S. cents (_New York Times,_ March 11, 1903). Assuming the same value in 1934, three million Mexican silver dollars then would be equal to about US$7 million in 2005, adjusting for inflation. While the total amount of hard currency the Shanghai CCP was able to smuggle into the Jiangxi soviet is uncertain, it likely was sufficient to play an important, perhaps a key role in the Long March's survival.

68. Edgar Snow was told that many weapons, much equipment, and "even much silver" had to be buried along the way. See Edgar Snow, _Red Star over China_ (1938; New York: Random House Modern Library, 1944), pp. 194–195. It seems doubtful that Mao would have left silver behind, but if so, he may have had even more than available documents indicate.

69. Cheng Siyuan, _Bai Chongxi Zhuan_ (Biography of Bai Chongxi) (Hong Kong: South China Press, 1989), pp. 195–180.

70. Chiang Diaries, Hoover, November 26, 1934, box 37, folder 13.

71. Dreyer, _China at War,_ p. 194; Stuart R. Schram, _Political Thought_ (Baltimore: Penguin Books, 1966), pp. 80–81.

72. Te-kong Tong and Li Tsung-jen (Li Congren), _The Memoirs of Li Tsung-jen_ (Boulder, Colo.: Westview, 1979), pp. 295–296. Li records that the Guangxi Army inflicted 10,000 CCP casualties and took 7,000 prisoners.

73. Chen Lifu, _Storm Clouds,_ pp. 114–115. Chen reports that the assassin was killed on the spot.

74. Wakeman, _Spymaster,_ pp. 182–186.

75. Chen Minzhong, "Shi lun 1935–1936 nian zhong ri hui tan" (On Sino-

Japanese Negotiations in 1935–1936), *Minguo dang an* (Nanking) 2, no. 16 (1989): 105–118.

76. Ibid.

77. Chen Minzhong, "Shi lun 1935–1936 nian zhong ri hui tan," pp. 105–118; "Material Concerning the Negotiations between China and Japan from December 1935 to February 1937," *Minguo dang an* 2, no. 12 (1988): 19–44.

78. See, for example, Marius B. Jansen, *Japan and China: From War to Peace, 1894–1972* (Chicago: Rand McNally, 1975), p. 390.

79. Chen Minzhong, "Shi lun 1935–1936 nian zhong ri hui tan," pp. 105–118; "Material Concerning the Negotiations between China and Japan from December 1935 to February 1937," pp. 19–44.

80. Jansen, *Japan and China*, pp. 390–391.

81. Chiang Diaries, Hoover, October 8, 1935, box 38, folder 6.

82. Sheng, *Battling Western Imperialism*, p. 25.

83. Chen Lifu, *Storm Clouds*, pp. 116–119. Chen provides a photocopy of the handwritten note from Zhou. Chiang Kai-shek, *Soviet Russia in China* (New York: Farrar, Strauss and Cudahay, 1957), p. 72, reports that Zhou first contacted a KMT representative in Hong Kong in the autumn and winter of 1935, declaring that the CCP wanted only to stop the fighting with the KMT and resist Japan together; there were no other conditions. Zhou then wrote directly to the Chen brothers. See also Wu T'ien-wei, *The Sian Incident* (Ann Arbor: University of Michigan Center for Chinese Studies, 1976), pp. 21–22.

84. June Chang and Jon Halliday, *Mao* (New York: Knopf, 2005), p. 167, citing Soviet foreign ministry files.

85. Chen Lifu, *Storm Clouds*, pp. 116–119.

86. Chiang Kai-shek speech to students and scholars, January 15, 1936, in Qin Xiaoyi, *Zong tong*, vol. 3, pp. 912–917.

87. Akira Iriye, *The Origins of the Second World War in Asia and the Pacific* (London: Longman, 1987), pp. 32–33.

88. Warren I. Cohen, *America's Response to China* (New York: Columbia University Press, 1989), pp. 112–113.

89. Zhang Guotao, *Rise of the Chinese Communist Party*, pp. 449–450.

90. Ibid., pp. 638–640; Jonathan D. Spence, *The Search for Modern China* (New York: W. W. Norton, 1990), p. 421.

91. Yu M. Ovichinnikov, *Stanovlenie I razvitie edunogo nationalnogo fronta sopreotvileniya Yaponii v Kitae* (The Formation and Development of the United National Front of the Resistance against Japan in China) (Moscow: Nauka, 1985), pp. 44–45.

92. Zhang Xueliang, Columbia interviews, vol. 84, p. 51-4192.

93. Alexander Dallin and F. I. Firsov, *Dimitrov and Stalin, 1934–1943: Letters from the Soviet Archives* (New Haven: Yale University Press, 2000), pp. 98–99.

94. Ibid., pp. 101–105.

95. Chiang public statement, August 25, 1932, in Qin Xiaoyi, *Zong tong,* vol. 3, p. 966.

96. Chiang Kai-shek, *Soviet Russia in China,* p. 68.

97. Chen Lifu, *Storm Clouds,* pp. 116–121; Clubb, *China and Russia,* pp. 297–298.

98. *New York Times,* February 12, 1936, p. 12.

99. Chiang Diaries, Hoover, September 24, October 1, October 7, 1936, box 39, folders 2, 3; Chen, *Storm Clouds,* pp. 114–115, 121–125.

100. Hollington K. Tong, *Chiang Kai-shek,* vol. 1 (Shanghai: China Publishing Company, 1938), p. 427.

101. Liu, *Military History,* pp. 101–102.

102. Ibid., p. 143.

103. Lloyd E. Eastman, *The Nationalist Era in China, 1927–1949,* paperback ed. (New York: Cambridge University Press, 1991), p. 46.

104. Franz Michael, "The Role of Law in Traditional, Nationalist, and Communist China," *China Quarterly* 9 (January–March 1962): 124–148.

105. Eastman, *Nationalist Era,* pp. 46–47.

106. *VKP (b), Komintern, I kitai Dokumenty* (The AUCP [All Union Communist Party][b], Comintern, and China Documents), vol. 4 (Moscow: AO Bulket, 2003), p. 892; L. M. Kaganovich and V. M. Molotov to I. V. Stalin, telegram, September 8, 1936, RGASPI Moscow, collection 495, inventory 184, file 36, sheet 263.

107. Soong Chingling to Wang Ming, January 26, 1937: "Not long ago answering Mao Zedong's letter in which he asked for money, I managed to send him some [later specified as '50,000 dollars'] three months ago." RGASPI collection 495, inventory 74, file 281, sheets 34–35, and collection 514, inventory 1, file 1037, sheets 90–94.

108. Chiang Kai-shek, *Soviet Russia in China,* p. 73.

109. Chen Lifu, *Storm Clouds,* p. 120; Sheng, *Battling Western Imperialism,* pp. 28–29; Ovichinnikov, *Stanovlenie I razvitie edunogo nationalnogo fronta sopreot- vileniya Yaponii v Kitae,* pp. 44–45.

110. Chiang Diaries, Hoover, October 19 and November 1, 1936, box 39, folder 4.

111. Zhang Xueliang, Columbia interviews, vol. 38, p. 25-189.

112. Ibid., vol. 38, p. 25-1900.

113. *Time,* November 9, 1936.

114. Chiang Diaries, Hoover, November 24, 1936, box 39, folder 4.

115. Zhang Xueliang, Columbia interviews, vol. 38, pp. 25-1892 to 25-1893. For "strong words," see Chiang Diaries, December 10, 1936, in Qin Xiaoyi, *Zong tong,* p. 1010.

116. Zhang Guotao, *Rise of the Chinese Communist Party,* pp. 478–479; Yang Kui- song, *Xi'an shibian xintan* (A New Study of the Xi'an Incident) (Taipei: Dongta tushu gongsi, 1995), cited by Chang and Halliday, *Mao,* pp. 181–182.

117. Chen Lifu, *Storm Clouds,* pp. 119–120.

118. T. V. Soong Papers, box 60, folder 3. In the 1950s when Soong gave the Hoover Institution Archives his journal of the Xi'an Incident and other selected private papers, he requested that they not be opened until after the death of Soong Mayling. T.V. was perhaps culturally and politically inclined to value objectivity in history more than the other participants who later wrote about the incident. In his negotiations with T. V. Soong in December 1936 over Chiang's release from captivity, Zhou Enlai revealed the number of troops to be allowed as agreed to by the two sides in Nanking. In his 1957 book *Soviet Russia in China,* on p. 73, Chiang said the agreement called for the CCP to "abolish the Red Army," not just its name, but the account in the Comintern archives records that the question was the size of the new Communist force. On page 81 of his book, Chiang repeats the four points of the CCP in the softer version, but then provides a statement he made in February 1937 welcoming the points but describing them as calling for the "abolition" of the Red Army. Chiang does not mention the condition spelled out in the autumn 1936 talks that called for Mao and others to go abroad.

119. Chen Lifu, *Storm Clouds,* pp. 119–120; Chiang Kai-shek, *Soviet Russia in China,* p. 73.

120. Chen Lifu, *Storm Clouds,* pp. 119–120.

121. Chiang Kai-shek, *Soviet Russia in China,* pp. 73, 81.

122. Zhang Xueliang, Columbia interviews, vol. 39, p. 25-1901.

123. Chiang Kai-shek, "A Fortnight," in *Sian: Extracts from a Diary* (Shanghai: China Publishing Company, 1937), pp. 58–63.

124. Brian Crozier, *The Man Who Lost China* (New York: Charles Scribner's Sons, 1976), pp. 182–183.

125. Chiang, "A Fortnight," pp. 54–55.

126. Earl Albert Selle, *Donald of China* (New York: Harper Brothers), p. 324.

127. Furuya, *Chiang Kai-shek,* p. 15.

128. Michael Gibson, "Chiang Kai-shek's Central Army, 1924–1938," Ph.D. diss., George Washington University, 1985, pp. 333–334.

129. Crozier, *Man Who Lost China,* pp. 184–185.

130. T. V. Soong Papers, box 10, folder 3, pp. 4–10. Madame Chiang's memoirs emphasize and probably exaggerate her role, but they strike me as probably an accurate account of her thoughts and actions as she remembered them. Her statements that Zhang Xueliang may have had "a reasonable grievance" and her attacks (cited later) on He Yingqin seem to vouch for her frankness.

131. Zhang Guotao, *Rise of the Chinese Communist Party,* pp. 479–482; Zhou Enlai to Mao, December 17, 1937, radiogram, in "Zhongguo gongchandang guanyu Xi'an shibian dangan shiliao xuanbian" (A Selection of CCP Archive Documents on the Xi'an Incident) (Peking: Zhongguo dangan chubanshe, 1997), p. 213.

132. Zhang Guotao, *Rise of the Chinese Communist Party,* pp. 482–483.

133. Han Suyin, *Elder Son: Zhou En-lai and the Making of Modern China* (New York: Hill and Wang, 1994), p. 152.

134. *Cheloviek meniyaet kozhu, ili zhizn I nieobichainiye prevrashchieniya giospodina Dzian Dzingo* (The Man Changes the Skin, or the Life and Extraordinary Metamorphoses of Mr. Ching-kuo), Russian Tele-Radio TV documentary produced by Samariy Zelikin, 1994.

135. Han Suyin, *Eldest Son,* p. 154.

136. Ibid., p. 153. Whether he actually used these words is uncertain, but the message was plain.

137. Zhang Xueliang, Columbia interviews, vol. 39, p. 25-1928.

138. Ibid.

139. Zhang Guotao, *Rise of the Chinese Communist Party,* pp. 479–487.

140. Zhang Xueliang, Columbia interviews, vol. 73, p. 42-3643.

141. Soong Mayling, *Sian: A Coup D'Etat* (Shanghai: China Publishing Company, 1937), pp. 15–17.

142. Cables referring to the Wang-Hitler meeting between Ambassador Trautmann and Berlin, German Foreign Office Archives 1928–1938: German Embassy Nanking radiogram October 1, 1937, AA/DB VIII 24/137442; and German Foreign Ministry radiogram, December 1, 1937, Nanking/zu Pol.VIII 24/137443. This citation was provided to me by Professor Chen Peng-jen. The German Foreign Ministry, when asked by reporters about what took place, said the reports of the meeting were "hearsay." Also see Clubb, *China and Russia,* p. 303.

143. T. V. Soong Papers, box 60, folder 3; Chiang, "Fortnight," pp. 54–55; Soong Mayling, *Xi'an,* pp. 54–55.

144. Chiang "Fortnight," p. 97.

145. In his journal, T.V. does not mention a meeting with Zhou until December 24. He says he spent the evening of December 20 "exploring a solution," but does not say with whom.

146. Soong Mayling, *Xi'an,* pp. 12–13.

147. Ibid., p. 28.

148. Wakeman, *Spymaster,* p. 234.

149. Soong Mayling, *Xi'an,* pp. 32–36.

150. Wang Chi interview, Washington, D.C., December 9, 1995, as told to him personally by Zhang Xueliang.

151. T. V. Soong Papers, box 60, folder 3, pp. 6–7.

152. Ibid.

153. Ibid., pp. 8–9.

154. Ibid., pp. 10–12.

155. Ibid., p. 12.

156. Selle, *Donald of China,* pp. 333–334.

157. Ibid., p. 13.

158. Ibid. T. V. Soong on page 13 of his journal also relates a comment by Chiang to Zhou that it "was long his intention that the Communists should be pushed north against Japan."

159. Han Suyin, *Elder Son*, p. 154. Han's source was a CCP member who, she reports, was listening outside the door. T.V., however, did not record this remark in his journal, possibly believing it was too personal a matter.

160. Soong Chingling complained of these indiscretions in a letter to Wang Ming in Moscow. See Soong Chingling to Wang Ming, January 26, 1937, RGASPI, collection 495, inventory 4, file 143, sheet 7.

161. Selle, *Donald*, pp. 333–334; Soong Mayling, *Xi'an*, pp. 47–51.

162. Chiang Kai-shek, "A Fortnight," pp. 109–115.

163. T. V. Soong Papers, box 60, folder 3, p. 15.

164. The anonymous journal of the Xi'an Incident apparently was written by a code clerk of T. V. Soong. See T. V. Soong Papers, box 60, folder 3.

165. Owen Lattimore, *China Memoirs* (Tokyo: University of Tokyo Press, 1990), p. 156.

166. On page 81 of Chiang Kai-shek's *Soviet Russia in China*, Chiang lists the four points.

167. Chiang article or talk titled "the lesson from the crucifixion of Jesus Christ," presented on Good Friday, March 26, 1937, in Qin Xiaoyi, *Zong tong*, vol. 3, p. 1073.

168. This paragraph was taken verbatim from my book *The Generalissimo's Son: Chiang Ching-kuo and the Revolutions in China and Taiwan* (Cambridge: Harvard University Press, 2000), p. 73, citing Chen Lifu, *Storm Clouds*, p. 126.

4. The Long War Begins

1. Edgar Snow, *Red Star over China* (1938; New York: Random House Modern Library, 1944), pp. 465, 471.

2. Anonymous journal of the Xi'an Incident apparently written by a code clerk for T. V. Soong, T. V. Soong Papers, box 60, folder 3.

3. Linda Chang, teleconference with author, May 30, 2003. Linda Chang is the niece of Zhang Xueliang.

4. Boorman, *Biographical Dictionary*, vol. 4, p. 7; Michael Gibson, "Chiang Kai-shek's Central Army, 1924–1938," Ph.D. diss., George Washington University, 1985, p. 336.

5. Zhang Guotao, *The Rise of the Chinese Communist Party* (Lawrence: University Press of Kansas, 1971), vol. 2, p. 497.

6. Ibid., p. 518.

7. Two Ping, "The Deployment of the Eighth Route Army and the New Fourth Army to the Front and Northern China and Their Strategic Expansion in the War of

Resistance against Japan," paper given at the Harvard University Conference on Wartime China, Maui, January 2004.

8. Snow, *Red Star,* p. 471.

9. Chiang's radiogram instructions to Gu Zhutong in Xi'an, January 31, 1927, in Qin Xiaoyi, *Zong tong,* vol. 4, p. 1061.

10. RGASPI, collection 495, inventory 74, file 281, sheet 28.

11. Zhang Guotao, *Rise of the Chinese Communist Party,* pp. 517–520.

12. Snow, *Red Star,* p. 474.

13. Chiang Diaries, Hoover, February 18, 1937, box 39, folder 8.

14. Akira Iriye, *The Origins of the Second World War in Asia and the Pacific* (New York: Longman, 1987), pp. 43–44; Donald S. Sutton, "German Advice and Residual War Lordism in the Nanking Decade: Influences on Nationalist Military Training and Strategy," *China Quarterly* 9, no. 91 (1982): 401.

15. Ibid., pp. 386–410.

16. Snow, *Red Star,* pp. 473–475.

17. Fenghua relatives and researchers, group interview, September 27, 1995.

18. *FRUS (1937),* vol. 3: *The Far East,* p. 87.

19. Chiang Diaries, Hoover, June 10, 1937, box 39, folder 12.

20. Kimittada I. Miwa, "Brief Notes on the Chinese Communists' Role in the Spread of the Marco Polo Bridge Incident into Full-Scale War," paper presented at the Harvard University Conference on Wartime China, Maui, January 2004, pp. 318–320.

21. Editor's note, in Qin Xiaoyi, *Zong tong,* vol. 4, pp. 1114–1115; "Chiang Zong tong mi lu" (The Secret Journal of President Chiang), in *Chung Yang jih pao yi lu* (Taipei, 1978), vol. 11, p. 12.

22. Editor's notes, in Qin Xiaoyi, *Zong tong,* vol. 4, p. 1119; Miwa, "Brief Notes," p. 321.

23. Chiang Diaries, Hoover, July 12, 1937, box 39, folder 13; Ma Chendu, "Analysis of the Strategy of the Chinese Troops during the Sino-Japanese War," paper presented at the Harvard University Conference on Wartime China, Maui, January 2004, p. 5.

24. Warren I. Cohen, *America's Response to China* (New York: Columbia University Press, 1989), pp. 118–120.

25. *FRUS (1937),* vol. 3: *The Far East,* p. 385. Four days later, an American embassy assessment concluded that while Japan had not deliberately provoked the clash of July 7, the Japanese military had decided shortly after the outbreak to use it as a pretext for extending Japanese influence in North China (p. 434).

26. Ibid., p. 397.

27. Marius B. Jansen, *Japan and China: From War to Peace, 1894–1972* (Chicago: Rand McNally, 1975), pp. 394–395.

28. Ibid., p. 395.

29. Chiang Ching-kuo, *Jiang Jingguo xian sheng zhuan ji* (Collected Works of Chiang Ching-kuo) (Taipei: Cultural and Educational Foundation, 1989), vol. 2, p. 271.

30. For "Lushan," see Miwa, "Brief Notes," p. 323. For "Military Council" see Chiang Diaries, Hoover, August 7, 1937, box 39, folder 14.

31. Yang Tienshi, "Chiang Kai-shek and the Battles of Shanghai and Nanking," paper presented at Harvard University Conference on Wartime China, Maui, January 2004, p. 8, quoting *Wang Shijie riji* (Diary of Wang Shijie) (Taipei: Academia Sinica, Modern History Institute, 1991), n.p.

32. Michael M. Sheng, *Battling Western Imperialism: Mao, Stalin, and the United States* (Princeton, N.J.: Princeton University Press, 1997), pp. 40–41.

33. Zhang Baijia, "China's Experience in Seeking Foreign Military Aid and Cooperation for Resisting Japanese Aggression," paper presented at Harvard University Conference on Wartime China, Maui, January 2004, pp. 13–14; Yang Tienshi, "Chiang Kai-Shek and the Battles of Shanghai," pp. 5–9.

34. Sutton, "German Advice," p. 403.

35. Ma Chendu, "Analysis of the Strategy of the Chinese Troops during the Sino-Japanese War," paper presented at Harvard University Conference on Wartime China, Maui, January 2004, p. 13.

36. John W. Garver, "Chiang Kai-shek's Quest for Soviet Entry into the Sino-Japanese War," *Political Science Quarterly* 102, no. 2 (Summer 1987): 304.

37. Barbara Tuchman, *Sand against the Wind: Stilwell and the American Experience in China* (London: Macmillan, 1971), p. 168.

38. The larger estimate comes from Ma Chendu, "Analysis," p. 19; the smaller is from Edward L. Dreyer, *China at War* (New York: Longman, 1995), p. 218.

39. Zhang Baijia, "China's Experience," pp. 12–20.

40. Chiang Diaries, Hoover, August 7, 1937, box 39, folder 15.

41. Chiang Diaries, Hoover, August 20, 1937, in Qin Xiaoyi, *Zong tong*, vol. 4, pp. 1151, 1159; Chiang Diaries, Hoover, September 17 and 18, 1937, box 39, folder 15.

42. Zhang Guotao, *Rise of the Chinese Communist Party*, pp. 537–539. At an earlier meeting in August, Mao described the CCP policy as superficial cooperation with the KMT, avoiding the real strength of the Japanese enemy, and enhancing the CCP's military strength (pp. 533–537).

43. Chiang Diaries, Hoover, October 25, 1937, box 39, folder 16.

44. Zhang Baijia, "China's Experience," pp. 18–20.

45. Ibid., p. 23. China would actually use about $173 million of the total aid commitment. In inflation-adjusted 2005 dollars, the commitment of US$250 million in 1937 would be approximately U.S. $3.34 billion, and in relative value to U.S. GDP, the equivalent in 2005 would be US$24.5 billion. See http://measuringworth. com.

46. Tuchman, *Sand,* p. 217.

47. Yang Tienshi, "Chiang Kai-Shek and the Battles of Shanghai," pp. 25–27.

48. Earl Albert Selle, *Donald of China* (New York: Harper and Brothers, 1948), p. 340.

49. According to one Central Army general, Kuo Zhukui, "several hundred thousand troops would not have fallen" if the retreat had been organized earlier. See Yang Tienshi, "Chiang Kai-Shek and the Battles of Shanghai," p. 31. But most of the casualties occurred in the battle for Shanghai, not during the retreat.

50. Zhang Baijia, "China's Experience," p. 30.

51. Sutton, "German Advice," p. 403.

52. Dreyer, *China at War,* p. 219.

53. Chiang Diaries, Hoover, November 20, 26, 27, 1937, box 39, folder 17.

54. Chiang Diaries, Hoover, November 20, 1937, box 39, folder 17.

55. Yang Tienshi, "Chiang Kai-Shek and the Battles of Shanghai," p. 40, citing a selected and abridged collection from Chiang Kai-shek's diaries called *Kunmian ji* (Anthology of Encouragement amid Difficulties) in the Archive of President Chiang Kai-shek, Bureau of National History, Taipei.

56. Garver, "Chiang Kai-shek's Quest," p. 309.

57. Yang Tienshi, "Chiang Kai-Shek and the Battles of Shanghai," pp. 39–40.

58. Iris Chang, *The Rape of Nanking* (New York: Penguin, 1997), pp. 81–105. Many Japanese scholars and some other historians say that Ms. Chang's book is exaggerated, but 10 percent of her figures would merit the title.

59. Qin Xiaoyi, *Zong tong,* vol. 4, pp. 1199–1202.

60. *Time,* January 3, 1938.

61. Ma Chendu, "Analysis," p. 28.

62. Chiang Diaries, Hoover, December 28, 1937, box 39, folder 18.

63. Chiang Diaries, Hoover, January 2, 1938, box 39, folder 20.

64. Yang Tianshi, *Jiang Jieshi midang yu Jiang Jieshi zhenxiang* (Facts about Chiang Kai-shek from his Secret Archives) (Beijing: Social Sciences Documentation Press, 2002), pp. 407–409.

65. Lloyd E. Eastman, "Relations between Chiang Kai-shek and Wang Jingwei during the War against Japan," *Republican China* 14, no. 2 (1989): 5–7.

66. Gibson, "Chiang Kai-shek's Central Army," p. 396.

67. Stephen MacKinnon, "Defense of the Central Yangtze and the Beginning of the War of Attrition," paper presented at Harvard University Conference on Wartime China, Maui, January 2004, pp. 22–27.

68. Te-kong Tong and Li Tsung-jen (Li Congren), *The Memoirs of Li Congren* (Boulder, Colo.: Westview, 1979), pp. 361, 366.

69. Sutton, "German Advice," p. 404.

70. Ibid., p. 402.

71. Ma Chendu, "Analysis," p. 33; Shen Jia-wen, "1938 nian huang he huayuankou jue di jing guo" (On the Bursting of the Banks of the Yellow River at Huayuankou in 1938), *Minguo dang an* 2, no. 4 (1986): 134–136.

72. Dana Lary, *China's Republic* (Cambridge, Eng.: Cambridge University Press, 2007), p. 120.

73. MacKinnon, "Defense of the Central Yangtze," p. 28.

74. Sutton, "German Advice," p. 409.

75. Mao Tse-tung, *Selected Works,* vol. 2 (New York: International Publishers, 1954), p. 140.

76. "Chiang Kai-shek, handwritten letter to Stalin, August 26, 1939," *Minguo dang an* 3, no. 45 (1996): 61–63.

77. Ibid., p. 59.

78. Jerrold Schecter and Leona Schecter, *Sacred Secret* (Washington, D.C.: Brassey's, 2002), pp. 15–16.

79. MacKinnon, "Defense of the Central Yangtze," pp. 29–35.

80. Editor's note, in Qin Xiaoyi, *Zong tong,* vol. 4, p. 1299.

81. Jerome Chen, *Mao and the Chinese Revolution* (New York: Oxford University Press, 1967), p. 215.

82. Qin Xiaoyi, *Zong tong,* vol. 4, p. 1299.

83. Chen, *Mao,* p. 235; Zhang Guotao, *Rise of the Chinese Communist Party,* pp. 533–539.

84. Chiang Diaries, November 18, 1938, box 40, folder 1.

85. Chiang Diaries, December 1938, box 40, folder 2.

86. On Chiang's proposal see Jin Chongji, "Kang ri zhan zheng zhu qi de guo gong guan xi wen ti" (Relationship between the Communists and the Nationalists in the Early Period of the Second Sino-Japanese War), *Minguo dang an* 1, no. 11 (1988): 76. Jin does not cite the specific source for this statement but his article is drawn from documents in the Second National (KMT) Archives in Nanking. On the CCP joining the KMT and other aspects of Chiang's merger proposal, see Alexander Dallin and F. I. Firsov, *Dimitrov and Stalin, 1934–1943, Letters from the Soviet Archives* (New Haven: Yale University Press, 2000), p. 118. On Mao's proposal, see Sheng, *Battling Western Imperialism,* p. 46. On Zhou's proposal, see Chiang Kaishek, *Soviet Russia in China* (New York: Farrar, Straus and Cudahy, 1957), p. 88.

87. Chen Lifu, *The Storm Clouds Clear over China* (Stanford, Calif.: Hoover Institution Press, 1994), p. 144.

88. Royal Leonard, *I Flew for China* (Garden City, N.J.: Doubleday, Doran, and Company, 1942), pp. 206–209.

89. In his memoirs published on the mainland in 1985, Zhang Zhizhong claimed that Chiang Kai-shek in a panic ordered the burning of Changsha. Chiang had just fled the key industrial city of Wuhan, where he had ordered the destruction of key

facilities, but not the burning down of the city. Zhang defected to the CCP in early 1949. MacKinnon, "Defense of the Central Yangtze," p. 39, cites the Zhang memoir.

90. Ruth Altman Greene, *Hsiang-ya Journal* (Hamden, Conn.: Archon, 1977), pp. 111–115.

91. Werner Gruhl, *Imperial Japan's World War II, 1931–1945* (Edison, N.J.: Transaction, 2007), p. 35.

92. Ma Chendu, "Analysis," pp. 40–41.

93. Chiang Diaries, Hoover, November 2 and 11, 1938, box 40, folder 1.

94. Chiang Diaries, Hoover, November 10, 1938, box 40, folder 1.

95. Robert Payne, *Chiang Kai-shek* (New York: Wright and Talley, 1969), pp. 233–234.

96. Ibid., p. 235.

97. "Documents Relating to the Dispute between H. H. Kung and T. V. Soong in the Early Years of the Sino-Japanese War," *Minguo dang an* 2, no. 52 (1998): 154.

98. MacKinnon, "Defense of the Central Yangtze," pp. 7–8.

99. Zhang Ruide, "The Central Army from Whampoa to 1949," in *A Military History of China,* ed. David Graff and Robin Hiphem (Boulder, Colo.: Westview, 2002), pp. 200–201.

100. Jonathan D. Spence, *The Search for Modern China* (New York: W. W. Norton, 1990), p. 461.

101. Chiang Diaries, Hoover, May 29, 1939, box 40, folder 8.

102. Yang Tianshi, *Jiang Jieshi,* pp. 415–420.

103. Payne, *Chiang Kai-shek,* pp. 233–234.

104. Laura Tyson Li, *Madame Chiang Kai-shek* (New York: Atlantic Monthly Press, 2006), p. 152.

105. Payne, *Chiang Kai-shek,* p. 236.

106. Chiang Diaries, Hoover, April 2, 1939, box 40, folder 7.

107. Akira Iriye, *Origins,* p. 76.

108. Chiang Diaries, Hoover, June 25, 1939, box 40, folder 9.

109. Zhou later presented an abstract of this report to the Comintern. See Abstract of Zhou Enlai's Report to the CCP Politburo, RGASPI, collection 495, inventory 10a, file 296, sheets 146–196.

110. Han Suyin, *Elder Son: Zhou Enlai and the Making of Modern China* (New York: Hill and Wang, 1994), p. 170.

111. Edwin P. Hoyt, *Japan's War: The Great Pacific Conflict* (New York: McGraw Hill, 1986), p. 187.

112. Lyman P. Van Slyke, ed., *The Chinese Communist Movement: A Report of the United States War Department, July 1945* (Stanford, Calif.: Stanford University Press, 1968), p. 212.

113. Chiang Kai-shek, handwritten letter to Stalin, August 26, 1939, *Minguo dang an* 3, no. 45 (1996): 63–64.

114. Chiang Diaries, Hoover, August 25, 1939, box 40, folder 11.

115. Chiang Diaries, Hoover, September 5, 12, and 30, 1939, box 40, folder 12.

116. Chiang Diaries, Hoover, August 2 and 26, 1939, box 40, folder 11.

117. Greene, *Hsiang-ya Journal*, pp. 122–126.

118. Chiang Diaries, Hoover, April 18 and 25, 1939, box 40, folder 7.

119. MacKinnon, "Defense of the Central Yangtze," p. 38.

120. Ma Chendu, "Analysis," p. 43.

121. See F. F. Liu, *A Military History of Modern China, 1924–1949* (Princeton, N.J.: Princeton University Press, 1956), p. 204.

122. Frank Dorn (Stilwell's assistant in China for four years), *The Sino-Japanese War, 1937–1941* (New York: Macmillan, 1974), pp. 304–322. Dorn and Stilwell ended their tours in China in September 1939.

123. Ma Chendu, "Analysis," pp. 46–49.

124. Dallin and Firsov, *Dimitrov and Stalin*, pp. 115, 120.

125. Ibid., pp. 116–117. Again, there is no reason to doubt that the cited documents are authentic.

126. Ibid., pp. 115, 116.

127. Eastman, "Relations," pp. 6–9. For an account of the assassination attempt, see Frederic Wakeman Jr., *Spymaster: Dai Li and the Chinese Secret Service* (Berkeley: University of California Press, 2003), pp. 337–338.

128. Editor's note of August 21, 1940, referring to a speech by Chiang on January 24, 1940, in Qin Xiaoyi, *Zong tong*, vol. 4, pp. 1616–1617.

129. Chiang Diaries, Hoover, December 30, 1939, box 40, folder 15.

130. Dallin and Firsov, *Dimitrov and Stalin*, pp. 119–121.

131. Budget submitted to the Comintern in February 1940 by the Central Committee of the CCP, printed in full in ibid., pp. 123–124. The CCP reported total monthly expenses equivalent to US$701,000, of which $600,000 was for military expenditures. In addition to the US$110,000 a month received from the Chinese government, the Communist armed forces collected approximately US$200,000 a month from "local government organs under the control of our party in the partisan zones of Northern China." The party organs collected about US$43,000 a month. It is not clear whether these collections included grain requisitions.

132. Ibid., pp. 123–125.

133. Chiang Diaries, Hoover, September 2, 1939, box 40, folder 12.

134. The file is in RGASPI, Comintern Executive Archival Collection no. 495, inventory 225, file 77.

135. Mao, *Selected Works*, vol. 2, pp. 204–210.

136. In his diary, Chiang only notes that he had a meeting with Zhou. See Chiang

Diaries, Hoover, July 17, 1940, box 40, folder 23. Later entries, however, make clear the nature of the proposal.

137. Han Suyin, *Elder Son,* p. 174.

138. Dallin and Firsov, *Dimitrov and Stalin,* p. 120.

139. William W. Whitson, *The Chinese High Command: A History of Chinese Communist Military Politics, 1927–1971* (New York: Praeger, 1973), pp. 70–74; Dreyer, *China at War,* p. 253.

140. Chiang Diaries, Hoover, September 29, 1940, box 40, folder 25.

141. Zhang Baijia, "China's Experience," pp. 40–42; Qin Xiaoyi, *Zong tong,* vol. 4, p. 1636.

142. Chiang Kai-shek's message to He Yingqin, October 19, 1940, in Qin Xiaoyi, *Zong tong,* vol. 4, p. 1637; Han Suyin, *Elder Son,* p. 174. Mao's coded messages to the Comintern made plain that Chiang Kai-shek had demanded the withdrawal of all CPP armed forces to areas north of the old Yellow River course—that is, totally outside of Jiangsu as well as most of Shandong. See Dallin and Firsov, *Dimitrov and Stalin,* pp. 125–134; Gregory Benton, "Maogate at Maolin? Pointing Fingers in the Wake of a Disaster, South Anhui, January 1941," *East Asian History* 4 (1992): 119–141.

143. Dallin and Firsov, *Dimitrov and Stalin,* pp. 131–134.

144. Ibid., pp. 125–134.

145. Han Suyin, *Elder Son,* p. 174.

146. Benton, "Maogate at Maolin?" p. 121. Gu Zhutong's men captured the New Fourth's chief of staff, Zhao Lingbo, who reputedly confessed that Xiang and Yeh were planning to move to southern Jiangsu and had sent 2,000 men ahead for organizing purposes. See Qin Xiaoyi, *Zong tong,* vol. 5, p. 1665.

147. Benton, "Maogate at Maolin?" p. 124.

148. Chiang Diaries, Hoover, January 28, 1940, box 41, folder 7; John W. Garver, *Chinese-Soviet Relations, 1937–1945* (Oxford, Eng.: Oxford University Press, 1988), p. 144.

149. Dallin and Firsov, *Dimitrov and Stalin,* p. 139; Garver, *Chinese-Soviet Relations,* p. 146.

150. Ibid., p. 139, which cites Mao's February 13, 1941, radiogram to Dimitrov. Maintaining the fiction that the CCP accepted military orders from the Military Council, Mao told Dimitrov that Chiang's requirement that the CCP forces move north was "not yet acceptable to us."

151. Dallin and Firsov, *Dimitrov and Stalin,* pp. 139–140.

152. Chiang Diaries, Hoover, April 24, 1941, box 41, folder 10.

153. Zhang Baijia, "China's Experience," pp. 43–44.

154. Sheng, *Battling Western Imperialism,* p. 70.

155. Schecter and Schecter, *Sacred Secret,* pp. 16–17, 42–43.

156. Dallin and Firsov, *Dimitrov and Stalin,* p. 188.

157. Chiang Diaries, Hoover, April 13, 1941, box 41, folder 10.

158. Garver, *Chinese-Soviet Relations,* p. 183.

159. Akira Iriye, *Origins,* p. 688.

160. Chiang Diaries, Hoover, April 13, 1941, box 41, folder 10.

161. Chiang Diaries, Hoover, June 19, 1941, box 41, folder 12.

162. Garver, *Chinese-Soviet Relations,* pp. 184–185.

163. Tobe Ryoici, "Japanese 11th Army's Operations in Central China, 1938–1941," paper presented at Harvard University Conference on Wartime China, Maui, January 2004, p. 29.

164. Dallin and Firsov, *Dimitrov and Stalin,* pp. 142–145.

165. Claire Lee Chennault, *The Way of a Fighter* (1949; Tucson, Ariz.: James Thorvaardson & Sons, 1991), pp. 82–83.

166. Robert Payne, *Chiang Kai-shek* (New York: Wright and Talley, 1969), pp. 239–241.

167. Arthur N. Young, *China and the Helping Hand, 1937–1945* (Cambridge: Harvard University Press, 1963), p. 257.

168. Ibid., pp. 17–18.

169. Owen Lattimore, *China Memoirs* (Tokyo: University of Tokyo Press, 1990), p. 87.

170. After the war, Senator Joseph McCarthy and his supporters would accuse Lattimore of being a Communist Party member and one of those Americans whose critical views of the KMT regime had brought about the "loss" of China. These charges seem patently false.

171. Lattimore, *China Memoirs,* pp. 135, 149, 155.

172. Ibid., p. 149.

173. Chiang Diaries, Hoover, August 16, 1941, box 41, folder 14.

174. Akira Iriye, *Origins,* p. 179.

175. Chiang Diaries, Hoover, November 9, 1941, box 41, folder 17.

176. Schecter and Schecter, *Sacred Secret,* pp. 42–43.

177. Akira Iriye, *Origins,* p. 151.

178. Chiang Wei-kuo interview, Taipei, June 5, 1996.

179. Tobe Ryoici, "Japanese 11th Army's Operations in Central China, 1938–1941," paper presented at Harvard University Conference on Wartime China, Maui, January 2004, pp. 29–30.

180. Chiang Diaries, Hoover, December 25, 1941, box 41, folder 17.

181. Lattimore, *China Memoirs,* p. 160. In Washington, the FBI likewise reported that the Japanese embassy was burning documents.

182. Chiang to Roosevelt, December 8, 1941, in Qin Xiaoyi, *Zong tong,* vol. 4, pp. 1816–1817.

183. Lattimore, *China Memoirs,* p. 161.

184. Ibid.

185. Te-kong Tong and Li Tsung-jen, *Memoirs,* pp. 428–429; Hauro Tohmatsu, "The Strategic Correlation between the Sino-Japanese and Pacific Wars," paper given at Harvard University Conference on Wartime China, Maui, January 2004, pp. 3–4; Liu, *Military History,* p. 209.

186. Haruo Tohmatsu, "Strategic Correlation," p. 3.

187. Ibid., pp. 3–4.

188. Chiang Diaries, December 10 and 11, 1941, January 31, 1942, box 41, folder 18; Chiang Diaries, January 31, 1942, in Qin Xiaoyi, *Zong tong,* vol. 5, p. 1855.

189. Chennault, *Way of a Fighter,* pp. 126–127.

190. Lattimore, *China Memoirs,* p. 164. He might have conceded, of course, that with overwhelmingly superior firepower the Japanese had conquered a quarter of China.

191. Chiang's radiogram to Roosevelt, January 7, 1942, in Qin Xiaoyi, *Zong tong,* p. 1847.

192. Chennault, *Way of a Fighter,* pp. 130–131.

193. Chiang Diaries, Hoover, December 31, 1941, box 42, folder 4; Qin Xiaoyi, *Zong tong,* vol. 5, p. 1856.

194. Tuchman, *Sand,* pp. 199–213.

195. Ibid., p. 243. Stilwell once said that in two generations China might produce good military officers (ibid., p. 172).

196. Ibid., p. 172.

197. Ibid., p. 153.

198. *FRUS (1937),* vol. 3: *The Far East,* p. 258.

199. Chiang's cables to Soong, January 22, 23, 1942, in Qin Xiaoyi, *Zong tong,* vol. 5, pp. 1852–1853.

200. Young, *China and the Helping Hand,* pp. 231–240.

5. Chiang and His American Allies

1. It was reported that for each truckload that departed on the journey, bad management and maintenance, as well as illegal diversion, reduced the final delivery to about one third of the original tonnage. See Zhang Baijia, "China's Experience in Seeking Foreign Military Aid and Cooperation for Resisting Japanese Aggression," paper presented at Harvard University Conference on Wartime China, Maui, January 2004, p. 46; Charles F. Romanus and Riley Sunderland, *Stilwell's Mission to China* (1952; Washington, D.C.: U.S. Army Center of Military History, 2002), p. 45.

2. Romanus and Sunderland, *Stilwell's Mission,* p. 45.

3. Editor's notes, February 4, 1942, in Qin Xiaoyi, *Zong tong,* vol. 5, p. 1857.

4. Alan K. Lathrop, "The Employment of Chinese Nationalist Troops in the First Burma Campaign," *Journal of Southeast Asia Studies* 12, no. 2 (September 1981): 409–410.

5. Qin Xiaoyi, *Zong tong*, vol. 5, p. 1857.

6. Text of Gandhi's letter to Chiang contained in Chiang's telegram to T. V. Soong, June 22, 1942, T. V. Soong Papers, box 36, folder 5; Chiang Diaries, Hoover, February 18, 1942, box 42, folder 7.

7. Chiang telegram to Soong, March 15, 2005, T. V. Soong Papers, box 36, folder 5.

8. Joseph W, Stilwell, *The Stilwell Papers,* ed. Theodore H. White (London: MacDonald, 1949), pp. 69, 70.

9. Chinese notes of Chiang's March 5, 1942, conversation with Stilwell, in Qin Xiaoyi, *Zong tong*, vol. 5, p. 1872.

10. Qin Xiaoyi, *Zong tong*, vol. 5, p. 1872.

11. Stilwell, *Papers,* pp. 94–95.

12. Field Marshall Viscount Slim, *Defeat into Victory: Battling Japan in Burma and India, 1942–1945* (New York: Cooper Square Press, 2000), p. 17; Zhang Ruide, "The Central Army from Whampoa to 1949," in *A Military History of China,* ed. David Graff and Robin Hiphem (Boulder, Colo.: Westview, 2002), pp. 201–210.

13. Telegram to T. V. Soong relating the transcript of the March 10 meeting between Chiang and Stilwell, T. V. Soong Papers, box 61, folder 11.

14. Romanus and Sunderland, *Stilwell's Mission,* p. 97.

15. Frank Dorn, *Walkout with Stilwell* (New York: Thomas Y. Crowell, 1971), pp. 71–72.

16. Romanus and Sunderland, *Stilwell's Mission,* p. 100.

17. Chiang Diaries, Hoover, March 20, 1942, box 42, folder 8.

18. Stilwell, *Papers,* p. 82.

19. Ibid.

20. Romanus and Sunderland, *Stilwell's Mission,* pp. 106–109.

21. Stilwell, *Papers,* p. 93.

22. Chiang Diaries, Hoover, April 1, 1942, box 42, folder 9.

23. Interview with Wang Chi, Washington, D.C., July 26, 2003.

24. Stilwell, *Papers,* pp. 93, 94; Editor's note, April 2, 1942, in Qin Xiaoyi, *Zong tong,* vol. 2, p. 1891.

25. Stilwell, *Papers,* p. 97.

26. Ibid., pp. 97, 99; Chiang message to Luo Zhuoying, April 15, 1942, T. V. Soong Papers, box 61, folder 2. According to Stilwell, Chiang also suggested as a morale booster giving each squad a watermelon.

27. Lathrop, "Employment of Chinese Nationalist Troops," pp. 417–418.

28. Ibid., pp. 418–419, citing U.S. Senate Committee on the Judiciary, Internal Security Subcommittee, *The Amerasia Papers: A Clue to the Catastrophe of China,* 2 vols. (Washington, D.C.: U.S. Government Printing Office, 1970), vol. 1, p. 187.

29. Claire Lee Chennault, *The Way of a Fighter* (1949; Tucson, Ariz.: James Thorvaardson and Sons, 1991), pp. 158–159.

30. Dorn, *Walkout with Stilwell,* p. 93.

31. Lathrop, "Employment of Chinese Nationalist Troops," p. 418.

32. Stilwell, *Papers,* p. 109.

33. Chennault, *Way of a Fighter,* p. 160.

34. Romanus and Sunderland, *Stilwell's Mission,* pp. 138–139.

35. Chiang's May 6, 1942, radiogram to Soong in Qin Xiaoyi, *Zong tong,* vol. 5, p. 1915.

36. Barbara Tuchman, *Sand against the Wind: Stilwell and the American Experience in China* (London: Macmillan, 1971), p. 372.

37. Romanus and Sunderland, *Stilwell's Mission,* pp. 138–139; Stilwell, *Papers,* p. 109.

38. Romanus and Sunderland, *Stilwell's Mission,* pp. 138–139.

39. Ibid., pp. 135–136.

40. Ray Huang, *Chiang Kai-shek and His Diary as a Historical Source* (Armonk, N.Y.: M. E. Sharpe, 1996), part 2, p. 19.

41. Chiang Diaries, Hoover, May 7, 1942, box 42, folder 10.

42. Stilwell, *Papers,* pp. 110, 111.

43. Huang, *Chiang Kai-shek,* part 1, p. 21.

44. Romanus and Sunderland, *Stilwell's Mission,* pp. 141, 143–146; Chennault, *Way of a Fighter,* p. 161.

45. Jack Belden, *Retreat with Stilwell* (New York: Alfred A. Knopf, 1949).

46. Stilwell, *Papers,* p. 109.

47. Lathrop, "Employment of Chinese Nationalist Troops," pp. 421–423.

48. Romanus and Sunderland, *Stilwell's Mission,* p. 139.

49. Chiang Diaries, Hoover, May 4, 1942, box 42, folder 10.

50. Lathrop, "Employment of Chinese Nationalist Troops," pp. 431, 432.

51. Carrol V. Clines, *Doolittle's Tokyo Raiders* (Princeton, N.J.: D. Van Nostrand, 1964), p. 6.

52. Haruo Tohmatsu, "The Strategic Correlation between the Sino-Japanese and Pacific Wars," paper presented at Harvard University Conference on Wartime China, Maui, January 2004, p. 6.

53. Stilwell, *Papers,* p. 121.

54. Romanus and Sunderland, *Stilwell's Mission,* pp. 153–154.

55. Stilwell, *Papers,* p. 121.

56. Romanus and Sunderland, *Stilwell's Mission,* p. 154.

57. Ibid., p. 152.

58. Chiang's June 18, 1942, radiogram to Soong, in Qin Xiaoyi, *Zong tong,* vol. 5, pp. 1952–1953.

59. Romanus and Sunderland, *Stilwell's Mission,* p. 157.

60. Ibid., p. 171; Qin Xiaoyi, *Zong tong,* vol. 5, pp. 1957–1959; Huang, *Chiang Kai-shek,* part 1, p. 26.

61. Stilwell, *Papers,* p. 128.

62. See a Theodore White article in *Life,* March 2, 1942, published in Edward T. Thompson, ed., *Theodore H. White at Large* (New York: Pantheon, 1992), p. 36.

63. Stilwell, *Papers,* pp. 131–132.

64. Radiogram from Chiang Kai-shek to T. V. Soong, July 6, 1942, passing the full text of the memorandum from Stilwell, T. V. Soong Papers, box 61, folder 2.

65. Ibid.

66. Chiang radiogram to T. V. Soong, July 5, 1942, T. V. Soong Papers, box 61, folder 2; Qin Xiaoyi, *Zong tong,* vol. 5, pp. 1969–1972.

67. Stilwell, *Papers,* p. 132.

68. Lauchlin Currie, "Report on Visit to China, August 24, 1942," in Currie Papers, box 4, folder "Currie 2nd trip to China, Interviews with Chiang Kai-shek."

69. *Washington Post,* July 22, 1942, p. 1, citing a report of the Office of War Information. Most of the missing would prove to be prisoners of war.

70. Chiang Diaries, Hoover, September 12, 1942, box 42, folder 14.

71. Yang Kuisong, "The Formation and Implementation of the Chinese Communists' Guerrilla Warfare Strategy in the Enemy's Rear during the Sino-Japanese War," paper presented at Harvard University Conference on Wartime China, Maui, January 2004, pp. 32–36. Yang Kuisong cites "Zhongyang geming junshi weiyuanhui guanyu kangri genjudi junshi jianshe de zhishi" (The Instruction of the Central Revolutionary Military Committee Concerning the Military Development in the Base Areas of Resistance, November 7, 1941).

72. Chiang Diaries, Hoover, July 26, 1942, box 42, folder 12.

73. Chiang Diaries, Hoover, July 30, 1942, box 42, folder 12; Romanus and Sunderland, *Stilwell's Mission,* pp. 153–154.

74. Currie Papers, box 4, folder "Report."

75. Chiang Diaries, Hoover, August 4, 1942, box 42, folder 12.

76. Stilwell, *Papers,* p. 137.

77. Currie Papers, box 4, folder "Report."

78. Stilwell, *Papers,* pp. 131, 132.

79. Chinese record of Chiang and Willkie meeting, October 5, 1942, in Qin Xiaoyi, *Zong tong,* vol. 5, p. 2045.

80. For "stupidity" see Chiang Diaries, Hoover, September 25, 1942, box 42, folder 14.

81. Chiang Kai-shek, *Resistance and Reconstruction: Messages during China's Six Years of War, 1937–1943* (New York: Harper, 1943), pp. 320–322.

82. Romanus and Sunderland, *Stilwell's Mission,* pp. 224–225.

83. Brian Crozier, *The Man Who Lost China* (New York: Charles Scribner's Sons, 1976), p. 253.

84. Gardner Cowles, *Mike Looks Back: The Memoirs of Gardner Cowles, Founder of "Look" Magazine* (New York: Gardner Cowles, 1985).

85. Ibid.

86. Drew Pearson, *Drew Pearson's Diaries: 1949–1959,* ed. Tyler Abell (New York: Holt, Rinehart, and Winston, 1974). On the legal maneuverings regarding the *Pearson Diaries,* see Luo Yizheng (a 1970s official in the Information Department of the GRC), *Wei chen wu li ke hui tian-Luo Yizheng de wai jiao sheng ya* (Valiant but Fruitless Endeavors: Memoirs of Yizheng Luo) (Taipei: Commonwealth Publishing Group, 2002), pp. 246–255.

87. Gardner Cowles, *Mike Cowles Looks Back* (New York: Gardner Cowles, 1985), pp. 87–91.

88. Currie to Mrs. Roosevelt, January 16, 1943, Currie Papers, box 1, folder "Eleanor Roosevelt."

89. Laura Tyson Li, *Madame Chiang Kai-shek* (New York: Atlantic Monthly Press, 2006), p. 194.

90. Ibid., pp. 194–195.

91. Chennault, *Way of a Fighter,* pp. 39, 41.

92. Tuchman, *Sand,* pp. 335–339; Chennault, *Way of a Fighter,* p. 216.

93. Tuchman, *Sand,* pp. 339–340.

94. Ibid.

95. *FRUS* (1942): *China,* pp. 99–102; *FRUS* (1943): *China,* pp. 193–199.

96. John Stewart Service, *Lost Chance in China* (New York: Random House, 1974), p. 169.

97. Harold Isaacs, *The Tragedy of the Chinese Revolution* (1938; Stanford, Calif.: Stanford University Press, 1951); Edgar Snow, *Red Star over China* (1938; New York: Random House, 1944). Another important book was Graham Peck, *Two Kinds of Time* (Boston: Houghton Mifflin, 1950).

98. Lucian W. Pye, *The Spirit of Chinese Politics* (Cambridge: MIT Press, 1968), p. 15.

99. Arthur N. Young, *China's Wartime Finance and Inflation* (Cambridge: Harvard University Press, 1965), pp. 286–298.

100. Robert A Kapp, "The Kuomintang and Rural China in the War of Resistance, 1937–1945," in F. Gilbert Chan, ed., *China at the Crossroads: Nationalists and Communists, 1927–1949* (Boulder, Colo.: Westview, 1980), p. 169.

101. Ibid.

102. Young, *China's Wartime Finance and Inflation,* pp. 263, 299–308, 348–349; Hsi-Hseng Ch'i, *Nationalist China at War: Military Defeats and Political Collapse, 1937–1945* (Ann Arbor: University of Michigan Press, 1982), p. 173.

103. Stilwell, *Papers,* p. 179.

104. Chiang Diaries, Hoover, November 3, 1942, box 42, folder 16.

105. Romanus and Sunderland, *Stilwell's Mission,* pp. 131–132.

106. Ibid., p. 245.

107. Stilwell, *Papers,* p. 245.

108. Chiang radiogram to Roosevelt, December 2, 1942, in Qin Xiaoyi, *Zong tong,* vol. 5, p. 2082.

109. Romanus and Sunderland, *Stilwell's Mission,* p. 249.

110. Winston Churchill, *The Second World War* (London: Cassell, 1952), p. 650.

111. Stilwell, *Papers,* pp. 179–180.

112. Romanus and Sunderland, *Stilwell's Mission,* p. 259.

113. Chinese record of meeting between Chiang and Arnold in Qin Xiaoyi, *Zong tong,* vol. 5, p. 2112.

114. Ibid.

115. Chiang Diaries, Hoover, February 7, 1942, box 43, folder 1; Romanus and Sunderland, *Stilwell's Mission,* p. 276.

116. Romanus and Sunderland, *Stilwell's Mission,* pp. 279–280.

117. Ibid., pp. 282, 287; Chennault, *Way of a Fighter,* p. 217.

118. Joseph W. Alsop, *I've Seen The Best* (New York: W. W. Norton, 1992), p. 212. Barbara Tuchman describes Alsop as "excitable," given to "cataclysmic opinions . . . opinionated," and "melodramatic"—characteristics that a biographer might also have applied to General Stilwell. See Tuchman, *Sand,* p. 358.

119. James C. Hsiung and Steven I. Levine, eds., *China's Bitter Victory* (Armonk, N.Y.: M. E. Sharpe, 1992), p. 161.

120. Tuchman, *Sand,* p. 366; Romanus and Sunderland, *Stilwell's Mission,* p. 335.

121. Li, *Madame Chiang,* p. 201.

122. *New York Times,* February 18, 1943.

123. Ibid.

124. Eleanor Roosevelt, *The Autobiography of Eleanor Roosevelt* (1961; New York: Da Capo Press, 1992), pp. 249–250.

125. Currie Papers, box 1, folder "John Carter Vincent."

126. John S. Service and Caroline Service, "Man across the Street," Georgetown University Foreign Affairs Oral History Project, vol. 1, pp. 180–182, cited by Li, *Madame Chiang,* p. 217.

127. Freedom of Information Act materials provided to Laura Tyson Li; see Li, *Madame Chiang,* p. 218.

128. Jerrold Schecter and Leona Schecter, *Sacred Secrets* (Washington, D.C.: Brassey's, 2002), pp. 115, 125, 128, 138. In postwar investigations Currie was never charged with espionage, but he was publicly accused by Bentley of being one of her contacts. Currie denied he was ever a Soviet agent.

129. Romanus and Sunderland, *Stilwell's Mission,* pp. 318–320.

130. Ibid., p. 320. Chiang's assertion that the Chinese Army could defend against a Japanese attack was hardly an expression—as Romanus and Sunderland assert—that he was satisfied with his army as it was and that there was no need to provide it new arms or improve its combat efficiency.

131. Chennault, *Way of a Fighter,* p. 220.

132. Tuchman, *Sand,* p. 367.

133. Churchill, *The Second World War and an Epilogue, 1945–1957* (London: Cassell, 1959), p. 664.

134. Romanus and Sunderland, *Stilwell's Mission,* p. 323. The army historians, in describing Stilwell's unusual behavior, stressed his alleged modesty: "Stilwell said little in his own behalf and slipped into the reserve that came so naturally to him."

135. Tuchman, *Sand,* pp. 367–368.

136. Ibid., p. 368.

137. Romanus and Sunderland, *Stilwell's Mission,* p. 323.

138. The army historians suggest that he may also have presented the points orally. See also Romanus and Sunderland, *Stilwell's Mission,* pp. 323–324.

139. Tuchman, *Sand,* p. 371.

140. Chennault, *Way of a Fighter,* p. 220; Tuchman, *Sand,* p. 371.

141. Chennault, *Way of a Fighter,* p. 245.

142. Huang, *Chiang Kai-shek,* part 2, pp. 36–37.

143. Chinese record of Soong's May 17 presentation to the Combined Chiefs of Staff, in Qin Xiaoyi, *Zong tong,* vol. 5, p. 2157; Romanus and Sunderland, *Stilwell's Mission,* p. 326, citing "summaries" of the Combined Chiefs meetings.

144. T. V. Soong memorandum re. conversation with Assistant Secretary of War McCoy, May 5, 1943, T. V. Soong Papers, box 61, folder 6.

145. Arthur N. Young, *China and the Helping Hand, 1937–1945* (Cambridge: Harvard University Press, 1963), p. 318.

146. Alsop, *I've Seen the Best,* pp. 218–223.

147. Tuchman, *Sand,* p. 489.

148. Memorandum re. General Stilwell, August 20, 1943, T. V. Soong Papers, box 61, folder 2.

149. Robert E. Sherwood, *Roosevelt and Hopkins* (1948; New York: Bantam Books, 1950), vol. 2, p. 352.

150. T. V. Soong, "Note on Conversation with Harry Hopkins on August 16, 1943," T. V. Soong Papers, box 61, folder 6.

151. Chiang Diaries, Hoover, June 17, 1943, box 43, folder 5.

152. Chiang's June 21, 1943, radiograms to his wife, in Qin Xiaoyi, *Zong tong,* vol. 5, pp. 2171–2172.

153. Chiang Diaries, Hoover, June 28, 1943, box 43, folder 5; Romanus and Sunderland, *Stilwell's Mission,* p. 341.

154. Chiang Diaries, Hoover, August 22, 1943, box 43, folder 7.

155. Hauro Tohmatsu, "The Strategic Correlation between the Sino-Japanese and Pacific Wars," paper given at Harvard University Conference on Wartime China, Maui, January 2004, p. 9.

156. Romanus and Sunderland, *Stilwell's Mission,* pp. 358–363.

157. Stilwell set out the scenario in a June 1943 note in his "Black Book." See Romanus and Sunderland, *Stilwell's Mission,* p. 341.

158. Tuchman, *Sand,* p. 399.

159. Chiang Diaries, Hoover, September 21, 1943, box 43, folder 8; Stilwell's plan in Qin Xiaoyi, *Zong tong,* p. 2239; Huang, *Chiang Kai-shek,* part 2, p. 45; Romanus and Sunderlund, *Stilwell's Mission,* p. 341.

160. Tuchman, *Sand,* pp. 372–373, 476–477, 493.

161. Chennault, *Way of a Fighter,* p. 226; Tuchman, *Sand,* p. 371.

162. Huang, *Chiang Kai-shek,* part 2, p. 47.

163. Stilwell, *Papers,* pp. 213–217.

164. Soong radiogram of September 16, 1943, in Qin Xiaoyi, *Zong tong,* vol. 5, p. 2236; Romanus and Sunderland, *Stilwell's Mission,* pp. 376–377.

165. T. V. Soong radiogram to Hopkins via China Defense Supplies, October 13, 1943, T. V. Soong Papers, box 61, folder 2.

166. Romanus and Sunderland, *Stilwell's Mission,* p. 377.

167. Huang, *Chiang Kai-shek,* part 2, p. 47.

168. Chiang Diaries, Hoover, October 15, 1943, box 43, folder 9.

169. Alsop, *I've Seen the Best,* pp. 224–225.

170. Ibid., p. 224; Huang, *Chiang Kai-shek,* part 1, pp. 46–47.

171. Editor's notes on the Stilwell-Mayling and Chiang-Stilwell meetings, October 17, 1943, in Qin Xiaoyi, *Zong tong,* vol. 5, p. 2253.

172. Stilwell, *Papers,* pp. 220–221.

173. Chinese notes on Stilwell's October 17, 1943, meeting with Chiang, in Qin Xiaoyi, *Zong tong,* vol. 5, p. 2253.

174. Alsop, *I've Seen the Best,* p. 225.

175. Leo Soong, February 21, 2005, memo "Background of T. V. Soong's 1943 Apology Letter to Chiang Kai-shek," a copy of which was provided to me by Mr. Leo Soong by email on April 11, 2006.

176. Alsop, *I've Seen the Best,* p. 225.

177. Romanus and Sunderland, *Stilwell's Mission,* pp. 378–379.

178. Louis Mountbatten, *Personal Diary of Admiral the Lord Louis Mounbatten, 1943–1946,* ed. Philip Ziegler (London: Collins, 1988), p. 14.

179. Ibid., pp. 11–17; Romanus and Sunderland, *Stilwell's Mission,* p. 380.

180. Stilwell, *Papers,* p. 221.

181. Chiang Diaries, Hoover, September 8, 1943, box 43, folder 8.

182. Message to Dimitrov from Gao Dong (aka Godunov) in Chungking, August 14, 1943, RGASPI, collection 595, inventory 74, file 333, pp. 3–13.

183. Peter Vladimirov, *The Vladimirov Diaries* (New York: Doubleday, 1975), p. 133.

184. Tuchman, *Sand,* pp. 388–389.

185. Chiang Diaries, Hoover, August 11, 1943, box 43, folder 7.

186. Ibid.

187. Vladimirov, *Diaries,* pp. 133–134.

188. Ibid., p. 133.

189. Gao reported to Dimitrov that he had just received information that somewhere in the CCP mission a KMT mole had disclosed the cipher key for decoding cables. Message to Dimitrov from Gao Dong in Chungking, August 14, 1943, RGASPI, collection 595, inventory 74, file 333, pp. 7–8; Message to Dimitrov from Gao Dong in Chungking, August 14, 1943, RGASPI, collection 595, inventory 74, file 333, p. 6.

190. Chiang radiogram to Soong, September 9, 1943, in Qin Xiaoyi, *Zong tong,* vol. 5, pp. 2213–2214.

191. Chiang Diaries, August 15, 1943, in Qin Xiaoyi, *Zong tong,* vol. 5, p. 2201.

192. Chiang radiogram to Soong, September 9, 1943, in Qin Xiaoyi, *Zong tong,* vol. 5, pp. 2210, 2213–2214.

193. Chiang radiogram to Soong, September 10, 1943, in Qin Xiaoyi, *Zong tong,* vol. 5, pp. 2214–2215.

194. Chiang radiogram to Soong, September 19, 1943, in Qin Xiaoyi, *Zong tong,* vol. 5, p. 2216.

195. Chiang Diaries, Hoover, October 17, 1943, box 43, folder 9; Huang, *Chiang Kai-shek,* part 2, p. 51.

196. Don Lohbeck, *Patrick J. Hurley* (Chicago: Henry Regnery Company, 1956), pp. 15–86, 159–164.

197. Tuchman, *Sand,* pp. 397–398.

198. Chiang Diaries, Hoover, November 13, 1943, box 43, folder 10; Lohbeck, *Hurley,* p. 206.

199. Chiang Diaries, Hoover, November 17, 1943, in Qin Xiaoyi, *Zong tong,* vol. 5, pp. 2270–2272.

200. Tuchman, *Sand,* pp. 399–400.

201. Romanus and Sunderland, *Stilwell's Mission,* vol. 2, p. 61.

202. Stilwell, *Papers,* p. 225.

203. Tuchman calls the term "horrific," but explains that it appears "only once or twice again" in Stilwell's diaries. See Tuchman, *Sand,* p. 398.

204. Forrest C. Pogue, *George C. Marshall Interviews and Reminiscences for Forrest C. Pogue,* ed. Larry I. Bland, 3d ed. (Lexington, Va.: George C. Marshall Foundation, 1996), p. 605. Marshall added: "He was writing worse things to his wife."

6. The China Theater

1. Winston S. Churchill, *The Second World War and an Epilogue on the Years 1945 to 1957* (London: Cassell, 1959), p. 727.

2. Field Marshall Lord Alanbrooke, *War Diaries,* ed. Alex Danchev and Dan Todman (London: Widenfeld and Nicolson, 2001), entry for November 23, 1943.

3. Chiang Diaries, Hoover, November 23, 1943, box 43, folder 10.

4. Barbara Tuchman, *Sand against the Wind: Stilwell and the American Experience in China* (London: Macmillan, 1971), p. 402.

5. Charles F. Romanus and Riley Sunderland, *Stilwell's Command Problem* (1956; Washington, D.C.: U.S. Army Center of Military History, 1978), pp. 62–63.

6. Robert E. Sherwood, *Roosevelt and Hopkins* (1948; New York: Bantam Books, 1950), vol. 2, p. 393.

7. *FRUS (1943): The Conferences,* p. 117.

8. The Chiangs had a formal introductory meeting with Roosevelt on November 22.

9. Ray Huang, *Chiang Kai-shek and His Diary as a Historical Resource* (Armonk, N.Y.: M. E. Sharpe, 1996), part 2, p. 53.

10. Chiang Diaries, Hoover, November 24, 1943, box 43, folder 10.

11. Chiang Diaries, Hoover, November 23, 1943, box 43, folder 10; *FRUS (1943): The Conferences,* pp. 322–325.

12. Elliot Roosevelt, *As He Saw It* (New York: Duell, Sloan, and Pearce, 1946), p. 142.

13. Ibid.

14. Sherwood, *Roosevelt and Hopkins,* p. 395.

15. Tuchman, *Sand against the Wind,* p. 404.

16. *FRUS (1943): The Conferences,* pp. 347–348.

17. Ibid., pp. 338–339.

18. In the Combined Chiefs meeting on November 26, Marshall was very strong on this issue. See *FRUS (1943): The Conferences,* p. 364.

19. Chiang Diaries, Hoover, November 24, 1943, box 43, folder 10.

20. *FRUS (1943): The Conferences,* p. 349.

21. Chiang Diaries, Hoover, November 26, 1943, box 43, folder 10.

22. Ibid.

23. Roosevelt, *As He Saw It,* p. 164. Roosevelt dodged a guarantee on Manchuria but said that the Soviet Union would respect the frontier of Manchuria. He suggested that Hong Kong be returned to China but become an open port, and Chiang agreed.

24. Chiang Diaries, Hoover, November 26, 1943, box 43, folder 10.

25. Romanus and Sunderland, *Stilwell's Command Problem,* p. 64.

26. The President's log reports variously that the Roosevelt-Chiang afternoon meeting lasted ninety minutes and that the President's next appointment was at 6:15. *FRUS (1943): The Conferences,* pp. 63, 298–299. For the Stilwell-Marshall meeting with Roosevelt, see Joseph W. Stilwell, *The Stilwell Papers* (London: Macdonald, 1949), p. 232, and Romanus and Sunderland, *Stilwell's Command Problem,* p. 64.

27. Stilwell, *Papers*, p. 232.

28. For "He's off again," see ibid., p. 231; for the 10:30 p.m. meeting see Roosevelt, *As He Saw It*, pp. 160, 162.

29. For "President's log" see *FRUS (1943): The Conferences*, pp. lxiii, 298–299.

30. For "low down" see Mountbatten, *Diary*, p. 35, and Stilwell, *Papers*, p. 32. The Defense Department historians state in one sentence that on the "evening" of November 25, Chiang met again with Roosevelt and "reversed himself on every point." They give no source at all for this statement but presumably took this exact phrase from Mountbatten's report of what Marshall told him Stilwell had apparently reported about what he thought Hopkins had said. The State Department historians simply note that the Pentagon history "indicates" that Chiang "reversed himself on every point," but knowing there was no evening meeting, they assume the reputed reversal took place at the 5:00 p.m. session, which was of course not true as President Roosevelt reported after the meeting. See Romanus and Sunderland, *Command Problems*, p. 65; *FRUS (1943): The Conferences*, p. 366.

31. For "fed up" see Stilwell, *Papers*, p. 232; for "abilities" see Chiang Diaries, Hoover, November 27, 1943, box 43, folder 10; for "tonnage target" see Stilwell, *Papers*, p. 233.

32. For "complete accord" see Chiang Diaries, November 27, 1943, box 43, folder 10; for "strong statement of support" see *FRUS (1943): The Conferences*, p. 364; for "agreement on every point" see *FRUS (1943): The Conferences*, p. 366.

33. Mountbatten, *Diary*, p. 35; Stilwell, *Papers*, p. 233.

34. Mountbatten, *Diary*, pp. 35, 36; Romanus and Sunderland, *Stilwell's Command Problem*, p. 65, quoting the SEAC War Diary, November 29, 1943.

35. Chiang Diaries, November 27, 1943, box 34, folder 10.

36. Tuchman, *Sand*, pp. 407, 521.

37. Sherwood, *Roosevelt and Hopkins*, p. 431.

38. *FRUS (1943): The Conferences*, pp. 705–710.

39. Stilwell, *Papers*, p. 238; Roosevelt, *As He Saw It*, pp. 164, 204; Qin Xiaoyi, *Zong tong*, vol. 5, p. 2282.

40. Sherwood, *Roosevelt and Hopkins*, pp. 395, 396.

41. *FRUS (1943): The Conferences*, p. 681.

42. Romanus and Sunderland, *Stilwell's Command Problem*, pp. 41–42. When referring to this and other failures by the headquarters of the CAI (Chinese Army in India), a headquarters commanded by Stilwell and staffed by Americans, the Army historians frequently use the Chinese term *Zhi hui bu* rather than the equivalent English word "headquarters." On their organization chart of the CAI, "headquarters" is written in these Chinese phonetics only. In the text, it is not made clear that *Zhu hui bu* meant Stilwell's CAI headquarters staffed entirely by American officers. Many readers might assume that the *Zhi hui bu* was a Chinese, specifically a Chiang Kai-shek, organization and that the intelligence failures were his.

43. Romanus and Sunderland, *Stilwell's Command Problem,* pp. 46, 123–124.

44. Huang, *Chiang Kai-shek,* pp. 53–54.

45. Chiang Diaries, Hoover, November 26 and 27, 1943, box 34, folder 10.

46. Chiang Diaries, Hoover, November 26, 1943, box 34, folder 10.

47. Stilwell, *Papers,* p. 237.

48. Tuchman, *Sand,* p. 410.

49. Stilwell, *Papers,* pp. 236–238.

50. Romanus and Sunderland, *Stilwell's Command Problem,* p. 72, and footnote 61. These notes were found in Stilwell's loose papers.

51. Roosevelt, *As He Saw It,* p. 207.

52. Chiang Diaries, December 4, 1943, box 43, folder 11.

53. Hsi-hseng Ch'i, *Nationalist China at War: Military Defeats and Political Collapse, 1937–1945* (Ann Arbor: University of Michigan Press, 1982), pp. 113–114.

54. Ibid.

55. Ibid., p. 114.

56. Editor's notes on exchange with Bai, in Qin Xiaoyi, *Zong tong,* vol. 5, pp. 2192–2193.

57. Abstract of Zhou Enlai "Report to the Politburo" of the CCP, August 1939 copy found in the Comintern archives, RGASPI, collection 495, inventory 10a, file 296, sheet 146-96.

58. Frank Dorn, *Walkout with Stilwell* (New York: Thomas Y. Crowell, 1971), pp. 75–76.

59. Ibid., pp. 77–79.

60. Thomas H. Moon and Carl F. Eifler, *The Deadliest Colonel* (New York: Vantage Press, 1975), pp. 145–146. Eifler, head of OSS espionage in the China Theater, infuriated Wild Bill Donovan by consistently claiming he was under the jurisdiction of Stilwell. Consequently, Eifler would have felt no need to inform OSS headquarters of this rather important order from Stilwell, apparently even when he returned to Washington and saw Donovan on another matter. See Maochun Yu, *OSS in China: Prelude to Cold War* (New Haven: Yale University Press, 1996), p. 113.

61. Moon and Eifler, *Deadliest Colonel,* pp. 146, 184, 193. Although Moon and Eifler do not give the day or month of the time in 1943 when Stilwell first brought up the subject with Eifler, it is apparent from the chronology of events before and after this meeting that it took place in the suggested timeframe.

62. Sherwood, *Roosevelt and Hopkins,* pp. 395, 396.

63. Roosevelt, *As He Saw It,* p. 154.

64. Stilwell, *Papers,* pp. 217–218.

65. Xu Longxun and Zhan Minggai, *History of the Sino-Japanese War (1937–1945)* (Taipei: Chung Wu Publishing, 1971), p. 412.

66. *FRUS (1943): China,* p. 168.

67. Huang, *Chiang Kai-shek,* p. 64.

68. Claire Lee Chennault, *The Way of a Fighter* (1949; Tucson, Ariz.: James Thorvaardson and Sons, 1991), pp. 262–263.

69. Mrs. Chas. E. Cowman, *Streams in the Desert* (Los Angeles: Oriental Missionary Society, 1931), p. 23.

70. Chiang Kai-shek, *China's Destiny and Economic Theory* (New York: Roy Publishers, 1947).

71. Ibid., pp. 36, 40, 94, 96, 146, 157, 208, 231, 234–235, 263, 277, 279, 282–284, 289.

72. Ibid., pp. 289–290.

73. Ibid., p. 43.

74. Owen Lattimore, *China Memoirs* (Tokyo: University of Tokyo Press, 1990), p. 186; Harvey Klehr and Ronald Radosh, *The Amerasia Spy Case* (Chapel Hill: University of North Carolina Press, 1996), pp. 29, 32–37, 42, 132.

75. Herbert Feis, *The China Tangle: The American Effort in China from Pearl Harbor to the Marshall Mission* (Princeton, N.J.: Princeton University Press, 1953), p. 120.

76. Chiang Diaries, Hoover, November 30 and 31 ("Monthly reflection"), 1943, box 43, folder 10.

77. Romanus and Sunderland, *Stilwell's Command Problem*, p. 74; Feis, *China Tangle*, pp. 120–121.

78. Romanus and Sunderland, *Stilwell's Command Problem*, pp. 79–80.

79. Chiang Kai-shek letter to President Roosevelt, transmitted January 16, 1944, in *White Paper*, pp. 492–493; Arthur N. Young, *China's Wartime Finance and Inflation* (Cambridge: Harvard University Press, 1965), p. 283.

80. Romanus and Sunderland, *Stilwell's Command Problem;* Arthur N. Young, *China and the Helping Hand, 1937–1945* (Cambridge: Harvard University Press, 1963), p. 400.

81. Chiang Diaries, Hoover, January 15, 1944, box 43, folder 13.

82. Roosevelt's January 15, 1944, radiogram, and editor's notes, in Qin Xiaoyi, *Zong tong,* vol. 5, p. 2312; Tuchman, *Sand,* pp. 412–413; Young, *China and the Helping Hand,* pp. 284–285; Romanus and Sunderland, *Stilwell's Command Problem,* p. 298.

83. Romanus and Sunderland, *Stilwell's Command Problem,* pp. 300–301; Feis, *China Tangle,* p. 127.

84. Xu Longxun and Zhan Minggai, *History,* pp. 416–417; Chiang Kai-shek radiogram, February 22, 1944, in Qin Xiaoyi, *Zong tong,* vol. 5, p. 2327; Hara Takeshi, "The Ichigo Offensive: The Circumstances Leading to Its Execution and Its Results," paper presented at Harvard University Conference on Wartime China, Maui, January 2004, pp. 1, 7.

85. Hara Takeshi, "Ichigo Offensive," pp. 1–7; Wang Qisheng, "The Hunan Bat-

tle: The Chinese Military Response to the Japanese 'Battle no. 1,'" paper presented at
Harvard University Conference on Wartime China, Maui, January 2004, p. 3.

86. Chiang Diaries, Hoover, March 12, 1944, box 43, folder 15.

87. Peter Vladimirov, *The Vladimirov Diaries* (New York: Doubleday, 1975),
p. 184.

88. Chiang Diaries, Hoover, February 13, 1944, box 43, folder 14.

89. Romanus and Sunderland, *Stilwell's Command Problem,* pp. 300–304; Editor's notes, February 13 and 22, 1944, in Qin Xiaoyi, *Zong tong,* vol. 5, pp. 2322,
2327.

90. Romanus and Sunderland, *Stilwell's Command Problem,* pp. 162–163,
180–171.

91. Churchill, *Second World War,* pp. 825–826; Stilwell, *Papers,* p. 265.

92. Romanus and Sunderland, *Stilwell's Command Problem,* pp. 176–177, 180,
304; Tuchman, *Sand,* p. 439.

93. Romanus and Sunderland, *Stilwell's Command Problem,* pp. 305, 307–308;
Tuchman, *Sand,* p. 441.

94. Chiang Diaries, Hoover, April 5, 1944, box 43, folder 16.

95. Romanus and Sunderland, *Stilwell's Command Problem,* p. 310; Qin Xiaoyi,
Zong tong, vol. 5, p. 2345.

96. Chiang Diaries, Hoover, April 5, 1944, box 43, folder 16.

97. Romanus and Sunderland, *Stilwell's Command Problem,* pp. 313–314, 329,
340–341.

98. Ibid., pp. 312–314.

99. Ibid., p. 322.

100. Ibid., p. 319.

101. Hsi-hseng Ch'i, *Nationalist China at War,* pp. 75–76; Romanus and Sunderland, *Stilwell's Command Problem,* pp. 314, 323, 325, 326. Another 200 planes of
the 14th were designated to defend the B-29s at Chengdu and another 150 to support the Salween offensive. See Chennault, *Way of a Fighter,* p. 290, and Romanus
and Sunderland, *Stilwell's Command Problem,* p. 370. The 500 total planes in the
14th Air Force (900 by the end of 1944) contrasted with the 21,000 aircraft and 18
million tons of supplies that the United States would provide the Soviet Union during the war.

102. Romanus and Sunderland, *Stilwell's Command Problem,* p. 254.

103. Ibid., pp. 355–360; Chennault, *Way of a Fighter,* p. 275.

104. Romanus and Sunderland, *Stilwell's Command Problem,* pp. 363–364; Chennault, *Way of a Fighter,* pp. 287–288, 292.

105. Romanus and Sunderland, *Stilwell's Command Problem,* pp. 362–364.

106. The Chindits and their commanders, who provided 17,000 British, Gurhka,
Nigerian, and Burmese special-forces troops, grew highly critical of Stilwell, clas-

sifying the battle for Myitkyina as a blunder and a fiasco. Stilwell's intelligence had claimed that there were only 350 Japanese troops in the town. See Shelford Bidwell, *The Chindit War* (New York: Macmillan, 1979), p. 280.

107. Chiang Diaries, Hoover, May 28, 1944, box 43, folder 17; Romanus and Sunderland, *Stilwell's Command Problem*, 365.

108. He Yingqin interview with Central News Agency reporters, Chungking, September 20, 1944, in "News of the Central News Agency," October 7, 1944, in Qin Xiaoyi, ed., *Chunghua minkuo chungyao shihliao chupian tui erh k'angchan Shihch'i* (Preliminary Compilation of Important Historical Material of the ROC—Resist Japan Period), part 3: *Chanshih Waichiao* (Wartime Diplomacy) (Taipei: KMT Historical Archives, 1981), vol. 1, pp. 512–514. Lend-Lease that China received from May 1941 to April 1942 before the Burma Road was cut off provided supplies that the War Ministry distributed or stored, including: airplanes, 1,657 tons; arsenals (equipment and material for arms manufacture), 24,000 tons; vehicles, 29,000 tons; ordnance (presumably bombs and shells), 11,000 tons; weapons, 1,300 tons; ammunition, 8,700 tons; road-building equipment, 19,000 tons. See Charles F. Romanus and Riley Sunderland, *Stilwell's Mission to China* (1952; Washington, D.C.: U.S. Army Center of Military History, 2002), p. 49. If not a "trickle," considering the circumstances, these were certainly small amounts.

109. Romanus and Sunderland, *Stilwell's Command Problem*, pp. 321, 322.

110. Ibid., p. 369; Alsop, *The Best*, p. 235.

111. Romanus and Sunderland, *Stilwell's Command Problem*, p. 368.

112. Chiang Diaries, Hoover, June 5, 1944, box 43, folder 18.

113. The Chinese had small arsenals of China-made weapons and ammunition. According to a later study by Wedemeyer's headquarters, from March 1941 through June 1945, Chinese arsenals—apparently with the assistance of U.S.-supplied non-ferrous metals—were able to produce a total of 263,000 rifles, 44,000 machine guns, 10,000 mortars, 16 million hand grenades, and 610 million rounds of various caliber ammunition. Except for the hand grenades, this is a relatively small supply of replacement weapons and ammunition for four years given the size of the Chinese Army and the combat and other losses that they suffered. Even so, Chiang probably had sufficient reserve supplies of this China-produced matériel that he could have provided Changsha and Hengyang with the supplies they needed, but Chennault required Stilwell's approval to fly airdrop operations. On June 7, Chiang's team in Washington reported that the U.S. Joint Chiefs had approved use of the Tenth Air Force heavy bombers in India to drop 2,000 to 2,500 tons of matériel in the China Theater, but neither Chiang nor Stilwell ever picked up on this offer. Message from General Shang Zhen in Washington, June 7, 1944, in Qin Xioayi, *Zong tong*, vol. 5, p. 2374.

114. Chiang clearly withheld some or perhaps all major airdrops of ordnance supplies from Xue, but a number of recent writings on Ichigo do not mention this aspect

of the Chinese response to the campaign, suggesting that possibly it was not a critical factor in the outcome of the battles for Changsha and Hengyang. These texts include those of a Peking scholar of the campaign, Wang Qisheng; a noted Chinese-American historian who was in the Nationalist Army at the time, Ray Huang; and a Japanese scholar, Hara Takeshi. Xue did receive some U.S. howitzers directly from the Americans; see Romanus and Sunderland, *Stilwell's Command Problem,* p. 372.

115. Chiang Diaries, Hoover, June 20, 1944, box 43, folder 18.

116. Feis, *China Tangle,* p. 145.

117. *New York Times,* June 21, 1944.

118. *New York Times,* September 24, 1951, citing Wallace's letter to Harry Truman, September 19, 1951, in which he refers to his 1944 China trip; Romanus and Sunderland, *Stilwell's Command Problem,* p. 376.

119. Feis, *China Tangle,* p. 160; *New York Times,* June 9, August 22, and October 6, 1944.

120. *White Paper,* pp. 64–65.

121. Feis, *China Tangle,* pp. 148–151.

122. Lattimore, *China Memoirs,* pp. 181–186.

123. Feis, *Tangle,* pp. 148–151.

124. *New York Times,* January 19, 1950, and September 24, 1951. Vincent, like many others associated with China policy, would after the war be unfairly accused of being a Communist. Vincent fully concurred in this 1944 recommendation by Wallace to replace Stilwell—a recommendation that Zhou Enlai would certainly have seen as highly unfavorable to the CCP.

125. John S. Service, *Lost Chance in China* (New York: Random House, 1974), p. 95.

126. Lin Bowen, *Kua shiji diyi furen Song Meiling* (Soong Mayling: The First Lady across Centuries) (Taipei: China Times, 2000), pp. 443–444. One rumor was that Chiang's longtime paramour, Chen Jieru, had returned secretly to Chungking and Chiang had renewed the relationship. But Jieru did not mention this renewed liaison in her memoirs, suggesting it did not happen.

127. Sterling Seagrave, *The Soong Dynasty* (New York: Harper & Row Perennial Library Paperback, 1986), pp. 412–413.

128. Laura Tyson Li, *Madame Chiang Kai-shek: China's Eternal First Lady* (New York: Atlantic Monthly Press, 2006), p. 258.

129. Huang, *Chiang Kai-shek,* pp. 112–113; Romanus and Sunderland, *Stilwell's Command Problem,* pp. 379–380.

130. Feis, *China Tangle,* p. 170.

131. Romanus and Sunderland, *Stilwell's Command Problem,* pp. 381–382.

132. Geoffery C. Ward, *Closest Companion* (Boston: Houghton Mifflin, 1995), p. 114.

133. Stilwell, *Papers,* pp. 281–283, 296.

134. Chiang Diaries, Hoover, July 7, 1944, box 43, folder 19.

135. The Englishman known as Chinese Gordon in the middle of the nineteenth century briefly commanded only a small force of Europeans and Asians called "The Ever Victorious Army."

136. Chiang Diaries, Hoover, July 7, 1944, box 43, folder 19.

137. Chiang cables to Roosevelt, Wallace, and H. H. Kung, July 8 and 11, 1944, in Qin Xiaoyi, *Zong tong,* vol. 5, pp. 2394, 2395, 2397.

138. Chiang Kai-shek, July 11 (1944) radiogram, in Qin Xiaoyi, *Zong tong,* vol. 5, p. 2397.

139. H. H. Kung, July 12, 1944, radiogram to Chiang, in Qin Xiaoyi, *Zong tong,* vol. 5, p. 2399.

140. Ibid.

141. Romanus and Sunderland, *Stilwell's Command Problem,* pp. 386–387. The army historians give the date of the memo from Roosevelt to Chiang Kai-shek as July 13, saying it was conveyed to Chiang in a memo of July 15 from Stilwell's headquarters in Chungking.

142. Chiang Diaries, Hoover, July 12, 1944, box 43, folder 19.

143. Chiang Diaries, Hoover, July 18, 1944, in Qin Xiaoyi, *Zong tong,* vol. 5, pp. 2398, 2399.

144. Chiang Diaries, Hoover, July 18, 1944, box 43, folder 19.

145. Chiang Diaries, Hoover, July 22, 1944, box 43, folder 19.

146. Chiang Diaries, Hoover, July 20, 1944, box 43, folder 19.

147. Chennault, *Way of a Fighter,* pp. 292–296; editor's note, in Qin Xiaoyi, *Zong tong,* vol. 5, p. 2369.

148. Huang, *Chiang Kai-shek,* part 1, pp. 97–104; Hsi-hseng Ch'i, *Nationalist China at War,* p. 77.

149. Chennault, *Way of a Fighter,* pp. 94, 300.

150. Romanus and Sunderland, *Stilwell's Command Problem,* p. 402.

151. Ibid., pp. 412–413.

152. Ibid.

153. Ibid., p. 405.

154. Chennault, *Way of a Fighter,* p. 304.

155. Chiang Diaries, Hoover, August 11, 1944, box 43, folder 20.

156. Service, *Lost Chance,* pp. 271, 179, 180, 181, 196, 312.

157. Ibid., p. 197.

158. Ibid., p. 308; David D. Barrett, *The Dixie Mission: The United States Army Observer Group in Yenna, 1944* (Berkeley: University of California Press, 1970), p. 90.

159. Lyman P. Van Slyke, ed., *The Chinese Communist Movement* (Stanford, Calif.: Stanford University Press, 1968), pp. 104, 251–253, 254.

160. Chiang Diaries, Hoover, August 26, 1944, box 43, folder 20.

161. Don Lohbeck, *Patrick J. Hurley* (Chicago: Henry Regnery Company, 1956), pp. 285–286.

162. Chiang Diaries, Hoover, September 7, 1944, in Qin Xiaoyi, *Zong tong*, vol. 5, p. 2426.

163. Chiang Diaries, Hoover, September 8, 1944, box 43, folder 21.

164. Ibid.; Romanus and Sunderland, *Stilwell's Command Problem*, pp. 422–423.

165. Editor's notes, September 8, 1944, in Qin Xiaoyi, *Zong tong*, vol. 5, p. 2428.

166. Editor's notes, September 15, 1944, in Qin Xiaoyi, *Zong tong*, vol. 5, p. 2435.

167. Stilwell, *Papers*, p. 303.

168. Romanus and Sunderland, *Stilwell's Command Problem*, pp. 435–436.

169. Huang, *Chiang Kai-shek*, part 2, p. 121.

170. Romanus and Sunderland, *Stilwell's Command Problem*, p. 437; Lohbeck, *Hurley*, p. 290.

171. Romanus and Sunderland, *Stilwell's Command Problem*, pp. 446–447. Information about the September 1944 meeting comes from an interview of Hurley by the Army historians. See Alsop, *I've Seen the Best*, p. 239.

172. Romanus and Sunderland, *Stilwell's Command Problem*, pp. 445–446.

173. Chiang Diaries, Hoover, September 19, 1944, box 43, folder 21; Lohbeck, *Hurley*, p. 292.

174. Lohbeck, *Hurley*, p. 292.

175. Ibid.

176. Alsop, *I've Seen the Best*, p. 39; Lohbeck, *Hurley*, p. 293.

177. Lohbeck, *Hurley*, p. 293.

178. Alsop, *I've Seen the Best*, p. 241. Romanus and Sunderland seem to ignore the rather clear conclusion in their own writing that it was Stilwell's message of September 15 that provoked the War Department into sending the President the draft ultimatum to Chiang. Romanus and Sunderland in fact report that Stilwell's alarming message of September 15 led the Combined Chiefs meeting in Quebec, with Roosevelt and Churchill present, to agree to a strong response urging Chiang not to carry through with his proposals regarding the Y Force on the Salween front. This resulted in the ultimatum drafted by Marshall's staff in Quebec that was also based on the incorrect assertion that Chiang was stalling on the command issue. See Romanus and Sunderland, *Stilwell's Command Problem*, p. 447.

179. Alsop, *I've Seen the Best*, p. 242.

180. Lohbeck, *Hurley*, pp. 293–294.

181. Alsop, *I've Seen the Best*, p. 242.

182. Chiang Diaries, Hoover, September 20, 1944, box 43, folder 21.

183. Romanus and Sunderland, *Stilwell's Command Problem*, p. 451.

184. Ibid., pp. 447, 448.

185. Stilwell, *Papers*, pp. 305–306. The army historians simply note that Stilwell "marked the occasion" with "bit of doggerel," explaining in a footnote that he wrote

nonsense verse and other material "for the entertainment of himself, his family, and a few friends." See Romanus and Sunderland, *Stilwell's Command Problem*, p. 448. Tuchman, by contrast, provides the whole verse on "the principle of warts and all." See Tuchman, *Sand*, p. 494.

186. Stilwell, *Papers*, pp. 305–306.

187. Romanus and Sunderland, *Stilwell's Command Problem*, p. 452.

188. Chiang records that Hurley told him this. See Chiang Diaries, Hoover, September 24, 1944, box 43, folder 21.

189. Editor's notes, September 24, 1944, in Qin Xiaoyi, *Zong tong*, vol. 5, pp. 2452–2453.

190. Editor's notes, September 23, 1944, in Qin Xiaoyi, *Zong tong*, vol. 5, pp. 2444–2458.

191. Lohbeck, *Hurley*, p. 296.

192. Chiang Kai-shek, September 26, 1944, cable to H. H. Kung, in Qin Xiaoyi, *Zong tong*, vol. 5, p. 2455.

193. Chiang's formal letter to Hurley, September 25, 1944, in Qin Xiaoyi, *Zong tong*, vol. 5, p. 2454; Lohbeck, *Hurley*, p. 298; Romanus and Sunderland, *Stilwell's Command Problem*, p. 452.

194. Chiang Diaries, Hoover, September 30, 1944, box 43, folder 21.

195. Feis, *China Tangle*, pp. 193, 194; Romanus and Sunderland, *Stilwell's Command Problem*, p. 457.

196. Feis, *China Tangle*, pp. 194, 195; Stilwell, *Papers*, pp. 312–313; Romanus and Sunderland, *Stilwell's Command Problem*, p. 459.

197. Lohbeck, *Hurley*, pp. 300–301; Romanus and Sunderland, *Stilwell's Command Problem*, p. 463.

198. Stilwell, *Papers*, pp. 315–316.

199. Chiang Diaries, Hoover, October 21, 1944, box 43, folder 22; Stilwell, *Papers*, p. 317.

200. Tuchman, *Sand*, p. 503. In 1946, Stilwell told Owen Lattimore about wishing "to get over there [in the Chinese Civil War] and shoulder a rifle with Zhu Teh." He repeated this phrase in a letter to someone else and the passage was circulated after his death on October 12, 1946.

201. Stilwell, *Papers*, pp. 318, 319.

202. *New York Times*, October 31, 1944.

203. Chiang Diaries, Hoover, November 4, 1944, box 43, folder 23.

7. Yalta, Manchuria, and Postwar Strategy

1. Charles F. Romanus and Riley Sunderland, *Time Runs Out in the CBI* (Washington: D.C.: Office of the Chief of Military History, Department of the Army, 1959), p. 16.

2. Ibid., p. 52.

3. Ibid.

4. Although the Americans now had air superiority over most of Free China, the Japanese Air Force was by no means out of business.

5. Albert C. Wedemeyer, *Wedemeyer Reports* (New York: Holt, 1958), pp. 277–278.

6. Herbert Feis, *The China Tangle: The American Effort in China from Pearl Harbor to the Marshall Mission* (Princeton, N.J.: Princeton University Press, 1953), pp. 195, 204.

7. Chiang Diaries, Hoover, December 2 and 6, 1944, box 43, folder 24.

8. Wang Chaoguang, "Wartime Rivalry and the Deliberation of Postwar Issues," paper presented at Harvard University Conference on Wartime China, Maui, January 2004; F. F. Liu, *A Military History of Modern China, 1924–1949* (Princeton, N.J.: Princeton University Press, 1956), p. 219.

9. RGASPI, collection 17, inventory 128, file 822, sheets 7–21.

10. Wedemeyer, *Reports,* p. 205.

11. Peter Vladimirov, *The Vladimirov Diaries* (New York: Doubleday, 1975), p. 289.

12. Chiang Diaries, Hoover, November 11, 1944, box 43, folder 23; Qin Xiaoyi, *Zong tong,* vol. 5, p. 2474.

13. Chiang Diaries, Hoover, November 22, 1944, box 43, folder 23.

14. Barbara Tuchman, *Notes from China* (New York: Collier Books, 1971), pp. 77–79.

15. Later, Mao wrote in an intraparty document that the CCP would of course "never do such a thing" and in January 1945 he would also tell that to Hurley. See Michael M. Sheng, *Battling Western Imperialism: Mao, Stalin, and the United States* (Princeton, N.J.: Princeton University Press, 1997), p. 90.

16. Editor's notes, January 14, 1945, in Qin Xiaoyi, ed., *Zong tong,* vol. 5, p. 2506; *White Paper,* p. 79.

17. Robert E. Sherwood, *Roosevelt and Hopkins* (New York: Harper and Brothers, 1950), p. 512; Romanus and Sunderland, *Time Runs Out,* pp. 331–332.

18. Sheng, *Battling Western Imperialism,* p. 93.

19. Feis, *China Tangle,* p. 236.

20. Ibid., pp. 226–239.

21. Ibid., p. 249.

22. Harry Harding and Yuan Ming, eds., *Sino-American Relations, 1945–1955* (Wilmington, Del.: SR Books, 1989), p. 67; Robert E. Sherwood, *Roosevelt and Hopkins* (1948; New York: Bantam Books, 1950), vol. 2, p. 511.

23. Sheng, *Battling Western Imperialism,* p. 93. Sheng cites a Mao to Zhou radiogram of February 3, 1944, in which Mao notes that Stalin would be meeting with Roosevelt and Churchill. From this, Sheng reasonably concludes that Stalin had sent a message to Mao about the meeting.

24. Ibid., p. 94; Sherwood, *Roosevelt and Hopkins,* pp. 512, 516; Feis, *China Tangle,* p. 240.

25. Chiang Diaries, Hoover, February 21, 1945, box 44, folder 3.

26. Romanus and Sunderland, *Time Runs Out,* p. 338.

27. Chiang Diaries, Hoover, March 15, 1945, box 44, folder 4.

28. Feis, *China Tangle,* p. 278.

29. Don Lohbeck, *Patrick J. Hurley* (Chicago: Henry Regnery Company, 1956), pp. 372–377.

30. Feis, *China Tangle,* p. 277.

31. *Liberation Daily,* April 9, 1945.

32. Lohbeck, *Hurley,* p. 370.

33. Chiang Diaries, Hoover, April 13, 1945, box 44, folder 5.

34. *White Paper,* p. 83.

35. Ibid., pp. 84–85; Feis, *China Tangle,* p. 276.

36. *White Paper,* pp. 268–270.

37. *Bai Chongxi xian sheng fangwen jilu* (The Reminiscences of General Bai Chongxi), ed. Guo Dingye, 2 vols., no. 4 in the Oral History Series (Taipei: Institute of Modern History, Academia Sinica, 1984), p. 475.

38. Ibid., pp. 475–478.

39. Jonathan D. Spence, *The Search for Modern China* (New York: W. W. Norton, 1990), p. 482.

40. Joseph J. Heinlein, "Political Warfare: The Chinese Nationalist Model," Ph.D. diss., American University, 1974, p. 482; *White Paper,* p. 101.

41. Conrad Brandt, Benjamin Swartz, and John K. Fairbank, *A Documentary History of Chinese Communism* (Cambridge: Harvard University Press, 1959), p. 419; Feis, *China Tangle,* pp. 290–291.

42. Romanus and Sunderland, *Time Runs Out,* pp. 350–352; Hsi-sheng Ch'i, "The Military Dimension, 1942–1945," in James C. Hsiung and Steven I. Levine, *China's Bitter Victory* (Armonk, N.Y.: M. E. Sharpe, 1992), pp. 165–166.

43. Wang Chaoguang, "Wartime Rivalry," p. 7; Haruo Tohmatsu, "The Strategic Correlation between the Sino-Japanese and Pacific Wars," paper presented at Harvard University Conference on Wartime China, Maui, January 2004, p. 17; Romanus and Sunderland, *Time Runs Out,* pp. 278, 287, 289; Feis, *China Tangle,* p. 297; Wedemeyer, *Reports,* pp. 301, 338.

44. Lohbeck, *Hurley,* pp. 370, 376–377; Chiang Diaries, Hoover, June 15, 1945, box 44, folder 7; Ray Huang, *Chiang Kai-shek and His Diary as a Historical Resource* (Armonk, N.Y.: M. E. Sharpe, 1996), part 2, p. 140.

45. Sheng, *Battling Western Imperialism,* pp. 105–106.

46. Theodore H. White and Annalea Jacoby, *Thunder Out of China* (New York: William Sloane Associates, 1946) p. 266; for "guarantee" see Chiang Diaries, Hoover, May 24, 1945, box 44, folder 6.

47. *Time,* December 24, 1945.

48. Ibid.; Qin Xiaoyi, *Zong tong,* vol. 5, pp. 2565–2566.

49. For "Japanese territory" see Sheng, *Battling Western Imperialism,* pp. 97, 103. For "across the Yangtze" see editor's note in Qin Xiaoyi, *Zong tong,* vol. 5, p. 2571. For "three articles" see Wang Chaoguang, "Wartime Rivalry," p. 27.

50. Chiang Diaries, Hoover, July 5, 1945, box 44, folder 8.

51. Chiang Ching-kuo, *Chiang Ching-kuo xian sheng zhuan zhi* (Biography of Chiang Ching-kuo) (Taipei: Government Information Office, 1989), vol. 2, pp. 272–273; Jay Taylor, *The Generalissimo's Son* (Cambridge: Harvard University Press, 2000), p. 126.

52. Feis, *China Tangle,* pp. 317–321.

53. Romanus and Sunderland, *Time Runs Out,* pp. 317–321, 365–366. Some 11,600 tons of fuel were delivered by the pipeline. The prediction of Churchill, Chennault, and others in 1943 that the war would end before the road could be completed was five months off.

54. Romanus and Sunderland, *Time Runs Out,* pp. 15, 341. In November 30, 1944, there were 27,739 U.S. military personnel in China, a number that increased substantially over the next eight months.

55. The capture of the airfield at Myitkyina did allow a shorter and safer air route for the Air Transport Command transports.

56. Chiang Diaries, Hoover, July 28, 1945 (weekly reflection), box 44, folders 8, 13.

57. Ibid.

58. Ibid.

59. Chiang Diaries, Hoover, July 31, 1945, box 44, folder 8; Feis, *China Tangle,* pp. 334–335; Romanus and Sunderland, *Time Runs Out,* p. 391.

60. Romanus and Sunderland, *Time Runs Out,* p. 359.

61. Jack Samson, *The Flying Tiger: The True Story of General Clair Chennault and the U.S. 14th Air Force* (Guilford, Conn.: Lyons Press, 1987), p. 265.

62. Romanus and Sunderland, *Time Runs Out,* pp. 368, 381.

63. Sheng, *Battling Western Imperialism,* p. 106.

64. Chiang Diaries, Hoover, August 10, 1945, box 44, folder 9.

65. Romanus and Sunderland, *Time Runs Out,* pp. 394, 395; Feis, *China Tangle,* p. 337.

66. Editor's notes, August 14, 1945, in Qin Xiaoyi, *Zong tong,* vol. 5, p. 2639.

67. Feis, *China Tangle,* pp. 342–344.

68. Ibid.

69. Ibid., pp. 348–350.

70. Sheng, *Battling Western Imperialism,* p. 102; Tang Tsou, *America's Failure in China, 1941–1950* (Chicago: University of Chicago Press, 1963), p. 303.

71. Tang Tsou, *America's Failure,* pp. 303–304.

72. Ibid., p. 305.

73. Chen Liwen, *Cong Dongbei dongwu fa zhan kan jiezhou* (A Study on the Return of Northeast China after the War from the Perspective of KMT Party Politics and Party Organizational Rebuilding) (Taipei: Northeast Historical Documents Publishing House, 2000), p. 302; Steven I. Levine, *Anvil of Victory: The Communist Revolution in Manchuria, 1945–1948* (New York: Columbia University Press, 1987), p. 103; Sheng, *Battling Western Imperialism*, p. 105.

74. Levine, *Anvil of Victory*, p. 102; Sheng, *Battling Western Imperialism*, pp. 100–102; Tang Tsou, *America's Failure*, p. 303.

75. Wang Chaoguang, "Wartime Rivalry," p. 35.

76. *Bai Chongxi xian sheng fangwen jilu*, p. 242.

77. Rira Mona, "The Chinese Utilization of the Japanese Army after the Victory of the Sino-Japanese War," paper presented at Harvard University Conference on Wartime China, Maui, January 2004, p. 6; ibid., p. 243. The CCP claimed that from August 11 to October 10, its forces captured and accepted the surrender of 200,000 puppet and Japanese troops and killed or wounded 10,000. The overwhelming majority of the captured were puppet troops, including local and village police and militia. See Tang Tsou, *America's Failure*, p. 311.

78. Levine, *Anvil of Victory*, p. 43. At the end of 1946 there were still "many" Japanese serving in Yan's army.

79. Sheng, *Battling Western Imperialism*, pp. 103–104; Romanus and Sunderland, *Time Runs Out*, p. 395; Tang Tsou, *America's Failure*, p. 308.

80. Dimitri Volkogonov, *Stalin: Triumph and Tragedy* (London: Forum, 1991), p. 531.

81. Zhang Baijia, "Zhou Enlai and the Marshall Mission," in Larry I. Bland, ed., *George C. Marshall's Mediation Mission to China, December 1945–January 1947* (Lexington, Va.: George C. Marshall Foundation, 1998), p. 203.

82. Levine, *Anvil of Victory*, p. 140; He Changgong, *He Changgong huiyi lu* (Memoirs of He Changgong) (Peking: Liberation Army Publishers, 1987), pp. 403–430. At the time, He Changgong was the CCP's minister for ordnance in the Northeast. Over the years, the CCP, furthering its argument that Stalin only decided to side with Mao in Manchuria in 1947 after the tide had turned, claimed that Stalin did not turn over a substantial amount of Japanese weapons until the fall of that year. See Sergei Goncharov, John Lewis, and Xue Litai, *Uncertain Partners: Stalin, Mao, and the Korean War* (Stanford, Calif.: Stanford University Press, 1993), p. 14. A full reading of He's memoirs makes clear that this was not the case—although tanks and heavy artillery were held back until the fall of 1947, presumably in order to diminish the U.S. reaction to the huge Soviet transfer of Japanese weapons under way should Washington learn of it. Also see Levine, *Anvil of Victory*, p. 104.

83. Tang Tsou, *America's Failure in China* (Chicago: University of Chicago Press, 1963), p. 331fn. Soviet sources cited by Chinese Communist publication, *Zhong-guo*

xin min zhu zhu yi ge ming shi can gao ci liao [not identified], p. 433. Hsu Long-hsuen and Chang Ming-kai, *History of the Sino-Japanese War (1937–1945),* (Taipei: Chung Wu, 1971), p. 571.

84. Sheng, *Battling Western Imperialism,* p. 106, citing Ding Xiaochun, *Chronology of the Liberation War in Manchuria* (Peking: Publishing House of CCP Historical Materials, 1987).

85. Feis, *China Tangle,* pp. 380, 381.

86. Mao Zedong, "On Peace Negotiations with the Kuomintang," in Mao Zedong, *Selected Works* (Peking: International Publishers, 1949), vol. 4, p. 49.

87. Chiang Diaries, Hoover, August 28, 1945, box 44, folder 9.

88. Henry Luce, "Chungking Diaries," October 1945, cited by Laura Tyson Li, *Madame Chiang Kai-shek* (New York: Atlantic Monthly Press, 2006), p. 265; Han Suyin, *Elder Son: Zhou Enlai and the Making of Modern China* (New York: Hill and Wang, 1994), p. 261.

89. Chiang Diaries, Hoover, September 2, 1945, box 44, folder 10.

90. Chiang Diaries, Hoover, September 4, 1945, box 44, folder 10.

91. Chiang Diaries, Hoover, September 9, 1945, box 44, folder 10.

92. Chiang Diaries, Hoover, September 10 and 20, 1945, box 44, folder 10.

93. Chiang Diaries, Hoover, September 7, 1945, box 44, folder 10.

94. Sheng, *Battling Western Imperialism,* p. 108, citing Yang Kuisong, "Zhongguo Gongchangdang dongbei de zhanlu yanbian yu Sulian" (The Soviet Union and the Evolution of the CCP's Strategy of Seizing the Northeast), *Zhonggong dangshi yanjiu* (Journal of Chinese Communist Party History, Peking), 1990 (additional issue), pp. 60–71. The Soviets supposedly promised that the Red Army would support the CCP directly if Chiang Kai-shek's government launched an offensive in Manchuria.

95. Sheng, *Battling Western Imperialism,* pp. 106–108.

96. Chiang Diaries, Hoover, September 13, 1945, box 44, folder 11; Feis, *China Tangle,* p. 382.

97. Editor's notes, September 18, 1945, in Qin Xiaoyi, ed., *Zong tong,* vol. 5, p. 2675.

98. Chiang Diaries, Hoover, October 9, 1945, box 44, folder 11.

99. Chiang Diaries, Hoover, October 11, 1945, box 44, folder 11.

100. Goncharov, Lewis, and Xue Litai, *Uncertain Partners,* p. 11.

101. Sheng, *Battling Western Imperialism,* pp. 111–112, citing Zhonggong zhongyang wenxian yanjiushi (The Archival Research Office of the Central Committee of the CCP), *Mao Zedong nianbu* (Chronology of Mao Zedong) (Peking: People's Publishing House, 1993), vol. 3, pp. 42–43.

102. Chiang Diaries, Hoover, November 4, 1945, box 44, folder 12.

103. Ibid.; Du Yuming, *Wo zai Lizo Shen zhanyi zhong de jingli* (My Experience in the Liao-Shenyang Campaign: Memoirs of Former KMT Generals) (Peking: Cultural and Historical Data Press, 1985), pp. 520–525.

104. Chiang Diaries, Hoover, November 9, 1945, box 44, folder 12.

105. Chiang Diaries, Hoover, November 6, 1945, box 44, folder 12.

106. Chiang Diaries, Hoover, November 12, 1945, box 44, folder 12.

107. Qin Xiaoyi, *Zong tong*, vol. 5, p. 2717.

108. Chang Kia-ngau, *Last Chance in Manchuria: The Diary of Chang Kia-ngau*, ed. Donald G. Gillin and Ramon H. Myers (Stanford, Calif.: Hoover Institution Press, 1989), p. 118.

109. Editor's notes, November 12, 1945, in Qin Xiaoyi, *Zong tong*, vol. 5, p. 2722.

110. Wedemeyer, *Reports*, pp. 359–361.

111. Ibid., pp. 346, 451.

112. Chiang Diaries, Hoover, November 15, 1945, box 44, folder 12.

113. Chiang Diaries, Hoover, November 17, 1945, box 44, folder 12. Chiang recalled this November 1945 talk in a diary entry for August 7, 1951—see Qin Xiaoyi, *Zong tong*, vol. 5, p. 4680. In his diary entry on November 16, 1945, he simply mentions that he had two meetings with military officers: see Chiang Diaries, Hoover, November 15, 1945, box 44, folder 12.

114. Chiang Diaries, Hoover, November 17, 1945, box 44, folder 12.

115. Chang Kia-ngau, *Last Chance in Manchuria*, p. 33.

116. Ibid., p. 158; Goncharov, Lewis, and Xue Litai, *Uncertain Partners*, p. 11.

117. Editor's notes, December 5, 1945, in Qin Xiaoyi, *Zong tong*, p. 2737.

118. Zhang Lingau, "Chiang Ching-kuo Zai Dongbei" (Chiang Ching-kuo in the Northeast), in Literature and Historical Materials Committee of the Political Consultative Conference of Zhejiang Province, *Jiang shi fu zi* (The Chiangs, Father and Son) (Hangzhou: Literature and Historical Materials Committee of the Political Consultative Conference of Zhejiang Province, 1994), pp. 211–240.

119. Chiang Kai-shek, *Soviet Russia in China* (New York: Farrar, Strauss and Cudahay, 1957), p. 232. See also Chiang Diaries, August 7, 1951, in Qin Xiaoyi, *Zong tong*, vol. 10, p. 4753.

120. Larry I. Bland, ed., *The Papers of George Catlett Marshall* (Baltimore: John Hopkins University Press, 2003), vol. 5, p. 372.

121. Sheng, *Battling Western Imperialism*, p. 120. Zhang Baijia, "Zhou Enlai and the Marshall Mission," pp. 208–209.

122. Chiang Diaries, Hoover, December 12, 1945, box 44, folder 13.

123. Feis, *China Tangle*, pp. 418–420; Dorothy Borg and Waldo Heinrichs, *Uncertain Years* (New York: Columbia University Press, 1980), pp. 13–15.

124. Ibid. Levine, *Anvil of Victory*, p. 53.

125. *FRUS (1945–1953)*, vol. 7: *The Far East: China*, pp. 767–769.

126. *White Paper*, pp. 606, 608; Feis, *China Tangle*, p. 420. John Carter Vincent was now director of the Office of Far Eastern Affairs (Feis, *China Tangle*, p. 351). About the same time, Dean G. Acheson became Under-Secretary of State and thus acting Secretary during the frequent absences of Secretary Byrnes.

127. Chiang Diaries, Hoover, December 18, 1945, box 44, folder 13.

128. Ibid.

129. Chiang, December 16, 1945 speech, in Qin Xiaoyi, *Zong tong*, vol. 5, pp. 2743–2744; Huang, *Chiang Kai-shek*, p. 159.

130. Ibid.

131. Conversations with nearly a hundred KMT members who as adults or children lived as internal refugees during the war years.

132. Chiang Diaries, Hoover, October 26, 1945, box 44, folder 11.

133. John Robinson Beal, *Marshall in China* (Toronto: Doubleday Canada, 1970), p. 114.

134. Arthur N. Young, *China's Wartime Finance and Inflation* (Cambridge: Harvard University Press, 1965), pp. 174, 182.

135. Tang Tsou, *America's Failure*, p. 313.

136. Ibid.

137. James C. Kirby, "The Chinese War Economy," in James C. Hsiung and Steven I. Levine, *China's Bitter Victory* (Armonk, N.Y.: M. E. Sharpe, 1992), p. 204.

138. Wedemeyer, *Reports*, p. 363.

139. Chen Lifu, *The Storm Clouds Clear over China* (Stanford, Calif.: Hoover Institution Press, 1994), pp. 184, 185.

140. I personally experienced Chiang's weak handshake at receptions. John F. Melby, an embassy officer in Chungking, reported the "shock" of the famous general's soft grip. He also noted that Marshall's eyes "don't meet yours," which was very unlike the Generalissimo's steely gaze. See John F. Melby, *The Mandate of Heaven* (Toronto: University of Toronto Press, 1968), p. 55.

141. Beal, *Marshall in China*, p. 125.

142. Wedemeyer, *Reports*, p. 382.

143. *FRUS (1945–1953)*, vol. 7: *The Far East: China*, pp. 795–797. Marshall also said that if the Communists did not compromise, "they too would lose the sympathy of the American people." See Bland, *Papers of George Catlett Marshall*, p. 400.

144. *FRUS (1945–1953)*, vol. 7: *The Far East: China*, pp. 797, 804; Bland, *Papers of George Catlett Marshall*, p. 400.

145. Forrest C. Pogue, *George Marshall: Ordeal and Hope* (New York: Viking, 1966), p. 367.

146. *New York Times*, April 26, 1970.

147. Beal, *Marshall in China*, pp. 400, 607.

148. Bland, *Papers of George Catlett Marshall*, p. 404; *FRUS (1945–1953)*, vol. 7: *The Far East: China*, pp. 848–849.

149. Feis, *China Tangle*, pp. 427–428.

8. Chimera of Victory

1. Chiang Diaries, Hoover, December 30, 1945, box 44, folder 13.

2. Ibid.

3. *White Paper,* p. 137; Larry I. Bland, ed., *George C. Marshall Interviews and Reminiscences for Forrest C. Pogue,* 3d ed. (Lexington, Va.: George C. Marshall Foundation, 1996), p. 409.

4. Chiang Diaries, Hoover, August 7, 1951, box 49, folder 3.

5. Michael M. Sheng, *Battling Western Imperialism: Mao, Stalin, and the United States* (Princeton, N.J.: Princeton University Press, 1997), p. 110.

6. Qin Xiaoyi, *Zong tong,* vol. 6, pp. 2760, 2766.

7. *FRUS (1949),* vol. 8: *The Far East: China,* pp. 137–140: Qin Xiaoyi, *Zong tong,* vol. 6, p. 2768.

8. Chiang Diaries, January 15 and 19, 1946, in Qin Xiaoyi, *Zong tong,* vol. 6, pp. 2759, 2773.

9. Memorandum on Economic Cooperation in Northeast China by Russia, January 21, 1946, in Qin Xiaoyi, *Zong tong,* vol. 6, pp. 2773, 2782.

10. Chang Kia-ngau, *Last Chance in Manchuria* (Stanford, Calif.: Hoover Institution Press, 1989), p. 208.

11. Truman to Secretary Byrnes, January 5, 1946, in Harry S. Truman, *Memoirs by Harry S. Truman, 1945: Year of Decisions* (New York: Konecky & Konecky Military Books, 1999) p. 552.

12. Chiang Diaries, Hoover, January 18, 1946, box 45, folder 2.

13. Larry I. Bland, ed., *The Papers of George Catlett Marshall* (Baltimore: John Hopkins University Press, 2003), vol. 5, p. 420 n.2. Zhou apparently used one-time code pads rather than encrypting machines; thus messages sent from his office to Yan'an and back were not decoded by the Americans.

14. Ibid., p. 444.

15. Chiang Diaries, Hoover, January 22 and 23, 1946, box 45, folder 2.

16. *White Paper,* pp. 139–140.

17. Chiang Diaries, Hoover, January 31 and February 2, 1946, box 45, folder 2.

18. Zhang Baijia, "Zhou Enlai and the Marshall Mission," in Larry I. Bland ed., *George C. Marshall's Mediation Mission to China, December 1945–January 1947* (Lexington, Va.: George C. Marshall Foundation, 1998), p. 203.

19. Bland, *Marshall's Mediation Mission,* pp. 215–218.

20. Tang Tsou, *America's Failure in China, 1941–1950* (Chicago: University of Chicago Press, 1963), p. 411.

21. Ibid., p. 411; *White Paper,* pp. 140–143.

22. Bland, *Papers of George Catlett Marshall,* pp. 434, 435.

23. Chiang Diaries, Hoover, January 22 and February 2, 1946, box 45, folders 2, 3.

24. According to Chiang's diary, Marshall told him he was satisfied with the trip but that Mao was "wiley." Chiang Diaries, Hoover, March 8, 1946, box 45, folder 4. In his official reports, Marshall said that his talk with Mao "was frank to an extreme," but that the Chairman had "promised complete cooperation."

25. Bland, *Papers of George Catlett Marshall,* p. 490.

26. Steven I. Levine, *Anvil of Victory* (New York: Columbia University Press, 1987), p. 73.

27. Editor's note, March 7, 1946, in Qin Xiaoyi, *Zong tong,* vol. 6, p. 2819.

28. Bland, *Papers of George Catlett Marshall,* pp. 497, 501.

29. Sheng, *Battling Western Imperialism,* p. 132.

30. Levine, *Anvil of Victory,* p. 80.

31. Sheng, *Battling Western Imperialism,* p. 132; Editor's note, March 19, 1946, in Qin Xiaoyi, *Zong tong,* vol. 5, p. 2828.

32. *New York Times,* March 17, 1946, p. 26.

33. Chiang Diaries, Hoover, March 13, 1946, box 45, folder 4.

34. Chang Kia-ngau, *Last Chance,* p. 300.

35. Dorothy Borg and Waldo Heinrichs, *Uncertain Years: Chinese American Relations, 1947–1950* (New York: Columbia University Press, 1980), p. 10.

36. Chiang Diaries, Hoover, March 31 and April 1, 1946, box 45, folders 4, 5.

37. Sheng, *Battling Western Imperialism,* p. 135.

38. *New York Times,* April 30, 1946.

39. Bland, *Papers of George Catlett Marshall,* pp. 525, 530.

40. *White Paper,* p. 149.

41. Bland, *Papers of George Catlett Marshall,* p. 528.

42. Ibid.

43. *White Paper,* p. 151.

44. Editor's notes, April 2 and 3, 1946, in Qin Xiaoyi, *Zong tong,* vol. 6, p. 2848.

45. Bland, *Papers of George Catlett Marshall,* p. 529; *White Paper,* p. 151.

46. Zhang Baijia, "Zhou Enlai and the Marshall Mission," p. 221.

47. Bland, *Papers of George Catlett Marshall,* p. 534; *White Paper,* 151.

48. Chiang Diaries, Hoover, April 19, 1946, box 45, folder 5.

49. Chiang Diaries, Hoover, April 26, 1946, box 45, folder 5.

50. Bland, *Papers of George Catlett Marshall,* p. 535; Chiang Diaries, Hoover, April 28, 1945, box 45, folder 5.

51. Bland, *Papers of George Catlett Marshall,* p. 5.

52. John Robinson Beal, *Marshall in China* (Toronto: Doubleday Canada, 1970), pp. 27–28.

53. Zhang Baijia, "Zhou Enlai and the Marshall Mission," p. 222.

54. Beal, *Marshall in China,* p. 34.

55. Bland, *Papers of George Catlett Marshall,* p. 556n.

56. Ibid., pp. 543, 566.

57. Chiang Diaries, Hoover, May 11, 1946, box 45, folder 6; Bland, *Papers of George Catlett Marshall,* pp. 552, 548–552.

58. Bland, *Papers of George Catlett Marshall,* p. 562.

59. Sheng, *Battling Western Imperialism,* p. 140.

60. *Bai Chongxi xian sheng fangwen jilu* (Reminiscences of General Bai Chongxi), ed. Guo Dingye, 2 vols., no. 4 in the Oral History Series (Taipei: Institute of Modern History, Academia Sinica, 1984), pp. 815–816.

61. Bland, *Papers of George Catlett Marshall,* pp. 586, 564–565.

62. Chiang's diary records the city's capture as being on May 19. Chiang Diaries, Hoover, May 23, 1946, box 45, folder 6.

63. *Bai Chongxi xian sheng fangwen jilu,* p. 166.

64. Beal, *Marshall in China,* p. 66.

65. Bland, *Papers of George Catlett Marshall,* p. 567.

66. *White Paper,* pp. 156–157.

67. Bland, *Papers of George Catlett Marshall,* p. 578.

68. Ibid., pp. 570, 574, 579, 586.

69. Beal, *Marshall in China,* p. 222.

70. Bland, *Marshall Interviews and Reminiscences,* p. 607.

71. John Leighton Stuart, *The Forgotten Ambassador: The Reports of John Leighton Stuart,* ed. Kenneth W. Rea and John C. Brewer (Boulder, Colo.: Westview, 1981), p. 99.

72. Chiang Diaries, Hoover, May 25, 1946, box 45, folder 6.

73. Chiang Diaries, Hoover, June 6, 1946, box 45, folder 7; Bland, *Papers of George Catlett Marshall,* p. 578.

74. Editor's notes, June 3 and 6, 1946, in Qin Xiaoyi, *Zong tong,* vol. 6, pp. 2922, 2924.

75. Chiang Kai-shek, *Soviet Russia in China* (New York: Farrar, Strauss and Cudahy, 1957), p. 168.

76. Chiang Diaries, Hoover, June 14, 1946, box 45, folder 7.

77. *White Paper,* p. 159.

78. Bland, *Papers of George Catlett Marshall,* p. 589.

79. Ibid., p. 590.

80. Chiang Diaries, Hoover, June 26, 1946, box 45, folder 7.

81. Bland, *Papers of George Catlett Marshall,* p. 614.

82. Beal, *Marshall in China,* p. 109.

83. Chiang Diaries, Hoover, June 30, 1946, box 45, folder 7.

84. Ramon H. Myers, "Frustration, Fortitude, and Friendship: Chiang Kai-shek's Reactions to Marshall's Mission," in Larry I. Bland, ed., *George C. Marshall's Mediation Mission to China, December 1945–January 1947* (Lexington, Va.: George C. Marshall Foundation, 1998), p. 160.

85. Chiang Diaries, Hoover, June 30, 1946, box 45, folder 7.

86. Bland, *Papers of George Catlett Marshall,* p. 618.

87. Chiang Diaries, Hoover, July 14, 1946, box 45, folder 8.

88. *FRUS (1946),* vol. 9: *The Far East: China,* pp. 1295–1297.

89. Bland, *Papers of George Catlett Marshall,* p. 635.

90. Ibid., pp. 634, 637.

91. Myers, "Frustration," p. 159.

92. E. R. Hooton, *The Greatest Tumult: The Chinese Civil War, 1936–1949* (London: Brassey's, 1991), pp. 69–70; Bland, *Papers of George Catlett Marshall,* p. 626.

93. Sheng, *Battling Western Imperialism,* pp. 155–156.

94. Bland, *Papers of George Catlett Marshall,* p. 696.

95. Beal, *Marshall in China,* pp. 122–123; *New York Times,* July 20, 1946, p. 26.

96. Beal, *Marshall in China,* p. 145.

97. Bland, *Papers of George Catlett Marshall,* pp. 632, 668–669. The description of Guling is that of Mrs. Marshall in a letter to a friend.

98. Bland, *Papers of George Catlett Marshall,* p. 635; Beal, *Marshall in China,* pp. 122–123.

99. Albert C. Wedemeyer, *Wedemeyer Reports* (New York: Holt, 1958), pp. 366–370; Bland, *Papers of George Catlett Marshall,* p. 627.

100. Bland, *Papers of George Catlett Marshall,* p. 634.

101. *FEER* 1, no. 4 (November 6, 1946).

102. Bland, *Papers of George Catlett Marshall,* p. 652.

103. Editor's note, August 16, 1946, in Qin Xiaoyi, *Zong tong,* vol. 5, p. 2996.

104. Bland, *Marshall Mission,* p. 229, citing Zhang Baijia.

105. Ibid.

106. Bland, *Papers of George Catlett Marshall,* p. 664.

107. Myers, "Frustration," pp. 162–163.

108. Bland, *Papers of George Catlett Marshall,* p. 687.

109. Beal, *Marshall in China,* pp. 176–177.

110. Ibid.

111. Chiang Diaries, Hoover, September 18, 1946, box 45, folder 10.

112. Bland, *Papers of George Catlett Marshall,* p. 701.

113. Ibid., p. 701.

114. Ibid., p. 703.

115. Myers, "Frustration," p. 165.

116. Bland, *Papers of George Catlett Marshall,* p. 710.

117. Chiang Diaries, Hoover, October 6, 1946, box 45, folder 11; Beal, *Marshall in China,* pp. 225–226; Bland, *Papers of George Catlett Marshall,* p. 710.

118. Bland, *Papers of George Catlett Marshall,* p. 714.

119. *White Paper,* p. 196.

120. Sun Qiming, "Heping tanpan yu neizhan de jiaoxiangqu: Erzhan hou chuqi de Mao Zedong yu Jiang Jieshi" (The Symphony of Peace Talk and Civil War: Mao Zedong and Chiang Kai-Shek during the Early Years of the Post-War Period) (Shanghai: Shanghai People's Press, 1992), pp. 355–364.

121. Bland, *Papers of George Catlett Marshall*, pp. 718–719.

122. Ibid., pp. 720–721; Beal, *Marshall in China*, pp. 246–247; *White Paper*, pp. 198–199.

123. Bland, *Papers of George Catlett Marshall*, p. 726.

124. Ibid., pp. 724–725. Marshall provides the description of the hall.

125. Chiang Diaries, Hoover, October 24, 1946, box 45, folder 11; Bland, *Papers of George Catlett Marshall*, p. 727.

126. Annual Government Report, in Qin Xiaoyi, *Zong tong*, vol. 5, p. 3117.

127. Chiang Diaries, October 26, 1946, in Qin Xiaoyi, *Zong tong*, vol. 6, pp. 3038–3042.

128. Bland, *Papers of George Catlett Marshall*, p. 742; *White Paper*, 206–207.

129. Beal, *Marshall in China*, pp. 279, 280.

130. Bland, *Papers of George Catlett Marshall*, pp. 750, 765.

131. Ibid., pp. 750–752.

132. Beal, *Marshall in China*, p. 313.

133. Bland, *Papers of George Catlett Marshall*, pp. 751–752; *FRUS (1946)* vol. 10: *The Far East: China*, p. 581; Levine, *Anvil of Victory*, p. 131.

134. Beal, *Marshall in China*, p. 315.

135. Chiang Diaries, Hoover, December 5, 1946, box 45, folder 13.

136. Bland, *Papers of George Catlett Marshall*, p. 761; *White Paper*, pp. 605–609.

137. Suzanne Pepper, *Civil War in China* (1978; Berkeley: University of California Press, 1980), pp. 54–57.

138. Beal, *Marshall in China*, pp. 333–334.

139. *White Paper*, p. 218.

140. Chiang Diaries, January, 9, 1947, in Qin Xiaoyi, *Zong tong*, vol. 6, pp. 3114–3115.

141. Bland, *Marshall Interviews and Reminiscences*, p. 575.

142. Chiang Diaries, Hoover, January 10, 1947, box 46, folder 4.

143. Editor's notes, January 12 and February 2, 1947, in Qin Xiaoyi, *Zong tong*, pp. 3115–3116, 3133.

144. Chiang Diaries, Hoover, January 4 and 5, 1947, box 46, folder 4; Odd Arne Westad, *Decisive Encounters* (Stanford, Calif.: Stanford University Press, 2003), p. 64; Edward L. Dreyer, *China at War* (New York: Longman, 1995), p. 330.

145. Westad, *Decisive Encounters*, p. 65.

146. Editor's notes, February 16, 1947, in Qin Xiaoyi, *Zong tong*, vol. 6, pp. 3139, 3143.

147. Chiang Diaries, Hoover, February 28, 1947, box 46, folder 5.

148. Editor's notes, February 16, 1947, in Qin Xiaoyi, *Zong tong*, vol. 6, pp. 3139–3141.

149. Beal, *Marshall in China*, pp. 360–361, Stuart, *Forgotten Ambassador*, p. 65.

150. Stuart, *Forgotten Ambassador*, p. 72.

151. Editor's notes, February 24, 1947, in Qin Xiaoyi, *Zong tong,* vol. 6, p. 3145.

152. Chiang Diaries, Hoover, February 27, 1947, box 46, folder 5.

153. Beal, *Marshall in China,* p. 247.

154. Levine, *Anvil of Victory,* p. 132.

155. *White Paper,* p. 238.

156. Westad, *Decisive Encounters,* p. 78.

157. Ibid., p. 76.

158. Levine, *Anvil of Victory,* p. 184.

159. Westad, *Decisive Encounters,* p. 182.

160. Chen Lifu, *The Storm Clouds Clear over China* (Stanford, Calif.: Hoover Institution Press, 1994), p. 197; *Time,* May 25, 1947.

161. This and the following paragraphs on the uprising are drawn from the balanced account by Lai Tse-han, Ramon H. Myers, and Wei Wou, *A Tragic Beginning: The Taiwan Uprising of February 28, 1947* (Stanford, Calif.: Stanford University Press, 1991); *White Paper,* p. 309.

162. Chiang Diaries, February 28, 1947, in Qin Xiaoyi, *Zong tong,* vol. 6, p. 3148.

163. Document on the Cause and Resolution of the Taiwan Incident, March 10, 1947, in Qin Xiaoyi, *Zong tong,* vol. 6, p. 3153.

164. *FRUS (1947),* vol. 7: *The Far East: China,* p. 442.

165. Editor's notes, March 5–17, 1947, in Qin Xiaoyi, *Zong tong,* vol. 6, pp. 3150–3158.

166. Beal, *Marshall in China,* p. 247.

167. *White Paper,* p. 243.

168. Stuart, *Forgotten Ambassador,* pp. 90–92; Chiang's Announcement on the State Council, May 18, 1947, in Qin Xiaoyi, *Zong tong,* vol. 6, p. 3188.

169. Chiang Diaries, Hoover, April 2, 1947, box 46, folder 7.

170. U.S. Central Intelligence Agency, "Chinese Capabilities for Control of All of China," ORE 77–48, December 10, 1948, p. 2, in *Tracking the Dragon, National Intelligence Estimates on China during the Era of Mao, 1948–1976,* (Pittsburgh: U.S. Government Printing Office, 2004); Levine, *Anvil of Victory,* p. 149; E. R. Hooton, *The Greatest Tumult: The Chinese Civil War, 1936–1949* (London: Brassey's, 1991), pp. 91, 94.

171. Dreyer, *China at War,* pp. 330–331; Levine, *Anvil of Victory,* p. 154.

172. Levine, *Anvil of Victory,* p. 240.

173. Pepper, *Civil War in China,* pp. 242–243.

174. Editor's note, April 30, 1947, in Qin Xiaoyi, *Zong tong,* vol. 6, p. 3197.

175. Chiang's speech commemorating Zhang Lingfu, May 24, 1947, in Qin Xiaoyi, *Zong tong,* vol. 6, p. 3218.

176. Chiang Diaries, Hoover, May 24, 1947, box 46, folder 8.

177. Pepper, *Civil War in China,* pp. 58–65, 89–93; Stuart, *Forgotten Ambassador,* pp. 136, 104, 106.

178. Pepper, *Civil War in China,* pp. 64–65. Pepper gives only the figure for Chungking.

179. Ibid., pp. 67–68.

180. In February 1947, Chiang said it was $300 million. Editor's note, February 21, 1947, in Qin Xiaoyi, *Zong tong,* vol. 6, p. 3393.

181. Stuart, *Forgotten Ambassador,* p. 175.

182. Hooten, *Tumult,* pp. 89–90; Dreyer, *China at War,* pp. 330–331.

183. Chiang's cable to Xiong Shihui, in Qin Xiaoyi, *Zong tong,* vol. 6, pp. 3231, 3263, 3281.

184. Hooten, *Tumult,* pp. 89–90; Dreyer, *China at War,* pp. 330–331; Wedemeyer, *Reports,* p. 382.

185. Yu-ming Shaw, *An American Missionary in China: John Leighton Stuart and Chinese-American Relations* (Cambridge: Harvard University Press, 1992), p. 206.

186. *White Paper,* p. 386.

187. Stuart, *Forgotten Ambassador,* p. 133; *White Paper,* p. 386.

188. Wedemeyer, *Reports,* p. 388.

189. *White Paper,* p. 257; Wedemeyer, *Reports,* p. 389.

190. Chiang Diaries, Hoover, August 19, 1948, box 46, folder 11.

191. Wedemeyer, *Reports,* pp. 397–398; *White Paper,* p. 260.

9. The Great Failure

1. Te-kong Tong and Li Tsung-jen (Li Congren), *The Memoirs of Li Tsung-jen* (Boulder, Colo.: Westview, 1979), p. 453.

2. Du Yuming, "Xing rung Liaoxi-Shenyang zhanyi" (Description of the West Liaoning–Mukden Campaign) in *Liaoxi-Shenyang zhanyi qinli ji: yuan guo min dang jiang ling hui yi lu* (Experiences in the West Liaoning–Mukden Campaign: Memoirs of Former Kuomintang Generals) (Peking: Cultural and Historical Data Press, 1985), pp. 1–3; E. R. Hooten, *The Greatest Tumult: The Chinese Civil War, 1936–1949* (London: Brassey's, 1991), p. 92; Edward L. Dreyer, *China at War* (New York: Longman, 1995), p. 331.

3. John Leighton Stuart, *The Forgotten Ambassador: The Reports of John Leighton Stuart,* ed. Kenneth W. Rea and John C. Brewer (Boulder, Colo.: Westview, 1981), p. 144.

4. Chiang cable to Xiong Shihui, August 5, 1947, in Qin Xiaoyi, *Zong tong,* vol. 6, p. 3281.

5. *White Paper,* pp. 261–262.

6. Ibid., pp. 324, 348, 371–377.

7. Dreyer, *China at War,* p. 93; Chiang Diaries, October 2, 1947, in Qin Xiaoyi, *Zong tong,* vol. 6, p. 3316.

8. Suzanne Pepper, "The KMT-CCP Conflict, 1945–1949: The Nationalist Era

in China," in Lloyd Eastman, ed., *The Nationalist Era in China* (Cambridge, Eng.: Cambridge University Press, 1991), pp. 340–341; Hooten, *Greatest Tumult,* p. 94.

9. Chiang Diaries, Hoover, November 10, 1947, box 46, folder 14.

10. Stuart, *Forgotten Ambassador,* p. 157.

11. Ibid., p. 154.

12. Amemb Nanking Radiogram, December 19, 1947, *FRUS (1947),* vol. 7: *The Far East: China,* p. 411.

13. Ibid.

14. Mao Zedong, *Selected Works* (Peking: Foreign Languages Press, 1961), p. 172.

15. Hooten, *Greatest Tumult,* pp. 94–95.

16. Du Yuming, "Xing rung Liaoxi-Shenyang zhanyi," pp. 5–6.

17. Ibid., pp. 5–9; Chiang Diaries, Hoover, January 11 and 12, 1948, box 41, folder 17.

18. Dreyer, *China at War,* p. 330; Hooten, *Greatest Tumult,* p. 96.

19. Chiang Diaries, Hoover, February 3, 1948, box 46, folder 18.

20. Wei Lihuang's report, February 5, 1948, in Qin Xiaoyi, *Zong tong,* vol. 7, pp. 3381, 3382.

21. Du Yuming, "Xing rung Liaoxi-Shenyang zhanyi," p. 9. According to Du, Chiang's order for a general retreat except for rear guard divisions was sent in February and then repeated.

22. Ibid., p. 8; Chiang Diaries, February 24, 1948, in Qin Xiaoyi, *Zong tong,* vol. 7, p. 3395.

23. Chiang Diaries, February 28, 1948, in Qin Xiaoyi, *Zong tong,* vol. 7, pp. 3397–3398; Du Yuming, "Xing rung Liaoxi-Shenyang zhanyi," p. 9.

24. Du Yuming, "Xing rung Liaoxi-Shenyang zhanyi," p. 9.

25. *White Paper,* p. 329. Although he had told Wei a week earlier to "move the best armies in the Northeast to Jinzhou," on March 1 Chiang wrote that it was time to make "the final decision regarding Manchuria," editor's note, March 1, 1948, in Qin Xiaoyi, *Zong tong,* vol. 7, p. 3399. Presumably, Chiang was referring to a complete evacuation of Manchuria including a retreat from Jinzhou to a point south of the Great Wall.

26. Stuart, *Forgotten Ambassador,* pp. 166–167.

27. *FEER* 4, no. 5 (February 4, 1948): 105; *FEER* 4, no. 6 (February 12, 1948): 121.

28. Stuart, *Forgotten Ambassador,* p. 189.

29. Odd Arne Westad, *Decisive Encounters* (Stanford, Calif.: Stanford University Press, 2003), p. 186; *FEER* 4, no. 13 (March 31, 1948): 304. Earlier, however, as a stopgap measure, the United States did provide twenty C-46 transport planes, one million rounds of submachine-gun ammunition, and some US$45 million in grain.

30. Stuart, *Forgotten Ambassador,* p. 200.

31. Du Yuming, "Xing rung Liaoxi-Shenyang zhanyi," p. 9. While General Barr

knew about Chiang's orders to Wei to evacuate his main forces to Jinzhou, he reported on one occasion that Chiang told him that "political considerations precluded the abandonment of Changchun, the ancient capital of Manchuria." Chiang's diaries and the memoirs of Wei, Du, and others confirm that Chiang by this time had definitely decided on a complete pullout (both statements documented in *White Paper,* pp. 325–326).

32. Chiang Diaries, Hoover, March 25, 1948, box 46, folder 19.

33. Chen Lifu, *The Storm Clouds Clear over China* (Stanford, Calif.: Hoover Institution Press, 1994), pp. 198–200; Stuart, *Forgotten Ambassador,* pp. 164–165.

34. Chiang speech to National Assembly, March 29, 1948, in Qin Xiaoyi, *Zong tong,* vol. 7, pp. 3416–3420.

35. *Time,* January 6, 1948.

36. Te-kong Tong and Li Tsung-jen, *Memoirs,* p. 465.

37. Stuart, *Forgotten Ambassador,* pp. 193–194.

38. *White Paper,* pp. 327–329.

39. Du Yuming, "Xing rung Liaoxi-Shenyang zhanyi," pp. 12–13.

40. Editor's note, August 7, 1951, in Qin Xiaoyi, *Zong tong,* vol. 10, pp. 4784–4785.

41. Sergei N. Goncharov, John W. Lewis, and Xue Litai, *Uncertain Partners: Stalin, Mao, and the Korean War* (Stanford, Calif.: Stanford University Press, 1993), p. 25.

42. Hooten, *Greatest Tumult,* p. 99.

43. Du Yuming, "Xing rung Liaoxi-Shenyang zhanyi," p. 15.

44. Ibid.

45. Ibid., p. 16.

46. Ibid., p. 14.

47. "General Barr's Report," in *White Paper,* p. 333.

48. Chiang Diaries, October 5, 1948, in Qin Xiaoyi, *Zong tong,* vol. 7, p. 3496.

49. Jonathan Spence, *The Search for Modern China* (New York: W. W. Norton, 1990), pp. 501–502.

50. See speech by Ching-kuo in Shanghai Municipal Archives, file Q6–7–90, n.d.

51. Interview with Chen Zhijing, an associate of Chiang Ching-kuo, Shanghai, October 2, 1995.

52. Du Yuming, "Xing rung Liaoxi-Shenyang zhanyi," p. 17.

53. American Consulate General Hong Kong, dispatch no. 45, September 25, 1948, National Archives, RG 59, General Records of the Department of State, decimal file 1945–1949, box 7275.

54. "General Barr's Report," p. 335.

55. Gu Chenhuang (chief of staff of the 130th Division), "Wu Shi san Lu zhun zai Dongbei," in *Liaoxi-Shenyang zhanyi qinli ji: yuan guo min dang jiang ling hui yi lu* (Experiences in the West Liaoning–Mukden Campaign: Memoirs of For-

mer Kuomintang Generals) (Peking: Cultural and Historical Data Press, 1985), pp. 600–602.

56. Chiang Diaries, Hoover, October 10, 1948, box 47, folder 5.

57. Chiang Diaries, Hoover, October 10–16, 1948, box 47, folder 5; Hooten, *Greatest Tumult,* p. 100; Du Yuming, "Xing rung Liaoxi-Shenyang zhanyi," pp. 17–20.

58. Liao Yaoxiang, "Shemma fa sheng zai Liaoxi zhanyi" (What Happened during the Western Liaoning Campaign), in *Liaoxi Shenyang Zhanyi qingli ji: Yuan guo min dang jiang ling hui yi lu* (Experiences in the West Liaoning–Mukden Campaign: Memoirs of Former Kuomintang Generals) (Peking: Cultural and Historical Data Press, 1985), p. 174.

59. Du Yuming, "Xing rung Liaoxi-Shenyang zhanyi," p. 19.

60. Ibid., p. 24. Du Yuming, in recalling the events of 1945, confirms that Chiang's original plan was as he stated.

61. Liao Yaoxiang, "Shemma fa sheng zai Liaoxi zhanyi," p. 174; Hooten, *Greatest Tumult,* pp. 101–102.

62. Chiang Diaries, Hoover, October 30, 1948, box 47, folder 5.

63. Levine, *Anvil of Victory,* p. 136.

64. Boorman, *Biographical Dictionary,* vol. 3, p. 406.

65. Editor's note, November 10, 1948, in Qin Xiaoyi, *Zong tong,* vol. 7, p. 3526.

66. Chiang Diaries, August 7, 1951, in Qin Xiaoyi, *Zong tong,* vol. 10, pp. 4814–4816.

67. *Time,* January 6, 1948.

68. *White Paper,* p. 321.

69. I documented and discussed this assumption in *The Generalissimo's Son* (Cambridge: Harvard University Press, 2000).

70. *White Paper,* p. 333.

71. Chiang record of conversation, October 29, 1948, in Qin Xiaoyi, *Zong tong,* vol. 7, p. 3514.

72. Dreyer, *China at War,* p. 338; Hooten, *Greatest Tumult,* pp. 146–148.

73. Chiang Diaries, Hoover, November 20, 23, and 27, 1948, box 47, folder 7.

74. Chiang Wei-kuo interview, Taipei, June 10, 1995.

75. Stuart, *Forgotten Ambassador,* p. 284.

76. Chen Bulei's letter, November 13, 1948, in Qin Xiaoyi, *Zong tong,* vol. 7, p. 3528.

77. Chiang's message to Truman of November 9, 1948, in Qin Xiaoyi, *Zong tong,* vol. 7, p. 3524; Dorothy Borg and Waldo Heinrichs, *Uncertain Years: Chinese American Relations, 1947–1950* (New York: Columbia University Press, 1980), p. 65.

78. Quoted in Qin Xiaoyi, ed., *Zong tong,* vol. 6, p. 3541; Stuart, *Forgotten Ambassador,* pp. 280, 291–292; Laura Tyson Li, *Madame Chiang Kai-shek* (New York: Atlantic Monthly Press, 2006), p. 297.

79. Stuart, *Forgotten Ambassador,* p. 284.

80. *Time,* January 6, 1948.

81. Editor's note, in Qin Xiaoyi, ed., *Zong tong,* vol. 6, p. 3543.

82. *White Paper,* p. 323; Chiang Diaries, December 13, 1948, in Qin Xiaoyi, ed., *Zong tong,* vol. 6, p. 3551.

83. Borg and Heinrichs, *Uncertain Years,* p. 76.

84. Chiang Diaries, Hoover, December 12 and 31, 1948, box 47, folder 7.

85. Hooten, *Greatest Tumult,* pp. 112, 113, 120.

86. Chiang Diaries, Hoover, December 6, 1948, box 47, folder 7.

87. Hooten, *Greatest Tumult,* p. 148; Chiang Diaries, Hoover, December 26, 1948, box 47, folder 7.

88. Chiang Diaries, Hoover, December 31, 1949, box 47, folder 7.

89. *New York Times,* January 1, 1949.

90. Chiang Diaries, Hoover, December 31, 1948, box 47, folder 7.

91. Stuart, *Forgotten Ambassador,* p. 294.

92. Chiang Diaries, January 1, 8, and 11, 1949, box 47, folder 7.

93. Central Intelligence Agency (CIA), "Probable Developments in China, ORE-45–49, June 16, 1949," in *Tracking the Dragon: National Intelligence Estimates on China during the Era of Mao, 1948–1976* (Pittsburgh: U.S. Government Printing Office, 2004), p. 15; Chiang Diaries, January 4, 1949, in Qin Xiaoyi, *Zong tong,* vol. 7, p. 3571.

94. Stuart, *Forgotten Ambassador,* pp. 297–298.

95. Michael M. Sheng, *Battling Western Imperialism: Mao, Stalin, and the United States* (Princeton, N.J.: Princeton University Press, 1997), p. 164.

96. A Chinese American who was a close friend of Zhang Xueliang told me about this experience.

97. Interview with Sha Gongchuan, Chiang Kai-shek's pilot and military aide, Taipei, May 22, 1996; interview with Nancy Chiang, daughter-in-law of Chiang Ching-kuo, Taipei, May 22, 1996.

98. Sha Gongchuan interview, May 22, 1996.

99. Ibid. See also the National Palace Museum's website at http://www.npm.gov.tw.

100. Chiang Diaries, Hoover, January 8, 1949, box 47, folder 9.

101. Chiang Diaries, Hoover, January 10, 1949, box 47, folder 9.

102. Chiang Diaries, Hoover, January 22, 1949, box 47, folder 9.

103. Brian Crozier, *The Man Who Lost China* (New York: Charles Scribner's Sons, 1976), p. 330.

104. Sha Gongchuan interview, May 22, 1996.

105. Ibid.

106. Interview with Wang Chi, Washington, D.C., November 20, 2002; Boorman, *Biographical Dictionary,* vol. 2, p. 51.

107. Boorman, *Biographical Dictionary,* vol. 2, p. 51; Chiang Diaries, Hoover, January 24, 1949, box 47, folder 9.

108. Boorman, *Biographical Dictionary,* vol. 2, p. 51.

109. Zhou Hongtao, *Jiang Gong yu wu* (The President in My Own Eyes) (Taipei: World Vision Publishing Company, 2003), p. 90.

110. "Memorandum of A. I. Mikoyan to the Presidium on His January and February Visit to China," doc. P2375, cited in Andrei Ledovsky, "Mikoyan's Secret Mission to China in January and February 1949," *Far Eastern Affairs,* vol. 2: *Moscow* (1995): 73–93; Goncharov, Lewis, and Xue Litai, *Uncertain Partners,* pp. 40–44; Sheng, *Battling Western Imperialism,* p. 166.

111. "Memorandum of A. I. Mikoyan to the Presidium on His January and February Visit to China."

112. Ibid.; Te-kong Tong and Li Tsung-jen, *Memoirs,* pp. 502–503, 508, 512.

113. Borg and Heinrichs, *Uncertain Years,* p. 79; David Finkelstein, *Washington's Taiwan Dilemma, 1949–1950* (Fairfax, Va.: George Mason University Press, 1993), p. 126.

114. Finkelstein, *Taiwan Dilemma,* pp. 120–146.

115. *Lian he bao,* Taipei, March 22, 1988. According to Professor Zhu Hongyuan, there is a record of the meeting in MacArthur's appointment book but no record of the conversation.

116. Interview with Professor Zhu Hongyuan, Taipei, October 21, 2003. Zhu, a Taiwan scholar specializing in Sun Liren, interviewed Sun's daughter. See also ibid.

117. Chiang Ching-kuo, *Chiang Ching-kuo xian sheng zhuan zhi* (Autobiography of Chiang Ching-kuo) (Taipei: Government Information Office, 1989), vol. 2, pp. 216–217.

118. Ibid., pp. 380–399.

119. Tang Tsou, *America's Failure in China, 1941–1950* (Chicago: University of Chicago Press, 1963), p. 497. Senator Tom Connally declared in a Senate debate on September 9, 1949, that the amount was US$300 million. Li Congren states that the total value of gold and U.S. notes held by the Chinese Treasury in Shanghai in August 1948 was US$350 million (see Te-kong Tong and Li Tsung-jen, *Memoirs,* pp. 506–507). According to Livingston T. Merchant, gold stock on the island in April 1949 was "reliably reported at some two million ounces" (Finkelstein, *Taiwan Dilemma,* p. 150). Zhou Hungtao Chiang's secretary at the time of the gold transfer, wrote that 200,000 liang or 10 million grams of the metal were left in Shanghai (Zhou Hongtao, *Jiang Gong yu wu,* n.p.).

120. Chiang Ching-kuo, *Chiang Ching-kuo Xi'ansheng zhuan ji,* vol. 2, p. 221.

121. Sha Gongchuan interview, May 22, 1996.

122. Chiang Diaries, Hoover, March 25, 1949, box 47, folder 11; April 22, 1949, box 47, folder 12.

123. Crozier, *Man Who Lost China,* p. 332.

124. Te-kong Tong and Li Tsung-jen, *Memoirs,* p. 515; Chiang Diaries, Hoover, April 22, 1949, box 47, folder 12.

125. Ibid.

126. Chen Jian, *Mao's China and the Cold War* (Chapel Hill: University of North Carolina Press, 2001), p. 70.

127. Sheng, *Battling Western Imperialism,* p. 166.

128. *FRUS (1949),* vol. 8: *The Far East: China,* pp. 357–360.

129. Warren Cohen, "Conversations with Chinese Friends: Zhou Enlai's Associates Reflect on Chinese-American Relations in the 1940s and the Korean War," *Diplomatic History* 2, no. 3 (1987): 288.

130. Dreyer, *China at War,* p. 345; Chiang Diaries, April 25, 1949, in Qin Xiaoyi, ed., *Zong tong,* vol. 7, p. 3633.

131. Sha Gongchuan interview, May 22, 1996.

132. Ibid.

133. Chiang Diaries, Hoover, May 2 and 3, 1949, box 47, folder 12.

134. The U.S. consulate general reported secondhand information that the Generalissimo and Ching-kuo were still in Shanghai as of May 18. See Radiogram to Department of State, May 19, 1949, *FRUS (1949),* vol. 8: *The Far East: China,* p. 334.

135. Tang Tsou, *America's Failure in China,* p. 451.

136. *Jiang Jingguo zi shu* (Chiang Ching-kuo's Diaries) (Changsha: Hunan People's Press, 1988), p. 216.

137. Sha Gongchuan interview, May 22, 1996. Governor Wei had ended martial law in 1948.

138. Interview with Mao Gaowen, Taipei, 2003.

139. American Consulate General Taipei radiogram to Secretary of State, May 18, 1949, National Archives, RG 59, box 7387.

10. Streams in the Desert

1. Chiang Diaries, Hoover, July 6, 1949, box 47, folder 15; Hung-mao Tien, *The Great Transition: Political and Social Change in the Republic of China* (Stanford, Calif.: Hoover Institution Press, 1989), pp. 66–67.

2. Interview with Sha Gongchuan, Taipei, May 22 and 29, 1997.

3. Ibid.; Qin Xiaoyi, *Zong tong,* vol. 7, p. 3661.

4. Denny Roy, *Taiwan: A Political History* (Ithaca, N.Y.: Cornell University Press, 2003), p. 76.

5. U.S. Central Intelligence Agency, "Probable Developments in China," ORE 45–49, June 16, 1949, in *Tracking the Dragon: National Intelligence Estimates on China during the Era of Mao, 1948–1976* (Pittsburgh: U.S. Government Printing Office, 2004), p. 37.

6. *FEER* 6, no. 16 (April 20, 1949): 495.

7. *FEER* 8, no. 4 (January 26, 1950): 116; *FEER* 9, no. 11 (September 14, 1950): 307; *FEER* 7, no. 21 (November 1950): 665; Boorman, *Biographical Dictionary,* vol. 4, p. 41.

8. David Finkelstein, *Washington's Taiwan Dilemma, 1949–1950* (Fairfax, Va.: George Mason University Press, 1993), p. 170.

9. *FEER* 6, no. 18 (May 4, 1949): 545; Hung-mao Tien, *Great Transition,* pp. 22–23.

10. Mao Zedong, *On People's Democratic Dictatorship* (Peking: Foreign Languages Press, 1952), p. 10.

11. Sergei N. Goncharov, John W. Lewis, and Xue Litai, *Uncertain Partners: Stalin, Mao, and the Korean War* (Stanford, Calif.: Stanford University Press, 1993), pp. 72–76.

12. Chiang Diaries, Hoover, December 31, 1949, box 47, folder 20.

13. Finkelstein, *Washington's Taiwan Dilemma,* p. 171, citing U.S. Consul General radiogram to Secretary of State, July 14, 1949.

14. Te-kong Tong and Li Tsung-jen (Li Congren), *The Memoirs of Li Tsung-jen* (Boulder, Colo.: Westview, 1979), pp. 529–541.

15. *White Paper,* pp. 311–359.

16. Chiang Diaries, Hoover, August 24, 26, 29, and 30, 1949, box 47, folder 16.

17. Boorman, *Biographical Dictionary,* vol. 4, p. 7.

18. American Embassy Taipei cable to Department of State, September 15, 1949, National Archives, RG 59, box 7387.

19. Consul General at Taipei cable, November 3, 1949, *FRUS (1949),* vol. 9: *The Far East: China,* pp. 406–407.

20. Consul General at Taipei cable, November 6, 1949, *FRUS (1949),* vol. 9: *The Far East: China,* pp. 411–412; Finkelstein, *Washington's Taiwan Dilemma,* pp. 191–192.

21. American Embassy Taipei cable to Department of State, November 5, 1949, National Archives, RG 59, box 7387.

22. Chiang Diaries, Hoover, November 9–13, 1949, box 37, folder 19.

23. Wang Sheng, answers to my written questions, spring 1996.

24. Chiang Diaries, Hoover, November 19, 1949, box 37, folder 19.

25. Chiang Ching-kuo, *Chiang Ching-kuo xian sheng zhuan zhi* (Autobiography of Chiang Ching-kuo) (Taipei: Government Information Office, 1989), vol. 1, p. 68.

26. Chiang Diaries, Hoover, December 12, 1949, box 47, folder 19.

27. Te-kong Tong and Li Tsung-jen, *Memoirs,* p. 475.

28. Chiang Diaries, Hoover, November 23 and 29, 1949, box 47, folder 19.

29. Chiang Diaries, Hoover, November 30, 1949, box 47, folder 19.

30. Boorman, *Biographical Dictionary,* vol. 2, p. 177.

31. Editor's note, December 9, 1949, in Qin Xiaoyi, *Zong tong,* vol. 7, p. 3847.

32. Sha Gongchuan interview, May 22, 1996.

33. Brian Crozier, *The Man Who Lost China* (New York: Charles Scribner's Sons, 1976), p. 344.

34. Tang Tsou, *America's Failure in China, 1941–1950* (Chicago: University of Chicago Press, 1963), p. 501.

35. Chiang Diaries, Hoover, December 25 and 31, 1949, box 47, folder 20.

36. Hollington K. Tong, *Chiang Kai-shek,* rev. ed. (Taipei: China Publishing Company, 1953), p. 477.

37. Tang Tsou, *America's Failure,* pp. 512–513.

38. Memorandum of Conversation, Dean Acheson, Omar N. Bradley, et al., December 29, 1949, National Archives, RG 59, box 7387.

39. Tang Tsou, *America's Failure,* p. 529; John W. Garver, *Chinese-Soviet Relations, 1937–1945* (New York: Oxford University Press, 1988), p. 20.

40. Chiang Diaries, Hoover, January 6 and 7, 1950, box 48, folder 2.

41. Chiang Diaries, Hoover, January 6, 1950, in Qin Xiaoyi, *Zong tong,* vol. 9, p. 4120.

42. Tang Tsou, *America's Failure,* p. 529; U.S. Central Intelligence Agency, "Prospects for an Early Successful Chinese Communist Attack on Taiwan," July 26, 1950, IM-312, D/FE, obtained by FOI request.

43. Chiang Diaries, Hoover, January 5 and March 13, 1950, box 48, folders 2, 4.

44. Chiang Diaries, Hoover, February 2, 13, 14, 16, and March 24, 1950, box 48, folders 3, 4.

45. Memo from Leo Soong to Dr. Elena Danielson, February 21, 2005, Hoover Institution Archives, provided to me by Mr. Soong.

46. Chiang Diaries, Hoover, January 26 and February 2, 3, and 20, 1950, box 48, folders 2, 3; Peter Wang, "A Bastion Created, a Regime Reformed, an Economy Re-Engineered, 1949–1970," in Murray A Rubinstein, ed., *Taiwan: A New History* (Armonk, N.Y.: M. E. Sharpe, 1999), p. 323.

47. Te-kong Tong and Li Tsung-jen, *Memoirs,* p. 493. In a May 25, 1996, interview in Taipei, Wang Sheng said that in the 1949–1951 period more than 2,700 Communist agents were found.

48. Wang Sheng interview, May 25, 1996.

49. Allen Whiting, "Mystery Man of Formosa," *Saturday Evening Post,* March 12, 1955, p. 117.

50. Interview with Zhu Hongyuan, Taipei, October 20, 2003. Also see Chiang Diaries, May 12, 1950, in Qin Xiaoyi, *Zong tong,* vol. 9, p. 4249.

51. Chiang Diaries, Hoover, January 12, 1950, box 48, folder 2.

52. Ibid., p. 4124; Roy, *Taiwan,* p. 11.

53. Tang Tsou, *America's Failure,* p. 532.

54. Chiang Diaries, Hoover, January 15, 16, and 18, 1950, box 48, folder 2.

55. Chiang Diaries, Hoover, January 18, 1950, box 48, folder 2.

56. Goncharov, Lewis, and Xue Litai, *Uncertain Partners,* p. 101. Goncharov, however, believes there was considerable uncertainty in Peking and Moscow about what the United States would do in either case. Tang Tsou describes the pulling and tugging in America on the Taiwan issue, but underscores that even the arch conservatives seemed to hesitate at the prospect of an actual war with China over Taiwan. See Tang Tsou, *America's Failure,* pp. 520–551.

57. Chen Jian, *Mao's China and the Cold War* (Chapel Hill: University of North Carolina Press, 2001), pp. 87–88.

58. Ibid., pp. 85–90; Odd Arne Westad, *Decisive Encounters* (Stanford, Calif.: Stanford University Press, 2003), p. 319.

59. Chiang speech at the Academy of Revolutionary Study and Practice, January 30, 1950, in Qin Xiaoyi, *Zong tong,* vol. 9, p. 4141.

60. Chiang Diaries, Hoover, February 14 and 16, 1950, box 48, folder 3.

61. Interview with Chiang Wei-kuo, Taipei, June 5, 1996.

62. Chiang Diaries, Hoover, February 14, 19, and March 1, 1950, box 48, folders 3, 4.

63. Boorman, *Biographical Dictionary,* vol. 4, pp. 29–31.

64. Chiang Diaries, Hoover, March 3, 1950, box 48, folder 4.

65. Westad, *Decisive Encounters,* p. 302; E. R. Hooton, *The Greatest Tumult: The Chinese Civil War, 1936–1949* (London: Brassey's, 1991), pp. 168–169.

66. Interview with Hao Bocun, Taipei, April 3, 2003.

67. Chiang Diaries, Hoover, May 1, 9, and 18, 1950, box 48, folder 6.

68. Chiang Diaries, Hoover, May 21, 1950, box 48, folder 6.

69. Hung-mao Tien, *Great Transition,* p. 67.

70. Bruce Dickson, "The Lessons of Defeat: The Reorganization of the Kuomintang on Taiwan, 1950–1952," *China Quarterly* 133 (March 1993): 56–84.

71. Chiang Diaries, Hoover, February 9, 14, May 16, 30, 31, and June 9, 1950, box 48, folders 3, 6, 7.

72. U.S. Central Intelligence Agency, "Prospects."

73. Bruce Cumings, *Origins of the Korean War* (Princeton, N.J.: Princeton University Press, 1981), p. 528.

74. U.S. Central Intelligence Agency, "Prospects."

75. Goncharov, Lewis, and Xue Litai, *Uncertain Partners,* p. 196; Chen Jian, *China's Road to the Korean War: The Making of the Sino-American Confrontation* (New York: Columbia University Press, 1994), pp. 120–125; Westad, *Decisive Encounters,* pp. 319–320.

76. In his impressive and much admired work *Decisive Encounters,* Westad inexplicably writes that Mao "had no alternative" but to agree to give priority to the attack on South Korea. According to Westad, this was simply because to have asked Kim for a year's delay would have violated the Chairman's revolutionary principles (p. 320).

77. Gregory Henderson, *Korea: The Politics of the Vortex* (Cambridge: Harvard University Press, 1968), p. 149.

78. Chen Jian, *Mao's China and the Cold War,* p. 102.

79. *FEER* 9, no. 11 (September 14, 1950): 307; *FEER* 8, no. 26 (June 29, 1950): 852.

80. Interview with Zhou Lianhua, Taipei, October 12, 2003.

81. CIA memorandum, May 11, 1950, file AOI, 878.OA12, obtained by FOI request.

82. *FEER* 8, no. 24 (June 15, 2006): 783.

83. Finkelstein, *Washington's Taiwan Dilemma,* pp. 307–311.

84. Cumings, *Origins of the Korean War,* p. 535.

85. Xu Yueshun, ed., *Chen Cheng's huiyilu: Taiwan de sheli* (Chen Cheng's Memoirs: The Establishment of Taiwan) (Taipei: Academia Historica, 2005); interview with Chen Lifu, Beitou, May 29, 1996.

86. *FRUS (1950),* vol. 7: *Korea,* pp. 359–361; Chiang Diaries, May 12, 1950, in Qin Xiaoyi, *Zong tong,* vol. 9, p. 4249.

87. Top Secret State Department Memorandum, "Hypothetical Development of the Formosan Situation, May 3, 1950." No indication of the office of origin or the addressee is given. It was, however probably written in the Office of Chinese Affairs or in INR. This copy was in INR files. National Archives, INR files, box 4195, doc. 793.00/5–350.

88. Cumings, *Origins of the Korean War,* p. 537.

89. Finkelstein, *Washington's Taiwan Dilemma,* p. 328.

90. Du Nianzhong, *Zhongguo shi bao zhou kan* (China Times Weekly), September 1–7, 1990, pp. 8–11. Du interviewed Rusk in Athens, Georgia, in 1990 (month and date not given). After the interview, Rusk expressed dismay upon learning that Sun was still alive in Taiwan and thus would be embarrassed by the revelations. The first report of Sun's secret message to Rusk was in Thomas J. Shoenbaum, *Waging Peace and War* (New York: Simon and Schuster, 1988), p. 209. In an October 2003 interview, Professor Zhu Hongyuan, an academic specialist on Sun Liren, said he interviewed Sun in 1988 and 1989 after his release from 33 years of house arrest. Sun denied that he had sent a letter to Rusk or had ever plotted against Chiang Kai-shek.

91. Leonard A. Kusnitz, *Public Opinion and Foreign Policy: America's China Policy, 1949–1979* (Westport, Conn.: Greenwood, 1984), p. 34.

92. Finkelstein, *Washington's Taiwan Dilemma,* pp. 315, 316.

93. Chiang Diaries, Hoover, June 25, 1950, box 48, folder 7.

94. Phillip C. Jessup, memo summarizing Blair House meeting with the President, June 25, 1950; website of the Truman Presidential Museum and Library, http://www.trumanlibrary.org.

95. George M. Elsey, memo of conversation with President Truman, June 26,

1950, website of the Truman Presidential Museum and Library, http://www.truman-library.org.

96. Chiang Diaries, Hoover, June 26, 1950, box 48, folders 7, 8.

97. *New York Times,* June 28, 1950.

98. Chiang Diaries, Hoover, June 28 and 29, 1950, box 48, folder 7.

99. Dean Rusk as told to Richard Rusk, *As I Saw It,* ed. Daniel S. Papp (New York: Norton, 1990), pp. 175–176. According to Rusk, the "very high [Taipei] official" told him this story. Chiang's offer was conditioned on the complete equipping by the United States of the 33,000 troops with modern weapons and providing two years of training. Chiang Diaries, Hoover, June 28, 1950, box 48, folder 7.

100. Chiang Diaries, Hoover, June 30, 1950, box 48, folder 7.

101. Chiang Diaries, Hoover, July 7, 1950, box 48, folder 8.

102. Jessup memo, June 25, 1950.

103. Chen Jian, *Mao's China and the Cold War,* pp. 126–130, 139.

104. *New York Times,* July 4, 1950.

105. Chiang Diaries, Hoover, July 4, 1950, box 48, folder 8.

106. Chiang Diaries, Hoover, July 7, 1950, box 48, folder 8.

107. Ibid.

108. Nancy Bernkopf Tucker, "A House Divided: The United States, the Department of State and China," in Warren I. Cohen and Akira Iriye, eds., *The Great Powers in East Asia, 1953–1960* (New York: Columbia University Press, 1990), pp. 36–38; *New York Times,* July 6, 1950.

109. Dean Acheson, *Present at the Creation: My Years in the State Department* (New York: Norton, 1969), p. 422.

110. Sha Gongchuan interview, May 22, 1996. Sha attended the briefing.

111. Memorandum of conversation, General MacArthur and A. W. Harriman, undated, website of the Truman Presidential Museum and Library, http://www.truman-library.org.

112. *New York Times,* August 1, 1950.

113. Chiang Diaries, Hoover, July 31, 1950, box 48, folder 8.

114. *New York Times,* August 5, 1950.

115. John W. Garver, *The Sino-American Alliance* (Armonk, N.Y.: M. E. Sharpe, 1997), p. 39.

116. Karl Lott Rankin, *China Assignment* (Seattle: University of Washington Press, 1964), p. 48.

117. Chiang Diaries, Hoover, July 10, 11, 12, and August 5, 1950, box 48, folders 8, 9; *FRUS (1950),* vol. 6: *East Asia and the Pacific,* p. 371; Garver, *Sino-American Alliance,* p. 115.

118. Chiang Diaries, Hoover, July 28 and August 18, 1950, box 48, folders 8, 9.

119. Chiang Diaries, Hoover, August 24, 1950, box 48, folder 9.

120. Xu Yueshun, *Chen Cheng's Huiyilu,* p. 576.

121. Dickson, "Lessons of Defeat," p. 67.

122. Ibid., p. 68.

123. Chiang Diaries, Hoover, July 22, 1950, box 48, folder 8.

124. Dickson, "Lessons of Defeat," p. 63.

125. Chiang Diaries, Hoover, February 1, 1951, box 48, folder 16.

126. The Education Ministry would assume direction of the corps in 1960.

127. Chiang Command Message to Chen Chang, November 14, 1950, in Qin Xiaoyi, *Zong tong,* vol. 10, p. 4404.

128. Dickson, "Lessons of Defeat," pp. 70, 72, 76, 79.

129. Ibid., p. 63.

130. Ibid., p. 64.

131. Chiang Diaries, Hoover, July 13 and 21, 1950, box 48, folder 8.

132. Chen Lifu interview, May 29, 1998.

133. Presidential interview, November 14, 1954, Papers of Harry S. Truman: Post-Presidential Files, website of the Truman Presidential Museum and Library, http://www.trumanlibrary.org.

134. Memorandum of Conversation, General MacArthur and A. W. Harriman, undated, website of the Truman Presidential Museum and Library, http://www.trumanlibrary.org.

135. Chiang Diaries, Hoover, August 30 and September 1, 1950, box 48, folders 9, 10.

136. Chiang Diaries, Hoover, September 7, 1950, box 48, folder 10.

137. Ibid.

138. Chiang Diaries, Hoover, September 2, 1950, box 48, folder 10.

139. Chiang Diaries, Hoover, September 12, 1950, box 48, folder 10.

140. Xu Yueshun, *Chen Cheng's huiyilu,* p. 580.

141. Chiang Diaries, Hoover, September 12 and 15, 1950, box 48, folder 10.

142. Chiang Diaries, Hoover, September 19, 1950, box 48, folder 10; Chen Jian, *Mao's China and the Cold War,* p. 161.

143. Goncharov, Lewis, and Xue Litai, *Uncertain Partners,* pp. 188–195.

144. Tong, *Chiang Kai-shek,* p. 526, citing a report by General Vandenberg.

145. George Kennan, *Memoirs, 1950–1963* (New York: Pantheon, 1983), p. 94.

146. Tang Tsou, *America's Failure,* p. 575.

147. Ibid., pp. 584, 585.

148. Garver, *Sino-American Alliance,* p. 43.

149. Chiang Diaries, Hoover, November 29, 1950, box 48, folder 12.

150. Christopher Andrew and Oleg Gordievsky, *KGB: The Inside Story of Its Foreign Operations from Lenin to Gorbachev* (New York: Harper Collins, 1990), pp. 393–397.

151. Chiang Diaries, Hoover, December 1, 1950, box 48, folder 13.

152. Chen Jian, *Mao's China and the Cold War,* pp. 91–92.

153. CBS interview, December 9, 1950, in Qin Xiaoyi, *Zong tong,* vol. 9, p. 4432.

154. Karl Rankin, *China Assignment* (Seattle: University of Washington Press, 1964), pp. 99–100.

155. *New York Times,* December 22, 1950.

156. *FRUS (1951),* vol. 7: *Korea and China,* pp. 42–43.

157. Ibid., p. 56.

158. A report from the Dutch Embassy in Peking, in ibid., p. 50.

159. Chiang speech to Reform Committee, January 8, 1951, in Qin Xiaoyi, *Zong tong,* vol. 10, pp. 4444–4445.

160. *New York Times,* January 12, 13, 18, and 19, 1951; *FRUS,* vol. 7: *Korea and China,* pp. 88, 89, 1518, 1519.

161. Chiang Diaries, Hoover, January 13, 1951, box 48, folder 15.

162. Acheson, *Present at the Creation,* p. 516.

163. Chiang Diaries, Hoover, January 17, 1951, box 48, folder 15.

164. Chiang Diaries, Hoover, January 20, 1951, box 48, folder 15.

165. Chiang Diaries, Hoover, January 20 and 21, 1951, box 48, folder 15.

166. Chiang Diaries, Hoover, January 31, 1951, box 48, folder 15.

167. Interview with Everett Drumwright, Oral Histories CD (Arlington, Va.: Association for Diplomatic Studies and Training, 2006), p. 31.

168. Chiang Diaries, Hoover, January 21, 1950, box 48, folder 15.

169. Chiang Diaries, Hoover, May 29, 1951, box 48, folder 19.

170. Chiang Diaries, Hoover, June 18, 1951, box 49, folder 1.

171. Chiang Diaries, Hoover, July 12 and 14, 1951, box 49, folder 2.

172. Chiang Diaries, Hoover, June 18, 1951, box 49, folder 1.

173. Rankin, *China Assignment,* p. 113.

174. Chiang Diaries, Hoover, April 10, 1951, box 49, folder 18.

175. Chiang Diaries, Hoover, July 5, 1951, box 49, folder 2.

176. Chiang Diaries, Hoover, July 8, 1951, box 49, folder 2.

177. Chiang Diaries, Hoover, July 5, 1951, box 49, folder 2.

178. Chiang Diaries, Hoover, July 31, 1951, box 49, folder 2.

179. Editor's note, February 9, 1951, in Qin Xiaoyi, *Zong tong,* vol. 10, pp. 4479–4480.

180. For this and other details on General Okamura and Taiwan, see the Axis History Forum website at http://forum.axishistory.com.

181. Chiang Diaries, Hoover, July 3, August 30 and 31, 1951, box 49, folder 2.

182. Chiang Diaries, Hoover, September 31 and October 11, 31, 1951, box 49, folder 4.

183. Chiang Diaries, Hoover, April 14, 18, 27, 1952, box 49, folder 2.

11. Managing the Protector

1. Interview with Republic of China Air Force officer familiar with these operations who wished not to be named, Taipei, May 1996.

2. James Lilley, *China Hands: Nine Decades of Adventure, Espionage, and Diplomacy in Asia* (New York: Public Affairs, 2004), pp. 79–80, 82–83, 85–86.

3. Alfred W. McCoy, *The Politics of Heroin in Southeast Asia* (New York: Harper and Row, 1972), pp. 171–178.

4. John W. Garver, *The Sino-American Alliance* (Armonk, N.Y.: M. E. Sharpe, 1997), p. 30.

5. Chiang Diaries, Hoover, April 15, 1951, box 49, folder 15.

6. Laura Tyson Li, *Madame Chiang Kai-shek* (New York: Atlantic Monthly Press, 2006), p. 340.

7. Ibid., pp. 343, 350.

8. Chiang Diaries, Hoover, February 12, 1952, box 49, folder 10.

9. Interview with a Soong relative, California, May 2004.

10. Chiang's cable to Mayling, September 2, 1952, in Qin Xiaoyi, *Zong tong,* vol. 11, p. 4702.

11. Chiang Diaries, Hoover, August 8, 1951, box 49, folder 3.

12. *FRUS (1951),* vol. 7: *Korea and China,* p. 1641; Robert P. Newman, "Clandestine Chinese Nationalist Efforts to Punish Their American Detractors," *Diplomatic History* 7, no. 3 (Summer 1983): 205–222.

13. *FRUS (1952),* vol. 14: *China and Japan,* pp. 76–77; Editor's note, January 31, 1951, in Qin Xiaoyi, *Zong tong,* vol. 10, p. 4463.

14. Chiang Diaries, Hoover, August 8, 1951, box 49, folder 3.

15. Chiang Diaries, Hoover, October 7 and 16, 1952, box 49, folder 18.

16. Tyson Li, *Madame Chiang,* p. 351.

17. Chiang Diaries, Hoover, November 9 and 29, 1952, box 49, folder 19.

18. Karl Rankin, *China Assignment* (Seattle: University of Washington Press, 1964), p. 155.

19. Chiang Diaries, Hoover, January 31, 1953, box 50, folder 2.

20. Ibid.

21. Tom Wicker, *Dwight D. Eisenhower* (New York: Henry Holt and Company, 2002), p. 30.

22. Nancy Bernkopf Tucker, *Taiwan, Hong Kong, and the United States, 1945–1992* (New York: Twayne, 1994), pp. 33–38.

23. Dwight D. Eisenhower, *The White House Years: Mandate for Change* (Garden City, N.Y.: Doubleday, 1963), p. 181.

24. Ibid., p. 180.

25. White House Memorandum of Conversation between President Johnson and former President Eisenhower, *FRUS (1964–1968),* vol. 2: *Vietnam,* p. 300. Ike told

Johnson that "shortly after I came to office, I had three messages passed to the [North] Koreans and Chinese. One through Nehru, one through Chiang Kai-shek and one through officials at a lower level who were participating in the armistice discussions."

26. Chen Jian, *Mao's China and the Cold War* (Chapel Hill: University of North Carolina Press, 2001), p. 171.

27. Zhou Ming, ed., *Lishi zai zheli chensi* (History Ponders Here), 3 vols. (Peking: Huaxia chubanshe, 1987), p. 290, cited by Jung Chang and Jon Halliday, *Mao* (New York: Knopf, 2005), p. 374.

28. Chen Jian, *Mao's China and the Cold War,* p. 113.

29. Chiang Diaries, Hoover, April 15, 1953, box 50, folder 5.

30. Chiang Diaries, Hoover, April 10, 18, and 20, 1953, box 50, folder 5.

31. Chiang Diaries, Hoover, May 25, 1953, box 50, folder 6.

32. Chiang Diaries, Hoover, June 23, 1953, box 50, folder 7.

33. Ibid.

34. Chiang Diaries, Hoover, June 25, 1953, box 50, folder 7.

35. Chiang Diaries, Hoover, June 30, 1953, box 50, folder 7.

36. Eisenhower, *White House Years,* pp. 185–187.

37. Chiang Diaries, Hoover, July 1, 1953, box 50, folder 8.

38. Chiang Diaries, Hoover, July 12, 1953, box 50, folder 8.

39. Chiang Diaries, Hoover, July 17 and 31, 1953, box 50, folder 8. A Chinese (PRC) Defense College publication in 1991 claimed that the United States had authorized the attack, 10,000 Nationalist troops had taken part, and 3,000 were killed. Garver, *Sino-American Alliance,* pp. 76–77.

40. Editor's note, June 19, 1953, in Qin Xiaoyi, *Zong tong,* vol. 12, p. 5268.

41. Stephen Ambrose, *Eisenhower,* vol. 2 (New York: Simon and Schuster, 1984), p. 99.

42. State Department Memo of NSC Meeting, August 14, 1958, *FRUS (1958–1960),* vol. 19: *China,* p. 53.

43. Chiang Diaries, Hoover, November 28 and 29, 1953, box 50, folder 12.

44. Boorman, *Biographical Dictionary,* vol. 3, p. 167.

45. Chiang Diaries, Hoover, March 9, 1953, box 50, folder 15.

46. Chiang Diaries, Hoover, March 11, 17, 31, and April 6, 1953, box 50, folder 15.

47. *New York Times,* August 30, 1951; September 15, 1961; and October 16, 1952.

48. Interview with Xie Congming, Taipei, June 4, 1996. According to Xie, a KMT legislator told him that the figure was much higher—60,000 to 70,000.

49. In 1954, the Peace Preservation Headquarters announced that 858 cases of subversion involving 1,745 persons "had been tabled" in the first three quarters of the year, resulting in the conviction of 597 of these individuals, or extrapolating for

the whole year, a figure of around 750. National Intelligence Estimate, "Morale on Taiwan," April 16, 1955, *FRUS (1955–1957)*, vol. 2: *China*, p. 484n.

50. K. C. Wu, "Formosa," *Look*, June 29, 1954, pp. 39–43.

51. Chiang Diaries, Hoover, January 17 and 19, 1952, box 51, folder 2.

52. Chiang Diaries, Hoover, May 4 and 6, 1953, box 51, folder 4.

53. Chiang Diaries, Hoover, April 9–11, 1953, box 51, folder 5.

54. "The K. C. Wu Story," *The Reporter*, April 27, 1954, pp. 18–20.

55. AmEmb Taipei cable to Department of State, April 21, 1954, National Archives, RG 59, U.S. State Department files, 1950–1954, box 4218.

56. Chiang Diaries, Hoover, April 20 and 29, 1954, box 50, folder 18.

57. *FRUS (1952–1954)*, vol. 14: *China and Japan*, p. 115.

58. Ibid., pp. 363–364.

59. Interviews during November and December 1995 with former American military and CIA officers who wished to remain anonymous.

60. Tucker, *Taiwan, Hong, Kong, and the United States*, p. 64.

61. Interview with a U.S. Marine officer who served on the Tachen islands, Arlington, Va., April 17, 1996.

62. Ibid.

63. Interviews during 1995 and 1996 in the Washington, D.C., area with several CIA and military intelligence officers who served in Taiwan in the 1950s and 1960s.

64. *FRUS (1952–1954)*, vol. 14: *China and Japan*, pp. 195–196.

65. Rankin, *China Assignment*, p. 162.

66. Richard Nixon, *The Memoirs of Richard Nixon* (New York: Grosser and Dunlap, 1978), p. 126; *FRUS (1952–1954)*, vol. 14: *China and Japan*, pp. 210, 126.

67. *New York Times*, January 1, 1954.

68. Chiang Diaries, Hoover, February 21 and April 3, 1953, box 51, folders 3, 5.

69. McCoy, *Politics of Heroin*, p. 173.

70. *FRUS (1952–1954)*, vol. 14: *China and Japan*, p. 335.

71. SNIE 43-1-57, *FRUS (1955–1957)*, vol. 2: *China*, pp. 515–518; NIE 43-2-57, *FRUS (1955–1957)*, vol. 2: *China*, pp. 585–593.

72. *FRUS (1952–1954)*, vol. 14: *China and Japan*, pp. 641, 642.

73. Eisenhower, *White House Years*, p. 338.

74. U.S. Embassy Taipei radiogram to SecState, November 30, 1953, *FRUS (1952–1954)*, vol. 14: *China and Japan*, p. 332n.

75. Chen Jian, *Mao's China and the Cold War*, pp. 134–135.

76. Ambrose, *Eisenhower*, p. 184.

77. Chiang Diaries, Hoover, April 2, 10 and 17, 1954, box 50, folder 18.

78. Chen Jian, *Mao's China and the Cold War*, p. 137.

79. Ibid., p. 139.

80. Chiang Diaries, Hoover, May 1, 1954, box 50, folder 19.

81. AmembTaipei radiogram to SecState, *FRUS (1952–1954)*, vol. 14: *China and Japan*, p. 490.

82. Garver, *Sino-American Alliance*, p. 115.

83. Chen Jian, *Mao's China and the Cold War*, pp. 168–169.

84. He Di and Gordan H. Chang, "The Absence of War in the U.S./China Confrontation over Quemoy and Matsu in 1954–1955: Contingency, Luck, Deterrence," *American Historical Review* 98 (December 1993); Tucker, *Taiwan*, pp. 38–42.

85. Chen Jian, *Mao's China and the Cold War*, pp. 168–169.

86. *FRUS (1952–1954)*, vol. 14: *China and Japan*, p. 562.

87. *New York Times*, September 5, 1954.

88. Among other activities while visiting Quemoy in 1961, my fellow Chinese-language students and I released propaganda balloons that were intended to land on the mainland carrying bars of soap and propaganda messages. When the wind changed, the "Chicoms" sent their own balloons toward Quemoy, also with bars of soap.

89. *New York Times*, September 13, 1954; *FRUS (1952–1954)*, vol. 14: *China and Japan*, p. 582.

90. Chiang Diaries, Hoover, September 9, 10, 11, and 30, 1954, box 51, folders 3, 4.

91. Rankin, *China Assignment*, p. 209.

92. *New York Times*, September 6, 7, and 8, 1954.

93. *FRUS (1952–1954)*, vol. 14: *China and Japan*, p. 829.

94. Ibid., pp. 833–835.

95. Ibid.

96. Eisenhower mentioned this report in his letter of February 1, 1955, to General Gruenther. See Ambrose, *Eisenhower*, p. 236.

97. Evgeny A. Negin and Yuri N. Smirnov (Russian nuclear physicists involved at the time in nuclear weapons), "Did the USSR Share Atomic Secrets with China?" Parallel History Project on Cooperative Security website, http://www.php.isn.ethz.ch, accessed March 15, 2008.

98. *New York Times*, October 13, 1954.

99. Chiang Diaries, Hoover, October 31, 1954, box 51, folder 4.

100. Chiang Diaries, Hoover, November 11 and December 13, 1954, box 51, folders 5, 6.

101. Eisenhower, *White House Years*, p. 466.

102. *New York Times*, December 26 and November 27, 1954.

103. Kenneth W. Condit, *History of the Joint Chiefs of Staff*, vol. 6: *The Joint Chiefs of Staff and National Policy, 1955–1956* (Washington, D.C.: Historical Office, Joint Chiefs, 1992), p. 194.

104. *FRUS (1955–1957)*, vol. 2: *China*, pp. 69–83; Eisenhower, *White House Years*, pp. 555–556.

105. Condit, *Joint Chiefs*, p. 197.

106. Ibid., pp. 196–199; *FRUS (1952–1954)*, vol. 14: *China and Japan*, p. 832; *FRUS (1955–1957)*, vol. 2: *China*, pp. 515–516.

107. Condit, *Joint Chiefs*, pp. 197–198.

108. *FRUS (1955–1957)*, vol. 2: *China*, p. 171; *FRUS (1952–1954)*, vol. 14: *China and Japan*, p. 832. Radford described Dulles's statement to Yeh in his April 25 conversation with Chiang; see *FRUS (1955–1957)*, vol. 2: *China*, pp. 514, 516.

109. *FRUS (1955–1957)*, vol. 2: *China*, pp. 167–168.

110. Both Radford and Chiang refer to this letter in their conversation of April 25, 1955. See *FRUS (1955–1957)*, vol. 2: *China*, pp. 514, 516.

111. Eisenhower, *White House Years*, pp. 470–471.

112. "March 3 Conversation between President Chiang and Secretary Dulles," *FRUS (1955–1957)*, vol. 2: *China*, pp. 321–328; Foreign Service Dispatch, Amembassy Taipei 444, March 15, 1955. Full text is in U.S. Embassy Manila, Foreign Service Dispatch no. 441, March 15, 1955, obtained by FOI request.

113. Condit, *Joint Chiefs*, pp. 203–204; Eisenhower, *White House Years*, p. 477.

114. Garver, *Sino-American Alliance*, p. 131; *New York Times*, March 17, 1955.

115. Ambrose, *Eisenhower*, p. 239.

116. Ibid., pp. 241–242.

117. Victor M. Gobarev, "Soviet Policy towards China: Developing Nuclear Weapons, 1949–69," *Journal of Slavic Military Studies* 12, no. 4 (1999): 21, cited by June Chang and Jon Halliday in *Mao* (New York: Knopf, 2005), p. 397.

118. *FRUS (1955–1957)*, vol. 2: *China*, pp. 510–513.

119. Condit, *Joint Chiefs*, p. 206.

120. *FRUS (1955–1957)*, vol. 2: *China*, pp. 510–513; Ambrose, *Eisenhower*, pp. 242–244.

121. Ibid.

122. Ibid.

123. *FRUS (1955–1957)*, vol. 2: *China*, pp. 510–513.

124. Ibid., pp. 510–513, 523–525.

125. Chiang Diaries, Hoover, April 25, 27, and 29, 1955, box 51, folder 11. He wrote that Robertson was "a son of a bitch," but Radford at least was a "gentleman."

126. Condit, *Joint Chiefs*, p. 208.

127. Harry Harding and Yuan Ming, eds., *Sino-American Relations, 1945–1955* (Wilmington, Del.: SR Books, 1989), pp. 276–277.

128. Ambrose, *Eisenhower*, p. 244.

129. *FRUS (1955–1957)*, vol. 2: *China*, pp. 519–520.

130. Condit, *Joint Chiefs*, p. 208.

131. Wendell L. Minnick, "Target Zhou Enlai," *FEER* 158, no. 28 (July 13, 1995): 54.

132. For the Zhou-Kissinger discussion in 1971, see *FRUS (1969–1972)*, vol. 17: *China*, pp. 503–504.

133. Chiang Diaries, Hoover, April 16, 1955, box 51, folder 11.

134. Chiang Diaries, Hoover, May 28, 1955, box 51, folder 12.

135. Wellington Koo, Reminiscences of Wellington Koo, Oral History, Butler Library, Columbia University, undated, pp. 287–288.

136. Rankin, *China Assignment,* p. 273.

137. Interview with Chiang Wei-kuo, Taipei, June 10, 1995.

138. Murray A. Rubinstein, ed., *Taiwan: A New History* (Armonk, N.Y.: M. E. Sharpe, 1999), p. 325.

139. Interview with K. T. Li, Taipei, September 7, 1995.

140. Hung-mao Tien, *The Great Transition: Political and Social Change in the Republic of China* (Stanford, Calif.: Hoover Institution Press, 1989), p. 23; *FEER* 27, no. 15 (October 8, 1959): 585; Rubenstein, *Taiwan,* pp. 325–328.

141. Rubinstein, *Taiwan,* p. 327.

142. *FEER* 29, no. 5 (August 4, 1960): 292.

143. *FEER* 27, no. 15 (October 8, 1959): 585.

144. Chiang Diaries, Hoover, January 29 and February 16, 1951, box 48, folder 15.

145. *FEER* 27, no. 15 (October 8, 1959): 585.

146. Hung-mao Tien, *Great Transition,* p. 29.

147. *FEER* 13, no. 10 (September 2, 1952): 132.

148. Hung-mao Tien, *Great Transition,* p. 27.

149. *FEER* 14, no. 18 (April 30, 1953): 567.

150. Ibid.

151. Chiang Diaries, Hoover, February 8, 1951, and May 30 and September 6, 1952, in Qin Xiaoyi, *Zong tong,* vol. 12, p. 4478.

152. Chiang Diaries, Hoover, February 27, 1951, box 48, folder 16. In this case, the American MAAG also opposed the arrangement, believing each service best knew its own needs.

153. Richard Hughes, "Portrait of Chiang on His Mountaintop," *New York Times Magazine,* September 28, 1958.

154. Rankin, *China Assignment,* p. 252.

155. U.S. Mission Geneva cable, Johnson to SecState, *FRUS (1955–1957),* vol. 3: *China,* p. 200.

156. In the written agreement, Peking was willing to say that the two sides should settle "disputes between the two countries in the Taiwan area without resorting to the use of force." See John King Fairbank, *Sino-American Relations, 1949–1971* (New York: Praeger, 1972), p. 127.

157. Chiang Diaries, Hoover, July 27, 1955, box 51, folder 14.

158. *FRUS (1955–1957),* vol. 3: *China,* p. 584.

159. Chen Jian, *Mao's China and the Cold War,* p. 171.

160. Chiang Kai-shek, *Soviet Russia in China* (New York: Farrar, Strauss and Cudahy, 1957), pp. 6–7.

161. Chiang Kai-shek, *Soviet Russia in China* (New York: Farrar, Strauss, and Cudahy, 1957), pp. 345–349.

162. Interview with Lee Huan, Taipei, May 18, 1996; interview with Ma Ying-jeou, Taipei, March 10, 1998.

163. Roderick MacFarquhar, ed., *The Hundred Flowers* (New York: Praeger, 1960).

164. Chen Jian, *Mao's China and the Cold War*, p. 173.

165. Memorandum of Conversation, Taipei, March 14, 1958, Dulles and Chiang Kai-shek, et al., *FRUS (1958–1960)*, vol. 19: *China*, p. 9.

166. Victor Marchetti and John D. Marks, *The CIA and the Cult of Intelligence* (New York: Knopf, 1980), p. 122.

167. American Embassy Taipei radiogram to Department of State, May 22, 1958, *FRUS (1958–1960)*, vol. 19: *China*, pp. 145–146.

168. Department of State memorandum of Conversation, Dulles, Casey, et al., September 9, 1958, *FRUS (1958–1960)*, vol. 19: *China*, p. 281.

169. Chen Jian, *Mao's China and the Cold War*, pp. 178–179. Mao was just receiving the first harvest reports since implementation of the Great Leap Forward, and they all recounted miraculous successes when in fact the rice and wheat crops were disasters.

170. Roy Medvedev, *China and the Superpowers* (Oxford, Eng.: Blackwell, 1986), p. 33; Chen Jian, *Mao's China and the Cold War*, p. 179.

171. Li Zhisui, *The Private Life of Chairman Mao* (New York: Random House, 1994), pp. 270–271.

172. Chen Jian, *Mao's China and the Cold War*, p. 188.

173. Alan J. Day, ed., Peter Jones and Siân Kevill, comps., *China and the Soviet Union, 1949–1984* (London: Facts on File, 1985), pp. 11–12.

174. From the journal of S. F. Antonov, chargé Soviet Embassy Peking, entry for October 21, 1959, "Summary of a Conversation with the Chairman of the CC CPC [Central Committee Communist Party of China] Mao Zedong on 14 October 1959." From the Cold War International History Project website, http://www.mtholyoke.edu/acad/intrel/maoconv.htm, accessed August 28, 2008.

175. Chen Jian, *Mao's China and the Cold War*, p. 193.

176. The Generalissimo's request remains classified but its denial is reported in *FRUS (1958–1960)*, vol. 19: *China*, pp. 509–510.

177. White House, Memorandum of Meeting on Taiwan Straits Situation, August 25, 1958, *FRUS (1958–1960)*, vol. 19: *China*, p. 73. See also p. 98 for Memorandum on the meeting of August 25; then it is Eisenhower who complains of Chiang Kai-shek, who having "ignored our advice, comes whining to us."

178. *FRUS (1958–1960)*, vol. 19: *China*, p. 98.

179. Day, *China*, pp. 11–12.

180. *FRUS (1958–1960)*, vol. 19: *China*, p. 121.

181. Tyson Li, *Madame Chiang*, p. 376. Tyson Li does not cite the date of this broadcast.

182. American Embassy Taipei cable to Department of State, September 19, 1958, *FRUS (1958–1960)*, vol. 19: *China*, p. 227.

183. Eisenhower, *White House Years*, pp. 691–692.

184. Ibid., p. 692.

185. *FRUS (1955–1957)*, vol. 3: *China*, p. 592.

186. Operations Coordinating Board Memorandum, "Report on Taiwan and the Government of the Republic of China (NSC 5723)," April 20, 1959, National Archives, Department of Defense File, 1959, box MNR2.

187. Department of State memorandum from Smith to Dulles, September 3, 1958, *FRUS (1958–1960)*, vol. 19: *China*, pp. 122–124.

188. Memorandum by Regional Planning Adviser in the Bureau of Far Eastern Affairs, "Taiwan Straits Crisis: Where Do We Go from Here?" September 18, 1958, *FRUS (1958–1960)*, vol. 19: *China*, p. 222. The intelligence document to which this memorandum refers has not been declassified, but the subject is clearly spelled out. Ten years later, Chiang Kai-shek would tell Dean Rusk that the United States "must never, ever think of using nuclear weapons against China"; see Dean Rusk, *As I Saw It* (New York: W. W. Norton, 1990), p. 288. But this was after Peking had tested its own nuclear bomb and Taipei had itself begun its own secret effort to develop such a weapon—clearly as a deterrent. In 1958 as in 1953, when the possibility seemed quite real that America might actually employ the bomb against the mainland and China had no such weapons with which it could hit Taiwan, there were no similar protestations from either the Generalissimo or his son.

189. Ambrose, *Eisenhower*, p. 484.

190. Chen Jian, *Mao's China and the Cold War*, pp. 192, 194.

191. Ambrose, *Eisenhower*, p. 485.

192. *New York Times*, October 1, 1958.

193. Ibid.

194. *New York Times*, October 3, 1958.

195. Chen Jian, *Mao's China and the Cold War*, p. 198.

196. Ibid., p. 199.

197. *New York Times*, October 6, 1958.

198. *FRUS (1958–1960)*, vol. 19: *China*, p. 379.

199. Ibid., p. 470.

200. Talking Paper Prepared by Secretary of State Dulles, Taipei, October 21, 1958, in *FRUS (1958–1960)*, vol. 19: *China*, p. 415.

201. American Embassy Taipei cable, October 21, 1958, in *FRUS (1958–1960)*, vol. 19: *China*, p. 416.

202. Ibid.

203. *FRUS (1958–1960)*, vol. 19: *China*, pp. 421–422.

204. Ibid., pp. 422–423.

205. Department of State Memorandum of Conversation, Taipei, Dulles, Chiang, et al., in ibid., pp. 431–432.

206. Fredrick Chien, *Qian Fu Hui I Lu* (The Memoirs of Fredrick Chien) (Taipei: Tian Xia Publishing Company, 2005), p. 80. That the missiles were Matadors is from National Security Archive Electronic Briefing Book no. 197 edited by William Burr —posted August 18, 2006 at http://www.gwu.edu/nsarchiv, doc. 7, pp. 64–66, accessed September 1, 2008.

207. *FRUS (1958–1960)*, vol. 19: *China,* pp. 440–441.

208. For the final text of the communiqué, see ibid., pp. 442–443; *New York Times,* October 28, 1958, p. 58.

209. Interview with Wang Chi, Washington, D.C., November 28, 1995. Wang, a distinguished Chinese American who at the time was head of the Chinese section of the Library of Congress, said that during a December 1994 visit to Peking, he met with Qiao Shi, chairman of the National Peoples Congress and longtime head of China's intelligence and security apparatus. Qiao told Wang of the Chiang Kai-shek letter to Zhou Enlai. Qiao would seem to have no reason thirty-six years later to have made up this story.

210. *FRUS (1969–1976)*, vol. 17: *China,* pp. 765–766. Zhou said that just by changing the shelling, Chiang "understood," but given the earlier quoted comment by Qiao Shi, it is likely that there was a secret exchange of views and that in the earlier remark to Kissinger, Zhou was trying to protect the secrecy of the Hong Kong contact with Chiang Kai-shek.

211. *FRUS (1958–1960)*, vol. 17: *China,* pp. 509–510. This clandestine program was revealed by Chiang Ching-kuo in a semi-annual report to the Legislative Yuan in 1975. See *China Quarterly* 64 (December 1975): 808.

12. Shifting Dynamics

1. Sun Lifan, *Chen Cheng wan nian* (Chen Cheng's Late Years) (Hofei: Anhui People's Press, 1996), p. 151.

2. Boorman, *Biographical Dictionary,* vol. 1, p. 364; Interview with Chiang Wei-kuo, Taipei, June 5, 1996.

3. Chen Pengren, *Chiang furen Soong Mayling nushi hua zhuan* (The Pictorial Biography of Madame Sung Mayling) (Taipei: Modern China, 1998), pp. 181–191.

4. Cited by Laura Tyson Li, *Madame Chiang Kai-shek* (New York: Atlantic Monthly Press, 2006), pp. 374, 376.

5. Chen Pengren, *Chiang furen,* pp. 181–191. On the White House lunch, see Tyson Li, *Madame Chiang,* pp. 374, 375.

6. Interviews with Chiang family members, Taipei, May 2002, April 2003; E-mail August 30, 2006, from one of those who joined "The Eight Immortals Club."

7. National Intelligence Estimate no. 43–64, March 11, 1964, p. 5, FOI request to the CIA.

8. Interviews with a CIA officer stationed in South Asia at the time, Washington, D.C., June 1996.

9. On May 3, 1959, Chiang Kai-shek complained that the United States refused to cooperate in exploiting the uprising. *FRUS (1958–1960),* vol. 19: *China,* p. 562; CIA officer interviews, June 1996.

10. *FRUS (1958–1960),* vol. 19: *China,* pp. 756–757.

11. *New York Times,* March 26, 1959.

12. *FRUS (1958–1960),* vol. 19: *China,* p. 755.

13. Status report on the program in *FRUS (1964–1968),* vol. 30: *China,* pp. 739–742; *FRUS (1958–1960),* vol. 19: *China,* p. 808.

14. From the journal of S. F. Antonov, Chargé Soviet Embassy Peking, entry for October 21, 1959, "Summary of a Conversation with Mao Zedong, October 14, 1959." From the Cold War International History Project website, http://www.mtholyoke.edu/acad/intrel/maoconv.htm.

15. *New York Times,* December 1, 1960.

16. *New York Times,* September 4, 1960.

17. *New York Times,* June 4, 1960.

18. Sun Lifan, *Chen Cheng,* pp. 122–123.

19. *FRUS (1958–1960),* vol. 19: *China,* pp. 724–726.

20. *Foreign Broadcast Information Service, Daily Report, Asia and Pacific,* September, 23, p. DDD.2, September 27, p. DDD.13; *New York Times,* October 9 and 22, 1960.

21. John Israel, "Politics on Formosa," *China Quarterly* 15 (July–September 1963): 6.

22. Stephen Ambrose, *Eisenhower,* vol. 2 (New York: Simon and Schuster, 1984), p. 580.

23. *New York Times,* June 19, 1960.

24. *FRUS (1958–1960),* vol. 19: *China,* pp. 677, 679, 680, 690.

25. Ibid., pp. 686, 687.

26. Ibid., pp. 688, 689, 748.

27. *New York Times,* October 14, 1960.

28. Ibid.; *New York Times,* November 12, 1960.

29. *FRUS (1961–1963),* vol. 22: *Northeast Asia,* p. 2n.

30. Fredrick Chien, *Qian Fu Hui I Lu* (The Memoirs of Fredrick Chien) (Taipei: Tian Xia Publishing Company, 2005), pp. 115–116.

31. CIA Field Information Report, Taipei, June 27, 1961, FOI request to the CIA; Enclosure to a State Department memo to the White House, February 22, 1961, *FRUS (1961–1963),* vol. 22: *Northeast Asia,* p. 94.

32. Alfred W. McCoy, *The Politics of Heroin in Southeast Asia* (New York: Harper and Row, 1972), p. 176.

33. *FRUS (1961–1963),* vol. 22: *Northeast Asia,* pp. 50–51.

34. Ibid., pp. 58, 60.

35. Ibid., pp. 76–79.

36. Ibid., pp. 76–78.

37. Ibid., pp. 102–103.

38. Ibid., pp. 89–91.

39. Http://www.state.gov/r/pa/ho/frus/ doc. 71–74.

40. Ibid., p. 148.

41. Ibid., p. 184.

42. Ibid., pp. 195, 196, 196n.

43. Ibid., p. 203.

44. Ibid., pp. 204–207.

45. Ibid., pp. 218, 218n.

46. *FEER* 36, no. 6 (May 10, 1962): 267.

47. *FRUS (1961–1963)*, vol. 22: *Northeast Asia,* pp. 220–221, 223–224.

48. Ibid., p. 220.

49. Ibid., p. 232n.

50. *FRUS (1961–1963)*, vol. 22: *Northeast Asia,* p. 228.

51. Ibid., pp. 247–248, 268, 270, 274.

52. Ibid., pp. 275, 297.

53. Ibid., pp. 283–284.

54. Ibid., pp. 285–288, 292.

55. Ibid.

56. Ibid., doc. 151.

57. Ibid.

58. Ibid., p. 313.

59. Interview with Ralph Clough, Washington, D.C., November 30, 1995.

60. *FRUS (1961–1963)*, vol. 22: *Northeast Asia,* p. 337 and p. 337n.

61. Interview with Xiong Yuan, Taipei, May 31, 1996. Shong implied in this interview that he himself witnessed the shaking hands. In his 1998 oral history, Xiong stated that Madame reported that the American doctor's hands shook before the operation. In a 1962 letter to T.V., Mayling said that Chiang had insisted on the American urologist while she had opposed the idea. See Tyson Li, *Madame Chiang,* p. 382. The exact date of the mishandled operation is uncertain, but it was clearly before 1962. In his oral history and his 1996 interview with me, Xiong mistakenly placed it after the auto accident in 1969. See Oral History Series no. 69, Institute of Modern History, Academia Sinica, Taipei, 1998.

62. Mayling's July 2, 1962, letter to T. V. Soong, cited by Tyson Li, *Madame Chiang,* p. 382.

63. Interviews in Taipei with various former secretaries and aides of Chiang Kai-shek, Taipei, 1995, 1996, 1998, 2003, 2004.

64. *FRUS (1961–1963)*, vol. 22: *Northeast Asia,* p. 330.

65. Ibid., p. 338, p. 338n, p. 334n.

66. Fredrick Chien, *Qian Fu Hui Yi Lu,* pp. 115–116.

67. Interviews with Ralph Clough, Washington, D.C., November 30, 1995, and

Fredrick Chien, Taipei, August 29, 1995. Clough reported on the Kirk-Chiang conversation in a letter to Averill Harriman dated September 23, 1963. This letter is in the Library of Congress Manuscript Division, Harriman Papers, Kennedy-Johnson-Administrations, subject files: Kirk.

68. *FRUS (1961–1963)*, vol. 22: *Northeast Asia*, pp. 342–346.

69. American Embassy Taipei Airgram no. A-649, February 22, 1963; and Airgram no. A-757, March 23, 1963, National Archives, RG 59, State Department Files, box 3669.

70. *FRUS (1961–1963)*, vol. 22: *Northeast Asia*, p. 352.

71. CIA Taipei report no. TDCS DB-3/654,567, May 9, 1963, FOI request to the CIA.

72. Top secret State Department memo, "Visit of Chiang Ching-kuo, US-GRC Consultations Concerning Possible Actions against the Mainland," background paper, September 17, 1965, Lyndon B. Johnson Library, National Security File (China), memos, vol. 4, 7/65–10/65, pp. 1–2.

73. Nancy Bernkopf Tucker, *Taiwan, Hong, Kong, and the United States, 1945–1992* (New York: Twayne, 1994), p. 65.

74. *FRUS (1961–1963)*, vol. 22: *Northeast Asia*, p. 405.

75. Http://www.state.gov/r/pa/ho/frus/ doc. 197.

76. Interview with Wen Huaxiong, Taipei, May 17, 1996.

77. *FRUS (1964–1968):* vol. 30: *China*, doc. 26.

78. K. T. Li, *Economic Transformation of Taiwan, ROC* (London: Shephrard-Walwyn, 1988), p. 111.

79. John Franklin Cooper, *Taiwan: Nation-State or Province?* (Boulder, Colo.: Westview, 2003), p. 95.

80. Richard Hughes, "Portrait of Chiang on His Mountaintop," *New York Times Magazine,* September 28, 1958.

81. Interviews with Cu Songqiu, Fredrick Chien, and Hao Beicun, Taipei, October 3, 2003.

82. Tyson Li, *Madame Chiang*, p. 385.

83. Interview with a relative who wishes to remain anonymous, Taipei, October 21, 2003.

84. Tyson Li, *Madame Chiang*, p. 424.

85. American Embassy Taipei cable to the Department of State, August 2, 1963, National Archives, RG 59, State Department Files, box 3669; American Embassy Taipei Airgram no. A-498, December 4, 1963, National Archives, RG 59, State Department Files, box 3867.

86. *FRUS (1964–1968)*, vol. 30: *China*, p. 22.

87. Ibid., p. 161.

88. Ibid., pp. 112–113, 116.

89. Ibid., p. 143.

90. Interviews with senior CIA officers who served in Taiwan in the 1960s, Arlington, Va., 1995. Confirmed in National Security Archive Electronic Briefing Book no. 197, http://www.gwu.edu/~nsarchiv, ed. William Burr, accessed August 18, 2006.

91. Chiang Kai-shek letter to President Johnson, November 23, 1964, FOI request to U.S. Department of State.

92. *FRUS (1964–1968)*, vol. 30: *China*, pp. 41–55.

93. George McT. Kahin, *Intervention: How America Became Involved in Vietnam* (New York: Doubleday, 1986), p. 332.

94. Joyce K. Kallgren, "Vietnam and Politics in Taiwan," *Asian Survey* 6, no. 1 (January 1966): 28.

95. Gabriel Kolko, *Anatomy of a War* (New York: New Press, 1985), p. 211.

96. American Embassy Taipei Airgram, 1963, National Archives, RG 59, State Department Files, box 3669.

97. Melvin Gurtov, "Recent Developments on Formosa," *China Quarterly* 31 (July–September 1967): 59–60.

98. Interview with Lu Yicheng, Taipei, April 11, 2003. Licheng, a former Nationalist official, accompanied Madame Chiang on much of her 1965–1966 tour.

99. State memcon, Rusk-Chiang Ching-kuo, September 22, 1965, NSF, China, 1/165–1/3/66, Lyndon B. Johnson Library, Austin, Tex.

100. Min S. Yee, *Boston Globe*, May 6, 1968.

101. *FRUS (1964–1968)*, vol. 30: *China*, p. 279.

102. Interview with Ralph Clough, Washington, D.C., November 30, 1995.

103. Interviews with senior CIA officers who served in Taiwan in the 1960s, Arlington, Va., 1995; *FRUS (1964–1968)*, vol. 30: *China*, p. 267.

104. For Chiang Kai-shek's views, I relied on interviews from 1995 to 2006 with his and Chiang Ching-kuo's associates, aides, and secretaries such as Li Huan, Qin Xiaoyi, Zhang Baoshu, Cu Songqiu, Yu Jizhong, Ma Yingjiu, Fredrick Chien, Ma Shuli, Song Chuyu, and others. See also Mark Plummer, "The New Look in Government," *Asian Survey* 9, no. 1 (January 1969): 18–22; Hung-mao Tien, *The Great Transition, Political and Social Change in the Republic of China* (Stanford, Calif.: Hoover Institution Press, 1989), p. 69. Seventeen years after CKS's retreat to Taiwan, there were no Taiwanese among the 24 police regional bureau directors and only 5 among the 120 sub-bureaus. Of the 22 *hsien* or county finance chiefs, 2 were Taiwanese and of the 22 revenue office directors only one was a provincial. Only one cabinet member was a native Taiwanese, and senior officials below the ministerial level were overwhelmingly mainlanders. No generals or admirals were Taiwanese. See Plummer, *New Look*, p. 21; Hung-mao Tien, *Great Transition*, p. 69.

105. Plummer, *New Look*, pp. 18–22.

106. *FEER* 89, no. 32 (August 8, 1975): 28.

107. *FRUS (1958–1960)*, vol. 19: *China*, p. 529.

108. Joseph J. Heinlein, "Political Warfare: The Chinese Nationalist Model," Ph.D. diss., American University, 1974, pp. 584–584.

109. *Christian Science Monitor,* May 7, 1986.

110. *FRUS (1964–1968),* vol. 30: *China,* pp. 351–352.

111. Ibid., p. 490.

112. During his meeting in Washington with President Johnson, C. K. Yen said this was Chiang Kai-shek's estimate. Ibid., p. 559.

113. Interview with David Dean, Fairfax, Va., April 30, 1996.

114. *FRUS (1964–1968),* vol. 30: *China,* p. 59.

115. Ibid., p. 491.

116. Ibid., p. 553. Melvin Gurtov, "Recent Developments on Formosa," *China Quarterly* 31 (July–September 1967): 61.

117. Richard Nixon, "Asia after Vietnam," *Foreign Affairs* 46 (October 1967).

118. Interview with Fredrick Chien (confidential secretary to Chiang Kai-shek in 1967), Taipei, April 19, 2008.

119. AmEmbassy Taipei Airgram, A-249, September 30, 1967, National Archives, RG59, /50/65/6.shelf 4, 1967–1969, China Policy File, China box 1984.

120. Ibid.

121. *FEER* 63, no. 9 (March 1, 1968): 352.

122. *FRUS (1964–1968),* vol. 30: *China,* pp. 638–640.

123. *FEER* 62, no. 43 (October 26, 1968): 184.

124. *FRUS (1964–1968),* vol. 30: *China,* pp. 661, 674–675.

125. Chen Jian, *Mao's China and the Cold War,* p. 240.

126. *Zhongguo shi bao* (China Times), Taipei, May 1995, series on the Victor Louis episode. Also my numerous interviews with Chiang Kai-shek subordinates and American officials in 1995 and 1996.

127. *FEER* 64, no. 17 (April 26, 1969): 240.

128. *FRUS (1964–1968),* vol. 30: *China,* p. 704.

129. Johnson, "Visit of Chiang Ching-kuo," pp. 5–6.

130. AmEmbassy Taipei Airgram A-1037, June 20, 1966, National Security Archive (George Washington University), Electronic Briefing Book no. 19, ed. William Burr, October 13, 1999, http:// www.gwu.edu/~nsachiv.

131. Fredrick Chien interview, April 19, 2008.

132. *FRUS (1969–1976),* vol. 17: *China,* pp. 7–8.

133. Ibid., p. 51.

134. Ibid., p. 399.

135. *FRUS (1969–1976),* vol. E-13: *Documents on China,* p. 4.

136. Fredrick Chien interview, April 19, 2008.

137. Ibid.

138. National Security Archive (George Washington University), Electronic Briefing Book no. 195, http://www.gwu.edu/~nsarchiv.

139. Fredrick Chien interview, April 19, 2008.

140. *FRUS (1969–1976)*, vol. 17: *China*, p. 52.

141. Ibid., pp. 67, 69.

142. *FEER* 65, no. 37 (September 7–13, 1969).

143. Interview with Li Guoding, Taipei, September 7, 1995; Ralph W. Huene-mann, "Family Planning in Taiwan," *Modern China* 16, no. 21 (April 1990): 173–189.

144. *FRUS (1969–1976)*, vol. 17: *China*, p. 53 n.3.

145. Ibid., pp. 53–54.

146. Ibid., pp. 55–56.

147. Fredrick Chien, *Qian Fu Hui Yi Lu*, p. 117.

148. For Chiang Kai-shek's views, I relied once again on interviews from 1995 to 2006 with his associates, aides, and secretaries cited previously.

149. *FEER* 60, no. 20 (May 12–18, 1968): 343.

150. Peter R. Moody, *Political Change on Taiwan: A Study of Ruling Party Adapt-ability* (New York: Praeger, 1992), p. 77; *FEER* 71, no. 10 (March 6, 1931): 31. On the CIA's role, see Fredrick Chien interview, April 19, 2008.

151. Interview with Xiong Yuan, Taipei, May 31, 1996; Xiong Yuan, *The Reminis-cences of Dr. Xiong Yuan,* Oral History Series no. 69, Chen Sanqing, interviewer (Tai-pei: Institute of Modern History, Academia Sinica, 1998), pp. 117–118.

152. Xiong Yuan interview, May 31, 1996; Xiong Yuan, *Reminiscences,* pp. 117–118; Weng Yuan, *Wo dzai Jiang Chieh-shih fu tse shen pian de chih tse* (The Days When I Served the Chiangs) (Taipei: Shu Hua Publisher, 1994), pp. 118, 128–131.

153. Xiong Yuan, *Reminiscences,* pp. 117–118; *FRUS (1969–1976)*, vol. 17: *China,* p. 146; Tyson Li, *Madame Chiang,* pp. 400–401.

154. Chen Jian, *Mao's China and the Cold War,* pp. 245–249.

155. *FRUS (1969–1976)*, vol. 17: *China,* pp. 88, 143.

156. Ibid., pp. 88–90.

157. Ibid., p. 105.

158. Ibid., p. 137.

159. Sheldon Appleton, "Taiwan Portents of Change," *Asian Survey* 11, no. 1 (Jan-uary 1971): 68.

13. Nixon and the Last Years

1. *FRUS (1969–1976)*, vol. 17: *China, 1969–1972,* pp. 147–149.

2. Ibid.

3. Ibid., p. 150.

4. Ibid., p. 198.

5. Ibid., p. 154.

6. James C. H. Shen, *The U.S. and China: How the U.S. Sold Out Its Ally* (Washington, D.C.: Acropolis Books, 1983), p. 67.

7. Roy Medvedev, *China and the Superpowers* (New York: Blackwell, 1986), p. 95; *FRUS* (1969–1976), vol. 17: *China, 1969–1972*, pp. 164, 169.

8. *FRUS (1969–1976)*, vol. 17: *China, 1969–1972*, p. 186; "misleading" comes from interview with Fredrick Chien, Taipei, April 19, 2008.

9. *FRUS (1969–1976)*, vol. 17: *China, 1969–1972*, p. 182.

10. Various conversations with the Foreign Service officers who interpreted for the meetings.

11. *FRUS (1969–1976)*, vol. 17: *China, 1969–1972*, p. 187.

12. Ibid., pp. 192–194. For the events of March 27, 1970, see pp. 193–196.

13. Ibid.

14. Interview with Yu Guohua, Taipei, August 28, 1995.

15. Fredrick Chien interview, Taipei, April 19, 2008.

16. *FRUS (1969–1976)*, vol. 17: *China, 1969–1972*, p. 197.

17. Richard M. Nixon, *Memoirs* (New York: Gosset and Dunlop, 1978), p. 547.

18. *FRUS (1969–1976)*, vol. 17: *China, 1969–1972*, p. 202.

19. Shen, *U.S. and China*, p. 439.

20. *FRUS (1969–1976)*, vol. 17: *China, 1969–1972*, p. 220.

21. Ibid., p. 225.

22. Chen Jian, *Mao's China and the Cold War* (Chapel Hill: University of North Carolina Press, 2001), p. 256.

23. *FRUS (1969–1976)*, vol. 17: *China, 1969–1972*, pp. 225–226.

24. Ibid., p. 228.

25. Ibid., p. 230.

26. Ibid., p. 232.

27. Ibid.

28. Ibid., p. 233.

29. Ibid., pp. 234–235.

30. *FEER* 71, no. 10 (March 6, 1971): 31.

31. *New York Times,* December 20, 1999.

32. *FRUS (1969–1976)*, vol. 17: *China, 1969–1972*, p. 237.

33. Ibid., p. 238.

34. Ibid.

35. Ibid., p. 241.

36. At the time, I was in the U.S. Consulate General in Hong Kong in charge of reporting on China's international, including U.S., relations.

37. Interview with a Soong family member, California, April 2004.

38. *FEER* 73, no. 31 (July 31, 1971): 6.

39. *FRUS (1969–1976)*, vol. 17: *China, 1969–1972*, p. 296.

40. Ibid., p. 254n.

41. *New York Times,* December 11, 1970.

42. *FRUS (1969–1976),* vol. 17: China, p. 255.

43. *FEER* 71, no. 2 (January 9, 1971): 26.

44. Chen Guying, "The Reform Movement among Intellectuals in Taiwan since 1970," *Bulletin of Concerned Asian Scholars* (July–September 1982): 34.

45. *FEER* 71, no. 10 (March 6, 1971): 31.

46. Interview with Xie Congming, Taipei, June 4, 1996.

47. Sheldon L. Appleton, "Taiwan Portents of Change," *Asian Survey,* 11, no. 1 (January 1971): 68–73.

48. Chen Jian, *Mao's China and the Cold War,* p. 261.

49. Shen, *U.S. and China,* pp. 58–59. For "check with the White House," see Fredrick Chien interview, April 19, 2008.

50. State cable to Taipei, April 30, 1971, National Archives, RG 59, China Pol, box 2202; Amembassy Taipei cable to SecState, 2537, April 30, 1971, National Archives, RG 59, SNF (1970–1973), China Pol, box 2203.

51. Y. C. Wang, *Chinese Intellectuals and the West, 1872–1949* (Chapel Hill: University of North Carolina Press, 1966), p. 440, quoting Arthur Salter, *Personality in Politics* (London: Faber and Faber, 1947).

52. John Robinson Beal, *Marshall in China* (Toronto: Doubleday Canada, 1970), pp. 360–361.

53. See Last Will and Testament in the T. V. Soong Collected Papers, Hoover Institution Archives, Stanford, Calif.

54. *FRUS (1969–1976),* vol. 17: *China, 1969–1972,* p. 293.

55. Ibid., p. 295.

56. Interview with Hao Beicun, Taipei, April 3, 2003.

57. *FRUS (1969–1976),* vol. 17: *China, 1969–1972,* p. 293.

58. Ibid., pp. 309–311.

59. Ibid., p. 300.

60. Ibid., p. 344.

61. Ibid., pp. 348–354.

62. Ibid., p. 355.

63. Ibid., p. 356.

64. Ibid., p. 394.

65. Ibid., p. 396.

66. Ibid., p. 403.

67. Ibid., p. 368. The reason Truman sent the Seventh Fleet into the Taiwan Strait was the existence of a unanimous and subsequently proven correct consensus in the U.S. leadership that the attack on Korea was part of a Sino-Soviet plan for the revolutionary transformation of East Asia guided, assisted, and if necessary backed up primarily by China.

68. Ibid., p. 369.

69. Ibid., p. 446.

70. Ibid., p. 445.

71. Ibid., pp. 370–372.

72. Ibid., p. 372.

73. Ibid.

74. Ibid., p. 383.

75. Ibid., p. 405.

76. Ibid., p. 447. Speaking of Chiang, Zhou also added without elaboration, "The United States must beware."

77. Ibid., pp. 291, 294, 348, 412, 448.

78. Chen Jian, *Mao's China and the Cold War,* p. 268.

79. *FRUS (1969–1976),* vol. 17: China, p. 422.

80. Interview with Fredrick Chien, Taipei, May 16, 1996.

81. Ibid.

82. *FEER* 73, no. 31 (July 31, 1971): 7.

83. *FRUS (1969–1976),* vol. 17: *China, 1969–1972,* pp. 456–457.

84. Ibid., p. 458.

85. Ibid., p. 602.

86. Ibid., p. 599.

87. Ibid., pp. 514–515.

88. Ibid., p. 602.

89. Ibid., pp. 514–515.

90. Ibid., p. 591.

91. Chen Jian, *Mao's China and the Cold War,* pp. 269–270.

92. *FRUS (1969–1976),* vol. 17: *China, 1969–1972,* pp. 454–455.

93. Ibid., p. 459.

94. Ibid., pp. 446, 527, 538.

95. Ibid., pp. 468–469: Shen, *U.S. and China,* p. 75.

96. *FRUS (1969–1976),* vol. 17: *China, 1969–1972,* p. 489.

97. Ibid., p. 586.

98. Ibid., p. 493.

99. Harvey Feldman, notes to the author, January 1999. According to Fredrick Chien (interview April 19, 2008), former foreign minister Shen Zhanghuan first suggested the axiom.

100. *Lingshou jinsheng wangu changqing-Zong tong Jiang gong aixi shilu* (The Vivid Spirits of the Leader through the Ages—A True Record of the Mourning for President Chiang), Taipei, special publication of the *Chong Yang ri bao* (Central Daily News), October 25, 1971.

101. *FEER* 74, no. 46 (November 13, 1971): 17; *FEER* 74, no. 50 (December 11, 1971): 60.

102. Sheldon Appleton, "Taiwan Portents of Change," *Asian Survey* 11, no. 1 (January 1971): 68, 37.

103. *FRUS (1969–1976),* vol. 17: *China, 1969–1972,* p. 560.

104. Ibid., p. 505.

105. In December, Washington passed the message to Yang that his views had been "given consideration at appropriate levels within the U.S. Government." Ibid., p. 629.

106. Ibid., pp. 599–601.

107. Ibid., pp. 582, 584.

108. Ibid., pp. 581, 591, 593.

109. Shen, *U.S. and China,* p. 77.

110. Ibid.

111. *FRUS (1969–1976),* vol. 17: *China, 1969–1972,* p. 593.

112. Ibid., pp. 635–636.

113. Ibid., pp. 668–669.

114. Ibid., p. 678.

115. Ibid., pp. 765, 766.

116. Ibid., p. 772.

117. Ibid., p. 765.

118. Ibid., pp. 766–768.

119. Ibid., pp. 768–770, 773.

120. *FRUS (1969–1973),* vol. E-13: *Documents on China,* doc. 100.

121. William Bader and Jeffery T. Bergner, *The Taiwan Relations Act* (Menlo Park, Calif.: SRI International, 1989), p. 159.

122. *FRUS (1969–1976),* vol. 17: *China 1969–1972,* p. 835.

123. Telephone interview with John Holdridge, Washington, D.C., October 10, 1997.

124. Chiang Ching-kuo quoted in *FEER* 102, no. 2 (January 12, 1979): 22.

125. *FRUS (1969–1976),* vol. 17: *China 1969–1972,* p. 858.

126. Ibid., pp. 837, 840.

127. Ibid., p. 626.

128. *FEER* 75, no. 11 (March 11, 1972): 6.

129. J. Bruce Jacobs, "Taiwan 1972: Political Season," *Asian Survey* 13, no. 1 (January 1973): 102–112.

130. Ibid.; Appleton, "Taiwan Portents," p. 37.

131. *FRUS, 1969–1976,* vol. 17: *China,* p. 115.

132. Fredrick Chien interview, May 16, 1996; Xiong Yuan, *The Reminiscences of Dr. Xiong Yuan* (Taipei: Institute of Modern History, Academia Sinica, 1998); interview with Xiong Yuan, Taipei, May 31, 1996.

133. Xiong Yuan, *Reminiscences;* Xiong Yuan interview, May 31, 1996.

134. Li Zhisui, *The Private Life of Chairman Mao* (New York: Random House, 1994), pp. 573–574.

135. Fredrick Chien interviews, Taipei, August 29, 1995, and May 16, 1996; interview with Chang Cuyi, Taipei, May 16, 1996.

136. Chen Guying, "The Reform Movement among Intellectuals in Taiwan since 1970," *Bulletin of Concerned Asian Scholars* (July–September 1982): 35.

137. Interviews with many Chiang Ching-kuo subordinates of the time, 1995, 1996; also interview with Chiang Hsiaoyung, Taipei, May 19, 1996; Xiong Yuan interview, May 31, 1996.

138. Xiong Yuan interview, May 31, 1996.

139. Xiong Yuan, *Reminiscences;* ibid.

140. *FEER* 82, no. 49 (December 10, 1973): 22.

141. William Burr, ed., *The Kissinger Transcripts: The Top Secret Talks with Beijing and Moscow* (New York: Free Press, 1999), pp. 114–115.

142. *FEER* 84, no. 19 (May 13, 1974): 30.

143. *FEER* 87, no. 4 (January 24, 1975): 22; *FRUS (1969–1976),* vol. 17: *China,* pp. 1119–1120.

144. See the National Security Archive Electronic Briefing Book, no. 18, at http://www.gwu.edu/~nsarchiv/NSAEBB/NSAEBB19/.

145. AmEmbassy Taipei cable 3505, November 22, 1974, p. 141.

146. Shong Yuan, *Reminiscences;* Shong Yuan interview, May 31, 1996.

147. Laura Tyson Li, *Madame Chiang Kai-shek* (New York: Atlantic Monthly Press, 2006).

148. I wrote this account of Chiang's last hours for *The Generalissimo's Son* (Cambridge: Harvard University Press, 2001), p. 321. My May 31, 1996, interview with Xiong Yuan, who witnessed the event, provided an authoritative and compelling account. Therefore, I have used it here mostly verbatim. In the interview, however, Xiong left out the fact that Ching-kuo had joined Madame Chiang at the bedside. Reaction to the storm is from *FEER* 88, no. 16 (April 18, 1975): 20. The government announcement stated that Chiang suffered a heart attack at 11:20 p.m., was taken to Veterans Hospital, and died at 11:50 p.m. with Madame Chiang and Ching-kuo at his side. *New York Times,* April 6, 1975. But Chiang's secretary, Fredrick Chien, confirmed he died at Shilin. Note to author, November 15, 2008.

149. *New York Times,* April 6, 1975. The English version substituted the nonsocialist "colleagues" for "comrades."

150. Taylor, *Generalissimo's Son,* p. 321; ibid.

151. *New York Times,* April 12 and 14, 1975.

152. *New York Times,* April 7, 1975.

153. *New York Times,* April 27, 1975.

154. This and the following paragraphs are drawn heavily from Richard Halloran's article in *New York Times,* April 17, 1975.

155. Ibid.

156. Wang Shoujia et al., *Mao Zedong wannian guoyan shiwenlu* (The Poems and Prose of Mao Zedong Read during His Later Years) (Hong Kong: Balong Shuwu,

1993), pp. 17, 871–874. Mao apparently did not, as reported elsewhere, add two lines dedicated to Chiang. See Xiong Xianghui, *Wo de Qinghao yu waijiao shengya* (My Intelligence and Diplomatic Career) (Beijing: Zhonggong dangshi chubanshe, 1998), pp. 289–290; and June Chang and Jon Halliday, *Mao* (New York: Alfred A. Knopf, 2005), p. 628.

Epilogue

1. A Soong relative's email to the author, July 16, 2008.

2. Albert C. Wedemeyer Papers, a memorial tribute given at Washington National Cathedral, April 16, 1975, box 1, folder 19, Hoover Institution Archives, Stanford, California. Wedemeyer may have visited the island in the 1960s. We don't know. But the quotation sounds like something that Chiang would have said at that time, not in 1947. The General and Chiang did exchange letters, but none with this quote are found in the Hoover collection.

Postscript to the Paperback Edition

1. Chiang Diaries, Hoover, October 22, 1958, box 67, folder 1.

2. Chiang Diaries, Hoover, October 23, 1958, box, 67, folder 1.

3. *FRUS (1958–1960),* vol. 17: *China,* pp. 509–510.

4. Chiang Diaries, Hoover, October 25, 1958, box 67, folder 1.

5. *New York Times,* October 25, 1958.

6. Chiang Diaries, Hoover, April 20, 27, 1960, box 67, folder 21; monthly reflection, December 31, 1960, box 68, folder 6.

7. Chiang Diaries, Hoover, January 20, 21, 1961, box 68, folder 8.

8. Chiang Diaries, Hoover, February 10, 18, 1960, box 68, folder 9.

9. Chiang Diaries, Hoover, April 22, 1961, box 68, folder 11.

10. Ibid., p. 160.

11. Chiang Diaries, Hoover, October 20, 1962, box 69, folder 16.

12. Chiang Diaries, Hoover, October 29, 1962, box 69, folder 16.

13. Chiang Diaries, Hoover, November 2 (weekly reflection), November 3, 1963, box 70, folder 10.

14. Chiang Diaries, Hoover, June 30, July 10, 1966, box 72, folder 12.

15. Chiang Diaries, Hoover, May 31, 1968, box 74, folder 5.

16. Chiang Diaries, Hoover, January 20, 1969, box 74, folder 17.

17. Ibid.

18. Chiang Diaries, Hoover, January 31, 1969, box 74, folder 17.

19. Ibid. Chiang Diaries, Hoover, July 2, 31 (monthly reflection), August 8, 1969, box 75, folders 5, 6.

20. Chien Fu interview, April 19, 2008.

21. Ibid. Chiang Diaries, Hoover, July 2, 31 (monthly reflection), August 8, 1969, box 75, folders 5, 6.

22. *FRUS (1969–1976),* vol. 17: *China,* pp. 55–56.

23. Chiang Diaries, Hoover, July 24, 1969, box 75, folder 5.

24. Chiang Diaries, Hoover, July 17, August 12, 1969, box 75, folders 5, 6.

25. Chiang Diaries, Hoover, October 30, 1970, box 76, folder 3.

26. Jay Taylor, *The Generalissimo's Son* (Cambridge: Harvard University Press, 2000), p. 289.

27. Chiang Diaries, Hoover, March 16, 18, 1970, box 75, folder 14.

28. Chiang Diaries, Hoover, March 18, 1970, box 75, folder 14.

29. Chiang Diaries, Hoover, May 31, 1970, box 75, folder 16. Taylor, *The Generalissimo's Son,* pp. 299–300.

30. Chiang Diaries, Hoover, July 27, 31, 1970, box 75, folder 18.

31. Chiang Diaries, Hoover, April 16, 1971, box 76, folder 10.

32. Chiang Diaries, Hoover, April 10, 18, 1971, box 76, folder 10.

33. Chiang Diaries, Hoover, July 16, 1971, box 76, folder 13.

34. Chiang Diaries, Hoover, July 16, 29, August 4, 1971, box 76, folders 13, 14.

35. *Lingshou jingsheng wangu changqing-Zong tong Jiang gong aixi shilu* (A leader's Enduring Spirit, A True Record of the Mourning for President Chiang), Taipei, special publication of the *Zhong yang ri bao* (Central Daily News), October 25, 1971. For "aspiration for years," see Chiang Diaries, Hoover, end of October reflection, 1971, box 76, folder 16.

36. Ibid., pp. 635–636. For "Granma Liu," see Chiang Diaries, Hoover, November 29, 1971, box 76, folder 17. Several diary entries convey Chiang's belief that Nixon bore a personal resentment, even "hatred," of him for supposedly not praising Nixon after his 1964 visit to Taiwan. See Chiang Diaries, Hoover, July 29, 1971, box 76, folder 13, and December 26, 1971, box 76, folder 18.

37. Chiang Diaries, Hoover, February 12, 1972, box 72, folder 21.

38. Chiang Diaries, Hoover, February 27, 28, 1972, box 76, folder 21.

39. Chiang Diaries, Hoover, March 11, 1972, box 76, folder 23.

40. Chiang Dairies, Hoover, April 10, 1972, box 76, folder 23.

41. Chiang Diaries, Hoover, April 20, 1972, box 76, folder 23.

42. Chiang Diaries, Hoover, July 20, 21, 1972, box 76, folder 26.

Index